DISCOVERING THE WESTERN PAST

COMBINED EDITION

MERRY E. WIESNER

UNIVERSITY OF WISCONSIN – MILWAUKEE

HOUGHTON MIFFLIN COMPANY

Boston New York

Senior Sponsoring Editor: Nancy Blaine
Editorial Assistant: Shoma Aditya
Senior Project Editor: Christina Horn
Senior Production/Design Coordinator: Carol Merrigan
Manufacturing Manager: Florence Cadran
Marketing Manager: Sandra McGuire
Custom Publishing Editor: Dan Luciano
Custom Publishing Production Manager: Kathleen McCourt
Project Coordinator: Harmony Flewelling

Cover Designer: Kyle Sarofeen

This book contains select works from existing Houghton Mifflin Company resources and was produced by Houghton Mifflin Custom Publishing for collegiate use. As such, those adopting and/or contributing to this work are responsible for editorial content, accuracy, continuity and completeness.

Printed in the United States of America.

ISBN: 0-618-15926-6
3-98937

6   7   8   9 – CCI – 04 03

Houghton Mifflin
Custom Publishing

222 Berkeley Street • Boston, MA 02116

Address all correspondence and order information to the above address.

CONTENTS

PREFACE

The first three editions of *Discovering the Western Past: A Look at the Evidence* elicited a very positive response from instructors and students alike, and that response encouraged us to proceed with this Fourth Edition. As authors, we were particularly gratified by the widespread acceptance of the central goal of *Discovering the Western Past*, that of making students active analysts of the past and not merely passive recipients of its factual record.

The title of this book begins with a verb, a choice that reflects our basic philosophy about history. History is not simply something one learns about; it is something one does. One discovers the past, and what makes this pursuit exciting is not only the past that is discovered but also the process of discovery itself. This process can be simultaneously exhilarating and frustrating, enlightening and confusing, but it is always challenging enough to convince those of us who are professional historians to spend our lives at it. And our own students, as well as many other students, have caught this infectious excitement.

The recognition that history involves discovery as much as physics or astronomy does is often not shared by students, whose classroom experience of history frequently does not extend beyond listening to lectures and reading textbooks. The primary goal of *Discovering the Western Past: A Look at the Evidence* is to allow students enrolled in the Western Civilization course to *do* history in the same way we as historians do—to examine a group of original sources in order to answer questions about the past. We feel that contact with original sources is an excellent means of communicating the excitement of doing history, but incorporating complete works or a collection of documents into a Western Civilization course can be problematic for many instructors.

The evidence in this book thus differs from that in most source collections in its variety. We have included visual evidence such as coins, paintings, aerial photographs, cartoons, buildings, architectural plans, maps, and political posters. In choosing written evidence we again have tried to offer a broad sample—songs, plays, poems, novels, court records, notarial contracts, statistical data, and work regulations all supplement letters, newspapers, speeches, autobiographies, and other more traditional sources.

For students to learn history the way we as historians do, they must not only be confronted with the evidence; they must also learn how to use that evidence to arrive at a conclusion. In other words, they must learn historical methodology. Too often methodology (or even the notion that historians *have* a methodology) is reserved for upper-level majors or graduate students; beginning students are simply presented with historical facts and interpretations without being shown how these were unearthed or formulated. Students may learn that historians hold different interpretations of the significance of an event or individual or different ideas about causation, but they are not informed of how historians come to such conclusions.

Thus, along with evidence, we have provided explicit suggestions about how one might analyze that evidence, guiding students as they reach their own conclusions. As they work through the various chapters, students will discover not only that the sources of historical information are wide-ranging but also that the methodologies appropriate to understanding and using them are equally diverse. By doing history themselves, students will learn how intellectual historians handle philosophical treatises, economic historians quantitative data, social historians court records, and political and diplomatic historians theoretical treatises and memoirs. They will also be asked to consider the limitations of their evidence, to explore what historical questions it cannot answer as well as those it can. Instead of passive observers, students become active participants.

Following an approach that we have found successful in many different classroom situations, we have divided each chapter into five parts: The Problem, Sources and Method, The Evidence, Questions to Consider, and Epilogue. The section called "The Problem" presents the general historical background and context for the evidence offered and concludes with the central question or questions explored in the chapter. The section titled "Sources and Method" provides specific information about the sources and suggests ways in which students might best study and analyze this primary evidence. It also discusses how previous historians have evaluated such sources and mentions any major disputes about methodology or interpretation. "The Evidence" forms the core of each chapter, presenting a variety of original sources for students to use in completing the central task. In "Questions to Consider," suggestions are offered about connections among the sources, and students are guided to draw deductions from the evidence. The final section, "Epilogue," traces both the immediate effects of the issue under discussion and its impact on later developments.

Within this framework, we have tried to present a series of historical issues and events of significance to the instructor as well as of interest to the student. We have also aimed to provide a balance among political, social, diplomatic, intellectual, and cultural history. In other words, we have attempted to create a kind of historical sampler that we believe will help students learn the methods and skills used by historians. These skills—analyzing arguments, developing hypotheses, comparing evidence, testing conclusions, and reevaluating material—will not only enable students to master historical content; they will also provide the necessary foundation for critical thinking in other college courses and after college as well.

Discovering the Western Past is designed to accommodate any format of the Western Civilization course, from the small lecture/discussion class of a liberal arts or community college to the large lecture with discussions led by teaching assistants at a sizable university. The chapters may be used for individual assignments, team projects, class discussions, papers, and exams. Each is self-contained, so that any combination may be assigned. The book is not intended to replace a standard textbook, and it was written to accompany any Western Civilization text the instructor chooses. The *Instructor's Resource Manual*, written by the authors of the text, offers suggestions for class discussions, suggestions for ways in which students' learning may be evaluated, and annotated lists of suggestions for further reading.

New to the Fourth Edition

The Fourth Edition of *Discovering the Western Past* incorporates the responses to the book that we have received from our own students, as well as from student and faculty users of the book around the country. Every chapter in the two volumes has received some reworking, and new chapters are included in each volume.

Volume I includes new chapters on ancient suicide, slave law in Roman and Germanic society, and peasant violence in the period 1500–1789. Volume II offers readers new chapters on the French Revolution (reinstated from the Second Edition), "New Women" of the 1920s, and immigration in Europe.

Acknowledgments

In the completion of this book, the authors received assistance from a number of people. Our colleagues and students at the University of Wisconsin—Milwaukee, Marquette University, and the University of Tennessee, Knoxville, have been generous with their ideas and time. Merry E. Wiesner (-Hanks) wishes especially to thank Judith Bennett, Judith Beall, Martha Carlin, Abbas Hamdani, and Marci Sortor for their critiques and suggestions, and Neil Wiesner-Hanks and Kai and Tyr Wiesner-Hanks for their help in maintaining the author's perspective. Julius Ruff acknowledges the assistance of two valued colleagues who aided in preparing all four editions of this work: the Reverend John Patrick Donnelly, S.J., of Marquette University and Michael D. Sibalis of Wilfrid Laurier University. He also wishes to thank Laura, Julia, and Charles Ruff for their continued support. William Bruce Wheeler wishes to thank Owen Bradley and John Bohstedt for their valuable assistance.

We wish to acknowledge particularly the following historians who read and commented on the manuscript of this Fourth Edition as it developed:

Marjorie K. Berman, *Red Rocks Community College*
Melissa Bokovoy, *University of New Mexico*
Richard Camp, *California State University, Northridge*

Phillip A. Cantrell II, *West Virginia University*

Victoria Chandler, *Georgia College & State University*

Rhonda L. Clark, *Mercyhurst College*

Christopher R. Corley, *Bloomsburg University*

Greg A. Eghigian, *University of Texas at Arlington*

Luci Fortunato-DeLisle, *Bridgewater State College*

Meredith A. Medler, *St. Cloud State University*

Catherine Patterson, *University of Houston*

Charles M. Radding, *Michigan State University*

Bernard Schlager, *University of New Hampshire*

Linda J. Simmons, *Northern Virginia Community College*

Phillip Thurmond Smith, *Saint Joseph's University, Philadelphia*

Finally, the authors extend their thanks to the staff of Houghton Mifflin Company for their enthusiastic support.

M.E.W.

J.R.R.

W.B.W.

CHAPTER ONE

THE NEED FOR WATER

IN ANCIENT SOCIETIES

THE PROBLEM

The title of the course for which you are using this book is probably a variant of "Western Civilization." Why do we use the term *civilization*? What distinguishes human cultures that are labeled civilizations from those that are not? Though great differences separate them, all civilizations share some basic characteristics. The most important of these similarities is the presence of cities; indeed, the word *civilization* comes from the Latin word *civilis* (meaning "civic"), which is also the root of *citizen* and *civil*. Historians and archaeologists generally define a city as a place inhabited by more than 5,000 people, and they have discovered the remains of the earliest communities of this size in ancient Mesopotamia, which is present-day Iraq.

Why should the presence of cities be the distinguishing mark of cultural development? It is not the cities themselves but what they imply about a culture that makes them so important. Any society in which thousands of people live in close proximity to one another must have some sort of laws or rules governing human behavior. These may be either part of an oral tradition or, as in ancient Mesopotamia, written down. A city must provide its residents with a constant supply of food, which means developing ways to transport food into the city from the surrounding farmland, to store food throughout the year, and to save it for years marked by poor harvests. Not only does the presence of cities indicate that people could transport and store food effectively, but it also reveals that they were producing enough surplus food to allow for specialization of labor. If all work time had been devoted to farming, it would not have been possible to build roads, produce storage bins, or enforce laws on which the city depended. This specialization of labor, then, allowed some members of society the opportunity and time to create and produce goods and artifacts that were not directly essential to daily survival. Urban residents in Mesopotamia began to construct large buildings and decorate them with sculptures, paintings, and mosaics; write poetry and history; and develop religious and philosophical ideas, all of which are pursuits we consider essential to a civilization. As the cities themselves grew, they required greater and greater amounts of food to feed their inhabitants, which led to further technological development.

Mesopotamia was in many ways an odd location for the beginning of a civilization. True, the soil is so rich that the region is called the Fertile Crescent, but it does not receive enough natural rainfall to grow crops steadily year after year. In fact, this region is not where agriculture began in the West; that happened closer to the Mediterranean, where the rainfall was more regular. Apparently, as techniques of planting and harvesting crops spread into Mesopotamia, the inhabitants realized that they would be able to use these techniques effectively only through irrigation. They needed to tap the waters flowing in the Tigris and Euphrates Rivers, a project requiring the cooperation of a great many people. Thus, rather than proving a block to further development, the need for irrigation in ancient Mesopotamia may have been one of the reasons that cities first arose there. We may never be able to know this with certainty, because irrigation systems were already in place when written records began and because cities and irrigation expanded at the same time. We do know, however, that in Mesopotamia, neither could have existed without the other; cities could survive only where irrigation had created a food surplus, and irrigation could survive only where enough people were available to create and maintain ditches and other parts of the system.

Building irrigation systems presented both technical and organizational problems. The Tigris and Euphrates were fast-flowing rivers that carried soil as well as water down from the highlands. This rich soil created new farmland where the rivers emptied into the Persian Gulf. (The ancient Persian Gulf ended more than 100 miles north of its present boundary; all that land was created as the rivers filled in the delta.) The soil also rapidly clogged up the irrigation ditches, which consequently required constant cleaning. Every year these deposits were excavated and piled on the banks until the sides of the ditches grew so tall that cleaning could no longer be easily accomplished. At this point the old ditch was abandoned and a new ditch was cut, tasks that required a great deal of work and the cooperation of everyone whose land was watered by that ditch.

Mesopotamian farmers used several types of irrigation. One technique, known as *basin irrigation,* was to level large plots of land fronting the rivers and main canals and build up dikes around them. In the spring and other times during the year when the water was high, farmers knocked holes in the dikes to admit water and fresh soil. Once the sediment had settled, they let the water flow back into the channel. They also built small waterways between their fields to provide water throughout the year, thereby developing a system of *perennial irri-*

gation. In the hillier country of northern Mesopotamia, farmers built *terraces* with water channels running alongside them. The hillside terraces provided narrow strips of flat land to farm, and the waterways were dug to connect with brooks and streams.

Farmers could depend on gravity to bring water to their fields during spring and flood seasons, but at other times they needed water-raising machines. They devised numerous types of machines, some of which are still in use today in many parts of the world. These solved some problems but created others, as farmers with machines could drain an irrigation ditch during times of low water, leaving their neighbors with nothing. How were rights to water to be decided? Solving this problem was crucial to human social organization, and the first recorded laws regarding property rights in fact concern not rights to land but rights to water. In Mesopotamia, land was useless unless it was irrigated.

Many of the irrigation techniques developed in Mesopotamia either spread to Egypt or were developed independently there. Because it received even less rainfall than Mesopotamia, Egypt was totally dependent on the Nile for watering crops. Fortunately, the Nile was a much better source of water than the Tigris and Euphrates because it flooded regularly, allowing easy basin irrigation. The rise and fall of the Nile was so regular, in fact, that the Egyptians based their 365-day calendar on its annual flooding. The Egyptians also constructed waterways and water-lifting machines to allow

for perennial irrigation. As in Mesopotamia, irrigation in Egypt both caused and resulted from the growth of cities. It contributed as well to the power of the kings, whom the Egyptian people regarded as responsible for the flood of the Nile.

Irrigation was more difficult in places that did not have flood-prone rivers, including many parts of North Africa and the Near East. Here people adapted techniques to conserve water from sporadic heavy rainfalls. They dammed the temporary lakes (termed *wadis*) created by these rainfalls and built ditches to convey the water to fields, rather than allowing it simply to flow off onto the desert. Sometimes this wadi irrigation involved a whole series of small dams down the course of rivers that ran only after storms. Besides providing water, wadi irrigation also built up terraces because the rivers carried soil with them.

The earliest water systems were for crop irrigation, but people also began to demand good drinking water. In many parts of the ancient world, the demand for drinking water led to the setting up of a second system because river water that is suitable for irrigation may be brackish, unpleasant, or even unhealthful to drink. In southern Europe, where lakes were often not far from growing cities, people solved the problem by building channels made of timber, stone, or clay earthenware to carry water from the lakes to the city. These channels might be open or closed, depending on the terrain and the level of technical development of the culture that built them. Generally they relied on gravity flow and fed into underground tanks or reservoirs in the city; the oldest known water channels are in Jerusalem and date from about 1000 B.C. The construction of such systems, which demanded even more technical expertise than the building of irrigation ditches, provoked additional legal problems about ownership of the right to this clean, cool water.

When lakes were not located close enough to make aboveground channels feasible, people had to rely on water from *aquifers,* underground water-bearing layers of gravel or porous rock. The water could be obtained from wells drilled in the ground, but wells could supply only a small amount of water at a time. Once an aquifer had been discovered, however, a horizontal channel could be dug to lead the water to an outside channel or reservoir. A horizontal channel worked only in hilly areas where the aquifer stood higher than a nearby valley, but such channels, called *qanats,* have been found in Iran, Syria, Egypt, and Turkey that are over 2,000 years old. If the amount of water it yielded was large enough, the qanat could be used for irrigation as well as drinking water.

When the Romans conquered the Middle East and North Africa in the second century B.C., they inherited irrigation systems that in some cases had already been in existence for more than 2,000 years. The Romans carried many ideas to other parts of their empire and made innovations as the terrain or distance required. Most of the European territory in the Roman Empire received adequate rainfall for farming without irrigation, but many Roman cities, especially Rome itself, experienced a chronic shortage of drinking water. The Romans solved this problem by building *aqueducts,* covered or uncovered channels that brought water into the cities from lakes and springs. The first of these in Rome was built in 312 B.C., and the system expanded continuously up to about A.D. 150. Over 300 miles of aqueducts served the city of Rome alone, with extensive systems in the outlying provinces as well. Although Roman engineers went to great lengths to avoid valleys, they were occasionally forced to construct enormous bridges to carry the aqueducts over valleys. Some of these bridges were over 150 feet high, and a few, such as the bridge-aqueduct in Segovia, Spain, still bring water to city residents. The Romans' sophisticated architectural and construction techniques—the arch and water-resistant cement, for example—enabled them to build water systems undreamed of in Mesopotamia and Egypt. Legal problems were not as easily solved, however, and disputes about water rights recur frequently throughout the long history of Rome.

Supplying cities with water was not simply a technological problem; it had economic, legal, and political implications. Through their solutions to these complex problems, ancient societies created what we call civilization. Your task in this chapter will be to use both visual and written evidence of ancient water systems to answer the question, How did the need for a steady supply of water shape civilization?

4

SOURCES AND METHOD

Historians use a wide variety of sources when examining ancient irrigation and water supply systems. Many of these systems were created before the development of writing, so archaeological evidence is extremely important, especially in examining technological development. This evidence may be the actual remains of ancient ditches, machines, or aqueducts, but in many areas these have completely disappeared. This does not mean that they have left no trace, however, for the ancient uses of modern landscapes are often revealed through patterns of depressions and discoloration.

The easiest way to see these patterns is through aerial photography. Analyzing aerial photographs can be a difficult task, however, and learning how to read ancient land-use patterns through the overlay of modern development takes a great deal of training. Occasionally the older patterns can be quite clear, however, and only a small amount of additional information is necessary for you to begin to decode them. The first piece of evidence, Source 1, is an aerial photograph of the site of a pre-Roman city in Italy. Examine the picture carefully. Can you see the old grid pattern of irrigation ditches, which shows up as light and dark marsh grass? The dark lines are the outlines of ancient irrigation ditches, the lighter squares are ancient fields, and the white parallel lines superimposed on the top are part of a modern drainage system. To examine the an-

cient system, you will need to strip away the modern system mentally. What do you think the broader black strip at the top left is? Does this system look like basin or perennial irrigation? Look at the flatness of the landscape. Would silting be a problem?

A more sophisticated type of aerial photography involves the use of satellites rather than airplanes. Satellites can take extremely detailed pictures of the earth's surface that reveal natural and artificially constructed features, both ancient and contemporary. The sharpest images are produced by high-resolution military satellites whose pictures are not available to the public. Low-power images produced by LANDSAT, the only U.S. commercial imaging satellite system, are adequate for most archaeological and historical purposes, however. Source 2 is a map of the major ancient irrigation ditches between the Tigris and Euphrates rivers that were identifiable in a recent LANDSAT image. What does the size of the system reveal about Mesopotamian technology? What does it imply about the political systems in this area—would you expect, for example, the cities in Mesopotamia to be hostile to one another? New technologies such as LANDSAT imagery not only provide answers to questions, but also guide future research. How could you use this map to plan further investigations of irrigation systems?

Aerial photography provides visual evidence of entire irrigation systems but not of the specific tools and machines used to lift water to the fields. For these we must look to the remains of the tools themselves or to depictions of them in tomb paintings, mosaics, and pottery. Comparing these pictures with machines still in use today shows that many techniques for lifting water have remained virtually unchanged for thousands of years.

Sources 3 through 6 show four different machines for raising water that we know were in use in ancient times and are still in use in many parts of the world today: the shaduf, saqiya, Archimedes' screw,[1] and noria. To assess their role and importance, you must consider a number of different factors while carefully examining the four diagrams. Some of these factors are technical: How complicated is the machine to build? Does it have many moving parts that must all be in good repair? How much water can it lift? How high can it lift the water? Can it work with both flowing and stationary water? Some factors are economic: Does the machine require a person to operate it, thus taking that person away from other types of labor? Does it require a strong adult, or can it be operated by a child? Does it require an animal, which must be fed and cared for? Some factors are both economic and political: Does the machine require a variety of raw materials to build, more than one family might possess? Does it require any raw materials, like metal, that would have to be imported? (Such questions are political because someone has to decide which families get the raw materials necessary for their fields.) Some factors are legal: Does the machine raise

1. Archimedes (287–212 B.C.) was a Greek mathematician and inventor who is credited with inventing this machine.

so much water that laws about distribution would become necessary? At this point, you may want to make a chart summarizing your assessment of the advantages and disadvantages of each machine, which will help you in making your final conclusions.

We will now turn from visual to written sources. Because water is such a vital commodity, mention of water systems appears very early in recorded human history. The next five sources are written accounts of the construction or operation of water systems. Source 7 contains sections from the Code of Hammurabi, a Babylonian legal code dating from 1750 B.C., that refer to irrigation. Source 8 is a description of the Roman aqueduct system written by Vitruvius during the first century B.C., and Source 9 is a description of the water-system projects undertaken by Emperor Claudius during his reign (A.D. 41–54), written by the Roman historian Suetonius. The next selection is a discussion of some of the problems associated with Rome's water system written about A.D. 100 by Frontinus, who was commissioner of the water supply. The last is a proclamation issued by Emperor Theodosius in 438 as part of his code of laws, an edict that had probably been in effect for many earlier decades as well.

As you read these sources, notice first of all the technical issues that the authors are addressing. What problems in tapping, transportation, and storage of water do they discuss? What solutions do they suggest? Then look at legal problems, which you can find most clearly stated in the selection by Frontinus and the law codes of Hammurabi and Theodosius. Keep in mind when you are reading the law codes that laws are generally written to address those problems that already exist, not those the lawmakers are simply anticipating. The presence of a law, especially one that is frequently repeated, is often a good indication that the prohibited activity was probably happening, and happening often. How did people misuse or harm the water systems? What penalties were provided for those who did? Who controlled the legal use of water, and who decided how water was to be distributed?

The written sources also include information about political and economic factors in ancient water supply systems that is nearly impossible to gain from archaeological evidence. Careful reading can reveal who paid for the construction of such systems and who stood to gain financially from them once they were built. What reasons, other than the simple need for water, might rulers have had for building water systems? What political and economic factors entered into decisions about the ways in which water was to be distributed?

THE EVIDENCE

Source 1 from Leo Deuel, Flights into Yesterday: The Story of Aerial Archeology *(New York: St. Martin's Press, 1969), p. 236. Photo by Fotoaerea Valvassori, Ravenna.*

1. Aerial Photograph of Pre-Roman City in Italy

Source 2 from Robert MaC. Adams, Heartland of Cities; Surveys of Ancient Settlements and Land Use on the Central Floodplains of the Euphrates *(Chicago: University of Chicago Press, 1981), p. 34.*

2. Major Ancient Levees Identifiable in LANDSAT Imagery

Sources 3 through 6 adapted from sketches by Merry E. Wiesner.

3. Shaduf

4. Saqiya

5. Archimedes' Screw

6. Noria

Source 7 from Robert F. Harper, The Code of Hammurabi *(Chicago: University of Chicago Press, 1904).*

7. Sections from the Code of Hammurabi Referring to Irrigation, 1750 B.C.

53. If a man neglects to maintain his dike and does not strengthen it, and a break is made in his dike and the water carries away the farmland, the man in whose dike the break has been made shall replace the grain which has been damaged.

54. If he is not able to replace the grain, they shall sell him and his goods and the farmers whose grain the water has carried away shall divide [the results of the sale].

55. If a man opens his canal for irrigation and neglects it and the water carries away an adjacent field, he shall pay out grain on the basis of the adjacent field.

56. If a man opens up the water and the water carries away the improvements of an adjacent field, he shall pay out ten *gur* of grain per *bur* [of damaged land]. . . .

66. If a man has stolen a watering-machine from the meadow, he shall pay five shekels of silver to the owner of the watering-machine.

Sources 8 and 9 from Naphtali Lewis and Meyer Reinhold, editors and translators, Roman Civilization *(New York: Columbia University Press, 1955), pp. 304–306; pp. 151–152. Reprinted with permission of Columbia University Press, 562 W. 113th St., New York, NY 10025, via Copyright Clearance Center, Inc.*

8. Vetruvius's Description of the Roman Aqueduct System, first century B.C.

The supply of water is made by three methods: by channels through walled conduits, or by lead pipes, or by earthenware pipes. And they are arranged as follows. In the case of conduits, the structure must be very solid; the bed of the channel must be leveled with a fall of not less than half a foot in 100 feet. The walled conduits are to be arched over so that the minimum amount of sun may strike the water. When it comes to the city walls, a reservoir is to be made. To this reservoir a triple distribution tank is to be joined to receive the water; and three pipes of equal size are to be placed in the reservoir, leading to the adjoining tanks, so that when there is an overflow from the two outer tanks, it may deliver into the middle tank. From the middle tank pipes will be laid to all basins and fountains; from the second tank to the baths, in order to furnish an annual revenue to the treasury; to avoid a deficiency in the public supply, private houses are to be supplied from the third, for private persons will not be able to divert the water, since they have their own limited supply from the distribution sources. Another reason why I have made these divisions is that those who take private supplies into their houses may by their taxes paid through tax farmers contribute to the maintenance of the water supply.

If, however, there are hills between the city and the source, we must proceed as follows: underground channels are to be dug and leveled to the fall mentioned above. If the bed is of tufa or stone, the channel may be cut in it; but if it is of soil or sand, the bed of the channel and the walls with the vaulting must be constructed, and the water should be thus conducted. Air shafts are to be so constructed that they are 120 feet apart.

But if the supply is to be by lead pipes, first of all a reservoir is to be built at the source. Then the opening of the pipe is to be determined in accordance with the amount of water, and these pipes are to be laid from the source reservoir to a reservoir which is inside the city.

When an aqueduct is to be made with lead pipes it is to have the following arrangement. If there is a fall from the source to the city and the intervening hills are not high enough to interrupt the supply, then if there are valleys, we must build substructures to bring it up to a level, as in the case of channels and conduits. If the way round the valley is not long, a circuit should be used; but if the valleys are expansive, the course will be directed down the hill, and when it reaches the bottom it is carried on a low substructure so that the level there may continue as far as possible. This will form a "belly," which the Greeks call *koilia*. When the "belly" comes to the hill opposite, and the long distance of the "belly" makes the water slow in welling up, the water is to be forced to the height of the top of the hill. . . .

Again, it is not without advantage to put reservoirs at intervals of 24,000 feet, so that if a break occurs anywhere neither the whole load of water nor the whole structure need be disturbed, and the place where it has occurred may be more easily found. But these reservoirs are to be neither in the descent nor on the level portion of the "belly," nor at risings, nor anywhere in a valley, but on unbroken level ground.

But if we wish to employ a less expensive method, we must proceed as follows. Earthenware pipes are to be made not less than two inches thick, but these pipes should be so tongued at one end that they can fit into and join one another. The joints are to be coated with quicklime mixed with oil. . . . Everything also is to be fixed as for lead pipes. Further, when the water is first let in from the source, ashes are to be put in beforehand, so that if any joints are not sufficiently coated they may be lined with the ashes.

Water supply by earthenware pipes has these advantages. First, in the construction: if a break occurs, anybody can repair it. Again, water is much more wholesome from earthenware pipes than from lead pipes. For it seems to be made injurious by lead, because white lead is produced by it; and this is said to be harmful to the human body. So if what is produced by anything is injurious, there is no doubt that the thing itself is not wholesome. We can take an example from the workers in lead who have complexions affected by pallor. For when lead is smelted in casting, the fumes from it settle on the members of the body and, burning them, rob the limbs of the virtues of the blood. Therefore it seems that water should by no means be brought in lead pipes if we desire to have it wholesome. Everyday life can be used to show that the flavor from earthenware pipes is better, because everybody (even those who load their table with silver vessels) uses earthenware to preserve the purity of water.

But if we are to create springs from which the water supplies come, we must dig wells.

But if the soil is hard, or if the veins of water lie too deep, then supplies of water are to be collected from the roofs or higher ground in concrete cisterns. . . . If the cisterns are made double or triple, so that they can be changed by percolation, they will make the supply of water much more wholesome. For when the sediment has a place to settle in, the water will be more limpid and will keep its taste without any smell. If not, salt must be added to purify it.

9. Suetonius's Description of the Water Projects Undertaken by Emperor Claudius (r. A.D. 41–54)

The public works which Claudius completed were great and essential rather than numerous; they were in particular the following: an aqueduct begun by Caligula; also the drainage channel of Lake Fucine and the harbor at Ostia, although in the case of the last two he knew that Augustus had refused the former to the Marsians in spite of their frequent requests, and that the latter had often been considered by the deified Julius but given up because of its difficulty. He brought to the city on stone arches the cool and abundant springs of the Claudian aqueduct . . . and at the same time the channel of the New Anio, distributing them into many beautifully ornamented fountains. He made the attempt on the Fucine Lake as much in the hope of gain as of glory, inasmuch as there were some who offered to drain it at their own cost provided the land that was drained be given them. He finished the drainage canal, which was three miles in length, partly by leveling and partly by tunneling a mountain, a work of great difficulty requiring eleven years, although he had 30,000 men at work all the time without interruption.

Source 10 from B. K. Workman, editor and translator, They Saw It Happen in Classical
Times *(New York: Barnes & Noble, 1964), pp. 179–181. Reprinted by permission of Littlefield,
Adams & Company and Basil Blackwell Publishers.*

10. Frontinus's Discussion of Rome's Water System, ca A.D. 100

The New Anio[2] is drawn from the river in the district of Sinbrinum, at about
the forty-second milestone along the Via Sublacensis. On either side of the
river at this point are fields of rich soil which make the banks less firm, so that
the water in the aqueduct is discoloured and muddy even without the damage done by storms. So a little way along from the inlet a cleansing basin was
built where the water could settle and be purified between the river and the
conduit. Even so, in the event of rain, the water reaches the city in a muddy
state. The length of the New Anio is about 47 miles, of which over 39 are underground and more than 7 carried on structures above the ground. In the
upper reaches a distance of about two miles in various sections is carried on
low structures or arches. Nearer the city, from the seventh Roman mile-stone,
is half a mile on substructures and five miles on arches. These arches are very
high, rising in certain places to a height of 109 feet.

. . . All the aqueducts reach the city at different levels. So some serve the
higher districts and some cannot reach loftier ground. For the hills of Rome
have gradually increased in height because of the rubble from frequent fires.
There are five aqueducts high enough at entrance to reach all the city, but they
supply water at different pressures. . . .

Anyone who wants to tap water for private consumption must send in an application and take it, duly signed by the Emperor, to the Commissioner. The latter
must take immediate action on Caesar's grant, and enroll one of the Imperial
freedmen to help him in the business. . . . The right to water once granted cannot
be inherited or bought, and does not go with the property, though long ago a
privilege was extended to the public baths that their right should last in perpetuity. . . . When grants lapse, notice is given and record made in the ledgers, which
are consulted so that future applicants can be given vacant supplies. The previous
custom was to cut off these lapsed supplies at once, to make some profit by a temporary sale to the landowners or even to outsiders. Our Emperor felt that property should not suddenly be left without water, and that it would be fairer to give
thirty days' notice for other arrangements to be made by the interested party. . . .

Now that I have explained the situation with regard to private supply, it
will be pertinent to give some examples of the ways in which men have broken these very sound arrangements and have been caught red-handed. In
some reservoirs I have found larger valves in position than had been granted,

2. An aqueduct completed under the emperor Claudius in A.D. 52.

14

and some have not even had the official stamp on them. When a stamped valve exceeds the legal dimensions, then the private advantage of the controller who stamped it is uncovered. When a valve is not even stamped, then both parties are clearly liable, chiefly the purchaser, but also the controller. Sometimes stamped valves of the correct dimensions open into pipes of a larger cross-section. The result is that the water is not kept in for the legal distance, but forced through a short, narrow pipe and easily fills the larger one which is joined to it. So care must be taken that, when a valve is stamped, the pipes connected to it should be stamped as of the correct length ordered by Senatorial decree. For then and only then will the controller be fully liable when he knows that only stamped pipes must be positioned.

When valves are sited, good care must be taken to see that they are placed in a horizontal line, not one above the other. A lower inlet gets a greater pressure of water, the upper one less, because the supply of water is taken by the lower. In some pipes no valves are positioned at all. These are called "free" pipes, and are opened and closed to suit the watermen.

Another of the watermen's intolerable practices is to make a new outlet from the cistern when a water-grant is transferred to a new owner, leaving the old one for themselves. I would say that it was one of the Commissioner's chief duties to put a stop to this. For it affects not only the proper protection of the supply, but also the upkeep of the reservoir which would be ruined if needlessly filled with outlets.

Another financial scheme of the watermen, which they call "puncturing," must also be abolished. There are long separate stretches all over the city through which the pipes pass hidden under the pavement. I found out that these pipes were being tapped everywhere by the "puncturers," from which water was supplied by private pipe to all the business premises in the area, with the result that only a meagre amount reached the public utilities. I can estimate the volume of water stolen in this way from the amount of lead piping which was removed when these branch pipes were dug up.

Source 11 from Naphtali Lewis and Meyer Reinhold, editors and translators, Roman Civilization *(New York: Columbia University Press, 1955), pp. 479–480. Reprinted with permission of Columbia University Press, 562 W. 113th St., New York, NY 10025, via Copyright Clearance Center, Inc.*

11. Proclamation of Emperor Theodosius, A.D. 438

It is our will that the landholders over whose lands the courses of aqueducts pass shall be exempt from extraordinary burdens, so that by their work the aqueducts may be cleansed when they are choked with dirt. The said landholders shall not be subject to any other burden of a superindiction,[3] lest they be occupied in other matters and not be present to clean the aqueducts. If they neglect this duty, they shall be punished by the forfeiture of their landholdings; for the fisc[4] will take possession of the landed estate of any man whose negligence contributes to the damage of the aqueducts. Furthermore, persons through whose landed estates the aqueducts pass should know that they may have trees to the right and left at a distance of fifteen feet from the aqueducts, and your[5] office shall see to it that these trees are cut out if they grow too luxuriantly at any time, so that their roots may not injure the structure of the aqueduct.

QUESTIONS TO CONSIDER

Now that you have looked at both visual and written evidence, you will need to put together the information you have gathered from each type of source to achieve a more complete picture. Because sources for the earliest period of human development are so scanty, we need to use every shred of information available and use it somewhat creatively, making speculations where no specific evidence exists.

Take all the evidence about technical problems first. Keeping in mind that the ancient world had no power equipment and no tools more elaborate than axes, hammers, saws, and drills (the Romans also had planes and chisels), what would you judge to be the most difficult purely technical problem involved in constructing water systems? In keeping them operating? The four diagrams of the water-raising machines are arranged in chronological order of their development: The shaduf may be as old as 2500 B.C., and the other three did not appear until 1,000 years later. Looking at your chart on the advantages and disadvantages of each machine, in what ways did the later machines improve on the shaduf? What additional problems might these improvements have produced? What types of technological experimentation did the need for water encourage?

Technological advance is not always an unmitigated blessing. For example, water standing in irrigation ditches can become brackish, providing a good breeding ground for mosquitoes and other carriers of disease. Cities that depend on irrigation suffer food shortages and famine when ditches cannot be kept clear or when river levels are low. The diversion of large quantities of water for irrigation makes rivers much smaller when they finally reach their deltas, which means

3. That is, any special taxes.

4. **fisc:** the imperial treasury.

5. This proclamation was addressed to the administrator of the water supply, the same office that Frontinus held earlier.

that the deltas become increasingly salty from seawater and unable to support the types of plant and animal life they originally fostered. Judging by the aerial photograph and the LAND-SAT map, would you expect any of these problems in ancient Italy or Mesopotamia? Do you find evidence in the written sources for problems in the later Roman water systems that were caused by technical advances? Do the written sources offer suggestions for solving these problems?

Now consider what you have learned about the economic issues associated with water systems. You have doubtless noticed that tremendous numbers of people were needed to construct irrigation ditches and aqueducts. Some of the written sources, such as the extract from Suetonius, provide exact figures. The size and complexity of the systems in the other sources also imply a substantial work force, given the lack of elaborate equipment. The rulers of Mesopotamia and Rome saw the need for a large labor force as no problem; it was, rather, a solution to the greater problem of unemployment. According to a story told about the Roman emperor Vespasian, when he was offered a labor-saving machine, he refused to allow its use because that would put people out of work and lead to social problems in Rome. We might regard this concern for full employment as a positive social attitude, but it should also tell you something about the value of labor in ancient societies. What would you expect wages to be for construction workers? What class of people would you expect to find working on these water systems?

Large numbers of workers were needed not only to build but also to maintain irrigation systems and to operate water-lifting machines. What does this fact tell you about the value of labor? What would happen with a sudden drop in the population, such as that caused by a famine or epidemic? How would a loss of workers affect the available food supply?

The sources also reveal information about political factors associated with water systems. What does the construction of these systems indicate about the power of rulers to coerce or hire labor? How do rulers control the building and maintenance of machines and ditches? How might their control affect the power and independence of local communities or of individual families? What does this tell you about the role of water in expanding centralized political power?

Finally, the sources provide evidence of alterations in the law made necessary by the search for water. Previously unrestricted and unregulated actions now came under the control of public authorities, which meant that the number of enforcement agents and courts had to increase. What would this do to taxation levels? In what ways would political concerns shape the regulations?

Political issues affect not only the types of laws to be passed, but also the stringency or selectivity with which those laws are enforced. We have very little information about how rigidly law codes were implemented in ancient societies, for few legal documents have survived; law codes were frequently recopied and reissued, but the outcome of individual cases was not. It is therefore dangerous to assume that the prescribed penalties were actually levied or that the law was regularly obeyed. (Think for a minute the mistake a person 2,000 years from now would make in describing traffic patterns in twentieth-century America if he or she assumed that the posted speed limit described the actual speed at which traffic moved!) Looking again at the law codes of Hammurabi and Theodosius, would you expect the penalties to be carried out, or do they appear to serve more as a strong warning? How would the penalties differ in their effects on poor and rich people?

You are now ready to answer the question posed at the beginning of the chapter. How did the need for a steady supply of water affect the development of civilization in the West?

EPILOGUE

The irrigation and water supply systems of the ancient world not only required huge amounts of labor, but also made necessary a strong central authority to coerce or hire that labor and to enforce laws to keep the channels flowing. At first, each Mesopotamian city managed its own irrigation system, but the wealthy and advanced cities were attractive targets for foreign conquerors. The political history of ancient Mesopotamia was one of wave after wave of conquerors coming down from the north—the Akkadians, Babylonians, Assyrians, Persians, Greeks, and finally the Romans. Most of these conquerors realized the importance of irrigation and ordered the conquered residents to maintain or expand their systems. When the Muslims invaded the region in the seventh century, they also learned Mesopotamian techniques and spread these westward into North Africa and Spain, where Roman irrigation systems had in many places fallen apart.

Irrigation could also be overdone, however, and during periods of political centralization many areas were overirrigated, which led to salinization, making the land useless for farming. This, combined with the rivers of Mesopotamia changing their courses, meant that many cities could not survive. Centuries of irrigation combined with too little fertilization made even land that was not salinized less and less productive.

The benefits and problems produced by irrigation are not limited to the ancient world, however; they can be seen in many modern societies. One of the best modern examples comes from the same part of the world we have been studying in this chapter. Throughout the twentieth century, Egypt has expanded its irrigation system watered by the Nile with a series of dams, culminating in the Aswan High Dam; this dam, begun in 1960, was designed to provide hydroelectric power and limit the free flow of water at the height of the flood season. The enormous reservoir formed by the dam can also be tapped at low-water times to allow for perennial irrigation. The Aswan Dam serves all its intended purposes very well, but it has also created some unexpected problems. The river's regular flooding had brought new fertile soil to the Nile Valley and carried away the salts that resulted from evaporation. Once the dam stopped the flooding, Egyptian fields needed artificial fertilizer to remain productive, a commodity many farmers could not afford. The soil of the Nile Valley has a high clay content, rendering drainage difficult, and a steady supply of water makes many fields waterlogged and unusable. The large reservoir created by the dam sits in the middle of the Sahara, allowing a tremendous amount of evaporation and significantly decreasing the total flow of water in the Nile; it has also put many acres of farmland under water and forced the relocation of tens of thousands of people. The drought in North Africa has further lowered the Nile's level, decreasing the amount of hydroelectric power the river can produce. Ending the flooding also allowed snails carrying bilharzia or schistosomiasis—an intestinal parasite that makes people very weak—to proliferate in the fields and irrigation ditches. The high water table resulting from the dam is destroying many ancient monuments, such as the temples of Luxor and Karnak, that have survived for millennia. Thus, like the lead pipes that brought water to the Romans, the Aswan High Dam has proved a mixed blessing in modern Egypt.

As you reflect on what you have discovered in this chapter, you may want to think about problems associated with the distribution of water in your own region. How does the need for water affect the political and economic structures of your city or state? What technological solutions has your region devised, and how have these worked?

CHAPTER TWO

THE IDEAL AND THE REALITY

OF CLASSICAL ATHENS

THE PROBLEM

Athens during the fifth century B.C. is often identified as one of the main sources of Western values and standards. Later Europeans and Americans regarded the Athenians as the originators of democracy, drama, representational or realistic art, history, philosophy, and science. At different times over the past 2,500 years they have attempted to imitate this "Golden Age" of classical Athens in everything from buildings to literature. Many U.S. state capitols and government buildings are modeled on the Parthenon or other temples, complete with statuary of former governers in the manner of Greek gods. We still divide drama into tragedies and comedies in the same way the Athenians did, though now we sometimes use a prerecorded laugh track instead of grinning masks to indicate that a given work is a comedy. During some historical periods, such as the Renaissance, thinkers and writers made conscious attempts to return to classical ideals in all areas of life, combing the works of Athenian authors for previously overlooked material in their quest to draw guidance and learn everything possible from this unique flowering of culture.

Even more than as a model for literature and art, classical Athens has continued to serve as a relevant source for answers to basic questions about human existence. Though all cultures have sought to identify the ultimate aim and meaning of human life, the ancient Greeks, especially the Athenians, were the first in the West to provide answers that were not expressed in religious or mythological terms. Their thoughts on these matters grew out of speculations on the nature of the universe made by earlier Greeks, particularly Thales and his followers Anaximander and Heraclitus. These thinkers, living in the seventh and sixth centuries B.C., theorized about how the universe had been formed and what it was made of by means of rational explanations drawn from observation rather than from myth or religious tradition. Because they believed the natural universe could be explained in other than supernatural terms, they are often termed the first true scientists or first philosophers.

During the fifth century B.C., several Athenian thinkers turned their attention from the world around them to the human beings living in that world. They used this new method of philosophical inquiry to question the workings of the human mind and the societies humans create. They asked such questions as, How do we learn things? What should we try to learn? How do we know what is right or wrong, good or bad? If we can know what is good, how can we create things that are good? What kind of government is best? This type of questioning is perhaps most often associated with Socrates (469–399 B.C.) and his pupil Plato (427?–347 B.C.), who are generally called the founders of Western philosophy. Thales and his followers are thus known as the pre-Socratics; and a twentieth-century philosopher, Alfred North Whitehead, noted—only half jokingly—that "the European philosophical tradition . . . consists of a series of footnotes to Plato."

Both Socrates and Plato believed that goodness is related to knowledge and that excellence could be learned. For Plato especially, true knowledge was gained not by observation of the world but by contemplation of what an ideal world would be like. In their view, to understand goodness, justice, or beauty, it is necessary to think about what pure and ultimate goodness, justice, or beauty means. Plato thus introduced into Western thought a strong strain of *idealism* and was the first to write works on what an ideal society or set of laws would look like. He also described the education required to train citizens for governing this ideal state and the social and economic structure necessary to keep them at their posts. Though he probably recognized that these standards could never be achieved, he believed that the creation of ideals was an important component of the discipline of philosophy, a sentiment shared by many Western thinkers after him.

Plato's most brilliant pupil, Aristotle (384–322 B.C.), originally agreed with his teacher but then began to depart somewhat from idealism. Like the pre-Socratics, Aristotle was fascinated by the world around him, and many of his writings on scientific subjects reveal keen powers of observation. Even his treatises on standards of human behavior, such as those concerning ethics and politics, are based on close observation of Athenian society and not simply on speculation. Aristotle further intended that these works should not only describe ideal human behavior or political systems, but also provide suggestions about how to alter current practice to conform more closely to the ideal. Thus, although Aristotle was still to some degree an idealist, both the source and the recipient of his ideals was the real world.

In classical Athens, human nature was a subject contemplated not only by scientists and philosophers, but also by historians, such as Herodotus and Thucydides. They, too, searched for explanations about the natural order that did not involve the gods. For Herodotus and Thucydides, the Persian and Peloponnesian wars were caused by human failings, not by actions of vengeful gods such as those that Homer, following tradition, depicted in the *Iliad* as causing the Trojan War. Like Aristotle, they were interested in describing real events and finding explanations for them; like Plato, they were also interested in the possible as well as the actual. History, in their opinion, was the best arena for observing the true worth of various ideals to human society.

To the Athenians, war was the ultimate test of human ideals, morals, and values, but these could also be tested and observed on a much smaller scale in the way people conducted their everyday lives. Although for Plato the basis of an ideal government was the perfectly trained ruler or group of rulers, for Aristotle and other writers it was the perfectly managed household, which they regarded as a microcosm of society. Observing that the household was the smallest economic and political unit in Athenian society, Aristotle began his consideration of

the ideal governmental system with thoughts on how households should be run. Other writers on politics and economics followed suit, giving advice after observing households they regarded as particularly well managed.

Whereas Plato clearly indicated that he was describing an ideal, in the case of Aristotle and other Athenians, it is sometimes difficult to determine whether they were attempting to describe reality, what they wished were reality, or a pure ideal. Your task in this chapter will be to examine the relationship between ideal and reality in the writings of several Athenian philosophers, historians, and commentators and in architectural diagrams of Athenian buildings and houses. What ideals do the writers set forth for the individual, the household, and the government? How are these ideals reflected in more realistic descriptions of life in Athens and in the way Athenians built their houses and their city?

SOURCES AND METHOD

All the written sources we will use come from Athenians who lived during the classical period and are thus what we term original or primary sources. They differ greatly from modern primary sources, however, in that their textual accuracy cannot be checked. Before the development of the printing press, the only way to obtain a copy of a work was to write it out by hand yourself or hire someone to do so. Therefore, each manuscript copy might be slightly differ-

ent. Because the originals of the works of Aristotle or Thucydides have long since disappeared, what we have to work with are translations of composites based on as many of the oldest copies still in existence after 2,500 years that the translators could find.

The problem of accuracy is further complicated with some of the authors we will read because they did not actually write the works attributed to them. Many of Aristotle's works, for instance, are probably copies of his students' notes combined with (perhaps) some of his own. If you think of the way in which you record your own instructors' remarks, you can see why we must be cautious about assuming that these secondhand works contain everything Aristotle taught exactly as he intended it. Socrates, in fact, wrote nothing at all; all his ideas and words come to us through his pupil Plato. Scholars have long debated how much of the written record represents Socrates and how much represents Plato, especially when we consider that Socrates generally spoke at social gatherings or informally while walking around Athens, when Plato was not taking notes. These problems do not mean that we should discount these sources, they simply mean that we should realize that they differ from the printed documents and tape-recorded speeches of later eras.

We will begin our investigation with what is probably the most famous description of classical Athens: a funeral speech delivered by Pericles. Pericles, one of the leaders of Athens when the Peloponnesian War opened, gave this speech in 430 B.C. in honor of those who had died during the first year of the war. It was recorded by Thucydides and, though there is some disagreement over who actually wrote it, reflects Pericles' opinions. Read the speech carefully. Is Pericles describing an ideal he hopes Athens will achieve or reality as he sees it? How does he depict Athenian democracy and the Athenian attitude toward wealth? How does he compare Athens with Sparta? How does Athens treat its neighbors? What role does Pericles see for Athenian women? Before going on to the next readings, jot down some words that you feel best describe Athens and the Atheni-

ans. Would you want to live in the Athens Pericles describes?

Source 2 comes from a later section of Thucydides' *Peloponnesian War,* and it describes Athenian actions in the sixteenth year of the war. As you read it, think about the virtues that Pericles ascribed to the Athenians. Are these virtues reflected in the debate with the Melians or in the actions against them? How do the Athenians justify their actions? After reading this selection, jot down a few more words that you think describe the Athenians. Would you now erase some entries from your first list?

Source 3 is taken from the first book of Aristotle's *The Politics.* In this selection, he describes the proper functioning of a household and the role of each person in it. As you read it, you will notice that Aristotle is concerned equally with the economic role of household members and their moral status. What qualities does he see as important in the ideal head of household? the ideal wife or child? the ideal slave? How does he justify the differences between household members? How do these qualities compare with those described by Pericles or exhibited by the Athenians in their contact with the Melians? Add a few more words to your list describing the Athenians.

The fourth selection, by an unknown author, presents another view of Athenian democracy and the Athenian empire. This passage was written about five years after the speech made by Pericles and about ten years before the Melian debate. How does this author view democracy and Athens's relations with its neighbors?

What words might he add to your list to describe his fellow Athenians? How do you think he would have responded had he been in the audience listening to Pericles' funeral speech?

The fifth selection is a discussion of household management cast in the form of a dialogue, from a treatise by Xenophon called *The Economist.* What does the main speaker, whose name is Ischomachus, see as the main roles of husband and wife? Would he have agreed with Aristotle's conclusions about the qualities necessary in an ideal husband and wife? What suggestions does he make for encouraging ideal behavior in wives and slaves? Does he appear to be describing an actual or an ideal marital relationship? What words would you now add to or subtract from your list?

The sixth selection is a very small part of *The Republic,* in which Plato sets out his views on the ideal government. Plato did not favor democracy; he advocated training a group of leaders, whom he called *guardians,* to work for the best interests of all. What qualities does Plato feel are most important in the guardians? What economic and family structures does he feel will help them maintain these qualities? How does his description of the ideal female guardian compare with Pericles' and Xenophon's descriptions of the ideal Athenian wife? Do the qualities he finds important in guardians match up with any of those on your list?

Once you have read all the selections carefully, go back to Pericles' speech and read it again. Do you still have the same opinion about whether he is describing ideal or reality? Which of the words describing Athens that were on your original list are left?

Now look at the two diagrams, which are based on archaeological discoveries. They are thus clear representations of physical reality in classical Greece, but they tell us something about ideals as well, for people construct the space they live in according to their ideas about how society should operate. The first diagram, Source 7, is the floor plan of a house from fifth-century B.C. Olynthus. Does the actual house correspond to the one described by Xenophon? How does the layout of the house reinforce the roles prescribed for the ideal husband and wife? The second diagram, the eighth selection, is a plan of the Athenian *agora,* the open square in the center of Athens that served as both the political and commercial center of the city. The west side of the agora was a line of government buildings, including the *bouleuterion,* where the council met. The agora was bordered by several *stoa,* roofed-over open colonnades in front of lines of shops and offices. Because the climate of Greece is mild a good part of the year, much business could take place outside or in one of the stoa. What qualities from your list does the openness of the agora encourage? As you can see from the diagram, the agora was bordered by buildings with religious, governmental, and commercial functions. What does the placement of these buildings indicate about how Athenians valued the different areas of their lives?

Sources 1 and 2 from Thucydides, History of the Peloponnesian War, *translated by Richard Crawley (New York: Modern Library, 1951), pp. 103–106; p. 109.*

1. Pericles' Funeral Speech,
430 B.C.

That part of our history which tells of the military achievements which gave us our several possessions, or of the ready valour with which either we or our fathers stemmed the tide of Hellenic or foreign aggression, is a theme too familiar to my hearers for me to dilate on, and I shall therefore pass it by. But what was the road by which we reached our position, what the form of government under which our greatness grew, what the national habits out of which it sprang; these are questions which I may try to solve before I proceed to my panegyric upon these men: since I think this to be a subject upon which on the present occasion a speaker may properly dwell, and to which the whole assemblage, whether citizens or foreigners, may listen with advantage.

Our constitution does not copy the laws of neighbouring states; we are rather a pattern to others than imitators ourselves. Its administration favours the many instead of the few; this is why it is called a democracy. If we look to the laws, they afford equal justice to all in their private differences; if to social standing, advancement in public life falls to reputation for capacity, class considerations not being allowed to interfere with merit; nor again does poverty bar the way, if a man is able to serve the state, he is not hindered by the obscurity of his condition. The freedom which we enjoy in our government extends also to our ordinary life. There, far from exercising a jealous surveillance over each other, we do not feel called upon to be angry with our neighbour for doing what he likes, or even to indulge in those injurious looks which cannot fail to be offensive, although they inflict no positive penalty. But all this ease in our private relations does not make us lawless as citizens. Against this fear is our chief safeguard, teaching us to obey the magistrates and the laws, particularly such as regard the protection of the injured, whether they are actually on the statute book, or belong to that code which, although unwritten, yet cannot be broken without acknowledged disgrace.

Further, we provide plenty of means for the mind to refresh itself from business. We celebrate games and sacrifices all the year round, and the elegance of our private establishments forms a daily source of pleasure and helps to banish the spleen; while the magnitude of our city draws the produce of the world into our harbour, so that to the Athenian the fruits of other countries are as familiar a luxury as those of his own.

If we turn to our military policy, there also we differ from our antagonists. We throw open our city to the world, and never by alien acts exclude foreigners from any opportunity of learning or observing, although the eyes of an enemy may occasionally profit by our liberality; trusting less in system and policy than to the native spirit of our citizens; while in education, where our rivals from their very cradles by a painful discipline seek after manliness, at Athens we live exactly as we please, and yet are just as ready to encounter every legitimate danger. In proof of this it may be noticed that the Lacedæmonians[1] do not invade our country alone, but bring with them all their confederates; while we Athenians advance unsupported into the territory of a neighbour, and fighting upon a foreign soil usually vanquish with ease men who are defending their homes. Our united force was never yet encountered by any enemy, because we have at once to attend to our marine and to despatch our citizens by land upon a hundred different services; so that, wherever they engage with some such fraction of our strength, a success against a detachment is magnified into a victory over the nation, and a defeat into a reverse suffered at the hands of our entire people. And yet if with habits not of labour but of ease, and courage not of art but of nature, we are still willing to encounter danger, we have the double advantage of escaping the experience of hardships in anticipation and of facing them in the hour of need as fearlessly as those who are never free from them.

Nor are these the only points in which our city is worthy of admiration. We cultivate refinement without extravagance and knowledge without effeminacy; wealth we employ more for use than for show, and place the real disgrace of poverty not in owning to the fact but in declining the struggle against it. Our public men have, besides politics, their private affairs to attend to, and our ordinary citizens, though occupied with the pursuits of industry, are still fair judges of public matters; for, unlike any other nation, regarding him who takes no part in these duties not as unambitious but as useless, we Athenians are able to judge at all events if we cannot originate, and instead of looking on discussion as a stumbling-block in the way of action, we think it an indispensable preliminary to any wise action at all. Again, in our enterprises we present the singular spectacle of daring and deliberation, each carried to its highest point, and both united in the same persons; although usually decision is the fruit of ignorance, hesitation of reflexion. But the palm of courage will surely be adjudged most justly to those, who best know the difference between hardship and pleasure and yet are never tempted to shrink from danger. In generosity we are equally singular, acquiring our friends by conferring not by receiving favours. Yet, of course, the doer of the favour is the firmer friend of the two, in order by continued kindness to keep the recipient in his debt; while the debtor feels less keenly from the very consciousness that the return he makes will be a payment, not a free gift. And it is only the Athenians who,

---

1. **Lacedæmonians:** Spartans.

fearless of consequences, confer their benefits not from calculations of expediency, but in the confidence of liberality.

In short, I say that as a city we are the school of Hellas; while I doubt if the world can produce a man, who where he has only himself to depend upon, is equal to so many emergencies, and graced by so happy a versatility as the Athenian. And that this is no mere boast thrown out for the occasion, but plain matter of fact, the power of the state acquired by these habits proves. For Athens alone of her contemporaries is found when tested to be greater than her reputation, and alone gives no occasion to her assailants to blush at the antagonist by whom they have been worsted, or to her subjects to question her title by merit to rule. Rather, the admiration of the present and succeeding ages will be ours, since we have not left our power without witness, but have shown it by mighty proofs; and far from needing a Homer for our panegyrist, or other of his craft whose verses might charm for the moment only for the impression which they gave to melt at the touch of fact, we have forced every sea and land to be the highway of our daring, and everywhere, whether for evil or for good, have left imperishable monuments behind us. Such is the Athens for which these men, in the assertion of their resolve not to lose her, nobly fought and died; and well may every one of their survivors be ready to suffer in her cause. . . .

[I]f I must say anything on the subject of female excellence to those of you who will now be in widowhood, it will be all comprised in this brief exhortation. Great will be your glory in not falling short of your natural character; and greatest will be hers who is least talked of among the men whether for good or for bad.

My task is now finished. I have performed it to the best of my ability, and in words, at least, the requirements of the law are now satisfied. If deeds be in question, those who are here interred have received part of their honours already, and for the rest, their children will be brought up till manhood at the public expense: the state thus offers a valuable prize, as the garland of victory in this race of valour, for the reward both of those who have fallen and their survivors. And where the rewards for merit are greatest, there are found the best citizens.

And now that you have brought to a close your lamentations for your relatives, you may depart.

2. The Melian Debate, 415 B.C.

The Athenians also made an expedition against the isle of Melos with thirty ships of their own, six Chian, and two Lesbian vessels, sixteen hundred heavy infantry, three hundred archers, and twenty mounted archers from Athens, and about fifteen hundred heavy infantry from the allies and the islanders. The

Melians are a colony of Lacedæmon[2] that would not submit to the Athenians like the other islanders, and at first remained neutral and took no part in the struggle, but afterwards upon the Athenians using violence and plundering their territory, assumed an attitude of open hostility. Cleomedes, son of Lycomedes, and Tisias, son of Tisimachus, the generals, encamping in their territory with the above armament, before doing any harm to their land, sent envoys to negotiate. These the Melians did not bring before the people, but bade them state the object of their mission to the magistrates and the few; upon which the Athenian envoys spoke as follows: . . .

ATHENIANS: We will now proceed to show you that we are come here in the interest of our empire, and that we shall say what we are now going to say, for the preservation of your country; as we would fain exercise that empire over you without trouble, and see you preserved for the good of us both.

MELIANS: And how, pray, could it turn out as good for us to serve as for you to rule?

ATHENIANS: Because you would have the advantage of submitting before suffering the worst, and we should gain by not destroying you.

MELIANS: So that you would not consent to our being neutral, friends instead of enemies, but allies of neither side.

ATHENIANS: No; for your hostility cannot so much hurt us as your friendship will be an argument to our subjects of our weakness, and your enmity of our power.

MELIANS: Is that your subjects' idea of equity, to put those who have nothing to do with you in the same category with peoples that are most of them your own colonists, and some conquered rebels?

ATHENIANS: As far as right goes they think one has as much of it as the other, and if any maintain their independence it is because they are strong, and that if we do not molest them it is because we are afraid; so that besides extending our empire we should gain in security by your subjection; the fact that you are islanders and weaker than others rendering it all the more important that you should not succeed in baffling the masters of the sea.

MELIANS: But do you consider that there is no security in the policy which we indicate? For here again if you debar us from talking about justice and invite us to obey your interest, we also must explain ours, and try to persuade you, if the two happen to coincide. How can you avoid making enemies of all existing neutrals who shall look at our case and conclude from it that one day or another you will attack them? And what is this but to make greater the enemies that you have already, and to force others to become so who would otherwise have never thought of it?

ATHENIANS: Why, the fact is that continentals generally give us but little alarm; the liberty which they enjoy will long prevent their taking precautions against us; it is rather islanders like yourselves, outside our empire, and sub-

2. **Lacedæmon:** Sparta.

jects smarting under the yoke, who would be the most likely to take a rash step and lead themselves and us into obvious danger.

MELIANS: Well then, if you risk so much to retain your empire, and your subjects to get rid of it, it were surely great baseness and cowardice in us who are still free not to try everything that can be tried, before submitting to your yoke.

ATHENIANS: Not if you are well advised, the contest not being an equal one, with honour as the prize and shame as the penalty, but a question of self-preservation and of not resisting those who are far stronger than you are. . . .

Of the gods we believe, and of men we know, that by a necessary law of their nature they rule wherever they can. And it is not as if we were the first to make this law, or to act upon it when made: we found it existing before us, and shall leave it to exist for ever after us; all we do is to make use of it, knowing that you and everybody else, having the same power as we have, would do the same as we do. . . . You will surely not be caught by that idea of disgrace, which in dangers that are disgraceful, and at the same time too plain to be mistaken, proves so fatal to mankind; since in too many cases the very men that have their eyes perfectly open to what they are rushing into, let the thing called disgrace, by the mere influence of a seductive name, lead them on to a point at which they become so enslaved by the phrase as in fact to fall wilfully into hopeless disaster, and incur disgrace more disgraceful as the companion of error, than when it comes as the result of misfortune. This, if you are well advised, you will guard against; and you will not think it dishonourable to submit to the greatest city in Hellas, when it makes you the moderate offer of becoming its tributary ally, without ceasing to enjoy the country that belongs to you; nor when you have the choice given you between war and security, will you be so blinded as to choose the worse. And it is certain that those who do not yield to their equals, who keep terms with their superiors, and are moderate towards their inferiors, on the whole succeed best. Think over the matter, therefore, after our withdrawal, and reflect once and again that it is for your country that you are consulting, that you have not more than one, and that upon this one deliberation depends its prosperity or ruin.

The Athenians now withdrew from the conference; and the Melians, left to themselves, came to a decision corresponding with what they had maintained in the discussion, and answered, 'Our resolution, Athenians, is the same as it was at first. We will not in a moment deprive of freedom a city that has been inhabited these seven hundred years; but we put our trust in the fortune by which the gods have preserved it until now, and in the help of men, that is, of the Lacedæmonians; and so we will try and save ourselves. Meanwhile we invite you to allow us to be friends to you and foes to neither party, and to retire from our country after making such a treaty as shall seem fit to us both. . . .

The Athenian envoys now returned to the army; and the Melians showing no signs of yielding, the generals at once betook themselves to hostilities, and drew a line of circumvallation[3] round the Melians, dividing the work among the different states. Subsequently the Athenians returned with most of their army, leaving behind them a certain number of their own citizens and of the allies to keep guard by land and sea. The force thus left stayed on and besieged the place. . . .

Meanwhile the Melians attacked by night and took the part of the Athenian lines over against the market, and killed some of the men, and brought in corn and all else that they could find useful to them, and so returned and kept quiet, while the Athenians took measures to keep better guard in future.

Summer was now over. The next winter . . . the Melians again took another part of the Athenian lines which were but feebly garrisoned. Reinforcements afterwards arriving from Athens in consequence, under the command of Philocrates, son of Demeas, the siege was now pressed vigorously; and some treachery taking place inside, the Melians surrendered at discretion to the Athenians, who put to death all the grown men whom they took, and sold the women and children for slaves, and subsequently sent out five hundred colonists and inhabited the place themselves.

Source 3 from Aristotle, The Politics, *translated by T. A. Sinclair and revised by Trevor J. Saunders (Baltimore: Penguin, 1962, 1981), pp. 26–27, 31, 34, 50–53. Copyright © the estate of T. A. Sinclair, 1962; revised material copyright © Trevor J. Saunders, 1981. Reprinted with permission.*

3. From Aristotle, *The Politics*

We shall, I think, in this as in other subjects, get the best view of the matter if we look at the natural growth of things from the beginning. . . .

It was out of the association formed by men with these two, women and slaves, that the first household was formed; and the poet Hesiod was right when he wrote, "Get first a house and a wife and an ox to draw the plough." (The ox is the poor man's slave.) This association of persons, established according to the law of nature and continuing day after day, is the household. . . .

Now property is part of a household and the acquisition of property part of the economics of a household; for neither life itself nor the good life is possible without a certain minimum standard of wealth. Again, for any given craft the existence of the proper tools will be essential for the performance of its task. Tools may be animate as well as inanimate; a ship's captain uses a lifeless rudder, but a living man for watch; for the worker in a craft is, from the point of view of the craft, one of its tools. So any piece of property can be regarded as a tool enabling a man to live; and his property is an assemblage of such tools, including his slaves; and a slave, being a living creature like any other servant, is a tool worth many tools. . . .

3. **circumvallation:** ramparts and walls.

The "slave by nature" then is he that can and therefore does belong to another, and he that participates in the reasoning faculty so far as to understand but not so as to possess it. For the other animals serve their owner not by exercise of reason but passively. The use, too, of slaves hardly differs at all from that of domestic animals; from both we derive that which is essential for our bodily needs. . . . It is clear then that in household management the people are of greater importance than the material property, and their quality of more account than that of the goods that make up their wealth, and also that free men are of more account than slaves. About slaves the first question to be asked is whether in addition to their value as tools and servants there is some other quality or virtue, superior to these, that belongs to slaves. Can they possess self-respect, courage, justice, and virtues of that kind, or have they in fact nothing but the serviceable quality of their persons?

The question may be answered in either of two ways, but both present a difficulty. If we say that slaves have these virtues, how then will they differ from free men? If we say that they have not, the position is anomalous, since they are human beings and capable of reason. Roughly the same question can be put in relation to wife and child: Have not these also virtues? Ought not a woman to be self-respecting, brave, and just? Is not a child sometimes naughty, sometimes good? . . .

This mention of virtue leads us straightaway to a consideration of the soul; for it is here that the natural ruler and the natural subject, whose virtue we regard as different, are to be found. In the soul the difference between ruler and ruled is that between the rational and the nonrational. It is therefore clear that in other connexions also there will be natural differences. And so generally in cases of ruler and ruled; the differences will be natural but they need not be the same. For rule of free over slave, male over female, man over boy, are all natural, but they are also different, because, while parts of the soul are present in each case, the distribution is different. Thus the deliberative faculty in the soul is not present at all in a slave; in a female it is inoperative, in a child undeveloped. We must therefore take it that the same conditions prevail also in regard to the ethical virtues, namely that all must participate in them but not all to the same extent, but only as may be required by each for his proper function. The ruler then must have ethical virtue in its entirety; for his task is simply that of chief maker and reason is chief maker. And the other members must have what amount is appropriate to each. So it is evident that each of the classes spoken of must have ethical virtue. It is also clear that there is some variation in the ethical virtues; self-respect is not the same in a man as in a woman, nor justice, nor courage either, as Socrates thought; the one is courage of a ruler, the other courage of a servant, and likewise with the other virtues.

If we look at the matter in greater detail it will become clearer. For those who talk in generalities and say that virtue is "a good condition of the soul," or that it is "right conduct" or the like, delude themselves. Better than those who look for general definitions are those who, like Gorgias, enumerate the different virtues. So the poet Sophocles singles out "silence" as "bringing credit to a woman," but that is not so for a man. This method of assessing virtue according to function is one that we should always follow. Take the child: he is not yet fully developed and his function is to grow up, so we cannot speak of his virtue as belonging absolutely to him, but only in relation to the progress of his development and to whoever is in charge of him. So too with slave and master; we laid it down that a slave's function is to perform menial tasks; so the amount of virtue required will not be very great, only enough to ensure that he does not neglect his work through loose living or mere fecklessness.

Source 4 from B. K. Workman, editor and translator, They Saw It Happen in Classical Times *(New York: Barnes & Noble, 1964), pp. 32–34. Reprinted by permission of Littlefield, Adams & Company and Basil Blackwell, Publishers.*

4. An Unknown Author's View of Athenian Democracy

Insolent conduct of slaves and resident aliens is everywhere rife in Athens. You cannot strike a slave there, and he will not get out of your way in the street. There is good reason for this being the local custom. If the law allowed a free-born citizen to strike a slave, an alien, or a freedman, then you would often strike an Athenian citizen in the mistaken impression that he was a slave. For the common people dress as poorly as slaves or aliens and their general appearance is no better. . . .

The common people take no supervisory interest in athletic or aesthetic shows, feeling that it is not right for them, since they know that they have not the ability to become expert at them. When it is necessary to provide men to put on stageshows or games or to finance and build triremes,[4] they know that impresarios come from the rich, the actors and chorus from the people. In the same way, organizers and ship-masters are the rich, while the common people take a subordinate part in the games and act as oarsmen for the triremes. But they do at least think it right to receive pay for singing or running or dancing or rowing in the fleet, to level up the incomes of rich and poor. The same holds good for the law courts as well; they are more interested in what profit they can make than in the true ends of justice. . . .

Of the mainland cities in the Athenian Empire, the large ones are governed by fear, the small ones by want. For all states must import and export, and this they cannot do unless they remain subject to the mistress of the seas.

4. **trireme:** standard Greek warship, about 120 feet long and rowed by 150 to 175 men; a ram on the bow was the trireme's main weapon.

Source 5 from Julia O'Faolain and Lauro Martines, editors, Not in God's Image: Women in History from the Greeks to the Victorians *(New York: Harper & Row, 1973), pp. 20–22. Adapted from several translations. Copyright © 1973 by Julia O'Faolain and Lauro Martines. Reprinted with permission of HarperCollins Publishers, Inc.*

5. From Xenophon, *The Economist*

"Here's another thing I'd like to ask you," said I. "Did you train your wife yourself or did she already know how to run a house when you got her from her father and mother?"

"What could she have known, Socrates," said he, "when I took her from her family? She wasn't yet fifteen. Until then she had been under careful supervision and meant to see, hear, and ask as little as possible. Don't you think it was already a lot that she should have known how to make a cloak of the wool she was given and how to dole out spinning to the servants? She had been taught to moderate her appetites, which, to my mind, is basic for both men's and women's education."

"So, apart from that," I asked, "it was you, Ischomachus, who had to train and teach her her household duties?"

"Yes," said Ischomachus, "but not before sacrificing to the gods. . . . And she solemnly swore before heaven that she would behave as I wanted, and it was clear that she would neglect none of my lessons."

"Tell me what you taught her first. . . ."

"Well, Socrates, as soon as I had tamed her and she was relaxed enough to talk, I asked her the following question: 'Tell me, my dear,' said I, 'do you understand why I married you and why your parents gave you to me? You know as well as I do that neither of us would have had trouble finding someone else to share our beds. But, after thinking about it carefully, it was you I chose and me your parents chose as the best partners we could find for our home and our children. Now, if God sends us children, we shall think about how best to raise them, for we share an interest in securing the best allies and support for our old age. For the moment we only share our home. . . .' "

"My wife answered, 'But how can I help? What am I capable of doing? It is on you that everything depends. My duty, my mother said, is to be well behaved.' "

" 'Oh, by Zeus,' said I, 'my father said the same to me. But the best behavior in a man and woman is that which will keep up their property and increase it as far as may be done by honest and legal means.' "

" 'And do you see some way,' asked my wife, 'in which I can help in this?' "

" '. . . It seems to me that God adapted women's nature to indoor and man's to outdoor work. . . . As Nature has entrusted woman with guarding the household supplies, and a timid nature is no disadvantage in such a job, it has endowed woman with more fear than man. . . . It is more proper for a woman to stay in the house than out of doors and less so for a man to be indoors instead of out. If anyone goes against the nature given him by God and leaves his appointed post . . . he will be punished. . . . You must stay indoors and send out the servants whose work is outside and supervise those who work indoors, receive what is brought in, give out what is to be spent, plan ahead what should be stored and ensure that provisions for a year are not used up in a month. When the wool is brought in, you must see to it that clothes are made from it for whoever needs them and see to it that the corn is still edible. . . . Many of your duties will give you pleasure: for instance, if you teach spinning and weaving to a slave who did not know how to do this when you got her, you double her usefulness to yourself, or if you make a good housekeeper of one who didn't know how to do anything. . . . ' Then I took her around the family living rooms, which are pleasantly decorated, cool in summer and warm in winter. I pointed out how the whole house faces south so as to enjoy the winter sun. . . . I showed her the women's quarters which are separated from the men's by a bolted door to prevent anything being improperly removed and also to ensure that the slaves should not have children without our permission. For good slaves are usually even more devoted once they have a family; but good-for-nothings, once they begin to cohabit, have extra chances to get up to mischief."

Source 6 from B. Jowett, translator, The Dialogues of Plato, *revised edition, vol. 3 (Oxford: Oxford University Press, 1895, revised 1924), pp. 58, 100–101, 103, 106, 140–142, 147–148, 151, 159.*

6. From Plato, *The Republic*

Is not the love of learning the love of wisdom, which is philosophy?

They are the same, he replied.

And may we not say confidently of man also, that he who is likely to be gentle to his friends and acquaintances, must by nature be a lover of wisdom and knowledge?

That we may safely affirm.

Then he who is to be a really good and noble guardian of the State will require to unite in himself philosophy and spirit and swiftness and strength?

Undoubtedly.

Then we have found the desired natures; and now that we have found them, how are they to be reared and educated? Is not this an enquiry which may be expected to throw light on the greater enquiry which is our final end—How do justice and injustice grow up in States?

Adeimantus thought that the enquiry would be of great service to us. . . .

Come then, and let us pass a leisure hour in storytelling, and our story shall be the education of our heroes.

By all means.

And what shall be their education? Can we find a better than the traditional sort?—and this has two divisions, gymnastic for the body, and music[5] for the soul.

True. . . .

Very good, I said; then what is the next question? Must we not ask who are to be rulers and who subjects?

Certainly.

There can be no doubt that the elder must rule the younger.

Clearly.

And that the best of these must rule.

That is also clear.

Now, are not the best husbandmen those who are most devoted to husbandry?

Yes.

And as we are to have the best of guardians for our city, must they not be those who have most the character of guardians?

Yes. . . .

Then there must be a selection. Let us note among the guardians those who in their whole life show the greatest eagerness to do what is for the good of their country, and the greatest repugnance to do what is against her interests.

Those are the right men.

And they will have to be watched at every age, in order that we may see whether they preserve their resolution, and never, under the influence either of force or enchantment, forget or cast off their sense of duty to the State. . . . And he who at every age, as boy and youth and in mature life, has come out of the trial victorious and pure, shall be appointed a ruler and guardian of the State; he shall be honoured in life and death, and shall receive sepulture[6] and other memorials of honour, the greatest that we have to give. But him who fails, we must reject. I am inclined to think that this is the sort of way in which our rulers and guardians should be chosen and appointed. I speak generally, and not with any pretension to exactness.

And, speaking generally, I agree with you, he said. . . .

Then let us consider what will be their way of life, if they are to realize our idea of them. In the first place, none of them should have any property of his own beyond what is absolutely necessary; neither should they have a private house or store closed against any one who has a mind to enter; their provisions should be only such as are required by trained warriors, who are men of temperance and courage; they should agree to receive from the citizens a fixed rate of pay, enough to meet the expenses of the year and no more; and

5. By "music," the Athenians meant all that was sacred to the **muses**, the patron goddesses of the arts and sciences.

6. **sepulture:** a special burial ceremony.

they will go to mess and live together like soldiers in a camp. Gold and silver we will tell them that they have from God; the diviner metal is within them, and they have therefore no need of the dross which is current among men, and ought not to pollute the divine by any such earthly admixture; for that commoner metal has been the source of many unholy deeds, but their own is undefiled. And they alone of all the citizens may not touch or handle silver or gold, or be under the same roof with them, or wear them, or drink from them. And this will be their salvation, and they will be the saviours of the State. But should they ever acquire homes or lands or moneys of their own, they will become housekeepers and husbandmen instead of guardians, enemies and tyrants instead of allies of the other citizens; hating and being hated, plotting and being plotted against, they will pass their whole life in much greater terror of internal than of external enemies, and the hour of ruin, both to themselves and to the rest of the State, will be at hand. For all which reasons may we not say that thus shall our State be ordered, and that these shall be the regulations appointed by us for our guardians concerning their houses and all other matters?

Yes, said Glaucon. . . .

The part of the men has been played out, and now properly enough comes the turn of the women. Of them I will proceed to speak, and the more readily since I am invited by you.

For men born and educated like our citizens, the only way, in my opinion, of arriving at a right conclusion about the possession and use of women and children is to follow the path on which we originally started, when we said that the men were to be the guardians and watchdogs of the herd.

True.

Let us further suppose the birth and education of our women to be subject to similar or nearly similar regulations; then we shall see whether the result accords with our design.

What do you mean?

What I mean may be put into the form of a question, I said: Are dogs divided into hes and shes, or do they both share equally in hunting and in keeping watch and in the other duties of dogs? or do we entrust to the males the entire and exclusive care of the flocks, while we leave the females at home, under the idea that the bearing and suckling their puppies is labour enough for them?

No, he said, they share alike; the only difference between them is that the males are stronger and the females weaker.

But can you use different animals for the same purpose, unless they are bred and fed in the same way?

You cannot.

Then, if women are to have the same duties as men, they must have the same nurture and education?

Yes. . . .

My friend, I said, there is no special faculty of administration in a state which a woman has because she is a woman, or which a man has by virtue of his sex, but the gifts of nature are alike diffused in both; all the pursuits of men are the pursuits of women also, but in all of them a woman is inferior to a man.

Very true.

Then are we to impose all our enactments on men and none of them on women?

That will never do.

One woman has a gift of healing, another not; one is a musician, and another has no music in her nature?

Very true.

And one woman has a turn for gymnastic and military exercises, and another is unwarlike and hates gymnastics?

Certainly.

And one woman is a philosopher, and another is an enemy of philosophy; one has spirit, and another is without spirit?

That is also true.

Then one woman will have the temper of a guardian, and another not. Was not the selection of the male guardians determined by differences of this sort?

Yes.

Men and women alike possess the qualities which make a guardian; they differ only in their comparative strength or weakness.

Obviously.

And those women who have such qualities are to be selected as the companions and colleagues of men who have similar qualities and whom they resemble in capacity and in character?

Very true. . . .

The law, I said, which is the sequel of this and of all that has preceded, is to the following effect—"that the wives of our guardians are to be common, and their children are to be common, and no parent is to know his own child, nor any child his parent."

Yes, he said, that is a much greater wave than the other; and the possibility as well as the utility of such a law are far more questionable. . . .

Both the community of property and the community of families, as I am saying, tend to make them more truly guardians; they will not tear the city in pieces by differing about "mine" and "not mine"; each man dragging any acquisition which he has made into a separate house of his own, where he has a separate wife and children and private pleasures and pains; but all will be affected as far as may be by the same pleasures and pains because they are all of one opinion about what is near and dear to them, and therefore they all tend towards a common end.

Certainly, he replied.

Source 7 adapted from Orestis B. Doumanis and Paul Oliver, editors, Shelter in Greece *(Athens: Architecture in Greece Press, 1974), p. 25.*

7. Floor Plan of a House from Olynthus, 5th century B.C.

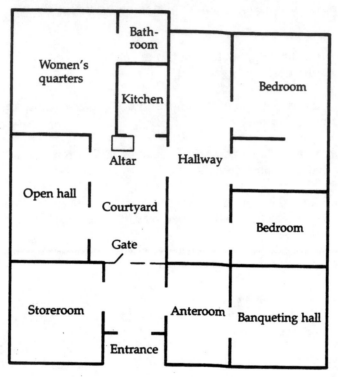

Source 8 adapted from A. W. Lawrence, Greek Architecture *(Baltimore: Penguin Books, 1957), p. 257.*

8. The Athenian Agora, 4th century B.C.

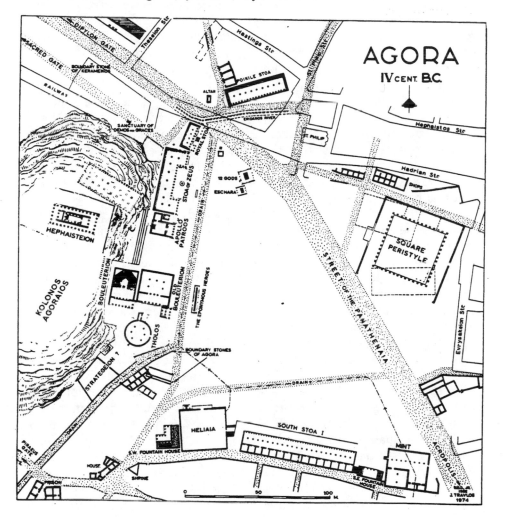

QUESTIONS TO CONSIDER

Before you start to think about the questions in this section, you may want to turn to your text to read (or reread) the section on Athens during the classical period. This can give you more background on the authors and on the political events that might have affected what they wrote.

Though some of the written selections in this chapter clearly describe ideals and others reality, still others blend realism and idealism, creating an idealized view of actual persons or situations. Which selections would you put in this last category? Why would these authors describe reality in an idealized manner? (To answer this question, you need to think about both the purpose of each selection and whether the author truly thought that what he was describing actually existed—in other words, whether this was a conscious or unconscious alteration of reality.)

Once you have labeled the written sources as ideals, reality, and idealizations of reality, go back to your list of the personal qualities of Athenians. Which qualities would you put in each of these three categories? Now that you know you are describing only an ideal or real characteristic, would you add any further qualities? The next step is to divide your list into categories of persons, for it is clear that most of the authors make great distinctions between male and female, adult and child, slave and free. Do all the authors agree on the qualities important in an ideal man, woman, or slave? Which authors have

opposing ideas? Why might this be so? Sometimes distinctions between categories are not clearly set out by the author; when Pericles, for instance, uses the words *person* and *people* in his funeral oration, one might think he was talking about all Athenians. Looking at your list divided into categories, of whom is Pericles speaking when he says "person" and "people"? Do any of the authors make distinctions between individuals of the same category based on such factors as wealth or education; for example, do they describe wealthy men differently from poor men, or set out different ideals for women who are interested in learning than for those who are not? If Athenians lived up to the ideals prescribed for them, what types of people would you expect to meet in the agora? What types of people would you not expect to meet?

Turning from the individual to social units, what qualities should the ideal Athenian household possess? How might real households work to emulate these ideals? Judging from information in the selections and in your text about Athenian marriage patterns, family life, and social life in general, did real Athenian households approach the ideal at all? How did their beliefs about the way households should be run affect the way Athenians designed their houses? How did the layout of a house work to make reality correspond with those ideals?

The qualities of governments as presented in the selections may also be classified as real, ideal, or idealized. Were any of the words you used to describe the Athenian government after first reading Pericles included in your final list? Does his idealized view of Athens come closer to the realistic view provided in the Melian debate or to the purely ideal view of Plato? After reading all the selections, would you put the quality "democracy" into the real or the ideal column for Athens? How would Athenians define democracy? How does the layout of the agora reflect this definition? Do all the authors agree that democracy is a desirable form of government? Judging from information in your text about politics in Athens in the fifth century, why would authors disagree on this matter? If you put democracy in the ideal column, what changes in existing conditions would have been necessary for it to become a reality?

The selections you have read offer varying opinions on a great many subjects, including the benefits of wealth and private property, the relationship between dominant and dependent states and between dominant and dependent individuals, the reasons for the differences between men and women, the role of naval power in foreign policy, and the causes of imperialism. All these issues have both ideal and real components, and you may want to think about them before you draw your final conclusions about classical Athens. How well did Athens live up to the ideals it set for itself? How did the different ideals held up for different categories of persons affect their participation in Athenian life?

EPILOGUE

We can find the ideals of the Athenians expressed not only in their philosophy, history, and architecture, as you have discovered here, but also in their drama, poetry, and sculpture. Indeed, most of the original sources we have from Athens are not realistic descriptions but either thoughts about ideals or idealizations of actual persons and episodes. That they are idealizations may be very clear to us as modern skeptical readers, but for a long time the statements in these sources were taken as literal truth. To give you an example, here is a quotation from Edith Hamilton, one of the

foremost historians of Greece, published in 1930:

> For a hundred years Athens was a city where the great spiritual forces that war in men's minds flowed together along in peace; law and freedom, truth and religion, beauty and goodness, the objective and the subjective—there was a truce to their eternal warfare, and the result was the balance and clarity, the harmony and completeness, that the word Greek has come to stand for.[7]

Given what you have just read, would you agree with her? Do you

7. Edith Hamilton, *The Greek Way* (New York: Norton, 1930), p. 206.

think everyone living in classical Athens would have agreed with her?

No matter how you have judged the relationship between ideal and reality in classical Athens, the ideals for the individual and state created there have significantly shaped the development of Western philosophy and social institutions. Roman philosophers closely studied Plato's *Republic*, and medieval philosophers were strongly influenced by Aristotle's *Politics*. Writers from the Renaissance to the present have invented ideal societies, "utopias" guided by wise leaders like Plato's guardians. Occasionally small groups of people have actually tried to set up working replicas of these ideal societies, frequently forbidding private property and the nuclear family as Plato did. Educational theorists have devised "perfect" school systems that, if not entirely successful when put into practice, have had their effect on real-life pedagogy. The Athenian ideal of

government by the people is reflected in the constitutions of modern democratic states, with the category "people" now including groups unthinkable to Pericles.

In terms of Athenian history, democracy was an extremely short-lived phenomenon. Widespread revolt broke out in the Athenian empire, and Sparta ultimately defeated Athens, bringing the Peloponnesian War to a close after twenty-seven years. This did not end warfare in Greece, however, as the city-states continued to battle among themselves. Finally, in 338 B.C., Greece was conquered by Philip of Macedon, and Athens became simply one small part of a much larger empire. From that point on, Athenian ideals of individual behavior would be emulated in Western culture, but democratic government would not again be attempted as an experiment in the real world for another 2,000 years.

CHAPTER THREE

THE ACHIEVEMENTS

OF AUGUSTUS

For many centuries, the seat of power in Rome was the senate, a body of men drawn from the most powerful and prominent Roman families that made all major political and military decisions. Under the leadership of the senate, Rome had gradually taken control of the entire Italian peninsula. It then conquered southern France and much of Spain, and, after defeating Carthage in the Punic Wars, occupied northern Africa. These territorial conquests altered the nature of power in Rome, however, because the armies that conquered and held the new territories pledged loyalty to their military leaders and not to the senate. During the first century before Christ, several of these semi-independent armies challenged the senate's power, and civil war erupted in many parts of the Roman territory. The city itself was plundered several times by rival legions, and trade and communications were frequently dis-

rupted. In 60 B.C., three army generals—Pompey, Crassus, and Julius Caesar—decided to form a political alliance, the triumvirate, leaving the senate intact but without much actual power.

All three of these generals were ambitious men who were unwilling to share power with anyone for very long. The senate was especially worried about Julius Caesar, who was gathering an increasingly larger army in Gaul (present-day France), and decided to put its trust in Pompey, whose base of power lay in Greece. (Crassus had meanwhile died in battle.) It ordered Caesar to disband his army and not to return to Rome, setting the Rubicon River near Ravenna in northern Italy as the line he must not cross. In 49 B.C., Caesar crossed the Rubicon (an expression we still use for an irrevocable decision), directly challenging the power of the senate and of Pompey. His armies quickly defeated those of the senate in Italy, and within a few months he held the entire Italian peninsula. From there Caesar turned his attention to Pompey's army, which his forces also defeated in 48 B.C., leaving him in control of all the Roman territory. Though he did not disband the senate, he did begin to shape the government to his liking, appointing officials and army officers and directly overseeing the administration of the provinces. He increased the size of the senate from 600 to 900 members by padding it with his followers, many of whom came from the provinces.

Caesar's meteoric and extralegal rise to power created great resentment among many Roman senators. Intensely proud of Roman traditions and of their own families' long-standing political power, they felt that Caesar was degrading the senate by adding unsophisticated rural representatives. A group of senators, led by Brutus and Cassius, decided to assassinate Caesar, which they did on the steps of the Roman senate on March 15, 44 B.C. The conspirators had not thought much beyond this act, however, and Caesar's death led not to peace but to a renewal of civil war. Some of the army was loyal to the assassins; some to Mark Antony, an associate of Caesar's; and some to Caesar's nephew and adopted son, Octavian. At first Mark Antony and Octavian cooperated to defeat the assassins, but then they turned against each other. The war dragged on for over a decade, with Octavian's forces gradually gaining more territory. Octavian won the support of many Romans by convincing them that Antony was plotting with Cleopatra, queen of Egypt, and in 31 B.C. his forces decisively de-

feated those of Antony at the naval battle of Actium. Antony and his ally Cleopatra committed suicide, leaving Octavian sole ruler of the Mediterranean world.

The problem now facing Octavian was the same one Julius Caesar had confronted twelve years earlier: how to transform a state won by military force into a stable political system. Caesar's answer—personal, autocratic rule—had led to his assassination at the hands of disgruntled senators. This lesson was not lost on Octavian, who realized that directly opposing the strong republican tradition in Rome could be very dangerous.

This tradition had arisen from both political reality—the senate had held actual power for many generations— and Roman political theory. The Romans held that their form of government had been given to them by the gods, who had conferred authority on Romulus, the mythical founder of Rome. That authority was later passed on to the senate, whose original function was to consult the gods about actions Rome should take. The senate in turn passed on authority to the rest of the government bureaucracy and to male heads of household, for in Rome households were considered, as in Athens, the smallest unit of government. Only male heads of household could sit in the senate, for only such individuals were regarded as worthy enough to consult the gods on matters of great importance to the state. This meant that Roman society was extremely patriarchal, with fathers having (at least in theory) absolute control over their wives, children, and servants.

This divinely ordained authority could always be distributed downward as the political bureaucracy grew, but to do away with existing institutions was extremely dangerous. Any radical transformation of the structure of government, especially any change in the authority of the senate, would have been regarded as impious.

Octavian had himself grown up in this tradition and at least to some degree shared these ideas about authority and the divine roots of the Roman political system. He realized that he could be more effective—and probably would live longer—if he worked through, rather than against, existing political institutions. Moreover, serious problems existed that had to be faced immediately, and after years of civil war, the government bureaucracy was no longer firmly in place to deal with them. Octavian needed to appoint officials and governors and reestablish law and order throughout Roman territory without offending the senate by acting like an autocrat or dictator.

In the eyes of many of his contemporaries, Octavian accomplished this admittedly difficult task very well. The senate conferred on him the name he is usually known by, Augustus, meaning "blessed" or "magnificent." Later historians regarded Augustus, rather than Julius Caesar, as the creator of the Roman Empire. Your task in this chapter will be to evaluate these judgments. How did Augustus transform the Roman republic into an empire? Why was he successful where Julius Caesar had not been?

SOURCES AND METHOD

As you think about these questions, you can see that they involve two somewhat different components: the process by which Augustus made changes and the results of these changes, or what we might term the *means* and the *ends*. Both are important to consider in assessing the achievements of any political leader, and both have been used by the contemporaries of Augustus, later Roman writers, and modern historians in evaluating the first Roman emperor's reign.

One of the best sources for observing the process of political change is laws, especially basic laws such as constitutions that set out governmental structure. Rome was a society in which law was extremely important and was explicitly written down, unlike many early societies, in which laws were handed down orally from generation to generation. As the Romans conquered Europe and the Mediterranean, they brought their legal system with them; consequently, Roman law forms the basis of most modern Western legal systems, with England and thus the United States the most notable exceptions.

We encounter some serious difficulties in using laws as our source material for the reign of Augustus, however. Given Roman ideas about authority and the strength of Roman tradition, would you expect him to have made major legal changes? Augustus, after all, described his aims and his actions as restoring republican government; if we use only the constitution of Rome as a source, we might be tempted to believe him. No new office was created for the emperor. Instead, he carefully preserved all traditional offices while gradually taking over many of them himself. Augustus was both a consul and a tribune, although the former office was usually reserved for a patrician and the latter for a plebeian. Later the senate appointed him *imperator*, or commander-in-chief of the army, and gave him direct control of many of the outlying provinces. These provinces furnished grain supplies essential to the people of Rome as well as soldiers loyal to Augustus rather than to the senate. The senate also gave him the honorary title of *princeps* (or "first citizen"), the title he preferred, which gradually lost its republican origins and gained the overtones of "monarch" evident in its modern English derivative, "prince." Augustus recognized the importance of religion to most Romans, and in 12 B.C. he had himself named *pontifex maximus*, or "supreme priest." He encouraged the building of temples dedicated to "Rome and Augustus," laying the foundations for the growth of a ruler cult closely linked with patriotic loyalty to Rome.

None of these innovations required any alteration in the basic constitution of Rome. What did change, however, was the tone of many laws, particularly those from the outlying provinces, where Augustus could be more open about the transformation he was working without bringing on the wrath of the senate. Our first two

selections, then, are decrees and laws from Roman territories, where we can perhaps see some hint of the gradual development of the republic into an empire.

Source 1 is a decree by Augustus himself, an inscription dated 4 B.C. from the Greek city of Cyrene. Like all laws, it was passed in response to a perceived problem. What problem does the decree confront? What procedure does it provide to solve this problem? What complications does it anticipate, and how does it try to solve them? You will notice that the decree itself is set within a long framework giving the reasons it was issued. This is true for many laws, including the American Constitution, which begins, "We the people of the United States, in order to form a more perfect union, establish justice, insure domestic tranquillity." Why does Augustus say he is passing this law? This framework can also give you clues to the relationship between Augustus and the senate. How is this relationship described, and what does Augustus's attitude appear to be?

The second law is an inscription dated A.D. 11 from an altar in the city of Narbonne in southern France. This law was passed by the local government, not the central Roman authorities. What does it order the population to do? Although the law itself does not state why it was passed, what might some reasons have been? What does the law indicate about attitudes toward Augustus and toward Roman authorities?

Another valuable source for examining the achievements of Augustus consists of the comments of his contemporaries and later Roman historians. Because Romans had such a strong sense of their own traditions, they were fascinated by history and were ever eager to point out how the hand of the gods operated in a way that allowed Rome to conquer most of the Western world. In the century before Augustus took over, it looked to many Romans as if the gods had forgotten Rome, leaving its citizens to kill each other in revolutions and civil wars. Augustus's military successes and political acumen seemed to show that he had the gods on his side, so writers delighted in extolling his accomplishments. Augustus's astuteness also extended to the world of literature and the arts, and he hired writers, sculptors, architects, and painters to glorify Rome, causing his own reputation no harm in the process. Many of the poems and histories are blatant hero worship, others communicate a more balanced view, and, because Augustus was not totally successful at winning everyone over to his side, some authors are openly critical.

Sources 3 through 6 are assessments by various Romans of Augustus's rule. As you read them, first try to gauge each author's basic attitude toward Augustus. What does he find to praise or blame? Does his judgment appear overly positive or negative? Does he sound objective? In answering these questions, you will need to pay attention not only to the content of the selection but also to the specific words each author chooses. What kinds of adjectives does he use to describe Augustus's person and political actions? Once you have as-

sessed the basic attitude of each author, identify what he regards as important in Augustus's reign. To what factors does he attribute Augustus's success? How does he describe the process by which the Roman republic was turned into an empire? What reasons does he give for Augustus's success and Julius Caesar's failure?

A bit of background on each of these selections will help you put them in better perspective. Source 3 was written by Horace, a poet living at the court of Augustus. This is an excerpt from his *Odes,* a literary rather than a primarily historical work. Source 4, an excerpt from Suetonius's biography of Augustus, was composed during the first half of the second century. Suetonius, private secretary to the emperor Hadrian, was keenly interested in the private as well as the public lives of the Roman emperors. Source 5 is taken from the long history of Rome by the politician and historian Dio Cassius (ca 150–235). Source 6 is drawn from the *Annals* of Tacitus, an orator and historian from a well-to-do Roman family. Sources 4 through 6 were written between one and two centuries after the events they present and are thus "history" as we know it, describing events after they happened.

Source 7 is a third type of evidence, namely, Augustus's own description of his rule. Usually called the *Res Gestae Divi Augusti,* it is an inscription he composed shortly before the end of his life. In this piece, following a long Roman tradition of inscriptions commemorating distinguished citizens, he describes the honors conferred on him as well as his accomplishments. Like all autobiographical statements, it is intended not simply as an objective description of a ruler's deeds but specifically as a vehicle for all that Augustus most wanted people to remember about this reign. Even though it is subjective, the *Res Gestae* is unique and invaluable as a primary source because it gives us Augustus's own version of the transformations he wrought in Roman society. As you read it, compare Augustus's descriptions of his deeds with those of the historians you have just read. What does Augustus regard as his most important accomplishments?

Many of the best sources for Augustus, of course, as for all of ancient history, are not written but archaeological. In fact, two of the sources we have looked at so far, the decree issued by Augustus and the inscription from Narbonne (Sources 1 and 2), are actually archaeological as well as written sources because they are inscriptions carved in stone. Thus, unlike other texts from the ancient world, including such basic ones as Plato's *Republic,* we have the original text and not a later copy.

Inscriptions are just one of many types of archaeological evidence. As the Romans conquered land after land, they introduced not only their legal code but their monetary system as well. Roman coins have been found throughout all of Europe and the Near East, far beyond the borders of the Roman Empire. *Numismatics,* the study of coins, can thus provide us with clues available from no other source, for coins have the great advantage of being both durable and valuable. Though their value sometimes

works to render them less durable—people melt them down to make other coins or to use the metal in other ways—it also makes them one of the few material goods that people hide in great quantities. Their owners intend to dig them up later, of course, but die or forget where they have buried them, leaving great caches of coins for later archaeologists and historians.

Roman coins differ markedly from modern coins in some respects. Though the primary function of both is to serve as a means of exchange, Roman coins were also transmitters of political propaganda. One side usually displayed a portrait of the emperor, chosen very carefully by the emperor himself to emphasize certain qualities. The reverse side often depicted a recent victory, anniversary, or other important event, or the personification of an abstract quality of virtue such as health or liberty. Modern coins also feature portraits, pictures, and slogans, but they tend to stay the same for decades, and so we pay very little attention to what is on them. Roman emperors, on the other hand, issued new coins frequently, expecting people to look at them. Most of the people who lived in the Roman Empire were illiterate, with no chance to read about the illustrious deeds of the emperor, but they did come into contact with coins nearly every day. From these coins they learned what the emperor looked like, what he had recently done, or what qualities to associate with him, for even illiterate people could identify the symbols for such abstract virtues as liberty or victory. Over one hundred different portraits of Augustus have been found on coins, providing us with additional clues about the achievements he most wanted to emphasize.

Once you have read the written documents, look at the two illustrations of coins, Sources 8 and 9. On the first, issued in 2 B.C., the lettering reads CAESAR AUGUSTUS DIVI F PATER PATRIAE, or "Augustus Caesar, son of a God, Father of the Fatherland." (Julius Caesar had been deified by the senate after his assassination, which is why Augustus called himself "son of a God.") Augustus is crowned with what appears to be a wreath of wheat stalks; this crown was the exclusive right of the priests of one of Rome's oldest religious groups that honored agricultural gods. The second coin, issued between 20 and 16 B.C., shows Augustus alongside the winged figure of the goddess Victory in a chariot atop a triumphal arch that stands itself on top of a viaduct; the inscription reads QUOD VIAE MUN SUNT, "because the roads have been reinforced." Think about the message Augustus was trying to convey with each of these coins. Even if you could not read the words, what impression of the emperor would you have from coins like these?

Issuing coins was one way for an emperor to celebrate and communicate his achievements; building was another. As you have read in Augustus's autobiography, he had many structures—stadiums, marketplaces, and temples—built for various purposes. He, and later Roman emperors, also built structures that were purely symbolic, the most impressive of which were celebratory arches,

built to commemorate an achievement or a military victory. The second coin shows Augustus standing on top of such an arch; Source 10 is a photograph of the arch of Augustus that still stands at Rimini. This arch was built at one end of the Flaminian Way, which Augustus reconstructed, as you have read in his autobiography; a similar arch was built at the other end in Rome. As you did when looking at the coins, think about the message such an arch conveys. It was put up with the agreement of the senate; does it give you a sense of republicanism or empire?

Roads are another prime archaeological source, closely related to the aqueducts we examined in Chapter 1. The Romans initially built roads to help their army move more quickly; once built, however, the road system facilitated trade and commerce as well. Roads are thus symbols of power as well as a means to maintain and extend it. Archaeologists have long studied the expansion of the Roman road system, and their findings can most easily be seen diagrammed on maps. Though maps do not have the immediacy of actual archaeological remains, they are based on such remains and enable us to detect patterns and make comparisons over time.

Selections 11 and 12 are maps of the major Roman roads existing before the reign of Augustus, those built or reconstructed during his reign, and the Roman road system at its farthest extent. Compare the first map with the information you have obtained from Augustus himself about his expansion of the frontiers of

49

Rome (Source 7, paragraph 26). Notice that he mentions only the western part of the Roman Empire; do the roads built during his reign reflect this western orientation? What do the later road-building patterns shown in Source 12 tell us about the goals and successes of later Roman emperors?

THE EVIDENCE

Sources 1 through 3 from Naphtali Lewis and Meyer Reinhold, editors and translators, Roman Civilization, *vol. 2, The Empire (New York: Columbia University Press, 1955), pp. 39–42; p. 62; p. 20. Reprinted with permission of Columbia University Press, 562 W. 113th St., New York, NY 10025, via Copyright Clearance Center, Inc.*

[handwritten: THEME: AUGUSTUS & AUTHORITIES (SENATE) & THE PEOPLE]

1. Decree Issued by Emperor Augustus, 4 B.C.

[handwritten: WHY IS AUGUSTUS PASSING THIS LAW?]

The Emperor Caesar Augustus, *pontifex maximus,* holding the tribunician power for the nineteenth year, declares:

A decree of the senate was passed in the consulship of Gaius Calvisius and Lucius Passienus, with me as one of those present at the writing. Since it affects the welfare of the allies of the Roman people, I have decided to send it into the provinces, appended to this my prefatory edict, so that it may be known to all who are under our care. From this it will be evident to all the inhabitants of the provinces how much both I and the senate are concerned that none of our subjects should suffer any improper treatment or any extortion.

DECREE OF THE SENATE

Whereas the consuls Gaius Calvisius Sabinus and Lucius Passienus Rufus spoke "Concerning matters affecting the security of the allies of the Roman people which the Emperor Caesar Augustus, our *princeps,* following the recommendation of the council which he had drawn by lot from among the senate, desired to be brought before the senate by us," the senate passed the following decree:

[handwritten: RECOVERING EXTORTED MONEY]

Whereas our ancestors established legal process for extortion so that the allies might more easily be able to take action for any wrongs done them and recover moneys extorted from them, and whereas this type of process is sometimes very expensive and troublesome for those in whose interest the law was enacted, because poor people or persons weak with illness or age are dragged from far-distant provinces as witnesses, the senate decrees as follows:

If after the passage of this decree of the senate any of the allies, desiring to recover extorted moneys, public or private, appear and so depose before one of the magistrates who is authorized to convene the senate, the magistrate—except where the extorter faces a capital charge—shall bring them before the senate as soon as possible and shall assign them any advocate they themselves request to speak in their behalf before the senate; but no one who has in accordance with the laws been excused from this duty shall be required to serve as advocate against his will. . . .

The judges chosen shall hear and inquire into only those cases in which a man is accused of having appropriated money from a community or from private parties; and, rendering their decision within thirty days, they shall order him to restore such sum of money, public or private, as the accusers prove was taken from them. Those whose duty it is to inquire into and pronounce judgment in these cases shall, until they complete the inquiry and pronounce their judgment, be exempted from all public duties except public worship. . . .

The senate likewise decrees that the judges who are selected in accordance with this decree of the senate shall pronounce in open court each his several finding, and what the majority pronounces shall be the verdict.

2. Inscription from the City of Narbonne, A.D. 11

In the consulship of Titus Statilius Taurus and Lucius Cassius Longinus, September 22. Vow taken to the divine spirit of Augustus by the populace of the Narbonensians in perpetuity: "May it be good, favorable, and auspicious to the Emperor Caesar Augustus, son of a god, father of his country, *pontifex maximus*, holding the tribunician power for the thirty-fourth year; to his wife, children, and house; to the Roman senate and people; and to the colonists[1] and residents of the Colonia Julia Paterna of Narbo Martius,[2] who have bound themselves to worship his divine spirit in perpetuity!"

The populace of the Narbonensians has erected in the forum at Narbo an altar at which every year on September 23—the day on which the good fortune of the age bore him to be ruler of the world—three Roman *equites*[3] from the populace and three freedmen shall sacrifice one animal each and shall at their own expense on that day provide the colonists and residents with incense and wine for supplication to his divine spirit. And on September 24 they shall likewise provide incense and wine for the colonists and residents. Also on January 1 they shall provide incense and wine for the colonists and residents. Also on January 7, the day on which he first entered upon the command of the world, they shall make supplication with incense and wine, and

1. The word *colonist* has a very specific meaning in Roman history. **Colonists** were Romans, often retired soldiers, who were granted land in the outlying provinces in order to build up Roman strength there. They were legally somewhat distinct from native residents, which is why this law uses the phrase "colonists and residents" to make it clear that both groups were required to follow its provisions.

2. The long phrase "Colonia Julia Pasterna of Narbo Martius" is the official and complete Roman name for the town of Narbo, which we now call Narbonne.

3. **equites:** cavalry of the Roman army.

shall sacrifice one animal each, and shall provide incense and wine for the colonists and residents on that day. And on May 31, because on that day in the consulship of Titus Statilius Taurus and Manius Aemilius Lepidus he reconciled the populace to the decurions,[4] they shall sacrifice one animal each and shall provide the colonists and residents with incense and wine for supplication to his divine spirit. And of these three Roman *equites* and three freedmen one . . . [The rest of this inscription is lost.]

3. From Horace, *Odes*

Thine age, O Caesar, has brought back fertile crops to the fields and has restored to our own Jupiter the military standards stripped from the proud columns of the Parthians;[5] has closed Janus' temple[6] freed of wars; has put reins on license overstepping righteous bounds; has wiped away our sins and revived the ancient virtues through which the Latin name and the might of Italy waxed great, and the fame and majesty of our empire were spread from the sun's bed in the west to the east. As long as Caesar is the guardian of the state, neither civil dissension nor violence shall banish peace, nor wrath that forges swords and brings discord and misery to cities. Not those who drink the deep Danube shall violate the orders of Caesar, nor the Getae, nor the Seres,[7] nor the perfidious Parthians, nor those born by the Don River. And we, both on profane and sacred days, amidst the gifts of merry Bacchus, together with our wives and children, will first duly pray to the gods; then, after the tradition of our ancestors, in songs to the accompaniment of Lydian flutes we will hymn leaders whose duty is done.

Source 4 from Suetonius, The Lives of the Twelve Caesars, *edited and translated by Joseph Gavorse (New York: Modern Library, 1931), p. 89.*

4. From Suetonius, *Life of Augustus*

The whole body of citizens with a sudden unanimous impulse proffered him the title of "father of his country"—first the plebs, by a deputation sent to

4. **decurion:** member of a town council.

5. The Parthians were an empire located in the region occupied by present-day Iraq. They had defeated Roman armies led by Mark Antony and had taken the Roman military standards, that is, the flags and banners of the army they defeated. Augustus recovered these standards, an important symbolic act, even though he did not conquer the Parthians.

6. This was a small temple in Rome that was ordered closed whenever peace reigned throughout the whole Roman Empire. During the reign of Augustus it was closed three times.

7. The Getae and the Seres were people who lived in the regions occupied by present-day Romania and Ukraine.

Antium, and then, because he declined it, again at Rome as he entered the theater, which they attended in throngs, all wearing laurel wreaths; the senate afterwards in the senate house, not by a decree or by acclamation, but through Valerius Messala. He, speaking for the whole body, said: "Good fortune and divine favor attend thee and thy house, Caesar Augustus; for thus we feel that we are praying for lasting prosperity for our country and happiness for our city. The senate in accord with the Roman people hails thee 'Father of thy Country.' " Then Augustus with tears in his eyes replied as follows (and I have given his exact words, as I did those of Messala): "Having attained my highest hopes, members of the senate, what more have I to ask of the immortal gods than that I may retain this same unanimous approval of yours to the very end of my life?"

Sources 5 through 7 from Naphtali Lewis and Meyer Reinhold, editors and translators, Roman Civilization, *vol. 2,* The Empire *(New York: Columbia University Press, 1955), pp. 4–8; p. 4; pp. 9–10, 12, 14–16, 17, 19. Reprinted with permission of Columbia University Press, 562 W. 113th St., New York, NY 10025, via Copyright Clearance Center, Inc.*

5. From Dio Cassius, *Roman History*

[handwritten: AUGUSTUS IS DEAD AS OF THIS WRITING]

[handwritten: Anti] In this way the power of both people and senate passed entirely into the hands of Augustus, and from this time there was, strictly speaking, a monarchy; for monarchy would be the truest name for it, even if two or three men later held the power jointly. Now, the Romans so detested the title "monarch" that they called their emperors neither dictators nor kings nor anything of this sort. Yet, since the final authority for the government devolves upon them, they needs must be kings. The offices established by the laws, it is true, are maintained even now, except that of censor; but the entire direction and administration is absolutely in accordance with the wishes of the one in power at the time. And yet, in order to preserve the appearance of having this authority not through their power but by virtue of the laws, the emperors have taken to themselves all the offices (including the titles) which under the Republic possessed great power with the consent of the people—with the exception of the dictatorship. Thus, they very often become consuls, and they are always styled proconsuls whenever they are outside the *pomerium*.[8] The title *imperator* is held by them for life, not only by those who have won victories in battle but also by all the rest, to indicate their absolute power, instead of the title "king" or "dictator." These latter titles they have never assumed since they fell out of use in the constitution, but the actuality of those offices is secured to them by the appellation *imperator*. By virtue of the titles named, they secure the right to make levies, collect funds, declare war, make peace, and

8. **pomerium:** the city limits of Rome.

rule foreigners and citizens alike everywhere and always—even to the extent of being able to put to death both *equites* and senators inside the *pomerium*—and all the other powers once granted to the consuls and other officials possessing independent authority; and by virtue of holding the censorship they investigate our lives and morals as well as take the census, enrolling some in the equestrian and senatorial orders and removing others from these orders according to their will. By virtue of being consecrated in all the priesthoods and, in addition, from their right to bestow most of them upon others, as well as from the fact that, even if two or three persons rule jointly, one of them is *pontifex maximus,* they hold in their own hands supreme authority over all matters both profane and sacred. The tribunician power, as it is called, which once the most influential men used to hold, gives them the right to nullify the effects of the measures taken by any other official, in case they do not approve, and makes their persons inviolable; and if they appear to be wronged in even the slightest degree, not merely by deed but even by word, they may destroy the guilty party as one accursed, without a trial.

Thus by virtue of these Republican titles they have clothed themselves with all the powers of the government, so that they actually possess all the prerogatives of kings without the usual title. For the appellation "Caesar" or "Augustus" confers upon them no actual power but merely shows in the one case that they are the successors of their family line, and in the other the splendor of their rank. The name "Father" perhaps gives them a certain authority over us all—the authority which fathers once had over their children; yet it did not signify this at first, but betokened honor and served as an admonition both to them to love their subjects as they would their children; and to their subjects to revere them as they would their fathers. . . .

The senate as a body, it is true, continued to sit in judgment as before, and in certain cases transacted business with embassies and envoys from both peoples and kings; and the people and the plebs, moreover, continued to come together for the elections; but nothing was actually done that did not please Caesar. At any rate, in the case of those who were to hold office, he himself selected and nominated some; and though he left the election of others in the hands of the people and the plebs, in accordance with the ancient practice, yet he took care that no persons should hold office who were unfit or elected as the result of factious combinations or bribery.

Such were the arrangements made, generally speaking, at that time; for in reality Caesar himself was destined to have absolute power in all matters for life, because he was not only in control of money matters (nominally, to be sure, he had separated the public funds from his own, but as a matter of fact he spent the former also as he saw fit) but also in control of the army. At all events, when his ten-year period came to an end, there was voted him another five years, then five more, after that ten, and again another ten, and then ten for the fifth time, so that by the succession of ten-year periods he continued to be sole ruler for life. And it is for this reason that the subsequent monarchs, though no longer appointed for a specified period but for their whole life once for all, nevertheless always held a celebration every ten years, as if then renewing their sovereignty once more; and this is done even at the present day.

Now, Caesar had received many privileges previously, when the question of declining the sovereignty and that of apportioning the provinces were under discussion. For the right to fasten laurels to the front of the imperial residence and to hang the civic crown above the doors was then voted him to symbolize the fact that he was always victorious over enemies and savior of the citizens. The imperial palace is called Palatium, not because it was ever decreed that this should be its name but because Caesar dwelt on the Palatine and had his military headquarters there.... Hence, even if the emperor resides somewhere else, his dwelling retains the name of Palatium.

And when he had actually completed the reorganization, the name Augustus was at length bestowed upon him by the senate and by the people.... He took the title of Augustus, signifying that he was more than human; for all most precious and sacred objects are termed *augusta*. For which reason they called him also in Greek *sebastos* ... meaning an august person.

6. From Tacitus, *Annals*

After the death of Brutus and Cassius, there was no longer any army loyal to the Republic.... Then, laying aside the title of triumvir and parading as a consul, and professing himself satisfied with the tribunician power for the protection of the plebs, Augustus enticed the soldiers with gifts, the people with grain, and all men with the allurement of peace, and gradually grew in power, concentrating in his own hands the functions of the senate, the magistrates, and the laws. No one opposed him, for the most courageous had fallen in battle or in the proscription. As for the remaining nobles, the readier they were for slavery, the higher were they raised in wealth and offices, so that, aggrandized by the revolution, they preferred the safety of the present to the perils of the past. Nor did the provinces view with disfavor this state of affairs, for they distrusted the government of the senate and the people on account of the struggles of the powerful and the rapacity of the officials, while the protection afforded them by the laws was inoperative, as the provinces were repeatedly thrown into confusion by violence, intrigue, and finally bribery....

At home all was peaceful; the officials bore the same titles as before. The younger generation was born after the victory of Actium, and even many of the older generation had been born during the civil wars. How few were left who had seen the Republic!

Thus the constitution had been transformed, and there was nothing at all left of the good old way of life. Stripped of equality, all looked to the directives of a *princeps* with no apprehension for the present, while Augustus in the vigorous years of his life maintained his power, that of his family, and peace.

EXAMPLE OF MASTER POLITICIAN

FACTION: MARK ANTONY

7. From Augustus, *Res Gestae Divi Augusti*

1. At the age of nineteen, on my own initiative and at my own expense, I raised an army by means of which I liberated the Republic, which was oppressed by the tyranny of a faction. For which reason the senate, with honorific decrees, made me a member of its order in the consulship of Gaius Pansa and Aulus Hirtius, giving me at the same time consular rank in voting, and granted me the *imperium*. It ordered me as propraetor, together with the consuls, to see to it that the state suffered no harm. Moreover, in the same year, when both consuls had fallen in the war, the people elected me consul and a triumvir for the settlement of the commonwealth.

2. Those who assassinated my father I drove into exile, avenging their crime by due process of law; and afterwards when they waged war against the state, I conquered them twice on the battlefield.

3. I waged many wars throughout the whole world by land and by sea, both civil and foreign, and when victorious I spared all citizens who sought pardon. Foreign peoples who could safely be pardoned I preferred to spare rather than to extirpate. . . . Though the Roman senate and people unitedly agreed that I should be elected soul guardian of the laws and morals with supreme authority, I refused to accept any office offered me which was contrary to the traditions of our ancestors. . . .

9. The senate decreed that vows for my health should be offered up every fifth year by the consuls and priests. In fulfillment of those vows, games were often celebrated during my lifetime, sometimes by the four most distinguished colleges of priests, sometimes by the consuls. Moreover, the whole citizen body, with one accord, both individually and as members of municipalities, prayed continuously for my health at all the shrines.

10. My name was inserted, by decree of the senate, in the hymn of the Salian priests. And it was enacted by law that I should be sacrosanct in perpetuity and that I should possess the tribunician power as long as I live. I declined to become *pontifex maximus* in place of a colleague while he was still alive, when the people offered me that priesthood, which my father had held. A few years later, in the consulship of Publius Sulpicius and Gaius Valgius, I accepted this priesthood, when death removed the man who had taken possession of it at a time of civil disturbance; and from all Italy a multitude flocked to my election such as had never previously been recorded at Rome. . . .

17. Four times I came to the assistance of the treasury with my own money, transferring to those in charge of the treasury 150,000,000 sesterces. And in the consulship of Marcus Lepidus and Lucius Arruntius I transferred out of my own patrimony 170,000,000 sesterces to the soldiers' bonus fund, which was

established on my advice for the purpose of providing bonuses for soldiers who had completed twenty or more years of service.

18. From the year in which Gnaeus Lentulus and Publius Lentulus were consuls, whenever the provincial taxes fell short, in the case sometimes of 100,000 persons and sometimes of many more, I made up their tribute in grain and in money from my own grain stores and my own patrimony. . . .

gave more $

20. I repaired the Capitol and the theater of Pompey with enormous expenditures on both works, without having my name inscribed on them. I repaired the conduits of the aqueducts which were falling into ruin in many places because of age, and I doubled the capacity of the aqueduct called Marcia by admitting a new spring into its conduit. I completed the Julian Forum and the basilica which was between the temple of Castor and the temple of Saturn, works begun and far advanced by my father, and when the same basilica was destroyed by fire, I enlarged its site and began rebuilding the structure, which is to be inscribed with the names of my sons; and in case it should not be completed while I am still alive, I left instructions that the work be completed by my heirs. In my sixth consulship I repaired eighty-two temples of the gods in the city, in accordance with a resolution of the senate, neglecting none which at that time required repair. In my seventh consulship I reconstructed the Flaminian Way from the city as far as Ariminum,[9] and also all the bridges except the Mulvian and the Minucian. . . .

Repaired & reconstructed many buildings

22. I gave a gladiatorial show three times in my own name, and five times in the names of my sons or grandsons; at these shows about 10,000 fought. Twice I presented to the people in my own name an exhibition of athletes invited from all parts of the world, and a third time in the name of my grandson. I presented games in my own name four times, and in addition twenty-three times in the place of other magistrates. On behalf of the college of fifteen, as master of that college, with Marcus Agrippa as my colleague, I celebrated the Secular Games[10] in the consulship of Gaius Furnius and Gaius Silanus. In my thirteenth consulship I was the first to celebrate the Games of Mars, which subsequently the consuls, in accordance with a decree of the senate and a law, have regularly celebrated in the succeeding years. Twenty-six times I provided for the people, in my own name or in the names of my sons or grandsons, hunting spectacles of African wild beasts in the circus or in the Forum or in the amphitheaters; in these exhibitions about 3,500 animals were killed.

He played games & gave things in the name of others.

9. Present-day Rimini, Italy.

10. The Secular Games were an enormous series of athletic games, festivals, and banquets that Augustus ordered held in 17 B.C. Though called "secular," they were held in honor of the gods and were directed by the College of Fifteen, a board that oversaw sacrifices to the gods. All adult Roman citizens were expected to view the games out of religious duty.

23. I presented to the people an exhibition of a naval battle across the Tiber where the grove of the Caesars now is, having had the site excavated 1,800 feet in length and 1,200 feet in width. In this exhibition thirty beaked ships, triremes or biremes, and in addition a great number of smaller vessels engaged in combat. On board these fleets, exclusive of rowers, there were about 3,000 combatants. . . .

26. I extended the frontiers of all the provinces of the Roman people on whose boundaries were peoples subject to our empire. I restored peace to the Gallic and Spanish provinces and likewise to Germany, that is, to the entire region bounded by the Ocean from Gades to the mouth of the Elbe River. I caused peace to be restored in the Alps, from the region nearest to the Adriatic Sea as far as the Tuscan Sea, without undeservedly making war against any people. My fleet sailed the Ocean from the mouth of the Rhine eastward as far as the territory of the Cimbrians,[11] to which no Roman previously had penetrated either by land or by sea. . . .

34. In my sixth and seventh consulships, after I had put an end to the civil wars, having attained supreme power by universal consent, I transferred the state from my own power to the control of the Roman senate and people. For this service of mine I received the title of Augustus by decree of the senate, and the doorposts of my house were publicly decked with laurels, the civic crown was affixed over my doorway, and a golden shield was set up in the Julian senate house, which, as the inscription on this shield testifies, the Roman senate and people gave me in recognition of my valor, clemency, justice, and devotion. After that time I excelled all in authority, but I possessed no more power than the others who were my colleagues in each magistracy.

35. When I held my thirteenth consulship, the senate, the equestrian order, and the entire Roman people gave me the title of "father of the country" and decreed that this title should be inscribed in the vestibule of my house, in the Julian senate house, and in the Augustan Forum on the pedestal of the chariot which was set up in my honor by decree of the senate. At the time I wrote this document I was in my seventy-sixth year.

11. Near present-day Hamburg, Germany.

Sources 8 and 9 from The American Numismatic Society, New York.

8. Roman Coin Issued 2 B.C.

9. Roman Coin Issued 20–16 B.C.

Source 10 from Alinari/Art Resource. Photo by Stab D. Anderson, 1931.

10. Arch of Augustus at Rimini

Source 11 adapted from sketches by Merry E. Wiesner.

11. Main Roman Roads, 31 B.C.–A.D. 14

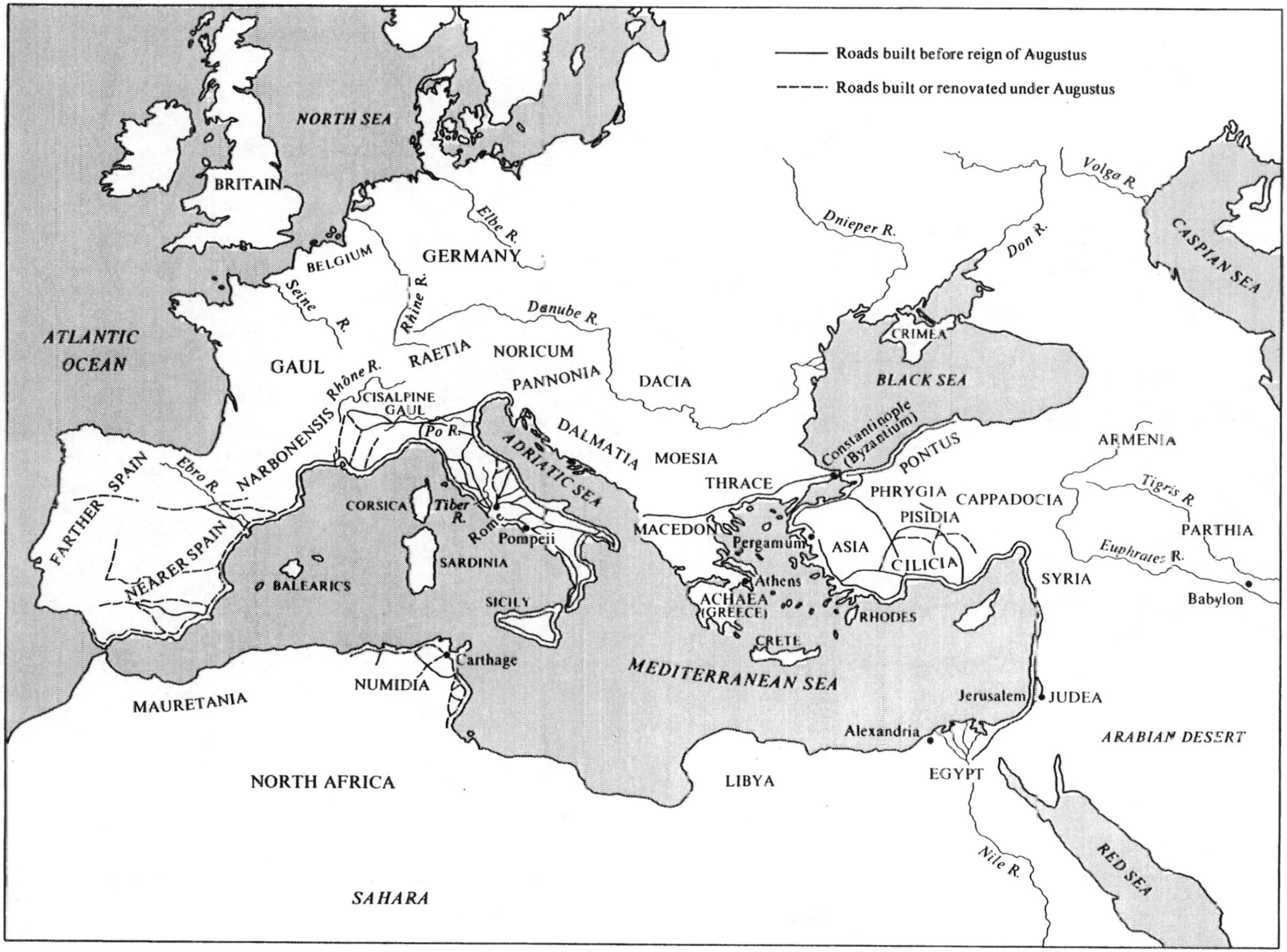

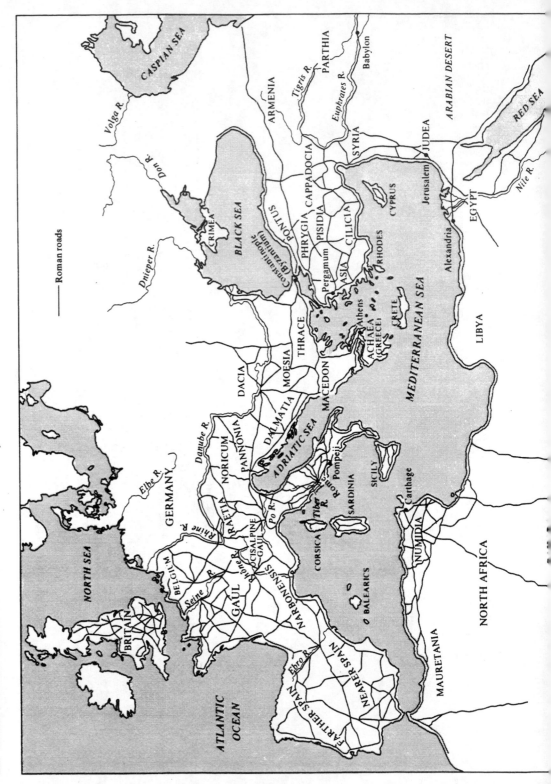

Source 12 from Victor W. Von Hagen, *The Roads That Led to Rome* (Cleveland and New York: World Publishing Co., © 1967 by George Weidenfeld and Nicolson, London), pp. 18–19.

12. Main Roman Roads at Their Greatest Extent, A.D. 180

Roman roads

QUESTIONS TO CONSIDER

Now that you have examined various pieces of evidence, you need to put them together to arrive at a conclusion that you can support. Do not worry about not having all the evidence you need; no historian can ever discover "all" the facts about an event or person. He or she makes conclusions on the basis of the evidence available, alters those conclusions when new material is discovered, and uses those conclusions as a framework for further research. In this respect, historians operate just like physicists learning how the universe works. Do not worry if some of your sources disagree; ten people who witness an auto accident often come up with ten quite contradictory accounts of the event. Why might accounts of Augustus's rule be even more contradictory?

The sources have made you aware of the operation of Roman government on two levels: that of the formal constitution, which remained a republic, and that of the actual locus of power, which was increasingly the emperor. The changes that Augustus instituted thus took place at the second level, and in many areas we can ignore the formal constitution of Rome in describing the process of change. Comparing all the sources, how would you describe the means by which Augustus transformed the republic into a different type of government? Which steps were most important? Which observers seemed to have the clearer view of this process, Augustus himself and those living during his lifetime, or later histori-

ans? In considering this last question, you need to think about the advantages and disadvantages of eyewitness reports versus later, secondary accounts.

The second question concerns results, not process: Why was Augustus successful? To answer this, we must consider not only the changes themselves, but people's perceptions of them. A ruler's place in history depends not only on real accomplishments but also on how these accomplishments are perceived and judged by later generations. Rulers perceived as good or successful are often given credit for everything good that happened during their reigns, even if they had nothing to do with it. Conversely, rulers regarded as unsuccessful, weak, or bad get blamed for many things that were not their fault. A reputation is generally based on actual achievements, but occasionally it is also determined by a ruler's successful manipulation of public opinion, and sometimes by that manipulation alone.

Augustus clearly recognized the importance of public opinion, which in Rome was tied to upholding tradition. How does he make use of Roman traditions in the laws and coins he issues? How do other observers judge his connection with tradition? Many of Rome's traditions were incorporated into public rituals and ceremonies. What sorts of ceremonies did Romans participate in or view? How did Augustus use these ceremonies to demonstrate his power or his personal connections with Roman tradition? Along with rituals, titles are also important demonstrations of power. What does Augustus call himself and what do others call him, both in the written documents and on the coins? Why is there so much discussion of his accepting or not accepting various titles?

Now that you have considered the opinions of a range of commentators, assessed some actual legal changes and road-building patterns, examined some coins, and heard from Augustus himself, you are ready to answer the questions: How did Augustus transform the Roman republic into an empire? Why was he successful? Once you have made your assessment, think about how you would use it to structure future research. What other evidence would be useful in supporting your conclusions? Where might you go to find that evidence?

EPILOGUE

Though Augustus said that his aim was a restoration of the republic, in reality he transformed Roman government into an empire ruled by one individual. His reign is generally termed the *Principate,* a word taken from Augustus's favorite title *princeps,* but the rulers of Rome after him did not hesitate to use the title *emperor.* Like him, they also retained the titles *pontifex maximus,* supreme priest, and *imperator,* commander-in-chief. It is interesting to see how many of our words denoting aspects of royal rule come from Augustus: not only *prince, emperor,* and *czar* (the Russian variant of "Caesar") but also *palace,* from Palatine, the hill where Augustus had his house.

The emperors who came after Augustus built on his achievements, both literally and figuratively. They extended the borders of the Roman Empire even farther, so that at its largest it would stretch from Scotland to the Sudan and from Spain to Syria. The Roman road system was expanded to over 50,000 miles, longer than the current interstate highway system in the United States; some of those roads are still usable today. Roman coins continued to be stamped with the emperor's picture and have been found as far away as southern India. Later emperors continued Augustus's building projects in Rome and throughout the empire. Vespasian built the Colosseum, which could seat 50,000 people; Trajan, the Forum with a number of different buildings and an enormous 125-foot column with his statue on top; Hadrian, the Pantheon and a wall dividing England and Scotland. The emperor Nero may have even ordered part of Rome burned to make room for his urban renewal projects.

Augustus's successors also continued his centralization of power. His stepson Tiberius stripped the assemblies of their right to elect magistrates, and later emperors took this power away from the senate as well. Bureaucrats appointed by the emperor oversaw the grain trade, the army, and the collection of taxes, with the senate gradually dwindling into a rubber stamp for the emperor's decisions. New territories were ruled directly by the emperor through governors and generals; in these jurisdictions, the senate did not have even the pretense of power.

The cult of ruler worship initiated somewhat tentatively in the provinces under Augustus grew enormously after his death, when, like Julius Caesar, he was declared a god. Though Romans officially deified only the *memory* of deceased emperors, some emperors were not willing to wait that long. Caligula declared himself a god at the age of twenty-five, spent much of his time in the temple of Castor and Pollux, and talked to the statue of Jupiter as an equal. Though Caligula was probably insane and later was stabbed to death, ruler worship in general was serious business for most Romans, closely linked as it was to tradition and patriotism. Groups like the Christians who did not offer sacrifices to the emperor or at least to the emperor's "genius" were felt to be unpatriotic, disloyal, and probably traitorous.

Thus in many ways Augustus laid the foundation for the success and durability of his empire. Historians have always been fascinated with the demise of the Roman Empire, but considering the fact that it lasted more than 400 years after Augustus in western Europe—and, in a significantly altered form, almost 1,500 years in eastern Europe—a more appropriate question might be why it lasted so long. Though the weaknesses that led to the empire's eventual collapse were also outgrowths of the reign of Augustus, the latter still represents a remarkable success story.

We must be careful of attributing too much to one man, however. As we have seen, Augustus had an extremely effective network of supporters and advisers, including Rome's most important men of letters. Their rendering of the glories of Roman civilization and the brilliance of Augustus has shaped much of what has been written about Rome since; you may only need to check the adjectives used in your text to describe Augustus to confirm this. Myths or exaggerations told about a ruler die hard, especially those that have been repeated for nearly 2,000 years.

CHAPTER FOUR

PHILOSOPHY AND FAITH:

THE PROBLEM OF ANCIENT SUICIDE

THE PROBLEM

Life itself is our most precious possession, and every civilization has viewed suicide, representing as it does the rejection of all human society, as an act of supreme importance, charged with religious, philosophical, and even legal significance. Indeed, the French philosopher Albert Camus (1913–1960) wrote, "There is only one truly philosophical problem, and that is suicide. Judging whether life is or is not worth living amounts to answering the fundamental question of philosophy."[1] Camus was only one of the most recent in a long line of thinkers, extending back at least to the civilization of ancient Egypt, who have written on the fundamental issues raised by the act of self-destruction. This extensive discourse on suicide can afford us a revealing glimpse of the intellectual life of past civilizations by allow-

ing us to compare the evolution of their thinkers' ideas on this important act.

In the twentieth century, for example, most of us understand suicide in terms defined by the modern social, psychological, and medical sciences. Emile Durkheim (1858–1917), the pioneering French sociologist, identified several kinds of suicide, but concentrated particularly on the role of modern society in eroding the integrative and regulative aspects of traditional society, resulting, he claimed, in an increase in suicide. We now know that Durkheim's statistical evidence for the increase in suicide in modern times was defective, but his conclusion that suicide is a particular side effect of modern society has endured, even though deprived of its statistical support. Sigmund Freud (1856–1940), the father of modern psychoanalysis, and others of his discipline focused modern attention on the psychological problems that often produce suicide. And since the work of the German physician Emil Kraepelin (1865–1926), medical professionals have sought to treat the organic

1. Albert Camus, *The Myth of Sisyphus and Other Essays,* translated by Justin O'Brien (New York: Vintage Books, 1991), p. 3.

causes of depressive disorders that can end in self-destruction.

The earliest Western societies, on the other hand, lacking our modern scientific knowledge, viewed the act of self-destruction in very different, often spiritual terms. Such societies certainly condemned suicide because it robbed their ranks of productive members. But primitive peoples also believed that the spirits of those who took their own lives would not rest in the world of the dead, but would return to haunt the realm of the living.

In the present chapter we will examine the thought of the ancient world on suicide. The practice was common for much of the period, and ancients seem to have taken their lives for a number of reasons. One had to do with personal honor. Examples abound of ancients extolled in the literature of their time for their nobility in ending their lives to preserve their honor. Perhaps the most famous of these suicides was that of Cato the Younger (95–46 B.C.), a leader of the senatorial opposition to Julius Caesar's attempt to control Rome. With his forces defeated in the field, and facing Caesar's imminent attack on Utica, the stronghold under his command, Cato assured the escape of his followers and took his own life rather than surrender to the man he regarded as a tyrant. Other ancients took their own lives to avoid the pains of old age, perhaps because they saw mental and physical decline as diminishing their honor. Thus, the Greek philosopher Zeno (ca 334–ca 262) took his own life at the age of seventy-two when breaking a bone in a minor accident seemed to convince

him of impending physical decline. Love for a dead spouse also led to suicide. Portia, the daughter of Cato and the wife of Caesar's assassin, Brutus, took her own life after her husband's suicide upon his defeat by Caesar's heir, Octavian, in 42 B.C. Ancients also took their lives in the belief that their deaths could advance a cause, and we will look at such an act in the death of Samson. Indeed, we will examine ancient thought on such acts of self-destruction among the Greeks, the Romans, the Hebrews of the Old Testament, and early Christians.

Historians date Hellenic, or classical Greek, civilization from about 800 B.C., when growing commercial wealth and the development of an efficient writing system promoted the economic and intellectual flowering of Greek city-states on the Greek mainland, the islands of the Aegean, Asia Minor (modern Turkey), and the shores of the Black Sea. The epics of Homer helped to shape early Hellenic culture, with the heroes providing role models for young Greeks and the tales of the gods forming the basis for early belief in a cluster of deities, presided over by Zeus, inhabiting the heights of Mount Olympus. These religious beliefs of the Greeks had little of the creedal structure of modern religion, but emphasized instead the duty of citizens of an independent city-state (as most Greeks were) to live in accord with the community. For the early Greeks, as for most Mediterranean peoples of that period, death simply represented the spirit's journey to a shadowy realm of the dead.

The greatest accomplishment of Hellenic intellectuals was to begin to transcend this traditional Greek religion—which explained events in this life in terms of divine action—and to apply reason to their understanding of natural phenomena and human events. As they replaced myth with reason, the Greeks first attempted to explain the physical world around them. The Cosmologists, thinkers concerned with the origins, structure, and operation of the universe, including Thales (ca 624–548 B.C.), Anaximander (ca 611–547 B.C.), and Pythagoras (ca 580–507 B.C.), sought natural explanations for the origins of the universe and advanced the concept that the physical world operates according to mathematical, scientific laws. Greek philosophers also evaluated human society, examining political and ethical problems through the use of reason. Socrates (ca 469–399 B.C.) and Plato (ca 429–347 B.C.), philosophers we will study in this chapter, in particular led the Greek inquiry into ethical problems.

A political event fundamentally transformed the Hellenic age, however. In 338 B.C. King Philip of Macedon (382–336 B.C.), a primitive state in northern Greece, conquered the city-states of Greece and ended their independence by subjecting them to the rule of his growing empire. Philip planned further military campaigns; these were carried out after his death by his son, Alexander the Great (356–323 B.C.). Alexander conquered Greece's historic enemy, the Persian Empire, and created an empire that stretched to the borders of India.

Although Alexander's empire dissolved into several smaller monarchies after his death, his conquests began a new Hellenistic age. Greek became the language of administration and intellectual life in the eastern Mediterranean world, and contact with eastern ideas reshaped Hellenic thought. Hellenistic philosophy reflected a search for intellectual peace for the individual in a world far less democratic and secure than that of the independent city-states of the Hellenic age.

Epicurus (342–270 B.C.) began to teach philosophy in Athens in the late fourth century, creating Epicureanism, one of the great schools of Hellenistic philosophy. Seeking intellectual tranquillity in a much less secure age, Epicurus urged his followers to withdraw from public affairs and civic responsibilities, which had been central to the earlier period of city-states. He also taught his students to abandon pursuit of worldly success. The wise person, Epicurus taught, would seek spiritual tranquillity instead, and he taught his students not to fear even divine interruptions of that peace. He affirmed the gods' existence, but held that they played no role in human affairs. Adopting the thought of the Cosmologist Democritus (ca 460–370 B.C.), Epicurus taught that the physical world consisted of matter made up of atoms governed by mechanical principles and unaffected by divine action. Death released the atoms making up the human form to constitute new matter, and so the peace Epicurus sought to instill in his followers was very much one of this world.

Zeno, who, as we have seen, committed suicide, founded a second school of Hellenistic philosophy. He taught on the *stoa poecile* (the "painted porch") near the agora, or marketplace, of Athens. As a consequence, his ideas came to be called Stoicism. Stoics accepted the new realities of the Greek and, later, Roman worlds by emphasizing the universality of human society. As expressed by Zeno, "All men should regard themselves as members of one city and people, having one life and order as a herd feeding together on a common pasture."[2] Stoics believed that the universe inhabited by such a society received order from divine reason, or Logos. Animals followed this divine order by instinct, and inanimate objects necessarily adhered to the physical laws of the universe— for example, those governing the regular movements of the heavenly bodies. Humans, however, had free will and could choose to reject the divine plan. But Stoics taught that the virtuous person could achieve happiness only by living in harmony with the Logos, subjecting personal emotions to reason, and accepting life's trials as part of the overall plan of the universe.

While Epicureans withdrew from the world and Stoics sought to live in accord with the Logos, the Cynics, a third group of Hellenistic philosophers led by Diogenes of Sinope (ca 412–323 B.C.), rejected social conventions. They urged their followers to

2. Quoted in D. Brendan Nagle, *The Ancient World: A Social and Cultural History* (Englewood Cliffs, N.J.: Prentice-Hall, 1979), p. 206.

give up material possessions and the complexities of human society and live lives of self-sufficiency and high personal ethics. Because material matters meant little to Cynics, they were prepared to commit suicide if anything blocked their quest for the virtuous life. Indeed, Diogenes reportedly said that the conduct of life required either reason or the noose.

Imperial expansion fundamentally shaped Roman civilization. Thus, in the fourth century B.C., the Romans came into contact with the Greek settlements in the south of their native Italy, and Roman equivalents of the Greek deities soon replaced traditional Roman religion, which was centered on the gods of home and family. In philosophy, the Romans similarly embraced Hellenistic Epicureanism and Stoicism. But, ultimately, the fundamental force reshaping Roman thought as the empire conquered the Mediterranean world was religious. Rome's world empire only increased the sense of alienation and personal insecurity that we identified in the Hellenistic age, and while educated Romans adopted Stoicism and other rational solutions to these problems, others often sought religious answers. Popular among such people were the mystery religions, so called because they involved secret rituals known only to initiates. These religions, whose attraction only grew as the Roman Empire weakened, offered their adherents spiritual immortality in · an afterlife. But the greatest religious force transforming Rome was Christianity, whose roots we must seek in the Jewish experience beginning in the Middle East in the late second millennium B.C.

The founders of this religious tradition, the Hebrews, originated a faith that was unique in the ancient Middle East. By the late second millennium B.C., their Judaism was a monotheistic religion centered on the deity Yahweh, who demanded ethical behavior of his followers. In this ethical monotheism of the early Hebrews, Yahweh enforced his laws by divine intervention in this life. There was no belief in a last judgment, and afterlife beliefs were quite similar to those of the Greeks; the Jews' Sheol was a dark underworld of the dead.

By the first century B.C., new ideas were taking root among the Jews of Palestine, dividing them into four main sects. The Sadducees, often drawn from the elite of Jewish society, maintained traditional beliefs and ceremonies and the letter of ancient religious law dating back to the days of the lawgiver Moses. The Pharisees, quite possibly representing the majority of Jews in Palestine, challenged the Sadducees by their willingness to admit the law to interpretation and by their acceptance of the eastern idea of a life after death, with the possibility of spiritual salvation through resurrection. The Essenes, the third group within first-century Judaism, also accepted the idea of resurrection, but formed a monastic-style community near the Dead Sea where they awaited the imminent establishment of the Kingdom of God on earth. The fourth sect, the Zealots, refused to accept Roman conquest of their homeland and engaged in violent resistance, culminat-

ing in a Jewish revolt in Palestine in A.D. 66.

A widely held belief among first-century Jews in Palestine was that they would be delivered from foreign domination by a Messiah. Many Jews conceived of the Messiah as a military leader, but when a peaceful figure, Jesus of Nazareth (ca 4 B.C.–ca A.D. 29), declared that he was the Messiah, many Jews saw him as fulfilling their expectation, and Jesus soon had a growing following. Grounded in Jewish monotheism, Jesus' teachings called on his followers to repent their sins in order to enter the Kingdom of God and thus achieve spiritual salvation in a life after death. But to conservative Jews like the Sadducees, Jesus was defying traditional religious law, and they turned him over to Roman authorities. In a difficult province of their empire, these officials certainly saw Jesus as an unsettling presence who counted Zealots among his closest followers, and they ordered his execution.

Jesus' followers proclaimed his resurrection three days after his death as fulfillment of his teachings, and the nature of his following shortly began to change. More and more Gentiles, or non-Jews, joined Jesus' original Jewish followers, as Saint Paul (ca 5–ca A.D. 67) emphasized that adherence to traditional Jewish law, including dietary rules and circumcision, was not required for membership in the Christian community. In the Hellenized culture of the Middle East, Jesus increasingly was referred to as "Christ," from the Greek *Christos*, or "the Anointed," a translation of the

Hebrew word *Messiah*. Thus, a new faith, Christianity, quite distinct from Judaism, emerged and grew steadily because of its promise of otherworldly rewards in a society already seeking such spiritual comfort in the mystery religions. Soon the Christian community grew large enough to attract the attention of Roman authorities to a faith that seemed subversive in its nonviolence and refusal even superficially to conform to the Roman civic practice of venerating the emperor. Imperial authorities responded with sporadic, often brutal, persecutions of Christians, beginning in A.D. 64. But the continued growth of the new faith led first to its legalization under Emperor Constantine in A.D. 313 and finally to its elevation to the status of Rome's official religion by Emperor Theodosius I in A.D. 392.

As it achieved legitimacy, Christianity also defined its belief system in an atmosphere of theological controversy. Many theologians whose ideas came to be viewed by the Church as false doctrines, or heresies, sought to promote their ideas in the Christian community. Thus, the followers of Arius (A.D. 250–326), a Greek priest of Alexandria, denied the absolute divinity of Christ, who had declared that he was the son of God. Arians, who taught that Christ was certainly no mere mortal but that

neither was he God's equal, received the Church's condemnation at the Council of Nicaea in A.D. 325. Another heretical group was the Donatists, who rejected the idea, held by the majority of Christians, that the Church should be a universal, or catholic, church embracing all, sinners as well as those meriting salvation. Donatists believed that the Church should include only the elect. Other heresies also spread, but the work of a group of theologians remembered as Church Fathers eventually imposed doctrinal uniformity on the early Church.

Your goal in this chapter is to analyze the thought of these ancient peoples on three levels defined by the central questions of this chapter. The first is very specific to the issue of suicide: What does the author of each selection say about suicide? The second asks you to place these ideas in their intellectual context: How do each author's ideas on self-destruction represent his own thought system and the intellectual outlook of the society in which he lived? The third requires that you perform one of the essential tasks of the historian and examine change over an extended period of time: What change in attitudes toward self-destruction do you see over the extended time period covered by these selections?

SOURCES AND METHOD

This chapter, like Chapter 2, offers us ancient primary sources that present certain analytical challenges. Again,

we must recognize that the absolute accuracy of these texts cannot be verified the way records of modern scholars' writings can be checked in their printed works or in recordings or transcripts of their lectures.

Products of a pre-print age, the handwritten originals of most of these sources have long ago disappeared, and students must rely on texts based on ancient scribes' transcriptions of the originals, which may not always be entirely faithful to the authors' precise words. Furthermore, because much ancient writing has failed to survive, it is often difficult to determine whether a given work represents all that its author had to say on a subject.

We also will encounter again sources that are not actually the work of those to whom they are attributed. As we saw in Chapter 2, we can know the thought of Socrates, who wrote nothing, only through the work of his student Plato, and scholars still disagree as to which ideas in the latter's writings are his own and which are those of his teacher. Such considerations require some analysis for all our sources in this chapter.

Source 1 is the work of Plato, an Athenian philosopher who, in the course of his long career, wrote on just about all the philosophical problems that have occupied Western thinkers since his death. His surviving works include letters and a number of dialogues. The dialogues replicate in written form the teaching method of Socrates. Socrates particularly concerned himself with the search for the values by which he and his fellow Athenians might live lives of moral excellence. Socrates believed that these values were not imparted to humanity by a deity, but rather that the individual could discover them through rational inquiry, and

he devised a mode of inquiry, dialectics, to facilitate that search. As practiced by Socrates and his followers, dialectics represented a logical discussion, propelled by the teacher's questions to the student, that forced the student to clarify and justify his thought. Thus, in Source 1, from Plato's dialogue *The Phaedo*, questions are posed by Socrates.

Many scholars divide Plato's dialogues into two chief categories, according to the order in which they probably were written. They call the earlier dialogues, including *The Apology, The Meno,* and *The Gorgias,* "Socratic" because they seem to express chiefly the ideas of Socrates. The later dialogues, including *The Phaedo,* seem more nearly to express the ideas of Plato himself.

Plato divided knowledge into two realms. One of these was knowledge of the material world, which can be gathered through sensory perceptions. The other, higher realm of knowledge was that of absolute reality and perfect virtues, the realm of forms or ideas for Plato, which could be achieved only intellectually.

In Source 1, one of the most dramatic episodes of ancient literature, Plato describes the execution of Socrates. Plato's teacher had employed his dialectic method not only with his students, but with his fellow citizens as well, in the hope of leading them to more ethical lives. Indeed, he became the Athenians' "gadfly," and he made more than a few enemies. When Athens lost the Peloponnesian War with Sparta, many of those enemies led Athenians who were seeking an explanation for their defeat to charge Socrates with having had a role in the military disaster. Indeed, several of Socrates' former students had betrayed their city in the war, and his enemies charged him with having led the youth of Athens away from the traditional gods and thereby contributed to the Spartan victory.

As was customary in Athens, the trial of Socrates took place before a jury with wide-ranging powers; the jury not only judged guilt or innocence but also determined the sentence. Plato's accounts of the procedure in *The Apology* make it clear that Socrates could have escaped serious penalty by going into voluntary exile before trial or, perhaps after conviction, by admitting error and promising to stop teaching. But when the jury found him guilty and asked him to suggest a punishment, Socrates almost mockingly proposed what amounted to civic honors. Even though he subsequently suggested a fine, the jury clearly took offense at his remarks; more jurors voted for the penalty of death by taking poison (hemlock) than had voted for the verdict of guilty.

Socrates' behavior at his trial and his subsequent refusal to approve the efforts of his friends Simmias and Cebes, who arrived with money to finance an escape from confinement, suggest to many scholars a sort of death wish. These scholars propose that the philosopher's end represented not so much an execution as a suicide. Indeed, self-destruction figures prominently in *The Phaedo*, which opens on Socrates' execution day (which had been delayed by Athenian religious observances). Socrates spent that day surrounded by friends, and one of these, Cebes, asked Socrates, on behalf of the poet Evenus, why he had lately taken to writing poetry. Socrates replied that he had no wish to rival Evenus, but simply wrote in response to a dream demanding that he "make music"; he wrote only so as to leave no duty undone as he met his end. Our selection from The Phaedo opens in the midst of the discussion of poetry. In that selection, why does Socrates think that philosophers in particular should welcome death? How should death open to philosophers the realm of ideas or forms? Does Socrates suggest any divine limitation on an individual's right to self-destruction? What suggests to you that Socrates believed that a divine necessity now permitted his death and that he welcomed his end as a remedy for the problems of this life? What in the thought of Socrates strikes you as characteristic of a philosopher who was a free citizen of a democratic city-state? What about Plato's thought might suggest to you that he was less optimistic than his teacher about finding perfection in this life?

While important portions of Plato's work have survived for modern study, the work of some other ancient philosophers comes to us less directly. This is the case with both Epicurus (ca 341–270 B.C.), of whose vast writings only fragments have survived, and Epictetus (ca 50–ca A.D.

73

138), whose thought survives only in writings of a disciple, Arrian, based on notes of Epictetus' words.

Much of what we know of the life and thought of Epicurus comes from *Lives of Eminent Philosophers* by Diogenes Laertius, an author about whom scholars know very little. He wrote this history of ancient philosophers in Greek, and the contents of the book suggest that he composed it early in the third century after the birth of Christ. *Lives of Eminent Philosophers* is a remarkable source for ancient history because Diogenes Laertius included many writings that subsequently were lost and, therefore, are available nowhere else. The author illustrated his accounts of philosophers' lives with quotations from their philosophical writings as well as from decrees, letters, wills, and epitaphs. Indeed, Source 2 opens with a letter from Epicurus and concludes with a brief portion of the maxims that he expected his students to memorize, all drawn from *Lives of Eminent Philosophers*.

In the excerpts from the works of Epicurus in Source 2, what aim in life does he urge on his followers? How are they to attain that goal? Why will death be "nothing" to Epicureans? How did his thought relate to self-destruction? Why did the Roman thinker Cicero (106–43 B.C.) write the following passage?

For my part I think that in life we should observe the rule which is followed at Greek banquets:—"Let him either drink," it runs, "or go!" And rightly; for either he should enjoy the pleasure of tippling along with the oth-

ers or get away early, that a sober man may not be a victim to the violence of those who are heated with wine. Thus by running away one can escape the assaults of fortune which one cannot face. This is the same advice as Epicurus gives.[3]

How does this quotation embody developments we have examined in the Hellenistic and Roman worlds?

Source 3 presents a selection from the *Discourses* of Epictetus recorded by Arrian (ca A.D. 95–175), who was a cosmopolitan figure indeed. A Greek born in Asia Minor, he entered Roman service and combined success as a governor and general with scholarship. Writing in Greek, he was the author of several histories, including one of Alexander the Great, and as a student of philosophy, Arrian wrote the only record of the thought of his teacher, Epictetus.

Like Arrian a Greek born in Asia Minor, Epictetus was the son of a slave woman and was a slave himself for many years. Taken to Rome as a youth, he studied philosophy there; once freed, perhaps at his master's death, he taught first in the imperial capital and then at Nicopolis in Greece. The teaching of Epictetus reflected this former slave's love of freedom and placed him in the ranks of the foremost Stoics.

Stoicism proved particularly attractive to the Romans, many of whom believed that their empire represented the Stoic ideal of a universal

3. Cicero, *Tusculan Disputations*, translated by J. E. King (Cambridge, Mass.: Harvard University Press, 1960), pp. 543–545.

human community. For Roman audiences, Epictetus called Logos "God" in Source 3. What evidence do you find of the philosopher's love of freedom? What is the concern of "the good and excellent man" in life? When may such a person terminate his life? What similarity do you find between these circumstances and those in which Plato found suicide justifiable? How does the thought of Epictetus perhaps reflect problems of the Roman world?

With Sources 4 through 9, we move from the classical tradition of Greece and Rome to the roots of the Judeo-Christian heritage in Palestine. Sources 4 through 8 are from the thirty-nine books of the Hebrew scriptures that Jews refer to as *Tanak* and that Christians call the Old Testament of the Bible. Written between the thirteenth and second centuries B.C., the Hebrew scriptures provide a remarkable record of the experience of the Jewish people before the birth of Christ, and we must examine their utility as a work of history.

The compilers of the Old Testament were not historians but religious thinkers concerned with Jewish faith, law, and literature, as well as history. The Old Testament thus is the foundation of the modern Jewish and Christian faiths. Students of history find the Old Testament an invaluable source, but they also find that this work of religious inspiration sometimes contains historical contradictions and occasional factual errors, and so scholars must verify biblical accounts of events against records in other sources. Nevertheless, the Old Testament, a collection of works by many authors, contains a consistent expression of values and belief and is our best source for understanding the religion of the Hebrews, and it is from that perspective that we will consider Sources 4 through 8.

We draw Sources 4 through 8 from the Hebrew scriptures' books of Judges, 1 and 2 Samuel, and 1 Kings, books that recount the teachings and careers of the great Hebrew prophets and leaders. These books contain all the acts of self-destruction that are found in the Hebrew scriptures. Sources 4 and 5 come from the Book of Judges, which describes the period in Hebrew history between the deaths of Moses and Joshua—who had led their people out of captivity in Egypt and into the promised land of Canaan—and the advent of kings as rulers among the Hebrews. Source 4 is from the Book of Judges' account of political instability among the Hebrews as they evolved from nomadic tribesmen into a more settled people who needed nontribal, permanent institutions of government. In search of that government, they offered the crown to the prophet Gideon, who rejected the overture, proclaiming that God alone should rule. After Gideon's death, his son Abimelech slew all but one of his brothers and seized the crown his father had rejected. Established as king, Abimelech brutally put down rebellions against his authority and, as told in Source 4, engaged in an attack on the rebellious city of Thebez. How did Abimelech meet his end? Why may we consider this suicide? Beyond the statement that Abimelech's death represented divine retribution, do you find any textual condemnation of the death of Abimelech?

Source 5 also comes from the Book of Judges; it is part of the account of the mighty Samson, a judge, or leader, of the Hebrews. According to this account, Samson possessed extraordinary strength, which he used against the pagan Philistines, who were enemies of the Hebrews. Samson's long hair represented his vows of devotion to God, and when the woman Delilah learned of this, she cut his hair, depriving Samson of his strength. The Philistines then captured Samson, blinded him, and enslaved him. But his hair grew back, and with it his strength, a fact unnoticed by the Philistines when they put him on display in a temple to their god, Dagon. What does Source 5 show Samson doing in the temple? While this is an act of martyrdom, why must it also be considered a suicide? Understanding that among many ancient peoples, burial in the family tomb was an honor, what can you conclude about the Hebrews' perception of Samson's death?

In Source 6 we have an account of the first anointed king of the Hebrews, Saul. Selected as king by the great judge Samuel, Saul disobeyed God's commands, and Samuel designated David as the new and rightful king. Nevertheless, Saul retained the crown, fighting David in a civil war, while continuing to battle the historic enemies of the Hebrews, the Philistines. What action did Saul, facing defeat by the Philistines atop Mount Gilboa, take in Source 6? Why must you conclude that Saul's death was a suicide? What is the reaction of

the Hebrews to Saul's death? How does the following response of David to the death of Saul and his son Jonathan reinforce your conclusion about the Hebrews' reaction to Saul's self-destruction?

Thy glory, O Israel, is slain upon
   thy high places!
How are the mighty fallen!
. . . . .
Saul and Jonathan, beloved and
   lovely!
In life and death they were not
   divided;
They were swifter than eagles,
   they were stronger than lions.[4]

Saul's death allowed David to gain the crown, but David's rule did not go unchallenged. He faced a rebellion by his son Absalom and his former counselor, Ahithophel. The advice of Ahithophel was highly esteemed, for "in those days the counsel which Ahithophel gave was as if one consulted the oracle of God."[5] Nevertheless, Absalom rejected the strategy proposed by Ahithophel, "For the Lord had ordained to defeat the good counsel of Ahithophel, so that the Lord might bring evil on Absalom."[6] What does Source 7 indicate was Ahithophel's response to Absalom's humiliating him by ignoring his advice? What happened to Ahithophel's remains? What response does this in-

4. 2 Samuel 1:19, 23, in *The Oxford Annotated Bible with the Apocrypha* (New York: Oxford University Press, 1965), p. 375.

5. 2 Samuel 16:23, in *The Oxford Annotated Bible*, p. 397.

6. 2 Samuel 17:14, in *The Oxford Annotated Bible*, p. 398.

dicate that Ahithophel's contemporaries had to his death?

After the death of King David's son and heir, Solomon, the Hebrew kingdom divided into Israel and Judah, and Source 8 recounts an event in Israel. Zimri, a powerful military leader, killed King Elah and seized the throne. Zimri's coup did not go unopposed, however, and the forces of the army commander, Omri, besieged the usurper in the city of Tirzah. What end overtook Zimri, according to Source 8? While the text certainly suggests that God's punishment was a factor in Zimri's death, did the author in any way condemn the act of suicide?

Source 9 also is a biblical selection, but it comes from the writings commonly known among Christians as the New Testament. These Christian scriptures consist of the twenty-seven books that recount the life of Jesus Christ and record his teachings and those of his followers. They are central to the belief of all Christians. Source 9 describes the death of one of the twelve apostles of Jesus, Judas Iscariot. For thirty silver coins, Judas had betrayed Jesus' location to priests of the Temple in Jerusalem who opposed his teachings. Christ was arrested and executed by crucifixion, a mode of punishment commonly employed by the Roman authorities. Source 9 describes the suicide of Judas. Why, according to this account, did Judas take his own life? Is there any textual condemnation of this act of self-destruction? What response to suicide seems common to both Hebrew and Christian texts?

Source 10 is the work of Josephus, one of the greatest ancient historians. Josephus (37–ca A.D. 100) was a complex individual, and we require an understanding of his background in order to interpret his writings. A Jew born in Jerusalem, his early studies led Josephus to join the Pharisees. When Palestine erupted in a Jewish rebellion against Roman rule in A.D. 66, the scholarly Josephus took an active role, commanding rebel forces in Galilee. Roman legions eventually crushed the rebellion, and Josephus won the favor of their commander, Titus Flavius Vespasian; he even added "Flavius" to his own name. Vespasian went on to become emperor of Rome, and Josephus Flavius enjoyed imperial patronage in the capital. There he wrote in Greek several important histories, including *Jewish Antiquities*, a history of the Jews from Adam and Eve to the first century A.D., and *The Jewish War*, a history of the Jewish rebellion against Roman rule in Palestine.

Scholars detect many influences on Josephus that we must identify before reading his work. Certainly he was a devout Jewish Pharisee whose work represented an apology of sorts for his people's rebellion. At the same time, Josephus was a Roman citizen who had been thoroughly imbued with the Greco-Roman culture of the first century A.D. And we must not forget that Josephus enjoyed an imperial pension, which might have affected his portrayal of events in his histories.

Source 10 presents perhaps the most famous event in the Jewish rebellion, the last stand of the Zealots at the mountain fortress of Masada in 73 A.D. Faced with inevitable defeat, what step did the Zealots' leader, Eleazar, urge upon them? How did the garrison respond? How many persons perished, according to Josephus? How does he portray this mass suicide? How does this portrayal replicate reactions to suicide in other ancient sources?

Our final source, Source 11, is the work of Saint Augustine (A.D. 354–430), one of the greatest early Church Fathers. Saint Augustine lived in turbulent times, when the Roman Empire in the West was in marked decline and heretical ideas challenged Christian doctrine. Raised as a Christian in his native North Africa, Augustine abandoned that faith during a rather dissolute period as a young man and adopted the Manichaean heresy, an eastern belief system founded upon the idea that the world was a battleground between the forces of good and evil deities. Eventually, in Milan, Italy, Augustine encountered the eloquent preaching of another Church Father, Saint Ambrose, bishop of Milan, which helped to win him back to Christianity.

Augustine returned to North Africa, became bishop of Hippo, and produced a large body of writings that helped to define Christian doctrine and to defend it against the numerous heresies of the day. *The City of God Against the Pagans*, excerpted in Source 11, is the most important of these. Saint Augustine wrote it in response to the sack of Rome by the Visigoths in 410. Non-Christians blamed this disaster on the Christianity that had won over much of the empire in the fourth century A.D. They saw the event as the revenge of the old gods that had been abandoned by many Romans and as the result of Christians' refusal to perform military service. Saint Augustine denied such charges and reasoned that, while imperial Rome was the greatest city that humanity could realize, the true object of the Christian life should be attainment to the heavenly City of God. In short, the rise and fall of empires was unimportant compared to the individual's spiritual journey to heavenly salvation.

Saint Augustine also used *The City of God* to further his mission of defending Christian doctrine. An issue that particularly concerned him was how his contemporaries, Christians and heretics alike, fulfilled Christ's injunction in Mark 8:34–35: "If any man would come after me, let him deny himself and take up his cross and follow me. For whoever would save his life will lose it; and whoever loses his life for my sake and the gospel's will save it."[7] Early Christians sometimes actually sought martyrdom at the hands of Roman officers assigned to enforce the superficial rites of official veneration of the emperor. Such suicidal self-sacrifice especially occurred among Donatists.

This enthusiastic martyrdom caused several early Christian thinkers to distinguish between true martyrdom and suicide. Saint Augustine takes up this theme in Source 11 as part of his discussion of the plunder of Rome in 410, when a number of women committed suicide rather than suffer sex-

7. *The Oxford Annotated Bible*, p. 1225.

ual assault by the Visigothic attackers. How does Saint Augustine view suicide? How does Saint Augustine's interpretation of the deaths of Samson and Judas differ from the accounts in Sources 5 and 9? In what circumstances would Saint Augustine permit suicide? What religious change did these conditions reflect? What new approach to suicide did Saint Augustine introduce?

Using this background on ancient philosophy and theology, now examine the evidence. As you read each source, you should seek answers for the central questions of this chapter. What does the author of each selection say about suicide? How do each author's ideas on self-destruction represent his own thought system and the intellectual outlook of the society in which he lived? What change in attitude toward self-destruction do you observe over the extended time period covered by these selections?

THE EVIDENCE

Source 1 from Plato with English Translation, *vol. 1,* Euthyphro, Apology, Crito, Phaedo, Phaedrus, *translated by Harold North Fowler (Cambridge, Mass.: Harvard University Press, 1953), pp. 213–233, 399–403. Reprinted with permission of the publishers and the Loeb Classical Library.*

1. Plato, *The Phaedo*

"So tell Evenus that, Cebes, and bid him farewell, and tell him, if he is wise, to come after me as quickly as he can. I, it seems, am going to-day; for that is the order of the Athenians."

And Simmias said, "What a message that is, Socrates, for Evenus! I have met him often, and from what I have seen of him, I should say that he will not take your advice in the least if he can help it."

"Why so?" said he. "Is not Evenus a philosopher?"

"I think so," said Simmias.

"Then Evenus will take my advice, and so will every man who has any worthy interest in philosophy. Perhaps, however, he will not take his own life, for they[8] say that is not permitted." And as he spoke he put his feet down on the ground and remained sitting in this way through the rest of the conversation.

Then Cebes asked him: "What do you mean by this, Socrates, that it is not permitted to take one's life, but that the philosopher would desire to follow after the dying?" . . .

---

8. **they:** Socrates refers here to the Pythagorean philosophers, including Philolaus, who opposed suicide. Pythagoreans believed that the soul was imprisoned in the body as punishment for sins in an earlier life. Thus, self-destruction was akin to a prison escape and was unacceptable to them.

"Why in the world do they say that it is not permitted to kill oneself, Socrates? I heard Philolaus, when he was living in our city, say the same thing you just said, and I have heard it from others, too, that one must not do this; but I never heard anyone say anything definite about it."

"You must have courage," said he, "and perhaps you might hear something. But perhaps it will seem strange to you that this alone of all laws is without exception, and it never happens to mankind, as in other matters, that only at some times and for some persons it is better to die than to live; and it will perhaps seem strange to you that these human beings for whom it is better to die cannot without impiety do good to themselves, but must wait for some other benefactor."

And Cebes, smiling gently, said, "Gawd knows it doos," speaking in his own dialect.

"It would seem unreasonable, if put in this way," said Socrates, "but perhaps there is some reason in it. Now the doctrine that is taught in secret about this matter, that we men are in a kind of prison and must not set ourselves free or run away, seems to me to be weighty and not easy to understand. But this at least, Cebes, I do believe is sound, that the gods are our guardians and that we men are one of the chattels of the gods. Do you not believe this?"

"Yes," said Cebes, "I do."

"Well, then," said he, "if one of your chattels should kill itself when you had not indicated that you wished it to die, would you be angry with it and punish it if you could?"

"Certainly," he replied.

"Then perhaps from this point of view it is not unreasonable to say that a man must not kill himself until god sends some necessity upon him, such as has now come upon me."

"That," said Cebes, "seems sensible. But what you said just now, Socrates, that philosophers ought to be ready and willing to die, that seems strange if we were right just now in saying that god is our guardian and we are his possessions. For it is not reasonable that the wisest men should not be troubled when they leave that service in which the gods, who are the best overseers in the world, are watching over them. A wise man certainly does not think that when he is free he can take better care of himself than they do. A foolish man might perhaps think so, that he ought to run away from his master, and he would not consider that he must not run away from a good master, but ought to stay with him as long as possible; and so he might thoughtlessly run away; but a man of sense would wish to be always with one who is better than himself. And yet, Socrates, if we look at it in this way, the contrary of what we just said seems natural; for the wise ought to be troubled at dying and the foolish to rejoice." . . .

. . . "I wish now to explain to you, my judges, the reason why I think a man who has really spent his life in philosophy is naturally of good courage when he is to die, and has strong hopes that when he is dead he will attain the greatest blessings in that other land. So I will try to tell you, Simmias, and Cebes, how this would be.

"Other people are likely not to be aware that those who pursue philosophy aright study nothing but dying and being dead. Now if this is true, it would be absurd to be eager for nothing but this all their lives, and then to be troubled when that came for which they had all along been eagerly practising."

And Simmias laughed and said, "By Zeus, Socrates, I don't feel much like laughing just now, but you made me laugh. For I think the multitude, if they heard what you just said about the philosophers, would say you were quite right, and our people at home would agree entirely with you that philosophers desire death, and they would add that they know very well that the philosophers deserve it."

"And they would be speaking the truth, Simmias, except in the matter of knowing very well. For they do not know in what way the real philosophers desire death, nor in what way they deserve death, nor what kind of a death it is. Let us then," said he, "speak with one another, paying no further attention to them. Do we think there is such a thing as death?"

"Certainly," replied Simmias.

"We believe, do we not, that death is the separation of the soul from the body, and that the state of being dead is the state in which the body is separated from the soul and exists alone by itself and the soul is separated from the body and exists alone by itself? Is death anything other than this?" "No, it is this," said he.

"Now, my friend, see if you agree with me; for, if you do, I think we shall get more light on our subject. Do you think a philosopher would be likely to care much about the so-called pleasures, such as eating and drinking?"

"By no means, Socrates," said Simmias.

"How about the pleasures of love?"

"Certainly not."

"Well, do you think such a man would think much of the other cares of the body—I mean such as the possession of fine clothes and shoes and the other personal adornments? Do you think he would care about them or despise them, except so far as it is necessary to have them?"

"I think the true philosopher would despise them," he replied.

"Altogether, then, you think that such a man would not devote himself to the body, but would, so far as he was able, turn away from the body and concern himself with the soul?"

"Yes."

"To begin with, then, it is clear that in such matters the philosopher, more than other men, separates the soul from communion with the body?"

"It is." . . .

"Now, how about the acquirement of pure knowledge? Is the body a hindrance or not, if it is made to share in the search for wisdom? What I mean is this: Have the sight and hearing of men any truth in them, or is it true, as the poets are always telling us, that we neither hear nor see anything accurately? And yet if these two physical senses are not accurate or exact, the rest are not likely to be, for they are inferior to these. Do you not think so?"

"Certainly I do," he replied.

"Then," said he, "when does the soul attain to truth? For when it tries to consider anything in company with the body, it is evidently deceived by it."

"True."

"In thought, then, if at all, something of the realities becomes clear to it?"

"Yes."

"But it thinks best when none of these things troubles it, neither hearing nor sight, nor pain nor any pleasure, but it is, so far as possible, alone by itself, and takes leave of the body, and avoiding, so far as it can, all association or contact with the body, reaches out toward the reality."

"That is true."

"In this matter also, then, the soul of the philosopher greatly despises the body and avoids it and strives to be alone by itself?"

"Evidently."

"Now how about such things as this, Simmias? Do we think there is such a thing as absolute justice or not?"

"We certainly think there is."

"And absolute beauty and goodness."

"Of course."

"Well, did you ever see anything of that kind with your eyes?"

"Certainly not," said he.

"Or did you ever reach them with any of the bodily senses? I am speaking of all such things, as size, health, strength, and in short the essence or underlying quality of everything. Is their true nature contemplated by means of the body? Is it not rather the case that he who prepares himself most carefully to understand the true essence of each thing that he examines would come nearest to the knowledge of it?"

"Certainly."

"Would not that man do this most perfectly who approaches each thing, so far as possible, with the reason alone, not introducing sight into his reasoning nor dragging in any of the other senses along with his thinking, but who employs pure, absolute reason in his attempt to search out the pure, absolute essence of things, and who removes himself, so far as possible, from eyes and ears, and, in a word, from his whole body, because he feels that its companionship disturbs the soul and hinders it from attaining truth and wisdom? Is not this the man, Simmias, if anyone, to attain to the knowledge of reality?"

"That is true as true can be, Socrates," said Simmias.

"Then," said he, "all this must cause good lovers of wisdom to think and say one to the other something like this: 'There seems to be a short cut which leads us and our argument to the conclusion in our search that so long as we have the body, and the soul is contaminated by such an evil, we shall never attain completely what we desire, that is, the truth. . . .

. . . "For, if pure knowledge is impossible while the body is with us, one of two thing[s] must follow, either it cannot be acquired at all or only when we are dead; for then the soul will be by itself apart from the body, but not before. And while we live, we shall, I think, be nearest to knowledge when we avoid, so far as possible, intercourse and communion with the body, except what is absolutely necessary, and are not filled with its nature, but keep ourselves pure from it until God himself sets us free. And in this way, freeing ourselves from the foolishness of the body and being pure, we shall, I think, be with the pure and shall know of ourselves all that is pure—and that is, perhaps, the truth. For it cannot be that the impure attain the pure.' Such words as these, I think, Simmias, all who are rightly lovers of knowledge must say to each other and such must be their thoughts. Do you not agree?"

"Most assuredly, Socrates."

"Then," said Socrates, "if this is true, my friend, I have great hopes that when I reach the place to which I am going, I shall there, if anywhere, attain fully to that which has been my chief object in my past life, so that the journey which is now imposed upon me is begun with good hope; and the like hope exists for every man who thinks that his mind has been purified and made ready." . . .

Thereupon Crito nodded to the boy who was standing near. The boy went out and stayed a long time, then came back with the man who was to administer the poison, which he brought with him in a cup ready for use. And when Socrates saw him, he said: "Well, my good man, you know about these things; what must I do?" "Nothing," he replied, "except drink the poison and walk about till your legs feel heavy; then lie down, and the poison will take effect of itself."

At the same time he held out the cup to Socrates. He took it, and very gently, Echecrates, without trembling or changing colour or expression, but looking up at the man with wide open eyes, as was his custom, said: "What do you say about pouring a libation[9] to some deity from this cup? May I, or not?" "Socrates," said he, "we prepare only as much as we think is enough." "I understand," said Socrates; "but I may and must pray to the gods that my departure hence be a fortunate one; so I offer this prayer, and may it be granted." With these words he raised the cup to his lips and very cheerfully and quietly drained it. Up to that time most of us had been able to restrain our tears fairly well, but when we watched him drinking and saw that he had drunk the poison, we could do so no longer. . . . He walked about and, when he said his legs were heavy, lay down on his back, for such was the advice of the attendant. The man who had administered the poison laid his hands on him and after a while examined his feet and legs, then pinched his foot hard and asked if he

---

9. **libation:** the ritual pouring out of wine or holy oil as an offering to a deity.

felt it. He said "No"; then after that, his thighs; and passing upwards in this way he showed us that he was growing cold and rigid. And again he touched him and said that when it reached his heart, he would be gone. The chill had now reached the region about the groin, and uncovering his face, which had been covered, he said—and these were his last words—"Crito, we owe a cock to Aesculapius.[10] Pay it and do not neglect it." "That," said Crito, "shall be done; but see if you have anything else to say." To this question he made no reply, but after a little while he moved; the attendant uncovered him; his eyes were fixed. And Crito when he saw it, closed his mouth and eyes.

Such was the end, Echecrates, of our friend, who was, as we may say, of all those of his time whom we have known, the best and wisest and most right-eous man.

Source 2 from Diogenes Laertius, Lives of Eminent Philosophers, *vol. 2, translated by Robert Drew Hicks (New York: G. P. Putnam's Sons, 1925), pp. 651–653, 657, 665.*

2. Epicurus on the Meaning of Death

[*From a letter*]

"Accustom thyself to believe that death is nothing to us, for good and evil imply sentience,[11] and death is the privation of all sentience; therefore a right understanding that death is nothing to us makes the mortality of life enjoyable, not by adding to life an illimitable time, but by taking away the yearning after immortality. For life has no terrors for him who has thoroughly apprehended that there are no terrors for him in ceasing to live. Foolish, therefore, is the man who says that he fears death, not because it will pain when it comes, but because it pains in the prospect. Whatsoever causes no annoyance when it is present, causes only a groundless pain in the expectation. Death, therefore, the most awful of evils, is nothing to us, seeing that, when we are, death is not come, and, when death is come, we are not. It is nothing, then, either to the living or to the dead, for with the living it is not and the dead exist no longer. But in the world, at one time men shun death as the greatest of all evils, and at another time choose it as a respite from the evils in life. The wise man does not deprecate life nor does he fear the cessation of life. The thought of life is no offence to him, nor is the cessation of life regarded as an evil. And even as men choose of food not merely and simply the larger portion, but the more pleas-

10. **Aesculapius:** sometimes also rendered "Asclepius," this was the chief god of healing. It was common in the ancient world to offer animal sacrifices to deities as part of prayerful entreaties or as offerings of thanks.
11. **sentience:** the capacity for feeling or sensation.

ant, so the wise seek to enjoy the time which is most pleasant and not merely that which is longest. . . .

"When we say, then, that pleasure is the end and aim, we do not mean the pleasures of the prodigal or the pleasures of sensuality, as we are understood to do by some through ignorance, prejudice, or wilful misrepresentation. By pleasure we mean the absence of pain in the body and of trouble in the soul. It is not an unbroken succession of drinking-bouts and of revelry, not sexual love, not the enjoyment of the fish and other delicacies of a luxurious table, which produce a pleasant life; it is sober reasoning, searching out the grounds of every choice and avoidance, and banishing those beliefs through which the greatest tumults take possession of the soul. Of all this the beginning and the greatest good is prudence. Wherefore prudence is a more precious thing even than philosophy; from it spring all the other virtues, for it teaches that we cannot lead a life of pleasure which is not also a life of prudence, honour, and justice; nor lead a life of prudence, honour, and justice, which is not also a life of pleasure. For the virtues have grown into one with a pleasant life, and a pleasant life is inseparable from them. . . .

[*From the maxims*]

Death is nothing to us; for the body, when it has been resolved into its elements, has no feeling, and that which has no feeling is nothing to us.

Source 3 from Epictetus, The Discourses as Reported by Arrian, the Manual, and Fragments, *vol. 2, translated by W(illiam) A(bbott) Oldfather (New York: G. P. Putnam's Sons, 1926), pp. 215–217.*

3. Epictetus on Ending Life

For this reason the good and excellent man, bearing in mind who he is, and whence he has come, and by whom he was created, centres his attention on this and this only, how he may fill his place in an orderly fashion, and with due obedience to God. "Is it Thy will that I should still remain? I will remain as a free man, as a noble man, as Thou didst wish it; for Thou hast made me free from hindrance in what was mine own. And now hast Thou no further need of me? Be it well with Thee. I have been waiting here until now because of Thee and of none other, and now I obey Thee and depart." "How do you depart?" "Again, as Thou didst wish it, as a free man, as Thy servant, as one who has perceived Thy commands and Thy prohibitions. But so long as I continue to live in Thy service, what manner of man wouldst Thou have me be? An official or a private citizen, a senator or one of the common people, a soldier or a general, a teacher or the head of a household? Whatsoever station and post Thou assign me, I will die ten thousand times, as Socrates says, or ever I abandon it.[12] And where wouldst Thou have me be? In Rome, or in Athens, or in Thebes, or in Gyara? Only remember me there. If Thou sendest me to a place where men have no means of living in accordance with nature, I shall depart this life, not in disobedience to Thee, but as though Thou wert sounding for me the recall. I do not abandon Thee—far be that from me! but I perceive that Thou hast no need of me. Yet if there be vouchsafed a means of living in accordance with nature, I will seek no other place than that in which I am, or other men than those who are now my associates."

Sources 4 through 9 from the Revised Standard Version of the Bible, pp. 307–308; p. 316; p. 373; p. 399; p. 441; p. 1209. Copyright 1946, 1952, 1971 by the Division of Christian Education of the National Council of the Churches of Christ in the U.S.A. Used by permission.

4. The Death of Abimelech
(Judges 9:50–56)

Then Abim'elech went to Thebez, and encamped against Thebez, and took it. But there was a strong tower within the city, and all the people of the city fled to it, all the men and women, and shut themselves in; and they went to the roof of the tower. And Abim'elech came to the tower, and fought against it, and drew near to the door of the tower to burn it with fire. And a certain woman threw an upper millstone upon Abim'elech's head, and crushed his skull. Then he called hastily to the young man his armor-bearer, and said to him, "Draw your sword and kill me, lest men say of me, 'A woman killed him.' " And his young man thrust him through, and he died. And when the men of Israel saw that Abim'elech was dead, they departed every man to his home. Thus God requited the crime of Abim'elech, which he committed against his father in killing his seventy brothers.

5. The Death of Samson
(Judges 16:23–31)

Now the lords of the Philistines gathered to offer a great sacrifice to Dagon their god, and to rejoice; for they said, "Our god has given Samson our enemy into our hand." And when the people saw him, they praised their god; for they said, "Our god has given our enemy into our hand, the ravager of our country, who has slain many of us." And when their hearts were merry, they said, "Call Samson, that he may make sport for us." So they called Samson out of the prison, and he made sport before them. They made him stand between the pillars; and Samson said to the lad who held him by the hand, "Let me feel

12. This is a paraphrase of the words of Socrates in Plato's dialogue *The Apology*, which recounts the philosopher's defense at his trial.

86

the pillars on which the house rests, that I may lean against them." Now the house was full of men and women; all the lords of the Philistines were there, and on the roof there were about three thousand men and women, who looked on while Samson made sport.

Then Samson called to the LORD and said, "O Lord GOD, remember me, I pray thee, and strengthen me, I pray thee, only this once, O God, that I may be avenged upon the Philistines for one of my two eyes." And Samson grasped the two middle pillars upon which the house rested, and he leaned his weight upon them, his right hand on the one and his left hand on the other. And Samson said, "Let me die with the Philistines." Then he bowed with all his might; and the house fell upon the lords and upon all the people that were in it. So the dead whom he slew at his death were more than those whom he had slain during his life. Then his brothers and all his family came down and took him and brought him up and buried him between Zorah and Esh'ta-ol in the tomb of Mano'ah his father. He had judged Israel twenty years.

6. The Deaths of Saul and His Armor-Bearer (1 Samuel 31:1–13)

Now the Philistines fought against Israel; and the men of Israel fled before the Philistines, and fell slain on Mount Gilbo'a. And the Philistines overtook Saul and his sons; and the Philistines slew Jonathan and Abin'adab and Mal'chishu'a, the sons of Saul. The battle pressed hard upon Saul, and the archers found him; and he was badly wounded by the archers. Then Saul said to his armor-bearer, "Draw your sword, and thrust me through with it, lest these uncircumcised come and thrust me through, and make sport of me." But his armor-bearer would not; for he feared greatly. Therefore Saul took his own sword, and fell upon it. And when his armor-bearer saw that Saul was dead, he also fell upon his sword, and died with him. Thus Saul died, and his three sons, and his armor-bearer, and all his men, on the same day together. And when the men of Israel who were on the other side of the valley and those beyond the Jordan saw that the men of Israel had fled and that Saul and his sons were dead, they forsook their cities and fled; and the Philistines came and dwelt in them.

On the morrow, when the Philistines came to strip the slain, they found Saul and his three sons fallen on Mount Gilbo'a. And they cut off his head, and stripped off his armor, and sent messengers throughout the land of the Philistines, to carry the good news to their idols and to the people. They put his armor in the temple of Ash'taroth; and they fastened his body to the wall of Beth-shan. But when the inhabitants of Ja'besh-gil'ead heard what the Philistines had done to Saul, all the valiant men arose, and went all night, and took the body of Saul and the bodies of his sons from the wall of

Beth-shan; and they came to Jabesh and burnt them there. And they took their bones and buried them under the tamarisk tree in Jabesh, and fasted seven days.

7. The Death of Ahithophel
(2 Samuel 17:23)

When Ahith'ophel saw that his counsel was not followed, he saddled his ass, and went off home to his own city. And he set his house in order, and hanged himself; and he died, and was buried in the tomb of his father.

8. The Death of Zimri
(1 Kings 16:18–19)

And when Zimri saw that the city was taken, he went into the citadel of the king's house, and burned the king's house over him with fire, and died, because of his sins which he committed, doing evil in the sight of the LORD, walking in the way of Jerobo'am,[13] and for his sin which he committed, making Israel to sin.

9. The Death of Judas
(Matthew 27:1–8)

When morning came, all the chief priests and the elders of the people took counsel against Jesus to put him to death; and they bound him and led him away and delivered him to Pilate the governor.

When Judas, his betrayer, saw that he was condemned, he repented and brought back the thirty pieces of silver to the chief priests and the elders, saying, "I have sinned in betraying innocent blood." They said, "What is that to us? See to it yourself." And throwing down the pieces of silver in the temple, he departed; and he went and hanged himself. But the chief priests, taking the pieces of silver, said, "It is not lawful to put them into the treasury, since they are blood money." So they took counsel, and bought with them the potter's field, to bury strangers in. Therefore that field has been called the Field of Blood to this day.

13. **Jeroboam:** a traitor and idolater in the Old Testament who led an unsuccessful revolt of the north of the Hebrew state against King David's son, Solomon. He later led a successful rebellion against Solomon's son, King Rehoboam, and established an independent state in which he encouraged the worship of idols, not Yahweh.

Source 10 from Josephus with English Translation, vol. 3, The Jewish War, Books IV–VII, translated by Henry St. John Thackeray (New York: G. P. Putnam's Sons, 1928), pp. 595–603, 613–619.

10. Josephus on Mass Suicide at Masada, 73 A.D.

However, neither did Eleazar himself contemplate flight, nor did he intend to permit any other to do so. Seeing the wall consuming in the flames, unable to devise any further means of deliverance or gallant endeavour, and setting before his eyes what the Romans, if victorious, would inflict on them, their children and their wives, he deliberated on the death of all. And, judging, as matters stood, this course the best, he assembled the most doughty of his comrades and incited them to the deed by such words as these:

"Long since, my brave men, we determined neither to serve the Romans nor any other save God, for He alone is man's true and righteous Lord; and now the time is come which bids us verify that resolution by our actions. At this crisis let us not disgrace ourselves; we who in the past refused to submit even to a slavery involving no peril, let us not now, along with slavery, deliberately accept the irreparable penalties awaiting us if we are to fall alive into Roman hands. For as we were the first of all to revolt, so are we the last in arms against them. Moreover, I believe that it is God who has granted us this favour, that we have it in our power to die nobly and in freedom—a privilege denied to others who have met with unexpected defeat. Our fate at break of day is certain capture, but there is still the free choice of a noble death with those we hold most dear. For our enemies, fervently though they pray to take us alive, we can no more prevent this than we can now hope to defeat them in battle. . . .

. . . Let our wives thus die undishonoured, our children unacquainted with slavery; and, when they are gone, let us render a generous service to each other, preserving our liberty as a noble winding-sheet. But first let us destroy our chattels and the fortress by fire; for the Romans, well I know, will be grieved to lose at once our persons and the lucre. Our provisions only let us spare; for they will testify, when we are dead, that it was not want which subdued us, but that, in keeping with our initial resolve, we preferred death to slavery."

Thus spoke Eleazar; but his words did not touch the hearts of all hearers alike. Some, indeed, were eager to respond and all but filled with delight at the thought of a death so noble,[14] but others, softer-hearted, were moved with

14. Scholars disagree about the precise translation of the original Greek text at this point. Some render "filled with delight at the thought of a death so noble" as "filled with pleasure supposing such a death to be noble." The latter translation significantly modifies the meaning of Josephus.

compassion for their wives and families, and doubtless also by the vivid prospect of their own end, and their tears as they looked upon one another revealed their unwillingness of heart. Eleazar, seeing them flinching and their courage breaking down in face of so vast a scheme, feared that their whimpers and tears might unman even those who had listened to his speech with fortitude. Far, therefore, from slackening in his exhortation, he roused himself and, fired with mighty fervour, essayed a higher flight of oratory on the immortality of the soul. Indignantly protesting and with eyes intently fixed on those in tears, he exclaimed:

"Deeply, indeed, was I deceived in thinking that I should have brave men as associates in our struggles for freedom—men determined to live with honour or to die. But you, it seems, were no better than the common herd in valour or in courage, you who are afraid even of that death that will deliver you from the direst ills, when in such a cause you ought neither to hesitate an instant nor wait for a counsellor. For from of old, since the first dawn of intelligence, we have been continually taught by those precepts, ancestral and divine—confirmed by the deeds and noble spirit of our forefathers—that life, not death, is man's misfortune. For it is death which gives liberty to the soul and permits it to depart to its own pure abode, there to be free from all calamity; but so long as it is imprisoned in a mortal body and tainted with all its miseries, it is, in sober truth, dead, for association with what is mortal ill befits that which is divine. . . .

. . . Unenslaved by the foe let us die, as free men with our children and wives let us quit this life together! This our laws enjoin, this our wives and children implore of us. The need for this is of God's sending, the reverse of this is the Romans' desire, and their fear is lest a single one of us should die before capture. Haste we then to leave them, instead of their hoped-for enjoyment at securing us, amazement at our death and admiration of our fortitude."

He would have pursued his exhortation but was cut short by his hearers, who, overpowered by some uncontrollable impulse, were all in haste to do the deed. Like men possessed they went their way, each eager to outstrip his neighbour and deeming it a signal proof of courage and sound judgement not to be seen among the last: so ardent the passion that had seized them to slaughter their wives, their little ones and themselves. . . . They had died in the belief that they had left not a soul of them alive to fall into Roman hands; but an old woman and another, a relative of Eleazar, superior in sagacity and training to most of her sex, with five children, escaped by concealing themselves in the subterranean aqueducts, while the rest were absorbed in the slaughter. The victims numbered nine hundred and sixty, including women and children; and the tragedy occurred on the fifteenth of the month Xanthicus.[15]

15. May 2, A.D. 73.

The Romans, expecting further opposition, were by daybreak under arms and, having with gangways formed bridges of approach from the earthworks, advanced to the assault. Seeing none of the enemy but on all sides an awful solitude, and flames within and silence, they were at a loss to conjecture what had happened. At length, as if for a signal to shoot, they shouted, to call forth haply any of those within. The shout was heard by the women-folk, who, emerging from the caverns, informed the Romans how matters stood, one of the two lucidly reporting both the speech and how the deed was done. But it was with difficulty that they listened to her, incredulous of such amazing fortitude; meanwhile they endeavoured to extinguish the flames and soon cutting a passage through them entered the palace. Here encountering the mass of slain, instead of exulting as over enemies, they admired the nobility of their resolve and the contempt of death displayed by so many in carrying it, unwavering, into execution.

Source 11 from Saint Augustine, The City of God Against the Pagans, *translated by George E. McCracken (Cambridge, Mass.: Harvard University Press, 1957), pp. 77–79, 91–101, 109–113. Reprinted by permission of the publishers and the Loeb Classical Library.*

11. Saint Augustine, *The City of God*, Book I

XVII
ON SUICIDE CAUSED BY FEAR OF PUNISHMENT OR DISGRACE.

For if it is not right on individual authority to slay even a guilty man for whose killing no law has granted permission, certainly a suicide is also a homicide, and he is guilty, when he kills himself, in proportion to his innocence of the deed for which he thought he ought to die. If we rightly execrate Judas' deed, and truth pronounces that when he hanged himself, he increased rather than expiated the crime of that accursed betrayal, since by despairing of God's mercy, though he was at death repentant, he left himself no place for a saving repentance, how much more should the man who has no guilt in him to be punished by such means refrain from killing himself!

When Judas killed himself, he killed an accursed man, and he ended his life guilty not only of Christ's death but also of his own, because, though he was killed to atone for his crime, the killing itself was another crime of his. Why, then, should a man who has done no evil do evil to himself, and in doing away with himself do away with an innocent man so as not to suffer from the crime of another, and perpetrate upon himself a sin of his own, so that another's may not be perpetrated on him?

XX
THAT THERE IS NO AUTHORITY THAT ALLOWS CHRISTIANS IN ANY CASE THE RIGHT TO DIE OF THEIR OWN WILL.

Not for nothing is it that in the holy canonical books no divinely inspired order or permission can be found authorizing us to inflict death upon ourselves, neither in order to acquire immortality nor in order to avert or divert some evil. For we must certainly understand the commandment as forbidding this when it says: "Thou shalt not kill,"[16] particularly since it does not add "thy neighbour," as it does when it forbids false witnessing. . . .

On this basis some try to extend this commandment even to wild and domestic animals and maintain that it is wrong to kill any of them. Why not then extend it also to plants and to anything fixed and fed by roots in the earth? For things of this kind, though they have no feeling, are said to live, and therefore can also die, and hence, when violence is exercised, be slain. Thus the Apostle, when he speaks of seeds of this sort, says: "That which thou sowest is not quickened except it die,"[17] and we find in a psalm, "He killed their vines with hail."[18] Do we from this conclude, when we hear "Thou shalt not kill," that it is wrong to pull up a shrub? Are we so completely deranged that we assent to the Manichaean error?

Hence, putting aside these ravings, if when we read, "Thou shalt not kill," we do not understand this phrase to apply to bushes, because they have no sensation, nor to the unreasoning animals that fly, swim, walk or crawl, because they are not partners with us in the faculty of reason, the privilege not being given them to share it in common with us—and therefore by the altogether righteous ordinance of the Creator both their life and death are a matter subordinate to our needs—the remaining possibility is to understand this commandment, "Thou shalt not kill," as meaning man alone, that is, "neither another nor thyself," for in fact he who kills himself kills what is no other than a man.

XXI
WHAT CASES OF HOMICIDE ARE EXCEPTED FROM THE CHARGE OF MURDER?

This very same divine law, to be sure, made certain exceptions to the rule that it is not lawful to kill a human being. The exceptions include only such persons as God commands to be put to death, either by an enacted law or by special decree applicable to a single person at the given time—but note that the man who is bound to this service under orders, as a sword is bound to be the tool of him who employs it, is not himself the slayer, and consequently there is no breach of this commandment, which says, "Thou shalt not kill," in the case of those who by God's authorization have waged wars, or, who, repre-

16. Exodus 20:16. Saint Augustine makes frequent biblical references in his text.
17. 1 Corinthians 15:36.
18. Psalms 78:46.

senting in their person the power of the state, have put criminals to death in accordance with God's law, being vested, that is, with the imperial prerogative of altogether righteous reason. Abraham too not only was not blamed for cruelty, but was even praised for piety, because he resolved to slay his son, not with criminal motives but in obedience to God. And it is properly a question whether we should regard it as equivalent to a command of God when Jephthah slew his daughter who ran to meet him after he had vowed to sacrifice to God the first victim that met him as he returned victorious from battle.[19] Nor is Samson acquitted of guilt on any other plea, inasmuch as he crushed himself by the collapse of the house along with his enemies, than the plea that the Spirit who through him had been working miracles,[20] had secretly ordered this. With these exceptions then, those slain either by application of a just law or by command of God, the very fount of justice, whoever kills a human being, either himself or no matter who, falls within the meshes of the charge of murder.

XXII
WHETHER SUICIDE IS EVER A SIGN OF GREATNESS OF MIND.

Those who have laid violent hands upon themselves are perhaps to be admired for the greatness of their souls, but not to be praised for the soundness of their wisdom. If, however, you take reason more carefully into account, you will not really call it greatness of soul which brings anyone to suicide because he or she lacks strength to bear whatever hardships or sins of others may occur. For the mind is rather detected in weakness, if it cannot bear whether it be the harsh enslavement of its own body, or the stupid opinion of the mob; and a mind might better be called greater that can endure instead of fleeing from a distressful life, and that can in the light of pure conscience despise the judgement of men, especially that of the mob, which as a rule is wrapped in a fog of error.

Therefore, if suicide can be thought to be a great-souled act, this quality of greatness of soul was possessed by that Theombrotus[21] of whom they say that, when he had read Plato's book containing a discussion of the immortality of the soul,[22] he hurled himself headlong from a wall and so departed from this life to that which he thought a better. He was not urged to this act by any calamity of fortune or accusation, false or true, that he had not strength to bear and so made away with himself. Nay, his sole motive for seeking death and breaking the sweet bonds of this life was his greatness of soul. Nevertheless, this Plato himself whom he had read could have borne witness that he

19. Judges 11:29–40.
20. Judges 16:28–30.
21. **Theombrotus:** a philosopher of Ambracia, Greece.
22. Plato's dialogue *The Phaedo*.

acted greatly rather than well, for assuredly Plato would have made this act the first step and the most important step he took himself, and might well have pronounced in favour of it too, had he not, with that intellect by which he saw the soul's immortality, reached the conclusion that suicide should not be committed, nay more, should be forbidden.

Yet in fact many have killed themselves to prevent falling into the hands of the enemy. We are not now asking whether this was done but whether it should have been done. Sound reasoning, naturally, is to be preferred even to precedents, but there are precedents for that matter not discordant with reason—such, be it noted, as are precedents the more worthy of imitation as they are more outstanding in piety. No case of suicide occurred among patriarchs, among prophets, among apostles, seeing that the Lord Christ himself, when he advised them, if they suffered persecution, to flee from city to city,[23] might then have advised them to lay hands upon themselves to avoid falling into the hands of their persecutors. Furthermore, granted that he gave no command or advice to His disciples to employ this means of departing from life, though he promised that he would prepare everlasting mansions for them when they departed, then, no matter what precedents are brought forward by heathen that know not God, it is obvious that suicide is unlawful for those who worship the one true God.

XXVI

WHAT EXPLANATION WE SHOULD ADOPT TO ACCOUNT FOR
THE SAINTS' DOING CERTAIN THINGS THAT THEY ARE KNOWN
TO HAVE DONE WHICH IT IS NOT LAWFUL TO DO.

But, they say, in time of persecution certain saintly women, to avoid the pursuers of their chastity, cast themselves into a river that would ravish and drown them, and in that way they died and their memorial shrines are frequented by great numbers who venerate them as martyrs in the Catholic Church.

With regard to these women I dare not give any rash judgement. I do not know whether the divine authority has counselled the church by some trustworthy testimonies to honour their memory in this, and it may be so. For what if the women acted as they did, not by human misconception, but by divine command, and they did not go astray in their act, but were obedient? Compare the case of Samson, where it would be sin to hold any other view. When God, moreover, gives a command and makes it clear without ambiguity that he gives it, who can summon obedience to judgement? Who can draw up a brief against religious deference to God? . . .

. . . Let anyone, therefore, who is told that he has no right to kill himself, do the deed if he is so ordered by him whose orders must not be slighted. There is just one proviso: he must be sure that his divine command is not made pre-

23. Matthew 10:5–15.

carious by any doubt. It is through the ear that we take note of men's thoughts; we do not arrogate to ourselves any right to judge such as are kept secret. No one "knows what goes on in a man except the spirit of the man that is in him."[24]

This we say, this we declare, this we by all means endorse: that no man ought to inflict on himself a voluntary death, thinking to escape temporary ills, lest he find himself among ills that are unending; that no one ought to do so because of another's sins, lest by the very act he bring into being a sin that is his own, when he would not have been polluted by another's; that on one ought to do so on account of any past sins, inasmuch as he needs this life the more to make possible their healing by repentance; that no one ought to do so thinking to satisfy his hunger for the better life for which we hope after death, inasmuch as the better life after death does not accept those who are guilty of their own death.

24. 1 Corinthians 2:11.

QUESTIONS TO CONSIDER

The evidence in this chapter all deals with the central issue of suicide, but it comes from sources originating over an extraordinarily long period, about a millennium and one-half of the ancient period. Our objective in spanning such a period is to examine the continuities and changes in ancient thought on the subject of self-destruction by asking you to address three progressively more probing central questions based on the sources.

The first question asks that you consider each of the selections individually by identifying every author's thought on the suicide that was common in much of the ancient world. How do all of the authors, except Saint Augustine, implicitly or more directly accept suicide as justifiable? What sort of ethical considera-

tions does the act raise for each author? What limitations, if any, does each place on self-destruction?

The second question requires that you place each of the sources in the intellectual context within which its author wrote. You must consider the religious beliefs and philosophical outlook of each period represented in the sources: the Hellenic and Hellenistic ages, the Roman Empire, Old and New Testament Palestine, and the early Christian era. How did the ideas of the various thinkers reflect the religious and philosophical orientations of their respective ages?

The third question asks that you examine the evolution of ancient ideas on suicide over an extended period of time. What basic continuities on this subject do you note in ancient thought? At what point did ancient thought on suicide change? What aspects of Christian doctrine and the controversies surrounding this faith in the third and fourth centuries A.D. promoted the viewpoint advanced by Saint Augustine? On what basis did he deny that the acts of self-destruction in the Bible were true suicides? Why might you assume that Saint Augustine's theology heavily influenced Western attitudes toward suicide in the Christian era that emerged from the decline and fall of the Roman Empire?

As you consider your answers to these questions, you should better comprehend the ancients' views on suicide, but even more importantly, you should understand the philosophical and theological foundations for those ideas.

EPILOGUE

Very few ancient thinkers unconditionally condemned the act of self-destruction, although as we have seen, Socrates noted one such group, the Pythagoreans. [We must add that Neoplatonists like Plotinus (205–270) also condemned suicide. They held that since one's standing in the afterlife rested on the state of one's soul at death, suicide was inadmissible because the possibility of moral improvement existed as long as life endured.] Thus, Saint Augustine's general condemnation of suicide reflected a distinct break with the past. Indeed, his dictum that suicide was murder, reaffirmed by later theologians, including Saint Thomas Aquinas (1225–1274), shaped the religious and legal response of the Christian West to the act of self-destruction into the twentieth century.[25]

Religiously, Saint Augustine's condemnation of all forms of suicide, perhaps reinforced by primitive suicide taboos among the Germanic tribes overwhelming late ancient Rome, became part of canon law. That law always relieved persons of diminished psychological capacity from the spiritual consequence of suicide. But for suicides of apparently sound mind, the act of self-destruction incurred severe spiritual penalties. Theologians believed suicides by such individuals represented despair and thus rejection of the Christian message, perhaps reflecting Satanic possession. Thus at the Council of Braga in 563, the Roman Catholic Church denied religious burial to these persons, a practice many Protestant groups perpetuated after the Reformation of the sixteenth century.

25. Indeed, the very word *suicide* did not exist in Western languages prior to the early seventeenth century, and some variation of the phrase "murder of oneself" described the act of self-destruction in most European tongues. The word *suicide* seems first to have appeared in a work of the Englishman Sir Thomas Browne, *Religio medici*, published in 1642. The use of the term slowly gained ground in English usage, and in the eighteenth century it found its way into French, Italian, Portuguese, and Spanish lexicons. Literally translated from its Latin roots as "to strike oneself mortally," the word itself is highly significant because it eschews the more condemnatory term *murder*.

Legally, most medieval and early modern Western states reflected canon law by adopting statutes recognizing suicide as a form of murder. Thus, persons taking their own lives might incur worldly as well as spiritual penalties if a postmortem judicial proceeding determined that they had, indeed, ended their own lives while in a sound mental state. Worldly penalties typically included two elements. The first was financial in nature. Under laws dating from at least as early as the thirteenth century in England and France, the state confiscated the property of the successful suicide. In the second form of punishment, the authorities desecrated the corpse of the suicide in ceremonies that included the spiritual penalty of denied burial. Thus, in Catholic France prior to the Revolution, judicial authorities dragged suicides' corpses through the streets, frequently displayed the remains to the public, and disposed of the bodies without burial rites, often as refuse. In England, after the Reformation, the authorities buried suicides' remains without religious sacraments at crossroads. Because of popular fears that the spirits of suicides might return to the world of the living, the authorities often drove stakes through the bodies and into the ground to prevent the return of the deceased from their graves. Other Western countries engaged in similar practices that long endured, and attempted suicide was a capital offense in many legal codes for centuries.

Only in the late seventeenth and eighteenth centuries, in a process that historians have called a "secularization of suicide,"[26] did many Western thinkers begin to view the act of self-destruction as a social, psychological, or medical problem rather than the moral and theological issue defined by Saint Augustine. Nevertheless, the law long reflected this earlier attitude, and the act of suicide persistently excited basic religious and philosophical controversies. Suicide remained a crime in France until 1791, and the last English crossroads burial occurred in 1823. Attempted suicide continued to be a crime in England until 1961, and until that same year, those of sound mind who took their own lives might be denied burial rites by the Church of England. Attempted suicide remains a criminal offense in a small number of American states today.

26. This terminology was introduced by the work of Michael MacDonald and Terence Murphy, *Sleepless Souls: Suicide in Early Modern England* (Oxford: Oxford University Press, 1990).

CHAPTER FIVE

THE DEVELOPMENT

OF ORTHODOXY

IN EARLY CHRISTIANITY

The world in which Christianity began was one in which people practiced many different religions. The Romans generally tolerated the religions of the people they conquered as long as they did not appear to be politically or socially revolutionary, and as long as the people would also participate in ceremonies that honored and appeased the Roman gods. Like most of the peoples of the ancient world, the Romans were *polytheists* who honored many gods and easily added new gods or goddesses to their belief systems. In fact, Romans often adopted the gods of conquered peoples, believing that additional gods would simply make the Roman state stronger. In their religious life, most people who lived in the Roman Empire were *syncretistic*, that is, they not only easily added new deities, but also combined parts of various religious and philosophical systems together in an individualized way.

One group living within the Roman Empire had very different religious ideas, however. These were the Jews, who were strictly *monotheistic*, believing that they were to worship only one single god, whom they termed *Yahweh*. They would thus not participate in events that honored other gods or those in which living or deceased Roman emperors were described as divine. Though one would think this would have led to trouble with Roman authorities, usually it did not, for the Romans recognized that Jewish monotheism had a long tradition behind it. The Romans' respect for their own traditions led them to make an exception in the case of the Jews; the Jews were also not actively seeking converts, so the Romans did not have to worry that Judaism would spread.

Though all Jews were monotheistic, during the lifetime of Jesus of Nazareth (ca 5 B.C.–A.D. 29), on whose ideas Christianity was based, there were a number of groups within Judaism that stressed different parts of the Jewish tradition or had slightly different ideas. Thus when Jesus' early followers—all of them Jews—began to talk about his ideas, they appeared to Roman authorities as simply another Jewish sect. In fact, many of Jesus' early followers, who regarded him as the Messiah (the one foretold in Jewish prophecy who would bring about a period of happiness for Jews), thought of their movement as one primarily to reform Judaism.

By the last half of the first century, this way of thinking began to change, as those who followed Jesus' ideas began to set themselves apart from other Jews by participating in a special commemorative meal and by aggressively preaching. Many of them began to preach to non-Jews (termed *Gentiles*), leading to disagreements about whether those who accepted Jesus' ideas first had to become Jews to become full members of the movement. This issue was resolved at a meeting in Jerusalem in favor of the more universalist position, for it was decided that Gentile followers should have equal status without having to be circumcised or follow Jewish laws and customs. This decision enabled the movement to spread much more widely, with men and women traveling as missionaries throughout the Roman Empire. Instead of being a group within Judaism, Jesus' followers were now a distinct religion, taking the name that the Romans had first given them, *Christians*, a word derived from Christ, a Greek translation of the Hebrew word *Messiah* and a title given to Jesus by his followers.

Though Christians separated themselves from Jews, they took many of their religious ideas from Judaism, most importantly its monotheism, moral standards, and refusal to honor other gods. Christians also refused to participate in public religious ceremonies or honor the emperor as divine, but because their ideas were new and not part of a long-standing tradition, Romans did not feel that they warranted the same respect that Jews did. Beginning with the reign of the emperor Nero (54–68), Roman authorities began to persecute Christians, decreeing the death penalty for any who would not recant. These persecutions were stepped up during periods of unrest in the Empire, when Christians were blamed for provoking the displeasure of the traditional gods by refusing to honor them, so that the gods allowed turmoil and crisis. Many Christian beliefs and practices also appeared to be suspect or dangerous to Roman eyes: They talked about their king, who sounded like a rival to the emperor, and held ceremonies in which they claimed to eat the body and blood of this king, which to Romans appeared to be cannibalism; husbands and wives called each other brother and sister, suggesting incest; Christians spoke of an imminent end of the world, which would of course mean the end of the Roman Empire, and so appeared to be preaching political revolution. Christians' refusal to participate in the state cult implied disloyalty to Rome. They held secret meetings, which only the initiates could attend; this suggested they had something to hide and contrasted sharply with the public religious ceremonies common in Roman polytheism.

Despite Roman suspicion, however, the campaigns against Christians were never very thorough. Most of the emperors and the governors of Roman provinces followed the advice of the emperor Trajan (98–117) that Christians were not to be sought out, but only arrested if a responsible citizen accused them, and only executed if they did not recant. He recommended that authorities avoid general investigations or listening to rumors, and called for the arrest of anyone who accused someone of being a Christian without clear proof. Trajan and many of the emperors who followed him thus did not take Christianity very seriously, and let local governors decide how to handle Christians in their territories. The persecutions that did take place often led to dramatic public martyrdoms, giving Christianity great publicity and convincing many people throughout the Roman Empire that this new religion offered something distinctive.

The heroism of the early martyrs combined with the sporadic nature of the persecutions gave Christianity breathing space to expand. The number of Christians, particularly in urban areas, grew slowly but steadily, and began to include highly educated people who were familiar with a wide variety of religious and philosophical ideas. This was a time in the Roman Empire when many people appear to have been dissatisfied with traditional religion, and a number of groups that offered salvation to converts gained in popularity. Because it combined a promise of life after death with a spirit of community and gave believers a sense of purpose in life, Christianity grew faster than most other religions. This growth created problems for Christianity, however, for there was great diversity among early Christian communities, with each interpreting the accounts of Jesus' life related to them by missionaries and the main points of his message slightly differently. Because they had been brought up in a tradition of religious syncretism, many people adopted only some of the ideas of Christianity or combined Christian ideas with those from other sources. The sayings of Jesus and the accounts of his preaching were often enigmatic, so that people were able to use them in support of widely differing ideas.

This diversity was troubling to many of the leaders of early Christianity, who thought it extremely important that there be unity among all those who called themselves Christians. They thus began to declare certain ideas as *orthodox,* that is, acceptable or correct, and others as *heretical,* that is, unacceptable or incorrect, breaking with the Greco-Roman tradition of religious syncretism and toleration. They realized this could not be done simply on their own authority, but that some type of standards needed to be devised by which to judge ideas and practices. The establishment of orthodox ideas and authoritative standards did not happen in a vacuum, however, but was shaped by the preconceptions of early Church leaders and the social and political situation of the Roman Empire in which they lived. Your task in this chapter will be to use the writings of both those authors judged orthodox and those judged heretical to assess the way in which early Christianity developed. How was the initial diversity of Christianity transformed into a split between orthodoxy and heresy? What ideas and institutions came to be the most important determinants of orthodoxy?

SOURCES AND METHOD

Studying the history of any religious movement poses special problems for historians, for sources are very rarely objective. Even in the tolerant Roman Empire, some religious ideas were judged dangerous or deviant, so the writings of these groups were destroyed or not preserved, and the only record we have of them is from hostile observers. This is even more the case with Christianity, for most of our records come from those whose ideas were later judged orthodox. It is thus important for us to remember when using such sources that orthodoxy and heresy are relative terms. Only those who don't accept a belief label it as a heresy; those who accept it regard it as correct, of course, so that in their minds the others are the heretics. What we now call heresies within Christianity are beliefs that were rejected as orthodoxy was established.

Along with problems created by subjective sources, we may also have more difficulties in achieving unbiased assessments of the history of religion than other historical topics because we have an intellectual, spiritual, or emotional commitment to certain religious ideas. This does not mean, however, that we should avoid religious topics, particularly when studying Western history in which Judaism, Christianity, and Islam have been key factors, but that we should be cognizant of our own prejudices. Our job as historians is to understand people's religious ideas within their historical context and to see how religious faith manifested itself in historically observable phenomena; it is not to judge whether certain religious ideas are right or wrong. The people we are studying (and perhaps we ourselves) may believe certain developments to be the result of divine will or action, but as historians, we must use the same standards about how or why something happened that we would use in evaluating any event in the past and concentrate on the human actors. Perhaps the most important part of our methodology in exploring religious topics is thus to approach them with both objectivity and respect.

Not only are many of our sources subjective, but very few of them were written simply to describe things that have happened. Rather, they were written to bolster the faith of other followers, to correct perceived errors, or to win converts. You can see this clearly in studying the earliest decades of Christianity. The only contemporary written sources that describe the events in the life of Jesus and in the lives of his first followers were recorded by those who regarded themselves as Christians.

These writings were later termed *gospels* (*evangelium* in Latin), a word that means "good news," and were written primarily to spread the "good news" of Jesus' message and not simply to record the biographical details of his life. We can extract historical information from them and compare them with one another, but we have no way of checking them against non-Christian sources except for their references to political events such as the reigns of emperors.

Because gospels are some of the earliest Christian writings that have survived, they are a good place to start our exploration of the development of orthodoxy. During the early centuries of Christianity, many different gospels circulated, but gradually four—those of Matthew, Mark, Luke, and John—came to be considered orthodox and the rest heretical, or at least not as central as Matthew, Mark, Luke, and John. By comparing these orthodox Gospels with those which were excluded, we can see some of the ideas that became central to orthodoxy very early.

The first two sources are from the Gospels of Luke and Matthew, and form the basis for the orthodox interpretation of the resurrection of Jesus and his handing on of authority. In Source 1, who first discovers the empty tomb? What are they told has happened to the body of Jesus? What was the reaction of Jesus' other followers to their report? What point is Jesus trying to make about his own resurrection in verses 36–43? According to Luke, is the resurrection physical or spiritual? Source 2 is the very end of the Gospel of Matthew, and

describes Jesus' final words to his followers. According to this account, to whom does Jesus give authority? What is the source and extent of the authority he is delegating? To whom does Jesus say his message should be communicated?

Sources 3 and 4 offer quite a different view of Jesus' resurrection and handing on of authority, though these were also written by people calling themselves Christians in the first two centuries after the death of Jesus. They come from a movement termed *gnosticism*, with which you may be less familiar than with Christian orthodoxy. Gnosticism was not an organized group, but a diffuse body of beliefs drawn from Greek philosophy, Judaism, Persian religions, and then Christianity. While gnostics disagreed with each other about many things and their beliefs are often very complex, they generally agreed that they had special knowledge, revealed to them by a messenger sent from the creative power or supreme being of the universe; the term *gnostic,* in fact, comes from the Greek word *gnosis,* which means "to know." This special knowledge would enable them to understand the world, and particularly the presence of evil in it, and teach them how to act in order to gain deliverance from the world and achieve salvation. Gnostics believed that the supreme being was totally spiritual and that the material world was either accidentally created or was evil; they were thus uninterested in the things of this world such as politics or human society and were very pessimistic about them. They did feel that a small group of humans would be able to return to the purely spiritual world on death—those who had been given the secret knowledge, which would enable the "pure" spirit to escape the "impure" body.

People who were interested in these ideas found much in Christian teachings that appealed to them, and many gnostics became Christian. They created their own body of literature slightly later than the gospels you have read so far, the bulk of which was lost or destroyed. Until quite recently scholars had only fragments of certain gnostic texts and discussions of gnostic ideas in the writings of orthodox thinkers, so that it was difficult to get an unbiased picture. This changed when in 1945 near the town of Nag Hammadi, an Egyptian peasant accidentally found a jar filled with gnostic books, copies made probably in 350–400 of texts first written down as much as three centuries earlier. These were gradually transcribed and translated, and turned out to be fifty-two texts, some of them also labeled "gospels." Sources 3 and 4 are from two of these Nag Hammadi texts, 3 from the gospel of Mary Magdalene and 4 from a text titled "The Wisdom of Jesus Christ."

Source 3 begins with the same event described in the Gospel of Matthew, but then goes on to relate a series of events not included in the orthodox Gospels. How do the instructions Jesus gives his followers differ from those included in Matthew? Who emerges as the strongest of Jesus' followers? What gives her special authority? What is the reaction of Jesus' other followers to this? Source 4 describes an appearance of Jesus to his followers after his crucifixion. How does its description of his appearance differ from that in the Gospel of Luke? How does the group to whom Jesus appears differ from that described in Matthew? Whom does Jesus say will receive true knowledge? How does this group differ from those whom Matthew describes as the audience of his message?

As you can see from your readings so far, there was great diversity among early Christians in regard to such basic things as the nature of Jesus' Resurrection, the intended audience for his message, and the nature of the group responsible for spreading this message. During the second century, however, many Church leaders felt that this diversity was dangerous, and began to declare certain ideas and interpretations orthodox. The remaining sources in this chapter all stem from second-century orthodox writers, and will help you discover both what ideas were rejected as heresy and the standards devised by Church leaders to make this rejection. We will focus on gnostic ideas, as these were regarded as the most divergent from what became orthodoxy, though the gnostics were not the only heretics in early Christianity. Indeed, many church leaders, including some bishops and the philosopher Origen (185?–254?) held ideas that were, either during their lifetimes or after they died, judged to be heretical. Because of the Nag Hammadi find, however, we have more direct access to gnostic ideas than those of most other heretical thinkers.

Source 5 comes from a work generally known as *Against Heresies,* written in the late second century by Irenaeus of Lyons (ca 130–ca 202), a Greek theologian who became bishop of Lyons in France and who was one of the first to systematize Christian doctrine. In *Against Heresies,* Irenaeus seeks to refute gnostic ideas. In this extract, he describes three different types of gnosticism, each of which had different ideas about who Jesus was and the relation between Jesus and the creator of the universe. As you read these three descriptions, it might be useful to write down the variant gnostic answers to the following questions: What was the nature of Jesus—spirit? Human? What actually happened at the crucifixion? What was Jesus' chief purpose while on earth? What is the nature of human salvation—spiritual? Bodily? Because of this, what is the proper attitude of humans toward their bodies—indifference? Rejection?

Though they spent much of their time describing and refuting gnostic ideas, Irenaeus and other leaders recognized that it was also important to devise a positive formulation of the ideas that would be considered orthodox. They took this from the words that many Christian groups were already using when they baptized new initiates, and put together what was termed the "symbol of the faith," or what we would call a creed. This second-century creed became the basis for what later came to be called the Apostles' Creed, first given

that name in a letter of St. Ambrose, the bishop of Milan, in about 390, and assuming its present form in about 650 (Source 6). As you read this source, note which clauses directly refute the various gnostic answers to the questions posed above. What is becoming the orthodox answer to these questions?

The sources thus far have mainly touched on the substance of orthodoxy—the second of the central questions for this chapter—but those remaining will address the first question, regarding the process of the establishment of orthodoxy, more directly. We have already seen, perhaps without noticing, one step in this process—the devising of a uniform statement of belief, with clauses that are unacceptable to most gnostics. Sources 7 and 8 describe another element of this process. Source 7 is another section of Irenaeus's *Against Heresies,* in which he describes the ideas of Marcion, a second-century religious leader influenced by the gnostics. What ideas does Marcion hold that disagree with the statement of faith in the Apostles' Creed? How does Marcion alter the works of other authors so that they support him? Marcion's alteration of Luke and Paul's works led other Church leaders to the realization that some decision needed to be made about which writings from the earliest followers of Jesus were to be accepted as authoritative, and what standards were to be used to make this decision. Source 8 is a fragment from a Greek text probably dating from the late second century, in which the unknown author sets out what he feels are the books and letters (termed *epistles*) that should have special status. This is the earliest known *canon*, or list of the books that later came to be included in the Christian New Testament, and is called the *Muratorian Canon* after the Italian historian who discovered the text. As you read this, note the reasons the author gives for including certain books and excluding others, or for why the authors of these books wrote what they did. How is Luke's authority to write a gospel established, considering that he was not one of the original disciples? What inspires John to write a gospel? In writing Acts, why does Luke exclude certain events? Why does the author feel that the personal letters he regards as written by Paul (to Philemon, Titus, and Timothy) should be included?

As you have probably discovered, the way in which this author judged which books should be included was the same way that orthodox leaders gave authority to their statement of faith—by linking it with the apostles, that is, with Jesus' early followers. As you remember from the first four readings, however, there were wide variations as to whom should be regarded as Jesus' closest followers; Mark speaks of eleven men, "The Wisdom of Jesus Christ" of twelve men and seven women. Mark represents what came to be the orthodox interpretation, which included as true apostles eleven of Jesus' original disciples plus a few other men—most notably Paul, as Source 7 makes clear. By this standard, the works of the gnostics were judged not to be orthodox not only because of their content, but also because they were generally not as old as the books included in the Christian New Testament. In addition, they did not always make a claim of connection with one of the apostles. The problem for orthodox leaders was now to affirm their own connection with this original group of men. Sources 9 through 11 give you the writings of three early orthodox leaders on this issue. Source 9 is from a letter of Clement of Rome, the bishop of Rome who was martyred about 97 A.D., to Christians at Corinth in Greece, written at the end of the first century. Source 10 is another section from Irenaeus of Lyons's *Against Heresies*, and Source 11 is a section from *Prescription Against the Heretics*, written by Tertullian (ca 160–ca 230), a theologian from North Africa. As you read these, note the ways in which the idea of apostolic succession, like the creed and canon, was also shaped by gnosticism. How would you compare Clement's discussion of the initial mood of the apostles with that described in the *Gospel of Mary*? How does the way in which Clement alters the Old Testament text of Isaiah help support his argument? How does Irenaeus use apostolic succession to refute the gnostic idea that there was a secret tradition revealed only to a few? Do the authors give evidence of events that contradict their notion of a unity among "true" churches? Whom exactly do they regard as the contemporary holders of apostolic authority?

Before you answer the central questions for this chapter, you may wish to reread all the sources to assess the ways in which the two questions are interrelated. How might the process by which orthodoxy was established have affected the content of orthodox ideas? And, conversely, how might the content of those ideas have shaped the institutions that established orthodoxy?

THE EVIDENCE

Sources 1 and 2 from New Oxford Annotated Bible *(Revised Standard Version) (New York: Oxford University Press, 1971), p. 1283; p. 1284.*

1. The Gospel of Luke, Chapter 24

But on the first day of the week, at early dawn, they went to the tomb, taking the spices which they had prepared. ²And they found the stone rolled away from the tomb, ³but when they went in they did not find the body. ⁴While they were perplexed about this, behold, two men stood by them in dazzling apparel; ⁵and as they were frightened and bowed their faces to the ground, the men said to them, "Why do you seek the living among the dead? ⁶Remember how he told you, while he was still in Galilee, ⁷that the Son of man must be delivered into the hands of sinful men, and be crucified, and on the third day rise." ⁸And they remembered his words, ⁹and returning from the tomb they told all this to the eleven and to all the rest. ¹⁰Now it was Mary Mag'-dalene and Jo-an-'na and Mary the mother of James and the other women with them who told this to the apostles; ¹¹but these words seemed to them an idle tale and they did not believe them. . . .

> [*Jesus then appeared to two men in a village near Jerusalem, who returned to Jerusalem to tell the disciples what they had seen.*]

³⁶As they were saying this, Jesus himself stood among them. ³⁷But they were startled and frightened, and supposed that they saw a spirit. ³⁸And he said to them, "Why are you troubled, and why do questionings rise in your hearts? ³⁹See my hands and my feet, that it is I myself; handle me, and see; for a spirit has not flesh and bones as you see that I have."[1] ⁴¹And while they still disbelieved for joy, and wondered, he said to them, "Have you any-

---

1. Other ancient authorities add verse 40, *And when he had said this, he showed them his hands and feet.*

thing here to eat?" [42]They gave him a piece of broiled fish, [43]and he took it and ate before them.

2. The Gospel of Matthew, *Cowel* Chapter 28

[16]Now the eleven disciples went to Galilee, to the mountain to which Jesus had directed them. [17]And when they saw him they worshiped him; but some doubted. [18]And Jesus came and said to them, "All authority in heaven and on earth has been given to me. [19]Go therefore and make disciples of all nations, baptizing them in the name of the Father and of the Son and of the Holy Spirit, [20]teaching them to observe all that I have commanded you; and lo, I am with you always, to the close of the age."

Sources 3 and 4 from James M. Robinson, editor, The Nag Hammadi Library in English, *3d edition (San Francisco: Harper and Row, 1988), pp. 525–527; pp. 222–224.*

3. The Gospel of Mary *Gnostic* Magdalene

When the blessed one[2] had said this, he greeted them all, saying, "Peace be with you. Receive my peace to yourselves. Beware that no one lead you astray, saying, 'Lo here!' or 'Lo there!' For the Son of Man is within you. Follow after him! Those who seek him will find him. Go then and preach the gospel of the kingdom. Do not lay down any rules beyond what I appointed for you, and do not give a law like the lawgiver lest you be constrained by it." When he had said this, he departed.

But they were grieved. They wept greatly, saying, "How shall we go to the gentiles and preach the gospel of the kingdom of the Son of Man? If they did not spare him, how will they spare us?" Then Mary stood up, greeted them all, and said to her brethren, "Do not weep and do not grieve nor be irresolute, for his grace will be entirely with you and will protect you. But rather let us praise his greatness, for he has prepared us and made us into men." When Mary said this, she turned their hearts to the Good, and they began to discuss the words of the [Savior].

Peter said to Mary, "Sister, we know that the Savior loved you more than the rest of women. Tell us the words of the Savior which you remember—which you know (but) we do not, nor have we heard them." Mary answered and said, "What is hidden from you I will proclaim to you." And she began to speak to them these words: "I," she said, "I saw the Lord in a vision and I said

2. **the blessed one:** Jesus.

to him, 'Lord, I saw you today in a vision.' He answered and said to me, 'Blessed are you, that you did not waver at the sight of me. For where the mind is, there is the treasure.' I said to him, 'Lord, now does he who sees the vision see it ⟨through⟩ the soul ⟨or⟩ through the spirit?' The Savior answered and said, 'He does not see through the soul nor through the spirit, but the mind which [is] between the two—that is [what] sees the vision and it is [. . .].'

[*The next several pages are lost, and then*
Mary goes on to describe the ascent of
the soul.]

"[. . .] it. And desire that, 'I did not see you descending, but now I see you ascending. Why do you lie, since you belong to me?' The soul answered and said, 'I saw you. You did not see me nor recognize me. I served you as a garment, and you did not know me.' When it had said this, it went away rejoicing greatly.

"Again it came to the third power, which is called ignorance. [It (the power)] questioned the soul saying, 'Where are you going? In wickedness are you bound. But you are bound; do not judge!' And the soul said, 'why do you judge me although I have not judged? I was bound though I have not bound. I was not recognized. But I have recognized that the All is being dissolved, both the earthly (things) and the heavenly.'

When the soul had overcome the third power, it went upwards and saw the fourth power, (which) took seven forms. The first form is darkness, the second desire, the third ignorance, the fourth is the excitement of death, the fifth is the kingdom of the flesh, the sixth is the foolish wisdom of flesh, the seventh is the wrathful wisdom. These are the seven [powers] of wrath. They ask the soul, 'Whence do you come, slayer of men, or where are you going, conqueror of space?' The soul answered and said, 'What binds me has been slain, and what surrounds me has been overcome, and my desire has been ended, and ignorance has died. In a [world] I was released from a world, [and] in a type from a heavenly type, and (from) the fetter of oblivion which is transient. From this time on will I attain to the rest of the time, of the season, of the aeon, in silence.' "

When Mary had said this, she fell silent, since it was to this point that the Savior had spoken with her. But Andrew answered and said to the brethren, "Say what you (wish to) say about what she has said. I at least do not believe that the Savior said this. For certainly these teachings are strange ideas." Peter answered and spoke concerning these same things. He questioned them about the Savior: "Did he really speak with a woman without our knowledge (and) not openly? Are we to turn about and all listen to her? Did he prefer her to us?"

Then Mary wept and said to Peter, "My brother Peter, what do you think? Do you think that I thought this up myself in my heart, or that I am lying about the Savior?" Levi answered and said to Peter, "Peter, you have always been hot-tempered. Now I see you contending against the woman like the adversaries. But if the Savior made her worthy, who are you indeed to reject her? Surely the Savior knows her very well. That is why he loved her more than us. Rather let us be ashamed and put on the perfect man and acquire him for ourselves as he commanded us, and preach the gospel, not laying down any other rule or other law beyond what the Savior said." When [. . .] and they began to go forth [to] proclaim and to preach.

4. "The Wisdom of Jesus Christ" GNOSTIC

The Sophia[3] of Jesus Christ.

After he rose from the dead, his twelve disciples and seven women continued to be his followers and went to Galilee onto the mountain called "Divination and Joy." When they gathered together and were perplexed about the underlying reality of the universe and the plan and the holy providence and the power of the authorities and about everything that the Savior is doing with them in the secret of the holy plan, the Savior appeared, not in his previous form, but in the invisible spirit. And his likeness resembles a great angel of light. But his resemblance I must not describe. No mortal flesh could endure it, but only pure (and) perfect flesh, like that which he taught us about on the mountain called "Of Olives" in Galilee. And he said: "Peace be to you! My peace I give to you!" And they all marveled and were afraid.

The Savior laughed and said to them: "What are you thinking about? (Why) are you perplexed? What are you searching for?" Philip said: "For the underlying reality of the universe and the plan."

The Savior said to them: "I want you to know that all men born on earth from the foundation of the world until now, being dust, while they have inquired about God, who he is and what he is like, have not found him. Now the wisest among them have speculated from the ordering of the world and (its) movement. But their speculation has not reached the truth. For it is said that the ordering is directed in three ways by all the philosophers, (and) hence they do not agree. For some of them say about the world that it is directed by itself. Others, that it is providence (that directs it). Others, that it is fate. But it is none of these. Again, of the three voices I have just mentioned, none is close to the truth, and (they are) from man. But I, who came from Infinite Light, I am here—for I know him (Light)—that I might speak to you about the precise nature of the truth. For whatever is from itself is a polluted life; it is self-made. Providence has no wisdom in it. And fate does not discern.

But to you it is given to know; and whoever is worthy of knowledge will receive (it), whoever has not been begotten by the sowing of unclean rubbing but by First Who Was Sent, for he is an immortal in the midst of mortal men."

---

3. **Sophia:** Greek word for "wisdom."

109

Source 5 from Henry Bettenson, editor and translator, Documents of the Christian Church,
2d edition (London: Oxford University Press, 1963), pp. 35–37.

5. Descriptions of the Ideas of
Several Gnostic Thinkers,
from Irenaeus of Lyons's
Against Heresies

Saturninus[4] was of Antioch.[5] . . . Like Menander,[4] he taught that there is one
Father, utterly unknown, who made Angels, Archangels, Virtues, Powers; and
that the world, and all things therein, was made by certain angels, seven in
number. . . .

The Saviour he declared to be unborn, incorporeal and without form, asserting that he was seen as a man in appearance only. The God of the Jews, he
affirms, was one of the Angels; and because all the Princes wished to destroy
his Father, Christ came to destroy the God of the Jews, and to save them that
believed on him, and these are they who have a spark of his life. He was the
first to say that two kinds of men were fashioned by the Angels, one bad, the
other good. And because the demons aid the worst, The Saviour came to destroy the bad men and the Demons and to save the good. But to marry and
procreate they say is of Satan. . . .

Basilides,[4] that he may seem to have found out something higher and more
plausible, vastly extends the range of his teaching, declaring that Mind was
first born of the Unborn Father, then Reason from Mind, from Reason, Prudence, from Prudence, Wisdom and Power, and from Wisdom and Power the
Virtues, Princes and Angels, whom he also calls "the First." By them the First
Heaven was made; afterwards others were made, derived from these, and
they made another Heaven like to the former, and in like manner others . . . [in
all, 365 Heavens].

4. Those Angels who hold sway over the later Heaven, which is seen by us,
ordered all things that are in the world, and divided among them the earth
and the nations upon the earth. And their chief is he who is held to be the God
of the Jews. He wished to subdue the other nations beneath his own people,
the Jews, and therefore all the other Princes resisted him and took measures
against him. . . . Then the Unborn and Unnamed Father . . . sent his First-be-
gotten Mind (and there is he they call Christ), for the freeing of them that believe in him from those who made the world. And he appeared to the nations
of them as a man on the earth, and performed deeds of virtue. Wherefore he
suffered not, but a certain Simon, a Cyrenian, was impressed to bear his cross
for him; and Simon was crucified in ignorance and error, having been trans-
figured by him, that men should suppose him to be Jesus, while Jesus himself

4. **Saturninus, Menander, Basilides,** and **Cerinthus:** gnostic thinkers.

5. **Antioch:** a city in Syria.

took on the appearance of Simon and stood by and mocked them. . . . If any therefore acknowledge the crucified, he is still a slave and subject to the power of them that made our bodies; but he that denies him is freed from them, and recognises the ordering of the Unborn Father.

A certain Cerinthus[4] also in Asia taught that the world was not made by the first God, but by a certain Virtue far separated and removed from the Principality which is above all things, a Virtue which knows not the God over all. He added that Jesus was not born of a virgin but was the son of Joseph and Mary, like other men, but superior to all others in justice, prudence and wisdom. And that after his baptism Christ descended upon him in the form of a dove, from that Principality which is above all things; and that then he revealed the Unknown Father and performed deeds of virtue, but that in the end Christ flew back, leaving Jesus, and Jesus suffered and rose again, but Christ remained impassible, being by nature spiritual.

6. The Apostles' Creed: Adapted from a Letter of St. Ambrose of Milan, 390

I believe in God, the Father Almighty, maker of heaven and earth, and in Jesus Christ his only Son our Lord, conceived by the Holy Spirit and born of the Virgin Mary. He suffered under Pontius Pilate, was crucified, died and was buried. He descended into hell. On the third day he rose again from the dead. He ascended into heaven and sits at the right hand of God the Father Almighty. From whence he shall come again to judge the quick and the dead. I believe in the Holy Spirit, the Holy catholic[6] church, the communion of saints, the forgiveness of sins, the resurrection of the body, and the life everlasting.

Sources 7 through 11 from Henry Bettenson, editor and translator, Documents of the Christian Church, *2d edition (London: Oxford University Press 1963), p. 37; pp. 28–29; p. 63; pp. 68–70; p. 71.*

7. Description of the Ideas of Marcion, from Irenaeus of Lyons's *Against Heresies*

Marcion of Pontus took his [Cerdon's[7]] place and amplified his teaching, impudently blaspheming him who is declared to be God by the Law and the Prophets; calling him a worker of evils, delighting in wars, inconstant in

6. "Catholic" in this instance means worldwide.

7. **Cerdon:** a gnostic thinker.

judgement and self-contradictory. While he alleges that Jesus came from the Father who is above the God that made the world; that he came to Judaea in the time of Pontius Pilate the governor, who was the procurator of Tiberius Caesar, and was manifest in the form of a man to all that were in Judaea, destroying the prophets and the Law and all the works of that God who made the world, whom he calls also the Ruler of the Universe. Moreover he mutilated the Gospel according to Luke, removing all the narratives of the Lord's birth, and also removing much of the teaching of the discourses of the Lord wherein he is most manifestly described as acknowledging the maker of this universe to be his father. Thus he persuaded his disciples that he himself was more trustworthy than the apostles, who handed down the Gospel; though he gave to them not a Gospel but a fragment of a Gospel. He mutilated the Epistles of the Apostle Paul in the same manner, removing whatever is manifestly spoken by the Apostle concerning the God who made the world, where he says that he is the father of our Lord Jesus Christ, and setting aside all the Apostle's teaching drawn from the Prophetic writings which predict the advent of the Lord.

2. And then he says that salvation will be of our souls only, of those souls which have learned his teaching; the body, because forsooth it is taken from the earth, cannot partake in salvation.

8. The Muratorian Canon

. . . The third book of the Gospel is that according to Luke. Luke, the physician, when, after the Ascension of Christ, Paul had taken him to himself as one studious of right [*or, probably,* as travelling companion] wrote in his own name what he had been told [*or* in order], although he had not himself seen the Lord in the flesh. He set down the events as far as he could ascertain them, and began his story with the birth of John.

The fourth gospel is that of John, one of the disciples. . . . When his fellow-disciples and bishops exhorted him he said, 'Fast with me for three days from to-day, and then let us relate to each other whatever may be revealed to each of us.' On the same night it was revealed to Andrew, one of the Apostles, that John should narrate all things in his own name as they remembered them. . . .

Moreover the Acts of all the Apostles are included in one book. Luke addressed them to the most excellent Theophilus, because the several events took place when he was present; and he makes this plain by the omission of the passion of Peter and of the journey of Paul when he left Rome for Spain.

For the Epistles of Paul . . . he wrote to not more than seven churches, in this order: the first to the Corinthians, the second to the Ephesians, the third to the Philippians, the fourth to the Colossians, the fifth to the Galatians, the sixth to the Thessalonians, the seventh to the Romans. . . . He wrote besides these one to Philemon, one to Titus, and two to Timothy. These were written in personal affection; but they have been hallowed by being held in honour by the Catholic Church for the regulation of church discipline. There are extant also a letter to the Laodiceans and another to the Alexandrians, forged under Paul's name to further the heresy of Marcion. And there are many others which cannot be received into the Catholic Church. For it is not fitting for gall to be mixed with honey.

The Epistle of Jude indeed, and two bearing the name of John, are accepted in the Catholic Church; also Wisdom, written by the friends of Solomon in his honour. We receive also the Apocalypse of John and that of Peter, which some of us refuse to have read in the Church. But the *Shepherd* was written very recently in our time by Hermas, in the city of Rome, when his brother, Bishop Pius, was sitting in the Chair of the Church of Rome. Therefore it ought also to be read; but it cannot be publicly read in the Church to the people, either among the Prophets, since their number is complete [?], or among the Apostles, to the end of time. . . .

9. Clement of Rome, Letter to the Christians at Corinth

. . . The Apostles for our sakes received the gospel from the Lord Jesus Christ; Jesus Christ was sent from God. Christ then is from God, and the Apostles from Christ. Both therefore came in due order from the will of God. Having therefore received his instructions and being fully assured through the Resurrection of our Lord Jesus Christ, they went forth with confidence in the word of God and with full assurance of the Holy Spirit, preaching the gospel that the Kingdom of God was about to come. And so, as they preached in the country and in the towns, they appointed their firstfruits (having proved them by the Spirit) to be bishops and deacons [overseers and ministers] of them that should believe. And this was no novelty, for of old it had been written concerning bishops and deacons; for the Scripture says in one place, 'I will set up their bishops in righteousness, and their deacons in faith' (Is. lx. 17).[8]

Our Apostles knew also, through our Lord Jesus Christ, that there would be strife over the dignity of the bishop's office. For this reason therefore, having received complete foreknowledge, they appointed the aforesaid, and after a time made provision that on their death other approved men should succeed to their ministry. . . .

8. Clement is here changing the original wording of Isaiah 60: 17, which reads *overseers* and *taskmasters* instead of *bishops* and *deacons*.

10. Discussion of Succession from Irenaeus's *Against Heresies*

... Those that wish to discern the truth may observe the apostolic tradition made manifest in every church throughout the world. We can enumerate those who were appointed bishops in the churches by the Apostles, and their successors [*or* successions] down to our own day, who never taught, and never knew, absurdities such as these men produce. For if the Apostles had known hidden mysteries which they taught the perfect in private and in secret, they would rather have committed them to those to whom they entrusted the churches. For they wished those men to be perfect and unblameable whom they left as their successors and to whom they handed over their own office of authority. But as it would be very tedious, in a book of this sort, to enumerate the successions in all the churches, we confound all those who in any way, whether for self-pleasing, or vainglory, or blindness, or evilmindedness, hold unauthorized meetings. This we do by pointing to the apostolic tradition and the faith that is preached to men, which has come down to us through the successions of bishops; the tradition and creed of the greatest, the most ancient church, the church known to all men, which was founded and set up at Rome by the two most glorious Apostles, Peter and Paul. For with this church, because of its position of leadership and authority, must needs agree every church, that is, the faithful everywhere; for in her the apostolic tradition has always been preserved by the faithful from all parts.

2. The blessed Apostles, after founding and building up the church, handed over to Linus the office of bishop. Paul mentions this Linus in his epistles to Timothy (2 Tim. iv. 21). He was succeeded by Anacletus, after whom, in the third place after the Apostles, Clement was appointed to the bishopric. He not only saw the blessed Apostles but also conferred with them, and had their preaching ringing in his ears and their tradition before his eyes. In this he was not alone; for many still survived who had been taught by the Apostles. Now while Clement was bishop there arose no small dissension among the brethren in Corinth, and the church in Rome sent a most weighty letter to the Corinthians urging them to reconciliation, renewing their faith and telling them again of the tradition which he had lately received from the Apostles. ...

3. Euarestus succeeded this Clement, Alexander followed Euarestus; then Sixtus was appointed, the sixth after the Apostles. After him came Telesphorus, who had a glorious martyrdom. Then Hyginus, Pius, Anicetus and Soter; and now, in the twelfth place from the Apostles, Eleutherus occupies the see. In the same order and succession the apostolic tradition in the Church and the preaching of the truth has come down to our time. ...

4. And then Polycarp, besides being instructed by the Apostles and acquainted with many who had seen the Lord, was also appointed by the Apos-

tles from Asia as bishop of the church in Smyrna.[9] Even I saw him in my early youth; for he remained with us a long time, and at a great age suffered a martyrdom full of glory and renown and departed this life, having taught always the things which he had learnt from the Apostles, which the Church hands down, which alone are true. There testify to these things all the churches throughout Asia, and the successors of Polycarp down to this day, testimonies to the truth far more trustworthy and reliable than Valentinus[10] and Marcion and the other misguided persons.

Polycarp, when staying in Rome in the time of Anicetus, converted many of the before-mentioned heretics to the Church of God, declaring that he had received this one and only truth from the Apostles, the truth which has been handed down by the Church. There are also some who heard him relate that John, the disciple of the Lord, went to the baths at Ephesus; and seeing Cerinthus[10] inside he rushed out without taking a bath, saying, 'Let us flee, before the baths fall in, for Cerinthus the enemy of the truth is inside.' . . .

iv. 1. Since therefore there are so many proofs, there is now no need to seek among others the truth which we can easily obtain from the Church. For the Apostles have lodged all that there is of the truth with her, as with a rich bank, holding back nothing. And so anyone that wishes can draw from her the draught of life. This is the gateway of life; all the rest are thieves and robbers. . . .

Therefore we ought to obey only those presbyters who are in the Church, who have their succession from the Apostles, as we have shown; who with their succession in the episcopate have received the sure gift of the truth according to the pleasure of the Father. The rest, who stand aloof from the primitive succession, and assemble in any place whatever, we must regard with suspicion, either as heretics and evil-minded; or as schismatics, puffed up and complacent; or again as hypocrites, acting thus for the sake of gain and vainglory. All these have fallen from the truth.

11. Discussion of Succession from Tertullian, *Prescription Against the Heretics*

But if any of these [heresies] are bold enough to insert themselves into the Apostolic age, in order to seem to have been handed down from the Apostles because they existed under the Apostles, we can say: Let them then produce the origins of their churches; let them unroll the list of their bishops, an unbroken succession from the beginning so that that first bishop had as his precursor and the source of his authority one of the Apostles or one of the apostolic men who, though not an Apostle, continued with the Apostles. This is how

9. **Smyrna:** a city in Asia Minor (present-day Turkey).
10. **Valentinus** and **Cerinthus:** gnostic thinkers.

the apostolic churches report their origins; thus the church of the Smyrnaeans relates that Polycarp was appointed by John, the church of Rome that Clement was ordained by Peter. . . .

QUESTIONS TO CONSIDER

As scholars have discovered more about the diversity of early Christian beliefs and practices, they have been increasingly interested in explaining not only *how*, but also *why* certain ideas became identified as orthodox and others were rejected, and why orthodoxy ultimately triumphed. Answers to these questions take us far beyond the sources included here, but you can use the sources, combined with information from your textbook about Roman society in the first centuries after Jesus, to begin to address them. Considering these questions will also allow you to deepen your understanding of the process of this change as you answer the questions for this chapter.

Thinking about gnostic ideas in general, why might the gnostic view that Jesus' true mission was to an elite group able to understand secret knowledge have reduced its popularity among early converts to Christianity? How did the gnostic notion that the inner experience or vision of Christ was what mattered, an experience that anyone could have, challenge Roman ideas of proper structures of authority? How did the gnostic idea that the true message of Jesus had primarily been communicated orally both allow for and limit the spread of gnostic ideas?

Taking some of the actions in the establishment of orthodoxy, why might orthodox views of the crucifixion, which emphasized its bodily nature, be especially appealing at a time when Christians were persecuted by Roman authorities? How did orthodoxy's setting up of objective criteria for membership (that is, taking in anyone who would accept orthodox doctrines and agree to be governed by bishops) increase its appeal as compared to gnosticism's demand for special spiritual insight? Once bishops were established as figures of authority, why would it be increasingly difficult to promote gnostic ideas? How did setting up the criterion of "apostolic" as the central determinant of orthodoxy limit the importance of visions such as that described by Mary Magdalene in Source 3? How would the idea of apostolic authority have worked against groups such as the gnostics who did not think it important to link themselves with the apostles?.

Once you begin to understand what ideas became central to orthodox Christianity, you can see that certain events surrounding the life of Jesus were somewhat problematic because they seemed to point to an alternative interpretation. One of these events is that related in Source 1, the fact that the empty tomb was discovered by women, not by the disciples, and that women first heard the message that Jesus had risen. How did this conflict with notions of authority being developed in orthodoxy? One solution for problems such as this was to alter the account somewhat, and, in fact, some ancient texts of Luke add an additional verse after verse 11 in Source 1, which reads: "But Peter rose and ran to the tomb; stooping and looking in, he saw the linen cloths by themselves; and he went home wondering at what had happened." How might this addition change one's interpretation of the event?

As we search for human reasons for the developments traced in this chapter, it is important not to forget that the people we are studying regarded these events as signs of divine providence, of God working in history. Early Christians and many non-Christian Romans expected God (or the gods) to act through human agents and so did not regard human explanations as disproof of the divine or miraculous. If the question of how and why orthodoxy triumphed had been put to someone like Irenaeus, how might he have answered? Comparing his hypothetical answer to yours, how have ideas of causation in history changed since ancient times?

EPILOGUE

The transformation of Christianity from its original diversity to a religion with clear lines between heresy and orthodoxy was not something that was accomplished by A.D. 200, but has continued to the present day. The original pattern set by the confrontation with gnosticism has been largely followed, however. Christianity generally defined what would be considered orthodoxy only when confronted by a group taking a firm alternative position; the development of Christian theology has thus been reactive rather than spontaneous, and Christianity has tolerated *heterodoxy*, or a range of opinions, on many issues for a long time.

Because of its many denominations, modern Christianity appears at first glance to be a return to diversity and heterodoxy, yet the ideas and institutions you have traced in this chapter are still present in many Christian denominations. Contemporary theological disputes, particularly within Roman Catholicism but also within Eastern Orthodoxy and many Protestant denominations, are still being decided upon by reference to apostolic authority and the texts of the New Testament. Bishops in many Christian denominations still have a great amount of power, and people still recite the Apostles' Creed. Though it would be hard to find an idea that all Christian denominations today regard as heresy, those of the gnostics would probably come the closest.

The ideas and interpretations put forth by gnostics did not completely die out in the second century, however. Not only did gnostic Christianity survive for several more centuries, but gnostic ideas reemerged in the Middle Ages and in many

Christian thinkers down to the present day. The gnostic texts rediscovered at Nag Hammadi have also become increasingly popular with people searching for spiritual answers today. Both those who wish to remain within a Christian tradition but are uncomfortable with the institutionalization and stress on authority that came to mark orthodoxy, and those who are again developing syncretistic personal religions from a variety of traditions have turned to gnosticism for inspiration.

CHAPTER SIX

SLAVE LAW IN ROMAN AND

GERMANIC SOCIETY

In all the cultures of the ancient Mediterranean, some people were slaves, owned as property by other people. In Mesopotamia and Egypt, people became slaves in a variety of ways, and the earliest law codes, such as that of Hammurabi (ca 1780 B.C.), include provisions regarding slavery. Many slaves were war captives, brought into the area from outside along with other types of booty. Some were criminals, for whom slavery was the punishment for a crime. Some had been sold into slavery by their parents or had sold themselves into slavery in times of economic hardship. Others became slaves to repay debts, a condition that was often temporary. In these cultures, slaves performed a variety of tasks, from farming to highly skilled professional and administrative work, but the proportion of slaves in the population was not very great and most work was carried out by free persons. Thus, historians describe Mesopotamia and Egypt as slave-using but not slave societies.

By contrast, republican Rome was truly a slave society, in which a significant proportion of the population were slaves—perhaps one-quarter or one-third by the second century B.C.—and in which slaves did much of the productive labor. The military conquests of Rome during the second and first centuries B.C. provided many new war captives and also increased the wealth of Rome's elite, who invested in huge agricultural estates (termed *latifundia*). These estates were too large to be worked by single peasant families—who were often migrating to the cities in any case—and so an increasing share of agricultural production was carried on by large labor gangs of slaves under the supervision of overseers, who might themselves be slaves. The owners of both the land and the slaves were often absentee, living in Rome or another urban center rather than out on the latifundia themselves. This system of agricultural slavery continued into the Roman Empire, although the influx of new slaves lessened somewhat as military expansion slowed and laws were passed prohibiting the enslavement of subjects of the Empire. In addition, urban slaves who worked as household servants, artisans, teachers, gladiators, or shopkeepers continued to be very common.

The Germanic tribes that gradually migrated into the Roman Empire beginning in the second century were also slave-owning cultures, although the relative number of slaves among them was probably less than that in Rome. When they conquered Roman lands, they generally took a proportion of the slaves and the land for themselves, leaving the rest to the existing Roman proprietors. However, the breakdown in communication and political control that accompanied the disintegration of the Roman Empire in the West made it increasingly difficult for absentee owners to control their estates and to ship their products safely to distant markets. Thus, like many other aspects of life during this period, slavery became increasingly localized and less economically significant than it had been earlier in these areas, although it did not disappear.

Slavery in both Roman and Germanic societies was based not on racial distinctions but on notions of personal freedom that could be very complex. At the heart of this complexity was the issue that a slave was both a person, able to engage in relationships with other persons and to act on his or her own, and a thing, owned by another person. Law codes developed by both Romans and Germans had to balance these two aspects of being a slave, as well as regulate other matters concerning slaves and slavery. They had to establish and protect the boundaries between slave and free, but also establish ways in which those boundaries could be crossed, as slavery was not necessarily a permanent status. Your task in this chapter will be to investigate Roman and Germanic laws regarding slavery during the period 400 to 1000, in order to answer the following questions: How were legal distinctions between slave and free established, structured, and maintained, and how could they be overcome? What similarities and differences are there in Roman and Germanic laws regarding slavery?

SOURCES AND METHOD

When historians investigate legal developments, they often use law codes in conjunction with court records and other documents to examine the actual workings of the law, or to contrast legal theory with reality. For the

period we are investigating in this chapter, sources describing actual legal practice in central and western Europe are virtually nonexistent, and so our focus will be strictly on the law codes. (Other sources regarding slavery in the Roman Empire do exist, such as economic treatises, histories of slave revolts, and philosophical discussions of slavery, but there are no parallel sources for early Germanic societies.) We must thus keep in mind that everything we read is essentially legal theory, describing what is supposed to happen rather than what actually does happen. Law codes are not written in a vacuum, however. They reflect not only the ideals of the legal and political authorities who were their authors, but also these authorities' assumptions about what people—in this case slaves, their owners, and people who came into contact with slaves and their owners—might actually do. In some cases laws also explicitly describe actual conduct, generally as a preamble to a prohibition of this conduct, or a succession of laws implies actual conduct, as prohibitions are made more specific or penalties are made more stringent.

It is important in this chapter, then, to keep in mind the limitations of using law codes as a source, and it is also important to recognize that the law codes we will be using come from two cultures that had very different notions concerning the origin, function, and purpose of law. Roman law began during the republican period as a set of rules governing the private lives of citizens, and was later expanded to include the handling of disputes between Romans and non-Romans and between foreigners under Roman jurisdiction. The first written codification, the Twelve Tables, was made in the middle of the fifth century B.C. and posted publicly, giving at least those Romans who could read direct access to it. Legal interpreters called *praetors* and judges

called *judices* made decisions based on explicit statutes and also on their own notions of what would be fair and equitable, which gave them a great deal of flexibility. Praetors generally followed the laws set by their predecessors, announcing publicly at the beginning of their terms of office that they would do this, but they also added to the body of law as new issues arose. Thus Roman law was adaptable to new conditions, with jurists in the Empire regarding their work as building on that of earlier centuries rather than negating it. Ultimately all those living within the boundaries of the Roman Empire were regarded as subject to the same law, the *ius gentium*, or "law of peoples."

Roman law regarding slavery—like all Roman law—for most of the republican and imperial periods was a mixture of senatorial statutes, edicts of elected officials, opinions of learned jurists, imperial decrees, and rulings by lesser officials. Under Emperor Theodosius II (r. 408–450), an attempt was made to compile some of the actual imperial decrees, and the resultant Theodosian Code promulgated in 435–438 contained all of the imperial laws issued since the time of the emperor Constantine (r. 311–337) that were still in effect, including those on slavery. Theodosius ruled the eastern half of the Roman Empire (which later came to be called the Byzantine Empire), but his laws were promulgated for both the eastern and western halves. The Theodosian Code was expanded under the direction of the Byzantine Emperor Justinian (r. 527–565), with older and newer laws and the opinions of jurists added. Justinian's Code, promulgated in 529–533 and officially termed the *Corpus Juris Civilis*, became the basis of Byzantine legal procedure for nearly a millennium.

In contrast to Roman written statutory law, Germanic law remained a body of traditions handed down orally for almost a thousand years after the first codification of Roman law. Like all systems of customary law around the world, it was regarded as binding because it represented the immemorial customs of a specific tribe. The ultimate authority in this legal system was not an abstract body of laws or a group of legal interpreters, but the king, whose chief legal function was to "speak the law"—that is, to decide cases based on existing oral tradition; neither the king nor anyone else could (at least in theory) make new laws. This body of custom was regarded as the inalienable possession of all members of a tribe, no matter where they happened to be, and was thus attached to persons rather than to geographic areas the way Roman (and today's) statutory law codes were.

At roughly the same time that codifications of Roman law were promulgated by the emperors Theodosius and Justinian, Germanic kings in western Europe supported the initial written codifications of what had been oral customary law. These codes usually bore the name of the tribe, such as the Lombard Law, the Burgundian Law, or the Salic Law (the law of the Salian Franks). On the continent of Europe, such law codes were written down in Latin, often by Roman jurists employed by Germanic kings, so that they sometimes included Roman legal tradition as well as Germanic customs, particularly in southern Europe, where Roman culture was strongest. In northern Europe and in England—where the laws were initially written in the West Saxon dialect that became Old English—Roman influences were weaker, making the codes of these areas, such as those of the Frisians and the Anglo-Saxons, more purely customary in origin.

When the Germanic tribes came into the Empire, these two notions of the law—statutory and geographic versus customary and personal—came into direct conflict. The problem was solved initially by letting Romans be judged according to written Roman law while non-Romans were judged by their own oral customs. As the Germanic kingdoms became more firmly established, their rulers saw the merits of a written code, but two legal systems—one for Romans and one for Germanic people—often existed side by side for centuries in these areas. Only in cases that involved a conflict between a Roman and a German was the former expected to follow the new Germanic code. As noted above, however, Roman principles did shape these Germanic codes to some degree. Though the initial codifications claimed to be simply the recording of long-standing customs, in reality the laws often modified customs that no longer fit the needs of the Germanic peoples as they became more settled and adopted some aspects of the more sophisticated Roman culture. Later kings were also not hesitant to make new laws when situations demanded it and to state explicitly that this is what they were doing. Thus Germanic codes gradually evolved from records of tribal customs based on moral sanctions and notions of a common tradition into collections of royal statutes based on the political authority of kings. They remained more closely linked to the ruler than Roman law and never included the opinions of legal commentators the way Justinian's Code did, but, like Roman law, they were eventually tied to a geographic area rather than to a group of people.

There were thus significant differences between Roman and Germanic societies in the function and complexity of law, but the legal codes of all these societies included provisions regarding slavery. The sources for this chapter come from seven different law codes, two from Roman tradition—the Theodosian Code and Justinian's Code—and five from Germanic tradition—Burgundian, Salic, Lombard, Alemannic, and Anglo-Saxon. Many of these law codes exist in multiple manuscript versions, with the earliest extant version often dating from centuries after the code was first compiled. This provides much fuel for scholarly disagreement about exactly when they were drawn up, exactly which sections date from the initial codification and which from later revisions, and exactly how certain sections are supposed to read. (Scholars can often trace the path manuscripts followed by noting which errors were recopied by subse-

quent scribes; often this does not help in determining which versions are more "authentic," however.) For this chapter, we have used the version of these codes most widely accepted by recent scholarship, but you should be aware that any edition or translation of texts like these from manuscript cultures involves a decision on the part of the editor as to which version to use.

To explore the legal definitions of and boundaries between slavery and freedom, we will be examining four basic issues in this chapter: (A) How could a person become a slave, or a slave become free? (B) How were slaves valued, in comparison to other things a person might own, and what limits were placed on the treatment of slaves by their owners? (C) How were personal relationships between slave and free regulated? (D) How were slaves differentiated from free persons in terms of criminal actions committed by them or against them? To assist you in working through the issues in this chapter, provisions in the laws have been grouped according to these four topics rather than being presented in the order in which they appear in the codes. (In many of these codes, particularly the Germanic ones, laws are arranged completely haphazardly in any case, so that the order makes no difference.) Thus, as you are taking notes on the sources, it would be a good idea to draw up a chart for each issue. Other than this, your basic method in this chapter is careful reading.

Source 1 includes selections from the Theodosian Code. According to the selections in Source 1A, what are some of the ways in which one could become a slave in the late Roman Empire? What are some ways in which slaves could become free? According to 1B, what would happen to a master who beat his slaves? According to 1C, what would happen to a woman who had sexual relations with or married one of her slaves? To a man who had sexual relations with one of his slaves? To a decurion (a man who was a member of a local municipal council) who did so? According to 1D, what would happen to rebellious slaves?

Source 2 contains selections from Justinian's Code, which was itself divided into three parts: the *Codex*, actual imperial legislation, including much that was contained in the Theodosian Code; the *Digest*, the opinions of various jurists from throughout the history of Rome; and the *Institutes*, an officially prescribed course for first-year law students, in which some of the opinions found in the *Digest* are repeated. The legal opinions included in the *Digest* sometimes refer to specific imperial statutes, and sometimes simply describe what the commentator saw as Roman tradition in regard to legal categories or procedures. Like legal opinions today, however, the judgments of these jurists shaped the handling of cases, for later judges and lawyers looked to earlier precedents and opinions when making their decisions. They are thus much more important than the opinion of a private person on an issue would be, and all the selections included here come from the *Digest*. According to Source 2A, what were some of the ways in which one could

become a slave or become free? Would becoming free remove all obligations a slave had toward his master? According to 2C, did slaves have family relationships? According to 2D, what would happen to someone who killed a slave? To slaves whose master was killed while they were within earshot? To runaway slaves and those who protected them?

Putting the information from Sources 1 and 2 together, you can begin to develop an idea about the legal status of slaves in the later Roman Empire. What are some of the ways one could cross from slave to free? From free to slave? Is this a hard boundary, as the writers of the *Digest* imply in 2A, or are there intermediate steps? How do restrictions on slave/free sexual relationships help to maintain the boundaries? Why do you think there are gender differences in such restrictions? In what ways do the laws in 1D and 2D regard the slave as a thing? In what ways as a person?

Sources 3 through 7 are selections from Germanic law codes, which were often written down under the reign of one king and then expanded under his successors. Compared with Roman law, Germanic codes were extremely short and consist solely of statements of law, with no juristic opinions such as those contained in the *Digest*. They thus offer a less full picture of slave life than does Roman law, but slaves are mentioned in many of their clauses. In Germanic society, murder, injuries, or insults to honor had resulted in feuds between individuals and families, but by the time the law codes were written down, a system of monetary compensatory payments—called *wergeld* in the case of murder or *composition* in the case of lesser injuries—was being devised as a substitute. These compensatory payments were set according to the severity of the loss or injury, and also according to the social status of the perpetrator and the victim.

Source 3 comes from one of the earliest Germanic law codes, the Law of Gundobad, drawn up for his Burgundian subjects by King Gundobad (r. 474–516), who ruled the Burgundian kingdom in what is now southeastern France. (Following the principle that customary law applied to persons and not territories, Gundobad also drew up a separate code for his Roman subjects, the *Lex Romana Burgundionem,* at about the same time.) According to the laws in Source 3A, what were some of the ways in which one could become a slave or be freed if one were a slave? According to 3C, what were the penalties for rape of freewomen and slaves? For women who willingly had sexual relations with slaves? According to 3D, what was the relative value of slaves as compared to that of free persons and freedmen (former slaves), at least in regard to their teeth and female honor?

Source 4 comes from the Germanic tribe known as the Franks, who conquered the Burgundian kingdom in 534. The original Frankish code, the *Pactus Legis Salicae,* was issued by King Clovis in about 510 and was amended and revised by many of his successors. (Like all Germanic codes,

it did not apply to everyone living under Frankish overlordship; Burgundians living within the Frankish kingdom continued to be judged by Burgundian law for centuries after the conquest.) It includes no laws on how one becomes a slave or is released from slavery, but it does include sections on sexual relations with slaves, and on slaves who steal or run away. According to the laws in Source 4C, in the first group, what would happen to a freeman or freewoman who marries or has sexual intercourse with a slave? To a slave who marries or has sexual intercourse with a free person or another slave? According to 4D, how were the slave's owners' rights balanced against those of the person from whom the slave stole? How were those who encouraged slaves to run away to be punished? How does this punishment compare with that set for slaves who steal?

Source 5 contains selections from the Lombard Laws, written down between 643 and 755 under the direction of various Lombard kings, including King Rothair (issued in 643), King Luitprand (issued 713–735), and King Aistulf (issued 750–755). The Lombards invaded Italy in 568, after the Franks, Burgundians, and other tribes had already established successor kingdoms in parts of the old Roman Empire, and established a kingdom in central and northern Italy that lasted until 774, when it was conquered by the Frankish ruler Charlemagne. Like Burgundian law, Lombard law remained in force for Lombards within Frankish territory for centuries—in fact, until the city-states of Italy began to adopt Roman legal principles and the *Corpus Juris Civilis* in the twelfth century. Lombard law was more comprehensive than the Burgundian and Frankish codes, and included provisions regarding all of the issues we are investigating in this chapter. According to the laws in Source 5A, what were some of the ways in which a person could become a slave in Lombard society? How could a slave be freed? According to 5B, what was the relative value of slaves as compared to horses? According to 5C, how were marriages between slaves, freed persons, and free people to be handled? According to 5D, how were fugitive slaves and slaves who revolted to be handled?

Source 6 comes from the Germanic tribe known as the Alamans, who settled in what is now southern Germany and Switzerland in the third century A.D. and wrote their law codes between 613 and 713. Like other Germanic codes, Alamannic law set compensatory payments for various injuries and actions, and also used slavery as a punishment for certain crimes. According to Source 6A, what was one of the ways in which people could become slaves? According to 6B, were there limits on a master's treatment of slaves? According to 6C, what would happen to a free-woman who married a slave? According to 6D, what were the relative values placed on men and women from the three basic social groups, free persons, freedpersons, and slaves? How was the rape of slaves to be compensated?

Source 7, the final source for this chapter, contains provisions from Anglo-Saxon law codes from the various kingdoms of England, dating from the sixth through the tenth centuries. These codes were written in Old English, not in Latin, and show no signs of Roman influence, although many of their provisions are similar to those we have seen in other Germanic codes. According to Source 7A, laws issued by Edward the Elder (dated between 901 and 925), what was one way in which a person could become a slave? According to 7B, from the laws of Ine (688–695), what were some of the limitations on a master's treatment of his slaves? According to 7D, laws of Aethelbert of Kent (565–604) and Alfred (890–899), what was the punishment for rape of a slave? How did this differ depending on the status of the slave and the perpetrator?

You now need to put together the Germanic material in the same way that you did the Roman. How could people in Germanic society move from free to slave? From slave to free? Are there intermediate steps between these two, and how do the rights of these people differ from those of free people and slaves? What are the consequences of various types of slave/free sexual relationships? Are there hierarchies of status and value among slaves? On what are these based? Do the laws regarding crimes against slaves and crimes committed by slaves tend to view slaves as things or as persons?

Source 1 from Clyde Pharr, editor, The Theodosian Code *(Princeton, N.J.: Princeton Univer-sity Press, 1952), Sections 3.3.1; 4.6.7; 5.6.3; 5.9.1; 7.13.16; 7.18.4; 9.12.1–2; 9.9.1–3, 6; 10.10.33; 14.18.1. Copyright © 1952 by Clyde Pharr, Princeton University Press. Renewed 1980 by Roy Pharr. Reprinted by permission of Princeton University Press.*

1. Theodosian Code

A. Slave to Free/Free to Slave

[3.3.1] All those persons whom the piteous fortune of their parents has con-signed to slavery while their parents thereby were seeking sustenance shall be restored to their original status of free birth. Certainly no person shall de-mand repayment of the purchase price, if he has been compensated by the slavery of a freeborn person for a space of time that is not too short.

INTERPRETATION: If a father, forced by need, should sell any freeborn child whatsoever, the child cannot remain in perpetual slavery, but if he has made compensation by his slavery, he shall be restored to his freeborn status with-out even the repayment of the purchase price.

[4.6.7] We sanction that the name of natural children shall be placed upon those who have been begotten and brought into this world as the result of a lawful union without an honorable performance of the marriage ceremony. But it is established that children born from the womb of a slave woman are slaves, according to the law . . . [I]f natural children have been born from a slave woman and have not been manumitted by their master, they are reck-oned among the slaves belonging to his inheritance.

[5.6.3] We have subjected the Scyrae, a barbarian nation, to Our power after We had routed a very great force of Chuni, with whom they had allied them-selves. Therefore We grant to all persons the opportunity to supply their own fields with men of the aforesaid race.

[5.9.1] If any person should take up a boy or a girl child that has been cast out of its home with the knowledge and consent of its father or owner, and if he should rear this child to strength with his own sustenance, he shall have the right to keep the said child under the same status as he wished it to have when he took charge of it, that is, as his child or as a slave, whichever he should prefer.

[14.18.1] If there should be any persons who adopt the profession of mendi-cancy[1] and who are induced to seek their livelihood at public expense, each of

1. **mendicancy:** begging.

them shall be examined. The soundness of body and the vigor of years of each one of them shall be investigated. In the case of those who are able, the necessity shall be placed upon them that the zealous and diligent informer shall obtain the ownership of those beggars who are held bound by their servile status, and such informer shall be supported by the right to the perpetual colonate[2] of those beggars who are attended by only the liberty of their birth rights, provided that the informer should betray and prove such sloth.

[7.13.16] In the matter of defense against hostile attacks,[3] We order that consideration be given not only to the legal status of soldiers, but also to their physical strength. Although We believe that freeborn persons are aroused by love of country, We exhort slaves[4] also, by the authority of this edict, that as soon as possible they shall offer themselves for the labors of war, and if they receive their arms as men fit for military service, they shall obtain the reward of freedom, and they shall also receive two solidi each for travel money. Especially, of course, do We urge this service upon the slaves of those persons who are retained in the armed imperial service, and likewise upon the slaves of federated allies and of conquered peoples, since it is evident that they are making war also along with their masters.

[7.18.4] [In the case of deserters,] if a slave should surrender such deserter, he shall be given freedom. If a freeborn person of moderate status should surrender such deserter, he shall gain immunity.[5]

B. Value and Treatment of Slaves

[9.12.1–2] If a master should beat a slave with light rods or lashes or if he should cast him into chains for the purpose of custody, he shall not endure any fear of criminal charges if the slave should die, for We abolish all consideration of time limitations and legal interpretation.[6] The master shall not, indeed, use his own right immoderately, but he shall be guilty of homicide if he should kill the slave voluntarily by a blow of a club or of a stone, at any rate if he should use a weapon and inflict a lethal wound or should order the slave to be hanged by a noose, or if he should command by a shameful order that he be thrown from a high place or should administer the virus of a poison or should lacerate his body by public punishments,[7] that is, by cutting through

---

2. **colonate:** forced labor on farms.

3. At this time the Roman Empire was gradually crumbling from the attacks of the barbarians.

4. In violation of long-established Roman custom.

5. From compulsory public services, including taxes.

6. The references seem to be to preceding laws, which specified distinctions depending on whether a slave died immediately or after a period of time, and which contained various technicalities.

7. Types of punishment that were inflicted for certain public crimes.

his sides with the claws of wild beasts[8] or by applying fire and burning his body, or if with the savagery of monstrous barbarians he should force bodies and limbs weakening and flowing with dark blood, mingled with gore, to surrender their life almost in the midst of tortures.

Whenever such chance attends the beating of slaves by their masters that the slaves die, the masters shall be free from blame if by the correction of very evil deeds they wished to obtain better conduct on the part of their household slaves. . . .

INTERPRETATION: If a slave should die while his master is punishing a fault, the master shall not be held on the charge of homicide, because he is guilty of homicide only if he is convicted of having intended to kill the slave. For disciplinary correction is not reckoned as a crime.

C. Slave/Free Relations

[9.9.1–6] If any woman is discovered to have a clandestine love affair with her slave, she shall be subject to the capital sentence, and the rascally slave shall be delivered to the flames. All persons shall have the right to bring an accusation of this public crime; office staffs shall have the right to report it; even a slave shall have permission to lodge information, and freedom shall be granted to him if the crime is proved, although punishment threatens him if he makes a false accusation. 1. If a woman has been so married[9] before the issuance of this law, she shall be separated from such an association, shall be deprived not only of her home but also of participation in the life of the province, and shall mourn the absence of her exiled lover. 2. The children also whom she bears from this union shall be stripped of all the insignia of rank. They shall remain in bare freedom, and neither through themselves nor through the interposition of another person shall they receive anything under any title of a will from the property of the woman. 3. Moreover, the inheritance of the woman, in case of intestacy, shall be granted either to her children, if she has legitimate ones, or to the nearest kinsmen and cognates, or to the person whom the rule of law admits, so that whatever of their own property her former lover and the children conceived from him appear by any chance to have had shall be joined to the property of the woman and may be vindicated by the aforesaid successors. . . .

6. For after the issuance of this law We punish by death those persons who commit this crime. But those who have been separated in accordance with this

---

8. Implements of torture, actually made of metal.

9. A loose use of the word *marriage*, as slaves could not enter legally recognized marriages (*conubia*) because those were contracts available only to free persons. Instead they were joined in less formal unions termed *contubernia*.

law and secretly come together again and renew the forbidden union and who are convicted by the evidence of slaves or that of the office of the special investigator or also by the information of nearest kinsmen shall sustain a similar penalty.

INTERPRETATION: If any freeborn woman should join herself secretly to her own slave, she shall suffer capital punishment. A slave also who should be convicted of adultery with his mistress shall be burned by fire. Whoever wishes shall have it in his power to bring accusation of a crime of this kind. Even slaves or maidservants, if they should bring an accusation of this crime, shall be heard, on this condition, however, that they shall obtain their freedom if they prove their accusation; that if they falsify, they shall be punished. The inheritance of a woman who defiles herself with such a crime shall be granted either to her children, if they were conceived from her husband, or to those near kinsmen who succeed according to law.

[12.1.6] Although it appears unworthy for men, even though not endowed with any high rank, to descend to sordid marriages with slave women, nevertheless this practice is not prohibited by law; but a legal marriage cannot exist with servile persons, and from a slave union of this kind, slaves are born. We command, therefore, that decurions shall not be led by their lust to take refuge in the bosom of the most powerful houses. For if a decurion should be secretly united with any slave woman belonging to another man and if the overseers and procurators should not be aware of this, We order that the woman shall be cast into the mines through sentence of the judge, and the decurion himself shall be deported to an island; his movable property and his urban slaves shall be confiscated; his landed estates and rustic slaves shall be delivered to the municipality of which he had been a decurion, if he had been freed from paternal power and has no children or parents, or even close kinsmen, who may be called to his inheritance, according to the order of the law. But if the overseers or procurators of the place in which the disgraceful act was committed were aware of it and were unwilling to divulge this crime of which they were aware, they shall be cast into the mines. But if the master permitted such offense to be committed of afterwards learned of the deed and concealed it, and if indeed, it was perpetrated on his farm, the farm with the slaves and flocks and all other things which are used in rural cultivation shall be [confiscated].

D. Criminal Actions
by/toward Slaves

[10.10.33] The lawful distinction between slavery and freedom shall stand firm. We sanction the rights of masters by the restitution of their slaves, who shall not rebel with impunity.

Source 2 from S. P. Scott, translator, Corpus Juris Civilis: The Civil Law *(Cincinnati, Ohio: The Central Trust, 1932), Sections 1.5.4–5; 9.2.2; 11.4.1; 29.5.1; 37.14.1, 19; 38.10.10; 40.1.5.*

2. Selections from the *Digest* of Justinian's Code

A. Slave to Free/Free to Slave

[1.5.4] Liberty is the natural power of doing whatever anyone wishes to do unless he is prevented in some way, by force or by law.

(1) Slavery is an institution of the Law of Nations by means of which anyone may subject one man to the control of another, contrary to nature.

(2) Slaves are so called for the reason that military commanders were accustomed to sell their captives, and in this manner to preserve them, instead of putting them to death.

(3) They are styled *mancipia,* because they are taken by the hands [*manus*] of their enemies.

[1.5.5] One condition is common to all slaves; but of persons who are free some are born such, and others are manumitted.

(1) Slaves are brought under our ownership either by the Civil Law or by that of Nations. This is done by the Civil Law where anyone who is over twenty years of age permits himself to be sold for the sake of sharing in his own price. Slaves become our property by the Law of Nations when they are either taken from the enemy, or are born of our female slaves.

(2) Persons are born free who are born from a free mother, and it is sufficient for her to have been free at the time when her child was born, even though she may have been a slave when she conceived; and, on the other hand, if she was free when she conceived, and was a slave when she brought forth, it has been established that her child is born free, nor does it make any difference whether she conceived in a lawful marriage or through promiscuous intercourse; because the misfortune of the mother should not be a source of injury to her unborn child.

(3) Hence the following question arose, where a female slave who was pregnant, has been manumitted, and is afterwards again made a slave, or, after having been expelled from the city, should bring forth a child, whether that child should be free or a slave? It was very properly established that it was born free; and that it is sufficient for a child who is unborn that its mother should have been free during the intermediate time.

[40.1.5] If a slave should allege that he was purchased with his own money, he can appear in court against his master, whose good faith he impugns, and complain that he has not been manumitted by him; but he must do this at Rome, before the Urban Prefect, or in the provinces before the Governor, in accordance with the Sacred Constitutions of the Divine Brothers; under the penalty, however, of being condemned to the mines, if he should attempt this and not prove his case; unless his master prefers that he be restored to him, and then it should be decided that he will not be liable to a more severe penalty.

(1) Where, however, a slave is ordered to be free after having rendered his accounts, an arbiter between the slave and his master, that is to say, the heir, shall be appointed for the purpose of having the accounts rendered in his presence.

[37.14.1] Governors should hear the complaints of patrons against their freedmen, and their cases should be tried without delay; for if a freedman is ungrateful, he should not go unpunished. Where, however, the freedman fails in the duty which he owes to his patron, his patroness, or their children, he should only be punished lightly, with a warning that a more severe penalty will be imposed if he again gives cause for complaint, and then be dismissed. But if he is guilty of insult or abuse of his patrons, he should be sent into temporary exile. If he offers them personal violence, he must be sentenced to the mines.

[37.14.19] A freedman is ungrateful when he does not show proper respect for his patron, or refuses to manage his property, or undertake the guardianship of his children.

C. Slave/Free Relations

[38.10.10] We make use of this term, that is to say, cognates, even with reference to slaves. Therefore, we speak of the parents, the children, and the brothers of slaves; but cognation is not recognized by servile laws.

D. Criminal Actions
by/toward Slaves

[11.4.1] He who conceals a fugitive slave is a thief.

(1) The Senate decreed that fugitive slaves shall not be admitted on land or be protected by the superintendents or agents of the possessors of the same, and prescribed a fine. But, if anyone should, within twenty days, restore fugitive slaves to their owners, or bring them before magistrates, what they had previously done will be pardoned; but it was afterwards stated in the same Decree of the Senate that immunity is granted to anyone who restores fugitive slaves to their masters, or produces them before a magistrate within the prescribed time, when they are found on his premises. . . .

(4) And the magistrates are very properly notified to detain them carefully in custody to prevent their escape. . . .

(7) Careful custody permits the use of irons.

[9.2.2] It is provided by the first section of the *Lex Aquilia* that, "Where anyone unlawfully kills a male or female slave belonging to another, or a quadruped included in the class of cattle, let him be required to pay a sum equal to the greatest value that the same was worth during the past year."

[29.5.1] As no household can be safe unless slaves are compelled, under peril of their lives, to protect their masters, not only from persons belonging to his family, but also from strangers, certain decrees of the Senate were enacted with reference to putting to public torture all the slaves belonging to a household in case of the violent death of their master . . . , for the reason that slaves are punished whenever they do not assist their master against anyone who is guilty of violence towards him, when they are able to do so. . . . Whenever slaves can afford assistance to their master, they should not prefer their own safety to his. Moreover, a female slave who is in the same room with her mistress can give her assistance, if not with her body, certainly by crying out, so that those who are in the house or the neighbors can hear her; and this is evident even if she should allege that the murderer threatened her with death if she cried out. She ought, therefore, to undergo capital punishment, to prevent other slaves from thinking that they should consult their own safety when their master is in danger.

Source 3 from Katherine Fischer Drew, translator, The Burgundian Code *(Philadelphia: University of Pennsylvania Press, 1972), Sections 26, 30, 33, 35, 88, Constitutiones Extravagentes 21.9. Copyright © University of Pennsylvania Press. Reprinted by permission of the publisher.*

3. Selections from
The Burgundian Code

A. Slave to Free/Free to Slave

[Constitutiones Extravagantes, 21.9] If anyone shall buy another's slave from the Franks, let him prove with suitable witnesses how much and what sort of price he paid and when witnesses have been sworn in, they shall make oath in the following manner: "We saw him pay the price in our presence, and he who purchased the slave did not do so through any fraud or connivance with the enemy." And if suitable witnesses shall give oaths in this manner, let him receive back only the price which he paid; and let him not seek back the cost of support and let him return the slave without delay to his former owner.

[88] Since the title of emancipation takes precedence over the law of possession, great care must be exercised in such matters. And therefore it should be observed, that if anyone wishes to manumit a slave, he may do so by giving him his liberty through a legally competent document; or if anyone wishes to give freedom to a bondservant without a written document, let the manumis-

sion thus conferred by confirmed with the witness of not less than five or seven native freemen, because it is not fitting to present a smaller number of witnesses than is required when the manumission is in written form.

C. Slave/Free Relations

[30] OF WOMEN VIOLATED.

1. Whatever native freeman does violence to a maidservant, and force can be proved, let him pay twelve solidi to him to whom the maidservant belongs.
2. If a slave does this, let him receive a hundred fifty blows.

[35] OF THE PUNISHMENT OF SLAVES WHO COMMIT A CRIMINAL ASSAULT ON FREEBORN WOMEN.

1. If any slave does violence to a native freewoman, and if she complains and is clearly able to prove this, let the slave be killed for the crime committed.
2. If indeed a native free girl unites voluntarily with a slave, we order both to be killed.
3. But if the relatives of the girl do not wish to punish their own relative, let the girl be deprived of her free status and delivered into servitude to the king.

D. Criminal Actions
by/toward Slaves

[26] OF KNOCKING OUT TEETH.

1. If anyone by chance strikes out the teeth of a Burgundian of the highest class, or of a Roman noble, let him be compelled to pay fifteen solidi.
2. For middle-class freeborn people, either Burgundian or Roman, if a tooth is knocked out, let composition be made in the sum of ten solidi.
3. For persons of the lowest class, five solidi.
4. If a slave voluntarily strikes out the tooth of a native freeman, let him be condemned to have a hand cut off; if the loss which has been set forth above has been committed by accident, let him pay the price for the tooth according to the status of the person.
5. If any native freeman strikes out the tooth of a freedman, let him pay him three solidi. If he strikes out the tooth of another's slave, let him pay two solidi to him to whom the slave belongs.

[33] OF INJURIES WHICH ARE SUFFERED BY WOMEN.

1. If any native freewoman has her hair cut off and is humiliated without cause (when innocent) by any native freeman in her home or on the road, and

this can be proved with witnesses, let the doer of the deed pay her twelve so-lidi, and let the amount of the fine be twelve solidi.

2. If this was done to a freedwoman, let him pay her six solidi.

3. If this was done to a maidservant, let him pay her three solidi, and let the amount of the fine be three solidi.

4. If this injury (shame, disgrace) is inflicted by a slave on a native free-woman, let him receive two hundred blows; if a freedwoman, let him receive a hundred blows; if a maidservant, let him receive seventy-five blows.

5. If indeed the woman whose injury we have ordered to be punished in this manner commits fornication voluntarily (i.e., if she yields), let nothing be sought for the injury suffered.

Source 4 from Katherine Fischer Drew, translator, The Laws of the Salian Franks *(Philadel-phia: University of Pennsylvania Press, 1991), Sections 25, 39, 40, 98. Copyright © 1991 Uni-versity of Pennsylvania Press. Reprinted by permission of the publisher.*

4. Selections from Salic Law

C. Slave/Free Relations

[25] ON HAVING INTERCOURSE WITH SLAVE GIRLS OR BOYS

1. The freeman who has intercourse with someone else's slave girl, and it is proved against him . . . , shall be liable to pay six hundred denarii (i.e., fifteen solid[i]) to the slave girl's lord.

2. The man who has intercourse with a slave girl belonging to the king and it is proved against him . . . , shall be liable to pay twelve hundred denarii (i.e., thirty solidi).

3. The freeman who publicly joins himself with (i.e., marries) another man's slave girl, shall remain with her in servitude.

4. And likewise the free woman who takes someone else's slave in marriage shall remain in servitude.

5. If a slave has intercourse with the slave girl of another lord and the girl dies as a result of this crime, the slave himself shall pay two hundred forty denarii (i.e., six solidi) to the girl's lord or he shall be castrated; the slave's lord shall pay the value of the girl to her lord.

6. If the slave girl has not died . . . , the slave shall receive three hundred lashes or, to spare his back, he shall pay one hundred twenty denarii (i.e., three solidi) to the girl's lord.

7. If a slave joins another man's slave girl to himself in marriage without the consent of her lord . . . , he shall be lashed or clear himself by paying one hun-dred twenty denarii (i.e., three solidi) to the girl's lord.

[98] CONCERNING THE WOMAN WHO JOINS HERSELF TO HER SLAVE

1. If a woman joins herself in marriage with her own slave, the fisc[10] shall acquire all her possessions and she herself will be outlawed.

2. If one of her relatives kills her, nothing may be required from that relative or the fisc for her death. The slave shall be placed in the most severe torture, that is, he shall be placed on the wheel. And if one of the relatives of the woman gives her either food or shelter, he shall be liable to pay fifteen solidi.

D. Criminal Actions by/toward Slaves

[40] CONCERNING THE SLAVE ACCUSED OF THEFT

1. In the case where a slave is accused of theft, if [it is a case where] a freeman would pay six hundred denarii (i.e., fifteen solidi) in composition, the slave stretched on a rack shall receive one hundred twenty blows of the lash.

2. If he [the slave] confesses before torture and it is agreeable to the slave's lord, he may pay one hundred twenty denarii (i.e., three solidi) for his back [i.e., to avoid the lashes]; and the slave's lord shall return the value of the property stolen to its owner. . . .

4. . . . If indeed he [the slave] confessed in the earlier torture, i.e., before the one hundred twenty lashes were completed, let him [the slave] be castrated or pay two hundred forty denarii (i.e., six solidi); the lord should restore the value of the property stolen to its owner.

5. If he [the slave] is guilty of a crime for which a freeman or a Frank would be liable to pay eight thousand denarii (i.e., two hundred solidi), let the slave compound fifteen solidi (i.e., six hundred denarii). If indeed the slave is guilty of a more serious offense—one for which a freeman would be liable to pay eighteen hundred denarii (i.e., forty-five solidi)—and the slave confessed during torture, he shall be subjected to capital punishment. . . .

11. If indeed it is a female slave accused of an offense for which a male slave would be castrated, then she should be liable to pay two hundred forty denarii (i.e., six solidi)—if it is agreeable for her lord to pay this—or she should be subjected to two hundred forty lashes.

[39] ON THOSE WHO INSTIGATE SLAVES TO RUN AWAY

1. If a man entices away the bondsmen of another man and this is proved against him . . . , he shall be liable to pay six hundred denarii (i.e., fifteen solidi) [in addition to return of the bondsmen plus a payment for the time their labor was lost] .

10. **fisc:** king's treasury.

Source 5 from Katherine Fischer Drew, translator, The Lombard Laws (Philadelphia: University of Pennsylvania Press, 1973), Sections Rothair 156, 217, 221, 222, 267, 280, 333, 334; Luitprand 55, 63, 80, 140, 152. Copyright © 1973 University of Pennsylvania Press. Reprinted with permission of the publisher.

5. Selections from Lombard Laws

A. Slave to Free/Free to Slave

[Rothair 156]   In the case of a natural son who is born to another man's woman slave, if the father purchases him and gives him his freedom by the formal procedure . . . , he shall remain free. But if the father does not free him, the natural son shall be a slave to him to whom the mother slave belongs.

[Luitprand 63] He who renders false testimony against anyone else, or sets his hand knowingly to a false charter, and this fraud becomes evident, shall pay his wergeld as composition,[11] half to the king and half to him whose case it is. If the guilty party does not have enough to pay the composition, a public official ought to hand him over as a slave to him who was injured, and he [the offender] shall serve him as a slave.

[Luitprand 80] In connection with thieves, each judge shall make a prison underground in his district. When a thief has been found, he shall pay composition for his theft, and then the judge shall seize him and put him in prison for two or three years, and afterwards shall set him free.

If the thief is such a person that he does not have enough to pay the composition for theft, the judge ought to hand him over to the man who suffered the theft, and that one may do with him as he pleases.

If afterwards the thief is taken again in theft, he [the judge] shall shave . . . and beat him for punishment as befits a thief, and shall put a brand on his forehead and face. If the thief does not correct himself and if after such punishment he has again been taken in theft, then the judge shall sell him outside the province, and the judge shall have his sale price provided, nevertheless, that it be a proved case for the judge ought not to sell the man without certain proof.

[Luitprand 152] If the man who is prodigal or ruined, or who has sold or dissipated his substance, or for other reasons does not have that with which to pay composition, commits theft or adultery or a breach of the peace . . . or injures another man and the composition for this is twenty solidi or more, then a public representative ought to hand him over as a slave to the man who suffered such illegal acts.

11. **composition:** restitution.

[Luitprand 55] If anyone makes his slave folkfree and legally independent . . . or sets him free from himself in any manner by giving him into the hand of the king or by leading him before the altar of a church, and if afterwards that freedman [continues] to serve at the will of his patron, the freedman ought at frequent intervals to make clear his liberty to the judge and to his neighbors and [remind them] of the manner in which he was freed.

Afterward the patron or his heirs may at no time bring complaints against him who was freed by saying that because [he continues to serve] he ought still to obey, for it was only on account of the goodness of his lord that the former slave continued to serve his commands of his own free will. He shall remain permanently free.

[Luitprand 140] If a freeman has a man and woman slave, or aldius and aldia,[12] who are married, and, inspired by hatred of the human race, he has intercourse with that woman whose husband is the slave or with the aldia whose husband is the aldius, he has committed adultery and we decree that he shall lose that slave or aldius with whose wife he committed adultery and the woman as well. They shall go free where they wish and shall be as much folkfree . . . as if they had been released by the formal procedure for alienation . . .—for it is not pleasing to God that any man should have intercourse with the wife of another.

B. Value and Treatment
of Slaves

[Rothair 333] On mares in foal. He who strikes a mare in foal and causes a miscarriage shall pay one solidus as composition. If the mare dies, he shall pay as above for it and its young.

[Rothair 334] On pregnant woman slaves. He who strikes a woman slave large with child and causes a miscarriage shall pay three solidi as composition. If, moreover, she dies from the blow, he shall pay composition for her and likewise for the child who died in her womb.

C. Slave/Free Relations

[Rothair 217] On the aldia who marries a slave. The aldia or freedwoman who enters another man's house to a husband and marries a slave shall lose her liberty. But if the husband's lord neglects to reduce her to servitude, then when her husband dies she may go forth together with her children and all the property which she brought with her when she came to her husband. But

12. **aldius** and **aldia**: freedman and freedwoman.

she shall have no more than this as an indication of her mistake in marrying a slave.

[Rothair 221] The slave who dares to marry a free woman or girl shall lose his life. With regard to the woman who consented to a slave, her relatives have the right to kill her or to sell her outside the country and to do what they wish with her property. And if her relatives delay in doing this, then the king's gastald or schultheis[13] shall lead her to the king's court and place her there in the women's apartments among the female slaves.

[Rothair 222] On marrying one's own woman slave. If any man wishes to marry his own woman slave, he may do so. Nevertheless he ought to free her, that is, make her worthy born . . . , and he ought to do it legally by the proper formal procedure. . . . She shall then be known as a free and legal wife and her children may become the legal heirs of their father.

D. Criminal Actions
by/toward Slaves

[Rothair 267] The boatman who knowingly transports fugitive bondsmen, and it is proved, shall search for them and return them together with any properties taken with them to their proper owner. If the fugitives have gone elsewhere and cannot be found, then the value of those bondsmen together with the sworn value of the property which they carried with them shall be paid by that ferryman who knowingly transported the fugitives. In addition, the ferryman shall pay twenty solidi as composition to the king's fisc.

[Rothair 280] On seditious acts committed by field slaves. If, for any reason, rustics[14] . . . associate together for plotting or committing seditious acts such as, when a lord is trying to take a bondsman or animal from his slave's house, blocking the way or taking the bondsman or animal, then he who was at the head of these rustics shall either be killed or redeem his life by the payment of a composition equal to that amount at which he is valued. And each of those who participated in this evil sedition shall pay twelve solidi as composition, half to the king and half to him who bore the injury or before whom he presumed to place himself. And if that one who was trying to take his property endures blows or suffers violence from these rustics, composition for such blows or violence shall be paid to him just as is stated above, and the rustics shall suffer such punishment as is noted above for this presumption. If one of the rustics is killed no payment shall be required because he who killed him did it while defending himself and in protecting his own property.

13. **gastald** and **schultheis:** royal officials.
14. **rustics:** field slaves.

Source 6 from Theodore John Rivers, translator, Laws of the Alamans and Bavarians *(Philadelphia: University of Pennsylvania Press, 1977), Alamannic Law, Sections 17, 18, 37, 39, 75. Copyright © 1977 University of Pennsylvania Press. Reprinted by permission of the publisher.*

6. Laws of the Alamans

A. Slave to Free/Free to Slave

[39] We prohibit incestuous marriages. Accordingly, it is not permitted to have as wife a mother-in-law, daughter-in-law, step-daughter, step-mother, brother's daughter, sister's daughter, brother's wife, or wife's sister. Brother's children and sister's children are under no pretext to be joined together. If anyone acts against this, let them [the married pair] be separated by the judges in that place, and let them lose all their property, which the public treasury shall acquire. If there are lesser persons who pollute themselves through an illicit union, let them lose their freedom; let them be added to the public slaves.

B. Value and Treatment of Slaves

[37] 1. Let no one sell slaves . . . outside the province, whether among pagans or Christians, unless it is done by the order of the duke.

C. Slave/Free Relations

[17] 1. Concerning maidservants.[15] If a freewoman was manumitted by a charter or in a church, and after this she married a slave, let her remain permanently a maidservant of the church.

2. If, however, a free Alamannic woman marries a church slave and refuses the servile work of a maidservant, let her depart. If, however, she gives birth to sons or daughters there, let them remain slaves and maidservants permanently, and let them not have the right of departure.

D. Criminal Actions by/toward Slaves

[18] 1. Concerning waylayers . . . , [if a man blocks the way of a freeman] , let him pay six solidi.

2. If it is a freedman [who is blocked] , let the perpetrator pay four solidi.

3. If it is a slave, three solidi.

4. If he does this to a free Alamannic woman, let him compensate with twelve solidi.

15. **maidservants:** here, female slaves.

5. If it is a freedwoman, let him compensate with eight solidi.

6. If it is a maidservant, let him pay four solidi.

7. If a man seizes her hair, [let him compensate similarly].

[75] 1. If anyone lies with another's chambermaid against her will, let him compensate with six solidi.

2. And if anyone lies with the first maid of the textile workshop against her will, let him compensate with six solidi.

3. If anyone lies with other maids of the textile workshop against their will, let him compensate with three solidi.

Source 7 from F. L. Attenborough, editor, Laws of the Earliest English Kings, *Laws of Edward the Elder, Section 6; Laws of Ine, Section 3. Laws of Aethelbert, Sections 10, 11, 16; Laws of Alfred, Section 25.*

7. Laws of Anglo-Saxon Kings

A. Slave to Free/Free to Slave

[Edward the Elder 6] If any man, through [being found guilty of] an accusation of stealing, forfeits his freedom and gives up his person to his lord, and his kinsmen forsake him, and he knows no one who will make legal amends for him, he shall do such servile labour as may be required, and his kinsmen shall have no right to his wergeld [if he is slain] .

B. Value and Treatment of Slaves

[Ine 3] If a slave works on Sunday by his lord's command, he shall become free, and the lord shall pay a fine of 30 shillings.

§1. If, however, the slave works without the cognisance of his master, he shall undergo the lash or pay the fine in lieu thereof.

§2. If, however, a freeman works on that day, except by his lord's command, he shall be reduced to slavery, or [pay a fine of] 60 shillings. A priest shall pay a double fine.

D. Criminal Actions
by/toward Slaves

[Aethelbert 10] If a man lies with a maiden belonging to the king, he shall pay 50 shillings compensation.

[Aethelbert 11] If she is a grinding slave, he shall pay 25 shillings compensation. [If she is of the] third [class], [he shall pay] 12 shillings compensation.

[Aethelbert 16] If a man lies with a commoner's serving maid, he shall pay 6 shillings compensation; [if he lies] with a slave of the second class, [he shall pay] 50 sceattas[16] [compensation] ; if with one of the third class, 30 sceattas.

[Alfred 25] If anyone rapes the slave of a commoner, he shall pay 5 shillings to the commoner, and a fine of 60 shillings.[17]
    §1. If a slave rapes a slave, castration shall be required as compensation.

16. 20 sceattas = one shilling.
17. The 60 shillings went to the king's treasury.

QUESTIONS TO CONSIDER

The central questions for this chapter ask you to do two things: investigate the boundaries between slave and free in various law codes, and then compare these issues in Roman and Germanic cultures. Your answers to the second question are based, of course, on your answers to the first, and the Sources and Method section suggests some of the questions you might ask yourself about slave law in each of these two cultures.

In addition to these, in the Roman codes, what role does military conquest play in the determination of slave and free? Does conquest simply provide slaves, or does it also offer them opportunities? What limitations were placed on a male owner's treatment of his slaves? On a female owner's treatment of her slaves? What obligations does—or could—the status of freedman or freedwoman entail? Do these obligations make this status appear closer to that of a slave or that of a free person? How are family relationships among slaves regarded legally? The provi-

sion in Justinian's Code (Source 2D) that slaves who did not prevent a master's being killed were to be killed themselves may seem very harsh. Why do you think this was part of Roman slave law? What other provisions strike you as especially harsh, and why might these have been enacted? Given the role of slavery in the Roman economy, why were there such strong provisions about runaway slaves? Other than the restrictions on those who aided runaways, what laws discuss actions by those who were neither owners nor slaves? How might these have shaped general attitudes toward slavery and slaves?

Turning now to the Germanic codes, what are the hierarchies you find among slaves based on? Given the nature of Germanic society, in which tribes often moved around a great deal, why do you think there was so much concern about not taking slaves away to other areas, even if it was their owners who were taking them? Historians often point out the importance of personal honor in Germanic societies. Do you find evidence of this? Do slaves have honor?

Do any of their actions affect the honor of others in ways that the actions of free people do not? A close examination of the laws indicates that the only nonpunishable sexual relation between slave and free was a man marrying his own slave among the Lombards, mentioned in Source 5C. Why do you think this was allowed? What must a man do before he does this, and why do you think this was important?

You are now ready to investigate some comparative questions: In what ways do the different notions of the law in Roman and Germanic cultures—territorial versus personal, statutory versus traditional—emerge in laws regarding slavery? When comparing Germanic culture to Roman, historians often point to the relative propensity to interpersonal violence and the importance of the family among the Germans. Do the laws regarding slavery from these two cultures provide evidence of these factors? What evidence do you see of the different economic structures in the two cultures, i.e., of the greater complexity of the Roman economic system?

Comparing two cultures involves exploring continuities along with contrasts. One of the issues in slave systems was how to punish slaves without harming their owners. How do the laws handle this? Do you see much difference between Roman and Germanic cultures in this? How do the laws handle the issue that slaves do not own property? How are the actions and obligations of freed slaves toward their former masters handled in both cultures? Why do you think it was important in both cultures to have an intermediate status between slave and free? Do you see much difference with regard to laws concerning sexual relations between slaves and free in the two cultures? Why might there have been continuity in this?

After putting all of this material together, you are now ready to answer the central questions for this chapter: How were legal distinctions between slave and free established, structured, and maintained, and how could they be overcome? What similarities and differences are there in Roman and Germanic law regarding slavery?

EPILOGUE

During the Renaissance, scholars and thinkers began to divide the history of Europe into three stages, ancient, medieval, and modern, a division that has persisted until today. They viewed the end of the Roman Empire as a dramatic break in history, and saw the Germanic successor states as sharply different from Rome. This view is increasingly being modified today as historians point to a number of continuities between late ancient and early medieval society.

As you have discovered in this chapter, the slave system was one of those continuities, for slavery did not disappear from the European scene with the fall of Rome, nor did the spread of Christianity lead to an end of slavery. (Christianity did not oppose slavery on moral grounds, although it did praise those who chose to free their slaves and pushed for slaves being allowed to marry in legally binding ceremonies.) Gradually, however, more people came to occupy the intermediate stage between slave and free that you have seen in these laws, which became known as serfdom. Serfdom was a legal condition in which people were personally free—not owned by another individual as slaves were—but were bound to the land, unable to move and owing labor obligations to their lord. For former slaves, serfdom was a step up; for others, however, it was a step down, for the bulk of the serfs in Europe probably came from families that had originally been free peasants, but had traded their labor and freedom to move in return for protection. In any case, serfdom did not immediately replace slavery; both continued side by side for centuries, and the laws you have seen here regarding slaves often shaped later laws regarding serfs. Law codes alone, of course, cannot tell us about relative numbers of slaves or serfs, and they sometimes hide major changes. The transformation of slave to serf was so gradual that it occasioned little comment in the codes, which had, as we have seen, long included discussion of intermediate stages between slave and free and of hierarchies among slaves.

The laws you have seen here also had great influence beyond Europe. As you have discovered, Germanic law did not break sharply with Roman on many issues regarding slavery, indicating that Justinian's Code probably influenced some early medieval Germanic codes. Justinian's Code was also rediscovered in western Europe in the eleventh century, and became the basis of legal education at the law schools that were established in southern Europe in the twelfth century. It influenced national and local codes in this era of expanding states and growing cities, and ultimately all of the legal systems of western Europe except for that of England became based on Roman law. When Portugal and Spain set up slave systems extending into the New World, Roman law was the basis of many provisions regarding slavery. Thus, two of the New World's most heavily slave societies—the French Caribbean and Brazil—based their systems on Roman law.

The other slave societies in the New World—the British Caribbean and the southern United States before the Civil War—did not base their laws as directly on those of Rome, but their laws did grow out of Germanic codes such as those you have seen here. Though these systems were different from the Roman and Germanic systems in that slavery came to be based on race, many of the laws—those concerning owners' freedom to treat slaves as they wished, sexual relations between slave and free, punishment of those who aided runaway slaves—were remarkably similar. Once slavery came to be racially based, however, the permeable boundary between slave and free that you have traced in this chapter, with slavery not necessarily being a permanent status, became much harder to cross. Poverty, begging, theft, debt, capture in war, false testimony, or incest did not make a white person a slave, nor did turning in deserters, marriage to an owner, or—except in rare instances—military service make a black person free.

CHAPTER SEVEN

THE DEVELOPMENT OF

THE MEDIEVAL STATE

THE PROBLEM

The governments of medieval Europe are generally described as *feudal,* a word that perhaps confuses more than it clarifies. The term *feudalism* was unknown in the Middle Ages; it was invented only later to describe the medieval system of landholding and government. Used correctly, feudalism denotes a system of reciprocal rights and obligations, in which individuals who fight (knights) promise their loyalty, aid, and assistance to a king or other powerful noble, becoming what were termed *vassals* of that lord. The lord in turn promises his vassals protection and material support, which in the Early Middle Ages was often board and room in the lord's own household. As their vassals became more numerous or lived farther away, lords increasingly gave them grants of land as recompense for their allegiance. This piece of land, termed a *fief* (*feudum* in Latin), theoretically still belonged to the lord, with the vassal obtaining only the use of it. Thus feudalism involved a mixture of personal and property ties. Unlike the systems of property ownership in the Roman Empire or most modern governments, it did not involve any ties to an abstract state or governmental system, but was simply a personal agreement between individuals.

This promise of allegiance and support could be made only by free individuals, so that the slaves we examined in the last chapter or serfs who were tied to the land were not actually part of the feudal system. In the economic structure of medieval Europe, estates or *manors* of various sizes were worked by slaves, serfs, and free peasants. The whole economic system is termed *manorialism.* Fiefs were generally made up of manors and included the peasants who lived on them, but manorialism and feudalism are not synonymous.

Though serfs were not included in the feudal system, Church officials were. Rulers rewarded Church officials with fiefs for their spiritual services or promises of allegiance. In addition, the Church held pieces of land on its own, and granted fiefs in return for promises of assistance from knightly vassals. Abbots and abbesses of monasteries, bishops, and archbishops were either lords[1] or vassals in many feudal arrangements. In addition, both secular and clerical vassals further subdivided their fiefs, granting land to people who became their vassals, a process known as *subinfeudation*. Thus the same person could be a lord in one relationship and a vassal in another.

This system could easily become chaotic, particularly as it was easy to forget, once a family had held a piece of land for several generations, that the land actually belonged to the lord. This is more or less what happened from 700 until 1050, with political power becoming completely decentralized and vassals ruling their fiefs quite independently. About 1050 this began to change, however, and rulers started to manipulate feudal institutions to build up rather than diminish their power.

The rulers of England after the Norman Conquest in 1066 were particularly successful at manipulating feudal institutions to build up their own power. William the Conqueror (1066–1087) and Henry II (1154–1189) dramatically increased royal authority, as did later rulers of France, especially Philip II Augustus (1180–

1223), and of Germany, especially Frederick Barbarossa (1152–1190). Gradually the feudal system was transformed into one that is sometimes termed *feudal monarchy*. Because monarchs in the High Middle Ages had so much more power than they had had in the Early Middle Ages, however, some historians no longer term such governments feudal at all, but simply monarchies, and see in them the origins of the modern state.

In asserting their power, the rulers of western Europe had to suppress or limit the independent powers of two groups in medieval society— their noble vassals and Church officials. The challenge provided by each group was somewhat different. Noble vassals often had their own armies, and the people living on their fiefs were generally more loyal to– or afraid of—them than to any faraway ruler. During the period before the mid-eleventh century, vassals often supervised courts, which heard cases and punished crimes, and regarded themselves as the supreme legal authority in their fief. Though they were vassals of the ruler, Church officials also owed allegiance to an independent, international power— the papacy in Rome. Throughout the Middle Ages, the pope and higher Church officials claimed that all Church personnel, down to village priests and monks, were not subject to any secular legal jurisdiction, including that of a ruler. They also argued that the spiritual hierarchy of Western Christianity, headed by the pope, was elevated by God over all secular hierarchies, so that

1. Because abbesses and, in some parts of Europe, noblewomen who inherited land could grant fiefs and have vassals, the word *lord* in the context of feudalism did not always mean a man. It simply means "the person who holds the rights of lordship."

every ruler was subject to papal authority.

In this chapter we will be exploring the ways in which medieval monarchs asserted their authority over their vassals and the Church. We will use both visual and written evidence in answering the question, How did the rulers of the High Middle Ages overcome challenges to their power and begin the process of recentralization of power?

SOURCES AND METHOD

Traditionally, political history has been seen as the history of politics, and has used as its sources laws, decrees, parliamentary debates, and other written documents that give information about political changes. These are still important, but recently political history has been seen more broadly as the history not only of politics but of all relations involving power, and a wider range of sources is now used to understand the power relationships in past societies. Picking up techniques from anthropologists, political historians now use objects as well as written documents to explore the ways in which power is externally expressed and symbolized as well as the ways in which it is manipulated in relationships. The rulers of medieval western Europe were aware of the power of symbols, and along with actual military and legal moves to increase their authority, they also demonstrated that authority symbolically.

A symbol is basically something that stands for something else, that has a meaning beyond the actual object or words. Symbols can be used consciously or unconsciously, and can be interpreted differently by different observers or readers. Anthropologists have pointed out that symbols can often be read at many different levels, so understanding them in all their meanings can be very complicated. The symbols we will be looking at here are less complicated than many, however, because they were consciously employed by rulers and officials who wanted to be very sure that their correct meaning was understood. Since many of the observers were not highly educated or even literate, rulers chose simple symbols and repeated them so that their meaning would certainly be grasped. Because many of these symbols have much the same meaning to us today, you will find them easier to analyze than the symbols from unfamiliar cultures that are often the focus of anthropologists' studies. As we explore the ways in which rulers asserted their authority, then, we must keep in mind both the tactical and the symbolic impact of their actions.

The first four sources all provide evidence of one of the ways in which William the Conqueror and his successors gained power over the English nobility. Source 1 is from a history of England written in the early twelfth century by Ordericus Vitalis, a monk who was half Anglo-Saxon and half Norman. The author provides a relatively unbiased account of William's reign, and here describes how William subdued one of the many rebellions against him. Read the selection carefully. Rather than simply sending out armies, what does William do to establish royal power? Why does Ordericus feel this was effective in ending the rebellion?

Visual depictions of Norman castles may help you judge whether Ordericus's opinion about their importance was valid, so turn to the next three sources. Sources 2 and 3 are photographs of castles built by English kings. The first was begun at Richmond in 1089, and the second was built at Harlech between 1283 and 1290. Source 4 is a map of all the castles built in England by William the Conqueror during his reign, from 1066 to 1087. Many of these were wooden fortifications rather than the enormous stone castles shown in Sources 2 and 3, but William's successors expanded these simpler castles into larger stone ones as quickly as time and resources permitted. As you look at these, try to imagine yourself as a vassal or subject confronted by castles that looked like these in all the places you see on the map. What message would you get about the power of the king? What strategic value is gained by placing a castle on a hill? How would this also increase the castle's symbolic value? What other features of the castles depicted increase either their strategic value as fortresses or their symbolic value? The map indicates that the castles built by William were not evenly distributed. Given what your text tells you about the Norman Conquest and the problems that William faced, why might he have built his castles where he did? Does this pattern of castle building surprise you? (A clue here is to keep in mind that castles are both symbols of power and a means to enforce that power, and that these castles may not all have been built for the same reason.)

Source 5 provides evidence of another way in which William and his successors both gained and demonstrated authority over their vassals. It is an excerpt from *The Anglo-Saxon Chronicle* describing William's requirement in 1086 that all vassals swear loyalty to him in what became known as the Salisbury Oath. Rulers such as William recognized that people regarded oaths as very serious expressions of their duties as Christians, and so they required their vassals to swear allegiance regularly in person in ceremonies of *homage* (allegiance) and *fealty* (loyalty). They expanded the ceremonies of knighthood, impressing on young knights their duties of obedience and loyalty. After you read this short selection, think about how the fact that the vassals had to leave their fiefs to swear the Oath might have also helped increase royal power.

After William, Henry II was the most innovative fashioner of royal power in medieval England. In 1166, he issued the Assize[2] of Clarendon (the location of the king's hunting lodge), which set up inquest juries to report to the king's sheriff or traveling judges the name of anyone sus-

2. **assize:** a decree made by an assembly.

pected of having committed a major crime. Source 6 gives you some of the clauses from the Assize of Clarendon. As you read it, note the ways in which the independent powers of the vassals in their territories are restricted. Who does it state is the ultimate legal authority? Who gains financially from these provisions?

Henry II directly limited not only the legal power of his vassals, but also that of the Church in England. Two years before the Assize of Clarendon, he issued the Constitutions of Clarendon, which purported to be a codification of existing practices governing relations between the Church and the state. Source 7 is an extract from this document. Read it carefully, noting first under whose authority Henry issues it. Who does he say has agreed to its provisions? How do these provisions limit the legal power of the Church over its own clergy? Over laypeople? What role is the king to play in the naming of Church officials? In hearing cases involving clergy? How are Church officials to be reminded of their duties as the king's vassals?

The Constitutions of Clarendon are perhaps the strongest statement of the power of a secular ruler over the Church to emerge from the Middle Ages, and, as we will see in the epilogue to this chapter, they were quickly opposed by the Church. This was not the only time a ruler asserted his power over the Church, however, for on the Continent German kings and emperors also claimed extensive powers over all aspects of Church life up to and including the papacy. Source 8 gives an example of this as-

sertion of power. It is a selection from the biography of the German emperor Frederick Barbarossa (1152–1190), begun by Bishop Otto of Freising. Otto was Frederick's uncle, so though he is a bishop of the Church, he is quite favorably inclined toward the emperor. In this selection, Otto describes Frederick's coronation and some later responses by the emperor to papal ambassadors. What roles do Church officials play in Frederick's coronation? What does Otto view as a further symbol of Frederick's right to rule? What role does Otto report that the pope claimed to have played in granting Frederick power? What, in contrast to this, does Frederick view as the source of his authority? What does he see to be his religious duties as emperor?

Along with actions such as constructing castles or requiring oaths of loyalty, both of which combined tactical with symbolic assertions of power, medieval rulers also demonstrated their power over vassals and the Church in purely symbolic ways. The final sources in this chapter provide examples of some of these. Source 9 is a description of the coronation ceremony of Richard the Lionhearted, Henry II's son, in 1189. More than the much shorter description of Frederick Barbarossa's coronation, which you have already read, it gives evidence of the way in which kings and other territorial rulers expanded their coronation ceremonies, turning them into long, spectacular celebrations of royal wealth and power. As you read it, look first for things that symbolize power relationships. What titles are used to

151

describe the participants? What objects are used in the ceremonies? Who is in attendance, and what roles do they play? What actions are required of the various participants, either during the ceremony or as part of their later duties?

Living in the media age as we do, we are certainly used to the manipulation of symbols to promote loyalty and allegiance. Indeed, given the barrage of symbols accompanying the celebrations of the anniversaries of the Constitution, the Statue of Liberty, and the Bill of Rights, we may even be a bit jaded by flag-waving and military bands. Medieval people did not live in a world as full of visual stimulation, so the ceremonies surrounding a monarch were truly extraordinary.

Coronation ceremonies were rare events, and rulers also used symbols in more permanent visual demonstrations of their power, such as paintings and statuary, which they commissioned or which were designed in a way to gain their approval. The next three sources all depict rulers. Source 10 is a manuscript-illumination portrait of the German emperor Otto III (983–1002) seated on his throne. Source 11 is a section of the Bayeux tapestry showing on the left King Harold of England (1053–1066) seated on the throne. In the center, Englishmen acclaim him as king and point up to Halley's Comet (identified in the tapestry as a star). Source 12 is a tomb sculpture of Duke Henry of Brunswick in Germany and his wife, Matilda, dating from about 1240, shortly after they died. The Church that Henry holds in his right hand is

Brunswick Cathedral, which he completed and which houses his tomb. Because we no longer live in a world of royal authority, you may need some assistance in interpreting the meaning of the objects shown with the rulers, although medieval people would have understood them immediately. Many of these objects had both a secular and a religious meaning: the crown represented royal authority (the points symbolized the rays of the sun) and the crown of thorns worn by Jesus before the Crucifixion; the orb (the ball surmounted by a cross) represented the ruler's domination of the land and protection of the Church; the scepter also represented Church and state power by being ornamented with both religious and secular designs. Seeing a monarch in full regalia or a portrait of a monarch would impress on anyone that this was not just the greatest of the nobles, but also someone considered sacred, whose authority was supported by Scripture. Monarchs also demonstrated the sacred aspects of their rule with purely religious symbols, such as crosses and chalices.

Now look carefully at the pictures. What symbols are used to depict the sources of royal authority? How do these communicate the ruler's secular and religious authority? What types of individuals are shown with the ruler? What does this indicate about the relationship between lord and vassal, and between Church and state? Why might the appearance of the heavenly body that came to be known as Halley's Comet have been viewed as an appropriate symbol of monarchy?

You have now examined evidence of a number of ways in which rulers increased their own authority, decreased that of their noble vassals and Church officials, and expressed their greater power symbolically. As you assess how all of these helped rulers overcome challenges to their authority, it will be useful to recognize that symbols are not just passive reflections of existing power relationships, but are actively manipulated to build up or decrease power. Therefore it is often difficult to separate what we might term the real or tactical effect of an action or legal change from the symbolic. As you answer the central question in this chapter, then, think about the ways in which symbols and real change are interwoven.

THE EVIDENCE

Source 1 from Ordericus Vitalis, The Ecclesiastical History of England and Normandy, *trans. Thomas Forester (London: Henry G. Bohn, 1854). This source taken from a reprint of this edition (New York: AMS Press, 1968), vol. 2, pp. 17–20.*

1. From Ordericus Vitalis's *Ecclesiastical History of England and Normandy*

The same year [1068], Edwin and Morcar, sons of Earl Algar, and young men of great promise, broke into open rebellion, and induced many others to fly to arms, which violently disturbed the realm of Albion.[3] King William, however, came to terms with Edwin, who assured him of the submission of his brother and of nearly a third of the kingdom, upon which the king promised to give him his daughter in marriage. Afterwards, however, by a fraudulent decision of the Normans, and through their envy and covetousness, the king refused to give him the princess who was the object of his desire, and for whom he had long waited. Being, therefore, much incensed, he and his brother again broke into rebellion, and the greatest part of the English and Welsh followed their standard. The two brothers were zealous in the worship of God, and respected good men. They were remarkably handsome, their relations were of high birth and very numerous, their estates were vast and gave them immense power, and their popularity great. The clergy and monks offered continual prayers on their behalf, and crowds of poor daily supplications. . . .

At the time when the Normans had crushed the English, and were overwhelming them with intolerable oppressions Blethyn, king of Wales, came to

3. **Albion:** England.

the aid of his uncles, at the head of a large body of Britons. A general assembly was now held of the chief men of the English and Welsh, at which universal complaints were made of the outrages and tyranny to which the English were subjected by the Normans and their adherents, and messengers were dispatched into all parts of Albion to rouse the natives against their enemies, either secretly or openly. All joined in a determined league and bold conspiracy against the Normans for the recovery of their ancient liberties. The rebellion broke out with great violence in the provinces beyond the Humber. The insurgents fortified themselves in the woods and marshes, on the estuaries, and in some cities. York was in a state of the highest excitement, which the holiness of its bishop was unable to calm. Numbers lived in tents, disdaining to dwell in houses lest they should become enervated; from which some of them were called savages by the Normans.

In consequence of these commotions, the king carefully surveyed the most inaccessible points in the country, and, selecting suitable spots, fortified them against the enemy's excursions. In the English districts there were very few fortresses, which the Normans call castles; so that, though the English were warlike and brave, they were little able to make a determined resistance. One castle the king built at Warwick, and gave it into the custody of Henry, son of Roger de Beaumont.[4] Edwin and Morcar, now considering the doubtful issue of the contest, and not unwisely preferring peace to war, sought the king's favour, which they obtained, at least, in appearance. The king then built a castle at Nottingham, which he committed to the custody of William Peverell.

When the inhabitants of York heard the state of affairs, they became so alarmed that they made hasty submission, in order to avoid being compelled by force; delivering the keys of the city to the king, and offering him hostages. But, suspecting their faith, he strengthened the fortress within the city walls, and placed in it a garrison of picked men. At this time, Archill, the most powerful chief of the Northumbrians, made a treaty of peace with the king, and gave him his son as a hostage. The bishop of Durham, also being reconciled to King William, became the mediator for peace with the king of the Scots, and was the bearer into Scotland of the terms offered by William. Though the aid of Malcolm had been solicited by the English, and he had prepared to come to their succour with a strong force, yet when he heard what the envoy had to propose with respect to a peace, he remained quiet, and joyfully sent back ambassadors in company with the bishop of Durham, who in his name swore fealty to King William. In thus preferring peace to war, he best consulted his own welfare, and the inclinations of his subjects; for the people of Scotland, though fierce in war, love ease and quiet, and are not disposed to disturb themselves about their neighbours' affairs, loving rather religious exercises than those of arms. On his return from this expedition, the king erected castles at Lincoln, Huntingdon, and Cambridge, placing in each of them garrisons composed of his bravest soldiers.

4. **Roger de Beaumont:** a Norman noble.

Source 2 from The British Tourist Authority.

2. Richmond Castle, Begun in 1089

Source 3: *Photograph courtesy of the British Tourist Authority. Ground plan courtesy of the Ministry of Public Building and Works.*

3. View and Ground Plan of Harlech Castle, Built by Edward I Between 1283 and 1290

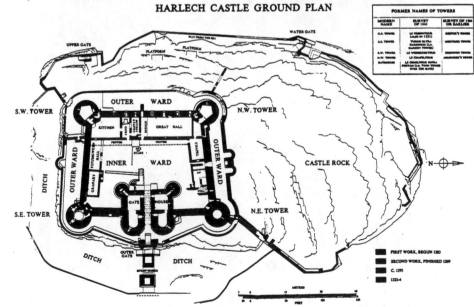

HARLECH CASTLE GROUND PLAN

Source 4 *adapted from map in H. C. Darby,* Domesday England *(Cambridge: Cambridge University Press, 1977), p. 316.*

4. Major Royal Castles Built During the Reign of William the Conqueror, 1066–1087

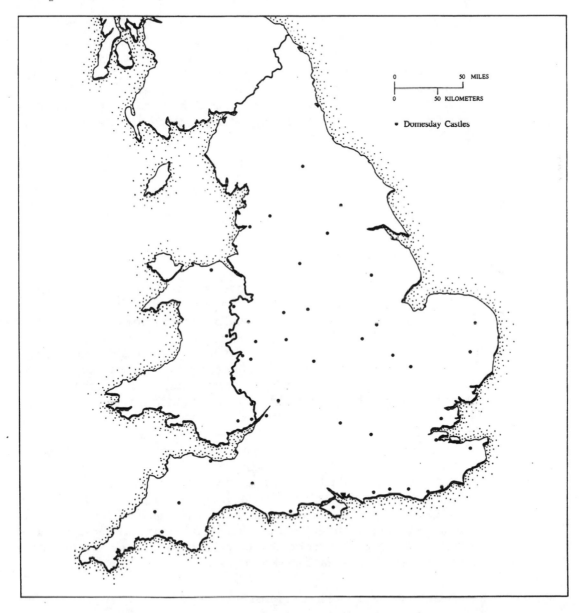

Source 5 from The Anglo-Saxon Chronicle *(London: Eyre and Spottiswoode, 1961, and New Brunswick, N.J.: Rutgers University Press), p. 162.*

5. From *The Anglo-Saxon Chronicle*

1086—In this year the king wore his crown and held his court at Winchester for Easter, and travelled so as to be at Westminster for Whitsuntide, and there dubbed his son, Henry, a knight. Then he travelled about so as to come to Salisbury at Lammas,[5] and there his councillors came to him, and all the people occupying land who were of any account all over England, no matter whose vassals they might be; and they all submitted to him and became his vassals, and swore oaths of allegiance to him, that they would be loyal to him against all other men. . . .

Sources 6 and 7 from Edward P. Cheyney, editor, "English Constitutional Documents," Translations and Reprints from the Original Sources of European History (Philadelphia: University of Pennsylvania, 1900), vol. I, no. 6, pp. 22–25; pp. 26–30.

6. Assize of Clarendon

Here begins the Assize of Clarendon, made by King Henry II, with the assent of the archbishops, bishops, abbots, earls and barons of all England.

1. In the first place, the aforesaid King Henry, with the consent of all his barons, for the preservation of the peace and the keeping of justice, has enacted that inquiry should be made through the several counties and through the several hundreds,[6] by twelve of the most legal men of the hundred and by four of the most legal men of each manor, upon their oath that they will tell the truth, whether there is in their hundred or in their manor, any man who has been accused or publicly suspected of himself being a robber, or murderer, or thief, or of being a receiver of robbers, or murderers, or thieves, since the lord king has been king. And let the justices make this inquiry before themselves, and the sheriffs before themselves.

2. And let any one who has been found by the oath of the aforesaid to have been accused or publicly suspected of having been a robber, or murderer, or thief, or a receiver of them, since the lord king has been king, be arrested and go to the ordeal of water and let him swear that he has not been a robber, or murderer, or thief, or receiver of them since the lord king has been king, to the value of five shillings, so far as he knows. . . .

5. **Lammas:** the wheat-harvest festival, August 1.
6. **hundred:** a division of a county.

4. And when a robber, or murderer, or thief, or receiver of them shall have been seized through the above-mentioned oath, if the justices are not to come very soon into that country where they have been arrested, let the sheriffs send word to the nearest justice by some intelligent man that they have arrested such men, and the justices will send back word to the sheriffs where they wish that these should be brought before them; and the sheriffs shall bring them before the justices; and along with these they shall bring from the hundred and the manor where they have been arrested, two legal men to carry the record of the county and of the hundred as to why they were seized, and there before the justice let them make their law.

5. And in the case of those who have been arrested through the aforesaid oath of this assize, no one shall have court, or judgment, or chattels,[7] except the lord king in his court before his justices, and the lord king shall have all their chattels. In the case of those, however, who have been arrested, otherwise than through this oath, let it be as it has been accustomed and ought to be. . . .

17. And if any sheriff shall have sent word to any other sheriff that men have fled from his county into another county, on account of robbery or murder or theft, or the reception of them, or for outlawry or for a charge concerning the forest of the king, let him arrest them. And even if he knows of himself or through others that such men have fled into his county, let him arrest them and hold them until he shall have secured pledges from them.

18. And let all sheriffs cause a list to be made of all fugitives who had fled from their counties; and let them do this in the presence of their county courts, and they will carry the written names of these before the justices when they come first before these, so that they may be sought through all England, and their chattels may be seized for the use of the king. . . .

7. Constitutions of Clarendon

In the year of the incarnation of the Lord, 1164, of the papacy of Alexander, the fourth year, of the most illustrious king of the English, Henry II, the tenth year, in the presence of the same king, has been made this memorial or acknowledgment of a certain part of the customs and franchises and dignities of his predecessors, that is to say of King Henry, his grandfather, and of other kings, which ought to be observed and held in the kingdom. And on account of the discussions and disputes which have arisen between the clergy and the justices of our lord and king and the barons of the kingdom concerning the customs and dignities, this acknowledgment is made in the presence of the archbishops and bishops and clergy and earls and barons and principal men of the kingdom. And these customs, acknowledged by

---

7. **chattels:** all items of property and goods except land.

the archbishops and bishops and earls and barons, and by the most noble and ancient of the kingdom, Thomas, archbishop of Canterbury, and Roger, archbishop of York, . . . [plus 12 bishops and 38 named barons] and many others of the principal men and nobles of the kingdom, as well clergy as laity.

Of these acknowledged customs and dignities of the realm, a certain part is contained in the present writing. Of this part the heads are as follows:

1. If any controversy has arisen concerning the advowson[8] and presentation of churches between laymen and ecclesiastics, or between ecclesiastics, it is to be considered or settled in the courts of the lord king.

2. Churches of the fee of the lord king cannot be given perpetually without his assent and grant.

3. Clergymen charged and accused of anything, when they have been summoned by a justice of the king shall come into his court, to respond there to that which it shall seem good to the court of the king for them to respond to, and in the ecclesiastical court to what it shall seem good should be responded to there; so that the justice of the king shall send into the court of holy church to see how the matter shall be treated there. And if a clergyman shall have been convicted or has confessed, the church ought not to protect him otherwise.

4. It is not lawful for archbishops, bishops, and persons of the realm to go out of the realm without the permission of the lord king. And if they go out, if it please the lord king, they shall give security that neither in going nor in making a stay nor in returning will they seek evil or loss to the king or the kingdom. . . .

7. No one who holds from the king in chief, nor any one of the officers of his demesnes shall be excommunicated, nor the lands of any one of them placed under an interdict, unless the lord king, if he is in the land, first agrees, or his justice, if he is out of the realm, in order that he may do right concerning him; . . .

8. Concerning appeals, if they should occur, they ought to proceed from the archdeacon to the bishop, from the bishop to the archbishop. And if the archbishop should fail to show justice, it must come to the lord king last, in order that by his command the controversy should be finally terminated in the court of the archbishop, so that it ought not to proceed further without the assent of the lord king. . . .

10. If any one who is of a city or a castle or a borough or a demesne manor of the lord king has been summoned by the archdeacon or the bishop for any offence for which he ought to respond to them, and is unwilling to make answer to their summons, it is fully lawful to place him under an interdict, but he ought not to be excommunicated before the principal officer of the lord

8. **advowson:** the right to recommend candidates for vacant church positions that carried with them capital assets.

king for that place agrees, in order that he may adjudge him to come to the answer. And if the officer of the king is negligent in this, he himself will be at the mercy of the lord king, and afterward the bishop shall be able to coerce the accused man by ecclesiastical justice.

11. Archbishops, bishops, and all persons of the realm, who hold from the king in chief, have their possessions from the lord king as a barony, and are responsible for them to the justices and officers of the king, and follow and perform all royal rules and customs; and just as the rest of the barons ought to be present at the judgment of the court of the lord king along with the barons, at least till the judgment reaches to loss of limbs or to death.

12. When an archbishopric or bishopric or abbacy or priorate of the demesne of the king has become vacant, it ought to be in his hands, and he shall take thence all its rights and products just as demesnes. And when it has come to providing for the church, the lord king ought to summon the more powerful persons of the church, and the election ought to be made in the chapel of the lord king himself, with the assent of the lord king and with the agreement of the persons of the realm whom he has called to do this. And there the person elected shall do homage and fealty to the lord king as to his liege lord, concerning his life and his limbs and his earthly honor, saving his order, before he shall be consecrated. . . .

This acknowledgment of the aforesaid royal customs and dignities has been made by the aforesaid archbishops, and bishops, and earls, and barons, and the more noble and ancient of the realm, at Clarendon, on the fourth day before the Purification of the Blessed Mary, perpetual Virgin, Lord Henry being there present with his father, the lord king. There are, however, many other and great customs and dignities of holy mother church and of the lord king, and of the barons of the realm, which are not contained in this writing. These are preserved to holy church and to the lord king and to his heirs and to the barons of the realm, and shall be observed inviolably forever.

8. Coronation of Emperor Frederick Barbarossa, 1152

[*From* Gesta Friderici]

In the year . . . 1152, after the most pious King Conrad had died in the spring . . . in the city of Bamberg . . . there assembled in the city of Frankfort from the vast expanse of the transalpine kingdom [Germany], marvellous to tell, the whole strength of the princes, not without certain of the barons from Italy, in one body, so to speak. Here, when the primates were taking counsel about the prince to be elected—for the highest honour of the Roman Empire claims this point of law for itself, as if by special prerogative, namely, that the kings do not succeed by heredity but are created by the election of the princes—finally Frederick, duke of Swabia, son of Duke Frederick, was desired by all, and with the approval of all, was raised up as king. . . .

When the king had bound all the princes who had assembled there in fealty and homage, he, together with a few whom he had chosen as suitable, having dismissed the others in peace, took ship with great joy on the fifth day and, going by the Main and Rhine, he landed at the royal palace of Sinzig. There, taking horse, he came to Aachen on the next Saturday; on the following day, Sunday [March 9th] . . . led by the bishops from the palace to the church of the blessed Virgin Mary, and with the applause of all present, crowned by Arnold, archbishop of Cologne, assisted by the other bishops, he was set on the throne of the Franks, which was placed in the same church by Charles the Great. Many were amazed that in such a short space of time not only so many of the princes and nobles of the kingdom had assembled but also that not a few had come even from western Gaul, where, it was thought, the rumour of this event could not yet have penetrated. . . .

Nor should I pass over in silence that on the same day in the same church the bishop-elect of Münster, also called Frederick, was consecrated as bishop by the same bishops who had consecrated the king; so that in truth the highest king and the priest believed this to be a sort of prognostication[9] in the present joyfulness that, in one church, one day saw the unction[10] of two persons, who

9. **prognostication:** prophecy.
10. **unction:** anointing.

alone are anointed sacramentally with the institution of the old and new dispensations and are rightly called the anointed of Christ. . . .

[*From "The Deeds of Frederick
Barbarossa"*]

In the middle of the month of October (1157) the emperor set out for Burgundy to hold a diet at Besançon. . . . We must speak of the ambassadors of the Roman pontiff, Hadrian. . . . The personnel of the embassy consisted of Roland, cardinal priest of the title of St. Mark and chancellor of the Holy Roman Church, and Bernard, cardinal priest of the title of St. Clement, both distinguished for their wealth, their maturity of view, and their influence, and surpassing in prestige almost all others in the Roman Church. . . . When this letter had been read and carefully set forth by Chancellor Rainald in a faithful interpretation, the princes who were present were moved to great indignation, because the entire content of the letter appeared to have no little sharpness and to offer even at the very outset an occasion for future trouble. But what had particularly aroused them all was the fact that in the aforesaid letter it had been stated, among other things, that the fullness of dignity and honor had been bestowed upon the emperor by the Roman pontiff, that the emperor had received from his hand the imperial crown, and that he would not have regretted conferring even greater benefits (*beneficia*) upon him. . . . And the hearers were led to accept the literal meaning of these words and to put credence in the aforesaid explanation because they knew that the assertion was rashly made by some Romans that hitherto our kings had possessed the imperial power over the City, and the kingdom of Italy, by gift of the popes, and that they made such representations and handed them down to posterity not only orally but also in writing and in pictures. . . .

They returned without having accomplished their purpose, and what had been done by the emperor was published throughout the realm in the following letter (October, 1157):

"Whereas the Divine Sovereignty, from which is derived all power in heaven and on earth, has entrusted unto us, His anointed, the kingdom and the empire to rule over, and has ordained that the peace of the churches is to be maintained by the imperial arms, not without the greatest distress of heart are we compelled to complain to Your Benevolence that from the head of the Holy Church, on which Christ has set the imprint of his peace and love, there seem to be emanating causes of dissentions and evils, like a poison, by which, unless God avert it, we fear the body of the Church will be stained, its unity shattered, and a schism created between the temporal and spiritual realms. . . . And since, through election by the princes, the kingdom and the empire are ours from God alone, Who at the time of the passion of His Son Christ subjected the world to dominion by the two swords, and since the apostle Peter taught the world this doctrine: 'Fear God, honor the king,' whosoever says that we received the imperial crown as a benefice (*pro beneficio*) from the lord pope contradicts the divine ordinance and the doctrine of Peter and is guilty of a lie. . . ."

Source 9 from J. A. Giles, translator and editor, Roger of Wendover's Flowers of History *(London: H. G. Bohn, 1849), vol. II, pp. 79–81.*

9. Coronation of Richard the Lionhearted, 1189

Duke Richard, when all the preparations for his coronation were complete, came to London, where were assembled the archbishops of Canterbury, Rouen, and Treves, by whom he had been absolved for having carried arms against his father after he had taken the cross. The archbishop of Dublin was also there, with all the bishops, earls, barons, and nobles of the kingdom. When all were assembled, he received the crown of the kingdom in the order following: First came the archbishops, bishops, abbots, and clerks, wearing their caps, preceded by the cross, the holy water, and the censers, as far as the door of the inner chamber, where they received the duke, and conducted him to the church of Westminster, as far as the high altar, in a solemn procession. In the midst of the bishops and clerks went four barons carrying candlesticks with wax candles, after whom came two earls, the first of whom carried the royal sceptre, having on its top a golden cross; the other carried the royal sceptre, having a dove on its top. Next to these came two earls with a third between them, carrying three swords with golden sheaths, taken out of the king's treasury. Behind these came six earls and barons carrying a chequer,[11] over which were placed the royal arms and robes, whilst another earl followed them carrying aloft a golden crown. Last of all came Duke Richard, having a bishop on the right hand, and a bishop on the left, and over them was held a silk awning. Proceeding to the altar, as we have said, the holy Gospels were placed before him together with the relics of some of the saints, and he swore, in presence of the clergy and people, that he would observe peace, honour, and reverence, all his life, towards God, the holy Church and its ordinances: he swore also that he would exercise true justice towards the people committed to his charge, and abrogating all bad laws and unjust customs, if any such might be found in his dominions, would steadily observe those which were good. After this they stripped him of all his clothes except his breeches and shirt, which had been ripped apart over his shoulders to receive the unction. He was then shod with sandals interwoven with gold thread, and Baldwin archbishop of Canterbury anointed him king in three places, namely, on his head, his shoulders, and his right arm, using prayers

11. **chequer:** a small table.

composed for the occasion: then a consecrated linen cloth was placed on his head, over which was put a hat, and when they had again clothed him in his royal robes with the tunic and gown, the archbishop gave into his hand a sword wherewith to crush all the enemies of the Church; this done, two earls placed his shoes upon his feet, and when he had received the mantle, he was adjured by the archbishop, in the name of God, not to presume to accept these honours unless his mind was steadily purposed to observe the oaths which he had made: and he answered that, with God's assistance, he would faithfully observe everything which he had promised. Then the king taking the crown from the altar gave it to the archbishop, who placed it upon the king's head, with the sceptre in his right hand and the royal wand in his left; and so, with his crown on, he was led away by the bishops and barons, preceded by the candles, the cross and the three swords aforesaid. When they came to the offertory of the mass, the two bishops aforesaid led him forwards and again led him back. At length, when the mass was chanted, and everything finished in the proper manner, the two bishops aforesaid led him away with his crown on, and bearing in his right hand the sceptre, in his left the royal wand, and so they returned in procession into the choir, where the king put off his royal robes, and taking others of less weight, and a lighter crown also, he proceeded to the dinner-table, at which the archbishops, bishops, earls, and barons, with the clergy and people, were placed, each according to his rank and dignity, and feasted splendidly, so that the wine flowed along the pavement and walls of the palace.

Source 10 from Hirmer Fotoarchiv.

10. Portrait of Emperor Otto III

Source 11 from Giraudon/Art Resource, NY.

11. **Portion of the Bayeux Tapestry Showing King Harold Seated on the Throne of England, with Halley's Comet Above**

Source 12 from Erwin Panofsky, Tomb Sculpture *(New York: Harry N. Abrams), fig. 222.*
Photograph from Foto Marburg/Art Resource, NY.

12. Tomb Sculpture of Duke Henry of Brunswick and His Wife, Matilda

QUESTIONS TO CONSIDER

The power relationships we have been investigating involve three main groups in medieval society: the nobles, the Church, and the rulers. To understand changes in the balance of power among them, you will need to extract information from each of the sources about them, and then compare your findings.

Take the nobles first. How would you compare the role of the nobles in the ceremonies of homage such as the Salisbury Oath with their role in the coronation ceremonies? How is their relationship to the ruler expressed in the pictures of Otto III and Harold? How does this compare with the way this relationship is expressed in the Assize of Clarendon? What differences do you see in the role of the nobles in Germany and those in England, as expressed in the coronation accounts?

Turning to the Church, what types of religious objects appear in the ceremonies and depictions of rulers? Do they serve to express the power of the Church as an institution or of someone else? What do they reveal to you about medieval religious beliefs and practices? What do the pictures of Otto III and Harold indicate about the relationship between the ruler and Church officials? How does this compare with the expression of this relationship in the Constitutions of Clarendon?

The most prominent group in the sources are rulers. How would you compare the three visual depictions of rulers? Might any of the differences you see be explained by differences in the function of these depictions, that is, the fact that the last one is a tomb sculpture? Why might rulers wish to express certain aspects of their rule while they are still living, and make sure others are stressed for posterity after they are dead?

The claim of rulers such as Henry II and Frederick Barbarossa to religious authority was accompanied in the High Middle Ages by changes in the theory underlying kingship. In the Early Middle Ages, the king was viewed as simply the greatest of the nobles, whose power derived from the agreements he had made with his vassals. This idea continued into the High Middle Ages, but alongside it developed the idea that the king got his power from God as well. Rulers were increasingly viewed not only as the apex of a pyramid of vassals, but also as the representative to God for their entire kingdom. They were not regarded as divine in the way that ancient rulers such as the Egyptian pharaohs and Roman emperors had been, for Christianity would not allow this, but they were considered sacred in some ways. What evidence of this new idea of kingship can you find in either the Constitutions of Clarendon or the statements of Frederick Barbarossa? The two coronation ceremonies, Sources 8 and 9, are from the period of the building up of the monarchy. What evidence do you see in them of both the older idea of the king as the greatest of the nobles, and the newer idea of the king as ordained by God?

Remember that most literate people in the Middle Ages were clerics, so that all of the documents included here were probably written by priests or monks. How might this have affected their account of the events?

EPILOGUE

The moves undertaken by rulers to increase their power during the High Middle Ages did not go unchallenged. The Constitutions of Clarendon were immediately opposed by Church officials, including Henry II's friend Thomas Becket, whom Henry had made the Archbishop of Canterbury. The controversy between them grew very bitter, and ended with Becket's murder by several of Henry's nobles. After this the Constitutions were officially withdrawn, but Henry continued to enforce many of their provisions anyway.

In the area ruled by the German emperors, the Church was better able to assert its independent power; in fact, constant disputes with the pope were one of the reasons that the German emperors were not successful at establishing a unified country. Church officials patterned themselves after secular rulers and began in the twelfth century to demand regular oaths of homage and loyalty. They made sure that Church power was clearly symbolized in any royal ceremony and in all ceremonies of knighthood. As rulers built castles, they built cathedrals, permanent monuments in stone to both the glory of God and the authority of the Church. The consecrations of churches and cathedrals rivaled the coronations of

Given what you have read and looked at here, what actions would you now regard as most significant in the creation of the medieval state?

monarchs in splendor and pomp. The Church was fortunate in this regard, for opportunities for special ceremonies and celebrations were much more frequent than they were for secular rulers. Even the regular mass could be used to convey the Church's might to all who observed it. The king may have had sacred authority, but Church officials wanted to make sure that everyone knew that they did as well.

Nobles in England also opposed the growth of royal power, and were more effective than the Church in enforcing limits to royal authority. The most famous of these was the Magna Carta in 1215, which King John was forced to sign at a meeting in Runnymede, giving the higher nobles of England the right to participate in government. This document said nothing about the rights of the vast majority of English people, but it is still unusual in its limitation of the power of the king, though John immediately refuted it once he left Runnymede.

Despite opposition, however, the expansion of royal power at the expense of the nobles and Church continued, for this expansion had only begun during the High Middle Ages. Monarchs in the later Middle Ages, the Renaissance, and the early modern period continued to build up their power, devising new methods of taxation to raise revenue, creating a centralized legal system under firm royal control, reducing the role of or doing away with feudal assemblies of nobles, hiring middle-class lawyers and bureaucrats as their advisers and officials, and forbidding the nobles to maintain their own armies while building up royal armies led by generals whom they chose for loyalty.

This expansion of royal power was made easier in many countries in the sixteenth century because of the Protestant Reformation. Many rulers, such as Henry VIII of England, resented any independent power of the Church; they thus found Protestant theology, which declared the papacy to be evil and the ruler the proper source of all religious authority, very attractive. Some rulers became Protestant out of sincere religious conviction, but for others the chance to take over Church property and appoint Church officials was the strongest motivation.

The growth of actual royal power was accompanied, as you would expect after working through this chapter, by changes in the theory underlying kingship and in the symbols used to portray the king. Political theorists developed the idea of the divine right of kings, whereby kings got their power directly and pretty much only from God, and so were not answerable to their subjects for their behavior. You can see this idea beginning in the documents you have just read, and it would be developed to its furthest extent in seventeenth-century absolutism.

Centralized monarchy did not develop in all parts of Europe, however. Germany and Italy remained divided, and in fact did not become unified nations until the late nineteenth century, just a little over a hundred years ago. From the description of Frederick Barbarossa's coronation, you can see one reason for this, the fact that the emperorship was elected rather than hereditary. The lack of strong central governments in Germany and Italy was one reason for their decreasing political importance in the early modern period. The rulers of western Europe had much greater financial resources, and so could field larger armies and encourage economic development. After the voyages of the Portuguese and Spanish revealed new lands and new ways to the East, these rulers also supported exploration and colonization, which further increased royal and national power. Some type of feudal structure existed in most parts of western Europe in the High Middle Ages, but it was the rulers of France, England, and Spain who were most successful at manipulating both actual power and the symbols of that power to build up their own authority and end the feudal system.

CHAPTER EIGHT

LIFE AT A

MEDIEVAL UNIVERSITY

Centers of learning grew up in several European cities—particularly Paris and Bologna, Italy—during the twelfth and thirteenth centuries. In Paris, scholars, drawn by excellent teachers such as Peter Abelard, gathered at the bishop's cathedral school. Because only an official of the bishop, called the *scholasticus* or chancellor, had the authority to issue licenses to teach, students and teachers clustered around the cathedral of Notre Dame, located on an island in the Seine. This educational community soon grew so large that it required additional housing on the left bank of the river, which came to be known as the "Latin Quarter" after the official academic language. Special residence halls for students, called *colleges*, were opened, though the teachers themselves had no classrooms and simply rented rooms on their own for lecturing.

As the number of students in Paris increased, the teachers joined together into a "universal society of teachers," or *university* for short. Be-

lieving that the chancellor often either granted the right to teach to unqualified parties or simply sold licenses outright, they began to require that prospective teachers pass an examination set by the university besides getting the chancellor's approval. This certificate to teach was the earliest form of academic degree, granting the holder one of the titles, *master* or *doctor*, that we still use today. (Bachelor's degrees were to come later.) Most of the students studied theology, and Paris became the model for later universities such as Oxford and Cambridge in England and Heidelberg in Germany.

Colleges at many universities changed their character over the centuries. Originally no more than residence halls, the colleges gradually began to sponsor lectures and arrange for courses, and the university became simply the institution that granted degrees. This process was especially noticeable at the English universities of Oxford and Cambridge. When colleges were first established in the United States, they generally modeled themselves on the colleges of Oxford and Cambridge; because they were not part of larger universities, the colleges also granted degrees themselves. Thus modern U.S. colleges may be either completely independent institutions or part of a university, such as the College of Engineering or the College of Letters and Science found at many universities. In most cases, colleges that are part of modern universities have completely lost their original function as residences.

The University of Bologna had somewhat different roots and a different emphasis. Professional schools for the training of notaries and lawyers had grown up in Bologna in the twelfth century because the city, located at the crossing of the main trade routes in northern Italy, was a center of commerce. The university developed from these professional schools, and consequently the students were older and more sophisticated than those at Paris. Here, the students themselves banded into a university; they determined the fees teachers would be paid, the hours of classes, and the content of lectures. The most important course of study at Bologna was law. Bologna became the model for European universities such as Orleans or Padua, where students have retained their traditional power through modern times.

Because all those associated with the universities were literate, a great many records survive detailing every aspect of university life, both inside and outside the classroom. We can observe the process by which universities were established, read the rules students were required to live by, and learn what they were supposed to be studying (as well as what they actually spent time doing!). Much of medieval university life will seem familiar to us, for modern colleges and universities have inherited a great deal from their medieval predecessors. Indeed, most of the universities that had their beginning in the Middle Ages are still thriving today, making universities one of the few medieval institutions we can evaluate to some extent as insiders, rather than the outsiders we are when we look at such vanished social forms as serfdom or feudalism.

Because of the many parallels between medieval and modern universities, your task in this chapter will be twofold. First, you will be asked to use a variety of records to answer this question: What was life like for students at a medieval university? You can then use this description and your own experiences as a student to answer the second question: How would you compare medieval with modern student life, and what factors might account for the differences?

SOURCES AND METHOD

You will be using four types of sources in this chapter. The first type (Sources 1 through 4) consists of rules for university or college life issued by the founders. These are prescriptive documents, setting forth standards of functioning and behavior. The second type (Sources 5 through 8), written by teachers at medieval universities, describes their methods of teaching or presents the area on which they concentrated. The third type (Source 9) is a critique of university teaching by an individual outside the university structure. These sources provide us with information about how and what students studied or were supposed to study and so have both prescriptive and descriptive qualities. Selections of the fourth type (Sources 10 through 13) describe actual student life or were written by students themselves. These sources are thus fully descriptive, recounting real events or the problems and desires of real students.

As you read each selection, keep in mind the identity of its author and his position in the university. (No women were allowed to attend medieval universities in any capacity, so we can be sure that all authors, even anonymous students, were male.) Then as now, the perspective of administrators, those who established and ran the universities, was very different from that of students and faculty. It is also important to identify the source as prescriptive or descriptive. Prescriptive rules were often written in response to real problems, but the standards they laid down should never be mistaken for reality.

Begin your analysis of medieval university life with a careful reading of Sources 1 through 4. Source 1 describes privileges granted to the students at the University of Paris by the king of France in 1200. Though the University of Paris was originally started by the teachers themselves, the king took the scholars under his special protection and guaranteed them certain extraordinary rights. What privileges are they granted in this document?

Source 2 consists of the statutes issued for the University of Paris by Cardinal Robert Courçon in 1215. Courçon, a representative of Pope Innocent III, took a special interest in the university and approved rules governing academic life. Innocent had been a student at Paris himself and wanted to ensure the university's tradition of theological orthodoxy and high levels of scholarship and behavior. As you read the selection, note the restrictions placed on those allowed to teach the arts. What restrictions are placed on teachers of theology? Why would Innocent be stricter about theology? What other areas did he believe important to regulate? What matters were the masters and students allowed to decide for themselves?

Source 3 contains further statutes issued for the University of Paris by Pope Gregory XI in 1231. What rules did he set for the chancellor's granting of teaching licenses? What issues was the university permitted to decide for itself? What special legal protections did students and teachers have? As pope, Gregory was particularly concerned with the manner in which theology was taught. What special restrictions did he lay down for students and teachers of theology? How would you compare these rules with the earlier ones established by Innocent III?

Source 4 is a series of rules governing life in one of the residential colleges, not the university as a whole. They were issued by Robert de Sorbon, the chaplain of King Louis IX, who established the college in the thirteenth century. This college was originally a residence hall for students of theology. By the sixteenth century, however, the word *Sorbonne* was used to describe the faculty of theology; since the nineteenth century the entire University of Paris has been called the Sorbonne.

As you can see from Source 4, Sorbon's establishment was simply a residence hall, with none of the broader functions that colleges later assumed. What aspects of student life did he regulate? What qualities did he attempt to encourage in the students living at his college?

By reading these four prescriptive sources, you have gained some information about the structure of one university (Paris), the hierarchy of authority, special student privileges, daily life in a residential college, and the handling of rule infractions. You have also learned something about the ideals held by authorities and patrons, for the popes and Sorbon established these rules because they held certain beliefs about how students should behave. What qualities would their ideal student exhibit? What did they see as the ultimate aim of the university? You can also use these sources to assess how church and secular leaders reacted to scholars, students, and the university in general. How would you describe their attitude—patronizing, respectful, hostile? How might their opinions about members of the university community have influenced other citizens of these university towns?

Besides informing us of standards, rules can also expose real-life problems because those who set the regulations were often responding to events in their environment. Which rules were specifically aimed at halting acts that were already taking place? Which rules seem most likely to have been a response to actual behavior? What kinds of acts did the authorities appear most upset about? Why do you think they believed these acts were important? Judging by the information in these sources, how would you describe relations between university students and the other residents of Paris? Before you go on to the next selections, write a brief description of medieval university life as you now see it. What types of sources would help you test whether your assumptions at this point are correct?

You have probably realized that so far you do not know very much about what or how students actually studied, other than those writings the popes recommended or forbade. The next four selections provide specific academic information. Sources 5 and 6 were written by teachers of theology and philosophy at Paris; Sources 7 and 8, by teachers of law at Bologna. Source 5 is the introduction to Peter Abelard's *Sic et Non,* a philosophical treatise introducing students and other readers to the *scholastic method* of inquiry, which applied logic to Christian theology. Source 6 is a demonstration of the scholastic method by one philosopher, Anselm of Canterbury, to prove the existence of God. If you are not familiar with philosophical works, you will need to read these excerpts very carefully, with special attention to the author's main points and the way in which logic is used to advance arguments. Because scholastic philosophers regarded logic as the most important aid to human understanding, it is fair for you to be critical if you see any flaws in their own logic. In making this analysis, you will be engaging in an activity that students in medieval universities both did themselves and were encouraged to do.

Begin with Abelard's introduction. How did he suggest to students that they read the works of the church fathers? How were they to handle seeming contradictions? Was all literature to be treated in this way? What, for Abelard, was the most important quality a student could possess? How was education supposed to strengthen this quality? Proceed to Anselm's proof, which you may need to read a number of times. Do you see any flaws in the logic? If you were a student disputing his proof, where would you begin?

Source 7 is an announcement of lectures in law by Odofredus, a teacher at the University of Bologna, written about 1250. Although later in the thirteenth century the city of Bologna began to pay teachers in order to control the university faculty more closely, at this point teachers were still paid directly by their students, and so Odofredus did not simply announce his course, he advertised it in a way that would make it attractive. What did he see as the positive qualities of his teaching method? How did he propose to handle a text? What specific skills was he trying to teach his students?

Source 8 is the introduction to the *Digest,* the main part of the collection of laws and commentaries made by the Emperor Justinian in the sixth century and one of the basic legal texts taught by Odofredus and his colleagues at Bologna. Like many textbooks, it opens with definitions of what would be taught. What distinctions among types of law does it present? What is the ultimate aim of legal education to be? Return to the description of university life you wrote after reading the first group of sources. What can you now add about the way teachers approached their subjects or the way in which material was taught? What do you now know about the content of courses in medieval universities?

Though teachers of theology and law used both logic and reason as means of analysis, there were some thinkers in the Middle Ages who questioned their value, particularly in matters of theology. Source 9 is an excerpt from two letters of St. Bernard of Clairvaux (1090–1153), a very influential French abbot, mystic, and adviser to the papacy. What does Bernard object to in Abelard's teaching? Why does he view Abelard's ideas as dangerous? What is his opinion of the scholastic method being developed at that time in the universities?

Students did not spend all their time studying, nor did they always behave in the ways popes or patrons hoped they would. The final group of sources come from students themselves or describe what might be termed their extracurricular activities. Source 10 is an anonymous account of a riot in Oxford in 1298, and Source 11 is a description of student life at Paris written by Jacques de Vitry, a high-minded scholar and historian who had studied at Paris himself. Source 12 consists of two letters, one from a student at Oxford to his father and another from a father to his son, a student at Orleans; Source 13 contains three anonymous short poems written originally in Latin by twelfth-century students.

The account of the riot is relatively straightforward and objective, like a story you might read in a newspaper today. What does this incident indicate about the relations between university scholars and townspeople? Whom did the two sets of disputants ask to decide the matter?

The other selections are more subjective than this account, so you must keep the point of view and the intent of the authors in mind as you read them. What kind of language does Vitry use to describe students? With what authority did he criticize their actions? How would you describe his general opinion of university life?

How would you compare his critique of logic and the philosophers who used it with Bernard's? What tactics did the student use to convince his father to send money? How would you compare the father's attitude with Vitry's?

Most medieval student poetry was written by young scholars who wandered from university to university and took much longer at their studies than normal, if they ever finished at all. It is important when reading from this genre to remember that the authors were not describing the daily grind but celebrating their wild escapades, in the same way you might talk about an academic year in terms of homecoming parties, weekend bashes, and early morning cramming for exams. This does not mean that we should reject their poetry as a valid historical source; rather, we must simply be aware of its intent and limitations. Keeping this in mind, how do the poets describe themselves and their problems? How does this description of student life reinforce or change what you have learned so far?

Return to your original description of university life. What would you add now?

███████ THE EVIDENCE ███████

Sources 1 through 3 from Dana Carleton Munro, editor and translator, Translations and Reprints from the Original Sources of European History, *vol. 2, no. 3 (Philadelphia: University of Pennsylvania Press, no date), pp. 4–5; pp. 12–15; pp. 7–11.*

1. Royal Privileges Granted to the University of Paris by the King of France, 1200

Protection of the students [handwritten]

In the Name of the sacred and indivisible Trinity, amen. Philip, by the grace of God, King of the French. . . .

Witnesses to crime [handwritten]

Concerning the safety of the students at Paris in the future, by the advice of our subjects we have ordained as follows: we will cause all the citizens of Paris to swear that if any one sees an injury done to any student by any layman, he will testify truthfully to this, nor will any one withdraw in order not to see [the act]. And if it shall happen that any one strikes a student, except in self-defense, especially if he strikes the student with a weapon, a club or a stone, all laymen who see [the act] shall in good faith seize the malefactor or malefactors and deliver them to our judge; nor shall they withdraw in order not to see the act, or seize the malefactor, or testify to the truth. Also, whether the malefactor is seized in open crime or not, we will make a legal and full examination through clerks or laymen or certain lawful persons; and our count and our judges shall do the same. And if by a full examination we or our judges are able to learn that he who is accused, is guilty of the crime, then we or our judges shall immediately inflict a penalty, according to the quality and nature of the crime; notwithstanding the fact that the criminal may deny the deed and say that he is ready to defend himself in single combat, or to purge himself by the ordeal by water. ~ *torture* [handwritten]

No one can touch a student [handwritten]

Also, neither our provost nor our judges shall lay hands on a student for any offence whatever; nor shall they place him in our prison, unless such a crime has been committed by the student, that he ought to be arrested. And in that case, our judge shall arrest him on the spot, without striking him at all, unless he resists, and shall hand him over to the ecclesiastical judge, who ought to guard him in order to satisfy us and the one suffering the injury. And if a serious crime has been committed, our judge shall go or shall send to see what is done with the student.

2. Statutes for the University of Paris Issued by Robert Courçon, 1215

R., servant of the cross of Christ, by the divine mercy cardinal priest of the title of St. Stephen in Monte Celio and legate of the apostolic seat, to all the masters and scholars at Paris—eternal safety in the Lord.

Let all know, that having been especially commanded by the lord pope to devote our energy effectively to the betterment of the condition of the students at Paris, and wishing by the advice of good men to provide for the tranquillity of the students in the future, we have ordered and prescribed the following rules:

No one is to lecture at Paris in arts before he is twenty-one years old. He is to listen in arts at least six years, before he begins to lecture. He is to promise that he will lecture for at least two years, unless he is prevented by some good reason, which he ought to prove either in public or before the examiners. He must not be smirched by any infamy. When he is ready to lecture, each one is to be examined according to the form contained in the letter of lord P. bishop of Paris (in which is contained the peace established between the chancellor and the students by the judges appointed by the lord pope, approved and confirmed namely by the bishop and deacon of Troyes and by P., the bishop, and J., the chancellor of Paris).

The treatises of Aristotle on logic, both the old and the new, are to be read in the schools in the regular and not in the extraordinary courses. The two Priscians,[1] or at least the second, are also to be read in the schools in the regular courses. On the feast-days nothing is to be read except philosophy, rhetoric, *quadrivialia*,[2] the Barbarism, the Ethics, if they like, and the fourth book of the Topics. The books of Aristotle on Metaphysics or Natural Philosophy, or the abridgements of these works, are not to be read, nor the writings of Master David of Dinant, the heretic Amauri, or the Spaniard Mauricius.[3]

In the promotions and meetings of the masters and in the confutations or arguments of the boys or youths there are to be no festivities. But they may call in some friends or associates, but only a few. We also advise that donations of garments and other things be made, as is customary or even to a greater extent, and especially to the poor. No master lecturing in arts is to

1. **Priscian:** a Roman grammarian whose two works presented models of correct letters and legal documents.
2. **quadrivialia:** the four more advanced fields of study within the seven liberal arts, arithmetic, geometry, astronomy, and music.
3. Aristotle's treatises on metaphysics and natural philosophy were forbidden by the pope because they stated that the world was eternal (rather than created by God) and that the human soul was not immortal. The last three authors the Church regarded as heretics.

dress code

wear anything except a cope,[4] round and black and reaching to the heels—at least, when it is new. But he may well wear a pallium.[5] He is not to wear under the round cope embroidered shoes and never any with long bands.

If anyone of the students in arts or theology dies, half of the masters of arts are to go to the funeral one time, and the other half to the next funeral. They are not to withdraw until the burial is completed, unless they have some good reason. If any master of arts or theology dies, all the masters are to be present at the vigils, each one is to read the psalter or have it read. Each one is to remain in the church, where the vigils are celebrated, until midnight or later, unless prevented by some good reason. On the day when the master is buried, no one is to lecture or dispute.

We fully confirm to them the meadow of St. Germain in the condition in which it was adjudged to them.

funerals of teachers & students

Each master is to have jurisdiction over his scholars. No one is to receive either schools or a house without the consent of the occupant, if he is able to obtain it. No one is to receive a license from the chancellor or any one else through a gift of money, or furnishing a pledge or making an agreement. Also, the masters and students can make among themselves or with others agreements and regulations, confirmed by a pledge, penalty or oath, about the following matters: namely, if a student is killed, mutilated or receives some outrageous injury—if justice is not done; for fixing the prices of lodgings; concerning the dress, burial, lectures and disputations; in such a manner, however, that the university is not scattered or destroyed on this account.

new lecture requirements

We decide concerning the theologians, that no one shall lecture at Paris before he is thirty-five years old, and not unless he has studied at least eight years, and has heard the books faithfully and in the schools. He is to listen in theology for five years, before he reads his own lectures in public. No one of them is to lecture before the third hour on the days when the masters lecture. No one is to be received at Paris for the important lectures or sermons unless he is of approved character and learning. There is to be no student at Paris who does not have a regular master.

3. Statutes for the University of Paris Issued by Pope Gregory XI, 1231

Gregory, the bishop, servant of the servants of God, to his beloved sons, all the masters and students of Paris—greeting and apostolic benediction. . . .

4. **cope:** a long cloak or cape.
5. **pallium:** a white stole usually worn by popes and archbishops as a symbol of their authority. In this case, a master teacher was allowed to wear one as an indication of his level of academic achievement and its corresponding institutional authority; the pallium thus served a function similar to the master's or doctoral hood.

Concerning the condition of the students and schools, we have decided that the following should be observed: each chancellor, appointed hereafter at Paris, at the time of his installation, in the presence of the bishop, or at the command of the latter in the chapter at Paris—two masters of the students having been summoned for this purpose and present in behalf of the university—shall swear that, in good faith, according to his conscience, he will not receive as professors of theology and canon law any but suitable men, at a suitable place and time, according to the condition of the city and the honor and glory of those branches of learning; and he will reject all who are unworthy without respect to persons or nations. Before licensing anyone, during three months, dating from the time when the license is requested, the chancellor shall make diligent inquiries of all the masters of theology present in the city, and of all other honest and learned men through whom the truth can be ascertained, concerning the life, knowledge, capacity, purpose, prospects and other qualities needful in such persons; and after the inquiries, in good faith and according to his conscience, he shall grant or deny the license to the candidate, as shall seem fitting and expedient. The masters of theology and canon law, when they begin to lecture, shall take a public oath that they will give true testimony on the above points. The chancellor shall also swear, that he will in no way reveal the advice of the masters, to their injury; the liberty and privileges being maintained in their full vigor for the canons at Paris, as they were in the beginning. Moreover, the chancellor shall promise to examine in good faith the masters in medicine and arts and in the other branches, to admit only the worthy and to reject the unworthy.

In other matters, because confusion easily creeps in where there is no order, we grant to you the right of making constitutions and ordinances regulating the manner and time of lectures and disputations, the costume to be worn, the burial of the dead; and also concerning the bachelors,[6] who are to lecture and at what hours, and on what they are to lecture; and concerning the prices of the lodgings or the interdiction of the same; and concerning a fit punishment for those who violate your constitutions or ordinances, by exclusion from your society. And if, perchance, the assessment of the lodgings is taken from you, or anything else is lacking, or an injury or outrageous damage, such as death or the mutilation of a limb, is inflicted on one of you; unless through a suitable admonition satisfaction is rendered within fifteen days, you may suspend your lectures until you have received full satisfaction. And if it happens that any one of you is unlawfully imprisoned, unless the injury ceases on a remonstrance from you, you may, if you judge it expedient, suspend your lectures immediately.

We command, moreover, that the bishop of Paris shall so chastise the excesses of the guilty, that the honor of the students shall be preserved and evil

---

6. **bachelor:** a student who had his first degree and could teach beginning-level subjects.

deeds shall not remain unpunished. But in no way shall the innocent be seized on account of the guilty; nay rather, if a probable suspicion arises against anyone, he shall be detained honorably and on giving suitable bail he shall be freed, without any exactions from the jailors. But if, perchance, such a crime has been committed that imprisonment is necessary, the bishop shall detain the criminal in his prison. The chancellor is forbidden to keep him in his prison. We also forbid holding a student for a debt contracted by another, since this is interdicted by canonical and legitimate sanctions. Neither the bishop, nor his official, nor the chancellor shall exact a pecuniary penalty for removing an excommunication or any other censure of any kind. Nor shall the chancellor demand from the masters who are licensed an oath, or obedience, or any pledge; nor shall he receive any emolument[7] or promise for granting a license, but be content with the above-mentioned oath.

Also, the vacation in summer is not to exceed one month, and the bachelors, if they wish, can continue their lectures in vacation time. Moreover, we prohibit more expressly the students from carrying weapons in the city, and the university from protecting those who disturb the peace and study. And those who call themselves students but do not frequent the schools, or acknowledge any master, are in no way to enjoy the liberties of the students.

Moreover, we order that the masters in arts shall always read one lecture on Priscian, and one book after the other in the regular courses. Those books on natural philosophy which for a certain reason were prohibited in a provincial council, are not to be used at Paris until they have been examined and purged of all suspicion of error. The masters and students in theology shall strive to exercise themselves laudably in the branch which they profess; they shall not show themselves philosophers, but they shall strive to become God's learned. And they shall not speak in the language of the people, confounding the sacred language with the profane. In the schools they shall dispute only on such questions as can be determined by theological books and the writings of the holy fathers.

It is not lawful for any man whatever to infringe this deed of our provision, constitution, concession, prohibition and inhibition or to act contrary to it, from rash presumption. If anyone, however, should dare to attempt this, let him know that he incurs the wrath of almighty God and of the blessed Peter and Paul, his apostles.

Given at the Lateran, on the Ides of April [April 13], in the fifth year of our pontificate.

---

7. **emolument:** fee.

Source 4 from Lynn Thorndike, editor and translator, University Records and Life in the Middle Ages *(New York: Columbia University Press, 1944), pp. 88–98. Reprinted with permission of Columbia University Press, 562 W. 113th St., New York, NY 10025, via Copyright Clearance Center, Inc.*

4. Robert de Sorbon's Regulations for His College, Before 1274

I wish that the custom which was instituted from the beginning in this house by the counsel of good men may be kept, and if anyone ever has transgressed it, that henceforth he shall not presume to do so.

No one therefore shall eat meat in the house on Advent, nor on Monday or Tuesday of Lent, nor from Ascension Day to Pentecost.

Also, I will that the community be not charged for meals taken in rooms. If there cannot be equality, it is better that the fellow eating in his room be charged than the entire community.

Also, no one shall eat in his room except for cause. If anyone has a guest, he shall eat in hall. If, morever, it shall not seem expedient to the fellow to bring that guest to hall, let him eat in his room and he shall have the usual portion for himself, not for the guest. If, moreover, he wants more for himself or his guest, he should pay for it himself. . . .

Also, the fellows should be warned by the bearer of the roll that those eating in private rooms conduct themselves quietly and abstain from too much noise, lest those passing through the court and street be scandalized and lest the fellows in rooms adjoining be hindered in their studies. . . .

Also, the rule does not apply to the sick. If anyone eats in a private room because of sickness, he may have a fellow with him, if he wishes, to entertain and wait on him, who also shall have his due portion. What shall be the portion of a fellow shall be left to the discretion of the dispenser. If a fellow shall come late to lunch, if he comes from classes or a sermon or business of the community, he shall have his full portion, but if from his own affairs, he shall have bread only. . . .

Also, all shall wear closed outer garments, nor shall they have trimmings of vair or grise[8] or of red or green silk on the outer garment or hood.

Also, no one shall have loud shoes or clothing by which scandal might be generated in any way.

Also, no one shall be received in the house unless he shall be willing to leave off such and to observe the aforesaid rules.

Also, no one shall be received in the house unless he pledges faith that, if he happens to receive books from the common store, he will treat them carefully as if his own and on no condition remove or lend them out of the

---

8. **vair:** squirrel fur. **grise:** any type of gray fur.

house, and return them in good condition whenever required or whenever he leaves town.

Also, let every fellow have his own mark on his clothes and one only and different from the others. And let all the marks be written on a schedule and over each mark the name of whose it is. And let that schedule be given to the servant so that he may learn to recognize the mark of each one. And the servant shall not receive clothes from any fellow unless he sees the mark. And then the servant can return his clothes to each fellow. . . .

Also, for peace and utility we propound that no secular person living in town—scribe, corrector, or anyone else—unless for great cause eat, sleep in a room, or remain with the fellows when they eat, or have frequent conversation in the gardens or hall or other parts of the house, lest the secrets of the house and the remarks of the fellows be spread abroad.

Also, no outsider shall come to accountings or the special meetings of the fellows, and he whose guest he is shall see to this.

Also, no fellow shall bring in outsiders frequently to drink at commons, and if he does, he shall pay according to the estimate of the dispenser.

Also, no fellow shall have a key to the kitchen.

Also, no fellow shall presume to sleep outside the house in town, and if he did so for reason, he shall take pains to submit his excuse to the bearer of the roll. . . .

Also, no women of any sort shall eat in the private rooms. If anyone violates this rule, he shall pay the assessed penalty, namely, sixpence.[9] . . .

Also, no one shall form the habit of talking too loudly at table. Whoever after he has been warned about this by the prior shall have offended by speaking too loudly, provided this is established afterwards by testimony of several fellows to the prior, shall be held to the usual house penalty, namely two quarts of wine.

The penalty for transgression of statutes which do not fall under an oath is twopence, if the offenders are not reported by someone, or if they were, the penalty becomes sixpence in the case of fines. I understand "not reported" to mean that, if before the matter has come to the attention of the prior, the offender accuses himself to the prior or has told the clerk to write down twopence against him for such an offence, for it is not enough to say to the fellows, "I accuse myself."

9. This was a substantial amount for most students to pay.

Source 5 from James Harvey Robinson, editor and translator, Readings in European History, vol. 1 (Boston: Ginn, 1904), pp. 450–452.

5. Introduction to Peter
Abelard's *Sic et Non*, ca 1122

There are many seeming contradictions and even obscurities in the innumerable writings of the church fathers. Our respect for their authority should not stand in the way of an effort on our part to come at the truth. The obscurity and contradictions in ancient writings may be explained upon many grounds, and may be discussed without impugning the good faith and insight of the fathers. A writer may use different terms to mean the same thing, in order to avoid a monotonous repetition of the same word. Common, vague words may be employed in order that the common people may understand; and sometimes a writer sacrifices perfect accuracy in the interest of a clear general statement. Poetical, figurative language is often obscure and vague.

[margin, handwritten: Reasons for contradictions]

Not infrequently apocryphal works are attributed to the saints. Then, even the best authors often introduce the erroneous views of others and leave the reader to distinguish between the true and the false. Sometime, as Augustine confesses in his own case, the fathers ventured to rely upon the opinions of others.

Doubtless the fathers might err; even Peter, the prince of the apostles, fell into error; what wonder that the saints do not always show themselves inspired? The fathers did not themselves believe that they, or their companions, were always right. Augustine found himself mistaken in some cases and did not hesitate to retract his errors. He warns his admirers not to look upon his letters as they would upon the Scriptures, but to accept only those things which, upon examination, they find to be true.

[margin, handwritten: Errors]

All writings belonging to this class are to be read with full freedom to criticise, and with no obligation to accept unquestioningly; otherwise the way would be blocked to all discussion, and posterity be deprived of the excellent intellectual exercise of debating difficult questions of language and presentation. But an explicit exception must be made in the case of the Old and New Testaments. In the Scriptures, when anything strikes us as absurd, we may not say that the writer erred, but that the scribe made a blunder in copying the manuscripts, or that there is an error in interpretation, or that the passage is not understood. The fathers make a very careful distinction between the Scriptures and later works. They advocate a discriminating, not to say suspicious, use of the writings of their own contemporaries.

In view of these considerations, I have ventured to bring together various dicta of the holy fathers, as they came to mind, and to formulate certain questions which were suggested by the seeming contradictions in the statements. These questions ought to serve to excite tender readers to a zeal-ous inquiry into truth and so sharpen their wits. The master key of knowledge is, indeed, a persistent and frequent questioning. Aristotle, the most clear-sighted of all the philosophers, was desirous above all things else to arouse this questioning spirit, for in his *Categories* he exhorts a student as follows: "It may well be difficult to reach a positive conclusion in these matters unless they be frequently discussed. It is by no means fruitless to be doubtful on particular points." By doubting we come to examine, and by examining we reach the truth.

> [*Abelard provides arguments for and*
> *against 158 different philosophical or*
> *theological propositions. The following are*
> *a few of the questions he discusses.*]

Should human faith be based upon reason, or no?
Is God one, or no?
Is God a substance, or no?
Does the first Psalm refer to Christ, or no?
Is sin pleasing to God, or no?
Is God the author of evil, or no?
Is God all-powerful, or no?
Can God be resisted, or no?
Has God free will, or no?
Was the first man persuaded to sin by the devil, or no?
Was Adam saved, or no?
Did all the apostles have wives except John, or no?
Are the flesh and blood of Christ in very truth and essence present in the
   sacrament of the altar, or no?
Do we sometimes sin unwillingly, or no?
Does God punish the same sin both here and in the future, or no?
Is it worse to sin openly than secretly, or no?

Source 6 from Roland H. Bainton, The Medieval Church *(Princeton, N.J.: D. VanNostrand, 1962), pp. 128–129.*

6. St. Anselm's Proof of the Existence of God, from His *Monologium*, ca 1070

I sought if I might find a single argument which would alone suffice to demonstrate that God exists. This I did in the spirit of faith seeking understanding. . . . Come now, O Lord my God, teach my heart where and how it may seek Thee. O Lord, if Thou art not here where shall I seek Thee absent, and if Thou art everywhere why do I not see Thee present? Surely Thou dwellest in light inaccessible. When wilt Thou enlighten our eyes? I do not presume to penetrate Thy profundity but only in some measure to understand Thy truth, which my heart believes and loves, for I seek not to understand that I may believe, but I believe in order that I may understand.

Now the fool will admit that there can be in the mind something than which nothing greater can be conceived. This, being understood, is in the mind, but it cannot be only in the mind, because it is possible to think of something which exists also in reality and that would be greater. If, therefore, that than which nothing greater can be conceived is only in the mind, that than which a greater cannot be conceived is that than which a greater can be conceived and this certainly cannot be. Consequently, without doubt, that than which nothing greater can be conceived exists both in the mind and in reality. This, then, is so sure that one cannot think of its not being so. For it is possible to think of something which one cannot conceive not to exist which is greater than that which cannot be conceived can be thought not to exist, it is not that a greater than which cannot be conceived. But this does not make sense. Therefore, it is true that something than which a greater cannot be conceived is not able to be conceived as not existing. This art Thou, O Lord, my God.

Source 7 from Lynn Thorndike, editor and translator, University Records and Life in the Middle Ages *(New York: Columbia University Press, 1944), pp. 66–67. Reprinted with permission of Columbia University Press, 562 W. 113th St., New York, NY 10025, via Copyright Clearance Center, Inc.*

7. Odofredus Announces His Law Lectures at Bologna, ca 1255

If you please, I will begin the *Old Digest*[10] on the eighth day or thereabouts after the feast of St. Michael[11] and I will finish it entire with all ordinary and extraordinary, Providence permitting, in the middle of August or thereabouts. The *Code*[12] I will always begin within about a fortnight of the feast of St. Michael and I will finish it with all ordinary and extraordinary, Providence permitting, on the first of August or thereabouts. The extraordinary lectures used not to be given by the doctors. And so all scholars including the

10. **Old Digest**: the first part of the *Digest*, the emperor Justinian's collation of laws, commentaries, and interpretations of laws by Roman jurists.

11. **feast of St. Michael**: September 29.

12. **Code**: another part of Justinian's collation of laws reflecting the additions to Roman law that came about after Christianity became the official religion of the empire.

unskilled and novices will be able to make good progress with me, for they will hear their text as a whole, nor will anything be left out, as was once done in this region, indeed was the usual practice. For I shall teach the unskilled and novices but also the advanced students. For the unskilled will be able to make satisfactory progress in the position of the case and exposition of the letter; the advanced students can become more erudite in the subtleties of questions and contrarieties. I shall also read all the glosses, which was not done before my time. . . .

For it is my purpose to teach you faithfully and in a kindly manner, in which instruction the following order has customarily been observed by the ancient and modern doctors and particularly by my master, which method I shall retain. First, I shall give you the summaries of each title before I come to the text. Second, I shall put forth well and distinctly and in the best terms I can the purport of each law. Third, I shall read the text in order to correct it. Fourth, I shall briefly restate the meaning. Fifth, I shall solve conflicts, adding general matters (which are commonly called *brocardica*) and subtle and useful distinctions and questions with the solutions, so far as divine Providence shall assist me. And if any law is deserving of a review by reason of its fame or difficulty, I shall reserve it for an afternoon review.

Source 8 from Anders Piltz, The World of Medieval Learning, *translated by David Jones (Totowa, N.J.: Barnes & Noble, 1981), p. 97.*

8. Introduction to *Digest* of Emperor Justinian, 6th century

Public law is the legislation which refers to the Roman state, *private law* on the other hand is of value to the individual. Common law contains statutes about sacrifices, the priesthood and civil servants. Private law can be divided into three parts: it comprises regulations based on natural law and regulations governing the intercourse of nations and of individuals. *Natural law* is what is taught to all living creatures by nature itself, laws which apply not only to mankind but to every living creature on the earth, in the heavens or in the seas. It is this that sanctions the union of man and woman, which is called marriage, and likewise the bearing and upbringing of children: we can see that other living creatures also possess understanding of this law. *International law* is the [commonly recognized set of] laws applied by every nation of the world. As can be seen it differs from natural law in that the latter is the same for all living creatures whereas the former only concerns human intercourse. . . . *Civil law* does not deviate completely from natural law but neither is it subordinate to it. . . . It is either written or unwritten. . . . Its sources are laws, popular decisions, decisions of the senate, the decrees of princes and the opinions of jurists. . . . *Justice* is the earnest and steadfast desire to give every man the rights he is entitled to. The injunctions of the law are these: live honestly, do no man injury, give to every man what he is entitled to.

Jurisprudence is knowledge of divine and human things, the study of right and wrong.

Source 9 from The Letters of St. Bernard of Clairvaux, *translated by Bruno Scott James (Chicago: Henry Regnery Company, 1953), pp. 321, 328.*

9. Extracts from the Letters of St. Bernard of Clairvaux, 1140

Master Peter Abelard is a monk without a rule, a prelate without responsibility. . . . He speaks iniquity openly. He corrupts the integrity of the faith and the chastity of the Church. He oversteps the landmarks placed by our Fathers in discussing and writing about faith, the sacraments, and the Holy Trinity; he changes each thing according to his pleasure, adding to it or taking from it. In his books and in his works he shows himself to be a fabricator of falsehood, a coiner of perverse dogmas, proving himself a heretic not so much by his error as by his obstinate defence of error. He is a man who does not know his limitations, making void the virtue of the cross by the cleverness of his words. Nothing in heaven or on earth is hidden from him, except himself. . . . He has defiled the Church; he has infected with his own blight the minds of simple people. He tries to explore with his reason what the devout mind grasps at once with a vigorous faith. Faith believes, it does not dispute. But this man, apparently holding God suspect, will not believe anything until he has first examined it with his reason. When the Prophet says, "Unless you believe, you shall not understand," this man decries willing faith as levity, misusing that testimony of Solomon: "He that is hasty to believe is light of head." Let him therefore blame the Blessed Virgin Mary for quickly believing the angel when he announced to her that she should conceive and bring forth a son. Let him also blame him who, while on the verge of death, believed those words of One who was also dying: "This day thou shalt be with me in Paradise."

Source 10 from Cecil Headlam, The Story of Oxford *(London: Dent, 1907), pp. 234–235.*

10. Anonymous Account of a Student Riot at Oxford, 13th century

They [the townsmen] seized and imprisoned all scholars on whom they could lay hands, invaded their inns, made havoc of their goods and trampled their books under foot. In the face of such provocation the Proctors[13] sent their bedels[14] about the town, forbidding the students to leave their inns. But all commands and exhortations were in vain. By nine o'clock next morning, bands of scholars were parading the streets in martial array. If the Proctors failed to restrain them, the mayor was equally powerless to restrain his townsmen. The great bell of S. Martin's rang out an alarm; oxhorns were sounded in the streets; messengers were sent into the country to collect rustic allies. The clerks,[15] who numbered three thousand in all, began their attack simultaneously in various quarters. They broke open warehouses in the Spicery, the Cutlery and elsewhere. Armed with bows and arrows, swords and bucklers, slings and stones, they fell upon their opponents. Three they slew, and wounded fifty or more. One band, led by Fulk de Neyrmit, Rector of Piglesthorne, and his brother, took up a position in High Street between the Churches of S. Mary and All Saints', and attacked the house of a certain Edward Hales. This Hales was a longstanding enemy of the clerks. There were no half measures with him. He seized his crossbow, and from an upper chamber sent an unerring shaft into the eye of the pugnacious rector. The death of their valiant leader caused the clerks to lose heart. They fled, closely pursued by the townsmen and country-folk. Some were struck down in the streets, and others who had taken refuge in the churches were dragged out and driven mercilessly to prison, lashed with thongs and goaded with iron spikes.

Complaints of murder, violence and robbery were lodged straight-way with the King by both parties. The townsmen claimed three thousand pounds' damage. The commissioners, however, appointed to decide the matter, condemned them to pay two hundred marks, removed the bailiffs, and banished twelve of the most turbulent citizens from Oxford. Then the terms of peace were formally ratified.

13. **proctor:** university official who maintained order and supervised examinations.

14. **bedel:** assistant to the proctor.

15. **clerks:** here, students and teachers.

Source 11 from Dana Carleton Munro, editor and translator, Translations and Reprints from the Original Sources of European History, *vol. 2, no. 3 (Philadelphia: University of Pennsylvania Press, no date), pp. 19–21.*

11. Jacques de Vitry's Description of Student Life at Paris, ca 1225

Almost all the students at Paris, foreigners and natives, did absolutely nothing except learn or hear something new. Some studied merely to acquire knowledge, which is curiosity; others to acquire fame, which is vanity; others still for the sake of gain, which is cupidity and the vice of simony. Very few studied for their own edification, or that of others. They wrangled and disputed not merely about the various sects or about some discussions; but the differences between the countries also caused dissensions, hatreds and virulent animosities among them, and they impudently uttered all kinds of affronts and insults against one another.

They affirmed that the English were drunkards and had tails; the sons of France proud, effeminate and carefully adorned like women. They said that the Germans were furious and obscene at their feasts; the Normans, vain and boastful; the Poitevins, traitors and always adventurers. The Burgundians they considered vulgar and stupid. The Bretons were reputed to be fickle and changeable and were often reproached for the death of Arthur. The Lombards were called avaricious, vicious and cowardly; the Romans, seditious, turbulent and slanderous; the Sicilians, tyrannical and cruel; the inhabitants of Brabant, men of blood, incendiaries, brigands and ravishers; those of Flanders, fickle, prodigal, gluttonous, yielding as butter, and slothful. After such insults, from words they often came to blows.

I will not speak of those logicians, before whose eyes flitted constantly "the lice of Egypt," that is to say, all the sophistical subtleties, so that no one could comprehend their eloquent discourses in which, as says Isaiah, "there is no wisdom." As to the doctors of theology, "seated in Moses' seat," they were swollen with learning, but their charity was not edifying. Teaching and not practicing, they have "become as sounding brass or a tinkling cymbal," or like a canal of stone, always dry, which ought to carry water to "the bed of spices." They not only hated one another, but by their flatteries they enticed away the students of others; each one seeking his own glory, but caring not a whit about the welfare of souls.

Having listened intently to these words of the Apostle, "If a man desire the office of a bishop, he desireth a good work," they kept multiplying the prebends,[16] and seeking after the offices; and yet they sought the work

---

16. **prebends:** that part of church revenues paid as a clergyman's salary.

decidedly less than the preëminence, and they desired above all to have "the uppermost rooms at feasts and the chief seats in the synagogue, and greetings in the market." Although the Apostle James said, "My brethren, be not many masters," they on the contrary were in such haste to become masters, that most of them were not able to have any students, except by entreaties and payments. Now it is safer to listen than to teach, and a humble listener is better than an ignorant and presumptuous doctor. In short, the Lord had reserved for Himself among them all, only a few honorable and timorous men, who had not stood "in the way of sinners," nor sat down with the others in the envenomed seat.

Sources 12 and 13 from Charles Homer Haskins, The Rise of Universities *(Ithaca, N.Y.: Cornell University Press, 1957), pp. 77–80; pp. 85–87.*

12. Two Letters, 13th century

B. to his venerable master A., greeting. This is to inform you that I am studying at Oxford with the greatest diligence, but the matter of money stands greatly in the way of my promotion,[17] as it is now two months since I spent the last of what you sent me. The city is expensive and makes many demands; I have to rent lodgings, buy necessaries, and provide for many other things which I cannot now specify. Wherefore I respectfully beg your paternity that by the promptings of divine pity you may assist me, so that I may be able to complete what I have well begun. For you must know that without Ceres and Bacchus Apollo[18] grows cold.

To his son G. residing at Orleans P. of Besançon sends greetings with paternal zeal. It is written, "He also that is slothful in his work is brother to him that is a great waster." I have recently discovered that you live dissolutely and slothfully, preferring license to restraint and play to work and strumming a guitar while the others are at their studies, whence it happens that you have read but one volume of law while your more industrious companions have read several. Wherefore I have decided to exhort you herewith to repent utterly of your dissolute and careless ways, that you may no longer be called a waster and your shame may be turned to good repute.

17. **promotion:** that is, attaining his degree.
18. **Ceres:** Roman god of grain. **Bacchus:** god of wine. **Apollo:** god of wisdom.

13. Three Anonymous
Student Poems, 12th century

I, a wandering scholar lad,
  Born for toil and sadness,
Oftentimes am driven by
  Poverty to madness.

Literature and knowledge I
  Fain would still be earning,
Were it not that want of pelf[19]
  Makes me cease from learning.

These torn clothes that cover me
  Are too thin and rotten;
Oft I have to suffer cold,
  By the warmth forgotten.

Scarce I can attend at church,
  Sing God's praises duly;
Mass and vespers both I miss,
  Though I love them truly.

Oh, thou pride of N——,
  By thy worth I pray thee
Give the suppliant help in need,
  Heaven will sure repay thee.

Take a mind unto thee now
  Like unto St. Martin;
Clothe the pilgrim's nakedness,
  Wish him well at parting.

So may God translate your soul
  Into peace eternal,
And the bliss of saints be yours
  In His realm supernal.

———————

We in our wandering,
Blithesome and squandering,
  Tara, tantara, teino!

Eat to satiety,
Drink with propriety;
  Tara, tantara, teino!

Laugh till our sides we split,
Rags on our hides we fit;
  Tara, tantara, teino!

Jesting eternally,
Quaffing infernally:
  Tara, tantara, teino!
                    etc.

———————

Some are gaming, some are drinking,
Some are living without thinking;
And of those who make the racket,
Some are stripped of coat and jacket;
Some get clothes of finer feather,
Some are cleaned out altogether;
No one there dreads death's invasion,
But all drink in emulation.

19. **pelf:** a contemptuous term for money.

QUESTIONS TO CONSIDER

You have now examined medieval universities and colleges from four points of view—those of the authorities who established them, the teachers who taught in them, the church officials who criticized them, and the students who attended them. In refining your description of university life, think first about points on which a number of sources agree. What role did religious and secular authorities play in the universities, both in their founding and in day-to-day operations? What privileges were extended to teachers and students, and how did these benefits affect their relationship with townspeople? Given these privileges along with student attitudes and actions, what opinion would you expect townspeople to have of students? Which of Sorbon's rules would you expect to have been frequently broken? What qualities did authorities and teachers alike see as vital to effective teaching? What qualities did both try to encourage in students? Would students have agreed about any of these? What problems did the authorities, teachers, and students all agree were most pressing for students?

Now turn to points on which you have contradictory information. How would you compare Abelard's beliefs about the role of logic in education with those of Bernard and de Vitry? How might Bernard and de Vitry have viewed Anselm's attempt to prove the existence of God through reason? Would Abelard have be-

lieved that the rules for students set out in Sources 1 through 4 helped or hindered the learning process? What suggestions for educational improvements might a philosopher like Abelard have made? A churchman like Bernard? Would Anselm and Odofredus have agreed about the proper methods and aims of education?

De Vitry's critique and the student poetry have pointed out that the rules for student life set out in Sources 1 through 4 were not always followed. The consequences of St. Bernard's criticism similarly demonstrate that Abelard's assertion of the need for free discussion of all topics was an ideal and not always the reality in medieval universities. In 1140, St. Bernard convinced the church leadership at the Council of Sens to condemn Abelard's teachings. Abelard appealed to the pope, who upheld the council's decision, and Abelard retired to a monastery, never to teach again. What does this incident indicate about where the ultimate authority in the university lay? Does this assertion of papal authority contradict any of the ideas expressed in other sources for this chapter besides Abelard's writings?

Some of the contradictions you have discovered are inherent in the highly different points of view of the four groups and are irreconcilable. You must, however, make some effort to resolve those contradictions that involve conflicting points of *fact* rather than simply conflicting *opinions*. Historians resolve contradictions in their sources by a variety of methods: by assessing the authors' intent and possible biases, giving weight to evidence that is likely to be most objective; by judging each source as partially valid, speculating on how each author's point of view might have affected his or her description; by trying to find additional information confirming one side or the other. At this point you can use the first two methods in your own thinking: Which observers do you judge to be most objective? Why did the students, teachers, and officials have different viewpoints in the first place? (You can also think about the third method historians use to resolve contradictions in their evidence: What other types of sources would you examine to confirm what you have discovered here?) Once you have made these judgments, you can complete your description of medieval university life.

Now move on to the second part of your task in this chapter, which is to compare medieval and modern university life. Some of the more striking contrasts have probably already occurred to you, but the best way to proceed is to think first about your evidence. What types of sources would give you the information for modern universities that you have unearthed for medieval ones? What are the modern equivalents of the medieval rules and ordinances? Of descriptions of student actions? Of student poetry? Of course announcements? Of philosophical treatises? Besides such parallel sources, where else can you find information about modern universities? What types of sources generated from modern universities, or from their students and teachers, have no medieval equivalent?

After considering these points of similarity and difference in sources, we are ready to make a specific comparison of university life in medieval and modern times. Because higher education in the United States is so diverse—some colleges and universities are public and some private, some religious and some nonsectarian, some residential and some commuter—it would be best if you compared your own institution with the more generalized description of medieval universities that you have developed. Do you see any modern equivalents to the privileges granted students by popes and kings? To the frequent clashes between universities and their surrounding communities? To the pope's restriction of "academic freedom" in the case of Abelard? How would you compare the relationship between religious and political authorities in medieval universities and in your own institution? The concern of authorities for the methods and content of higher education? How would you compare student residential life? Student problems? The students themselves? Relations between students and their parents? How would you compare the subjects taught? The method of teaching? The status of the faculty? Relations between students and teachers? Teachers' and students' views of the ultimate aims of education?

Once you have drawn up your comparison, you will need to perform what is often the most difficult task of any historical inquiry, which is to suggest reasons for what you have discovered. In doing this, you need to speculate not only about why some things have changed, but also about why others have remained the same. In your view, what is the most important difference between medieval and modern universities, and why?

EPILOGUE

The pattern set by Paris and Bologna was a popular one; by 1500, more than eighty universities were in existence throughout Europe. Often a dispute at one university, particularly among the faculty of theology, would lead a group of teachers and students to move elsewhere to form their own university. Sometimes they left one city because they felt the townspeople were overcharging them for food and lodging. Students often traveled from university to university in search of the best teachers or most amenable surroundings; because there were no admission forms or credits required for graduation, transferring from school to school was much easier in the Middle Ages than it is today.

As you have deduced from the sources, medieval students and teachers were criticized for all the seven deadly sins: greed, sloth, pride, lust, gluttony, envy, and anger. Toward the end of the Middle Ages, the university system itself came under increasing attack for being too remote from worldly concerns, providing students only with useless philosophical information that would never help them in the real world of politics and business. Especially in Italy, independent teachers of speech and writing began

to offer young men who wanted an education an alternative to universities, setting up academies to teach practical rhetorical and literary skills for those who planned to engage in commerce, banking, or politics. This new program of study, called *humanism*, emphasized language and literature rather than theology and philosophy.

Though the universities initially opposed the humanist curriculum, by the sixteenth century a considerable number, especially the newer ones, began to change their offerings. They established endowed chairs for teachers of Latin, Greek, and Hebrew, particularly because students who had trained at humanist secondary schools demanded further language training. Some of the oldest universities, such as Paris, were the slowest to change, but eventually they modified their program to keep students from going elsewhere.

The gradual introduction of humanism set a pattern that universities were to follow when any new body of knowledge or subject matter emerged. Innovative subjects and courses were at first generally taught outside the universities in separate academies or institutes, then slowly integrated into the university curriculum. In the seventeenth and eighteenth centuries, natural science was added in this way; in the nineteenth century, the social sciences and modern languages; and in the twentieth, a whole range of subjects, such as agriculture, engineering, and the fine arts. (The University of Paris continued to be the slowest to change well into the twentieth century; for example, it did not add sociology as a discipline until the 1960s. Moderniza-tion of the curriculum was one of the demands of the 1968 student revolt in Paris.) Thus, even though the university has survived since the Middle Ages, Peter Abelard or Robert de Sorbon might have difficulty recognizing the institution in its present-day form.

CHAPTER NINE

CAPITALISM AND CONFLICT

IN THE MEDIEVAL CLOTH TRADE

During the early Middle Ages, western Europe was largely a rural society. Most of the cities of the Roman Empire had shrunk to villages, and the roads the Romans had built were allowed to fall into disrepair. Manors and villages were relatively self-sufficient in basic commodities such as grain and cloth, and even in times of famine they could not import the food they needed because the cost of transportation was too high. Much local trade was carried out by barter, and any long-distance trade that existed was handled by Jews, Greeks, and Syrians, who imported luxury goods like spices, silks, and perfumes from the Near East. These extremely expensive commodities were purchased only by nobles and high-ranking churchmen. The lack of much regional trade is reflected in the almost complete absence of sources about trade before the tenth century. Commercial documents are extremely rare, and both public and private records testify to the agrarian nature of early medieval society.

This situation began to change in the tenth century, when Vikings in the north and Italians in the south revived long-distance European commerce. The Vikings initially raided and plundered along the coasts of northern Europe, but they soon turned to trading with the very people whose lands they had threatened. At the same time, merchants from the cities of Genoa, Pisa, and Florence were taking over former Muslim trade routes in the western Mediterranean. These Italian merchants began to keep increasingly elaborate records of their transactions and devised new methods of bookkeeping to keep track of their ventures. They developed new types of partnerships to share the risks and found ways to get around the medieval Christian church's prohibition of the lending of money at interest (termed *usury*). These changes, combined with the growth in trade, led to a transformation of the European economy often called the *Commercial Revolution*.

Once western European merchants began to trade more extensively with the East, particularly after the Crusades in the twelfth century, it became clear that the balance of trade favored the East; Eastern luxuries such as spices and silks were paid for primarily in gold. Gradually, however, western European merchants began to add high- and medium-quality woolen cloth, with Italian merchants trading cloth made in Flanders (modern-day Belgium and northeast France) to Asia and Africa, carrying it all the way to the court of Genghis Khan. They also shipped increasing quantities of cloth to other locations in Europe, eventually importing raw wool from England to supply the Flemish clothmakers and handling both long-distance and regional trade.

The reinvigoration of trade in the Commercial Revolution came with, and was one of the causes of, a rebirth of town life. Especially in Italy and the Low Countries, but in many other parts of Europe as well, towns began to spring up around cathedrals, monasteries, and castles or at locations favorable for trade, such as ports or major crossroads. Many of these became cloth-producing centers, as weavers and other artisans involved in the many stages of cloth production gathered together to manufacture goods for regional and long-distance traders. Cloth merchants in these towns—sometimes in combination with the merchants of other types of products—joined together to form a merchants' guild that prohibited nonmembers from trading in the town. These same merchants often made up

the earliest town government, serving as mayors and members of the city council, so that a town's economic policies were determined by its merchants' self-interest. Acting through the city council, the merchants' guilds determined the hours that markets would be open, decided which coins would be accepted as currency, and set prices on imported and local goods. Foreign affairs were also guided by the merchants, and cities formed alliances, termed *hanses*, with other cities to gain trading benefits.

From its beginnings, the trade in fine cloth was organized as a capitalist enterprise. Cloth merchants, called *drapers*, purchased raw materials, hired workers for all stages of production, and then sold the finished cloth; they rarely did any production themselves, and in some parts of Europe they were actually forbidden to do so. Some stages of production might be carried out in drapers' homes or in buildings that they owned, but more often production was carried out in the houses of those that they hired, who were paid by the piece rather than by the hour or day; these workers, especially those who wove cloth, might in turn hire several people to weave alongside them.

Cloth went through many stages from sheep to finished cloth. Once the sheep were sheared, the wool was sorted, beaten, and washed; it was then carded and spun by women using either hand spindles or, after the thirteenth century, spinning wheels. Next, the thread was prepared for weaving by *warpers*, who wound the long threads for the warp (warp threads are those that run lengthwise on a piece of cloth), and by *spoolers,* who wound woof threads (woof threads are those that run crosswise). The prepared thread went to the weavers, who used horizontal treadle looms. After the cloth was woven, it went to *fullers,* who stamped the cloth with their feet in troughs full of water, alkaline earth, and urine to soften it and fill in the spaces between the threads. (In the thirteenth century in some parts of Europe, fulling began to take place in water-powered fulling mills.) The cloth was then cleaned, hung to dry on wooden frames called *tenters,* and stretched to the correct width. The cloth was finished by repeatedly brushing it with thistle-like plants called *teasles* set in rows on a frame and then shearing the resulting fuzz off with large shears. It could be dyed at any stage in this process, as wool, thread, or whole cloth.

Some of these processes, such as dyeing, weaving, and shearing, required great skill and were usually reserved for men; others, such as spinning, sorting, and stretching on the tenter, called for less skill and were often carried out by women or young people. Once the cloth had been sheared for the final time, it went to the drapers, who monopolized all cutting of bolts of cloth and, thus, all retail sales. In areas where merchants organized production on a huge scale, such as Florence, there was a distinction between merchants and drapers, with the major merchants doing no actual cloth cutting themselves but simply hiring drapers; in most parts of Europe, however, merchants cut as

well as sold, and were often called merchant-drapers.

Especially in Flanders and Florence, the merchants who controlled the cloth trade attempted to regulate everything down to the smallest detail. They set up precise standards of quality with severe penalties for those who did not meet them, regulated the length of the workday and the wages of all workers, and sent out inspectors regularly to enforce the ordinances and handle disputes. At first there was little opposition, but, beginning in the twelfth and thirteenth centuries in many areas, cloth workers challenged the merchants' control through strikes and revolts, and attempted to form their own organizations, called *craft guilds.* (At the same time, those who produced or handled many other sorts of products, such as shoemakers, butchers, and blacksmiths, were also forming separate craft guilds.) In some areas, such as Florence, the cloth merchants were successful at stopping all organizing and suppressing all rebellions, but in others, such as many cities in Flanders, the merchants lost, and the wool workers were able to form their own guilds and even become part of the city government for at least a short period of time. In some places, those artisans who were highly skilled and who owned some of their own equipment, such as weavers, fullers, dyers, and shearers, were able to form guilds, whereas the less-skilled spinners and sorters were not.

In periods during which they were able to form independently, the craft guilds took over the regulation of production from the merchant guilds. They set quality standards for their particular product and regulated the size of workshops, the training period, and the conduct of members. In most cities, individual guilds, such as those of weavers or dyers, achieved a monopoly in the production of one particular product, forbidding nonmembers to work. The craft guild then chose some of its members to act as inspectors and set up a court to hear disputes between members, although the city court remained the final arbiter, particularly in cases involving conflict between merchants and artisans or between members of craft guilds and those who were not members.

Each guild set the pattern by which members were trained. If one wanted to become a dyer, for instance, one spent four to seven years as an apprentice and then at least that long as a journeyman, working in the shop of a master dyer, after which one could theoretically make one's masterpiece. If the masterpiece was approved by the other master dyers and if they thought the market in their town was large enough to allow for another dyer, one could then become a master and start a shop. Though the amount of time a candidate had to spend as an apprentice and a journeyman varied slightly from guild to guild, all guilds—both those in the cloth industry and those in other sorts of production—followed this same three-stage process. The apprentices and journeymen generally lived with the master and his family, and were often forbidden to marry. Conversely, many guilds required that masters be married, as they believed a wife was absolutely essential to the running of the shop and the household, and also felt that married men were likely to be more stable and dependable.

The master's wife assisted in running the shop, often selling the goods her husband had produced. Their children, both male and female, also worked alongside the apprentices and journeymen; the sons were sometimes formally apprenticed, but the daughters generally were not, since many guilds limited formal membership to males. Most guilds did allow a master's widow to continue operating a shop for a set period of time after her husband's death, for they recognized that she had the necessary skills and experience. Such widows paid all guild dues, but did not vote or hold office in the guilds because they were not considered full members. The fact that women were not formally guild members did not mean that they did not work in guild shops, however, for alongside the master's wife and daughters, female domestic servants often performed the less-skilled tasks. In addition, there were a few all-female guilds in several European cities, particularly Cologne and Paris, in which girls were formally apprenticed in the same way boys were in regular craft guilds.

Both craft and merchants' guilds were not only economic organizations, but also systems of social support. Though they were harsh against outsiders, they were protective and supportive of their members. They took care of elderly masters who could no longer work, and often supported masters' widows and orphans. They maintained an altar at a city church, and provided for the funerals of members and baptisms of their children. Guild members marched together in city parades, and reinforced their feelings of solidarity with one another by special ceremonies and distinctive dress.

Whether workers were able to form separate craft guilds or not, conflicts between merchants and workers over the cloth trade were a common feature of medieval town life in the major centers of cloth production. These conflicts often disrupted cloth production from a certain area, allowing other areas to expand their trade. In the late fourteenth century, for example, mass rebellions in Florence and Flanders benefited English weavers, who began to turn a greater percentage of English wool into cloth rather than exporting it as raw wool to the Continent. Government policy in England also helped the English weavers, as the crown in 1347 imposed a 33 percent tariff on the export of raw wool, while setting only a 2 percent tariff on the export of finished cloth. The crown also ordered people to wear English cloth (a provision that was very difficult to enforce) and en-

couraged Flemish cloth-makers displaced by unrest in their own towns to settle in England. Flemish cloth-makers also migrated to many towns in Germany, and by the sixteenth century the production of wool cloth was more dispersed throughout Europe than it had been several centuries earlier.

Often the change from the medieval to the modern economy is described as "the rise of capitalism," a change accompanied by "the rise of the middle class." Though specialists in the period disagree about many aspects of the development of capitalism, they agree that cloth production and trade was the earliest and most important capitalist enterprise in medieval Europe. Thus we can see in the cloth trade many of the issues that would emerge later in other parts of the economy, and that are still issues facing business and governments today. Your task in this chapter will be to use a variety of sources regarding cloth production from several parts of Europe to answer these questions: What were the key economic and social goals of governments, merchant-capitalists, and artisans regarding the cloth trade, and how did they seek to achieve these aims? What economic and social conflicts emerged as the cloth trade grew and changed?

SOURCES AND METHOD

In analyzing the development of the cloth trade, historians have a wide variety of documents at their disposal. Because cloth was regarded by

city and national governments as so important, their records include many laws that refer to the cloth trade, and often describe royal or municipal actions that encouraged cloth production. Some of the earliest attempts by governments to gather statistical information also refer to wool and cloth. The merchants' and later craft guilds themselves kept records—both regulations and ordinances, and records of judgments against those who broke these ordinances. Private business documents and personal documents such as contracts also often refer to aspects of the cloth trade.

In general, these sources can be divided into two basic types, a division that holds equally for sources from many other historical periods. The first type is *prescriptive*—laws, regulations, and ordinances that describe how the cloth trade was supposed to operate and how the guild or government officials who wrote the ordinances hoped things would be. These documents do not simply describe an ideal, however; they were generally written in response to events already taking place, so they can tell us about real problems and the attitudes of guilds and officials toward these problems. It is sources such as these that will allow us to answer the first of our questions, for they tell us specifically about goals and efforts to achieve them. What they cannot tell us is if any of these efforts worked, or what problems these efforts might have caused. For this we need to turn to a second type of primary evidence, *descriptive* documents such as court records and statistical information. Through these records we can observe how regulations were actually enforced, and assess—to a limited degree, because medieval statistics must always be used very carefully— the results of government and guild efforts to build up the cloth trade. As you are reading the sources, then, the first question you have to ask yourself is whether the record is prescriptive or descriptive, for confusing the two can give a very skewed view of medieval economic and social issues. (This kind of discrimination must be applied to any historical source, of course, and is not always an easy task. Sometimes even prominent historians have built a whole pyramid of erroneous theories about the past by assuming prescriptive sources accurately described reality. We investigated one example of this in Chapter 2 on classical Athens.)

The first three selections are all laws regarding the wool trade issued by territorial rulers. Source 1 comes from what are termed the laws of King Edward the Confessor of England (though they were written after his reign, sometime after 1115), setting out what were termed the "Liberties of London," or what we would term the rights accorded the citizens of London by the king. Source 2 is a similar law of the Count of Holland regarding the city of Dortrecht. Read each of these carefully. What special privileges were granted to the citizens of these towns by their rulers? Source 3 is a proclamation of the Countess of Flanders in 1224. What extra inducement did she offer to encourage wool production in the town of Courtrai? At this point you may want to begin a three-column list or chart, one column for the goals stated either explicitly or implicitly in the sources, a second for the actions taken to achieve those goals, and a third for the conflicts alluded to or discussed.

The next three sources are regulations regarding those who worked in cloth production issued by merchants' guilds or by the city councils, which were usually dominated by the merchants. Source 4 is from the English town of Winchester, Source 5 from the German town of Stendal, and Source 6 from the Flemish town of Arras. Read each of these sources carefully and add the information there to your three-column list. What were the most important aims of the merchants? What punishments did they set for those who broke the regulations, and how did they otherwise enforce their rules? Do the kinds of distinctions they make between groups—citizens and foreigners; those who make cloth and those who cut and sell it; members of artisans' families and non-members; masters, journeymen, and apprentices in a shop—suggest or perhaps contribute to social conflicts? What other types of conflicts are mentioned explicitly? (In all of these sources, the word *guest* or *foreigner* is used for someone who comes from a different town or village, and not necessarily from a different country.)

Though in many cities we do not have complete records of how well the provisions set forth in the ordinances were actually carried out, we can get glimpses from court records and similar sources from some cities. Through these we can see some instances of the enforcement of regulations and of the conflicts that this could cause. Sources 7 through 11 are examples of actual cases involving disputes in the cloth trade; Sources 7 and 8 are from fourteenth-century Flanders, and Sources 9 through 11 from sixteenth-century Germany. In Source 7, what is Jacquemars des

Mares' aim? That of the cloth inspectors and the city council? How well do the actions of the city councils in Sources 7, 8, and 9 reinforce the aims of the merchants as set out in Sources 4, 5, and 6? Though the ultimate decision of the city councils in Sources 10 and 11 is not known, from the supplications themselves we can get a good idea of actions taken by members of the weavers' guild. Do these fit with the aims of the merchants, or are the aims of these artisans somewhat different? Why might the women have appealed to the city council, made up largely of merchants, to rectify actions taken against them by artisans?

Along with government records, private records can give us additional information about the cloth trade. Most private business documents are primarily descriptive in nature, although they can also contain information about the aims of those who drew them up. Source 12 contains two apprenticeship contracts from the thirteenth century. What were the aims of the parents involved and of the master weavers? Can we get any hints of potential conflicts that arose in apprenticeships? Source 13 contains several insurance contracts for wool and cloth shipments from a fourteenth-century Italian merchant. Why would wool traders have wanted to enlist his services? How does their using an insurer fit with others of their actions?

The final sources for this chapter are statistical and rely on both official and private records. Source 14 consists of two charts of the total number of cloths produced in Florence and

Ypres in Flanders, based on guild records. Source 15 consists of two charts of the export of raw wool and wool cloth from England, based on customs records that began after customs duties were imposed in 1347. These records do not include cloth made for use in England and report *only* exports that went through the customs office (there was a great deal of smuggling, so they may significantly underreport the total amounts exported), but we can use them in conjunction with the charts of Source 14 to ascertain general trends. How would you compare the trends in cloth production for the three areas? How would you assess the success of English government policies that encouraged weaving? How might the decline in the amount of raw wool exported from England have affected weaving in Florence, Ypres, and other areas, despite the efforts there of governments or merchants?

THE EVIDENCE

Source 1 from Benjamin Thorpe, Ancient Laws and Institutes of England *(London: Eyre and Spottiswoode, 1840), p. 462.*

1. Laws Regarding Foreign Merchants Under King Edward the Confessor of England, after 1115

And after he has entered the city, let a foreign merchant be lodged wherever it please him. But if he bring dyed cloth, let him see to it that he does not sell his merchandise at retail, but that he sell not less than a dozen pieces at a time. And if he bring pepper, or cumin, or ginger, or alum, or brasil wood, or resin, or incense, let him sell not less than fifteen pounds at a time. But if he bring belts, let him sell not less than a thousand at a time. And if he bring cloths of silk, or wool or linen, let him see that he cut them not, but sell them whole.

Also a foreign merchant may not buy dyed cloth, nor make the dye in the city, nor do any work which belongs by right to the citizens.

Source 2 from C. Gross, The Gild Merchant *(Oxford: Clarendon, 1890), vol. I, p. 293.*

2. Law Regarding Cloth Cutting Under the Count of Holland, 1200

I, Theodore, by the grace of God, Count of Holland, and Adelaide, Countess of Holland, my wife, wish it to be known to all, both present and future, that we decree that our townsmen of Dortrecht may enjoy in their own right the following freedom in the said town, namely, that it is permitted to no one in Dortrecht to cut cloth for retail sale except to those who are designated by this trade, being called cutters of cloth, and except they be in the hanse[1] and fraternity of the townsmen belonging to Dortrecht. And that this charter, instituted by us, may forever be secure and intact, we corroborate it by affixing our seals thereto, and the signatures of witnesses.

These are the witnesses. . . .

Source 3 from Roy C. Cave and Herbert H. Coulson, A Source Book for Medieval Economic History *(New York: Biblo and Tannen, 1965), p. 374.*

3. Proclamation Regarding Taxes by the Countess of Flanders, 1224

I, Joan, Countess of Flanders and Hainault, wish it to be known to all both now and in the future, that I and my successors cannot and ought not to take any tax or payment from the fifty men who shall come to live at Courtrai, for as long as they remain here, to work in the woolen industry from this day on. But their heirs, after the decease of their parents, shall serve me just as my other burgesses do. Given at Courtrai, in the year of the Lord 1224, on the feast of St. Cecilia.

1. **hanse:** in this instance, the merchants' guild.

Source 4 from Beverley Town Documents, *edited by A. F. Leach, Publications of the Selden Society, vol. XIV (London: Selden Society, 1900), appendix II, pp. 134–135.*

4. City Ordinances Regarding Weavers in Winchester, England, ca 1209

This is the law of the Fullers and Weavers of Winchester: Be it known that no weaver or fuller may dry or dye cloth nor go outside the city to sell it. They may sell their cloth to no foreigner, but only to merchants of the city. And if it happens that, in order to enrich himself, one of the weavers or fullers wishes to go outside the city to sell his merchandise, he may be very sure that the honest men of the city will take all his cloth and bring it back to the city, and that he will forfeit it in the presence of the aldermen and honest men of the city. And if any weaver or fuller sell his cloth to a foreigner, the foreigner shall lose his cloth, and the other shall remain at the mercy of the city for as much as he has. Neither the weaver nor the fuller may buy anything except for his trade but by making an agreement with the mayor. No free man[2] can be accused by a weaver or a fuller, nor can a weaver or a fuller bear testimony against a free man. If any of them become rich, and wish to give up his trade, he may forswear it and turn his tools out of the house, and then do as much for the city as he is able in his freedom.

Sources 5 and 6 from Roy C. Cave and Herbert H. Coulson, A Source Book for Medieval Economic History *(New York: Biblo and Tannen, 1965), pp. 246–248; pp. 250–252.*

5. City Ordinances Regarding Guilds in Stendal, Germany, 1231 and 1233

We make known . . . that we, . . . desiring to provide properly for our city of Stendal, have changed, and do change, for the better, the laws of the gild [*sic*] brethren, and of those who are called cloth-cutters, so that they might have the same laws in this craft as their gild brethren the garment-cutters in Magdeburg have been accustomed to observe in the past.

These are the laws:

1. No one shall presume to cut cloth, except he be of our craft; those who break this rule will amend to the gild with three talents.[3]

2. **free man:** a citizen of Winchester. The weavers and fullers were not fully citizens at this point, but probably came from outside Winchester.
3. **talents, denarii, solidi:** different coins in circulation in Stendal. A mark was worth about 160 denarii; a solidus was worth about 25 denarii. The value of a talent varied widely.

2. Thrice a year there ought to be a meeting of the brethren, and whoever does not come to it will amend according to justice.

3. Whoever wishes to enter the fraternity whose father was a brother and cut cloth will come with his friends to the meeting of the brethren, and if he conduct himself honestly, he will be able to join the gild at the first request on payment of five solidi, and he will give six denarii to the master. And if he be dishonest and should not conduct himself well, he should be put off until the second or third meeting. But any of our citizens who wish to enter the gild, if he be an honest man, and worthy, will give a talent to the brethren on entry into the gild, and will present a solidus to the master. But if a guest who is an honest man should decide to join our fraternity, he will give thirty solidi to the gild on his entry, and eighteen denarii to the master. . . . But if any brother should make cloth against the institutions of the brethren, and of their decrees, which he ought on the advice of the consuls to observe, he will present to the consuls by way of emendation one talent for each offense or he will lose his craft for a year.

4. But if any one be caught with false cloth, his cloth will be burned publicly, and verily, the author of the crime will amend according to justice. . . .

9. If any one should marry a widow whose husband was of the craft, he will enter the fraternity with three solidi.

6. Shearers' Charter from Arras, Flanders, 1236

Here is the Shearers' Charter, on which they were first founded.

This is the first ordinance of the shearers, who were founded in the name of the Fraternity of God and St. Julien, with the agreement and consent of those who were at the time mayor and aldermen.

1. Whoever would engage in the trade of a shearer shall be in the Confraternity of St. Julien, and shall pay all the dues, and observe the decrees made by the brethren.

2. That is to say: first, that whoever is a master shearer shall pay 14 solidi to the Fraternity. And there may not be more than one master shearer working in a house. And he shall be a master shearer all the year, and have arms for the need of the town.

3. And a journeyman shall pay 5 solidi to the Fraternity.

4. And whoever wishes to learn the trade shall be the son of a burgess or he shall live in the town for a year and a day; and he shall serve three years to learn this trade.

5. And he shall give to his master 3 *muids*[4] for his bed and board; and he ought to bring the first *muid* to his master at the beginning of his apprenticeship, and another *muid* a year from that day, and a third *muid* at the beginning of the third year.

---

4. **muid:** a silver coin in circulation in Arras.

6. And no one may be a master of this trade of shearer if he has not lived a year and a day in the town, in order that it may be known whether or not he comes from a good place. . . .

9. And whoever does work on Saturday afternoon, or on the Eve of the Feast of Our Lady, or after Vespers on the Eve of the Feast of St. Julien, and completes the day by working, shall pay, if he be a master, 12 denarii, and if he be a journeyman, 6 denarii. And whoever works in the four days of Christmas, or in the eight days of Easter, or in the eight days of Pentecost, owes 5 solidi. . . .

11. And an apprentice owes to the Fraternity for his apprenticeship 5 solidi. . . .

13. And whoever does work in defiance of the mayor and aldermen shall pay 5 solidi. . . .

16. And those who are fed at the expense of the city shall be put to work first. And he who slights them for strangers owes 5 solidi: but if the stranger be put to work he cannot be removed as long as the master wishes to keep him. . . . And when a master does not work hard he pays 5 solidi, and a journeyman 2 solidi. . . .

18. And after the half year the mayor and aldermen shall fix such wages as he ought to have. . . .

20. And whoever maligns the mayor and aldermen, that is while on the business of the Fraternity, shall pay 5 solidi. . . .

23. And if a draper or a merchant has work to do in his house, he may take such workmen as he wishes into his house, so long as the work be done in his house. And he who infringes this shall give 5 solidi to the Fraternity. . . .

25. And each master ought to have his arms when he is summoned. And if he has not he should pay 20 solidi. . . .

32. And if a master does not give a journeyman such wage as is his due, then he shall pay 5 solidi.

33. And he who overlooks the forfeits of this Fraternity, if he does not wish to pay them when the mayor and aldermen summon him either for the army or the district, then he owes 10 solidi, and he shall not work at the trade until he has paid. Every forfeit of 5 solidi, and the fines which the mayor and aldermen command, shall be written down. All the fines of the Fraternity ought to go for the purchase of arms and for the needs of the Fraternity.

34. And whatever brother of this Fraternity shall betray his confrère for others shall not work at the trade for a year and a day. . . .

36. And should a master of this Fraternity die and leave a male heir he may learn the trade anywhere where there is no apprentice.

37. And no apprentice shall cut to the selvage[5] for half a year, and this is to obtain good work. And no master or journeyman may cut by himself because

---

5. **selvage:** very edge of the cloth.

no one can measure cloth well alone. And whoever infringes this rule shall pay 5 solidi to the Fraternity for each offense.

38. Any brother whatsoever who lays hands on, or does wrong to, the mayor and aldermen of this Fraternity, as long as they work for the city and the Fraternity, shall not work at his trade in the city for a year and a day.

And if he should do so, let him be banished from the town for a year and a day, saving the appeal to Monseigneur the King and his Castellan. . . .

Sources 7 and 8 from Carolly Erickson, The Records of Medieval Europe *(Garden City, New York: Anchor, 1971), p. 238. Translated by Carolly Erickson.*

7. Judgment Against a Draper in Flanders, mid-14th century

When Jacquemars des Mares, a draper, brought one of his cloths to the great cloth hall of Arras and sold it, the aforesaid cloth was examined by the *espincheurs*[6] as is customary, and at the time they had it weighed, it was half a pound over the legal weight. Then, because of certain suspicions which arose, they had the cloth dried, and when it was dry, it weighed a half pound less than the legal weight. The *espincheur* brought the misdeed to the attention of the Twenty;[7] Jacquemars was fined 100 shillings.

8. Dispute Between Master Fullers and Their Apprentices in Flanders, 1345

A point of discussion was mooted between the apprentice fullers on the one hand, and the master fullers on the other. The apprentices held that, as they laid out in a letter, no one could have work done in his house without taking apprentices. . . . For they complained of fulling masters who had their children work in their houses, without standing [for jobs] in the public square like the other apprentices, and they begged that their letter be answered. The fulling masters stated certain arguments to the contrary. The aldermen sent for both parties and for the Twenty also and asked the masters if indeed they kept their children as apprentices; each master said he did. It was declared by the aldermen that every apprentice must remain in the public square, as reason demanded.

Done in the year of 1344 [1345], in the month of February, and through a full sitting of the aldermen.

6. **espincheur:** cloth inspector.
7. **Twenty:** court of twenty men, made up of members of the city council.

Source 9 from Merry E. Wiesner, translator, unpublished decisions in Nuremberg Stadtarchiv, Quellen zur Nürnbergische Geschichte, Rep. F5, no. 68/I, fol. 58 (1577).

9. Decision by the
Nuremberg City Council, 1577

The honorable city council has decided to deny the request of Barbara Hansmesser that she be allowed to dye wool because the blanketweavers' guild has so adamantly opposed it. Because her husband is not a citizen, they are both ordered to get out of the city and find work in some other place, with the warning that if they are found in the vicinity of this city, and are doing any work here, work will be taken from them and the yarn cut to pieces. They can count on this.

Sources 10 and 11 from Merry E. Wiesner, translator, unpublished supplications in Frankfurt Stadtarchiv, Zünfte, Ugb. C-50, Ss, no. 4; Ugb. C-32, R, no. 1.

10. Widow's Supplication to
the Frankfurt City Council,
late 16th century

Distinguished and honorable sirs, I, a poor and distressed widow, wish to respectfully report in what manner earlier this year I spun some pounds of yarn, 57 to be exact, for the use of my own household. I wanted to take the yarn to be woven into cloth, but didn't know whom I should give it to so that I could get it worked into cloth the quickest and earliest.

Therefore I was talking to some farm women from Bornheim, who were selling their produce in front of the shoemakers' guild house, and they told me about a weaver that they had in Bornheim who made good cloth and could also make it quickly. I let him know—through the farmers' wives—that I wanted him to make my cloth. I got the yarn together and sent my children to carry it to him; as they were on their way, the weavers here grabbed the yarn forcefully from my children, and took it to their guild house. They said they had ordinances which forbade taking yarn to foreigners to weave, and told me they would not return it unless I paid a fine.

I then went to the lord mayors, asking them about this ordinance that would let people confiscate things without warning from the public streets. They said they didn't known about any such ordinance, and that my yarn should have long been returned to me. I then went to the overseer of the guild, master Adlaff Zimmermann who lives by the Eschenheimer tower, who answered me with rough, harsh words that they would in no way return my yarn to me, and that the guild did have such an ordinance.

Therefore I respectfully request, if they do have such an ordinance, I didn't know anything about it, and so ask you humbly and in God's name to tell the weavers to return my yarn. If, according to this ordinance, I am supposed to pay a fine, they should take it from the yarn, and give the rest back. I ask this of your honorable sirs, as the protectors of widows and orphans, and pray that you will help me.

Your humble servant, Agatha, the widow of the late Conrad Gaingen.

11. Widow's Supplication to the Frankfurt City Council, late 16th century

Most honorable and merciful gentlemen, you certainly know what a heavy and hard cross God has laid on me, and in what a miserable situation I find myself, after the much too early death of my late husband, with my young children, all of them still minors and some still nursing. This unfortunate situation is well known everywhere.

Although in consideration of my misfortune most Christian hearts would have gladly let me continue in my craft and occupation, and allowed me to earn a little piece of bread, instead the overseers of the woolweavers' guild came to me as soon as my husband had died, in my sorrow and even in my own house. Against all Christian charity, they began to order changes in my workshop with very harsh and menacing words. They specifically ordered that my apprentice, whom I had raised and trained at great cost and who had just come to be of use to me in the craft, leave me and go to them, which would be to their great advantage but my greater disadvantage. They ordered this on the pretense that there was no longer a master here so he could not finish his training.

Honorable sirs, I then humbly put myself under the protection of the lord mayors here, and asked that the two journeymen and the apprentice be allowed to continue on in their work as they had before unimpeded until a final judgment was reached in the matter. Despite this, one of the weavers began to shout at my journeymen whenever he saw them, especially if there were other people on the street. In his unhindered and unwarranted boldness, he yelled that my workshop was not honorable, and all journeymen who worked there were thieves and rascals. After doing this for several days, he and several others came into my workshop on a Saturday, and, bitter and jealous, pushed my journeymen out. They began to write to all places where this craft is practiced to tell other masters not to accept anyone who had worked in my workshop.

I now humbly beg you, my honorable and gracious sirs, protect me and my hungry children from such abuse, shame, and insult. Help my journeymen, who were so undeservedly insulted, to regain their honor. I beg you, as the protector of humble widows, to let my apprentice stay with me, as apprentices are allowed to stay in the workshops of widows throughout the entire Holy Roman Empire, as long as there are journeymen, whether or not there is a master present. Protect me from any further insults of the woolweavers' guild, which does nothing to increase the honor of our city, which you, honorable sirs, are charged to uphold. I plead with you to grant me my request, and allow me to continue my workshop.

Source 12 from Roy C. Cave and Herbert H. Coulson, A Source Book for Medieval Economic History *(New York: Biblo and Tannen, 1965), pp. 256–257.*

12. Two Apprenticeship Contracts, 13th century

Be it known to present and future aldermen that Ouede Ferconne apprentices Michael, her son, to Matthew Haimart on security of her house, her person, and her chattels,[8] and the share that Michael ought to have in them, so that Matthew Haimart will teach him to weave in four years, and that he (Michael) will have shelter, and learn his trade there without board. And if there should be reason within two years for Michael to default she will return him, and Ouede Ferconne, his mother, guarantees this on the security of her person and goods. And if she should wish to purchase his freedom for the last two years she may do so for thirty-three solidi, and will pledge for that all that has been stated. And if he should not free himself of the last two years let him return, and Ouede Ferconne, his mother, pledges this with her person and her goods. And the said Ouede pledges that if Matthew Haimart suffers either loss or damage through Michael, her son, she will restore the loss and damage on the security of herself and all her goods, should Michael do wrong.

April the ninth. I, Peter Borre, in good faith and without guile, place with you, Peter Feissac, weaver, my son Stephen, for the purpose of learning the trade or craft of weaving, to live at your house, and to do work for you from the feast of Easter next for four continuous years, promising you by this agreement to take care that my son does the said work, and that he will be faithful and trustworthy in all that he does, and that he will neither steal nor take anything away from you, nor flee nor depart from you for any reason, until he has completed his apprenticeship. And I promise you by this agreement that I will reimburse you for all damages or losses that you incur or sustain on my behalf, pledging all my goods, etc.; renouncing the benefit of all

8. **chattels:** personal property.

laws, etc. And I, the said Peter Feissac, promise you, Peter Borre, that I will teach your son faithfully and will provide food and clothing for him.

Done at Marseilles, near the tables of the money-changers. Witnesses, etc.

Source 13 from Robert S. Lopez and Irving W. Raymond, editors and translators, Medieval Trade in the Mediterranean World *(New York: Columbia University Press, 1955), pp. 263–265, no. 138.*

13. Insurance Contracts from Pisa, 1384

This is a book of Francesco of Prato and partners, residing in Pisa, and we shall write in it all insurances we shall make in behalf of others. May God grant us profit from these and protect us from dangers.

[*Seal of Francesco son of Marco*]

A memorandum that on September 7, 1384, in behalf of Baldo Ridolfi and partners we insured for 100 gold florins wool in the ship of Guilhem Sale, Catalan, [in transit] from Peñiscola to Porto Pisano. And from the said 100 florins we received 3 gold florins in cash, and we insured against all risks, as is evident by a record by the hand of Gherardo d'Ormanno which is under-signed by our hand.

Said ship arrived safely in Porto Pisano and unloaded on . . . October, 1384, and we are free from the insurance.

A memorandum that on September 10 in behalf of Ambrogio, son of Bino Bini, we insured for 200 gold florins Milanese cloth in the ship of Bartolomeo Vitale, [in transit] from Porto Pisano to Palermo. And from the said 200 florins we received 8 gold florins, charged to the debit account of Ambrogio on *c.* 174, and no other record appears [written] by the hand of any broker.

Arrived in Palermo safely.

First graph in Source 14 from R. S. Lopez, "Hard Times and Investment in Culture," The Renaissance: Medieval or Modern (Boston: D.C. Heath, 1959); second graph from H. van Werveke, "De omgang van de Ieperse lakenproductie in de veertiende eeuw," Medelelingen, K. Vlaamse Acad. voor Wetensch., Letteren en schone Kunsten van Belgie (1947). Both reprinted in Harry A. Miskimin, The Economy of Early Renaissance Europe, 1300–1460 (Englewood Cliffs, N.J.: Prentice-Hall, 1969), p. 94.

14. Trends in the Cloth Trade in Florence and Ypres

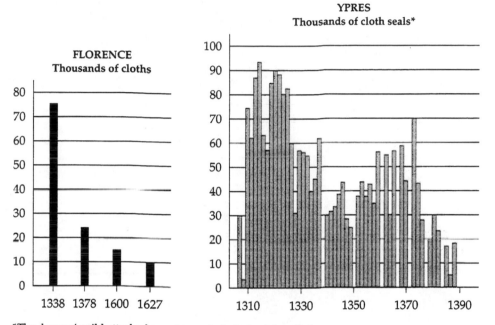

*The drapers' guild attached a seal to each cloth that it handled.

Table in Source 15 from A. R. Bridbury, Economic Growth: England in the Later Middle Ages *(London: G. Allen and Unwin, 1962), p. 32. Used by permission of the author; graphs adapted from H. C. Darby, editor,* A New Historical Geography of England *(Cambridge, England: Cambridge University Press, 1973), p. 219. Reprinted with permission of Cambridge University Press.*

15. English Exports of Raw Wool and Cloth, Based on Customs Records, ca 1350–1550

Years	Raw wool (sacks)	Woollen cloths (as equivalent to sacks of raw wool)
1361–70	28,302	3,024
1371–80	23,241	3,432
1381–90	17,988	5,521
1391–1400	17,679	8,967
1401–10	13,922	7,651
1411–20	13,487	6,364
1421–30	13,696	9,309
1431–40	7,377	10,051
1441–50	9,398	11,803
1471–80	9,299	10,125
1481–90	8,858	12,230
1491–1500	8,149	13,891

1 **Raw Wool Exports**

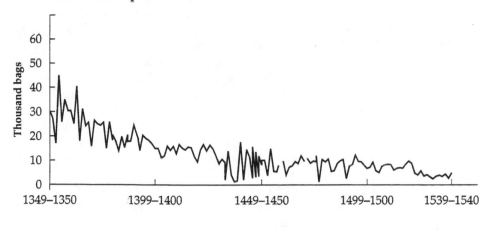

2 **Cloth Exports**

The records you have read shed some light on a wide variety of issues in the medieval cloth trade, as well as providing information on other social and economic matters. To draw some general conclusions and answer the questions for this chapter, you will need to go back to your list of goals, actions, and conflicts, and put together the information from the various sources. Because our focus here is on cloth production and sales, you will also need to leave aside what you have learned about other issues, though this may be very interesting to you. Investigating social and economic questions often involves not only uncovering sources that deal with your problem directly, but also extracting small bits of information from sources that cover a great many other areas, such as the city council records of Sources 9 through 11. Being a social historian requires that you discipline yourself to stick to the topic; though it may be fascinating to read every entry about every issue, this will not help with the completion of your research project.

Going back, then, to your list: How would you describe the key aims of territorial rulers regarding the cloth trade? Of local ruling bodies such as city councils? Do the sources you have read here lead you to support the thesis that city ordinances generally reflect the aims of cloth merchants? How might the aims of territorial rulers and merchants come into conflict? (For one example, how might cloth merchants or artisans already working in cloth production in Courtrai feel about the tax breaks that the Countess of Flanders gave to immigrants into the city in Source 3? What might cloth merchants do in response to this to maintain their monopoly on the cloth trade? For another, how might merchants in raw wool have regarded the changing nature of English exports as traced in Source 15 and the government tariff policies that were responsible for this?) In addition to shaping government policies, what private actions do you find merchants engaging in to achieve their goals?

Turning to the relationship of the merchants—or the city councils, usually dominated by merchants—to the artisans: What actions by artisans are explicitly prohibited in city ordinances or guild charters? (See Sources

4, 5, and 6.) How do these prohibitions reflect merchant aims? How would you describe the attitudes of merchants toward artisans—suspicious, friendly, hostile, paternalistic, fraternal? How did groups or individuals use the conflicts between these two to their own advantage? (The best examples here are the supplications quoted in Sources 10 and 11 and the dispute recorded in Source 8. To whom did the women and the apprentices turn to for help, and about which groups were they complaining? In the women's supplications, what sort of language do they use to persuade authorities to help them?)

Turning to the workplace itself: How would you characterize the atmosphere in the houses of most woolworkers—collegial and friendly, or divided and somewhat hostile? As you have no doubt noticed, ordinances regulated not simply individual workers, but their families as well. What special privileges were given to members of the master's family? Who objected to these privileges, and why? How did the guilds treat widows of their members? Do you see any discrepancy in the discussion of widows in the ordinances and in the actual treatment of a member's widow in Source 11? How do the guilds react to women working who were not the wives or widows of guild members? Would you regard the guilds as generally helpful to families or helpful to only certain types of families? Along with the privileges accorded to the master's family members, what other sources of dispute between masters and journeymen, and between masters and apprentices, are mentioned in the sources? How might the goals of the craft guild masters and those of the merchants come into conflict in the handling of these disputes?

You are now ready to answer the questions posed by this chapter: What were the key economic and social goals of governments, merchant-capitalists, and artisans regarding the cloth trade, and how did they seek to achieve these aims? What economic and social conflicts emerged as the cloth trade grew and changed?

EPILOGUE

Because of its capitalist organization and complex division of labor, the medieval cloth trade is often seen as a harbinger of modern economic developments. As you have read the sources for this chapter, you have probably discovered other areas in which there are parallels between the medieval cloth trade and the modern economy. Many of the goals of governments, merchants, and artisans that we have seen expressed in the medieval sources are shared by modern governments, corporations, and unions: the expansion of domestic production, the maintenance of order in the workplace, the limitation of risk, the highest level of profit, steady wages and job security, protection from foreign competition, the replacement of exports of raw materials with exports of manufactured products. As they were in the Middle Ages, these goals are often contradictory, if not mutually exclusive.

Many of the actions taken by medieval authorities and individuals continue to appear on the evening news as it reports economic developments: protectionist legislation, tax breaks to promote the development of industry and job creation, preferential treatment for certain groups, the transfer of jobs to places where wages are lower or workers are less likely to strike, immigration policies that promote the immigration of workers with specific skills, fraud and falsification of merchandise in an attempt to increase profits.

Many of the conflicts we have seen here still beset workplaces in the twentieth century: disputes over wage levels and the right to work; disagreements between labor and management over who controls certain aspects of the workplace; conflicts between older and younger workers, now often expressed as issues of seniority; and demands that employers pay more attention to the family responsibilities of their employees and make the workplace more "family friendly." Methods of enforcing aims and resolving conflicts that were tried in the Middle Ages are still often tried today, such as turning to outside authorities or arbitrators, revolts and strikes, and blacklisting and fines.

Though in the contemporary economy production of many types of goods often faces conflicts—automobiles, electronic and computer equipment, and agricultural products usually gain the most headlines—cloth and clothing production is still an important issue for many nations, corporations, and unions. Many of the commercials promoting the retail giant Wal-Mart's policy of buying products made in the United States highlight cloth and clothing manufacturers. The attempts by U.S. immigration authorities to make employers responsible for making sure their foreign-born employees have the necessary work permits have targeted sportswear makers in New York and California who hire undocumented aliens. Lawsuits by U.S. companies charging copyright infringement are often brought against foreign manufacturers of such items as T-shirts and beach towels. Just as cloth production in the Middle Ages was a harbinger of trends and conflicts in the modern economy, cloth production at the end of the twentieth century may also be a harbinger of the future. The internationalization of the marketplace and work force that it points to perhaps would not seem so strange to the Countess of Flanders or Francesco of Prato, nor would the difficulties that can result from this seem so strange to the woolworkers of Florence or Ypres.

CHAPTER TEN

LAY PIETY AND

HERESY IN

THE LATE MIDDLE AGES

During the late Middle Ages, the Christian church went through a period of turmoil and disunity, with corruption and abuse evident at all levels of its hierarchy. Though the Church was officially an independent institution, many of its officials, such as bishops and archbishops, were actually chosen by secular nobles and rulers, who picked their own relatives or others who would do as they were told. Officials who were elected or appointed from within the Church itself were often selected for their administrative and legal skills, not for their piety, high moral standards, or religious devotion. These problems extended all the way to the papacy, which for much of the fourteenth century was located not in Rome but in Avignon in southern France, where it was dominated by the French monarchy. During this time

the papacy lost its stature as an international power and had difficulty raising revenue from many parts of Europe, especially from the English, who rightly suspected that money sent to the pope might end up in the coffers of the French king, with whom they were at war. The Avignon popes had ever-increasing needs for revenue because they had to hire mercenaries to keep the Papal States in Italy under control, build palaces and churches in Avignon that reflected the power and prestige of the papacy, and pay the salaries of a growing corps of lawyers and bureaucrats who administered the papal empire.

The papacy devised a number of ways to meet its increasing need for money. Though the outright selling of Church offices, termed *simony*, was strictly forbidden, the popes required all candidates to pay for the privilege of taking over a vacant office, then hand over a large share of their first year's revenues directly to the papacy. Official prohibitions, such as those against priests having concubines or giving Church land to family members, could be ignored if the cleric paid the pope for a special dispensation. The papacy also collected money directly from laypeople, charging fees for clerical services such as marriage or baptism and for dispensations that legitimized children born out of wedlock.

The most lucrative source of income for the papacy proved to be the granting of *indulgences*. Indulgences were based on three doctrines developed by the medieval Church—the sacrament of penance, the concept of Purgatory, and the Treasury of Merit. To partake of the sacrament of penance, a believer was to confess all sins to a priest and be truly sorry, or contrite, for them, after which the priest absolved the believer, often requiring him or her to carry out certain acts as penance for these sins, such as saying prayers or going on pilgrimages. According to Church doctrine, penance did not end with death but might be extended into Purgatory, where Christians spent time atoning for the sins for which they had not done earthly penance. Only after a set time in Purgatory could most Christians be admitted to heaven. (Those who were going to hell, on the other hand, went directly there.)

Along with the doctrines of penance and Purgatory, the Church also developed the idea of the Treasury of Merit. This treasury was seen as a collection of all the superlative good deeds and meritorious acts that the apostles, saints, and other good people had done during their lives, which the pope as head of the Church could dispense as he wished through the granting of indulgences. The recipient of an indulgence received a share in the Treasury of Merit that took the place of having to do individual penance. Originally granted to people who performed special services for the Church, such as participating in crusades, indulgences gradually came to be exchanged for cash contributions. Though official theology taught that priestly absolution and true contrition were still necessary, unscrupulous indulgence peddlers often sold indulgences outright as easy substitutes for penance. Indulgences also began to be granted to relieve people of time in Purgatory and even to allow believers to shorten deceased relatives' time in Purgatory. To many people, it seemed that the Church was teaching that one could buy one's way into heaven, though this was not actually so.

Because Church officials at all levels were often chosen for their family connections or their legal and financial skills, they also bent official doctrines and saw their posts primarily in terms of income rather than spiritual duties. Bishops spent much of their time at the papal court trying to win the pope's favor and squeezed all possible revenues out of their dioceses in order to pay for their offices. These absentee officials, who left the affairs of the diocese in the hands of substitutes, often had very little idea about the needs or problems of their territory. Those who were successful in gaining papal backing might be appointed to many different offices simultaneously; they collected the income from all their posts, appointed badly paid proxies to carry out their duties, and might actually never even visit the diocese over which they were bishop.

With so little supervision, parish priests and monks were sometimes lax in their standards of morality and spiritual observance. Frequently parish priests were poor and badly educated, for most of the Church's wealth stayed in the hands of higher officials, who provided no opportunity for priests to gain an education; some priests did not even know Latin, but simply recited the Mass by rote without understanding what they were saying. During the week they farmed just as their parishioners did, for the income from tithes was not sufficient to support them. Some of the monasteries and convents maintained high standards, but others, caught in the squeeze for revenue, admitted any applicant who would pay the entrance fee, without determining if the person was fit for the monastic life.

With the Church embroiled in these problems, we might expect that people would turn away from religion to concentrate on other aspects of life, but this was not the case. Religion continued to dominate the lives of people in the late Middle Ages, which was in fact perhaps the most religious period in all of European history. What did change, however, was how people expressed and experienced their Christian faith. Not surprisingly, they turned away somewhat from the institutional Church and sought more direct paths to God through individual actions.

Much of this lay piety was supported by the Church hierarchy because it did not question basic theological doctrines such as life after death; the importance of the sacraments of baptism, communion, and penance; the honor owed to saints and their relics; and the right of the pope to grant indulgences, collect taxes, and determine correct doctrine. Pious laypeople also made frequent donations, which swelled the Church's revenue. Some individuals and groups went beyond personal piety, however, to question the Church's wealth and many of its central doctrines. The Church declared such people heretics and set up inquisitorial courts to investigate, try, and condemn them.

Your task in this chapter will be to examine late medieval lay piety and religious practices, both those approved by the institutional Church and those condemned as heresy. How did common people in the Middle Ages experience and express their religious faith? How did the Church as an institution respond to laypeople's ideas and actions?

SOURCES AND METHOD

Medieval Christianity, multifaceted in nature, may be explored from a number of angles. Christianity was a faith shared by most people living in Europe, whether they were highly educated or uneducated, wealthy or poor. We can find information about how educated men understood and interpreted Christianity fairly easily by reading theological treatises and official Church decisions, but these may not accurately reflect the religious views of the majority. For this perspective, we must turn to a much smaller group of sources that throw light on the religious beliefs of the common people.

Learning about and reconstructing the ideas of common people in the premodern period is extremely difficult, for such people were by and large illiterate. The surviving written records of their thoughts and actions thus all come through the filter of literate observers, whose perspective and understanding of events might differ radically from the participants'. This is especially a problem when we are examining religious ideas, for most people who could read and write in the Middle Ages were clerics and thus part of the institutional Church. It was often hard for such observers to be objective about criticism directed against the Church, or even to comprehend how uneducated people interpreted and understood theological concepts.

Because of these problems, we must ask several questions before turning to any written source about popular religious belief. Who actually wrote the document? Was the writer recording the words of an illiterate person or simply describing actions he or she had observed? Why was this piece written? If the writer is recording the words of someone else, did he or she clearly understand the language being spoken, or might there be some problems because of dialect? Is the writer translating a vernacular language such as English or French into Latin, and so possibly mistranslating religious ideas? Why were this person's thoughts recorded—did that person wish it or did the authorities, as was the case with trial records?

Artistic evidence might seem more direct, for people who could not read or write sculpted, painted, and made stained-glass windows. They did not always choose their own subject matter or sign their works, however, so medieval art does not directly express the individual personality and concerns of the artist in the way that modern art does. What it does reveal, however, is how common people learned about religion from windows and statues depicting biblical and other Christian scenes. We can also use frequently recurring images as a rough guide to popular religious sentiments, for individuals and groups commissioned art that reflected their own concerns. The dominance of certain images shifted throughout the Middle Ages as people's attitudes toward the Church and the right way to approach God changed.

Using artistic evidence as a source of information about popular belief requires a different set of initial questions from those needed for written evidence. Where and when was the piece probably made? Can we learn anything about the artist or patron, such as his or her identity? Where was the piece originally displayed? Are the materials simple enough that the piece could have been ordered or purchased by someone who was not wealthy? Is the image common or unusual?

Keeping in mind the limitations we have noted, turn now to the written sources. The first two are *sermon stories*, tales of miracles that learned preachers used in their public sermons; later they were collected by many different preachers and used widely in sermons all over Europe. These stories are consequently not written *by* laypeople but *for* them and reflect official Church doctrines. They do not present sophisticated theology, however, but show us how common people learned about Christianity. As you read, note the kinds of people who appear as main characters. Why would preachers use characters like these?

In the first sermon, to whom does the woman turn for assistance? When her prayers are not answered immediately, what does she do? Why would the preacher condone such a dramatic action? (To answer this question, think about the impact this story would have on the female members of the audience; Mary may not have responded instantly to prayer, but, like most mothers, she did so immediately once her child

was taken from her.) What qualities of Mary does this story emphasize?

The second sermon discusses an important element in lay piety, the belief in saints and relics. Does the author support or condemn these beliefs? Is it the relics themselves or faith in them that is important? Why would the author, himself a priest, describe the priest in the story as "wily" and "wicked"? (Again, keep in mind the audience. Given the problems most people recognized in the Church, how would a lay audience respond to a story in which the hero is also a layperson?)

Though most laypeople in the Middle Ages could not read, some of them could, and one of the most popular types of reading material was stories about the lives of saints, termed *hagiography*. Like sermon stories, hagiography often presented quite ordinary people whose lives were touched by God and who could serve as an inspiration. Source 3 comes from the best-known collection of saints' lives, *The Golden Legend*, first composed in the late thirteenth century by an Italian bishop, and then translated and recopied throughout Europe during the late Middle Ages. It describes events from the life of St. Nicholas (the original Santa Claus) and miracles attributed to him after his death, and would have been familiar even to those who could not read because they would have heard this story from those who could. What type of people does Nicholas assist? What sort of problems does he solve for them?

Taking these three sources together, what types of actions do you think preachers and writers of hagiography were trying to encourage in people? What traits of lay piety did they praise?

The remaining written sources directly record the thoughts and actions of laypeople, some of whom the Church supported and some of whom it condemned. None could read or write Latin, and so they qualified as unlearned by medieval standards, though some could read their own vernacular language. Source 4 is taken from the *Revelations* of Bridget of Sweden, a noblewoman who lived from 1303 to 1373. After her husband's death, Bridget traveled to Rome, where she began to see visions and give advice based on these visions to both laypeople and Church officials. Because she could not speak Latin, she wrote or dictated her visions in Swedish; these were later translated by her confessors and eventually were published in Latin. At the end of her life, Bridget made a pilgrimage to Jerusalem, where she had the visions reprinted here. How would you describe these visions? How did the fact that she was a woman shape her religious experience?

Source 5 is drawn from the first autobiography ever written in English, that of Margery Kempe, who was probably born in 1373, the same year Bridget died. Kempe, a middle-class woman from the town of King's Lynn, was illiterate in English as well as Latin. Although she was married and had fourteen children, she began to see visions in which Christ demanded that she set herself apart from most women. At the end of her most unusual life, she dictated her autobiography to several male scribes, who wrote it down in English. As you read, note how Kempe describes her actions and behavior. What made her most open to criticism? How does she defend her actions? She refers to herself, always in the third person, as "this creature." What does this practice indicate about her self-consciousness? Do her actions reflect this self-image? What aspects of Christianity most inspire or disturb her? How was the official reaction to her influenced by the fact that she was a woman?

The last two written sources come from trial records. Source 6 contains six testimonies from the Inquisition carried out between 1318 and 1325 by Jacques Fournier, Bishop of Pamiers in southern France. All six accused were illiterate peasants who spoke Occitan, a regional dialect; their words were translated by scribes into Latin. Fournier launched the Inquisition because he suspected large numbers of people in his district to be *Albigensians* (also called Cathars), followers of a heretical movement that rejected many basic Church doctrines. Albigensians regarded the material world as evil and not made by God and did not believe in the possibility of eternal life. They denied the power of many Church ceremonies and rituals and urged that any Church leader, including the pope, should not be obeyed if he did not live up to rigorous moral standards.

As you read the testimonies, note which specific Christian beliefs were being challenged. Given their statements, would you call the peasants who were being questioned Christians? How might problems of translation have affected the records? How might the fact that this was a trial have affected what the individuals said?

Source 7 comes from a heresy trial of sixty people suspected of Lollard beliefs, conducted in the diocese of Norwich, England, between 1428 and 1431. Lollards followed the ideas of John Wyclif, an English scholar who lived in the fourteenth century; the selection itself presents all of the basic Lollard beliefs. Most of the trial record is in Latin because it was conducted by ecclesiastical authorities and recorded by clerics, but a few of the confessions were written down in English. The selection here is one of those, with the spelling modernized. What does the accused admit to having believed? The list of unacceptable beliefs in many heresy trials reflects not only the ideas of the person confessing but also those the inquisitors thought were especially dangerous and in need of suppression. What did the inquisitors in this case appear particularly concerned about? How would this emphasis have shaped the confession? How was the accused to prove he had given up his heresy? Given his beliefs, would you call the person under questioning a Christian?

Now examine the two visual sources. Both are wooden statues carved in the fourteenth or fifteenth centuries by unknown artists and originally placed in churches in southern Germany. They are examples of the two most common religious images of the late Middle Ages. What aspects of popular belief that you have identified from the written sources do they reflect? Mary is shown wearing a crown and holding an orb, a sphere representing the world that normally was carried by monarchs. What qualities are emphasized through this depiction? Christ is shown in a dramatic pose of suffering. What does this attitude emphasize about his nature? Given what you now know about how common people understood Christianity, why would these two subjects be the most popular? Why do you think there is no depiction of God the Father?

227

Source 1 from C. C. S. Bland, editor and translator, Miracles of the Blessed Virgin Mary *(London: Routledge, 1928), p. 118.*

1. A Sermon Story About the Virgin Mary, 13th century

A certain woman of simple and upright life used to worship the Holy Mary, Mother of God, often strewing flowers and herbs before her image.

Now it chanced that the woman's only son was taken prisoner. And the mother weeping for him would not be comforted, and prayed with all her heart to the Blessed Virgin Mary for her son's deliverance. But seeing it was all in vain, she entered the church and thus addressed the image of the Blessed Virgin, "O Blessed Virgin Mary, often have I asked thee for the deliverance of my son and thou hast not heard me. Therefore, as my son was taken from me, so will I take away thine and will put him in durance as hostage for mine."

And taking the image of the Child from the bosom of Mary, she went home, wrapped him up in a clean cloth, and shut him up carefully in a chest. And, behold, the following night the Blessed Mary appeared to the captive youth bidding him to go forth and said to him: "Tell your mother to give me my Son." And he coming to his mother, described how he had been set free. But she with great rejoicing carried back the image of Jesus to Mary and gave her thanks.

Source 2 from Dana Carleton Munro, editor and translator, Translations and Reprints from the Original Sources of European History, *vol. 2, no. 4 (Philadephia: University of Pennsylvania Press, no date), p. 14.*

2. A Sermon Story About Relics, 13th century

A certain knight loved most ardently the above-mentioned martyr, St. Thomas of Canterbury,[1] and sought everywhere to obtain some relic of him. When a certain wily priest, in whose house he was staying, heard of this he said to him, "I have by me a bridle which St. Thomas used for a long time,

---

1. **Thomas Becket:** the Archbishop of Canterbury who was murdered on the steps of the cathedral on the orders of Henry II for opposing the king's wishes. He was quickly made a saint, and Canterbury became the most popular pilgrimage site in England.

and I have often experienced its virtues." When the knight heard this, and believed it, he joyfully paid the priest the money which the latter demanded and received the bridle with great devotion.

God truly, to whom nothing is impossible, wishing to reward the faith of the knight and for the honor of his martyr, deigned to work many miracles through the same bridle. The knight seeing this founded a church in honor of the martyr and in it he placed as a relic the bridle of that most wicked priest.

Source 3 from Iacobus de Voragine, The Golden Legend, *included in* Lives of the Saints, *translated by William Caxton and selected and edited by George V. O'Neill, S.J. (Cambridge: Cambridge University Press, 1914), pp. 62–71.*

3. Extracts from the Life of St. Nicholas, *The Golden Legend*, ca 1270

Nicholas, citizen of the city of Patras, was born of rich and holy kin, and his father was Epiphanes and his mother Johane. In his young age he eschewed the plays and japes[2] of other young children. He used and haunted gladly holy Church; and all that he might understand of holy Scripture he executed it in deed and work after his power. And when his father and mother were departed out of this life, he began to think how he might distribute his riches, and not to the praising of the world but to the honor and glory of God. And it was so that one, his neighbor, had then three daughters, virgins, and he was a nobleman: but for the poverty of them together, they were constrained and in very purpose to abandon them to sin. And when the holy man Nicholas knew hereof he had great horror of this, and threw by night secretly into the house of the man a mass of gold wrapped in a cloth. And when the man arose in the morning, he found this mass of gold, and rendered to God therefor great thankings, and therewith he married his oldest daughter. And a little while after this holy servant of God threw in another mass of gold; which the man found, and thanked God, and purposed to wake for to know him that so had aided him in his poverty. And after a few days Nicholas doubled the mass of gold, and cast it into the house of this man. He awoke by the sound of the gold, and followed Nicholas, which fled from him, and he said to him: "Sir, flee not away so but that I may see and know thee." Then he ran after him more hastily, and knew that it was Nicholas; and anon he kneeled down, and would have kissed his feet, but the holy man would not, but required him not to tell nor discover this thing as long as he lived.

2. **japes:** toys.

It is read in a chronicle that the blessed Nicholas was at the Council of Nice; and on a day, as a ship with mariners were in perishing on the sea, they prayed and required devoutly Nicholas, servant of God, saying: "If those things that we have heard of thee said to be true, prove them now." And anon a man appeared in his likeness, and said: "Lo! see ye me not? ye called me"; and then he began to help them in their exploit of the sea, and anon the tempest ceased. And when they were come to his church, they knew him without any man to show him to them, and yet they had never seen him. And then they thanked God and him of their deliverance. And he bade them to attribute it to the mercy of God and to their belief, and nothing to his merits.

It was so on a time that all the province of S. Nicholas suffered great famine, in such wise that vitaille[3] failed. And then this holy man heard say that certain ships laden with wheat were arrived in the haven. And anon he went thither and prayed the mariners that they would succor the perished at least with an hundred muyes of wheat of every ship. And they said: "Father, we dare not, for it is meted and measured, and we must give reckoning thereof in the garners[4] of the emperor in Alexandria." And the holy man said to them: "Do this that I have said to you, and I promise, in the truth of God, that it shall not be lessed or minished when ye shall come to the garners." And when they had delivered so much out of every ship, they came into Alexandria and delivered the measure that they had received. And then they recounted the miracle to the ministers of the emperor, and worshipped and praised strongly God and his servant Nicholas. Then this holy man distributed the wheat to every man after that he had need, in such wise that it sufficed for two years, not only for to sell but also to sow. . . .

And when it pleased Our Lord to have him depart out this world, he prayed Our Lord that he would send him his angels; and inclining his head he saw the angels come to him, whereby he knew well that he should depart, and began this holy Psalm: "In te domine speravi," unto "in manus tuas," and so saying: "Lord, into thine hands I commend my spirit," he rendered up his soul and died, the year of Our Lord three hundred and forty-three. . . .

There was a Jew that saw the virtuous miracles of S. Nicholas, and did do make an image of the saint, and set it in his house, and commanded him that he should keep well his house when he went out, and that he should keep well all his goods, saying to him: "Nicholas, lo! here be all my goods, I charge thee to keep them, and if thou keep them not well, I shall avenge me on thee in beating and tormenting thee." And on a time, when the Jew was out, thieves came and robbed all his goods, and left unborne away only the image. And when the Jew came home he found him robbed of all his goods. He areasoned the image, saying these words: "Sir Nicholas, I had set you in my house for to keep my goods from thieves, wherefore have ye not kept them? Ye shall receive sorrow and torments, and shall have pain for the thieves. I shall

3. **vitaille:** food.

4. **garners:** storehouses for grain.

avenge my loss and refrain my woodness in beating thee." And then took the Jew the image, and beat it, and tormented it cruelly. Then happed a great marvel, for when the thieves departed the goods, the holy saint, like as he had been in his array, appeared to the thieves, and said to them: "Wherefore have I been beaten so cruelly for you and have so many torments? See how my body is hewed and broken; see how that the red blood runneth down by my body; go ye fast and restore it again, or else the ire of God Almighty shall make you as to be one out of his wit, and that all men shall know your felony, and that each of you shall be hanged." And they said: "Who art thou that sayest to us such things?" And he said to them: "I am Nicholas the servant of Jesu Christ, whom the Jew hath so cruelly beaten for his goods that ye bare away." Then they were afeared, and came to the Jew, and heard what he had done to the image, and they told him the miracle, and delivered to him again all his goods. And thus came the thieves to the way of truth, and the Jew to the way of Jesu Christ.

A man, for the love of his son, that went to school for to learn, hallowed,[5] every year, the feast of S. Nicholas much solemnly. On a time it happed that the father had to make ready the dinner, and called many clerks to this dinner. And the devil came to the gate in the habit of a pilgrim for to demand alms; and the father anon commanded his son that he should give alms to the pilgrim. He followed him as he went for to give to him alms, and when he came to the quarfox[6] the devil caught the child and strangled him. And when the father heard this he sorrowed much strongly and wept, and bare the body into his chamber, and began to cry for sorrow, and say: "Bright sweet son, how is it with thee? S. Nicholas, is this the guerdon[7] that ye have done to me because I have so long served you?" And as he said these words, and other semblable,[8] the child opened his eyes, and awoke like as he had been asleep, and arose up tofore all, and was raised from death to life.

Source 4 from Katharina M. Wilson, editor, Medieval Women Writers *(Athens: University of Georgia Press, 1984), p. 245. Selection translated by Barbara Obrist.*

4. Two Visions of Bridget of Sweden, 1370s

After this the Virgin Mary appeared again to me, in the same place, and said: it has been a long time since in Rome I promised you that I would show you here in Bethlehem how my offspring had been born. And although in Naples I showed you something of it, that is to say the way I was standing when I gave

5. **hallowed:** honored.
6. **quarfox:** crossroads.
7. **guerdon:** reward.
8. **semblable:** similar ones.

birth to my son, you still should know for sure that I stood and gave birth such as you have seen it now—my knees were bent and I was alone in the stable, praying; I gave birth to him with such exultation and joy of my soul that I had no difficulties when he got out of my body or any pain. Then I wrapped him in swaddling clothes that I had prepared long ago. When Joseph saw this he was astonished and full of joy and happiness, because I had given birth without any help.

At the same place where the Virgin Mary and Joseph were adoring the boy in the cradle, I also saw the shepherds, who had been watching their flocks, coming so that they could look at the child and adore it. When they saw the child, they first wanted to find out whether it was a male or a female, for angels had announced to them that the savior of the world had been born, and they had not said that it was a savioress. Then the Virgin Mary showed to them the nature and the male sex of the child. At once they adored him with great awe and joy. Afterward they returned, praising and glorifying God for all they had heard and seen.

Source 5 from W. Butler-Bowdon, editor, The Book of Margery Kempe *(London: Oxford University Press, 1936), pp. 41–42, 86–88, 161–165, 167–168. Reprinted by permission of Oxford University Press.*

5. From the Autobiography of Margery Kempe, ca 1430

This creature, when Our Lord had forgiven her her sin, as has been written before, had a desire to see those places where He was born, and where He suffered His Passion,[9] and where He died, with other holy places where He was in His life, and also after His resurrection.

As she was in these desires, Our Lord bade her, in her mind, two years ere she went, that she should go to Rome, to Jerusalem and to Saint James,[10] and she would fain have gone but she had no money.

And then she said to Our Lord:—"Where shall I get money to go with to these Holy Places?"

Our Lord answered to her:—"I shall send thee friends enough in divers countries of England to help thee. And, daughter, I shall go with thee in every country and provide for thee, I shall lead thee thither, and bring thee back again in safety. And no Englishman shall die in the ship that thou art in. I shall

9. **Passion:** the crucifixion.
10. **St. James of Compostella:** a cathedral in northwestern Spain.

keep thee from all wicked men's power. And, daughter, I say to thee that I will that thou wearest clothes of white and no other colour, for thou shalt be arrayed after My will."

"Ah! Dear Lord, if I go arrayed in other manner than other chaste women do, I dread the people will slander me. They will say I am a hypocrite and wonder at me."

"Yea, daughter, the more ridicule that thou hast for My love, the more thou pleasest Me."

Then this creature durst not otherwise do than she was commanded in her soul. . . .

So they went forth into the Holy Land till they could see Jerusalem. And when this creature saw Jerusalem, riding on an ass, she thanked God with all her heart, praying Him for His mercy that, as He had brought her to see His earthly city of Jerusalem, He would grant her grace to see the blissful city of Jerusalem above, the city of Heaven. Our Lord Jesus Christ, answering her thought, granted her to have her desire.

Then for the joy she had, and the sweetness she felt in the dalliance with Our Lord, she was on the point of falling off her ass, for she could not bear the sweetness and grace that God wrought in her soul. Then two pilgrims, Duchemen, went to her, and kept her from falling; one of whom was a priest, and he put spices in her mouth to comfort her, thinking she had been sick. And so they helped her on to Jerusalem, and when she came there, she said:—

"Sirs, I pray you be not displeased though I weep sore in this holy place where Our Lord Jesus Christ was quick and dead."

Then went they to the temple in Jerusalem and they were let in on the same day at evensong time, and abode there till the next day at evensong time. Then the friars lifted up a cross and led the pilgrims about from one place to another where Our Lord suffered His[11] . . . and His Passion, every man and woman bearing a wax candle in one hand. And the friars always, as they went about, told them what Our Lord suffered in every place. The aforesaid creature wept and sobbed as plenteously as though she had seen Our Lord with her bodily eye, suffering His Passion at that time. Before her in her soul she saw Him verily by contemplation, and that caused her to have compassion. And when they came up on to the Mount of Calvary,[12] she fell down because she could not stand or kneel, and rolled and wrested with her body, spreading her arms abroad, and cried with a loud voice as though her heart would have burst asunder; for, in the city of her soul, she saw verily and clearly how Our Lord was crucified. Before her face, she heard and saw, in her ghostly sight, the mourning of Our Lady, of Saint John, and Mary Magdalene and of many others that loved Our Lord.

11. Word missing in manuscript.
12. **Calvary:** where Jesus is believed to have been crucified.

And she had such great compassion and such great pain, at seeing Our Lord's pain that she could not keep herself from crying and roaring though she should have died for it. And this was the first cry[13] that ever she cried in any contemplation. And this manner of crying endured many years after this time, for aught any man might do, and therefore, suffered she much despite and much reproof. The crying was so loud and so wonderful that it made the people astounded unless they had heard it before, or unless they knew the cause of the crying. And she had them so often that they made her right weak in her bodily might, and especially if she heard of Our Lord's Passion. . . .

[*She returned to England, where her crying upset many people and she was called to appear before the Archbishop of York.*]

On the next day she was brought into the Archbishop's Chapel, and there came many of the Archbishop's retinue, despising her, calling her "Lollard" and "heretic" and swearing many a horrible oath that she should be burnt.

And she, through the strength of Jesus, spoke back to them:—

"Sirs, I dread ye shall be burnt in Hell without end, unless ye amend in your swearing of oaths, for ye keep not the Commandments of God. I would not swear as ye do for all the money in this world."

Then they went away, as if they had been shamed. She then, making her prayer in her mind, asked grace so to be demeaned that day as was most pleasure to God, and profit to her own soul, and good example to her fellow Christians.

Our Lord, answering her, said it should be right well. At the last, the said Archbishop came into the chapel with his clerks, and sharply he said to her:—

"Why goest thou in white? Art thou a maiden?"

She kneeling on her knees before him, said:—

"Nay, sir, I am no maiden. I am a wife."

He commanded his retinue to fetch a pair of fetters and said she should be fettered, for she was a false heretic.

Then she said:—"I am no heretic, nor shall ye prove me one."

The Archbishop went away and left her standing alone. Then she made her prayers to Our Lord God Almighty to help her and succour her against all her enemies, ghostly and bodily, a long while, and her flesh trembled and quaked wonderfully, so that she was fain to put her hands under her clothes, so that it should not be espied.

Afterwards the Archbishop came again into the Chapel with many clerks, amongst whom was the same doctor who had examined her before, and the monk that had preached against her a little time before in York. Some of the

13. **cry:** outcry, scream.

people asked whether she were a Christian woman or a Jew; some said she was a good woman; some said "Nay."

Then the Archbishop took his seat and his clerks also, each of them in his degree, many people being present.

And during the time while the people were gathering together and the Archbishop taking his seat, the said creature stood all behind, making her prayers for help and succour against her enemies with high devotion, so long that she melted all into tears.

And at the last she cried aloud therewith, so that the Archbishop and his clerks and many people had great wonder of her, for they had not heard such crying before. When her crying was passed, she came before the Archbishop and fell down on her knees, the Archbishop saying full boisterously unto her:—

"Why weepest thou, woman?"

She, answering, said:—"Sir, ye shall wish some day that ye had wept as sore as I."

Then anon, the Archbishop put to her the Articles of our Faith,[14] to which God gave her grace to answer well and truly and readily without any great study, so that he might not blame her. Then he said to the clerks:—

"She knoweth her Faith well enough. What shall I do with her?"

The clerks said:—"We know well that she can say the Articles of Faith, but we will not suffer her to dwell amongst us, for the people hath great faith in her dalliance, and, peradventure, she might pervert some of them.". . .

Then said the Archbishop to her:—"Thou shalt swear that thou wilt neither teach nor challenge the people in my diocese."

"Nay, sir, I shall not swear," she said, "for I shall speak of God, and rebuke those that swear great oaths wheresoever I go, unto the time that the Pope and Holy Church hath ordained that no man shall be so bold as to speak of God, for God Almighty forbiddeth not, sir, that we shall speak of Him. And also the Gospel maketh mention that, when the woman had heard Our Lord preach, she came before Him with a loud voice and said: 'Blessed be the womb that bore Thee, and the teats that gave Thee suck.' Then Our Lord again said to her, 'Forsooth, so are they blessed that hear the word of God and keep it.' And therefore, sir, methinketh that the Gospel giveth me leave to speak of God."

"Ah! Sir," said the clerks, "here wot we well that she hath a devil within her, for she speaketh of the Gospel."

As quickly as possible, a great clerk brought forth a book and laid Saint Paul, for his part, against her, that no woman should preach.[15]

---

14. **Articles of Faith:** a standard series of questions, in which a person suspected of heresy was asked if he or she believed in the central doctrines of Christianity—the Trinity, the Virgin Birth, the efficacy of the sacraments, heaven and hell, the power of the Pope.

15. The first letter to Timothy in the New Testament, which until recently was believed to have been written by the apostle Paul, orders women to keep silent in church.

She answering thereto said:—"I preach not, sir; I come into no pulpit, I use but communication and good words, and that I will do while I live." . . .

She, kneeling down on her knees, asked his blessing. He, praying her to pray for him, blessed her and let her go.

Then she, going again to York, was received by many people and full worthy clerks, who rejoiced in Our Lord, Who had given her, unlettered, wit and wisdom to answer so many learned men without disgrace or blame, thanks be to God.

Source 6 from Edward Peters, editor, Heresy and Authority in Medieval Europe: Documents in Translation *(Philadelphia: University of Pennsylvania Press, 1980), pp. 259–261. Selection translated by Steven Sargent. Reprinted by permission.*

6. Testimony from the Inquisition Led by Jacques Fournier, Bishop of Pamiers, 1318–1325

Testimony of Arnaud de Savinhan

"He said that as long as he could remember, which might be about thirty years since he was then about forty-five years old, he had believed completely that God had not made the world, namely heaven, earth, and the elements, but that it had always been existing in and of itself, and was not made by God nor by anyone else. Nevertheless he always had believed that Adam was the first man and that God had made him, and thereafter there had been human generation. But before God had made Adam, the world had lasted infinitely into the past; and he [the witness] did not believe that the world had had a beginning.

"He also said that he had believed for all that time up to the beginning of May in the present year that the world had never had a beginning, and thus that it would never end, and that the world would go on in the same way in the future as it did now; and that just as men were generated now and as they had been generated from Adam onward, there would always be in the future the generation of men, and of vines, and of the other plants, and of all animals; nor would that generation ever end. He believed that there was no other world except the present one."

Testimony of Raimond de l'Aire, of Tignac

An older man told him that a mule has a soul as good as a man's "and from this belief he had by himself deduced that his own soul and those of other men are nothing but blood, because when a person's blood is taken away, he dies. He also believed that a dead person's soul and body both die, and that after death nothing human remains, because he didn't see anything leave the mouth of a person when he dies. From this he believed that the human soul after death has neither good nor evil, and that there is no hell or paradise in another world where human souls are rewarded or punished."

Testimony of Guillemette Benet

"Asked if, since she believed that human souls died with the bodies, she also believed that men would be resurrected and would live again after death, she answered that she did not believe that the resurrecting of the human body would happen, since she believed that as the dead body was buried, the soul was buried with the body; and since she saw that the body putrefied, she believed that it would never be resurrected. . . .

"Asked if she believed that the soul of Jesus Christ, who died on the cross, had died with his body, she answered yes, because although God is not able to die, nevertheless Jesus Christ died and therefore, even though she believed that God always existed, nevertheless she did not believe that Christ's soul lived and existed. . . .

"Asked if she believed that Christ was resurrected, she said yes and that God had done this."

Testimony of Arnaud Gelis, of Pamiers

Arnaud's beliefs

Roman Catholic orthodoxy

1. The souls of dead people do not do any other penance except to wander from church to church, some faster, some slower according to their sinfulness.

1. All souls of dead people go to purgatory, where they do the penance they had not completed on earth. And when this is done they go to the heavenly paradise where Christ, Mary, the angels, and the saints reside.

2. After they are finished going around to churches through the streets, the souls go to the place of rest, which is on this earth. They stay there until the judgment day.

2. When their penance is done, the souls of the dead go to the joy of the celestial paradise, which is no place of rest on earth, but rather in heaven.

3. No soul of any man except the most saintly goes directly to heaven or the heavenly kingdom. Souls do this on the day of judgment.

3. All souls of the dead, when their penance is done in purgatory (if they had need of it), enter the heavenly kingdom.

4. Souls of children who died before baptism go to an obscure place until the judgment day. There they feel neither pain nor pleasure. After the judgment day they enter paradise.

5. No soul of a dead person, no matter how evil, has entered or will enter hell.

6. At the last judgment God will have mercy on all who held the Christian faith and no one will be damned, no matter how evil he was.

7. Christ will have mercy on the souls of all heretics, Jews, and pagans; therefore none of them will be damned.

8. Human souls, both before the body's death and after, have their own bodily form just like their external body. And the souls have distinct members like hands, eyes, feet, and the rest.

9. Hell is a place only for demons.

4. The souls of unbaptized children will never be saved or enter the kingdom of heaven.

5. The souls of all evil persons— i.e., those who perpetrate great crimes that they do not confess or do penance for—go immediately after death to hell, where they stay and are punished for their sins.

6. All souls that held the Christian faith and accepted its sacraments and obeyed its commandments will be saved; but those who, even though holding the faith and accepting the sacraments, did not live according to the commandments will be damned.

7. All souls of heretics, pagans, and Jews, who did not want to believe in Christ, will be damned. They will be punished eternally in hell.

8. Human souls, both while in the body and after its death, because they are spirits, are not corporeal, nor do they have corporeal members, nor do they eat or drink, nor do they suffer such corporeal necessities.

9. Hell is a place for demons and for wicked people, where each is punished eternally as he deserves.

Disbelief in Indulgences: Testimony of Guillelme Cornelhano

"He also said that about two years before around the feast of Pentecost . . . a seller of indulgences passed by [him and Guillelma Vilara, wife of Arnald Cuculli] who had with him many indulgences. And after he had left them, Guillelma said, "Do you believe that any man is able to indulge or absolve anyone of his sins? Don't believe it, because no one can absolve anyone except God." And when he himself said that the pope and all priests could absolve man from sins, Guillelma answered that it was not so, only God could [do that]."

Testimony of Peter Sabatier

"When questioned, Peter said and confessed willingly that about three years ago on a certain day in the village of Varillis . . . when he returned from the church [to his house], he said that whatever things the priests and clerics were chanting and singing in the church were lies and tricks; but he never doubted, rather always believed, that the sacraments of the church and its articles of faith were true."

He persisted in this belief "for about a year, and believed out of silliness that priests and clerics, in singing and chanting those things in the church while performing the divine offices, sang and chanted in order to have the contributions, and that there was no good effect wrought by those divine offices."

Source 7 from Norman P. Tanner, editor, Heresy Trials in the Diocese of Norwich, 1428–1431, *Camden Fourth Series, vol. 20 (London: Royal Historical Society, 1977), pp. 111–113. Selection translated by Merry E. Wiesner.*

7. A Norwich Heresy Trial, 1428–1431

In the name of God, before you, the worshipful father in Christ, William, by the grace of God bishop of Norwich, I, John Reve, a glover from Beccles in your diocese, your subject, feeling and understanding that I have held, believed, and affirmed errors and heresies which be counted in this confession, that is to say:

That I have held, believed, and affirmed that the sacrament of baptism done in water in the form customary to the church is of no avail and not to be demanded if the father and mother of the child are christened and of Christian beliefs.

Also that the sacrament of confirmation done by a bishop is not profitable or necessary to man's salvation.

Also that confession ought not to be made to any priest, but only to God, for no priest has the power to forgive a man of sin.

Also that I have held, believed and affirmed that no priest has the power to make God's body in the sacrament of the altar, and that after the sacramental words said by a priest at mass nothing remains except a loaf of material bread.

Also that only consent of love in Jesus Christ between a man and woman of Christian beliefs is sufficient for the sacrament of matrimony, without any contract of words or solemnizing in church.

Also that I have held, believed and affirmed that only God has power to make the sacraments, and no other creature.

Also that I have held, believed and affirmed that no creature of Christian belief is required to fast in Lent, on the Umber Days, Fridays, vigils of saints nor any other times which the Church commands should be fasted, but it is lawful for people of Christian beliefs to eat meat at all such times and days. And in affirming this opinion I have eaten meat on Fridays and the other aforementioned days.

Also I have held, believed and affirmed that it is lawful for all Christ's people to do all bodily work on Sundays and all other days which the Church has commanded to be held holy, if people keep themselves from other sins at such days and times.

Also I have held, believed and affirmed that every man may lawfully and without sin withhold and withdraw his tithes and offerings from churches and curates, if it is done prudently.

Also I have held, believed and affirmed that it is lawful for God's people to act contrary to the precepts of the Church.

Also that censures of the Church and sentences of cursing whether from bishops, prelates, or other ordinaries are not to be taken into account or dreaded, for as soon as such bishops or ordinaries curse any man, Christ himself assails him.

Also that I have believed, held, and affirmed that no manner of worship ought to be done to any images of the crucifix, of Our Lady or of any other saints.

Also that no manner of pilgrimages ought to be done to any places of saints, but only to poor people.

Also that I have held and believed that it is not lawful to swear in any case.

Also that I have held, believed, and affirmed that the pope of Rome is the Antichrist and has no power in the Holy Church as St. Peter had unless he follows in the steps of Peter in his manner of living.

Also that all bishops, prelates and priests of the Church are the Antichrist's disciples.

Also that I have held, believed and affirmed that it is as meritorious and as profitable to all Christ's people to be buried in meadows or in wild fields as it is to be buried in churches or churchyards.

Because of which and many other errors and heresies which I have held, believed, and affirmed within your diocese, I am called before you, worshipful father, who has the cure of my soul. And you are fully informed that the said my holding, believing, and affirming are judged errors and heresies and contrary to the Church of Rome, wherefore I willingly follow the doctrine of holy Church and depart from all manner of heresy and error and turn with good heart and will to the unity of the Church. Considering that holy Church will not spare her bosom to him that will return nor God will the death of a sinner but rather that he be returned and live, with a pure heart I confess, detest and despise my said errors and heresies, and the said opinions I confess as heretical and erroneous and repugnant to the faith of the Church at Rome and all

universal holy Church. And for as much as I showed myself corrupt and un-
faithful through the said things that I so held, believed, and affirmed, from
henceforth I will show myself uncorrupt and faithful, and I promise to keep
the faith and doctrine of the holy Church truly. And I abjure and forswear all
manner of error and heresy, doctrine and opinion against the holy Church and
the determination of the Church of Rome—namely the opinions listed before—and swear by these holy gospels which I am bodily touching that from
henceforth I shall never hold error nor heresy nor false doctrine against the
faith of holy Church and the determination of the Church of Rome. No such
things shall I obstinately defend. I shall defend no person holding or teaching
such things openly or privately. I shall never after this time be an assistor,
counselor, or defender of heretics or of any person suspected of heresy. I shall
never ally myself with them. I shall not wittingly show fellowship to them,
nor give them counsel, gifts, succor, favor, or comfort. If I know any heretics
or any persons suspected of heresy, or people who counsel, assist or defend
them, or any persons holding private conventicles or meetings, or holding
any singular opinions different from the common doctrine of the Church, I
shall let you, worshipful father, or your vicar general in your absence or the
diocesans of such persons know soon and immediately. So help me God at
holy doom and these holy gospels.

In witness of which things I subscribe here with my own hand a cross—X.
And to this part intended to remain in your register I set my sign. And that
other part I receive with your seal to keep with me until my life's end. Given
at Norwich in the chapel of your palace, xviii day of the month of April in the
year of our Lord one thousand four hundred and thirty.

Source 8 from Bavarian National Museum, Munich.

8. Madonna, Germany, ca 1430

9. Crucifix, Germany, 14th century

QUESTIONS TO CONSIDER

The written sources and the religious statues have provided you with evidence for the two central questions of this chapter. Looking again at those questions, you can see that the first concerns the religious beliefs and practices of laypeople, and the second the official Church reaction to those beliefs and practices. You now need to sort through the sources to separate the information you have gained about each question.

Look first at lay piety itself. Which Christian beliefs were numbers of people attracted to? Why were these beliefs especially appealing? Why might it have been difficult for most people to respond to more esoteric points of theology such as the Trinity? Many of the sources have described or depicted the extremely important role of the Virgin Mary in lay piety. Why do you think people turned to her, rather than to God the Father, in their prayers and devotions? In official Christian theology, Mary is not a goddess but completely human, and believers were urged to honor but not to worship her. From the sources, do you think most laypeople understood this distinction? Looking at the first sermon story, which relates beliefs and practices approved of by the Church, was this distinction always made clear to laypeople?

You have seen that religion was not simply a matter of belief for most people but also of real-world practices and acts. What practices were most popular? How did people see these as contributing to their spiritual lives? One of the sermon stories, the life of St. Nicholas, and the works of Bridget and Margery Kempe refer matter-of-factly to visions and miracles. What does this imply about the divisions between the natural and supernatural in most people's minds?

The two heresy trials record beliefs that deviated from those officially accepted. Do you find evidence of similar beliefs, though perhaps not carried so far, in any of the other sources? For example, what religious beliefs and practices of Margery Kempe opened her to the accusation of heresy? How would you compare the two heresies from the sources reprinted here? Does either appear to deviate further from official Church teachings than the other? Which teachings do both dispute? Can you make any generalizations about late medieval heresy from these examples, or are the differences between them more striking than the similarities?

Now turn to the second question. Official Church reaction to lay piety was both positive and negative. Positive reactions included attempts by preachers and priests to shape popular belief and to encourage certain actions that they felt strengthened the Church. Judging by the sermon stories and the life of St. Nicholas, what beliefs and practices were preachers and hagiographers trying to encourage? Did the religious statuary encourage similar ideas? How did the archbishop try to influence Margery Kempe? Negative reactions included the Church's attempts to eradicate unacceptable beliefs and behavior, with sanctions ranging from mild scoldings to execution for heresy. Judging from the heresy trials and Margery Kempe's autobiography, what kinds of beliefs were Church officials especially worried about? Did they appear to be more concerned with beliefs or with behavior?

Many of those charged with heresy or with suspect beliefs in the late Middle Ages were women, and the Church hierarchy was of course totally male. Thinking particularly of the experience of Margery Kempe, do you find evidence of gender differences in official attitudes toward lay piety? Even women whose ideas were initially accepted could later be judged heretical. For example, Bridget of Sweden was made a saint less than twenty years after her death, but only forty years later the authenticity of her visions was questioned and she was dismissed by some Church officials as a chatterbox deluded by the devil. Do you find anything in the visions printed here that might have been disturbing to the all-male clerical establishment?

Both lay piety and official reaction to it were shaped by political and economic factors as well as by theology and doctrine. From your sources, which beliefs and practices encouraged or condemned by the Church would have had economic repercussions? Especially in the Norwich heresy trial, which ideas did the Church view as a political threat? Why would the ideas expressed in that trial have been seen as more dangerous than those of Margery Kempe? Reread the discussion in your text of the political and economic changes that late medieval Europe experienced. How was the Church involved in these changes? Do your sources provide evidence for any of the developments described in your text?

You are now ready to answer the two central questions of this chapter: How did common people in the Middle Ages experience and express their religious faith? How did the Church as an institution respond to laypeople's beliefs and practices? Are your answers more complex or less complex than you expected?

EPILOGUE

Most of the strong lay piety in the late Middle Ages remained inside the boundaries judged acceptable by the Church. Groups branded as heretics were usually small, and they were quite successfully wiped out by intensive inquisitions and campaigns of persecution such as those carried out against the Albigensians and Lollards.

Persecution did not put an end to dissatisfaction with the institutional Church, however, nor were preachers and priests ever able to exert total control over the beliefs or activities of common people. Indeed, the more historians study the beliefs of "unlearned" people, the more they discover that people do not passively absorb what they are told but add to it their own ideas. Illiteracy does not preclude imagination or intelligence, and influence between the learned elite and the common people runs in both directions.

Though lay dissatisfaction persisted, it did not cause the institutional Church to change or initiate reforms during the late Middle Ages. In 1377, the papacy returned to Rome, and when the pope died the following year the Roman people forced the college of cardinals, the body of church officials who chose the popes, to elect an Italian pope. This pope, Urban VI, tried to reform some of the Church's problems but did so in such a belligerent way that he set most of the college of cardinals against him. They responded by declaring that the pope's election was invalid because they had been put under duress and, calling for his resignation, elected another pope. Urban did not step down, however, and a forty-year power split began in which two and later three popes simultaneously excommunicated the others, collected taxes, made appointments, and granted indulgences. The Great Schism, as this period is called, was probably the low point in the history of organized Christianity in the West, but the eventual reunification of the Church in 1417 did not resolve all problems. For the next century, the popes con-

centrated their energies on artistic patronage and expansion of their political power in Italy. Despite several major attempts at reform and increasing recognition of internal problems by many Church officials and scholars throughout Europe, low standards of discipline and morality, and high levels of corruption, persisted.

Martin Luther's break with the Catholic church in the early sixteenth century began as yet another attempt at reform but quickly grew into a revolution that split Western Christianity from that time on. The swift and widespread acceptance of Luther's ideas gave vivid testimony to the depth of popular dissatisfaction with the Church. At the very beginning, at least, common people in many parts of Germany saw the Protestant Reformation as the change they had been looking for, a movement that emphasized personal piety and played down the priest's role in the individual's salvation. Supporting Luther initially, they quickly realized that he was not the leader they had hoped for and that he attacked many of the practices, such as pilgrimages or the veneration of Mary, that were dearest to them. Thus the strong lay piety movement of the late Middle Ages is an important factor in understanding not just medieval Christianity in all its complexity but the roots of the Reformation as well.

CHAPTER ELEVEN

THE RENAISSANCE

MAN AND WOMAN

THE PROBLEM

The age we know as the Renaissance had its beginnings in the fourteenth century as a literary movement among educated, mostly upper-class men in northern Italian cities, notably Florence. Such writers as Petrarch attempted to emulate as closely as possible the literary figures of ancient Rome, believing that these men, especially Cicero, had attained a level of style and a command of the Latin language that had never since been duplicated. Petrarch's fascination with antiquity did not stop with language, however, but also included an interest in classical architecture and art; he spent long hours wandering around the large numbers of Roman ruins remaining in Italy. His obsession with the classical past also led him to reject the thousand-year period between his own time and that of Rome, viewing this as a "dark," "gothic," or at best "middle" age—a deep trough between two peaks of

civilization. Though Petrarch himself did not call his own period the *Renaissance*—a word that means "rebirth"—he clearly believed he was witnessing the dawning of a new age. Writers and artists intending to recapture the glory that was Rome would have to study Roman models, and Petrarch proposed an appropriate course of study or curriculum termed the *studia humanitates,* or simply "liberal studies" or the "liberal arts." Like all curricula, it contained an implicit philosophy, a philosophy that came to be known as *humanism.* Humanism was not a rigorous philosophical system like Aristotelianism, nor an all-encompassing belief system like Christianity, but what we might better call an attitude toward learning and toward life.

This new attitude had a slow diffusion out of Italy, with the result that the Renaissance "happened" at very different times in different parts of Europe. Because it was not a single historical event in the same sense as the French Revolution or the

Peloponnesian War, the Renaissance is difficult to date. Roughly, we can say it began in Italy in the fourteenth century; spread to France, Germany, and Spain by the end of the fifteenth century; to England by the early part of the sixteenth century; and not until the seventeenth century to Scandinavia. Thus the Renaissance preceded the Reformation—which *was* an event—in most of Europe, took place at the same time as the Reformation in England, and came after the Reformation in Scandinavia. Shakespeare, for example, is considered a "Renaissance" writer even though he lived 250 years after Petrarch.

Though the chronology may be somewhat confusing, there are certain recurring features of humanism through the centuries. One of these is a veneration of the classical past. Petrarch concentrated primarily on Latin and ancient Rome, but during the mid-fifteenth century humanists also began to emphasize Greek language, art, architecture, philosophy, and literature. Though they disagreed about the relative merits of the classical philosophers and writers, all agreed that classical philosophy and literature were of paramount importance to their own culture.

Another feature of humanism is its emphasis on individualism. Medieval society was corporate—that is, oriented toward, and organized around, people acting in groups. Medieval political philosophy dictated that the smallest component of society was not the individual but the family. An individual ruler stood at the top of medieval society, but this ruler was regarded as tightly bound to the other nobles by feudal alliances and, in some ways, as simply the greatest of the nobles. Workers banded together in guilds; pious people formed religious confraternities; citizens swore an oath of allegiance to their own city. Even art was thought to be a group effort, with the individual artist feeling no more need to sign a work than a baker did to sign each loaf of bread. (We know the names of some medieval artists from sources such as contracts, bills of sale, and financial records, but rarely from the paintings or sculptures themselves.)

Christianity encouraged this sense of community as well. Though Christians were baptized and participated in most other sacraments as individuals, the priest represented the whole community when he alone drank wine at communion, and Christ was believed to have embodied all of Christianity when he died. Christians were encouraged to think of themselves as part of one great "Christendom" and to follow the example of Christ by showing humility and meekness rather than the self-assurance that draws attention to the individual.

These attitudes began to shift during the Renaissance. The family, the guild, and other corporate groups remained important social forces, but some individuals increasingly viewed the group as simply a springboard to far greater individual achievement that could be obtained through talent or hard work. Rather than defining themselves primarily within the context of the group, some prized their own sense of uniqueness and individuality, hiring artists to paint or sculpt their portraits and writers to produce verbal likenesses. Caught up in this new individualism, artists and writers themselves began to paint their own self-portraits and write autobiographies. Visual artists, believing that their skill at painting or sculpture was a result not simply of good training but of individual genius, began to sign their works. Rather than the vices they were to medieval Christians, self-confidence and individualism became virtues for many people. Humanists wrote not only biographies of prominent individuals but also treatises that described the attributes of the ideal person. In their opinion, that person should be well rounded and should also exhibit the quality of *virtù*—a word that does not mean virtue but rather the ability to make an impact in one's chosen field of endeavor.

The notion of individualism includes a belief that the people and objects of this world are important, at least important enough to warrant a picture or a verbal description. This belief, usually called *secularism,* is also a part of humanism. Secularism is a highly charged word in modern American political jargon—even more so when expanded to *secular humanism*—and may be too strong a term to apply to Renaissance thinkers. No one in the Renaissance denied the existence of God or the central importance of religion in human life. What they did reject was the idea that it was necessary to forsake the material world and retire to a life of contemplation in order to worship God. God had created this world full of beauty, including the human body, to be appreciated. The talents of each person should be developed to their fullest through education and then displayed to the world because those talents came from God. Studying pre-Christian philosophers such as Plato or Aristotle could enhance an understanding of Christianity because God could certainly have endowed these thinkers with great wisdom even though they were not Christian.

The basis for all these features of humanism—classicism, individualism, secularism—was learning, and humanists all agreed on the importance of education, not just for the individual but also for society as a whole. During the mid-fifteenth century many humanists, such as Leonardo Bruni, began to stress that a proper liberal education was based on training for service to society as well as on classical models. Medieval education had been primarily an organ of the Church, oriented to its needs. Church and cathedral schools trained students to read and write so that they could copy manuscripts, serve as church lawyers, and write correspondence. Monks, priests, and nuns also used their education to honor the glory of God by reciting prayers, studying the Bible and other religious works, composing and singing hymns, or simply speculating on the nature of God. In the Middle Ages the ultimate aim of human life was to *know,* and particularly to know God, so medieval education was often both inwardly directed and otherworldly, helping individuals to come to a better understanding of God. The Renaissance humanists, on the other hand, believed the ultimate aim of human life was to *act*, so humanist education was resoundingly outwardly directed and this-worldly, emphasizing practical skills such as public speaking and writing that would benefit any politician, diplomat, military leader, or businessman. This education was not to be used in a monastery where only God could see it, but in the newly expanding cities and towns of northern Italy, cities that were growing steadily richer thanks to the development of trade we examined in Chapter 8. The primarily classical humanism of the fourteenth century was gradually transformed into civic humanism as humanists took employment as city secretaries and historians and as merchants and bankers sent their sons to humanist schools.

Humanism underwent a further transformation in the sixteenth century, when the governing of the cities of northern Italy was taken over by powerful noblemen. These rulers hired humanists as secretaries, tutors, diplomats, and advisers, and they established humanist academies in their capital cities. Unlike medieval rulers, who saw themselves primarily as military leaders, Renaissance rulers saw themselves as the leaders of all facets of life in their territories. Thus they supported poets and musicians as well as generals, learned several languages, and established their court as the cultural as well as political center of the territory.

Reflecting this new courtly milieu, humanists began to write biographies of rulers and to reflect on the qualities that were important in the ideal ruler and courtier. The trait of *virtù*, so vital in an individual, was even more critical in a ruler. For a ruler, *virtù* meant the ability to shape society as a whole and leave an indelible mark on history. Humanists held up as models worthy of emulation such classical rulers as Alexander the Great and Julius Caesar.

In many ways, then, Renaissance thinkers broke with the immediate medieval past in developing new ideals for human behavior. For one group, however, this break was not so complete. When humanists described the ideal woman, she turned out to be much more like her medieval counterpart than the "Renaissance man" was. The problem of female education was particularly perplexing for humanists. Medieval women, like medieval men, had been educated to serve and know God. Renaissance men were educated to serve the city or the state, which no humanist felt was a proper role for women. If women were not to engage in the type of public activities felt to be the proper arena for displaying talent and education, why should they be educated at all? Should the new virtues of self-confidence and individualism be extended to include women? Or should women be the link with the older Christian virtues of modesty and humility? How could women properly show *virtù*—a word whose roots lie in the word *vir*, which meant "man"—when to do so required public actions? Should women, perhaps, be even more encouraged to remain within the private sphere of home and family, given the opinions of classical philosophers such as Aristotle (which we saw in Chapter 2) about the proper role of women? In their consideration of the proper "Renaissance woman," humanists often exhibited both the tension between, and their attempts to fuse, the pagan classical and medieval Christian traditions.

In this chapter, you will examine the writings of several humanists describing the ideal educational program for boys and girls, the ideal male and female courtier, and the ideal ruler. In addition, you will read one short section from the autobiography of a humanist and another from the biography of a ruler written by a humanist; you will also look at several portraits. How do these authors describe the ideal man, woman, and ruler? How were these ideals expressed in written descriptions and visual portraits of actual Renaissance people?

SOURCES AND METHOD

The written sources in this chapter are primarily prescriptive; in other words, they present ideals that their humanist authors hoped people would emulate. In Chapter 2 we used prescriptive literature to compare ideals and reality in classical Athens, but here we will explore only the ideals themselves. Our questions and methodology are those of intellectual historians, who are interested in the development of ideas as well as in how those ideas relate to other types of changes. Intellectual history is an especially important dimension of the Renaissance, which was primarily an intellectual rather than a political or social movement. The questions you need to keep most in mind, then, relate to the ideas set forth here: What qualities was the ideal man, woman, or ruler supposed to possess? How were these qualities to be inculcated in young people? On the basis of these qualities, what did humanists think was most important in human existence? How did authors and artists portraying real people—in biographies, autobiographies, or portraits—express similar ideas?

Whenever we use prescriptive literature as our historical source, we must first inquire into the author's motives. Why did our Renaissance writers believe that people had to be instructed in matters of behavior? Were they behaving badly, or were they confronting new situations in which they would not know how to act? The intentions of these humanist authors were fairly straightforward because they believed themselves to be living in a new age, a rebirth of classical culture. In their minds, people needed to be informed about the values of this new age and instructed in the means for putting these values into practice. The humanist authors were thus attempting to mold new types of people to fit a new world, not simply correcting attitudes and behavior they felt were wrong or misguided. Consequently, humanist prescriptive literature concentrates on the positive, telling people what to do rather than what not to do (unlike much other prescriptive literature, such as the Ten Commandments).

Before you read the written selections, look at the three portraits. The first is a self-portrait by the German artist Albrecht Dürer; the second a portrait of an Italian woman known simply as Simonetta, by the Italian artist Sandro Botticelli or a member of his workshop; the third a sculpture of the Venetian general Bartolommeo Colleoni by Andrea del Verrocchio. How would you describe the expressions of the subjects in each of these portraits? Do any of them exhibit the qualities prized by the humanists—individualism, *virtù*, self-confidence? What other traits did the artist choose to emphasize? What differences do you see in the portrait of the woman compared with those of the two men? Now proceed to the written evidence.

Sources 4 and 5 are letters from humanists to members of the nobility. The first, discussing the proper education for men, is from Peter Paul Vergerius to Ubertinus, the son of the ruler of Padua, Italy; the second, discussing the proper education for women, is from Leonardo Bruni to Lady Baptista Malatesta, the daughter of the Duke of Urbino. As you read them, note both the similarities and the differences in the two courses of study. What factors might account for this? What is the ultimate purpose of the two educational programs?

Sources 6 and 7 are taken from one of the most popular advice manuals

ever written, Baldassare Castiglione's *The Courtier*. Castiglione was himself a courtier in Urbino, Mantua, and Milan, and he wrote this discussion of the perfect courtier and court lady in the form of a dialogue between noblemen. As you did for Sources 4 and 5, compare the qualities prescribed for men and women, respectively. How do these relate to the educational program discussed in Sources 4 and 5?

Source 8 comes from one of the most widely read pieces of political advice ever written, Machiavelli's *The Prince*. Like Castiglione, Niccolo Machiavelli had served various governments and had watched rulers and states rise and fall in late-fifteenth- and early-sixteenth-century Italy. What does he believe is the most critical factor or factors in the training of a prince? What qualities should a ruler possess to be effective and display *virtù*?

The first five documents are all straightforward prescriptive literature, as the authors' frequent use of such words as "ought" and "should" indicates. This was not the only way humanists communicated their ideals, however; biographies of real people also expressed these ideals. To use biographies as a source of ideas, we must take a slightly more subtle approach, identifying those personal characteristics the author chose to emphasize, those that might have been omitted, and the way in which each biographer manipulated the true personality of his subject to fit the humanist ideal. These are points to consider as you read the next two documents. Source 9 is from the autobiography of Leon Battista Alberti, which you will note is written in the third person. How does Alberti describe himself? How did his life reflect the new humanist ideals? Why might he have chosen to write in the third person instead of saying "I"? Source 10 is Polydore Vergil's description of Henry VII of England, who ruled from 1485 to 1509. What does it tell us about Renaissance monarchs and also about the author?

Once you have read the written selections, return to the portraits. Do you find anything there that you did not see before?

THE EVIDENCE

Source 1 from German Information Center.

1. Albrecht Dürer, *Self-Portrait in a Fur Coat*, 1500

Source 2 from Staatliche Museen zu Berlin—Preussischer Kulturbesitz Gemaldegalerie. Photograph: Jorg P. Anders.

2. Workshop of Botticelli (ca 1444–1510), so-called *Simonetta*

Source 3 from Venice (Alinari/Art Resource, NY).

3. Andrea del Verrocchio (ca 1435–1488), Sculpture of General Bartolommeo Colleoni

Sources 4 and 5 from W. H. Woodward, editor and translator, Vittorino da Feltre and Other Humanist Educators (London: Cambridge University Press, 1897), pp. 102, 106–107, 109, 110; pp. 126–129, 132, 133

4. Peter Paul Vergerius, Letter to Ubertinus of Padua, 1392

3. We call those studies *liberal* which are worthy of a free man; those studies by which we attain and practice virtue and wisdom; that education which calls forth, trains, and develops those highest gifts of body and of mind which ennoble men, and which are rightly judged to rank next in dignity to virtue only. For to a vulgar temper gain and pleasure are the one aim of existence, to a lofty nature, moral worth and fame. It is, then, of the highest importance that even from infancy this aim, this effort, should constantly be kept alive in growing minds. . . .

We come now to the consideration of the various subjects which may rightly be included under the name of "Liberal Studies." Amongst these I accord the first place to History, on grounds both of its attractiveness and of its utility, qualities which appeal equally to the scholar and to the statesman. Next in importance ranks Moral Philosophy, which indeed is, in a peculiar sense, a "Liberal Art," in that its purpose is to teach men the secret of true freedom. History, then, gives us the concrete examples of the precepts inculcated by Philosophy. The one shows what men should do, the other what men have said and done in the past, and what practical lessons we may draw therefrom for the present day. I would indicate as the third main branch of study, Eloquence, which indeed holds a place of distinction amongst the refined arts. By philosophy we learn the essential truth of things, which by eloquence we so exhibit in orderly adornment as to bring conviction to differing minds. And history provides the light of experience—a cumulative wisdom fit to supplement the force of reason and the persuasion of eloquence. For we allow that soundness of judgment, wisdom of speech, integrity of conduct are the marks of a truly liberal temper. . . .

4. The principal "Disciplines" have now been reviewed. It must not be supposed that a liberal education requires acquaintance with them all: for a thorough mastery of even one of them might fairly be the achievement of a lifetime. Most of us, too, must learn to be content with modest capacity as with modest fortune. Perhaps we do wisely to pursue that study which we find most suited to our intelligence and our tastes, though it is true that we cannot rightly understand one subject unless we can perceive its relation to the rest. The choice of studies will depend to some extent upon the character of individual minds. . . .

Respecting the general place of liberal studies, we remember that Aristotle would not have them absorb the entire interests of life: for he kept steadily in

257

view the nature of man as a citizen, an active member of the State. For the man who has surrendered himself absolutely to the attractions of Letters or of speculative thought follows, perhaps, a self-regarding end and is useless as a citizen or as prince.

5. Leonardo Bruni, Letter to Lady Baptista Malatesta, ca 1405

There are certain subjects in which, whilst a modest proficiency is on áll accounts to be desired, a minute knowledge and excessive devotion seem to be a vain display. For instance, subtleties of Arithmetic and Geometry are not worthy to absorb a cultivated mind, and the same must be said of Astrology. You will be surprised to find me suggesting (though with much more hesitation) that the great and complex art of Rhetoric should be placed in the same category. My chief reason is the obvious one, that I have in view the cultivation most fitting to a woman. To her neither the intricacies of debate nor the oratorical artifices of action and delivery are of the least practical use, if indeed they are not positively unbecoming. Rhetoric in all its forms—public discussion, forensic argument, logical fence, and the like—lies absolutely outside the province of women.

What Disciplines then are properly open to her? In the first place she has before her, as a subject peculiarly her own, the whole field of religion and morals. The literature of the Church will thus claim her earnest study. Such a writer, for instance, as St. Augustine affords her the fullest scope for reverent yet learned inquiry. Her devotional instinct may lead her to value the help and consolation of holy men now living; but in this case let her not for an instant yield to the impulse to look into their writings, which, compared with those of Augustine, are utterly destitute of sound and melodious style, and seem to me to have no attraction whatever.

Moreover, the cultivated Christian lady has no need in the study of this weighty subject to confine herself to ecclesiastical writers. Morals, indeed, have been treated of by the noblest intellects of Greece and Rome. What they have left to us upon Continence, Temperance, Modesty, Justice, Courage, Greatness of Soul, demands your sincere respect. . . .

But we must not forget that true distinction is to be gained by a wide and varied range of such studies as conduce to the profitable enjoyment of life, in which, however, we must observe due proportion in the attention and time we devote to them.

First amongst such studies I place History: a subject which must not on any account be neglected by one who aspires to true cultivation. For it is our duty to understand the origins of our own history and its development; and the achievements of Peoples and of Kings.

For the careful study of the past enlarges our foresight in contemporary affairs and affords to citizens and to monarchs lessons of incitement or warning in the ordering of public policy. From History, also, we draw our store of examples of moral precepts. . . .

The great Orators of antiquity must by all means be included. Nowhere do we find the virtues more warmly extolled, the vices so fiercely decried. From them we may learn, also, how to express consolation, encouragement, dissuasion or advice. . . .

I come now to Poetry and the Poets—a subject with which every educated lady must shew herself thoroughly familiar. For we cannot point to any great mind of the past for whom the Poets had not a powerful attraction. . . . Hence my view that familiarity with the great poets of antiquity is essential to any claim to true education. For in their writings we find deep speculations upon Nature, and upon the Causes and Origins of things, which must carry weight with us both from their antiquity and from their authorship. Besides these, many important truths upon matters of daily life are suggested or illustrated. All this is expressed with such grace and dignity as demands our admiration.

But I am ready to admit that there are two types of poet: the aristocracy, so to call them, of their craft, and the vulgar, and that the latter may be put aside in ordering a woman's reading. A comic dramatist may season his wit too highly: a satirist describe too bluntly the moral corruption which he scourges: let her pass them by. . . .

But my last word must be this. . . . All sources of profitable learning will in due proportion claim your study. None have more urgent claim than the subjects and authors which treat of Religion and of our duties in the world; and it is because they assist and illustrate these supreme studies that I press upon your attention the works of the most approved poets, historians and orators of the past.

Sources 6 and 7 from Baldassare Castiglione, The Book of the Courtier, *trans. Charles S. Singleton, ed. Edgar Mayhew (Garden City, New York: Doubleday, 1959), pp. 32, 34, 70–71; pp. 206–208, 211–212. Copyright © 1959 by Charles S. Singleton and Edgar de N. Mayhew. Used by permission of Doubleday, a division of Random House, Inc.*

6. From Baldassare Castiglione, *The Courtier,* 1508–1516

"I hold that the principal and true profession of the Courtier must be that of arms which I wish him to exercise with vigor; and let him be known among the others as bold, energetic, and faithful to whomever he serves. And the repute of these good qualities will be earned by exercising them in every time and place, inasmuch as one may not ever fail therein without great blame.

And, just as among women the name of purity, once stained, is never restored, so the reputation of a gentleman whose profession is arms, if ever in the least way he sullies himself through cowardice or other disgrace, always remains defiled before the world and covered with ignominy. Therefore, the more our Courtier excels in this art, the more will he merit praise." . . .

Then signor Gasparo replied: "As for me, I have known few men excellent in anything whatsoever who did not praise themselves; and it seems to me that this can well be permitted them, because he who feels himself to be of some worth, and sees that his works are ignored, is indignant that his own worth should lie buried; and he must make it known to someone, in order not to be cheated of the honor that is the true reward of all virtuous toil. Thus, among the ancients, seldom does anyone of any worth refrain from praising himself. To be sure, those persons who are of no merit, and yet praise themselves, are insufferable; but we do not assume that our Courtier will be of that sort."

Then the Count said: "If you took notice, I blamed impudent and indiscriminate praise of one's self: and truly, as you say, one must not conceive a bad opinion of a worthy man who praises himself modestly; nay, one must take that as surer evidence than if it came from another's mouth. I do say that whoever does not fall into error in praising himself and does not cause annoyance or envy in the person who listens to him is indeed a discreet man and, besides the praises he gives himself, deserves praises from others; for that is a very difficult thing." . . .

"I would have him more than passably learned in letters, at least in those studies which we call the humanities. Let him be conversant not only with the Latin language, but with Greek as well, because of the abundance and variety of things that are so divinely written therein. Let him be versed in the poets, as well as in the orators and historians, and let him be practiced also in writing verse and prose, especially in our own vernacular; for, beside the personal satisfaction he will take in this, in this way he will never want for pleasant entertainment with the ladies, who are usually fond of such things. And if, because of other occupations or lack of study, he does not attain to such a perfection that his writings should merit great praise, let him take care to keep them under cover so that others will not laugh at him, and let him show them only to a friend who can be trusted; because at least they will be of profit to him in that, through such exercise, he will be capable of judging the writing of others. For it very rarely happens that a man who is unpracticed in writing, however learned he may be, can ever wholly understand the toils and industry of writers, or taste the sweetness and excellence of styles, and those intrinsic niceties that are often found in the ancients.

"These studies, moreover, will make him fluent, and (as Aristippus said to the tyrant) bold and self-confident in speaking with everyone. However, I would have our Courtier keep one precept firmly in mind, namely, in this as in everything else, to be cautious and reserved rather than forward, and take care not to get the mistaken notion that he knows something he does not know."

7. From Baldassare Castiglione, *The Courtier*, 1508–1516

I think that in her ways, manners, words, gestures, and bearing, a woman ought to be very unlike a man; for just as he must show a certain solid and sturdy manliness, so it is seemly for a woman to have a soft and delicate tenderness, with an air of womanly sweetness in her every movement. . . .

[Again] . . . many virtues of the mind are as necessary to a woman as to a man; also, gentle birth; to avoid affectation, to be naturally graceful in all her actions, to be mannerly, clever, prudent, not arrogant, not envious, not slanderous, not vain, not contentious, not inept, to know how to gain and hold the favor of her mistress [queen or presiding lady at court] and of all others, to perform well and gracefully the exercises that are suitable for women. And I do think that beauty is more necessary to her than to the Courtier, for truly that woman lacks much who lacks beauty. . . . I say that, in my opinion, in a Lady who lives at court a certain pleasing affability is becoming above all else, whereby she will be able to entertain graciously every kind of man with agreeable and comely conversation suited to the time and place and to the station of the person with whom she speaks, joining to serene and modest manners, and to that comeliness that ought to inform all her actions, a quick vivacity of spirit whereby she will show herself a stranger to all boorishness; but with such a kind manner as to cause her to be thought no less chaste, prudent, and gentle than she is agreeable, witty, and discreet: thus, she must observe a certain mean (difficult to achieve and, as it were, composed of contraries) and must strictly observe certain limits and not exceed them.

Now, in her wish to be thought good and pure, this Lady must not be so coy, or appear so to abhor gay company or any talk that is a little loose, as to withdraw as soon as she finds herself involved, for it might easily be thought that she was pretending to be so austere in order to hide something about herself which she feared others might discover; for manners so unbending are always odious. Yet, on the other hand, for the sake of appearing free and amiable she must not utter unseemly words or enter into any immodest and unbridled familiarity or into ways such as might cause others to believe about her what is perhaps not true; but when she finds herself present at such talk, she ought to listen with a light blush of shame. . . .

And to repeat briefly a part of what has already been said. I wish this Lady to have knowledge of letters, of music, of painting, and know how to dance and how to be festive, adding a discreet modesty and the giving of a good impression of herself to those other things that have been required of the

Courtier. And so, in her talk, her laughter, her play, her jesting, in short in everything, she will be most graceful and will converse appropriately with every person in whose company she may happen to be, using witticisms and pleasantries that are becoming to her.

Source 8 from Niccolo Machiavelli, The Prince and the Discourses, *translated by Luigi Ricci, revised by E. R. P. Vincent (New York: Random House, 1950), pp. 4, 53, 55, 56, 61–62. Reprinted by permission of Oxford University Press.*

8. From Niccolo Machiavelli, *The Prince*, 1513

I desire no honour for my work but such as the novelty and gravity of its subject may justly deserve. Nor will it, I trust, be deemed presumptuous on the part of a man of humble and obscure condition to attempt to discuss and direct the government of princes; for in the same way that landscape painters station themselves in the valleys in order to draw mountains or high ground, and ascend an eminence in order to get a good view of the plains, so it is necessary to be a prince to know thoroughly the nature of the people, and one of the populace to know the nature of princes. . . .

A prince should therefore have no other aim or thought, nor take up any other thing for his study, but war and its organisation and discipline, for that is the only art that is necessary to one who commands, and it is of such virtue that it not only maintains those who are born princes, but often enables men of private fortune to attain to that rank. And one sees, on the other hand, that when princes think more of luxury than of arms, they lose their state. The chief cause of the loss of states, is the contempt of this art, and the way to acquire them is to be well versed in the same. . . .

But as to exercise for the mind, the prince ought to read history and study the actions of eminent men, see how they acted in warfare, examine the causes of their victories and defeats in order to imitate the former and avoid the latter, and above all, do as some men have done in the past, who have imitated some one, who has been much praised and glorified, and have always kept his deeds and actions before them. . . .

It now remains to be seen what are the methods and rules for a prince as regards his subjects and friends. . . .

From this arises the question whether it is better to be loved more than feared, or feared more than loved. The reply is, that one ought to be both feared and loved, but as it is difficult for the two to go together, it is much safer to be feared than loved, if one of the two has to be wanting. For it may be said of men in general that they are ungrateful, voluble, dissemblers, anxious to avoid danger, and covetous of gain; as long as you benefit them, they are entirely yours; they offer you their blood, their goods, their life, and their children, as I have before said, when the necessity is remote; but when it approaches, they revolt. And the prince who has relied solely on their words, without making other preparations, is ruined; for the friendship which is gained by purchase and not through grandeur and nobility of spirit is bought but not secured, and at a pinch is not to be expended in your service. And men have less scruple in offending one who makes himself loved than one who makes himself feared; for love is held by a chain of obligation which, men being selfish, is broken whenever it serves their purpose; but fear is maintained by a dread of punishment which never fails.

Still, a prince should make himself feared in such a way that if he does not gain love, he at any rate avoids hatred; for fear and the absence of hatred may well go together, and will be always attained by one who abstains from interfering with the property of his citizens and subjects or with their women. And when he is obliged to take the life of any one, let him do so when there is a proper justification and manifest reason for it; but above all he must abstain from taking the property of others, for men forget more easily the death of their father than the loss of their patrimony. Then also pretexts for seizing property are never wanting, and one who begins to live by rapine will always find some reason for taking the goods of others, whereas causes for taking life are rarer and more fleeting.

But when the prince is with his army and has a large number of soldiers under his control, then it is extremely necessary that he should not mind being thought cruel; for without this reputation he could not keep an army united or disposed to any duty.

Source 9 from James Bruce Ross and Mary Martin McLaughlin, editors, The Portable Renaissance Reader *(New York: Viking, 1953), pp. 480–485, 490–492. Selection translated by James Bruce Ross. Copyright 1953, renewed 1981 by Viking Penguin Inc. Used by permission of Viking Penguin, a division of Penguin Books USA Inc.*

9. From Leon Battista Alberti, *Autobiography,* after 1460(?)

In everything suitable to one born free and educated liberally, he was so trained from boyhood that among the leading young men of his age he was considered by no means the last. For, assiduous in the science and skill of dealing with arms and horses and musical instruments, as well as in the pursuit of letters[1] and the fine arts, he was devoted to the knowledge of the most strange and difficult things. And finally he embraced with zeal and forethought everything which pertained to fame. To omit the rest, he strove so hard to attain a name in modelling and painting that he wished to neglect

1. **letters:** Alberti means the humanist program of study, primarily the study of languages and literature.

nothing by which he might gain the approbation of good men. His genius was so versatile that you might almost judge all the fine arts to be his. Neither ease nor sloth held him back, nor was he ever seized by satiety in carrying out what was to be done.

He often said that not even in letters had he noticed what is called the satiety of all things among mortals; for to him letters, in which he delighted so greatly, seemed sometimes like flowering and richly fragrant buds, so that hunger or sleep could scarcely distract him from his books. At other times, however, those very letters swarmed together like scorpions before his eyes, so that he could see nothing at all but books. Therefore, when letters began to be displeasing to him, he turned to music and painting and exercise.

He played ball, hurled the javelin, ran, leaped, wrestled, and above all delighted in the steep ascent of mountains; he applied himself to all these things for the sake of health rather than sport or pleasure. . . .

At length, on the orders of his doctors, he desisted from those studies which were most fatiguing to the memory, just when they were about to flourish. But in truth, because he could not live without letters, at the age of twenty-four he turned to physics and the mathematical arts. He did not despair of being able to cultivate them sufficiently, because he perceived that in them talent rather than memory must be employed. At this time he wrote for his brother *On the Advantages and Disadvantages of Letters,* in which booklet, taught by experience, he discussed whatever could be thought about letters. And he wrote at this time for the sake of his soul several little works: *Ephebia, On Religion, Deiphira,* and more of this sort in prose; then in verse, *Elegies* and *Eclogues,* and *Discourses,* and works on love of such a kind as to inculcate good habits in those who studied them and to foster the quiet of the soul. . . .

Although he was affable, gentle, and harmful to no one, nevertheless he felt the animosity of many evil men, and hidden enmities, both annoying and very burdensome; in particular the harsh injuries and intolerable insults from his own relatives. He lived among the envious and malevolent with such modesty and equanimity that none of his detractors or rivals, although very hostile towards him, dared to utter a word about him in the presence of good and worthy men unless it was full of praise and admiration. Even by these envious ones he was received with honour face to face. But, in truth, when he was absent, those who had pretended to love him most slandered him with every sort of calumny, wherever the ears of the fickle and their like lay open. For they took it ill to be exceeded in ability and fame by him who, far inferior to them in fortune, had striven with such zeal and industry. There were even some among his kinsmen (not to mention others) who, having experienced his humanity, beneficence, and liberality, conspired against him most ungratefully and cruelly in an evil domestic plot, and those barbarians aroused the boldness of servants to strike him with a knife, blameless as he was.

He bore injuries of this kind from his kinsmen with equanimity, more in silence than by indignantly resorting to vengeance or permitting the shame and ignominy of his relatives to be made public. . . .

He could endure pain and cold and heat. When, not yet fifteen, he received a serious wound in the foot, and the physician, according to his custom and skill, drew together the broken parts of the foot and sewed them through the skin with a needle, he scarcely uttered a sound of pain. With his own hands, though in such great pain, he even aided the ministering doctor and treated his own wound though he was burning with fever. And when on account of a pain in his side he was continually in an icy sweat, he called in musicians, and for about two hours he strove by singing to overcome the force of the malady and the agony of the pain. His head was by nature unable to endure either cold or wind; but by persistence he learned to bear them, gradually getting used to riding bareheaded in summer, then in winter, and even in raging wind. By some defect in his nature he loathed garlic and also honey, and the mere sight of them, if by chance they were offered to him, brought on vomiting. But he conquered himself by force of looking at and handling the disagreeable objects, so that they came to offend him less, thus showing by example that men can do anything with themselves if they will. . . .

When his favourite dog died he wrote a funeral oration for him.

Source 10 from Denys Hay, editor and translator, The Anglia Historia of Polydore Vergil, AD 1485–1537, *book 74 (London: Camden Society, 1950), p. 147.*

10. From Polydore Vergil, *Anglia Historia,* ca 1540

Henry reigned twenty-three years and seven months. He lived for fifty-two years. By his wife Elizabeth he was the father of eight children, four boys and as many girls. He left three surviving children, an only son Henry prince of Wales, and two daughters, Margaret married to James king of Scotland, and Mary betrothed to Charles prince of Castile. His body was slender but well built and strong; his height above the average. His appearance was remarkably attractive and his face was cheerful, especially when speaking; his eyes were small and blue, his teeth few, poor and blackish; his hair was thin and white; his complexion sallow. His spirit was distinguished, wise and prudent; his mind was brave and resolute and never, even at moments of the greatest danger, deserted him. He had a most pertinacious memory. Withal he was not devoid of scholarship. In government he was shrewd and prudent, so that no one dared to get the better of him through deceit or guile. He was gracious and kind and was as attentive to his visitors as he was easy of access. His hospitality was splendidly generous; he was fond of having foreigners at his court and he freely conferred favours on them. But those of his subjects who were indebted to him and who did not pay him due honour or who were generous only with promises, he treated with harsh severity. He well knew how to maintain his royal majesty and all which appertains to kingship at every time and in every place. He was most fortunate in war, although he was constitutionally more inclined to peace than to war. He cherished justice above all things; as a result he vigorously punished violence, manslaughter and every other kind of wickedness whatsoever. Consequently he was greatly regretted[2] on that account by all his subjects, who had been able to conduct their lives peaceably, far removed from the assaults and evil doing of scoundrels. He was the most ardent supporter of our faith, and daily participated with great piety in religious services. To those whom he considered to be worthy priests, he often secretly gave alms so that they should pray for his salvation. He was particularly fond of those Franciscan friars whom they call Observants, for whom he founded many convents, so that with his help their rule should continually flourish in his kingdom. But all these virtues were obscured latterly only by avarice, from which (as we showed above) he suffered. This avarice is surely a bad enough vice in a private individual, whom it forever torments; in a monarch indeed it may be considered the worst vice, since it is harmful to everyone, and distorts those qualities of trustfulness, justice and integrity by which the state must be governed.

QUESTIONS TO CONSIDER

The first step in exploring the history of ideas is to focus on and define the ideas themselves. Once you have done that by reading the selections and thinking about the questions proposed in Sources and Method, you need to take the next step, which is to compare the ideas of various thinkers. In this way you can trace the development of ideas, how they originate and mature and change in the mind of one thinker after another. First, ask specific questions, such as: What would Bruni think of Castiglione's court lady? How would Leon Battista Alberti be judged by Castiglione's standards? Did Polydore Vergil and Machiavelli have the same ideas about the personal qualities of a ruler? Would a man educated according to the ideas of Vergerius have fitted into Castiglione's ideal court? Would a ruler have wanted him? Would Bruni's learned lady have made a good member of Castiglione's court? Would Botticelli's Simonetta? Does Machiavelli's prince display the qualities Vergerius envisioned in a liberally educated man? How do the main qualities of Machiavelli's prince compare with those of Castiglione's courtier? Why might they be quite different? From the portrait, how might Dürer have been judged by each of the writers? Could we think of Verrocchio's sculpture of Colleoni as a portrait of a Machiavellian ruler? How did the artists' ideals for men, women, and rulers differ from the writers'?

Once you have made these specific comparisons, you can move on to broader comparisons of the basic assumptions of the authors and artists: What was the underlying view of

2. **regretted:** missed after he died.

human nature for these writers? Was this the same for men and women? You have probably noticed that all the writers and artists presented here are male. Given what you have now learned about ideals for men and women, would you have expected most Renaissance writers to be male?

Many intellectual historians are interested not only in the history of ideas themselves but also in their social and political origins. These historians want to know what people thought and why they thought the way they did. This type of intellectual history is called the *sociology of knowledge* because it explores the societal context of ideas in the same way that sociology examines past and present social groups. The sociology of knowledge is a more speculative field than the history of ideas alone because it attempts to discover the underlying reasons that cause people to develop different ways of thinking in different historial periods—a process that can be quite difficult to discern. Nevertheless, from the information your text provides about the social and political changes occurring during the Renaissance, you can also consider some sociology of knowledge questions: Why did humanism first arise in northern Italy and not elsewhere in Italy? Why was religion regarded as especially important for women? How did Castiglione's career affect his view of poli-

tics? How did Machiavelli's? What transformation of the status of artists during the Renaissance allowed both Alberti and Dürer to depict themselves in the ways they did? Given that the documents range from 1392 to 1540, what political changes might have accounted for the varying ideals proposed for the individual? How did the ideals proposed for rulers reflect the actual growth of centralized political power? How might the growth of that power have shaped the ideals set forth by Machiavelli and Polydore Vergil? Questions such as these take us somewhat beyond the scope of our original enquiry, but they are important to ask in looking at any ideological change, particularly a sensibility as far-reaching as the Renaissance. Humanism did not spring up in a vacuum but at a very specific time and place.

We must also be careful, however, not to overemphasize social and political background in tracing the development of ideas. Intellectual historians prefer to speak of "necessary conditions" or "background factors" rather than "causes." A movement as diffuse and long lasting as humanism necessarily stemmed from a wide variety of factors, so do not feel concerned if you find yourself qualifying your answers to the questions in the last paragraph with such words as "might," "perhaps," and "possibly."

Scholars and writers throughout Western history have attempted to revive the classical past, but none of these efforts before or after were to produce the long-lasting effects of the Italian Renaissance. In many ways Petrarch was right: It was the dawn of a new age. As the ideas and ideals of humanism spread, writers all over Europe felt that they had definitely broken with the centuries-long tradition that directly preceded them. It was at this point that historians began the three-part division of Western history that we still use today: antiquity, the Middle Ages or medieval period, and the modern period. (If you pause to reflect on what "middle" implies, you will see that no one living in the tenth century would have described him- or herself as living in the "Middle Ages.")

The effects of the Renaissance were eventually felt far beyond the realms of literature and art. Humanist schools and academies opened throughout Europe, and eventually the older universities changed their curricula to add courses in Latin, Greek, and Hebrew language and literature. In northern Europe, humanists became interested in reforming the Church, bringing it back to the standards of piety and morality they believed had been present in the early Church, in the same way that Petrarch had tried to return the Latin language to its ancient standards. This movement, termed *Christian humanism,* would be one of the background factors behind the Protestant Reformation, as learned people began to realize from their studies that the Church was now far removed from the ideas and standards of the early Christians. The intense Renaissance interest in the physical world, combined with monetary greed and missionary impulses, led to the exploration and eventual colonization of much of the non-European world. This secular spirit was also important in setting the stage for the Scientific Revolution of the seventeenth century.

Humanist ideas about the perfect man, woman, and ruler were originally directed at the upper classes but would eventually find a much larger audience. Castiglione's *The Courtier* was translated into every European language, and the personal characteristics he outlined for the ideal courtier became those expected of the middle-class gentleman. Echoes of the Renaissance ideal for women are still with us; a glance at women's magazines or at contemporary advice manuals for girls will show you that physical beauty, morality, femininity, and religion are often still seen to be the most important personal qualities a woman can possess. Machiavelli's *The Prince* has more dramatic echoes, as many modern dictators clearly would agree that it is more important to be feared than loved.

We should not overemphasize the effects of the intellectual changes of the Renaissance on people living during that period, however. Only a very small share of the population, primarily wealthy, urban, and, as we have seen, male, participated at all in cultural life, whether as consumers or as producers. Most people's lives were shaped much more during this period by economic changes and by religious practices than by the cultural changes we looked at in this chapter. In fact, in their efforts to stress the elitism of Renaissance culture, some historians have questioned whether the term *Renaissance* itself is a valid one, and prefer simply to use the more neutral phrase "late medieval and early modern period."

Even among the elites, many aspects of the Middle Ages continued during the Renaissance. Despite the emergence of individualism, family background remained the most important determinant of a person's social and economic standing. Despite an emphasis on the material, secular world, religion remained central to the lives of the elite as well as the common people. Though some artists were recognized as geniuses, they were still expected to be dependable, tax-paying members of society—that is, members of the community like everybody else. The fact that so many humanists felt it necessary to set standards and describe ideal behavior gives us a clue that not everyone understood or accepted that they were living in a new age: People have no need to be convinced of what they already believe is true.

CHAPTER TWELVE

THE SPREAD

OF THE REFORMATION

In 1517, an Augustinian monk in the German province of Saxony named Martin Luther (1483–1546) began preaching and writing against papal *indulgences*, those letters from the pope that substituted for earthly penance or time in Purgatory for Christians who earned or purchased them. Luther called for an end to the sale of indulgences because this practice encouraged people to believe that sins did not have to be taken seriously but could be atoned for simply by buying a piece of paper. In taking this position he was repeating the ideas expressed more than one hundred years earlier by John Hus (1369?–1415), a Czech theologian and preacher. Many of Luther's other ideas had also been previously expressed by Hus, and even earlier by John Wyclif (1328–1384), an English philosopher and theologian. All three objected to the wealth of the Church and to the pope's claims to earthly power; called for an end to pilgrimages and the veneration of saints;

said that priests were no better than other people, and that in fact all believers were priests; and believed that the Bible should be available for all people to read for themselves in their own language.

Though Luther's beliefs were quite similar to those of Wyclif and Hus, their impact was not. Wyclif had gained a large following and died peacefully in his bed; less than twenty years after his death, however, English rulers ordered anyone espousing his beliefs to be burned at the stake as a heretic and so the movement he started was more or less wiped out. Hus himself was burned at the stake in 1415 at the Council of Constance, which ordered the bones of Wyclif to be dug up and burned as well. Hus's followers were not as easily steered back to the fold or stamped out as Wyclif's had been, but his ideas never spread beyond Bohemia (modern-day Czech Republic). Martin Luther's actions, on the other hand, led to a permanent split in Western Christianity, dividing an institution that had existed as a unified body for almost 1,500 years.

Within only a few years, Luther gained a huge number of followers in Germany and other countries, inspiring other religious reformers to break with the Catholic church in developing their own ideas. This movement has come to be known collectively as the "Protestant Reformation," though perhaps *Revolution* might be a more accurate term.

To understand why Luther's impact was so much greater than that of his predecessors, we need to examine a number of factors besides his basic set of beliefs. As with any revolution, social and economic grievances also played a role. Many different groups in early-sixteenth-century German society were disturbed by the changes they saw around them. Peasants, wanting the right to hunt and fish as they had in earlier times, objected to new taxes their landlords imposed on them. Bitter at the wealth of the Church, they believed the clergy were more interested in collecting money from them than in providing spiritual leadership. Landlords, watching the price of manufactured goods rise even faster than they could raise taxes or rents, blamed urban merchants and bankers, calling them greedy and avaricious. Those with only small landholdings were especially caught in an inflationary squeeze and often had to sell off their lands. This was particularly the case for the free imperial knights, a group of about 3,000 individuals in Germany who owed allegiance directly to the emperor but whose landholdings were often less than one square mile. The knights were also losing their reason for exis-

tence because military campaigns increasingly relied on infantry and artillery forces rather than mounted cavalry. All these groups were becoming nationalistic and objected to their church taxes and tithes going to the pope, whom they regarded as primarily an Italian prince rather than an international religious leader.

Political factors were also important in the Protestant Revolution. Germany was not a centralized monarchy like France, Spain, and England, but a collection of hundreds of semi-independent territories loosely combined into a political unit called the Holy Roman Empire, under the leadership of an elected emperor. Some of these territories were ruled by nobles such as princes, dukes, or counts; some were independent cities; some were ecclesiastical principalities ruled by archbishops or bishops; and some were ruled by free imperial knights. Each territory was jealous of the power of its neighbors and was equally unwilling to allow the emperor any strong centralized authority. This effect usually worked to the benefit of the individual territories, but it could also work to their detriment. For example, the emperor's weakness prevented him from enforcing such laws against alleged heretics as the one the English king had used against Wyclif's followers, with the result that each territory was relatively independent in matters of religion. On the other hand, he was unable to place limits on papal legal authority or tax collection in the way the stronger kings of western Europe could, with the result that Germany supported many more indulgence peddlers than England or Spain.

The decentralization of the Holy Roman Empire also left each territory more vulnerable than before to external military threats, the most significant of which in the early sixteenth century was the Ottoman Turks. Originating in central Asia, the Turks had adopted the Muslim religion and begun a campaign of conquest westward. In 1453 they took Constantinople and by 1500 were nearing Vienna, arousing fear in many German rulers. The Turkish threat combined with social and economic grievances among many sectors of society to make western Europeans feel the end of the world was near or to look for a charismatic leader who would solve their problems.

Technological factors also played a role in the Protestant Revolution. The printing press was developed in Germany around 1450, and by Luther's time there were printers in most of the major cities in Europe. The spread of printing was accompanied by a rise in literacy, so that many more people were able to read than in the time of Wyclif or Hus. They were also more able to buy books and pamphlets, for the rag paper used by printers was much cheaper than the parchment or vellum used by copyists in earlier centuries. Owning a Bible or part of a Bible to read in one's own language was now a realistic possibility.

In many ways, then, the early sixteenth century was a favorable time for a major religious change in west-

ern Europe. Your task in this chapter will be to assess how that change occurred. How were the ideas of Luther disseminated so widely and so quickly? How were they made attractive to various groups within German society?

SOURCES AND METHOD

Before you look at the evidence in this chapter, think about how ideas are spread in modern American society. What would be the best ways to reach the greatest number of people if you wanted to discuss a new issue or present a new concept? You might want to use health issues as an example, for these often involve totally new ideas and information on one hand and are regarded as vitally important on the other. Think, for example, about the means by which the dangers of cigarette smoking or information about the spread of AIDS are communicated. To answer the first question, we will need to examine the sixteenth-century equivalents of these forms of communication. Health is an appropriate parallel because the most important such issue for many people in the sixteenth century was the health of their souls, a problem directly addressed by Luther and the other reformers.

The spread of the Reformation was perhaps the first example of a successful multimedia campaign; in consequence, as you might imagine, we will be using a wide variety of sources. As you read the written sources and look at the visual evidence, keep in mind that people were seeing, hearing, and reading all these materials at once. As in any successful advertising or propaganda campaign, certain ideas were reinforced over and over again to make sure the message was thoroughly communicated. You will need to pay particular attention, then, to those points that come up in more than one type of source.

Though they were seeing, hearing, or reading the same message, different groups within German society interpreted Protestant ideas differently. They latched on to certain concepts which had relevance for their own situations and often attached Protestant ideas to existing social, political, or economic grievances. Artists and authors spreading the Protestant message often conveyed their ideas in ways they knew would be attractive to various social groups. In answering the second question, it is important to note the portrayal of various social groups and pay attention to the frequency with which these portrayals appear. Thus as you look at the visual sources and read the written ones, jot down one list of the ideas expressed and another of the ways in which various types of people are depicted. In this way you will begin to see which ideas are central and perceived as popular, and which might be interpreted differently by different people.

Source 1 is a sermon delivered in 1521 by Martin Luther in Erfurt on his way to the Diet of Worms, a meeting of the leaders of the territories in the Holy Roman Empire. It is not based on Luther's own notes but was written down by a person in the audience who then gave the transcript to a local printer. This sermon is thus a record of both how the Reformation message was spread orally—so many people wanted to hear him that the church where Luther preached could not hold them all—and how it was spread in written form, for seven editions of the sermon appeared in 1521 alone. What teachings of the Catholic church did Luther criticize, and what ideas of his own did he emphasize? In assessing how ideas are spread, we have to pay attention not only to the content of the message but also to the form. In what sorts of words and images did Luther convey his ideas to his large audience?

The next sources—three hymns—also serve as both oral and written evidence. Martin Luther believed congregational hymn singing was an important part of a church service and an effective way to teach people about theology. In this tactic he anticipated modern advertisers, who recognize the power of a song or jingle in influencing people's choices. The first two hymns were written by Luther and the third by Paul Speratus, an early follower. As you read them, pay attention both to their content and their images. What ideas from Luther's sermon are reinforced in the hymns? What sorts of mental pictures do the words produce? (Keep in mind that you are reading these simply as poetry, whereas sixteenth-century people sang them. You may know the tune of "A Mighty Fortress," which is still sung in many Protestant congregations today, and can use your knowledge of its musical setting to help your assessment of the impact of the hymn and its message.)

The Lutheran message would certainly not have spread as widely as it did if church services were its only forum. The remaining sources are those people might have encountered anywhere. The woodcuts all come from Protestant pamphlets—small, inexpensive paperbound booklets written in German that were readily available in any city with a printer— or *broadsheets*—single-sheet posters that were often sold alone or as a series. These documents are extremely complex visually and need to be examined with great care. Most of the images used would have been familiar to any sixteenth-century person, but they may not be to you. Here, then, are some clues to help guide your analysis.

In Source 5, the person on the right wearing the triple crown with money on the table in front of him is the pope. The devils in front of the table are wearing the flat hats worn by cardinals; the pieces of paper with seals attached that they are handing out are indulgences. At the bottom are the flames of hell; at the top, heaven with a preacher and people participating in the two Church sacraments that the Protestants retained, baptism and communion.

Source 6, another heaven and hell image, shows Christ at the top deciding who will stay in heaven and two linked devils at the bottom dragging various people to hell. The right-hand devil wears the triple-crowned papal tiara, the left-hand the rolled turban worn by Turks. Included in the hell-bound group on the right are men wearing the flat cardinal's hat, the pointed hat of bishops, and the distinctive haircut of monks.

Source 7 comes from a series of woodcut contrasts. The left pictures show biblical scenes and the right the contemporary Church. The top left picture shows Christ with his disciples; the top right, the pope. From their hats and haircuts you can recognize some of the people gathered in front of the pope; those kneeling are wearing crowns, which in the sixteenth century were worn only by rulers. The bottom left picture shows Christ and the moneylenders at the temple at Jerusalem; the bottom right, the pope and indulgences.

Source 8 is the cover of a pamphlet called "The Wolf's Song." By now you recognize the hats and haircuts of the wolves at the top and sides; some of the geese wear crowns, and many carry jeweled necklaces. The choice of animals is intentional. Wolves were still a threat to livestock in sixteenth-century Europe, and geese were regarded as foolish, silly creatures willing to follow their leader blindly into dangerous situations.

Source 9 is a woodcut by the well-known German artist Lucas Cranach whom Luther commissioned to illustrate his pamphlet "Against the Papacy at Rome, Founded by the Devil" (1545). It shows two men defecating into the papal triple crown.

Taking all of the images into account, what message do the woodcuts convey about the pope and other Catholic clergy? About the Protestant clergy?

Which images and ideas are frequently repeated? How do these fit in with what was preached or sung in church?

The last source is a pamphlet by an unknown author printed in 1523. It is written in the form of a dialogue, a very common form for these Reformation printed materials. Read it, as you did the sermon and the hymns, for both content and tone. Why do you think the author chose these two characters to convey his message? What do they criticize about Catholic practices? How do the ideas expressed here compare with those in Luther's sermon? Which of the woodcuts might have served as an illustration for this pamphlet?

THE EVIDENCE

Source 1 from John W. Doberstein, editor, Luther's Works, *vol. 51 (Philadelphia: Fortress, 1959), pp. 61–66.*

1. Sermon Preached by Martin Luther in Erfurt (Germany), 1521

Dear friends, I shall pass over the story of St. Thomas this time and leave it for another occasion, and instead consider the brief words uttered by Christ: "Peace be with you" [John 20:19] and "Behold my hands and my side" [John 20:27], and "as the Father has sent me, even so I send you" [John 20:21]. Now, it is clear and manifest that every person likes to think that he will be saved and attain to eternal salvation. This is what I propose to discuss now.

You also know that all philosophers, doctors and writers have studiously endeavored to teach and write what attitude man should take to piety. They have gone to great trouble, but, as is evident, to little avail. Now genuine and true piety consists of two kinds of works: those done for others, which are the right kind, and those done for ourselves, which are unimportant. In order to find a foundation, one man builds churches; another goes on a pilgrimage to St. James'[1] or St. Peter's;[2] a third fasts or prays, wears a cowl, goes barefoot, or does something else of the kind. Such works are nothing whatever and must be completely destroyed. Mark these words: none of our works have any power whatsoever. For God has chosen a man, the Lord Christ Jesus, to crush death, destroy sin, and shatter hell, since there was no one before he came who did not inevitably belong to the devil. The devil therefore thought he would get a hold upon the Lord when he hung between the two thieves and

1. St. James of Compostella, a cathedral in northern Spain.
2. A cathedral in Rome.

was suffering the most contemptible and disgraceful of deaths, which was cursed both by God and by men [cf. Deut. 21:23; Gal. 3:13]. But the Godhead was so strong that death, sin, and even hell were destroyed.

Therefore you should note well the words which Paul writes to the Romans [Rom. 5:12–21]. Our sins have their source in Adam, and because Adam ate the apple, we have inherited sin from him. But Christ has shattered death for our sake, in order that we might be saved by his works, which are alien to us, and not by our works.

But the papal dominion treats us altogether differently. It makes rules about fasting, praying, and butter-eating, so that whoever keeps the commandments of the pope will be saved and whoever does not keep them belongs to the devil. It thus seduces the people with the delusion that goodness and salvation lies in their own works. But I say that none of the saints, no matter how holy they were, attained salvation by their works. Even the holy mother of God did not become good, was not saved, by her virginity or her motherhood, but rather by the will of faith and the works of God, and not by her purity, or her own works. Therefore, mark me well: this is the reason why salvation does not lie in our own works, no matter what they are; it cannot and will not be effected without faith.

Now, someone may say: Look, my friend, you are saying a lot about faith, and claiming that our salvation depends solely upon it; now, I ask you, how does one come to faith? I will tell you. Our Lord Christ said, "Peace be with you. Behold my hands, etc." [John 20:26–27]. [In other words, he is saying:] Look, man, I am the only one who has taken away your sins and redeemed you, etc.; now be at peace. Just as you inherited sin from Adam—not that you committed it, for I did not eat the apple, any more than you did, and yet this is how we came to be in sin—so we have not suffered [as Christ did], and therefore we were made free from death and sin by God's work, not by our works. Therefore God says: Behold, man, I am your redemption [cf. Isa. 43:3], just as Paul said to the Corinthians: Christ is our justification and redemption, etc. [I Cor 1:30]. Christ is our justification and redemption, as Paul says in this passage. And here our [Roman] masters say: Yes, *Redemptor,* Redeemer; this is true, but it is not enough.

Therefore, I say again: Alien works, these make us good! Our Lord Christ says: I am your justification. I have destroyed the sins you have upon you. Therefore only believe in me; believe that I am he who has done this; then you will be justified. For it is written, *Justicia est fides,* righteousness is identical with faith and comes through faith. Therefore, if we want to have faith, we should believe the gospel, Paul, etc., and not the papal breves,[3] or the decretals,[4] but rather guard ourselves against them as against fire. For everything that comes from the pope cries out: Give, give; and if you refuse, you are of

3. **breve:** letter of authority.
4. **decretal:** decree on matters of doctrine.

the devil. It would be a small matter if they were only exploiting the people. But, unfortunately, it is the greatest evil in the world to lead the people to believe that outward works can save or make a man good.

At this time the world is so full of wickedness that it is overflowing, and is therefore now under a terrible judgment and punishment, which God has inflicted, so that the people are perverting and deceiving themselves in their own minds. For to build churches, and to fast and pray and so on has the appearance of good works, but in our heads we are deluding ourselves. We should not give way to greed, desire for temporal honor, and other vices and rather be helpful to our poor neighbor. Then God will arise in us and we in him, and this means a new birth. What does it matter if we commit a fresh sin? If we do not immediately despair, but rather say within ourselves, "O God, thou livest still! Christ my Lord is the destroyer of sin," then at once the sin is gone. And also the wise man says: *Septies in die cadit iustus et resurgit.*" "A righteous man falls seven times, and rises again" [Prov. 24:16].

The reason why the world is so utterly perverted and in error is that for a long time there have been no genuine preachers. There are perhaps three thousand priests, among whom one cannot find four good ones—God have mercy on us in this crying shame! And when you do get a good preacher, he runs through the gospel superficially and then follows it up with a fable . . . or he mixes in something of the pagan teachers, Aristotle, Plato, Socrates, and others, who are all quite contrary to the gospel, and also contrary to God, for they did not have the knowledge of the light which we possess. Aye, if you come to me and say: The Philosopher says: Do many good works, then you will acquire the habit, and finally you will become godly; then I say to you: Do not perform good works in order to become godly; but if you are already godly, then do good works, though without affectation and with faith. There you see how contrary these two points of view are.

In former times the devil made great attacks upon the people and from these attacks they took refuge in faith and clung to the Head, which is Christ; and so he was unable to accomplish anything. So now he has invented another device; he whispers into the ears of our Junkers[5] that they should make exactions from people and give them laws. This way it looks well on the outside; but inside it is full of poison. So the young children grow up in a delusion; they go to church thinking that salvation consists in praying, fasting, and attending mass. Thus it is the preacher's fault. But still there would be no need, if only we had right preachers.

The Lord said three times to St. Peter: *"Petre, amas me? etc.; pasce oves meas"* [John 21:15–17]. "Peter, feed, feed, feed my sheep." What is the meaning of *pascere*? It means to feed. How should one feed the sheep? Only by preaching the Word of God, only by preaching faith. Then our Junkers come along and

---

5. **junker:** member of the landowning nobility.

say: *Pascere* means *leges dare,* to enact laws, but with deception. Yes, they are well fed! They feed the sheep as the butchers do on Easter eve. Whereas one should speak the Word of God plainly to guide the poor and weak in faith, they mix in their beloved Aristotle, who is contrary to God, despite the fact that Paul says in Col. [2:8]: Beware of laws and philosophy. What does "philosophy" mean? If we knew Greek, Latin, and German, we would see clearly what the Apostle is saying.

Is not this the truth? I know very well that you don't like to hear this and that I am annoying many of you; nevertheless, I shall say it. I will also advise you, no matter who you are: If you have preaching in mind or are able to help it along, then do not become a priest or a monk, for there is a passage in the thirty-third and thirty-fourth chapters of the prophet Ezekiel, unfortunately a terrifying passage, which reads: If you forsake your neighbor, see him going astray, and do not help him, do not preach to him, I will call you to account for his soul [Ezek. 33:8; 34:10]. This is a passage which is not often read. But I say, you become a priest or a monk in order to pray your seven canonical hours and say mass, and you think you want to be godly. Alas, you're a fine fellow! It [i.e., being a priest or monk] will fail you. You say the Psalter, you pray the rosary, you pray all kinds of other prayers, and say a lot of words; you say mass, you kneel before the altar, you read confession, you go on mumbling and maundering; and all the while you think you are free from sin. And yet in your heart you have such great envy that, if you could choke your neighbor and get away with it creditably, you would do it; and that's the way you say mass. It would be no wonder if a thunderbolt struck you to the ground. But if you have eaten three grains of sugar or some other seasoning, no one could drag you to the altar with red-hot tongs.[6] You have scruples! And that means to go to heaven with the devil. I know very well that you don't like to hear this. Nevertheless, I will tell the truth, I must tell the truth, even though it cost me my neck twenty times over, that the verdict may not be pronounced against me [i.e., at the last judgment].

Yes, you say, there were learned people a hundred or fifty years ago too. That is true; but I am not concerned with the length of time or the number of persons. For even though they knew something of it then, the devil has always been a mixer, who preferred the pagan writers to the holy gospel. I will tell the truth and must tell the truth; that's why I'm standing here, and not taking any money for it either. Therefore, we should not build upon human law or works, but rather have true faith in the One who is the destroyer of sin; then we shall find ourselves growing in Him. Then everything that was bitter before is sweet. Then our hearts will recognize God. And when that happens we shall be despised, and we shall pay no regard to human law, and then the

---

6. Because of the rule that the priest must say mass fasting.

pope will come and excommunicate us. But then we shall be so united with God that we shall pay no heed whatsoever to any hardship, ban, or law.

Then someone may go on and ask: Should we not keep the man-made laws at all? Or, can we not continue to pray, fast, and so on, as long as the right way is present? My answer is that if there is present a right Christian love and faith, then everything a man does is meritorious; and each may do what he wills [cf. Rom. 14:22], so long as he has no regard for works, since they cannot save him.

In conclusion, then, every single person should reflect and remember that we cannot help ourselves, but only God, and also that our works are utterly worthless. So shall we have the peace of God. And every person should so perform his work that it benefits not only himself alone, but also another, his neighbor. If he is rich, his wealth should benefit the poor. If he is poor, his service should benefit the rich. When persons are servants or maidservants, their work should benefit their master. Thus no one's work should benefit him alone; for when you note that you are serving only your own advantage, then your service is false. I am not troubled; I know very well what man-made laws are. Let the pope issue as many laws as he likes, I will keep them all so far as I please.

Therefore, dear friends, remember that God has risen up for our sakes. Therefore let us also arise to be helpful to the weak in faith, and so direct our work that God may be pleased with it. So shall we receive the peace he has given to us today. May God grant us this every day. Amen.

Source 2 from Ulrich Leupold, editor, Luther's Works, *vol. 53 (Philadelphia: Fortress, 1965), p. 305.*

2. Luther, *Lord, Keep Us Steadfast in Thy Word,* hymn, 1541–1542

1. Lord, keep us steadfast in thy Word,
And curb the pope's and Turk's vile sword,
Who seek to topple from the throne
Jesus Christ, thine only Son.

2. Proof of thy might, Lord Christ, afford,
For thou of all the lords art Lord;
Thine own poor Christendom defend,
That it may praise thee without end.

3. God Holy Ghost, who comfort art,
Give to thy folk on earth one heart;

Stand by us breathing our last breath,
Lead us to life straight out of death.

Sources 3 and 4 from Lutheran Book of Worship *(Minneapolis: Augsburg, 1978), hymn 229;
hymn 297.*

3. Luther, *A Mighty Fortress Is Our God,* hymn, 1527–1528

1. A mighty fortress is our God,
A sword and shield victorious;
He breaks the cruel oppressor's rod
And wins salvation glorious.
The old satanic foe
Has sworn to work us woe!
With craft and dreadful might
He arms himself to fight.
On earth he has no equal.

2. No strength of ours can match his might!
We would be lost, rejected.
But now a champion comes to fight,
Whom God himself elected.
You ask who this may be?
The Lord of hosts is he!
Christ Jesus, mighty Lord,
God's only Son, adored.
He holds the field victorious.

3. Though hordes of devils fill the land
All threat'ning to devour us,
We tremble not, unmoved we stand;
They cannot overpow'r us,
Let this world's tyrant rage;
In battle we'll engage!
His might is doomed to fail;
God's judgment must prevail!
One little word subdues him.

4. God's Word forever shall abide,
No thanks to foes, who fear it;
For God himself fights by our side
With weapons of the Spirit.
Were they to take our house,

Goods, honor, child, or spouse,
Though life be wrenched away,
They cannot win the day.
The Kingdom's ours forever!

4. Paul Speratus, *Salvation unto Us Has Come*, hymn, 1524

1. Salvation unto us has come
By God's free grace and favor;
Good works cannot avert our doom,
They help and save us never.
Faith looks to Jesus Christ alone,
Who did for all the world atone;
He is our mediator.

2. Theirs was a false, misleading dream
Who thought God's law was given
That sinners might themselves redeem
And by their works gain heaven.
The Law is but a mirror bright
To bring the inbred sin to light
That lurks within our nature.

3. And yet the Law fulfilled must be,
Or we were lost forever;
Therefore God sent his Son that he
Might us from death deliver.
He all the Law for us fulfilled,
And thus his Father's anger stilled
Which over us impended.

4. Faith clings to Jesus' cross alone
And rests in him unceasing;
And by its fruits true faith is known,
With love and hope unceasing.
For faith alone can justify;
Works serve our neighbor and supply
The proof that faith is living.

5.   All blessing, honor, thanks, and praise
To Father, Son, and Spirit,
The God who saved us by his grace;
All glory to his merit.
O triune God in heav'n above,
You have revealed your saving love;
Your blessed name we hallow.

Source 5 from Kupferstichkabinett Staatliche Museen zu Berlin, Preussischer Kulturbesitz,
Berlin. Photograph by Jorg P. Anders.

5. Matthias Gerung, Broadsheet, Lauingen (Germany), 1546

6. Matthias Gerung, Broadsheet, Lauingen, 1546

Source 7 from The Pierpont Morgan Library, New York/Art Resource NY.

7. Lucas Cranach, Pamphlet, Wittenberg (Germany), 1521

Source 8 from Herzog August Bibliothek, Wolfenbüttel.

8. Unknown Artist, Pamphlet, Augsburg (Germany), 1522

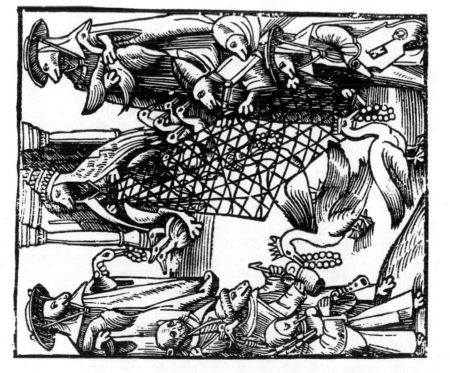

Source 9 from Brieg Gymnasialbibliothek.

9. Lucas Cranach, Pamphlet, Wittenberg, 1545[7]

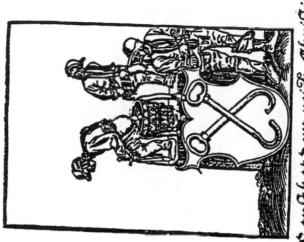

Bapst hat dem reich Christi gethon
Wie man hie handelt seine Cron.
Machts je zweifeltig: spricht der geist
S Denckt getrost ein:Gott ists ders heist.
Matt.Luth.

7. The lines below the woodcut read, "The pope has done to the king-dom of Christ/What is here being done to his own crown."

Source 10 from Oskar Schade, Satiren und Pasquille aus der Reformationszeit, *vol. 2, no. 15 (Hannover: 1863). Selection translated by Merry E. Wiesner.*

10. Anonymous German Pamphlet, 1523

A dialogue between two good friends named Hans Tholl and Claus Lamp, talking about the Antichrist[8] and his followers.

They are in a good mood while drinking wine and sit and discuss some ideas from the letters of Paul.

PREFACE

Dear Christians and brothers, if we want to recognize and know the Antichrist, we have to go to the brothers who can read, so that they will read us the second chapter of the second letter of Paul to the Thessalonians. There we will clearly find him, with his gestures and manners, how he acted and still acts, how he is now revealed so that we do not have to wait any longer but can know him despite his masks. How the devil sends his followers to knock us down, and how the old women and bath maids see him. We have long been blind to the lies and deceits of Satan, the devil. Because we have not paid attention to the divine warnings from Daniel, Paul, Christ, Peter, and the apocalypse of John, God has tormented us with ghosts and apparitions who will take us all with them to hell. Why should this cause God to suffer when He has offered you His holy word? If you don't want it, then go to the devil, for he is here now. He sees, finds, and possesses.

It happened that Hans Tholl and Claus Lamp were looking for each other and finally found each other in the evening.

CLAUS: My friend Hans, where have you been all day? I've been looking for you. The innkeeper has a good wine for two cents, and I wanted to drink a glass of wine with you.

HANS: Dear friend, I've been in a place that I wouldn't take six glasses of wine for.

CLAUS: So tell me where you have been.

HANS: I've got exciting news.

CLAUS: Well, what is it then? Tell me!

HANS: I was in a place where a friend read to four of us from the Bible. He read in the second chapter of the second letter of Paul to the Thessalonians about the Antichrist and how one is to recognize him.

CLAUS: Oh I would have given a penny to have been there.

8. **Antichrist:** the devil.

HANS: I want you to believe that I haven't heard anything like this in my whole life; I wouldn't have given three pennies to miss it.

CLAUS: Can't you remember anything, Hans? Can you tell me something about it?

HANS: I think I can tell you about almost the whole chapter, and only leave a little out.

CLAUS: So tell me! But let's get some wine first. I'll pay for yours.

HANS: Here's to your money!

CLAUS: Innkeeper, bring some wine.

HANS: What does he get for it?

CLAUS: He gets two cents. Now, tell me! I really want to hear what you will say about the Antichrist.

HANS: I'll tell you, but it will seem strange to you.

CLAUS: Why?

HANS: It seemed strange and odd to me, too, that people or states are the Antichrist.

CLAUS: Go ahead, then, you're boring me.

HANS: Stop that. All right, here's what the chapter says: "Dear brothers," Paul writes to the Thessalonians, "We ask you in the name of the coming of Christ and our coming together for the same, that you not be moved in your senses (or from your senses), or frightened by the spirit or the word or by letters supposedly coming from us, saying that the day of the Lord has come or will be coming soon. Let no one deceive you in any way, it will come only when there is disagreement and disunity (even though they all say they are preaching and believing nothing but the Gospel and Christianity) and the man of lawlessness will be disclosed, the son of damnation, who is against the gospel. Then he will be raised up (here Claus Lamp began to understand) above everything that is called a god (or is worshipped as a god) until he sits in the temple of God and lets himself be prayed to as if he were God." Claus, what are you thinking about? Do you know this man of lawlessness?

CLAUS: Now all the devils will come for you! He is no other beast than the Pope and his realm. I would never in my whole life have realized that if you hadn't been there [to hear it]. I'll buy you a second glass of wine!

HANS: Be quiet! I want to tell you more.

CLAUS: My dear friend, still more?

HANS: Of course. First I'll tell you the reason why I was talked to for so long.

CLAUS: My friend, for God's sake keep talking!

HANS: So listen! Here is the text: Paul says: "Don't you remember the things that I told you when I was with you? And now you know what is holding him (or what you should pay attention to), and that he will be revealed in his time. I tell you, that now he is doing so many evil and underhanded things, that only those who stop it now will stop it when his time comes fully. And then he will be revealed, the lawless one"—listen here, Claus—"who the lord Jesus Christ will slay with the breath of His mouth and will totally destroy with the light of His coming. But the coming of the Antichrist is through the activity of Satan, the devil, with great power and supposed signs and wonders, and with misguided celebration of the evil of those who will be destroyed. Because they would not accept the love of truth" (this clearly refers to the Gospel) "and be saved, God sends them the results of their errors, a great delusion, so that they believe the lies and are all condemned who did not believe the truth but agreed to the evil (and took it on themselves)." See that, Claus! Now you have heard why God has allowed error. Even though we have long wanted not to do wrong, we still hard-headedly keep doing it.

CLAUS: That says a lot. I would set my life on it, if it were only half as important. Now I hear and see that God allows very little understanding.

HANS: Yes, and why? People don't want to know very much and don't go to the Bible. God has hardened them and we are so godless. God will make us suffer because we don't ask about the truth. If we only had half as much concern about the health of our souls as we have about material goods, we wouldn't have come so far from the right path. As you have just heard, it isn't God who sent the so-called preachers [to lead us astray]. Here, I'll say it to you straight: Paul goes on to say: "Dear brothers, we should give thanks to God at all times because he chose you from the beginning, and he called you through the Gospel" (and not through other fairy-stories, as people are now saying).

CLAUS: Unfortunately you are right. Right now I hear strange things about the beast of the Antichrist from priests and monks. God help us!

HANS: Yes, we need to pray earnestly to God to send us good preachers, that preach the pure Gospel and leave the fairy-stories at home.

CLAUS: My friend, I am still thinking about the Antichrist, that he has begun so many devilish things and made the whole world to be his fool.

HANS: That astonishes me, too. But you have now heard from Paul, when he says: "God has allowed them to be deluded because they have not accepted the truth." We haven't noticed this, and the priests have hidden it from us.

CLAUS: I believe that the devil has possessed them all so that they haven't preached to us about these things.

HANS: They are afraid that people would recognize that their God, the Pope, is the Antichrist. People are supposed to honor and pray to him, just like Paul says about the Antichrist. So they are afraid.

CLAUS: That's really true. They've thought: If we tell the lay people this, they will notice and think about how they have to kiss the Pope's foot and call him "most holy." And some know-it-alls even say: The Pope can't do any wrong; he can't sin.

HANS: It's amazing that God has allowed this to happen for so long, that it hasn't been made clear that we have been so blind. What really matters is that we have deserted the truth, my dear Claus. Let's ask God for the true faith! I see clearly that everything will soon be over, that the Last Judgment stands right before the door!

CLAUS: My dear brother Hans, I've thought that for a long time. Shall we go home?

HANS: Yes, let's drink up and go.

CLAUS: I don't want to drink any more, because I have been so seized by pity and compassion. I see that things will end soon. My dear Hans, I want to take this thing to its end with you, so I have to ask: what do you think about the fact that there is such a commotion now about Luther and his writings?

HANS: I think it's because he has discovered the Antichrist. He can't stand it, and I believe he will make many martyrs. I've heard that it has already started in some places; in Antwerp three people have been burnt because of his teachings. And I've heard that in some places they are imprisoning people and hunting them down.

CLAUS: If that's true, that's what's supposed to happen. I have always heard that the Antichrist will make martyrs and will pay money so that people will kill those who do not believe in him but instead preach the word of God.

HANS: I've heard that, too. Now to the next thing: when I want to hear more things read, I'll tell you.

CLAUS: My dear friend, I'll let everything be open to you, because I see clearly what will come out of it. I see clearly, if I want to be saved, I have to come back to the true faith, from which without a doubt the Antichrist and his horde have led us. God give you a good night!

HANS: Same to you! See that you don't forget what I've said.

CLAUS: I won't for the rest of my life. God be praised.

QUESTIONS TO CONSIDER

In exploring how the Reformation movement grew and took root throughout Europe, many scholars point to the printing press as the key factor in explaining why Luther's reforms had a much greater impact than those of Wyclif and Hus. After examining the sources, would you agree? What difference did it make that Luther's sermons were not only delivered but also printed? That hymns were not simply taught to choirs of monks or clergymen but to congregations of laypeople, out of hymnals that were printed and might be purchased by any fairly well-to-do member? That small pamphlets such as the one reproduced here were written in German and appeared in paperback?

Several historians have also pointed to the opposite effect, that the Protestant emphasis on individual reading of the Bible dramatically increased the demand for books. Judging by the language, what sort of person might have bought Luther's sermon or the pamphlet? What effects would you expect the Protestant Reformation to have had on literacy? The religious conflict itself was also a spur to book production and book buying, and religious works were the best sellers of the sixteenth century. What techniques did the pamphlet writer use to make his work more appealing to a buyer? How might including some of the woodcuts have affected sales?

Of course, the great majority of people in the sixteenth century could not read, so it may be wrong to overemphasize written sources of communication. As you noticed in the dialogue, however, people who could not read often turned to their neighbors who could, so that printed pamphlets were often heard by many who could not read them themselves. This dialogue itself was probably read out loud and may even have been acted out, which we know was the case with more elaborate dialogues containing stage directions and a whole cast of characters. Do you think this dialogue would have been effective read aloud rather than silently? The printing press also increased the circulation of visual images; woodcuts such as those reproduced here often became best sellers. Why did so many people purchase these woodcuts? If a person's only contact with Protestant thinking were images such as these, how would his or her beliefs have differed from those of a person who could read Luther's words as well?

To answer the second question—how the Protestant message was made attractive to people—look at your list of frequently repeated ideas and images. Which seem directed to all Christians? For example, what do the sources say about the role of good works in helping a person achieve salvation? The role of faith? Why might these ideas have been appealing? What was wrong with the Catholic clergy? In contrast, what did "good preachers" do and emphasize? Why might the contrast have made Luther's ideas attractive?

Though ideas and images were often repeated, not everyone understood them in the same way nor was attracted to them for the same reasons. Groups within German society responded to different parts of the Protestant message and must be examined separately. Begin with the peasants. How are they depicted in the various sources? Why did the pamphlet writer and the artist of Source 9 choose to make their characters peasants? In the heaven and hell woodcuts, where are peasants and poor people? Why would peasants have been particularly attracted to the criticism of indulgences? Why would Luther's ideas about the value of good works have appealed to them? Source 5 shows nobles in fancy feathered hats near hell and Source 8 depicts rulers as geese; how would peasants have responded to these images? In the dialogue, Claus and Hans both agree that the Last Judgment is near. Why might sixteenth-century peasants have accepted this idea of the imminence of the end of the world?

Now consider the nobles and rulers. We have already noted that several of the woodcuts portray them negatively. How did Luther portray them in his sermon? Though hostility to nobles and rulers is evident in the Protestant message, many of the movement's ideas and images appealed to this class. Look, for example, at the upper right picture in Source 7. How does this scene reflect the hostility of rulers to the papacy? The noble class was primarily responsible for military actions in sixteenth-century Germany. How would they have responded to the language of the hymns? What effect might linking the Turks and the pope in the second hymn and the woodcut of Source 6 have had? Luther's sermon, the second and third hymns, Source 6, and the final dialogue all include devils attacking people or dragging them to hell at the Last Judgment. Why might nobles have been attracted to such imagery? What message would they have gotten from imagery linking such devils with the pope? In what ways did the reasons why Luther's ideas appealed to nobles contradict the reasons they appealed to peasants?

Other groups in German society appear only rarely in the sources given here, so you will not be able to discover as much about the ways in which the Protestant message attracted them as you can in the case of peasants and nobles. You may, however, want to review the sources for evidence relating to the middle class, which you can find most easily in the woodcuts. Which of your answers about the reasons certain ideas were appealing to peasants or nobles would also apply to middle-class people?

You are now ready to answer both questions posed in this chapter. How were the basic concepts of the Reformation communicated to a wide range of the population? How were these concepts made attractive to different groups?

EPILOGUE

Though Luther's initial message was one of religious reform, people quickly saw its social, economic, and political implications. The free imperial knights used Luther's attack on the wealth of the Church and his ideas about the spiritual equality of all Christians to justify their rebellion in 1521. Quickly suppressed, this uprising was followed by a more serious rebellion by peasants in 1525. Peasants in south Germany added religious demands, such as a call for "good pastors" and an end to church taxes, to their long-standing economic grievances and took up arms. The Peasants' War spread eastward and northward but was never unified militarily, and it was brutally put down by imperial and noble armies later the same year.

Given some of Luther's remarks about rulers and human laws (as you read in the sermon), the peasants expected him to support them. He did not and urged them instead to obey their rulers, for in his opinion religion was not a valid justification for political revolution or social upheaval. When the peasants did not listen and continued their rebellion, Luther turned against them, calling them "murdering and thieving hordes." He supported the rulers in their slaughter of peasant armies, and his later writings became much more conservative than the sermon you read here.

The nobles and rulers who accepted Luther's message continued to receive his support, however. Many of the German states abolished the Catholic church and established their own Protestant churches under their individual ruler's control. This expulsion led to a series of religious wars between Protestants and Catholics that were finally ended by the Peace of Augsburg in 1555. The terms of the peace treaty allowed rulers to choose between Catholicism and Lutheran Protestantism; they were further given the right to enforce religious uniformity within their territories. By the middle of the sixteenth century, then, the only people who could respond as they chose to the Protestant message were rulers.

Achieving religious uniformity was not as simple a task as it had been earlier, however. Though rulers attempted to ban materials they did not agree with and prevent their subjects from reading or printing forbidden materials, religious literature was regularly smuggled from city to city. Because printing presses could produce thousands of copies of anything fairly quickly, ideas of all types spread much more quickly than they did earlier. Once people can read, it is much more difficult to control the information they take in; though rulers could control their subjects' outward religious activities, they could not control their thoughts.

Rulers were not the only ones who could not control thinking and the exchange of ideas during the sixteenth century. As Luther discovered to his dismay, once ideas are printed and widely disseminated, they take on a life of their own; no matter how much one might wish, they cannot be called back nor be made to conform to their original meaning. Not only did German knights and peasants interpret Luther's message in their own way, but other religious reformers, building on what he had written, developed their own interpretations of the Christian message. They used the same variety of methods that had been so successful in spreading Luther's ideas to communicate their own, and the Protestant Reformation became a multifaceted movement with many different leaders and numerous plans for action.

The Catholic church, learning from Protestant successes, began to publish its own illustrated pamphlets with negative images of Luther and other Protestant leaders along with explanations of its theology in easy-to-understand language. In this chapter we have looked exclusively at Lutheran propaganda, but the oral, written, and visual techniques of communication presented here were employed by all sides in the sixteenth-century religious conflict. Later they would be adapted for other political and intellectual debates.

CHAPTER THIRTEEN

STAGING ABSOLUTISM

THE PROBLEM

The "Age of Absolutism" is the label historians often apply to the history of Europe in the seventeenth and eighteenth centuries. In many ways it is an appropriate description because, with the exception of England where the Civil War (1642–1648) and the Glorious Revolution (1688) severely limited royal power and created parliamentary government, most European states had monarchs in this era who aspired to absolute authority in their realms.

The royal absolutism that evolved in seventeenth-century Europe represents an important step in governmental development. In constructing absolutist states, monarchs and their ministers both created new organs of administration and built on existing institutions of government to supplant the regional authorities of the medieval state with more centralized state power. In principle, this centralized authority was subject to the absolute authority of the monarch; in practice, royal authority was nowhere as encompassing as that of a modern dictator. Poor communication sys-

tems, the persistence of traditional privileges that exempted whole regions or social groups from full royal authority, and other factors all set limits on royal power. Nevertheless, monarchs of the era strove for the ideal of absolute royal power, and France was the model in their work of state building.

French monarchs of the seventeenth and early eighteenth centuries more fully developed the system of absolute monarchy. In these rulers' efforts to overcome impediments to royal authority we can learn much about the creation of absolutism in Europe. Rulers in Prussia, Austria, Russia, and many smaller states sought not only the real power of the French kings but also the elaborate court ceremony and dazzling palaces that symbolized that power.

Absolutism in France was the work of Henry IV (r. 1589–1610), Louis XIII (r. 1610–1643) and his minister Cardinal Richelieu, and Louis XIV (r. 1643–1715). These rulers established a system of centralized royal political authority that destroyed many remnants of the feudal monarchy. The reward for their endeavors was great: with Europe's largest population and immense wealth, France was potentially the mightiest country on the continent in 1600 and its natural leader, if only these national strengths could be unified and directed by a strong government. Creation of such a government around an absolute monarch was the aim of French rulers, but they confronted formidable problems, common to many early modern states, in achieving their goal. Nobles everywhere still held considerable power, in part a legacy of the system of feudal monarchy. In France they possessed military power, which they used in the religious civil wars of the sixteenth century and in their Fronde revolt against growing royal power in the mid-seventeenth century. Nobles also exercised considerable political power through such representative bodies as the Estates General and provincial assemblies, which gave form to their claims for a voice in government. Moreover, nobles served as the judges of the great law courts, the *parlements*, that had to register all royal edicts before they could take effect.

A second obstacle to national unity and royal authority in many states, in an age that equated national unity with religious uniformity, was the presence of a large and influential religious minority. In France the Protestant minority was known as the Huguenots. Not only did they forswear the Catholic religion of the king and the majority of his subjects, but they possessed military power in their rights, under the Edict of Nantes,[1] to fortify their cities.

A third and major impediment to unifying a country under absolute royal authority lay in regional differences. The medieval monarchy of France had been built province by province over several centuries, and the kingdom was not well integrated. Some provinces, like Brittany in the north, retained local estates or assemblies with which the monarch actually had to bargain for taxes. Many provinces had their own cultural heritage that separated them from the king's government centered in Paris. These differences might be as simple as matters of local custom, but also as complex as unique systems of civil law. A particular problem was the persistence of local dialects, which made the French of royal officials a foreign and incomprehensible tongue in large portions of the kingdom.

The only unifying principle that could overcome all these centrifugal forces was royal authority. The task in the seventeenth century was to build a theoretical basis for a truly powerful monarch, to endow the king with tangible power that gave substance to theory, and to place the sovereign in a setting that would never permit the country to forget his new power.

To establish an abstract basis for absolutism, royal authority had to be strengthened and reinforced by a veritable cult of kingship. Seventeenth-

1. **Edict of Nantes:** In this 1598 decree, King Henry IV sought to end the civil warfare between French Catholics and Huguenots. He granted the Protestants basic protection, in the event of renewed fighting, by allowing them to fortify some 200 of their cities. The edict also accorded the Protestants freedom of belief with some restrictions and civil rights equal to those of Catholic Frenchmen.

century French statesmen built on medieval foundations in this task. Medieval kings had possessed limited tangible authority but substantial religious prestige; their vassals had rendered them religious oaths of loyalty. French monarchs since Pepin the Short had been anointed in a biblically inspired coronation ceremony in which they received not only the communion bread the Catholic church administered to all believers, but also the wine normally reserved for clerics; once crowned, they claimed to possess mystical religious powers to heal with the royal touch. All these trappings served to endow the monarch with almost divine powers, separating him from and raising him above his subjects. Many seventeenth-century thinkers emphasized this traditional divine dimension of royal power. Others, as you will see, found more practical grounds for great royal power.

To achieve greater royal power, Henry IV reestablished peace after the religious civil warfare of the late sixteenth century and Cardinal Richelieu curbed the military power of the nobility. With the creation of loyal provincial administrators, the *intendants,* and a system of political patronage that he directed, the cardinal also established firmer central control in the name of Louis XIII. Richelieu, moreover, ended Huguenot political power by crushing their revolt in 1628, and he intervened in the Thirty Years' War to establish France as a chief European power.

The reign of Louis XIV completed the process of consolidating royal authority in France. Louis XIV created much of the administrative apparatus necessary to centralize the state. The king brought the nobility under even greater control, building in Europe's largest army a force that could defeat any aristocratic revolt and creating in Versailles a court life that drew nobles near to the king, away from provincial plotting, where their actions could be observed. The king also sought to extend royal authority by expanding France's borders through a series of wars and to eliminate completely the Huguenot minority by revoking their religious freedoms embodied in the Edict of Nantes.

The king supplemented his military and political work of state building with other projects to integrate France more completely as one nation. With royal patronage, authors and scholars flourished and, by the example of their often excellent works, extended the French dialect in the country at the expense of provincial tongues. In the king's name, his finance minister, Jean-Baptiste Colbert (1619–1683) sought to realize a vision of a unified French economy. He designed mercantilist policies to favor French trade and to build French industry, and he improved transportation to bind the country together as one unit. The result of Louis's policies, therefore, was not only a stronger king and a more powerful France but a more unified country as well.

Far more than previous French monarchs, Louis XIV addressed the third task in establishing absolutism. In modern terms it consisted of effective public relations, which required visible evidence of the new royal authority. The stage setting for the royal display of the symbols of absolute authority was Versailles, the site of a new royal palace. Built between 1661 and 1682, the palace itself was massive, with a façade one-quarter mile long pierced by 2,143 windows. It was set in a park of 37,000 acres, of which 6,000 acres were embellished with formal gardens. These gardens contained 1,400 fountains that required massive hydraulic works to supply them with water, an artificial lake one mile long for royal boating parties, and 200 statues. The palace grounds contained various smaller palaces as well, including Marly, where the king could entertain small, select groups, away from the main palace that was the center of a court life embracing almost 20,000 persons (9,000 soldiers billeted in the town; and 5,000 royal servants, 1,000 nobles and their 4,000 servants, plus the royal family, all housed in the main palace). Because the royal ministers and their secretaries also were in residence, Versailles was much more than a palace: it was the capital of France.

Royal architects deliberately designed the palace to impart a message to all who entered. As a guidebook of 1681 by Laurent Morellet noted regarding the palace's art:

> The subjects of painting which complete the decorations of the ceilings are of heroes and illustrious men, taken from history and fable, who have deserved the titles of Magnanimous, of Great, of Fathers of the People, of Liberal, of Just, of August and Victorious, and who have possessed all the Virtues which we have seen appear in the Person of our Great Monarch during the fortunate course of his reign; so that everything remarkable which one sees in the Château and in the garden always has some relationship with the great actions of His Majesty.[2]

The court ritual and etiquette enacted in this setting departed markedly from the simpler court life of Louis XIII and were designed to complement the physical presence of the palace itself in teaching the lesson of a new royal power.

In this chapter we will analyze royal absolutism in France. What was the theoretical basis for absolute royal authority? What was traditional and what was new in the justification of royal power as expressed in late sixteenth- and seventeenth-century France? How did such early modern kings as Louis XIV communicate their absolute power in the various ceremonies and symbols of royal authority presented in the evidence that follows?

SOURCES AND METHOD

This chapter assembles several kinds of sources, each demanding a different kind of historical analysis. Two works of political theory that were influential in the formation of abso-

2. Laurent Morellet, *Explication historique de ce qu'il y a de plus remarquable dans la maison royale de Versailles et en celle de Monsieur à Saint-Cloud* (Paris, 1681), quoted in Robert W. Hartle, "Louis XIV and the Mirror of Antiquity" in Steven G. Reinhardt and Vaughn L. Glasgow, eds., *The Sun King: Louis XIV and the New World* (New Orleans: Louisiana State Museum Foundation, 1984), p. 111.

lutism open the evidence. To analyze these works effectively, you will need some brief background information on their authors and on the problems these thinkers discussed.

Jean Bodin (1530–1596) was a law professor, an attorney, and a legal official. His interests transcended his legal education, however. He brought a wide reading in Hebrew, Greek, Italian, and German to the central problem addressed in his major work, *The Six Books of the Republic* (1576), that of establishing the well-ordered state. Writing during the religious wars of the sixteenth century when government in France all but broke down, Bodin offered answers to this crisis. Especially novel for the sixteenth century was his call for religious toleration. Although he was at least formally a Catholic[3] and recognized unity in religion as a strong unifying factor for a country, Bodin was unwilling to advocate force in eliminating Protestantism from France. He believed that acceptance was by far the better policy.

Bodin's political thought was also significant, and his *Republic* immediately was recognized as an important work. Published in several editions and translated into Latin, Italian, Spanish, and German, the *Republic* influenced a circle of men, the *Politiques*,

who advised Henry IV. Through the process of seeking to explain how to establish the well-ordered state, Bodin contributed much to Western political theory. Perhaps his most important idea was that there was nothing divine about governing power. Men created governments solely to ensure their physical and material security; to meet those needs, the ruling power had to exercise a sovereignty on which Bodin placed few limits.[4] Indeed, Bodin's concept of the ruler's power is his most important contribution to political thought. In the brief selection from Jean Bodin's complex work, examine his conception of the sovereign power required to establish a well-ordered state in France and contrast this conception with the feudal state still partially existing in his time.

The second work of political theory was written by Jacques Bénigne Bossuet (1627–1704), Bishop of Meaux. A great orator who preached at the court of Louis XIV, Bossuet was entrusted with the education of the king's son and heir, the Dauphin. He wrote three works for that prince's instruction, including the one excerpted in this chapter, *Politics Drawn from the Very Words of the Holy Scripture* (1678).

As tutor to the Dauphin and royal preacher, Bossuet expressed what has been called the *divine right* theory of kingship: that is, the king was God's deputy on earth, and to oppose him was to oppose divine law. Here, of

---

3. Bodin's religious thought evolved in the course of his life. Although he was brought up a Catholic and was briefly a Carmelite friar, his knowledge of Hebrew and early regard for the Old Testament led some to suspect he was a Jew. Writings of his middle years indicate some Calvinist leanings. Later in life, his thought seems to have moved beyond traditional Catholic and Protestant Christianity. He was nevertheless deeply religious.

4. Bodin saw the sovereign power limited by natural law and the need to respect property (which meant that the ruler could not tax without his subjects' consent) and the family.

course, the bishop was drawing on those medieval beliefs and practices imputing certain divine powers to the king. Because Bossuet was an influential member of the court of Louis XIV, his ideas on royal authority carried considerable weight. Trained as a theologian, he buttressed his political theories with scriptural authority. In this selection, determine the extent of the royal link to God. Why might such a theory be particularly useful to Louis XIV?

Source 3 is a selection from the *Memoirs* of Louis de Rouvroy, Duke of Saint-Simon (1675–1755). Saint-Simon's memoirs of court life are extensive, comprising forty-one volumes in the main French edition. They constitute both a remarkable record of life at Versailles and, because of their style, an important example of French literature. As useful and important as the *Memoirs* are, however, they must be read with care. All of us, consciously or unconsciously, have biases and opinions, and memoirists are no exception. In fact, memoir literature illustrates problems of which students of history should be aware in all they read. The way in which authors present events, even what they choose to include or omit from their accounts, reflects their opinions. Because memoir writers often recount events in which they participated, they may have especially strong views about what they relate. Thus, to use Saint-Simon's work profitably, it is essential to understand his point of view. We must also ask if the memoir writer was in a position to know firsthand what he or she is relating or is simply recounting less reliable rumors.

Saint-Simon came from an old noble family recently risen to prominence when his father became a royal favorite. Ironically, no one was more deeply opposed to the policies of Louis XIV, which aimed at destroying the traditional feudal power of the nobility in the name of royal authority, than this man whose position rested on that very authority. Saint-Simon was, quite simply, a defender of the older style of kingship in which sovereignty was limited by the monarch's need to consult with his vassals. His memoirs reflect this view and are often critical of the king. But even with his critical view of the king and his court, Saint-Simon was an important figure there, an individual privy to state business and court gossip, who gives us a remarkable picture of life at Versailles. Analyze the court etiquette and ritual Saint-Simon describes as a nonverbal message from the king to his most powerful subjects. For example, what message did the royal waking and dressing ceremony convey to the most powerful and privileged persons in France, who crowded the royal bedroom and vied for the privilege of helping the king dress? What message did their very presence convey in turn to Louis XIV? Recall Bossuet's ideas of kingship. Why might public religious ritual such as that attending the royal rising be part of the agenda of a king not particularly noted for his piety during the first half of his life?

Studied closely, the three different kinds of written evidence presented—the work of a sixteenth-century political theorist, the writings of a contemporary supporter, and the memoirs of one of the king's opponents—reveal much about the growing power of the French monarchy. What common themes do you find in these works? What were the sources of the king's political authority? From these written sources we move on to pictorial evidence of the symbols of royal authority. Symbols are concrete objects possessing a meaning beyond what is immediately apparent. We are all aware of the power of symbols, particularly in our age of electronic media, and we all, perhaps unconsciously, analyze them to some extent. Take a simple example drawn from modern advertising: the lion appears frequently as an image in advertisements for banks and other financial institutions. The lion's presence is intended to convey to us the strength of the financial institution, to inspire our faith in the latter's ability to protect our funds. Using this kind of analysis, you can determine the total meaning of the symbols associated with Louis XIV.

Consider the painting presented as the fourth piece of evidence, *Louis XIV Taking Up Personal Government in 1661*. Louis XIV had been king in name since the age of five after his father's death in 1643, but only in 1661, as an adult, did he assume full power. Remember that such art was generally commissioned by the king and often had an instructional purpose. What do the following elements symbolize: the portrayal of Louis XIV as a Roman emperor; the positioning of a figure representing France on his right; the crowning of

the king with a wreath of flowers; the figure of Time (note the hourglass and scythe) holding a tapestry over the royal head; and the presence of herald angels hovering above?

Now go on to the other pictures and perform the same kind of analysis, always trying to identify the symbolic message the painter or architect wished to convey. For Source 5 study the royal pose and such seemingly superficial elements in the picture as the king's dress and the background details. Ask yourself what ideas these were intended to convey. Source 6 presents the insignia Louis XIV chose as his personal symbol, which decorated much of Versailles. Reflect on Louis's reasons for this choice in reading his explanation:

The symbol that I have adopted and that you see all around you represents the duties of a Prince and inspires me always to fulfill them. I chose for an emblem the Sun which, according to the rules of this art [heraldry], is the noblest of all, and which, by the brightness that surrounds it, by the light it lends to the other stars that constitute, after a fashion, its court, by the universal good it does, endlessly promoting life, joy, and growth, by its perpetual and regular movement, by its constant and invariable course, is assuredly the most dazzling and most beautiful image of the monarch.[5]

With Sources 8 through 13, we turn to analysis of architecture, which of course also served to symbolize royal power. You must ask yourself how great that concept of royal power was

5. Quoted in Reinhardt and Glasgow, *The Sun King*, p. 181.

as you look at the pictures of Versailles. The palace, after all, was not only the royal residence but also the setting for the conduct of government, including the king's reception of foreign ambassadors. At the most basic level, notice the scale of the palace. What impression might its size have been intended to convey? At a second level, examine decorative details of the palace. Why might the balustrade at the palace entry have been decorated with statuary symbolizing Magnificence, Justice, Wisdom, Prudence, Diligence, Peace, Europe, Asia, Renown, Abundance, Force, Generosity, Wealth, Authority, Fame, America, Africa, and Victory?

Observe the views of the palace's interior, considering the functions of the rooms and their details. Source 10 offers a view of the royal chapel at Versailles. Richly decorated in marble and complemented with ceiling paintings such as that depicting the Trinity, the chapel was the site of daily masses as well as of royal marriages and celebrations of victories. Note that the king attended mass in the royal gallery, joining the rest of the court on the main floor only when the mass celebrant was a bishop. Why might such a magnificent setting be part of the palace? More important, what significance do you place on the position the king chose for himself in this grand setting?

Sources 11 and 12 present the sites of the royal rising ceremony described by Saint-Simon. The royal bedroom, Source 11, was richly decorated in gilt, red, and white, and was complemented by paintings of biblical scenes. Notice the rich decoration of

the Bull's Eye Window Antechamber, just outside the bedroom, where the courtiers daily awaited the king's arising. Why were the rooms decorated in such a fashion?

Source 13 offers an artist's view of Marly. Again, notice the scale of this palace, reflecting that it was, according to Saint-Simon, a weekend getaway spot for Louis XIV and selected favorites. How might the king have used invitations to this château with the closeness to the royal person they entailed? Examine details of the palace. The central château had twelve apartments, four of which were reserved for the royal family, the others for its guests. The twelve pavilions around the lake in the center of the château's grounds each housed two guest apartments and represented the twelve signs of the zodiac. What symbolic importance might you attach to this?

Finally, return to Source 7, which recreates the pageant known as the Carousel of 1662, one of many such entertainments at court. The scale of such festivals could be huge. In 1662, 12,197 costumed people took part in a celebration that included a parade through the streets of Paris and games. Costumed as ancient Romans, Persians, and others, the participants must have made quite an impression on their audience. What kind of impression do you think it was?

What common message runs through the art and architecture you have analyzed? As you unravel the message woven into this visual evidence, combine it with the evidence you derived from Saint-Simon's portrayal of court life and the political theory of absolutism. Remember, too, the unstated message: that the monarchy of Louis XIV possessed in Europe's largest army the ultimate means for persuading its subjects to accept the divine powers of the king.

You should be able to determine from all this material what was new in this conception of royal authority and the ways in which the new authority was expressed.

THE EVIDENCE

Source 1 from Francis William Coker, editor, Readings in Political Philosophy *(New York: Macmillan, 1926), pp. 235–236.*

1. From Jean Bodin, *The Six Books of the Republic*, Book I, 1576

The first and principal function of sovereignty is to give laws to the citizens generally and individually, and, it must be added, not necessarily with the consent of superiors, equals, or inferiors. If the consent of superiors is required, then the prince is clearly a subject; if he must have the consent of equals, then others share his authority; if the consent of inferiors—the people or the senate—is necessary, then he lacks supreme authority. . . .

It may be objected that custom does not get its power from the judgment or command of the prince, and yet has almost the force of law, so that it would seem that the prince is master of law, the people of custom. Custom, insensibly, yet with the full compliance of all, passes gradually into the character of men, and acquires force with the lapse of time. Law, on the other hand, comes forth in one moment at the order of him who has the power to command, and often in opposition to the desire and approval of those whom it governs. Wherefore, Chrysostom[6] likens law to a tyrant and custom to a king. Moreover, the power of law is far greater than that of custom, for customs may be superseded by laws, but laws are not supplanted by customs; it is within the power and function of magistrates to restore the operation of laws which by custom are obsolescent. Custom proposes neither rewards nor penalties; laws carry one or the other, unless it be a permissive law which nullifies the penalty of some other law. In short, a custom has compelling force only as long as the prince, by adding his endorsement and sanction to the custom, makes it a law.

It is thus clear that laws and customs depend for their force upon the will of those who hold supreme power in the state. This first and chief mark of sovereignty is, therefore, of such sort that it cannot be transferred to subjects,

6. **Chrysostom:** Saint John Chrysostom (ca 347–407), an early Father of the Greek church whose religion led him into conflict with the Eastern Roman emperor.

though the prince or people sometimes confer upon one of the citizens the power to frame laws (*legum condendarum*), which then have the same force as if they had been framed by the prince himself. The Lacedæmonians bestowed such power upon Lycurgus, the Athenians upon Solon;[7] each stood as deputy for his state, and the fulfillment of his function depended upon the pleasure not of himself but of the people; his legislation had no force save as the people confirmed it by their assent. The former composed and wrote the laws, the people enacted and commanded them.

Under this supreme power of ordaining and abrogating laws, it is clear that all other functions of sovereignty are included; that it may be truly said that supreme authority in the state is comprised in this one thing—namely, to give laws to all and each of the citizens, and to receive none from them. For to declare war or make peace, though seeming to involve what is alien to the term law, is yet accomplished by law, that is by decree of the supreme power. It is also the prerogative of sovereignty to receive appeals from the highest magistrates, to confer authority upon the greater magistrates and to withdraw it from them, to allow exemption from taxes, to bestow other immunities, to grant dispensations from the laws, to exercise power of life and death, to fix the value, name and form of money, to compel all citizens to observe their oaths: all of these attributes are derived from the supreme power of commanding and forbidding—that is, from the authority to give law to the citizens collectively and individually, and to receive law from no one save immortal God. A duke, therefore, who gives laws to all his subjects, but receives law from the emperor, Pope, or king, or has a co-partner in authority, lacks sovereignty.

Source 2 from Richard H. Powers, editor and translator, Readings in European Civilization Since 1500 *(Boston: Houghton Mifflin, 1961), pp. 129–130.*

2. From Jacques Bénigne Bossuet, *Politics Drawn from the Very Words of the Holy Scriptures,* 1678

TO MONSEIGNEUR LE DAUPHIN

God is the King of kings. It is for Him to instruct and direct kings as His ministers. Heed then, Monseigneur, the lessons which He gives them in His Scriptures, and learn . . . the rules and examples on which they ought to base their conduct. . . .

---

7. **Lacedæmonians:** the Spartans of ancient Greece. **Lycurgus:** traditional author of the Spartan constitution. **Solon:** sixth-century B.C. Athenian lawgiver.

BOOK II: OR AUTHORITY . . .

CONCLUSION: Accordingly we have established by means of Scriptures that monarchical government comes from God. . . . That when government was established among men He chose hereditary monarchy as the most natural and most durable form. That excluding the sex born to obey[8] from the sovereign power was only natural. . . .

BOOK III: THE NATURE OF ROYAL AUTHORITY . . .

FIRST ARTICLE: Its essential characteristics. . . . First, royal authority is sacred; Second, it is paternal; Third, it is absolute; Fourth, it is subject to reason. . . .

SECOND ARTICLE: Royal authority is sacred.

FIRST PROPOSITION: God establishes kings as his ministers and reigns over people through them.—We have already seen that all power comes from God. . . .

Therefore princes act as ministers of God and as His lieutenants on earth. It is through them that he exercises His empire. . . .

Thus we have seen that the royal throne is not the throne of a man, but the throne of God himself. So in Scriptures we find "God has chosen my son Solomon to sit upon the throne of the kingdom of Jehovah over Israel." And further, "Solomon sat on the throne of Jehovah as king."

And in order that we should not think that to have kings established by God is peculiar to the Israelites, here is what Ecclesiastes says: "God gives each people its governor; and Israel is manifestly reserved to Him.". . .

SECOND PROPOSITION: The person of the king is sacred.—It follows from all the above that the person of kings is sacred. . . . God has had them anointed by His prophets with a sacred ointment, as He has had His pontiffs and His altars anointed.

But even before actually being anointed, they are sacred by virtue of their charge, as representatives of His divine majesty, delegated by His providence to execute His design. . . .

The title of *christ* is given to kings, one sees them called *christs* or the Lord's *anointed* everywhere.

Bearing this venerable name, even the prophets revered them, and looked upon them as associated with the sovereign empire of God, whose authority they exercise on earth. . . .

THIRD PROPOSITION: Religion and conscience demand that we obey the prince.—After having said that the prince is the minister of God Saint Paul concluded: "Accordingly it is necessary that you subject yourself to him out of fear of his anger, but also because of the obligation of your conscience. . . ."

And furthermore: "Servants, obey your temporal masters in all things. . . ." Saint Peter said: "Therefore submit yourselves to the order established among

---

8. **Sex born to obey:** women. The Salic Law, mistakenly attributed to the medieval Salian Franks, precluded women from inheriting the crown of France.

men for the love of God; be subjected to the king as to God . . . be subjected to those to whom He gives His authority and who are sent by Him to reward good deeds and to punish evil ones."

Even if kings fail in this duty, their charge and their ministry must be respected. For Scriptures tell us: "Obey your masters, not only those who are mild and good, but also those who are peevish and unjust."

Thus there is something religious in the respect which one renders the prince. Service to God and respect for kings are one thing. . . .

Thus it is in the spirit of Christianity for kings to be paid a kind of religious respect. . . .

BOOK IV: CONTINUATION OF THE CHARACTERISTICS OF ROYALTY

FIRST ARTICLE: Royal authority is absolute.

FIRST PROPOSITION: The prince need render account to no one for what he orders. . . .

SECOND PROPOSITION: When the prince has judged there is no other judgment. . . . Princes are gods.

Source 3 from Bayle St. John, translator, The Memoirs of the Duke of Saint-Simon on the Reign of Louis XIV and the Regency, *8th ed. (London: George Allen, 1913), vol. 2, pp. 363–365, vol. 3, pp. 221–227.*

3. The Duke of Saint-Simon on the Reign of Louis XIV

[*On the creation of Versailles and the
nature of its court life*]

He [Louis XIV] early showed a disinclination for Paris. The troubles that had taken place there during the minority made him regard the place as dangerous;[9] he wished, too, to render himself venerable by hiding himself from the eyes of the multitude; all these considerations fixed him at St. Germains[10] soon after the death of the Queen, his mother. It was to that place he began to attract the world by fêtes and gallantries, and by making it felt that he wished to be often seen.

---

9. During the Fronde revolt of 1648–1653, the royal government lost control of Paris to the crowds and the royal family was forced to flee the city. Because Louis XIV was a minor (only ten years of age) when the revolt erupted, the government was administered by his mother, Anne of Austria, and her chief minister, Cardinal Mazarin.

10. **St. Germain-en-Laye:** site of a royal château, overlooking the Seine and dating from the twelfth century, where Louis XIV was born. The court fled there in 1649 during the Fronde.

His love for Madame de la Vallière,[11] which was at first kept secret, occasioned frequent excursions to Versailles, then a little card castle, which had been built by Louis XIII—annoyed, and his suite still more so, at being frequently obliged to sleep in a wretched inn there, after he had been out hunting in the forest of Saint Leger. That monarch rarely slept at Versailles more than one night, and then from necessity; the King, his son, slept there, so that he might be more in private with his mistress; pleasures unknown to the hero and just man, worthy son of Saint Louis, who built the little château.[12]

These excursions of Louis XIV by degrees gave birth to those immense buildings he erected at Versailles; and their convenience for a numerous court, so different from the apartments at St. Germains, led him to take up his abode there entirely shortly after the death of the Queen.[13] He built an infinite number of apartments, which were asked for by those who wished to pay their court to him; whereas at St. Germains nearly everybody was obliged to lodge in the town, and the few who found accommodation at the château were strangely inconvenienced.

The frequent fêtes, the private promenades at Versailles, the journeys, were means on which the King seized in order to distinguish or mortify the courtiers, and thus render them more assiduous in pleasing him. He felt that of real favours he had not enough to bestow; in order to keep up the spirit of devotion, he therefore unceasingly invented all sorts of ideal ones, little preferences and petty distinctions, which answered his purpose as well.

He was exceedingly jealous of the attention paid him. Not only did he notice the presence of the most distinguished courtiers, but those of inferior degree also. He looked to the right and to the left, not only upon rising but upon going to bed, at his meals, in passing through his apartments, or his gardens of Versailles, where alone the courtiers were allowed to follow him; he saw and noticed everybody; not one escaped him, not even those who hoped to remain unnoticed. He marked well all absentees from the court, found out the reason of their absence, and never lost an opportunity of acting towards them as the occasion might seem to justify. With some of the courtiers (the most distinguished), it was a demerit not to make the court their ordinary abode; with others 'twas a fault to come but rarely; for those who never or scarcely ever came it was certain disgrace. When their names were in any way mentioned, "I do not know them," the King would reply haughtily. Those who presented themselves but seldom were thus characterized: "They are people I never see;" these decrees were irrevocable. . . .

11. **Madame de la Vallière:** Louise de la Baume le Blanc, Duchesse de la Vallière (1644–1710), the king's first mistress.

12. Saint-Simon greatly admired Louis XIII, whom he had never met, and for over half a century attended annual memorial services for the king at the royal tombs in the basilica of St. Denis.

13. Anne of Austria (1601–1666), the mother of Louis XIV.

Louis XIV took great pains to be well informed of all that passed everywhere; in the public places, in the private houses, in society and familiar intercourse. His spies and tell-tales were infinite. He had them of all species; many who were ignorant that their information reached him; others who knew it; others who wrote to him direct, sending their letters through channels he indicated; and all these letters were seen by him alone, and always before everything else; others who sometimes spoke to him secretly in his cabinet, entering by the back stairs. These unknown means ruined an infinite number of people of all classes, who never could discover the cause; often ruined them very unjustly; for the King, once prejudiced, never altered his opinion or so rarely, that nothing was more rare.

[*On the royal day and court etiquette*]

[*The royal day begins*]

At eight o'clock the chief valet de chambre on duty, who alone had slept in the royal chamber, and who had dressed himself, awoke the King. The chief physician, the chief surgeon, and the nurse (as long as she lived), entered at the same time. The latter kissed the King; the others rubbed and often changed his shirt, because he was in the habit of sweating a great deal. At the quarter, the grand chamberlain was called (or, in his absence, the first gentleman of the chamber), and those who had, what was called the *grandes entrées.* The chamberlain (or chief gentleman) drew back the curtains which had been closed again, and presented the holy water from the vase, at the head of the bed. These gentlemen stayed but a moment, and that was the time to speak to the King, if any one had anything to ask of him; in which case the rest stood aside. When, contrary to custom, nobody had aught to say, they were there but for a few moments. He who had opened the curtains and presented the holy water, presented also a prayer-book. Then all passed into the cabinet of the council. A very short religious service being over, the King called, they re-entered. The same officer gave him his dressing-gown; immediately after, other privileged courtiers entered, and then everybody, in time to find the King putting on his shoes and stockings, for he did almost everything himself and with address and grace. Every other day we saw him shave himself; and he had a little short wig in which he always appeared, even in bed, and on medicine days. He often spoke of the chase, and sometimes said a word to somebody. No toilette table was near him; he had simply a mirror held before him.

As soon as he was dressed, he prayed to God, at the side of his bed, where all the clergy present knelt, the cardinals without cushions, all the laity remaining standing; and the captain of the guards came to the balustrade during the prayer, after which the King passed into his cabinet.

He found there, or was followed by all who had the entrée, a very numerous company, for it included everybody in any office. He gave orders to each for the day; thus within a half a quarter of an hour it was known what he meant to do; and then all this crowd left directly. The bastards, a few favourites, and the valets alone were left. It was then a good opportunity for talking with the King; for example, about plans of gardens and buildings; and conversation lasted more or less according to the person engaged in it.

All the Court meantime waited for the King in the gallery, the captain of the guard being alone in the chamber seated at the door of the cabinet.

[*The business of government*]

On Sunday, and often on Monday, there was a council of state; on Tuesday a finance council; on Wednesday council of state; on Saturday finance council. Rarely were two held in one day or any on Thursday or Friday. Once or twice a month there was a council of despatches[14] on Monday morning; but the order that the Secretaries of State took every morning between the King's rising and his mass, much abridged this kind of business. All the ministers were seated according to rank, except at the council of despatches, where all stood except the sons of France, the Chancellor, and the Duc de Beauvilliers.[15]

[*The royal luncheon*]

The dinner was always *au petit couvert*,[16] that is, the King ate by himself in his chamber upon a square table in front of the middle window. It was more or less abundant, for he ordered in the morning whether it was to be "a little," or "very little" service. But even at this last, there were always many dishes, and three courses without counting the fruit. The dinner being ready, the principal courtiers entered, then all who were known; and the first gentlemen of the chamber on duty, informed the King.

I have seen, but very rarely, Monseigneur[17] and his sons standing at their dinners, the King not offering them a seat. I have continually seen there the Princes of the blood and the cardinals. I have often seen there also Monsieur,[18] either on arriving from St. Cloud to see the King, or arriving from the council of despatches (the only one he entered), give the King his napkin and remain standing. A little while afterwards, the King, seeing that he did not go away, asked him if he would not sit down; he bowed, and the King ordered a seat to be brought for him. A stool was put behind him. Some moments after the

14. **Council of Despatches:** the royal council in which ministers discussed the letters from the provincial administrators of France, the *intendants*.
15. **Duc de Beauvilliers:** Paul de Beauvilliers, Duc de St. Aignan (1648–1714), friend of Saint-Simon and tutor of Louis XIV's grandsons, the dukes of Burgundy, Anjou, and Berry.
16. **Au petit couvert:** a simple table setting with a light meal.
17. **Monseigneur:** Louis, Dauphin de France (1661–1711), son of Louis XIV and heir to the throne.
18. **Monsieur:** Philippe, Duc d'Orléans (1640–1701), Louis XIV's only sibling. His permanent residence was at the Château de St. Cloud near Paris.

King said, "Nay then, sit down, my brother." Monsieur bowed and seated himself until the end of the dinner, when he presented the napkin.

[*The day ends*]

At ten o'clock his supper was served. The captain of the guard announced this to him. A quarter of an hour after the King came to supper, and from the ante-chamber of Madame de Maintenon[19] to the table again, any one spoke to him who wished. This supper was always on a grand scale, the royal household (that is, the sons and daughters of France), at table, and a large number of courtiers and ladies present, sitting or standing, and on the evening before the journey to Marly all those ladies who wished to take part in it. That was called presenting yourself for Marly. Men asked in the morning, simply saying to the King, "Sire, Marly." In later years the King grew tired of this, and a valet wrote up in the gallery the names of those who asked. The ladies continued to present themselves.

After supper the King stood some moments, his back to the balustrade of the foot of his bed, encircled by all his Court; then, with bows to the ladies, passed into his cabinet, where on arriving, he gave his orders. He passed a little less than an hour there, seated in an arm-chair, with his legitimate children and bastards, his grandchildren, legitimate and otherwise, and their husbands or wives. Monsieur in another arm-chair; the princesses upon stools, Monseigneur and all the other princes standing.

The King, wishing to retire, went and fed his dogs; then said good night, passed into his chamber to the *ruelle*[20] of his bed, where he said his prayers, as in the morning, then undressed. He said good night with an inclination of the head, and whilst everybody was leaving the room stood at the corner of the mantelpiece, where he gave the order to the colonel of the guards alone. Then commenced what was called the *petit coucher*, at which only the specially privileged remained. That was short. They did not leave until he got into bed. It was a moment to speak to him. Then all left if they saw any one buckle to the King. For ten or twelve years before he died the *petit coucher* ceased, in consequence of a long attack of gout he had had; so that the Court was finished at the rising from supper.

19. **Madame de Maintenon:** Françoise d'Aubigné, Marquise de Maintenon (1635–1719), married Louis XIV after the death of his first wife, Marie Thérèse of Spain.
20. **ruelle:** the area in the bedchamber in which the bed was located and in which the king received persons of high rank.

Sources 4 and 5 from Château de Versailles/Cliché des Musées Nationaux-Paris.

4. **Charles Le Brun, *Louis XIV Taking Up Personal Government*, ca 1680, from the Ceiling of the Hall of Mirrors at Versailles**

5. Hyacinthe-François-Honoré-Pierre-André Rigaud, *Louis XIV, King of France and Navarre*, 1701

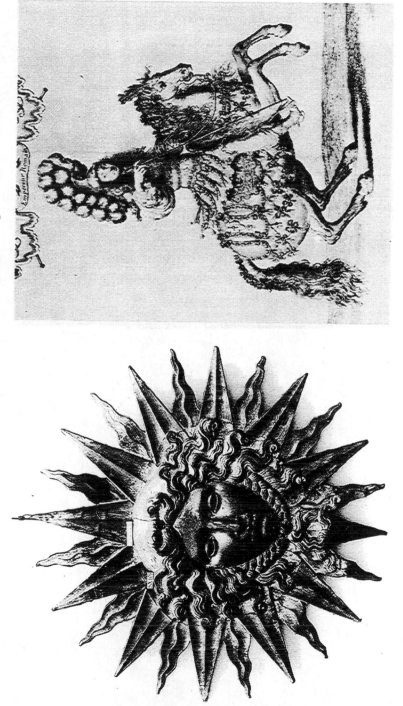

7. Rousselet, Louis XIV as "Roman Emperor" in an engraving from the Carousel of 1662

6. Mask of Apollo, God of Light, 17th century

313

Sources 8 and 9 from French Government Tourist Office.

8. Garden Façade of Versailles

9. Aerial View of Versailles

Sources 10 through 13 from Château de Versailles/Cliché des Musées Nationaux—Paris.

10. The Royal Chapel at Versailles

11. Reconstruction of the King's Chamber at Versailles, after 1701

12. Antechamber of the Bull's Eye Window at Versailles

13. Pierre Denis Martin, *Château of Marly,* **1724**

QUESTIONS TO CONSIDER

Louis XIV is reputed to have said, "I am the state." Whether the king actually uttered those words is immaterial for our purpose; they neatly summarize the unifying theme in all this chapter's evidence, which demonstrates how royal power was defined as absolute and how that authority was expressed in deeds, art, and architecture.

Consider first the theories of royal authority, comparing the political ideas of Bodin and Bossuet. What are the origins of sovereignty for Bodin and Bossuet? How do they differ? Why can Bodin be said to have justified absolutism on the basis of expediency, that is, that absolute royal power was the only way to ensure order? Do the two thinkers ultimately arrive at the same conclusions? What is the difference between Bodin's conclusion that the royal power permitted the king to hand down laws to his subjects and receive them from no one and Bossuet's definition of the king as virtually a god on earth?

Royal ceremony and etiquette enforced this view of the king. Consider Saint-Simon's *Memoirs* again. The selection describes only limited aspects of court etiquette, but it conveys to us a vivid image of court life. Who was the center of this court made up of the country's most prominent nobles? Analyze individual elements of court ceremony. How does each contribute to a consistent message? Consider the royal dining ritual. To reinforce the lesson of royal power,

who was kept standing during the king's luncheon? Who had the task, for most commoners performed by an ordinary waiter, of handing the king his napkin? A message of royal power is being expressed here in a way that is almost theatrical.

Indeed, the image of theater can be useful in further structuring your analysis. The stage setting for this royal display, the palace of Versailles, shows the work of a skilled director in creating a remarkably uniform message in landscape and architecture alike. Who do you suppose that director was? Examine his statement at Versailles. Look first at the exterior views of both Versailles (Sources 8 and 9) and Marly (Source 13). How do the grounds add to the expression of royal power? What view of nature might they suggest to a visitor? How did the stage set enhance the play described by Saint-Simon? How did it encourage the French to accept the authority of Louis XIV?

Look next at the interior of the palace. It was, of course, a royal residence. But do you find much evidence of its function as a place to live in? Examine the royal bedroom and its outer room (Sources 11 and 12). Modern bedrooms are generally intimate in size and decoration; how does the king's differ? Why? Notice, too, the art and use of symbols in the palace. Why might the king's artists and architects have decorated the palace so richly with biblical and classical heroes and themes (Sources 8, 9, 10, 11, 12)?

Finally, consider the principal actor, Louis XIV. Notice how his self-presentation is consistent with the trappings of the stage set. We find him consciously acting a role in Source 7, portraying an emperor in the Carousel of 1662. That engraving embodies a great deal of indirect information. What details reinforce the aura of royal power? Why should the king be mounted and in Roman costume? What strikes you about the king's attitude atop the prancing horse? Compare this picture with the Le Brun (Source 4) and Rigaud (Source 5) paintings. What elements do you find these pictures to have in common? How does the royal emblem of the sun (Source 6) contribute to the common message?

With these considerations in mind, return now to the central questions of this chapter. What was the theoretical explanation of royal power expressed in late sixteenth- and seventeenth-century France? How did such early modern kings as Louis XIV communicate their absolute power in the various ceremonies, displays, and symbols of royal authority presented in the evidence?

EPILOGUE

We all know that any successful act produces imitators. In the seventeenth century the monarchy of Louis XIV for a long time looked like the most successful regime in Europe. Royal absolutism had seemingly unified France. Out of that unity came a military power that threatened to overwhelm Europe; an economic strength, based on mercantilism, that increased French wealth; and an intellectual life that gave the culture of seventeenth-and eighteenth-century Europe a distinctly French accent. Imitators of Louis XIV's work were therefore numerous. At the very least, kings sought physically to express the unifying and centralizing monarchical principle of government in palaces recreating Versailles.[21]

But the work of such monarchs as Louis XIV involved far more than the construction of elaborate palaces in which to stage the theater of their court lives. The act of focusing the state on the figure of the monarch began the transition to the centralized modern style of government and marked the beginning of the end of the decentralized medieval state that bound subjects in an almost contractual relationship to their ruler. The king now emerged as theoretically all-powerful and also as a symbol of national unity.

The monarchs of the age did their work of state building so effectively that the unity and centralization they created often survived the monarchy itself. The French monarchy, for example, succumbed to a revolution in 1789 that in large part stemmed from the bankruptcy of the royal government after too many years of overspending on wars and court life in

21. Palaces consciously modeled on Versailles multiplied in the late seventeenth and early eighteenth centuries. They included the Schönbrunn Palace in Vienna (1694), the Royal Palace in Berlin (begun in 1698), Ludwigsburg Palace in Württemberg, Germany (1704–1733), the Würzburg Residenz in Franconia, Germany (1719–1744), and the Stupinigi Palace (1729–1733) near Turin, Italy.

the name of royal glory. But the unified state endured, strong enough to retain its sense of unity despite challenges in war and changes of government that introduced a new politics of mass participation.

The methods employed by Louis XIV and other monarchs also transcended their age. Modern governments understand the importance of ritual, symbolism, and display in creating the sense of national unity that was part of the absolute monarch's goal. Ritual may now be centered on important national observances. The parades on such days as July 4 in the United States, July 14 in France (commemorating one of the earliest victories of the Revolution of 1789), and the anniversary of the October 1917 Revolution as it was celebrated until 1990 in the former Soviet Union all differ in form from the rituals of Louis XIV. They are designed for a new political age, one of mass participation in politics, in which the loyalty of the whole people, not just an elite group, must be won. But their purpose remains the same: to win loyalty to the existing political order.

Modern states also use symbolism to build political loyalty. Artwork on public buildings in Washington, D.C., and the capital cities of other republics, for example, often employs classical themes. The purpose of such artwork is to suggest to citizens that their government perpetuates the republican rectitude of Athens and Rome. Display also is part of the political agenda of modern governments, even among governments of new arrivals in the community of nations. This is why newly independent, developing nations of the twentieth century expend large portions of their meager resources on such things as grand new capital cities, the most sophisticated military weaponry, and the latest aircraft for the national airline. These are symbols of their government's successes and thus the basis for these regimes' claims on their peoples' loyalty. These modern rituals, symbols, and displays perform the same function for modern rulers as Versailles did for the Sun King.

CHAPTER FOURTEEN

A DAY IN

THE FRENCH REVOLUTION:

JULY 14, 1789

THE PROBLEM

Tuesday, July 14, 1789, dawned cool and cloudy in Paris. Leaden skies threatening heavy rainfall cast little light into the narrow, crowded streets of the capital. But the rain held off until evening, thereby providing the opportunity for events to occur in the city's streets and squares that set off a fundamental change in the political history of France and the West as a whole. When rain finally fell, sending Parisians scurrying home, the forces of King Louis XVI had lost control of the capital, and, in hindsight, the principle of royal absolutism was clearly in decline.

On that Tuesday, the people of Paris seized the great fortress and prison on the city's eastern edge known as the Bastille. Construction of the Bastille had begun in 1370 as part of the eastern defenses of Paris. The fortress had eight towers, set in walls about 80 feet high and 10 feet thick. Its only entrance was by two drawbridges across a moat that was dry in 1789; by

that date the Bastille had been obsolete as a fort for several centuries. Developments in modern artillery had rendered its walls vulnerable, and the growth of Paris meant that the Bastille was no longer on the city's periphery, but instead was surrounded by the streets of the suburb known as the Faubourg Saint-Antoine.

As early as the fifteenth century, the monarchy had confined prisoners in the Bastille, but the systematic use of the old fort as a prison began during the ministry of Cardinal Richelieu in the early seventeenth century. The Bastille confined persons whose offenses were not punishable under the regular criminal laws of France, and received political prisoners held without trial under royal orders known as *lettres de cachet*. Religious dissenters joined the prison's inmates during the reign of Louis XV (1715–1774). The nature of this prison made it a symbol of despotism in the eighteenth century, but such notoriety was little warranted by 1789. Although the Bastille had a capacity for forty-two prisoners in cells, with room for additional inmates in a dungeon that had been unused for twenty years, it held only seven prisoners on July 14, 1789. These seven—four forgers, two noblemen locked away at the behest of their families for immoral behavior, and one murder suspect—hardly seemed victims of royal injustice. Indeed, the monarchy was considering plans to demolish this outdated structure when the Paris crowd captured it.

The origins of the crowd's storming of the Bastille, the first—but not the last—mass action of its kind in Paris during the Revolution, may be found in a political and economic crisis that had kept France in turmoil during the preceding thirty months. As a consequence of the costly wars of the eighteenth century and a system of taxation that largely exempted the clergy and nobility from fiscal obligations, the French monarchy faced bankruptcy by 1787.[1] Several finance ministers struggled with the crown's fiscal problems, but all eventually arrived at the same solution: fundamental financial reform that would tax the Church and the nobility, not simply the commoners. In proposing such changes, however, the royal ministers encountered constitutional problems. The proposed reforms violated traditional rights of the clergy and nobility, and the king was forced to call for the meeting of a

French representative body—the Estates General, which had not met since 1614—to consider reform.[?]

The election campaign for the Estates General stirred up the country, creating expectations of change. Election regulations enfranchised almost all male taxpayers, and these voters did not return a legislature prepared simply to approve tax reform and go home. Some representatives of the clergy and nobility resisted any change. More seriously, the monarchy confronted the defiant members of the Third Estate, representing the commoners, who demanded tax reform and greater political equality.[3] They declared themselves a National Assembly, the rightful representatives of the French people, and then, on June 20, 1789, in their Tennis Court oath, called for a constitution to limit royal power. This defiance of royal authority really had been the first act of revolution.

The king vacillated at first in the face of such defiance but then resolved on two steps. On June 22, 1789, he signed orders for the movement of troops into the region of Paris and Versailles to regain control of events. Those assigned were largely foreign soldiers (Swiss and German regiments especially) in French service, who presumably

1. France's successful intervention in the American War of Independence played no small part in this situation. The American war cost France 2 billion livres, a figure about four times the government's tax receipts in 1788. By that year, interest payments on the government's debts consumed 51 percent of its receipts.

2. Royal failure to call the Estates General was deliberate; the body was an obstacle to royal absolutism.

3. Representatives of the clergy constituted the First Estate of the Estates General; representatives of the nobility made up the Second Estate of what had been traditionally a three-house legislature. In 1789 the king required this traditional style of meeting, which gave great voice to the small minority of the population who were clerics and nobles.

would be more willing to use force on civilians than would French soldiers. Such troop movements, however, could not be kept secret. There was growing fear in Versailles and Paris of a royal coup in early July directed against the defiant National Assembly and its supporters in the capital.

The king's second step was the dismissal of Jacques Necker as royal finance minister on July 11, 1789. Popular opinion regarded Necker as a liberal financial genius whose skills kept the government solvent, stabilized financial markets, and kept Paris supplied with food. But he and the ministers associated with him were replaced with officials more fully committed to Louis's impending use of force to reestablish royal authority.

Political events of the preceding months and a rapid rise in bread prices caused by recent bad harvests had heightened tension in Paris even before the king reached this decision. The concurrence of political and economic unrest already had led to large-scale rioting on April 27–28, 1789, when rumors spread that a wallpaper manufacturer, Reveillon, had advocated reduction of workers' wages.[4] Troops had been needed to

restore order in the capital in April. News of Necker's firing reached Paris about 9:00 A.M. on July 12, a Sunday, when the population's release from normal weekday duties favored the spread of rumor and political agitation. One of the agitators, the demagogic Camille Desmoulins, effectively directed the thoughts of many Parisians to action when he said to his listeners at the popular gathering place, the Palais Royal:

> Citizens, you know that the Nation had asked for Necker to be retained, and he has been driven out! Could you be more insolently flouted? After such an act they will dare anything, and they may perhaps be planning and preparing a Saint-Bartholomew massacre of patriots for this very night! . . . To arms! To arms![5]

Demonstrations broke out in Paris by the middle of the day on July 12, bolstered by the adherence of the French Guards, a unit charged with keeping order in the city, to the cause of the crowds. By evening, fighting was taking place between demonstrators and units of the foreign troops ordered to Paris by the king, and their commanders withdrew royal forces from the city. Unrest continued through the night without opposition. At about 1:00 A.M. on July 13, crowds began to burn the tax stations along the wall surrounding Paris, since the majority of the commoners blamed the tax on goods en-

---

4. Reveillon was one of Paris's largest manufacturers; his wallpaper works employed about 300 persons. He had not, however, precisely advocated a reduction of wages in a speech he gave at his local assembly to elect representatives to the Estates General. On April 23, Reveillon had said that if the price of bread could be reduced, workers' wages would follow, resulting in a lower cost for the goods they produced. Sources vary widely on the human cost of the rioting. Jacques Godechot, *The Taking of the Bastille: July 14, 1789* (trans. Jean Stewart; New York: Scribner's, 1970, p. 147), accepts a figure of 300 dead.

5. Quoted by Godechot, pp. 187–188. **Saint-Bartholomew Massacre:** on August 24, 1572, Catholic forces killed several thousand Protestants all over France during the French wars of religion.

tering the capital for higher food prices. At 6:00 A.M., crowds attacked a monastery where they believed food was stored.

As disorder grew in the capital, on the morning of July 13, the men who had served as electors of the Parisian deputies to the Estates General assembled at the Paris city hall and implemented two important decisions.[6] First, they constituted a committee from their ranks to administer the city, in effect creating a revolutionary municipal government; second, they called for the founding of a "civic militia." The militia's stated purpose was to keep order in the capital, but the formation of such an armed force, obeying the orders of the electors rather than the king, was another revolutionary act.

The creation of the militia, soon to be called the *National Guard*, required arms, and the search for guns and ammunition became the next object of crowd action. On the morning of July 14, a crowd estimated at 80,000 persons forced its way into the *In-*

valides, an old soldiers' home/barracks, and seized all of the 32,000 muskets stored there. Muskets were of little value without gunpowder and musket balls, however, and the crowd found few of these commodities at the Invalides. They surged on that morning to the Bastille, to which royal officers earlier had transferred 250 barrels of powder for safekeeping as Paris grew restive. Defending the fortress against a growing crowd were eighty-two *invalides* (older or partially disabled soldiers fit only for garrison duty) and thirty-two soldiers of the Swiss regiments in French service. After two deputations from the crowd failed to secure the commander's surrender, the attack began around 1:30 P.M. By 5:00 P.M. the Bastille and its supplies had fallen to the crowd.

You now have a summary of what the crowd did on July 14, 1789. Such mass actions were common in early modern Europe, as we have seen in Chapter 1. Your task in this chapter is to analyze the evidence presented here to answer basic questions about the crowd. Why were the people of Paris angry in mid-July 1789? How were Parisians mobilized for action? Who made up the crowd that stormed the Bastille?

---

6. Rules for Estates General elections in Paris required that voters in each of the city's sixty electoral districts select electors, who in turn would vote for representatives to the Estates General.

SOURCES AND METHOD

This chapter presents a variety of evidence to assist you in answering the basic questions about the atmosphere in Paris in July 1789 that produced the attack on the Bastille. The first pieces of evidence you encounter in the chapter are visual. You already have analyzed such sources in Chapter 2, and you should examine the pictures presented in this chapter to reconstruct the physical setting for the events of 1789. In analyzing the evidence, your objective should be to derive answers to this question: What features of the physical layout of Paris were conducive to the spread of rumors and agitation?

Sources 1 and 2 offer views of the Palais Royal, the property of the Duke of Orléans, a member of the royal family. On the grounds of this palace, the duke developed a commercial and entertainment area lined with shops and cafés. The palace and its grounds were outside of police jurisdiction because they belonged to the duke and so attracted political agitators, prostitutes, and criminals such as pickpockets. Much of the politically active population of Paris would have been familiar with the grounds of the Palais Royal. What role might such a site have played on July 14, 1789? Why might the significance of the Palais Royal for the political climate of 1789 have been so great that a few historians have seen it as evidence of a plot by its owner to foment a revolution that might benefit his own political ambitions?

Source 3 shows the rue du Fer-à-Moulin, a street typical of many of those of eighteenth-century Paris at the time of the Revolution. In 1789 much of the Parisian population of about 600,000 still lived in such streets, crowded inside the boundaries set by the city's former medieval fortifications. To accommodate this dense population, residential buildings were six or seven stories high and crowded, with an average of almost thirty residents in each one. Try to imagine life in these buildings and streets. Do you think people would have spent a great deal of time in the streets? Why? What sorts of exchanges of information might have occurred in streets like these?

Source 4 introduces a new form of evidence, architectural drawings of residential buildings, to enhance your understanding of the physical aspect of Paris in 1789. The floor plan for 18, rue Contrescarpe is of a house very near the Bastille. Such multistoried structures typically had a ground floor that was rented out to a merchant or craftsman who maintained a shop that opened on the street. A craftsman might also have rented a workshop behind the shop on the ground floor. Access to the residential upper floors was through the gate opening onto the street at the end of the passage leading to the interior courtyard. Each building's numerous residents would cross the courtyard daily going in and out or fetching water from the well. All would have needed to mount the staircase to rooms whose prices decreased as the number of steps separating them from the ground increased. As a consequence of this pricing procedure, a master craftsman might occupy a large apartment on the first floor up these stairs; his employees, the tiny rooms in the attic. Reflect on this living situation. How might news and rumor have spread in such a setting? How might a crowd be mobilized there? Why might the economic power of an employer and his residential proximity to his workers in such buildings permit an employer who was committed to a political cause to draw his workers along with him?

This chapter also presents quantitative data similar to those that you analyzed in Chapter 4, in the form of graphs, tables, and a map. The information presented here is essential to understanding which social groups participated in the events of July 14, 1789, and why. As we found in Chapter 4, the largely illiterate majority of pre-nineteenth-century Europe left few conventional written records, like letters and diaries, that might allow historians to interpret their thought. Historians' ingenuity, however, has allowed them to understand these people through other sources. In constructing the data sets on food prices in this chapter, historians drew on a rich source for understanding seventeenth- and eighteenth-century life. Because early modern governments recognized a correlation between high food prices during periods of dearth on one hand and riots and other acts of public disorder on the other, they kept close watch on such prices. Their effort generated excellent records of food prices, especially of the cost of wheat, the essential ingredient for the bread that was the staple of early modern diets. Look at the graphs numbered 5 and 6 among the evidence for this chapter. Although the two researchers used slightly different measures of wheat in assembling their data, you are presented with significant price trends: Long-term trends in wheat prices for France as a whole are in Source 5 and short-term trends for Paris alone are in Source 6. Analyze the price trends presented here. Between the 1730s and mid-1780s, the highest prices were the result of failed harvests in the early 1770s. During that period, the rural poor in some regions of the country resorted at times to eating boiled grass or acorns when bread became too scarce and costly. The high food prices resulting from harvest failures also generated popular fear that the elevated cost of food was the result not of dearth, but of speculators unscrupulously hoarding large quantities of grain to artificially drive up prices and increase their own profits. Such fears, indeed, earlier had caused widespread rioting in the Paris region in the 1770s. How did prices in 1789 in Paris and France compare with those of the 1770s? Imagine yourself a Frenchman aged forty in 1789. What would your memory of food prices be? How would those of 1789 strike you? Consult Source 7, a table. How would price trends in 1788–1789 have affected your family's income? Reflect, too, on the fact that women did their families' marketing in the eighteenth century. Why would you not be surprised to find women protesting food prices and other issues? Why might you have been concerned about the preservation of order in Paris in July 1789 if you had been a police official?

Historians drew on a second kind of source—tax data—in formulating the map presenting the composition of the various Paris sections by income (Source 8). These data are your basis for understanding the economic structure of Paris's population and, most important for our purposes, the economic background of the crowd members who stormed the Bastille. For centuries, historians and government officials held that the lowest and most criminal elements composed these crowds. Indeed, eighteenth-century French police records use a phrase that may be translated as "the scum of the people" in describing the composition of crowds. What do we find about the Bastille crowd, however? Notice that the map in Source 8 provides data on the taxes paid by residents of the forty-eight sections into which early revolutionary Paris was divided. From those data we may judge each section's relative wealth because, of course, wealthier citizens paid more taxes. To completely analyze the data you need to know that "active" citizens under the 1791 constitution were those who could vote by virtue of paying taxes worth three days' labor (nationally, 41 percent of citizens did not meet this minimum standard). "Eligible" citizens were "active" citizens qualified for administrative office by paying taxes worth at least ten days' labor. Using this information, ascertain from the table in Source 8 the sections of Paris that housed those who made up the Bastille crowd. Why do you think that the police would have erred had they characterized that crowd in their usual manner?

Other data might also allow historians further to identify the members of the crowd, if not by name, at least by social group. Police records of those arrested in unsuccessful rebellions that provide personal data on participants have been systematically exploited only recently by historians. But the Bastille attack began a successful revolution, and the crowd members became heroes and hero-ines who received the title *Vainqueurs de la Bastille* ("Conquerors of the Bastille") and state pensions if they had been disabled in the attack. The list of these persons is one among many functions of the administrative and fiscal record keeping of a modern state, but it provides you, in the table that is Source 9, with an occupational listing of the Bastille's conquerors. From a distance of two hundred years, it is probably impossible to reconstruct the precise income of each conqueror. Moreover, each trade, like the cabinetmaking common in the Faubourg Saint-Antoine, would have shown a variety of incomes within the ranks of its practitioners—another frustration. We do know, however, that in skilled trades the self-employed tended to be masters of their trades and therefore probably more affluent than journeymen wage earners or apprentices employed by others. Examine the table. What were the most common trades of the Bastille's attackers? Who predominated, wage earners or the self-employed? What conclusion do you draw from the fact that most of the conquerors had definite trades and were not unskilled or poor?

Written sources can supplement quantitative evidence and supply historians with information on public opinion in Paris during the month of July 1789. This chapter presents several types of such evidence, which you have not previously analyzed. Source 10 is another part of the massive bureaucratic record generated by modern states, in this case a petition addressed to the French national legislature by a woman seeking compensation for herself and her husband as conquerors of the Bastille. In reading her petition, ask yourself how her account further contributes to your knowledge of the crowd's composition. Remember that the division of household labor in the eighteenth century gave housewives the major marketing responsibility. Why might women be involved in crowd actions in 1789 or at other points in the Revolution?

Next you will read a travel account, a literary form very common in the early modern period. Europe's curiosity about the outside world grew with the Age of Exploration during the sixteenth century, and a large reading audience developed for accounts by European travelers. The usefulness of such works in reconstructing a society varies, however, according to the intelligence and observational skills of their authors. In the case of Arthur Young, whose Paris report is excerpted as Source 11, we have the work of a master of the travel genre.

Arthur Young (1741–1820) was a wealthy and educated Englishman who sought out and publicized the latest agricultural techniques. Before visiting France to examine French farming, a journey that produced the selection here, Young, who was well known as an agricultural expert and as an economist, published descriptions of his travels through England, Wales, and Ireland. The record of his travels in France is valuable, therefore, for several reasons. Young's fame and his knowledge of the French language gained him access to many prominent Frenchmen. The

observational skills he had honed on earlier trips allowed him quickly to appreciate the economic problems of France and to assess public reaction to them. Finally, as luck would have it, his journey took him through France in the years 1787, 1788, and 1789, so that he was present in the country during the early days of the Revolution. His account, consequently, is extremely useful in understanding the events of the year 1789. Young tells us a great deal about modern politics and the spread of revolution. Thanks to parish schools that offered inexpensive elementary education, the population of Paris was much more literate than the rural population of France. How did Young find this literacy affecting politics in the capital? How did political news spread to provincial cities like Metz? Do you find in any of this description a political life that in some ways presages that of our modern age? Recall, too, the fears many Frenchmen had about having adequate food supplies in the eighteenth century. Why did Young believe that troop movements would renew such fears?

The third kind of written evidence presented in this chapter is diplomatic correspondence. The letters of ambassadors to their home governments long have been useful sources for historians. Their utility derives from the very functions of ambassadors. Since the posting of the first permanent ambassadors by Italian Renaissance states, these officials performed several roles. First, they represented their countries' interests to foreign courts, and thus we can identify the policies of their states in ambassadors' correspondence with their superiors. Additionally, from their earliest days ambassadors kept their governments informed of conditions in their host countries that might affect international relations; they functioned almost like spies, gathering all available information for use by their governments. In this regard, the British ambassador's reports to his superiors in the Foreign Office are extremely important. In 1789 France was a major power that had long been in conflict with England and one most influential in achieving American victory over the English in the War of Independence. As a result, information on political events in France was crucial to English policymakers, and their ambassador supplied detailed reports on France. As with all sources, however, the historian must approach such correspondence with a critical eye. Was the ambassador writing from firsthand knowledge of events? Is his information verified by other sources? How would you assess the reliability of the Duke of Dorset, the English ambassador to France, whose letters are Source 12 among the evidence? What do they tell you about events in Paris?

The fourth written source in this chapter is an excerpt from the journal and diary literature written by many educated persons in the centuries before our own. The historical utility of such sources again depends on their authors' activities and abilities to record accurately events of their times. In the journal of the Parisian bookseller Siméon-Prosper Hardy we have the work of a reasonably well-educated man who was something of a busybody, alert for all news. Hardy was also a cautious man who took no part in the dangerous events of July 14 and whose residence was far from the Bastille, however. He can therefore be relied on only for noting general trends in Paris, not for details on the Bastille attack. What picture of general events does the selection in Source 13 from his journal present?

All these sources should fit together in your mind like the pieces of a puzzle, allowing you to reconstruct the state of public opinion in Paris in July 1789, to determine how crowds were mobilized, and to understand who stormed the Bastille on July 14.

Source 1 from Musée Carnavalet, Paris. © Photothèque des Musées de la Ville de Paris.

1. Henri Monnier, *The Palais Royal*

Source 2 from Bibliothèque Nationale, Paris; Vinck Collection.

2. Camille Desmoulins Speaking to the Crowds at the Palais Royal, July 12, 1789

Source 4 adapted from David Garrioch, Neighborhood and Community in Paris, 1740–1790 (New York: Cambridge University Press, 1986), p. 222. Reprinted by permission.

4. Plan of a Typical Parisian Residential Building, 18, Rue Contrescarpe, Faubourg St.-Antoine

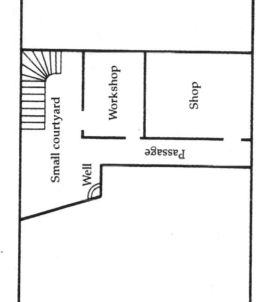

Source 3 from Musée Carnavalet, Paris. © Photothèque des Musées de la Ville de Paris.

3. Rue du Fer-à-Moulin, 1870

333

Source 5 adapted from Ernest Labrousse, Ruggiero Romano, and F.-G. Dreyfus, Le prix du
froment en France au temps de la monnaie stable (1726–1913) *(Paris: Ecole des Hautes
Études en Sciences Sociales, 1970), p. xiv.*

5. Average Price of a Hectoliter (100 liters) of Wheat in France, 1726–1790

Source 6 from Jacques Godechot, The Taking of the Bastille, July 14, 1789 *(New York: Scribner's, 1970), p. 13. Used by permission.*

6. Price of 100 Kilograms of Wheat in Paris, 1770–1790

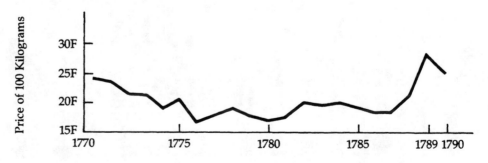

Source 7 from George Rudé, "Prices, Wages and Popular Movements in Paris During the French Revolution," Economic History Review, 2nd ser., vol. 6 (1953), p. 248. Used by permission of Basil Blackwell Ltd.

7. Bread and the Wage Earner's Budget[a]

Occupation	Effective Daily Wage in Sous (s)[b]	Expenditure on Bread as Percentage of Income with Bread at	
		9s (Aug 1788)	14½s (Feb–July 1789)
Laborer in Reveillon wallpaper works	15	60	97
Builder's laborer	18	50	80
Journeyman mason	24	37	60
Journeyman, locksmith, carpenter, etc.	30	30	48
Sculptor, goldsmith	60	15	24

[a]The price of the 4-pound loaf consumed daily by a workingman and his family as the main element in their diet.
[b]"Effective" wage represents the daily wage adjusted for 111 days of nonwork per calendar year for religious observation, etc.

Source 8 map from Marcel Reinhard, Nouvelle histoire de Paris: La Révolution *(Paris: Distributed by Hachette for the Association pour la publication d'une Histoire de Paris, 1971), pp. 66–67. Key and table from George Rudé,* The Crowd in the French Revolution *(New York: Oxford University Press, 1959), pp. 244–245. Copyright © 1959. Used by permission of Oxford University Press.*

8. Map of Paris by Economic Circumstances of Residents, 1790

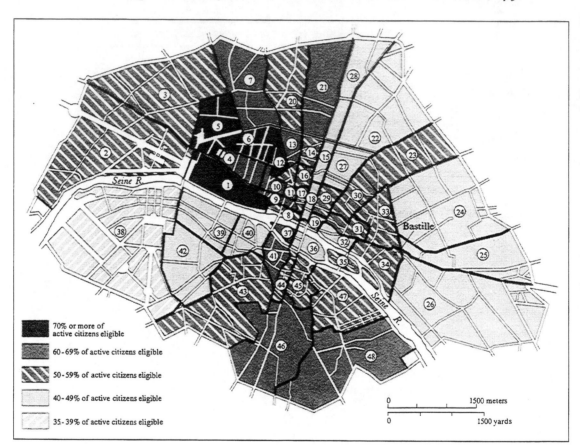

70% or more of active citizens eligible

60-69% of active citizens eligible

50-59% of active citizens eligible

40-49% of active citizens eligible

35-39% of active citizens eligible

Section[a]	Bastille July[b]	Section	Bastille July	Section	Bastille July
1. Tuileries	2	17. Marché des Innocents	6	34. Arsenal	23
2. Champs Élysées	—	18. Lombards	5	35. Île Saint-Louis	—
3. Roule	2	19. Arcis	3	36. Notre Dame	1
4. Palais Royal	1	20. Faubourg Montmartre	—	37. Henri IV	2
5. Vendôme	1	21. Poissonière	1	38. Invalides	5
6. Bibliothèque	2	22. Bondy	4	39. Fontaine de Grenelle	2
7. Grange Batelière	2	23. Temple	9	40. Quatre Nations	6
8. Louvre	1	24. Popincour	87	41. Théâtre Français	6
9. Oratoire	2	25. Montreuil	139	42. Croix Rouge	2
10. Halle au Blé	6	26. Quinze Vingts	193	43. Luxembourg	7
11. Postes	4	27. Gravilliers	3	44. Thermes de Julien	3
12. Louis XIV	—	28. Faubourg St. Denis	1	45. Sainte-Geneviève	10
13. Fontaine Montmorency	—	29. Beaubourg	5	46. Observatoire	3
14. Bonne Nouvelle	—	30. Enfants Rouges	2	47. Jardin des Plantes	3
15. Ponceau	3	31. Roi de Sicile	3	48. Gobelins Outside Paris	3
16. Mauconseil	4	32. Hôtel de Ville	18		
		33. Place Royale	17	*Total*	602

[a]Names of sections are as in 1790–1791.
[b]Numbers arrested, killed, wounded, or participated in the attack on the Bastille.

9. Trades of the Bastille Insurgents, 1789

Trade	Participants (no.)	Trade	Participants (no.)	Trade	Participants (no.)
1. Food, Drink		Cabinet makers	48 (9)	*9. Leather*	
Bakers	5	Chandlers	—	Curriers	—
Brewers	2 (1)[a]	Fancy ware	9 (1)	Leather, skin dressers	2
Butchers	5 (3)	Joiners	49 (8)	*10. Print and Paper*	
Cafés, restaurants	4	Upholsterers	4 (1)	Bookbinders	—
Chocolate	—	*5. Transport*		Booksellers	—
Cooks	2 (2)	Bargemen	3 (3)	Papermakers	1
Fruit vendors	—	Blacksmiths	—	Printers	8 (4)
Grocers	—	Carters	5 (5)	*11. Glass, Pottery*	
Innkeepers	2	Coachmen	2 (1)	Earthenware	1
Pastry chefs	4	Farriers	4 (1)	Potters	7
Tobacco	—	Harness, saddlers	5	Royal Glass factory	1 (1)
Wine merchants	11	Porters	16 (16)	*12. Miscellaneous*	
2. Building, Roads		Riverside workers	5 (5)	Actors, artists, musicians, etc.	—
Carpenters	3	Shipyard workers	5 (5)	Beggars	—
Glaziers	—	Wheelwrights	—	Bourgeois	—
Locksmiths	41 (8)	*6. Metal*		Businessmen	4
Monumental masons	9 (1)	Braziers	7 (1)	Charcoal burners	3
Navvies	2 (2)	Buttonmakers	3	Civil servants	—
Painters	4	Cutlers	—	Clerks	5
Paviors	—	Edge-tool makers	2	Domestic servants, cleaners	—
Plasterers	—	Engravers, gilders	13	Deputies	—
Quarrymen	—	Founders	9 (2)	Fishermen	2 (1)
Sawyers	4 (1)	Goldsmiths	6 (1)	Housewives	—
Sculptors	20 (1)	Instrument makers	—	Journalists, publishers	—
Stonecutters	4 (4)	Jewelers	5	Laborers	2 (2)
Stonemasons	7 (5)	Mechanics	—	Launderers	3 (1)
Surveyors	—	Nailsmiths	9 (1)	Newsagents, vendors	—
Tilers	—	Pewterers	2	Peasants	—
3. Dress		Stovemakers	5 (3)	Priests	—
Beltmakers	—	Tinsmiths	5 (2)	Professional (lawyers, doctors)	—
Boot and shoe	28 (5)	Watchmakers	3	Shopkeepers, assistants	22 (1)
Dressmakers	—	*7. Wood*		"Smugglers"	—
Dyers, cleaners	3	Coopers	3 (1)	Teachers	1
Florists, gardeners	6 (3)	Turners	10	Trades	56 (1)
Furriers	2 (1)	*8. Textiles*		Army, police, National Guard:	
Hairdressers	10	Cotton	—	a. Officers	—
Hatters	9 (4)	Gauze	22 (22)	b. Others	77
Ribbon weavers	3 (3)	Silk	1 (1)		
Stocking weavers	4 (4)	Weavers	1	*Total*	662 (149)
Tailors	7 (1)				
4. Furnishing					
Basketmakers	2				
Boxmakers	1				

[a]Figures in parentheses represent insurgents who probably were wage-earners (i.e., not self-employed).

Source 10 from Darline Gay Levy, Harriet Branson Applewhite, and Mary Durham Johnson, editors and translators, Women in Revolutionary Paris, 1789–1795 *(Urbana: University of Illinois Press, 1979), pp. 29–30. Copyright © 1979 by the Board of Trustees of the University of Illinois. Used with permission of the University of Illinois Press.*

10. Petition Addressed by Marguerite Pinaigre to the French National Assembly

Legislators:

The person named here, Margueritte Piningre [*sic*], wife of Sieur Bernard Vener, one of the Vainqueurs de la Bastille, has the honor of appearing today before your august assembly to reclaim the execution of the decree issued by the Constituent Assembly in his [her husband's] favor in 1789. This intrepid citizen, who has the misfortune of being crippled for the rest of his days without ever being able to work again in his life because of wounds received on all parts of his body, yes, Legislators, not only has this dear citizen fought in the conquest of the Bastille with the greatest courage, but furthermore, his *citoyenne*[7] wife, who is present here, worked equally hard with all her might, both of them having resolved to triumph or to die. It is she who ran to several wineshops to fill her apron with bottles, both broken and unbroken, which she gave to the authorities to be used as shot in the cannon used to break the chain on the drawbridge of the Bastille. Therefore, by virtue of these legitimate claims the petitioner believes herself justified in coming before the National Assembly today to advise it concerning the nonexecution of laws relative to conquerors who were severely maimed, as was the petitioner's husband. This law awards a pension to those who are really crippled and without the means for earning their living. Such is the situation of the latter, who is offering to provide evidence in the form of authentic statements. Nevertheless, he still has not been awarded this pension which he so richly deserves, he as well as his wife, as a consequence of the dangers they faced. The only gratification which this citizen has received is a small sum of four hundred *livres,* which since 1789 has barely sufficed to care for him and to help him get over the severe wounds he suffered.

Under these circumstances, and in the light of such a compelling account, the petitioner dares hope, Messieurs, for your justice and your usual generosity. May you be willing to take under urgent consideration the object of a request which is becoming as pressing as it is urgent—assuming that surely you would not allow one of the most zealous and intrepid Vainqueurs de la Bastille to languish any longer bent under the weight of the indigence to which he is presently reduced, along with his wife and his children, who ex-

---

7. **citoyenne:** citizeness. As an expression of revolutionary equality, during the Revolution, the terms of address "citizen" and "citizeness" replaced the traditional "Monsieur" and "Madame," based as they were on "My Lord" and "My Lady."

pect his every minute to be his last—because from this period [July 14, 1789] on he has always been ill and continues to suffer cruelly every day. The petitioner expects the favor of the representatives of the French nation, to whom she will never cease to offer her most heart-felt gratitude.

[signed] Marguerite Pinaigre

Source 11 from Arthur Young, Travels in France During the Years 1787, 1788 and 1789, edited by Jeffry Kaplow (Gloucester, MA: Peter Smith, 1976), pp. 104–105, 130, 145–146.

11. Arthur Young's Report from France

[June 1789 (in Paris)]

THE 9TH.—The business going forward at present in the pamphlet shops of Paris is incredible. I went to the Palais Royal to see what new things were published, and to procure a catalogue of all. Every hour produces something new. Thirteen came out to-day, sixteen yesterday, and ninety-two last week. We think sometimes that Debrett's or Stockdale's shops at London are crouded, but they are mere deserts, compared to Desenne's, and some others here, in which one can scarcely squeeze from the door to the counter. The price of printing two years ago was from 27 liv. to 30 liv.[8] per sheet, but now it is from 60 liv. to 80 liv. This spirit of reading political tracts, they say, spreads into the provinces, so that all the presses of France are equally employed. Nineteen-twentieths of these productions are in favour of liberty, and commonly violent against the clergy and nobility; I have to-day bespoken[9] many of this description, that have reputation; but enquiring for such as had appeared on the other side of the question, to my astonishment I find there are but two or three that have merit enough to be known. Is it not wonderful,[10] that while the press teems with the most levelling and even seditious principles, which put in execution would overturn the monarchy, nothing in reply appears, and not the least step is taken by the court to restrain this extreme licentiousness of publication? It is easy to conceive the spirit that must thus be raised among the people. But the coffee-houses in the Palais Royal present yet more singular and astonishing spectacles; they are not only crouded within, but other expectant crouds are at the doors and windows, listening *à gorge déployée*[11] to certain orators, who from chairs or

8. **livre:** the main unit of Old Regime currency, made up of 20 sous (s). Each sou contained 12 deniers (d); 6 livres equaled 1 écu.

9. **bespoken:** Young employs an archaic usage of this word, whose meaning here may most clearly be rendered as "encountered."

10. **wonderful:** another older usage. Young does not state approval here but indicates that the contents of the press were surprising.

11. **à gorge déployée:** enthusiastically.

tables harangue each his little audience: the eagerness with which they are heard, and the thunder of applause they receive for every sentiment of more than common hardiness or violence against the present government, cannot easily be imagined. I am all amazement at the ministry permitting such nests and hot-beds of sedition and revolt, which disseminate amongst the people, every hour, principles that by and by must be opposed with vigour, and therefore it seems little short of madness to allow the propagation at present.

THE 10TH.—Every thing conspires to render the present period in France critical: the want of bread is terrible: accounts arrive every moment from the provinces of riots and disturbances, and calling in the military, to preserve the peace of the markets. The prices reported are the same as I found at Abbeville and Amiens 5s. (2½d.) a pound for white bread, and 3½s. to 4s. for the common sort, eaten by the poor: these rates are beyond their faculties, and occasion great misery.

THE 26TH.—Every hour that passes seems to give the people fresh spirit: the meetings at the Palais Royal are more numerous, more violent, and more assured; and in the assembly of electors, at Paris, for sending a deputation to the National Assembly, the language that was talked, by all ranks of people, was nothing less than a revolution in the government, and the establishment of a free constitution: what they mean by a free constitution, is easily understood—*a republic*; for the doctrine of the times runs every day more and more to that point; yet they profess, that the kingdom ought to be a monarchy too; or, at least, that there ought to be a king. In the streets one is stunned by the hawkers of seditious pamphlets, and descriptions of pretended events, that all tend to keep the people equally ignorant and alarmed. The supineness, and even stupidity of the court, is without example: the moment demands the greatest decision—and yesterday, while it was actually a question, whether he should be a Doge of Venice,[12] or a King of France, the King went a hunting! The spectacle of the Palais Royal presented this night, till eleven o'clock, and, as we afterwards heard, almost till morning, is curious. The croud was prodigious, and fireworks of all sorts were played off, and all the building was illuminated: these were said to be rejoicings on account of the Duc d'Orléans[13] and the nobility joining the commons; but united with the excessive freedom,

---

12. **Doge of Venice:** in principle the head of Venetian government, the Doge in reality was a figurehead.

13. **Duc d'Orléans:** Louis Philippe Joseph, Duke of Orléans (1747–1793), was a member of the royal family who played an equivocal role in the Revolution's early years. As a member of the Assembly of Notables, he opposed new royal taxing authority. On June 25, 1789, the duke answered the call of the Third Estate of the Estates General for noblemen to join it, in defiance of royal order, as the National Assembly. This is the event celebrated in Young's account. The duke's ownership of the Palais Royal has led generations of historians to accuse him of inciting the revolutionary agitation that took place there. Before his death in the Reign of Terror, he served as a member of the legislature and in 1792 cast his vote for the death of Louis XVI.

and even licentiousness of the orators, who harangue the people; with the general movement which before was threatening, all this bustle and noise, which will not leave them a moment tranquil, has a prodigious effect in preparing them for whatever purposes the leaders of the commons shall have in view; consequently they are grossly and diametrically opposite to the interests of the court;—but all these are blind and infatuated.

[*July 1789 (on the road at Metz, a city about 150 miles east of Paris)*]

THE 14TH.—They have a *cabinet littéraire*[14] at Metz, something like that I described at Nantes, but not on so great a plan; and they admit any person to read or go in and out for a day, on paying 4s. To this I eagerly resorted, and the news from Paris, both in the public prints, and by the information of a gentleman, I found to be interesting. Versailles and Paris are surrounded by troops: 35,000 men are assembled, and 20,000 more on the road, large trains of artillery collected, and all the preparations of war. The assembling of such a number of troops has added to the scarcity of bread; and the magazines[15] that have been made for their support are not easily by the people distinguished from those they suspect of being collected by monopolists. This has aggravated their evils almost to madness; so that the confusion and tumult of the capital are extreme.

Source 12 from Keith Michael Baker, editor, Readings in Western Civilizations, *vol. 7,* The Old Regime and the Revolution *(Chicago: University of Chicago Press, 1987), pp. 193–196.*

12. Report of the British Ambassador, the Duke of Dorset, to the Foreign Office in London

(*25th June, 1789*.) The reports concerning the scarcity of corn[16] in the neighbourhood of Paris have but too much foundation: the deficiency of this material article extends to the distance of 15 leagues[17] round the City and is so severely felt that Administration has been obliged to supply the different great Markets, by sending corn from the Magazines of the *Ecole Militaire*[18] originally

---

14. **cabinet littéraire:** reading room.

15. **magazines:** storage depots.

16. **corn:** in British usage, this word refers to grain, not American corn or maize.

17. **league:** a unit of distance equal to 2.764 miles in English-speaking countries.

18. **Ecole Militaire:** the Military School in Paris.

intended for the consumption of the Capital: in regard to the other Provinces of the Kingdom there is no further apprehension, as they are sufficiently supplied 'till the ensuing harvest which has every appearance of being very plentifull. . . .

The French Guards have, in some few instances within these few days, shewn a great reluctance to act and some of the men have declared that if they should be called upon to quell any disturbance they will, if compelled to fire, take care not to do any mischief. The Archbishop of Paris was very ill-treated last night by the mob at Versailles: his coach was broke to pieces and his horses much bruised: if the Guards had not protected him he must himself have been inevitably destroyed.

The people now are disposed to any desperate act of violence in support of the *Assemblée Nationale.*[19] I shall not fail to send Your Grace immediate intelligence of any momentous occurrence during this critical state of affairs. . . .

(*16th July, 1789.*) I wrote to Your Grace on the 12th Inst. by a messenger extraordinary to inform you of the removal of M. Necker from His Majesty's Councils: I have now to lay before Your Grace an account of the general revolt, with the extraordinary circumstances attending it, that has been the immediate consequence of that step. On Sunday evening a slight skirmish happened in the Place de Louis XV, in which two Dragoons[20] were killed, and two wounded of the Duc de Choiseuil's Regiment: after which all the troops left the Capital, and the populace remained unmolested masters of everything: much to their credit however, uncontrouled as they now were, no material mischief was done; their whole attention being confined to the burning of some of the Barriers. Very early on Monday morning the Convent of St. Lazare was forced, in which, besides a considerable quantity of corn, were found arms and ammunition supposed to have been conveyed thither as a place of security, at different periods from the Arsenal: and now a general consternation was seen throughout the Town: all shops were shut; all public and private works at a stand still and scarcely a person to be seen in the Streets excepting the armed *Bourgeoisie,* a temporary police for the protection of private property, to replace the established one which no longer had any influence.

In the morning of Tuesday the Hospital of Invalids was summonsed to surrender and was taken possession of after a very slight resistance: all the cannon, small arms and ammunition were immediately seized upon, and every one who chose to arm himself was supplied with what was necessary . . . in the evening a large detachment with two pieces of cannon went to the Bastille

---

19. **Assemblée Nationale:** the National Assembly.
20. **Dragoon:** cavalryman equipped with both a sabre and a short musket and therefore capable of fighting either mounted or on foot.

to demand the ammunition that was there, the *Gardes Bourgeoises*[21] not being then sufficiently provided: a flag of truce was sent on before and was answered from within, notwithstanding which the governor (the Marquis de Launay) contrary to all precedent fired upon the people and killed several: this proceeding so enraged the populace that they rushed to the very gates with a determination to force their way through if possible: upon this the Governor agreed to let in a certain number of them on condition that they should not commit any violence: these terms being acceded to, a detachment of about 40 in number advanced and were admitted, but the drawbridge was immediately drawn up again and the whole party instantly massacred: this breach of honor aggravated by so glaring an act of inhumanity excited a spirit of revenge and tumult such as might naturally be expected: the two pieces of cannon were immediately placed against the Gate and very soon made a breach which, with the disaffection that as is supposed prevailed within, produced a sudden surrender of that Fortress: M. de Launay, the principal gunner, the tailer, and two old invalids who had been noticed as being more active than the rest were seized and carried to the *Hôtel de Ville*[22] where, after a very summary trial before the tribunal there, the inferior objects were put to death and M. de Launay had also his head cut off at the Place de Grève, but with circumstances of barbarity too shocking to relate. . . . In the course of the same evening the whole of the *Gardes Françoises*[23] joined the Bourgeoisie with all their cannon, arms and ammunition: the Regiments that were encamped in the *Champ de Mars*,[24] by an Order from Government left the ground at 2 o'Clock yesterday morning and fell back to Sêve, leaving all their camp equipage behind them; the magazines of powder and corn at the *Ecole Militaire* were immediately taken possession of and a *Garde Bourgeoise* appointed to protect them. Nothing could exceed the regularity and good order with which all this extraordinary business has been conducted: of this I have myself been a witness upon several occasions during the last three days as I have passed through the streets, nor had I at any moment reason to be alarmed for my personal safety.

21. **Gardes Bourgeoises:** the civic militia formed by the Parisian electors on July 13.
22. **Hôtel de Ville:** the Paris city hall.
23. **Gardes Françoises:** the French Guards, the unit normally charged with Parisian security, whose loyalty to the king had begun to erode as early as June 18, 1789.
24. **Champ de Mars:** the large parade ground in Paris in front of the Military School (Ecole Militaire).

Source 13 from Marcel Le Clère, editor, Paris de la préhistoire à nos jour (Paris: Editions Bordessoules, 1985), p. 411. Translated by Julius R. Ruff.

13. The Bookseller Hardy on the Background of the Bastille Attack

On Sunday, July 12, between five and six in the evening the news arrived from Versailles that Monsieur Necker, Minister of State and Director General of Finances, at the king's order had given up his office and had left incognito for Switzerland the previous night at one hour past midnight. If one believed the rumors, his departure came after he had told His Majesty that he deplored the disasters with which France was going to be overwhelmed, and warned him that before long there would, perhaps, not be a single *écu* left in the treasury. The resulting public outcry that worthy ministers had been dismissed and had been replaced by others who had no merit at all in public opinion led to the cancellation of all theatrical performances and the refunding of ticket prices to their audiences. This unexpected event causes a great clamor and spreads dread to all minds. In the Palais Royal, the Tuileries,[25] and in the Champs Elysées occurs an astonishing meeting of citizens of all social stations which results in the movements of large numbers of troops and guards charged with the city's security. People reported that various tragic events, of which I was unable to get precise details, had occurred in the Place Louis XV and on the Tuileries terrace. All the residents of the capital and its suburbs spend most of the night in the greatest anxiety.

QUESTIONS TO CONSIDER

Crowd violence was not uncommon in early modern Europe, and historians have recently shown that such violence, rather than reflecting blind rage, often represented the expression of very definite ideas. Recall the political crisis of June and July 1789. The National Assembly was defying the king, and many Parisians supported this stand. Both the legislators at Versailles and the people of Paris knew that royal troops were moving in the latter's direction. They correctly connected these military steps with Necker's dismissal and believed that the king was beginning a coup to suppress demands for change in France. How might political problems coinciding with other difficulties have helped to produce the Bastille attack? Your problem in this chapter is to reconstruct the nature and spread of certain ideas in Paris on July 14, 1789, by bringing together the various pieces of evidence presented here.

25. **Tuileries:** the gardens of the Tuileries Palace, open to the public. To their west was the Place Louis XV (now the Place de la Concorde) and an area still undeveloped in the eighteenth century, the Champs Elysées.

Consider first the physical setting of this historical drama. Examine the picture of the Palais Royal. How many people could congregate here in fair weather like that experienced on July 12–14? What effect did Camille Desmoulins appear to have on the crowd? If political agitation and rumors spread beyond the Palais Royal, what physical features of Paris, visible in the city's streets and residences, would have been conducive to their dispersion throughout the city? What conditions did Parisians encounter in the streets? How would these conditions affect the spread of news? What features of the floor plans of typical Parisian houses might have permitted the mobilization of all residents in a political cause? Combine all these facts and you should have an idea of the nature of political activity in the city in 1789.

Next, consider the prices for wheat in Paris. You need to know what these prices represented to Parisians in terms of daily survival. How might food prices have inspired the agitation made possible by the city's physical layout? Examine both national and Parisian trends in wheat prices. What impact did rising bread prices have on the budgets of even skilled workers like journeymen masons and locksmiths? What do you suppose their response to such prices might have been? Remember that Jacques Necker, who was widely regarded as an important factor in keeping Paris supplied with food, was dismissed on July 11.

Examine next the social background of the Bastille's attackers. Refer to the map and the table showing the trades and residences of Bastille insurgents to determine which groups felt the problems of 1789 most acutely. What social groups were represented in the crowd? What was their economic standing? What parts of the city did they come from? Why do you suppose such groups, rather than other residents of the city, were moved to action? What factors conducive to the mobilization of the insurgents would you expect to find among them? Why would you expect them to be accustomed to organization in trades still governed by guilds? Why would you expect them to have been involved in the business activities of Parisian streets and markets?

As you complete this analysis, you should have an understanding of the composition of the Bastille crowd, how it was mobilized, and why the population might be agitated by food problems in 1789. Remember that the food price crisis coincided with a political crisis. Consult the written sources to understand the conjunction of these problems. How does Arthur Young show the response of Parisian public opinion to all of this? Were the effects of the crisis felt beyond Paris? Look at the works of the British ambassador and the bookseller Hardy. What do they tell us about developments in Paris? Considering that the Bastille fell to a group of armed rebels, how do you account for the ambassador's assurances that he felt safe? Refer to your findings on the crowd's composition in answering this question and remember the creation of a civil guard made up of middle-class citizens.

What social group controlled Paris by the time rain fell on July 14?

By combining these sources, both the traditional written accounts long used by historians and the sociological material that establishes the composition of the crowd, you should be able now to answer the central questions of this chapter. What stirred Parisians to mass action? Who was in that crowd on July 14, 1789?

EPILOGUE

The fall of the Bastille to a popular attack whose genesis you have analyzed in this chapter was an event charged with both practical and symbolic significance. On the practical level, capturing the Bastille provided the crowd with the gunpowder it sought and made regaining control of Paris virtually impossible for the royal army. In consequence, the king's resolve to oppose the National Assembly evaporated along with his hopes of controlling Paris. Louis XVI announced to the National Assembly on July 15 that troops would be removed from the region of the capital; on July 16 he recalled Necker as finance minister. On the following day, July 17, the king went to Paris, where his actions publicly confirmed royal recognition and acceptance of the events of the preceding days. First he received the keys to the city from its new mayor, Jean-Sylvan Bailly, representative of the electors of Paris who now controlled the capital. At the city hall he affixed to his hat the blue, white, and red cockade,[26] composed of the blue and red of the Paris coat of arms and the white of the monarchy. That cockade would become the symbol of the Revolution, and its colors would come to form a new national flag.

With these actions, Louis XVI effectively surrendered control of events to the citizen rebels of Paris. Although we now know that his private sentiments remained steadfastly opposed to the widening Revolution, his public acquiescence was plain to Frenchmen of all political persuasions. The king's brother, the Count of Artois, left the country on the evening of July 16, the first of thousands who would flee the growing Revolution out of fear or hatred for what it represented. At the same time, towns and cities all over France imitated Paris by forming revolutionary governments and National Guards to consolidate the overthrow of the old regime in municipal administration. Disorder spread among peasants in the countryside, prompting the National Assembly on August 4, 1789, to end the distinct privileges of the nobility and clergy; henceforth, all citizens would be equal before the law, pay taxes, and enjoy equal rights and opportunities. The Revolution had won its first great victory, a fact that even the king later recognized. Planning an escape in 1792, Louis said that, in hindsight, he should

26. **cockade:** a rosette of ribbons often worn on the hat as a kind of badge in the eighteenth century.

have fled Paris on July 14, 1789, to rally his forces and undo the Revolution. He stated, "I know I missed my opportunity: that was on July 14th. I ought to have gone away then. . . . I missed my opportunity, and I've never found it again."[27]

The symbolic importance of the Bastille's fall also was great. Despite its small prisoner census by 1789, the old fortress-prison symbolized royal power to eighteenth-century Frenchmen. The Paris government conferred the job of physically smashing this symbol of the Old Regime on a patriotic contractor, Pierre-François Palloy (1755–1834). In his hands, the transformation of the Bastille into another sort of symbol began. Palloy demolished the prison and transformed its remains into physical symbols of liberty's victory. In 1790 he had stones of the prison carved into eighty-three small replicas of the Bastille and sent one to each of France's new administrative units, the *départements*. In 1793 he sent

27. Quoted in Godechot, p. 257.

stones from the Bastille to the 544 districts of France and a number of political clubs and prominent citizens. He also had the prison's irons struck into commemorative medals and sponsored festivals celebrating the prison's fall. Others followed his lead. Masonry taken from the prison was used in a Parisian bridge so that citizens could tread on the "stone of tyranny." Lafayette sent a key to the Bastille to George Washington as a symbol of the victory of liberty. This key hangs today at Mount Vernon. And on July 14, 1790, the city of Paris honored 954 citizens who had taken part in the prison's capture as conquerors of the Bastille.

Eighteenth-century Frenchmen recognized the great symbolic importance of July 14, 1789, and France commemorated the anniversary of the Bastille's fall throughout its Revolution. Future generations recognized the event's importance, too. In 1880 the Third Republic made July 14 the great national holiday, observed in France with as much patriotic fervor as Americans observe July 4.

CHAPTER FIFTEEN

LABOR OLD AND NEW:

THE IMPACT OF

THE INDUSTRIAL REVOLUTION

THE PROBLEM

The main difficulty did not ... lie so much in the invention of a proper self-acting mechanism for drawing and twisting cotton as in the distribution of the different members of the apparatus into one cooperative body, in impelling each organ with its appropriate delicacy and speed, and above all, in training human beings to renounce their desultory habits of work, to identify themselves with the unvarying regularity of work of the complex automation. It requires in fact a man of Napoleonic nerve and ambition to subdue refractory tempers of work people accustomed to irregular spasms of diligence, and to urge on his multifarious and intricate constructions in the face of prejudice, passion, and envy.

This is how Andrew Ure, an early and enthusiastic analyst of the Industrial Revolution, characterized the problems of industrial management in his book *The Philosophy of Manufacturers* (1835). In these few sentences,

Ure identified the essence of the Industrial Revolution. As most Western Civilization courses correctly emphasize, the period of history this label describes did indeed represent an economic and technological revolution of the greatest magnitude. The manner in which the West produced its goods changed more in the century from 1750 to 1850 than in all the previous centuries of human history, making necessary, as Ure says, the solution of tremendous problems of technology and integration of industrial processes.

But the Industrial Revolution had another impact, one that Ure did not neglect, though he approached it from the managerial point of view in emphasizing the manager's need to train his employees. That Ure thought the disciplining of the work force was perhaps the manager's chief problem suggests the broad social impact of industrialization. The first generations of factory laborers encountered a world of work dramatically transformed from that of their fathers and mothers, a laboring situation with which most were totally unfamiliar.

The work life of the preindustrial laborer certainly was not easy. Workdays were long, typically dawn to dusk, six days per week, and it was common for wives and children to labor alongside their husbands and fathers as part of a household economy. Indeed, for agricultural workers and craftsmen alike, labor took up so much of their time that little remained for other daily activities. The material rewards of labor often were meager, too; we saw the mass poverty of preindustrial Europe in Chapter 4. But preindustrial work, however long, hard, and unrewarding, had characteristics that distinguished it from early industrial labor.

Preindustrial work usually was conducted in and around the worker's residence. Such labor afforded the worker occasional variety and, in some instances, a measure of control over the pace of work. We may see this effect if we examine the various types of preindustrial workers. Agricultural workers certainly experienced periods of intensive labor, especially at spring plowing and at harvest time, but periods of less intensive labor, especially in the winter months, punctuated their work year and brought them a bit of respite from their duties.

Many of the skilled craftsmen who produced the consumer goods of preindustrial Europe were organized by trade into local, professional groups known as guilds. Guilds performed many functions for their members. By controlling the size of their member-

ship, guilds could limit the number of practitioners of a trade in their cities because practice of a trade often required guild membership. Such limitation of membership aimed at protecting the livelihoods of guild members by assuring that there would be sufficient work, and thus income, for each one. Guilds set prices for their products as well, always at a level that would assure an adequate income to guild members and prevent ruinous price competition. Guilds gave the consumer a measure of protection, too. Guilds regulated the quality of their members' output and, through a system of training known as *apprenticeship,* guaranteed consumers that producers had sufficient skills in their trades to produce a fine product. Apprenticeship gave a craftsman the essential skills of his trade, and most men followed apprenticeship with employment as *journeymen,* that is, as workers who were sufficiently skilled to command a daily wage in the shop of a guild master. Full guild membership, and the right to open one's own production unit in his trade, was reserved for those journeymen who completed a *masterpiece,* a fine example of their skills in their chosen profession, which won for them the title of guild master.

The production unit of a guild master afforded him some measure of freedom in plying his trade within guild regulations. The master supervised a production unit that often included members of his family, apprentices, and sometimes journeymen. The master set the pace for himself and his workers, who, particularly in Catholic countries, might look forward to a number of religious holidays, civic festivals, and fairs to interrupt their year's labor.

In the later centuries of the preindustrial age, another kind of labor began to emerge. Called the *putting-out system,* this form of employment became common in textile production. A merchant would purchase raw material, often wool, and deliver it to various rural workers, who would spin, weave, dye, and finish the cloth, using traditional methods. Often workers were farm families who took in textile work to supplement their incomes. Merchants sought such rural workers because they worked cheaply and because they were beyond the jurisdiction of urban authorities, who limited textile production to guild members. The putting-out system allowed merchants to gather large numbers of workers under their control and thus organize production more efficiently. Even workers in this more disciplined mode of production enjoyed some freedom in organizing their work, however, despite the low wages that often kept them in poverty. For example, consider a weaver employed as part of the putting-out system. The weaver might enjoy "holy Monday," that is, a prolongation of the Sabbath, by taking the first day of the week off. The weaver might also take a few hours off on Tuesday and Wednesday as well, completing the week's required production only by working all night Thursday and Friday. No matter how he or she scheduled his or her work time, however, the choice was the weaver's. The worker had some control over the labor.

Indeed, all these factors that somewhat lessened the intensity of preindustrial labor have led some historians to idealize preindustrial work. It is important that we do not follow their example. By perhaps the most important measure of a laborer's work life—the standard of living it supports—it is by no means certain that early industrial employment represented an overall worsening of workers' living conditions. Historians continue to debate the issue of standard of living, examining diverse data on wages, diet, and housing; the problem clearly is a complex one. Whereas the preindustrial skilled craftsman was generally well rewarded for his work, the agricultural laborer and putting-out worker usually were not, and peasant families on the Continent sometimes lived a subsistence existence. For some rural workers, early industrial labor may actually have improved their standard of living.

Industrial labor, however, definitely brought all those employed in the new mills, factories, and mines a new style of work. Hours in the new establishments remained long, and the work year was interrupted by fewer holidays because factory owners could maximize returns on their massive investments in plants and machines only by using them to their fullest. Labor by whole families often continued, too, but the factory system separated them from their homes, and the tasks and workplaces of family members were very different. Husbands endured the heaviest labor in textile mills or mines. Their wives, research has shown, most often remained at home, keeping house, caring for young children, and often laboring many hours in low-paying tasks that could be done at home—"slop work," that is, needle trades, bookbinding, millinery, or other such occupations. Only a minority of married women worked in early mills and mines. Children and unmarried women, however, went out to work in mills, where their hands were better suited to intricate machinery than men's, or in mines, where their small statures allowed them to move through low mine tunnels more easily than men. Their wages always were very low.

Most significantly, perhaps, the worker lost control over the pace of his or her work. Modern factory production dictated that workers serve these new machines that had taken over the productive role. Barring breakdowns, the machine's pace never varied; the new work was monotonous. Workers found themselves endlessly repeating the same tasks in the production process with little autonomy. In addition, industrial work imposed a new punctuality on workers. For the factory system to function smoothly, all had to be at their work stations on time and remain there except during scheduled breaks. "Holy Monday" and unscheduled leisure time threatened the smooth operation of an industrial establishment. Early mines and factories posed significant safety problems, too, as we will see.

How did the first generations of industrial workers respond to such fundamental changes? Some adapted. Others proved incapable of adjusting to the new working conditions, and absenteeism (especially on Mondays), chronic tardiness, and workers' inability to keep pace with machines plagued many early mills. Many other workers experienced a growing inner alienation, identified by such observers of industrialism as Karl Marx, that manifested itself in various forms of asocial behavior. When economic conditions were good and jobs were plentiful, early mills had problems with frequent employee resignations. Some mills experienced as much as 100 percent annual employee turnover.

Other new social problems also accompanied industrialization. Urban expansion accompanied the factory system (see Chapter 8), reflecting the movement of many rural families to growing cities in search of factory employment. Such moves separated the new arrivals from friends and from the social controls of village life. In the city they often found not only the poverty of early industrial work but also the anonymity of urban life and the wealth of modern society displayed by the privileged classes. The result was a rapid rise of crimes against property accompanying urban growth. Older social problems persisted, too. Preindustrial workers frequently consumed alcohol in excess as an escape from their tedious work lives. Indeed, "holy Monday" often reflected the effects of a worker's weekend of alcohol abuse. The early industrial age was little different. One English clergyman described to a committee of Parliament the sight of twelve-year-old coal miners staggering with drink.

The human response to this fundamental change in work thus assumed many forms; however, these did not include organized resistance to the machine age by industrial workers. Those employed in early mills and mines often were illiterate and consequently difficult to mobilize for collective actions such as strikes. Moreover, laws like the English Combination Acts (1799, 1800) and the French Le Chapelier Law (1791) actually forbade worker organizations; the few early unions were illegal and secretive. The only overt resistance to industrialization, therefore, came not from industrial workers but from one group of preindustrial laborers, namely, the artisans. Members of this class had a high rate of literacy and thus were aware that the new machines ultimately threatened both their livelihoods and their work autonomy. They lashed out with acts of machine smashing. English machine smashers were called *Luddites* after one Ned Ludd, who supposedly originated their movement.

Machine smashing, of course, could not stop industrialization, and workers in early mines and mills became the objects of an increasingly stringent discipline aimed at forcing their acceptance of the new labor. Overseers beat child laborers. Managers fined or dismissed adults and sometimes blacklisted particularly difficult workers to deny them any employment.

In this chapter you will be asked to contrast the working conditions of the preindustrial and industrial ages. How did industrial labor differ from preindustrial work? How did such labor evolve? What effects did the new labor have on the first generations of men, women, and children in Europe's mills and mines?

SOURCES AND METHOD

The central questions of this chapter require your analysis of both preindustrial and industrial labor. As an aid to this analysis, the evidence for this chapter is accordingly divided into two groups, one relating to the preindustrial age (the "old labor") and the other to the industrial era (the "new labor").

Let us begin our consideration of the old labor with its most traditional form, agricultural labor. Source 1 is the work of Sébastien Le Prestre de Vauban (1633–1707). Vauban was a brilliant military engineer whose skill in designing fortifications and conducting sieges for the army of Louis XIV of France propelled him to the highest rank in the army, Marshal of France. But Vauban's interests were not narrowly military in scope. This highly intelligent and observant man wrote extensively on a variety of problems; he was the author of treatises on agriculture, construction, and the need for religious toleration in an age of widespread persecution of religious minorities. The selection from Vauban's writings presented in Source

1 is drawn from one of his last works, a proposal for reforming the tax system of early-eighteenth-century France with the goals of both greater equity in assessing the tax burden and increased revenues to balance the royal budget. To adequately present his ideas, Vauban undertook a description of the economic situations of his fellow Frenchmen in this work, which gives the student of the eighteenth century a number of insights into the lot of common people who left little other record of their activities. In reading this source, pay particular attention to the agricultural workers Vauban describes. This group owned little property, but instead worked the lands of others. Lacking land of their own, this group of workers possessed a certain mobility, which would lead many of their number to factory employment a century after Vauban's analysis of their situation. How long was the agricultural work year of this group? Why were the earnings of such people from agriculture insufficient? What sort of nonagricultural employment did members of the family unit undertake?

In Source 2, you encounter further evidence on agricultural labor, this time on working conditions of farm workers in England almost a century and a half after Vauban wrote. Source 2 offers you for the first time a type of evidence you will analyze several times in this chapter, the record of hearings on early industrial working conditions conducted by legislative committees. From such records, committee members drew up recommendations, which often resulted in legislation to improve working conditions in early mills, factories, and mines.

These records have a great advantage for the historian because they also offer a glimpse into the world of the illiterate laboring poor of an earlier age. Secretaries to the investigating committees often took down the testimony of witnesses verbatim, providing an enduring record of all the difficulties of labor in the early industrial era. Mrs. Britton labored in the old style as an agricultural worker, but she brought a unique perspective to her testimony to a committee of the British Parliament because she once had worked in a factory also. What were the work conditions and the standard of living of agricultural workers like Mrs. Britton and her husband? How did agricultural labor compare with factory labor for Mrs. Britton?

With Source 3 we turn to the labor of the preindustrial craftsman. The evidence on craftsmen's labor opens with a summary of holidays in a textile-producing city, Lille, France, in the seventeenth century. How would you characterize the pace of labor in Lille, a city whose work calendar was not unusual in Catholic Europe?

Source 4 presents excerpts from guild regulations in the Prussian woolen industry. The Industrial Revolution began in England in the mid-eighteenth century but affected the Continent much later, only in the first decades of the nineteenth century. Thus, these guild regulations dating from 1797 describe the traditional labor of many Europeans. In reading them, ask yourself what sort of labor conditions these regulations sustained. A worker's demonstration of his mastery of all the processes of producing wool cloth won him the "freedom of the guild" and its privileges. The latter involved the right to establish his own production unit and market his goods, as well as guild assistance when old age or illness prevented work. What sort of limits on the activities of guild members accompanied these freedoms? What do you think were the reasons for these restrictions? What efforts to protect both the consumer and the guild members' market can you discern in these restrictions? Why was the putting-out system explicitly forbidden to guild members? What specifically in all these restrictions seems intended to create a protected monopoly for producers?

Source 5 describes another facet of the old style of labor in textile production, namely, the putting-out system. It is the work of François-Alexandre Frédéric, Duke of La Rochefoucauld-Liancourt (1747–1827), an astute observer of the social and economic problems of his day who applied his energy and wealth to various reform schemes, including experimental farms and an early cotton mill. La Rochefoucauld wrote persuasively on the need for improved poor relief and better education for all Frenchmen. Here, to support his call for social change, La Rochefoucauld provides a good description of the putting-out system in his travel account of 1781 to 1783, based on his visit to Rouen, the capital of the northern French province of Normandy. Who was employed in textiles in Rouen? What does the duke tell you about the quantity of production in Rouen, despite the continued use of hand looms? How did the organization of this work, the quantity

of production, and the destinations of its products foreshadow certain features of the industrial age?

Source 6, "The Clothier's Delight," is a popular song, a type of source you have not yet studied in Volume II. Historians examine songs as evidence of popular culture to understand the attitudes and lives of men and women who were often illiterate. We must understand that such songs may exaggerate their message a bit to achieve their desired effect among unsophisticated audiences. Nevertheless, we do have in this song some evidence of broad trends in the putting-out system and the concerns of those employed in it by English clothiers. Who controlled the material in this production process? Were the weavers and other textile workers the independent producers described in the guild regulations? Why did the workers view the clothiers as adversaries? How did the clothiers control the workers?

Next, consider the evidence on the new labor, that is, the work of the industrial age. Sources 7 and 8 in this section are regulations governing the conditions of work in early industrial enterprises. In using this material, the historian must remember that such regulations describe the behavior prescribed by persons in authority; they may not describe the actual comportment of those whose behavior the statutes aimed to control. Indeed, we can assume that there was frequent conflict between the prescribed rules and the actual behavior of working people as workers adapted to the new conditions of industrial work.

Examine the work code for the foundry and engineering works in

Moabit, an industrial suburb of Berlin, Germany, in 1844 (Source 7). What sort of habits did these regulations seek to inculcate in the foundry workers? Notice also the pay practices described in paragraph 18. Why would management have adopted these? What disadvantages did they represent for the worker?

The apprenticeship agreement for girls as silk workers in rural Tarare, France (Source 8), retains the terminology of the old labor in designating new workers as apprentices, but it lays down industrial-age work rules for the young women. Examine the agreement carefully, noting its disciplinary features. How long was the apprenticeship? When were wages paid? What happened if a girl left before the completion of her apprenticeship? What were the work hours? In what ways did management seek to increase production? Such mills as this were established in rural areas, away from cities like Lyons, where male preindustrial silk weavers had a centuries-long history of guild organization (and of unrest). Given that information, can you discern why the mill's location was chosen and why a female work force was sought? What attractions did the mill, with its long workday, offer unmarried rural women who otherwise would have been reluctant to seek industrial employment away from home?

The testimony of William Cooper to the Sadler Committee of the British Parliament (Source 9) provides dramatic evidence about the conditions of industrial labor in early textile mills. What effect did mill labor have on Cooper? What were the hours of work? How did overseers enforce punctuality and a faster work pace by young workers? Were conditions within the mills conducive to good health? Compare Cooper's height to that of his father. What could have accounted for Cooper's shorter stature? When he had health problems and was unable to work, what recourse did Cooper have?

Source 10 also describes the condition of labor in the textile industry, but it records the lot of women fifty or more years after William Cooper's experiences in the mills. Had working conditions improved very much since Cooper's day? How long was the workday? Did the work demand exceptional energy or skill from the workers? How did management impose discipline in such matters as punctuality?

With the selections brought together as Source 11, you will once more analyze the records of English parliamentary inquiries, but this time the committees examined coal mine labor in the 1840s. Read first the testimony of Joseph Staley. Note his position in the mine. How might this have affected his conclusion about his miners' health? How many boys did he employ, and what ages were they? What sort of labor did the boys do? What were their hours? Analyze the testimony of William Jagger. What age was he? How long had he worked in the mine? What were his hours? What do his testimony and the comment by the investigator following that testimony tell you about work conditions and mine safety?

With the testimony of Patience Kershaw we have a record of women's labor in the mines. What sort of labor did Kershaw do? What weight of coal did she move daily? What health effects did such labor have on women like Kershaw and her sisters? What impression did she make on the parliamentary investigator, as indicated in his comment following her testimony?

Industrialization transformed the Western world in many ways, and we will examine aspects of its consequences in other chapters of this book as well (see especially Chapters 8 and 14). Your analysis of the evidence presented here should aid you in understanding one aspect of that transformation: the emergence of a new world of industrial labor and how it affected men and women of the eighteenth and nineteenth centuries.

THE EVIDENCE

THE OLD LABOR

Source 1 from Sébastien Le Prestre de Vauban, Project d'une Dixme royale, *ed. by E. Coornaert (Paris: Alcan, 1933) reprinted in Pierre Goubert,* The Ancien Régime: French Society, *1600–1750, trans. by Steve Cox (New York: Harper and Row, 1974), pp. 116–118. Copyright © 1973 by George Weidenfield & Nicholson Ltd. Reprinted with permission of HarperCollins Publishers, Inc.*

1. Agricultural Labor Described by Vauban, about 1700

. . . It only remains to take stock of two million men[1] all of whom I suppose to be day-laborers or simple artisans scattered throughout the towns, *bourgs*[2] and villages of the realm.

What I have to say about all these workers . . . deserves serious attention, for although this sector may consist of what are unfairly called the dregs of the people, they are nonetheless worthy of high consideration in view of the services which they render to the State. For it is they who undertake all the great tasks in town and country without which neither themselves nor others could live. It is they who provide all the soldiers and sailors and all the serving women; in a word, without them the State could not survive. It is for this reason that they ought to be spared in the matter of taxes, in order not to burden them beyond their strength. . . .

---

1. Vauban wrote in an age that had no modern census data for accurately assessing the size of a population. His figures here, at best, are an estimate. Indeed, modern demographic historians generally find Vauban's population data highly inaccurate.

2. **bourgs:** market towns.

Among the smaller fry, particularly in the countryside, there are any number of people who, while they lay no claim to any special craft, are continually plying several which are most necessary and indispensable. Of such a kind are those we call *manoeuvriers,* who, owning for the most part nothing but their strong arms or very little more, do day- or piece-work for whoever wants to employ them. It is they who do all the major jobs such as mowing, harvesting, threshing, woodcutting, working the soil and the vineyards, clearing land, ditching, carrying soil to vineyards or elsewhere, labouring for builders and several other tasks which are all hard and laborious. These men may well find this kind of employment for part of the year, and it is true that they can usually earn a fair day's wage at haymaking, harvesting and grape-picking time, but the rest of the year is a different story. . . .

It will not be inappropriate [to give] some particulars about what the country day-laborer can earn.

I shall assume that of the three-hundred and sixty-five days in the year, he may be gainfully employed for one hundred and eighty, and earn nine *sols*[3] a day. This is a high figure, and it is certain that except at harvest and grape-picking time most earn not more than eight *sols* a day on average, but supposing we allow the nine *sols,* that would amount to eighty-five *livres* and ten *sols,* call it ninety *livres,* from which we have to deduct his liabilities (taxes plus salt[4] for a family of four, say 14l. 16s.) . . . leaving seventy-five *livres* four *sols.*

Since I am assuming that his family . . . consists of four people, it requires not less than ten *septiers*[5] of grain, Paris measure, to feed them. This grain, half wheat, half rye . . . commonly selling at six *livres* per *septier* . . . will come to sixty *livres,* which leaves fifteen *livres* 4 *sols* out of seventy-five *livres* four *sols,* out of which the labourer has to find the price of rent and upkeep for his house, a few chattels, if only some earthenware bowls, clothing and linen, and the needs of his entire family for one year.

But these fifteen *livres* four *sols* will not take him very far unless his industry[6] or some particular business supervenes and his wife contributes to their income by means of her distaff,[7] sewing, knitting hose or making small quan-

3. **sol:** sou.

4. Salt was subject to a form of tax in France before 1789. Tax farmers purchased the exclusive right to sell this dietary necessity to the public. The public was required by law to buy a certain amount of salt per year from these monopolists; in paying the price of the salt, buyers also paid a salt tax, the *gabelle,* to the tax farmers, who turned the proceeds of this over to the government. This form of taxation kept salt prices artificially high in much of France and was deeply resented by many taxpayers.

5. **septier:** a unit of measure in use in France prior to the Revolution of 1789. Its precise size varied from one district to another; hence here Vauban must specify that he is using the Parisian *septier.* Ten Parisian *septiers* would have equaled about 15.5 hectoliters or 43 bushels.

6. Many rural workers would have been employed in some phase of textile production, such as weaving.

7. **distaff:** a staff that holds unspun flax or wool during the process of spinning such material into thread. The word can also refer to women's work or interests, because spinning was women's work.

tities of lace . . . also by keeping a small garden or rearing poultry and perhaps a calf, a pig or a goat for the better-off . . . ; by which means he might buy a piece of larding bacon and a little butter or oil for making soup. And if he does not additionally cultivate some small allotment, he will be hard pressed to subsist, or at least he will be reduced, together with his family, to the most wretched fare. And if instead of two children he has four, that will be worse still until they are old enough to earn their own living. Thus however we come at the matter, it is certain that he will always have the greatest difficulty in seeing the year out. . . .

Source 2 from British Parliamentary Papers: Reports of Special Assistant Poor Law Commissioner on the Employment of Women and Children in Agriculture *(London: William Clowes and Sons for Her Majesty's Stationery Office, 1843), pp. 66–67.*

2. Testimony of an Agricultural Worker's Wife and Former Factory Worker, 1842[8]

Mrs. *Britton*, Wife of _____ *Britton*, of *Calne, Wiltshire*, Farm-labourer, examined.

I am 41 years old; I have lived at Calne all my life. I went to school till I was eight years old, when I went out to look after children. At ten years old I went to work at a factory in Calne, where I was till I was 26. I have been married 15 years. My husband is an agricultural labourer. I have seven children, all boys. The oldest is fourteen, the youngest three-quarters of a year old. My husband is a good workman, and does most of his work by the lump, and earns from 9s. to 10s. a-week pretty constantly, but finds his own tools,—his wheelbarrow, which cost 1l., pickaxe, which cost 3s., and scoop, which cost 3s.[9]

I have worked in the fields, and when I went out I left the children in the care of the eldest boy, and frequently carried the baby with me, as I could not

8. This testimony was delivered before a parliamentary committee studying the employment of women and children in British agriculture.

9. **by the lump:** Mr. Britton was paid by the job rather than by the hour or day. English coinage mentioned in this and following selections (with the abbreviations for each denomination where appropriate) includes:
   £ or l.: pound sterling.
   s.: shilling; 20 shillings to 1 pound sterling.
   d.: pence (from Latin *denari*); 12 pence to 1 shilling.
   crown: a coin worth 5 shillings.
   groat: a coin worth 4 pence.

go home to nurse it. I have worked at hay-making and at harvest, and at other times in weeding and keeping the ground clean. I generally work from half-past seven till five, or half-past. When at work in the spring I have received 10*d.* a-day, but that is higher than the wages of women in general; 8*d.* or 9*d.* is more common. My master always paid 10*d.* When working I never had any beer, and I never felt the want of it. I never felt that my health was hurt by the work. Hay-making is hard work, very fatiguing, but it never hurt me. Working in the fields is not such hard work as working in the factory. I am always better when I can get out to work in the fields. I intend to do so next year if I can. Last year I could not go out, owing to the birth of the baby. My eldest boy gets a little to do; he don't earn more than 9*d.* a-week; he has not enough to do. My husband has 40 lugs[10] of land, for which he pays 10*s.* a-year. We grow potatoes and a few cabbages, but not enough for our family; for that we should like to have forty lugs more. We have to buy potatoes. One of the children is a cripple, and the guardians[11] allow us two gallons of bread a-week for him.[12] We buy two gallons more, according as the money is. Nine people can't do with less than four gallons of bread a-week. We could eat much more bread if we could get it; sometimes we can afford only one gallon a-week. We very rarely buy butcher's fresh meat, certainly not oftener than once a-week, and not more than sixpenny worth. I like my husband to have a bit of meat, now he has left off drinking. I buy $\frac{1}{2}$ lb. butter a-week, 1 oz. tea, $\frac{1}{2}$ lb. sugar. The rest of our food is potatoes, with a little fat. The rent of our cottage is 1*s.* 6*d.* a-week; there are two rooms in it. We all sleep in one room, under the tiles. Sometimes we receive private assistance, especially in clothing. Formerly my husband was in the habit of drinking, and everything went bad. He used to beat me. I have often gone to bed, I and my children, without supper, and I have had no breakfast the next morning, and frequently no firing.[13] My husband attended a lecture on teetotalism one evening about two years ago, and I have reason to bless that evening. My husband has never touched a drop of drink since. He has been better in health, getting stouter, and has behaved like a good husband to me ever since. I have been much more comfortable, and the children happier. He works better than he did. He can mow better, and

10. **lug:** an old English measure of area equal to 49 square yards. The Brittons' 40 lugs would, therefore, have equaled 1,960 square yards, less than half of a full acre, which is 4,840 square yards.

11. **guardian:** Poor Law official.

12. **two gallons of bread:** the gallon as a gauge of wheat and other dry material is an archaic English measure, the weight of which was far from standard in the British Isles. Sources refer to gallons of wheat weighing anywhere from 8 to almost 10 pounds. If we assume a gallon to have been 9 pounds in the case of the Brittons, we find that the family claims to have required a minimum of 36 pounds of bread per week. For this time, in which bread was the basic dietary element of the poor, demographic historians assume an adult to have consumed 2 pounds per day. Even if the family comprised only two adults and the rest children, these were extremely short rations.

13. **firing:** that is, no morning hearth fire for want of the cost of fuel.

that is hard work, and he does not mind being laughed at by the other men for not drinking. I send my eldest boy to Sunday school, them that are younger go to the day school. My eldest boy never complains of work hurting him. My husband now goes regularly to church: formerly he could hardly be got there.

Source 3 from Alain Lottin, Chavatte, ouvrier lillois. Un contemporain de Louis XIV *(Paris: Flammarion, 1979), pp. 323–324. Reprinted with permission.*

3. The Work Year in 17th-century Lille, France

Holidays in Seventeenth-Century Lille

January	Monday following Epiphany (January 6)
22 January	Feast of St. Vincent
25 January	Feast of St. Paul's Conversion
February	Ash Wednesday
22 February	Feast of the Chair of St. Peter
March or April	Tuesday of Holy Week until the Thursday after Easter (eight working days)
3 May	Feast of the Finding of the True Cross
9 May	Feast of St. Nicholas
May or June	Feast of Pentecost (seventh Sunday after Easter): Pentecost eve through the following Thursday (five days)
5 June	Corpus Christi
9 June or second Sunday in June	Municipal procession accompanied by banquets
11 June	Feast of St. Barnabas
June	Thursday after municipal procession is a holiday
2 July	Feast of the visitation of the Virgin
1 August	Feast of St. Peter in Chains
3 August	Feast of St. Stephen
29 August	Feast of the Beheading of St. John the Baptist, followed by five days off
1 October	Feast of St. Remy
18 October	Feast of St. Luke
1 November	All Saints Day
24–31 December	Christmas (eight days)

This represents a total of forty-four days off, in addition to Sundays.

*Sources 4 and 5 from Sidney Pollard and Colin Holmes, editors, Documents in European
Economic History, vol. 1, The Process of Industrialization, 1750–1870 (New York: St.
Martin's, 1968), pp. 45–48, pp. 91–92. Copyright © 1968 by St. Martin's Press. Reprinted
with permission of St. Martin's Press, Inc., and Sidney Pollard.*

4. Guild Regulations in the Prussian Woolen Industry, 1797

§ 760

Although it is laid down in the General Privilege (8 Nov. 1734) that it shall
not be necessary to produce a masterpiece in order to gain the master's freedom; yet it was ruled afterwards: that anyone aspiring to the freedom of the
gild, shall (22 November 1772) apart from being examined by the Inspector of
Manufactures and the Gild Master whether he be properly experienced in
sorting and fulling, wool shearing and preparing and threading the looms,
also weave a piece of cloth of mixed colour from wool dyed by himself.

§ 765–§ 771

The woollen weavers may sell by retail and cutting-up home produced cloths
and baizes[14] on condition that they and their fellow gild members may not
only sell in their own town the goods made locally, but may also offer them
for sale at fairs and annual markets. The latter, however, is limited to this extent (1772 and 1791): that a gild member may not take part in any market or
fair unless he has at least 12 pieces of cloth for sale, though it is permissible
(18 December 1791) for two of them to enter a fair and to offer cloth for sale if
they have at least 12 pieces of cloth between them; at the same time, this privilege is extended also to weavers (1772) who are no longer practising their
trade themselves.

The woollen weavers of Salzwedel, however, may not sell the cloths produced by themselves, by retail and cutting-up, even in their own town, because the local cloth cutters' and tailors' gild enjoys, according to its old privilege (1233, 1323 and last confirmed on 26 January 1715) the sole right of
cutting up woollen and similar cloth for sale, so that neither the local merchants, nor the mercers, nor the woollen weavers of the town, whose rights
were recently confirmed, have the right to cut up woollen cloth for sale.

Woollen weavers may not trade in woollen cloths made outside their own
town, unless they have been specially granted this right, because this would
infringe the privileges granted to the merchants. . . .

---

14. **baize:** a soft woolen fabric.

Neither finishers nor croppers,[15] dyers or other craftsmen (1772) are permitted to trade in woollen cloths or undertake putting-out agencies on pain of losing their craft privileges.

In the countryside (28 August 1723, 14 November 1793) neither linen (?) weavers, nor vergers[16] or schoolmasters, nor husbandmen themselves, are permitted to manufacture woollen or worsted cloth not even for their own use. Neither are town linen weavers permitted to make goods wholly of wool.

Woollen weavers are permitted to dye their own cloths, but neither they nor the merchants are permitted to have the cloths made in the Electoral Mark finished or dyed in foreign towns, on pain of confiscation of the goods. While the export of unfinished and undyed cloths is permissible (1772), merchants and woollen weavers should be persuaded (26 October and 10 November 1791) to export only dyed and finished cloths.

Woollen weavers may not (1772) keep their own tenting frame and stretch their own cloths, but must leave this finishing process to the cloth finishers. They have however the concession (28 October and 11 November 1773) that they may keep 10–12 frames, but on these they may only stretch $\frac{3}{4}$ widths, and twill flannels. . . .

§ 798

On pain of requisition and, for repeated offences, on pain of loss of the freedom of the gild, better yarn may not be used for the ends of pieces of cloth than is used for the middle. No weaver is permitted to keep frames of his own, on pain of loss of his gild freedom, and he is obliged to take his cloths to the master shearmen; tanned wool and wool-fells may not be woven into pieces, but must be made only into rough goods and horse blankets. Finally it is laid down in detail how each type of woollen and worsted cloth shall be manufactured; and weavers have been advised several times to observe closely the detailed rules and regulations of the woollen and worsted order (20 September 1784, 9 September and 8 October 1787). . . .

§ 800

It is further laid down as a general rule, that all cloths shall be viewed by sworn aulnagers,[17] of whom eight shall be elected in large companies, six in medium sized ones, and two to four among small ones, and they shall be viewed three times, and sealed accordingly after each time. The first viewing shall determine that the piece is woven with sufficient and satisfactory yarn, woven sufficiently closely and without flaws, and of the correct length and

15. **cropper:** a craftsman who sheared the nap from woolen cloth.

16. **verger:** a parish official generally charged with care of the interior of a church.

17. **aulnager:** an official charged with measuring and inspecting woolen cloth.

width. The second, held on the frame, shall determine whether the cloth is overstretched, and has wholly pure wool, is fulled cleanly and free of errors in fulling, and the third, held on the frame after dyeing, whether it has suffered by the dyeing.

5. La Rochefoucauld Describes the Putting-Out System in Rouen, France, 1781–1783

I then saw the material called cotton check (*cotonnades*). There are all sorts of cotton manufacture made up at Rouen and in the area 15 leagues[18] around it. The peasant who returns to the plough to work his fields, sits at his cotton frame and makes either *siamoises*[19] or ticking or even white, very fine, cotton cloth. One must admire the activity of the Normans. This activity does not interfere at all with their daily work. Land is very dear and consequently very well cultivated. The farmer works on the land during the day and it is in the evening by the light of the lamp that he starts his other task. His workers and his family have to help. When they have worked all week they come into the town with horses or carts piled up with material. Goods are sold in the Hall, which is all that remains of the palace of the former Dukes of Normandy, on Thursdays. It is a truly wonderful sight. It takes place at a surprising speed. Almost 800,000 francs worth of business is transacted between 6.00 and 9.00 in the morning. Among those who do the buying there are many agents who buy for merchants and then the goods pass to America, Italy and Spain. The majority goes to America. I have seen many pieces destined to become shirts for negroes; but their skin will be seen through the material, since the cloth is thin and almost sufficiently coarse to make ticking. It costs 17, 20 and even 25 francs per aune[20] in the Hall.

18. **league:** a league equals 2.764 miles.
19. **siamoises:** common cotton goods.
20. **aune:** an old French measurement unit for textiles; equal to 45 inches.

Source 6 from James Burnley, The History of Wool and Wool Combing *(London: Sampson Low, Marston, Searle and Rivington, Ltd., 1889), pp. 160–163.*

6. "The Clothier's Delight; or, the Rich Men's Joy, and the Poor Men's Sorrow, Wherein Is Exprest the Craftiness and Subtility of Many Clothiers in England by Beatting Down Their Workmen's Wages," Song, 18th century

Of all sorts of callings that in England be,
There is none that liveth so gallant as we;
Our trading maintains us as brave as a knight,
We live at our pleasure, and take our delight;
We heapeth up riches and treasure great store,
Which we get by griping and grinding the poor.
   And this is a way for to fill up our purse,
   Although we do get it with many a curse.

Throughout the whole kingdom, in country and town,
There is no danger of our trade going down,
So long as the Comber[21] can work with his comb,
And also the Weaver weave with his lomb;[22]
The Tucker[23] and Spinner[24] that spins all the year,
We will make them to earn their wages full dear.
   And this is the way, &c.

In former ages we us'd to give,
So that our work-folks like farmers did live;
But the times are altered, we will make them know
All we can for to bring them all under our bow;

21. **comber:** the person who performed one of the processes in finishing raw wool, the combing out of the wool.
22. **lomb:** archaic spelling of *loom*.
23. **tucker:** in the processing of wool, the person who performed the task of *fulling* the wool, that is, cleaning, shrinking, and thickening the fabric with moisture, heat, and pressure.
24. **spinner:** the person who spun the raw wool into thread on a spinning wheel or other device.

We will make to work hard for sixpence a day,[25]
Though a shilling they deserve if they had their just pay.
   And this is the way, &c.

And first for the Combers, we will bring them down
From eight groats a score unto half a crown.
If at all they murmur, and say 'tis too small,
We bid them choose whether they will work at all:
We'll make them believe that trading is bad;
We care not a pin, though they are ne'er so sad.
   And this is the way, &c.

We'll make the poor Weavers work at a low rate;
We'll find fault where there's no fault, and so we will bate;[26]
If trading grows dead, we will presently show it;
But if it grows good, they shall never know it;
We'll tell them that cloth beyond sea will not go,
We care not whether we keep clothing or no.
   And this is the way, &c.

Then next for the Spinners we shall ensue,
We'll make them spin three pound instead of two;
When they bring home their work unto us, they complain,
And say that their wages will not them maintain;
But if that an ounce of weight they do lack,
Then for to bate threepence we will not be slack.
   And this is the way, &c.

But if it holds weight, then their wages they crave,
We have got no money, and what's that you'd have?
We have bread and bacon and butter that's good,
With oatmeal and salt that is wholesome for food;
We have soap and candles whereby to give light,[27]
That you may work by them so long as you have light.
   And this is the way, &c.

---

25. There were 12 pence to a shilling; hence sixpence represented a 50 percent pay cut. In the next verse, the value of 8 groats was 32 pence, and half a crown was worth 30 pence. Thus the song portrays the clothiers as seeking to reduce wages a small and perhaps unnoticed amount, 2 pence.

26. **bate:** to beat back or reduce a worker's wages.

27. This whole verse refers to a practice, theoretically illegal in England after 1701, of paying putting-out workers in textiles with goods, not cash. This practice kept workers dependent on their employers because they lacked hard currency when they were paid in such commodities as bread, bacon, butter, oatmeal, salt, soap, and candles. That the practice endured despite the law is indicated by additional laws directed against it as late as 1779.

We will make the Tucker and Shereman understand
That they with their wages shall never buy land;
Though heretofore they have been lofty and high
Yet now we will make them submit humbly;
We will lighten their wages as low as may be,
We will keep them under in every degree.
    And this is the way, &c.

And thus we do gain all our wealth and estate,
By many poor men that work early and late;
If it were not for those that do labour full hard,
We might go and hang ourselves without regard;
The Combers, the Weavers, the Tuckers also,
With the Spinners that work for wages full low.
    By these people's labour we will up our purse, &c.

Then hey for the Clothing Trade, it goes on brave;
We scorn for to toyl and moyl,[28] nor yet to slave.
Our workmen do work hard, but we live at ease;
We go when we will, and come when we please;
We hoard up our bags of silver and gold;
But conscience and charity with us are cold.
    By poor people's labour, &c.

THE NEW LABOR

Source 7 from Sidney Pollard and Colin Holmes, editors, Documents in European Economic History, *vol. 1,* The Process of Industrialization, 1750–1870 *(New York: St. Martin's, 1968), pp. 534–536. Copyright © 1968 by St. Martin's Press. Reprinted with permission of St. Martin's Press, Inc., and Sidney Pollard.*

7. Rules for Workers in the Foundry and Engineering Works of the Royal Overseas Trading Company, Berlin, 1844

In every large works, and in the co-ordination of any large number of workmen, good order and harmony must be looked upon as the fundamentals of success, and therefore the following rules shall be strictly observed.

Every man employed in the concern named below shall receive a copy of these rules, so that no one can plead ignorance. Its acceptance shall be deemed to mean consent to submit to its regulations.

28. **toyl and moyl:** archaic spellings of *toil* and *moil*—that is, work and drudgery.

(1) The normal working day begins at all seasons at 6 a.m. precisely and ends, after the usual break of half an hour for breakfast, an hour for dinner and half an hour for tea, at 7 p.m., and it shall be strictly observed.

Five minutes before the beginning of the stated hours of work until their actual commencement, a bell shall ring and indicate that every worker employed in the concern has to proceed to his place of work, in order to start as soon as the bell stops.

The doorkeeper shall lock the door punctually at 6 a.m., 8.30 a.m., 1 p.m. and 4.30 p.m.

Workers arriving 2 minutes late shall lose half an hour's wages; whoever is more than 2 minutes late may not start work until after the next break, or at least shall lose his wages until then. Any disputes about the correct time shall be settled by the clock mounted above the gatekeeper's lodge.

These rules are valid both for time- and for piece-workers, and in cases of breaches of these rules, workmen shall be fined in proportion to their earnings. The deductions from the wage shall be entered in the wage-book of the gatekeeper whose duty they are: they shall be unconditionally accepted as it will not be possible to enter into any discussions about them.

(2) When the bell is rung to denote the end of the working day, every workman, both on piece- and on day-wage, shall leave his workshop and the yard, but is not allowed to make preparations for his departure before the bell rings. Every breach of this rule shall lead to a fine of five silver groschen to the sick fund. Only those who have obtained special permission by the overseer may stay on in the workshop in order to work.—If a workman has worked beyond the closing bell, he must give his name to the gatekeeper on leaving, on pain of losing his payment for the overtime.

(3) No workman, whether employed by time or piece, may leave before the end of the working day, without having first received permission from the overseer and having given his name to the gatekeeper. Omission of these two actions shall lead to a fine of ten silver groschen payable to the sick fund.

(4) Repeated irregular arrival at work shall lead to dismissal. This shall also apply to those who are found idling by an official or overseer, and refuse to obey their order to resume work.

(5) Entry to the firm's property by any but the designated gateway, and exit by any prohibited route, e.g., by climbing fences or walls, or by crossing the Spree, shall be punished by a fine of fifteen silver groschen to the sick fund for the first offences, and dismissal for the second.

(6) No worker may leave his place of work otherwise than for reasons connected with his work.

(7) All conversation with fellow-workers is prohibited; if any worker requires information about his work, he must turn to the overseer, or to the particular fellow-worker designated for the purpose.

(8) Smoking in the workshops or in the yard is prohibited during working hours; anyone caught smoking shall be fined five silver groschen for the sick fund for every such offence.

(9) Every worker is responsible for cleaning up his space in the workshop, and if in doubt, he is to turn to his overseer.—All tools must always be kept in good condition, and must be cleaned after use. This applies particularly to the turner, regarding his lathe.

(10) Natural functions must be performed at the appropriate places, and whoever is found soiling walls, fences, squares, etc., and similarly, whoever is found washing his face and hands in the workshop and not in the places assigned for the purpose, shall be fined five silver groschen for the sick fund.

(11) On completion of his piece of work, every workman must hand it over at once to his foreman or superior, in order to receive a fresh piece of work. Pattern makers must on no account hand over their patterns to the foundry without express order of their supervisors. No workman may take over work from his fellow-workman without instruction to that effect by the foreman.

(12) It goes without saying that all overseers and officials of the firm shall be obeyed without question, and shall be treated with due deference. Disobedience will be punished by dismissal.

(13) Immediate dismissal shall also be the fate of anyone found drunk in any of the workshops.

(14) Untrue allegations against superiors or officials of the concern shall lead to stern reprimand, and may lead to dismissal. The same punishment shall be meted out to those who knowingly allow errors to slip through when supervising or stocktaking.

(15) Every workman is obliged to report to his superiors any acts of dishonesty or embezzlement on the part of his fellow workmen. If he omits to do so, and it is shown after subsequent discovery of a misdemeanour that he knew about it at the time, he shall be liable to be taken to court as an accessory after the fact and the wage due to him shall be retained as punishment. Conversely, anyone denouncing a theft in such a way as to allow conviction of the thief shall receive a reward of two Thaler, and, if necessary, his name shall be kept confidential.—Further, the gatekeeper and the watchman, as well as every official, are entitled to search the baskets, parcels, aprons etc. of the women and children who are taking the dinners into the works, on their departure, as well as search any worker suspected of stealing any article whatever. . . .

(18) Advances shall be granted only to the older workers, and even to them only in exceptional circumstances. As long as he is working by the piece, the workman is entitled merely to his fixed weekly wage as subsistence pay; the extra earnings shall be paid out only on completion of the whole piece contract. If a workman leaves before his piece contract is completed, either of his own free will, or on being dismissed as punishment, or because of illness, the partly completed work shall be valued by the general manager with the help

of two overseers, and he will be paid accordingly. There is no appeal against the decision of these experts.

(19) A free copy of these rules is handed to every workman, but whoever loses it and requires a new one, or cannot produce it on leaving, shall be fined $2\frac{1}{2}$ silver groschen, payable to the sick fund.

Moabit, August, 1844.

Source 8 from Erna Olafson Hellerstein, L. P. Hume, and K. M. Offen, editors, Victorian Women: A Documentary Account of Women's Lives in Nineteenth-Century England, France, and the United States *(Stanford, Calif.:Stanford University Press, 1981), pp. 394–396. Used by permission of Stanford University Press.*

8. Apprenticeship Contract for Young Women Employed in the Silk Mills of Tarare, France, 1850s

MILLING, REELING, AND WARP-PREPARATION OF SILKS

Conditions of Apprenticeship

Art. 1. To be admitted, young women must be between the ages of thirteen and fifteen, of good character and in good health, intelligent and industrious, and must have been vaccinated. They must present their birth certificate, a certificate of vaccination, and a trousseau.

Art. 2. Girls who are accepted by the establishment will be placed in milling, reeling, or warp[29] preparation by the director, according to the needs of the establishment and their intelligence.

Art. 3. During the apprenticeship period, the pupil will be paid wages, fed, lodged, given heat and light, and laundry *for her body linen only*; she will also be furnished with aprons.

Art. 4. The pupil promises to be obedient and submissive to the mistresses charged with her conduct and instruction, as well as to conform to the rules of the establishment.

Art. 5. In case of illness the director will notify the father or guardian of the sick apprentice, and if her state necessitates a leave, it will be granted until her recovery.

Art. 6. If the sick pupil remains in the establishment, every care necessitated by her condition will be given to her.

---

29. **warp:** in the weaving process, threads placed lengthwise in the loom. They were woven with threads called the *weft* or *woof* placed perpendicularly to them.

Art. 7. In case of illness or any other serious cause that warrants her leaving, the apprentice who must absent herself from the establishment will be obligated to prolong her apprenticeship during a time equal to that of her absence.

Art. 8. The director alone has the right to authorize or refuse leaves. They will be granted only on the request of the father or guardian of the pupil.

Art. 9. Apprenticeship is for three consecutive years, *not including an obligatory trial month.* In order to encourage the pupil, she will be paid:

1st year:	a wage of 40 to 50 francs
2nd year:	" " " 60 to 75 "
3rd year:	" " " 80 to 100 "

After the apprenticeship the wage will be established according to merit.

At the end of the apprenticeship, a gratuity of 20 francs will be given to the apprentice to reward her for her exactitude in fulfilling her engagements.

Art. 10. The effective work time is twelve hours. Summer and winter, the day begins at 5 o'clock and ends at 7:15.

Breakfast is from 7:30 to 8:15; lunch is from 12:00 to 1:00; snack is from 5:00 to 5:30; supper is at 7:15.

After the second year, pupils will receive lessons in reading, writing, and arithmetic. They will be taught to sew and do a little cooking.

Art. 11. As a measure of encouragement and with no obligation, it is established that at the end of each month the young people will be graded as follows:

1st class, gift for the month 1 fr.	50 c.
2nd class	1 " —
3rd class	50 c.
4th class	—30

Each month a new classification will take place, and the young person will rise or fall according to her merit. This classification will be based on an overall evaluation of conduct, quantity and quality of work, docility and diligence, etc.

Art. 12. Wages are not due until the end of the year. They will be paid during the month following their due date. Gifts, incentive pay, and compensation for extra work will be paid each month.

Art. 13. Any apprentice who leaves the establishment before the end of her term, or who has been dismissed for bad conduct, conspiracy, rebellion, laziness, or a serious breach of the rules loses her rights to wages for the current

30. Abbreviations for French currency.
    fr.: franc.
    c.: centime, 100 centimes to 1 franc.

year; beyond this, in such a case, the father or guardian of the pupil agrees to pay the director of the establishment the sum of one hundred francs to indemnify him for the non-fulfillment of the present agreement: half of this sum will be given to the *bureau de bienfaisance*[31] in the pupil's parish.

Art. 14. If, during the first year, apprentice is recognized as unfit, despite the agreement and in the interest of both parties the director reserves the right to send her away without indemnity.

Art. 15. The apprentice who leaves the establishment at the end of the first month under the pretext that she cannot get used to the place, will pay 50 centimes per day toward the costs she has occasioned, as well as her travel expenses.

Art. 16. On her arrival, the apprentice will submit to inspection by the house doctor. Any girl who has a skin disease or who is found to be sickly will not be accepted and will be sent away immediately at her own expense.

Contract

The undersigned _____ the manufacturer, and have made the following contract:

M. _____, having read and understood the conditions of apprenticeship stipulated above in sixteen articles, declares that he accepts them for _____ aged _____, present and consenting, and pledges to execute them and have them executed in all their contents by _____. M. _____, manufacturer, pledges likewise to execute the above conditions insofar as they concern him.

The present agreement is consented to for *Three years* beginning on _____ .

Made and signed in duplicate _____

_____   _____
Father or Guardian   Director

P.S. Girls will not be admitted on Sundays or holidays.[32]

---

31. **bureau de bienfaisance:** Catholic social welfare organization.

32. That is, girls were not admitted to employment in the mill on Sundays or holidays.

Source 9 from British Parliamentary Papers: Reports from Committees, *vol. 15*, Labour of Children in Factories *(London: House of Commons, 1832), pp. 6–13.*

9. Report of the Sadler Committee, 1832[33]

William Cooper, called in; and Examined.

What is your business?—I follow the cloth-dressing at present.

2. What is your age?—I was eight-and-twenty last February.

3. When did you first begin to work in mills or factories?—When I was about 10 years of age.

4. With whom did you first work?—At Mr. Benyon's flax[34] mills, in Meadowland, Leeds.

5. What were your usual hours of working?—We began at five, and gave over at nine; at five o'clock in the morning.

6. And you gave over at nine o'clock?—At nine at night.

7. At what distance might you have lived from the mill?—About a mile and a half.

8. At what time had you to get up in the morning to attend to your labour?—I had to be up soon after four o'clock.

9. Every morning?—Every morning.

10. What intermissions had you for meals?—When we began at five in the morning, we went on until noon, and then we had 40 minutes for dinner.

11. Had you no time for breakfast?—No, we got it as we could, while we were working.

12. Had you any time for an afternoon refreshment, or what is called in Yorkshire your "drinking?"—No; when we began at noon, we went on till night; there was only one stoppage, the 40 minutes for dinner.

13. Then as you had to get your breakfast, and what is called "drinking" in that manner, you had to put it on one side?—Yes, we had to put it on one side; and when we got our frames doffed, we ate two or three mouthfuls, and then put it by again.[35]

14. Is there not considerable dust in a flax mill?—A flax mill is very dusty indeed.

---

33. **Sadler Committee:** the Committee on the Bill to Regulate the Labour of Children in the Mills and Factories of the United Kingdom.

34. **flax:** a plant whose fiber is manufactured into linen for thread or weaving into fabrics.

35. Vocabulary of the textile mill:
   frame: the water frame, an early spinning machine.
   doff: the task, in the industrial spinning process, of removing spindles filled with yarn from the spinning machine.
   bobbin: a reel, cylinder, or spoollike apparatus on which thread is wound.

15. Was not your food therefore frequently spoiled?—Yes, at times with the dust; sometimes we could not eat it, when it had got a lot of dust on.

16. What were you when you were ten years old?—What is called a bobbin-doffer; when the frames are quite full, we have to doff them.

17. Then as you lived so far from home, you took your dinner to the mill?—We took all our meals with us, living so far off.

18. During the 40 minutes which you were allowed for dinner, had you ever to employ that time in your turn in cleaning the machinery?—At times we had to stop to clean the machinery, and then we got our dinner as well as we could; they paid us for that.

19. At these times you had no resting at all?—No.

20. How much had you for cleaning the machinery?—I cannot exactly say what they gave us, as I never took any notice of it.

21. Did you ever work even later than the time you have mentioned?—I cannot say that I worked later there: I had a sister who worked up stairs, and she worked till 11 at night, in what they call the card-room.

22. At what time in the morning did she begin to work?—At the same time as myself.

23. And they kept her there till 11 at night?—Till 11 at night.

24. You say that your sister was in the card-room?—Yes.

25. Is not that a very dusty department?—Yes, very dusty indeed.

26. She had to be at the mill at five, and was kept at work till eleven at night?—Yes.

27. During the whole time she was there?—During the whole time; there was only 40 minutes allowed at dinner out of that.

28. To keep you at your work for such a length of time, and especially towards the termination of such a day's labour as that, what means were taken to keep you awake and attentive?—They strapped us at times, when we were not quite ready to be doffing the frame when it was full.

29. Were you frequently strapped?—At times we were frequently strapped.

30. What sort of strap was it?—About this length [*describing it*].

31. What was it made of?—Of leather.

32. Were you occasionally very considerably hurt with the strap?—Sometimes it hurt us very much, and sometimes they did not lay on so hard as they did at others.

33. Were the girls strapped in that sort of way?—They did not strap what they called the grown-up women.

card: a tool used to comb out textile fibers (wool, flax, etc.) in preparation for spinning them into thread.

gigger: a person who worked in the gigging process, a step in dressing wool cloth in which loose fibers are drawn off of the fabric and in which the fabric's nap is raised. The process used **teasles,** thistlelike plants that hooked the fabric and raised it.

boiler: part of the processing of wool involved boiling and scrubbing to remove oils.

primmer, brusher: workers involved in the final preparation of woolen cloth.

34. Were any of the female children strapped?—Yes; they were strapped in the same way as the lesser boys. . . .

44. Were your punishments the same in that mill as in the other?—Yes, they used the strap the same there.

45. How long did you work in that mill?—Five years.

46. And how did it agree with your health?—I was sometimes well, and sometimes not very well.

47. Did it affect your breathing at all?—Yes; sometimes we were stuffed.

48. When your hours were so long, you had not any time to attend to a day-school?—We had no time to go to a day-school, only to a Sunday-school,[36] and then with working such long hours we wanted to have a bit of rest, so that I slept till the afternoon, sometimes till dinner, and sometimes after.

49. Did you attend a place of worship?—I should have gone to a place of worship many times, but I was in the habit of falling asleep, and that kept me away; I did not like to go for fear of being asleep.

50. Do you mean that you could not prevent yourself from falling asleep, in consequence of the fatigue of the preceding week?—Yes. . . .

85. After working at a mill to this excess, how did you find your health at last?—I found it very bad indeed; I found illness coming on me a long time before I fell down.

86. Did you at length become so ill as to be unable to pursue your work?—I was obliged to give it up entirely.

87. How long were you ill?—For six months.

88. Who attended?—Mr. Metcalf and Mr. Freeman.

89. What were you told by your medical attendants was the reason of your illness?—Nothing but hard labour, and working long hours; and they gave me up, and said no good could be done for me, that I must go into the country.

90. Did this excessive labour not only weaken you, but destroy your appetite?—It destroyed the appetite, and I became so feeble, that I could not cross the floor unless I had a stick to go with; I was in great pain, and could find ease in no posture.

91. You could drink in the meantime, if you could not eat?—Yes, I could drink.

92. But you found that did not improve your health?—No.

93. Has it been remarked that your excessive labour from early life has greatly diminished your growth?—A number of persons have said that such was the case, and that I was the same as if I had been made of iron or stone.

94. What height are you?—About five feet. It is that that has hindered me of my growth.

95. When you were somewhat recovered, did you apply for labour?—I applied for my work again, but the overlooker said I was not fit to work; he was

---

36. **Sunday-school:** churches often ran schools for mill children on their day off (Sunday) to teach the rudiments of reading and writing along with religious instruction.

sure of that, and he would not let me have it. I was then obliged to throw my-self on the parish.[37]

96. Have you subsisted on the parish ever since?—Yes.

97. Have you been always willing and anxious to work?—I was always willing and anxious to work from my infancy.

98. Have you been on the parish since your severe illness?—Yes.

99. How long is that ago?—Six months. When I was ill I got something from the Society; they relieved me then, but when I became better I received no benefit from it.

100. Yours is not what is called a Friendly Society?—No, it is what we call Odd Fellows.[38]

101. And they do not extend relief after a certain period?—Not after you get better. . . .

124. You say that you had no time to go to school during the week, but that you went on Sunday?—I went on Sunday; I had no time to go to a day-school.

125. Can you read or write?—I can read, but I cannot write. . . .

142. If you had refused to work over-hours, would they have turned you off altogether?—Yes, they would have turned us off. If one will not do it, another will.

143. At this particular period, when you were thus over-worked, were there not a great number of able-bodied individuals in Leeds totally out of employment?—A great number. A few individuals have it all, and the rest, of course, are obliged to apply to the parish.

144. If you had refused to work the over-work, there were plenty of others willing to undertake it?—That is very true.

145. And they were people able to perform the sort of work you were engaged in?—They were.

146. You of course know your trade?—Yes.

147. Were those people out of work persons who could have undertaken your situation?—They were out of work.

148. At the time that you were working these over-hours were there a great many out of work in Leeds?—Yes.

149. And were they capable of doing your work?—Yes, capable of doing the same work.

150. Do you work anywhere now?—I have not worked anywhere for rather more than a year. I have been constantly out to seek for employment since I have been better.

37. **on the parish:** under existing English laws, poor relief was the responsibility of the local parish.

38. **Friendly Society, Odd Fellows Society:** organizations founded to benefit workers through "self-help." They took up small weekly sums from their members and used the funds thus collected to aid sick or injured members who were unable to work, or to assist the widows and orphans of members.

151. How are you supported?—By the town.

152. Do you mean by the parish? Yes.

153. Of what place?—Leeds. . . .

184. How did you contrive to be awake so early in the morning?—My father used to call me up.

185. Did he get up so early as that for his own business?—He got up on purpose to call me.

186. How many hours did he work in a day at his own business?—Sometimes from five in the morning till eight at night.

187. You say he was a shoemaker?—Yes.

188. Then, according to this, he worked more hours than you did?—I think not so long.

189. Did your father take his regular intervals for his meals?—I should think so.

190. And walked about to market for his family; had he not many pauses in his labour?—He worked at home, and therefore could do as he pleased. . . .

198. Has your health improved since you left off working long hours?—I am a deal better than I was; but I believe that if I could have got work, and have had something to support me, I should have recruited my health better. I have been very poorly kept for these last six months, having been out of work. I have only half a crown a week allowed from the parish for my wife and myself.

199. When you were working the long hours, were there any people in the same employment, when you were a gigger, for instance, who were working the short hours?—Yes; some mills were working short hours in the same line; there were none in the same room that worked less hours than I did.

200. That did not depend on your choice, did it?—They would not let us have it of our own choice; we might either do it or leave it.

201. Suppose it was left to you, would you prefer a moderate degree of labour with lower wages, to high wages with this excessive labour?—I would rather have short hours and moderate wages, than great wages and long hours. I should be a great deal better.

202. Of course you do not mean to say that these long hours have continued in mills and factories when trade has slackened; has not the excessive labour somewhat abated when there is not such a brisk trade?—It has abated when there was not a brisk trade; when there was, it was again increased for those that were working, who were not willing to lose their employment, and so they submitted, or they must have gone travelling about the streets, and applied to the parish. But if the hours of work had not been then so much increased, more hands would have got employment. There would have been not so many over-worked, and not so many without any thing to do; it would have been share and share alike. . . .

206. When you were working these very long hours in a mill as a gigger and boiler, had you the liberty, if you wished to be away for a day or part of a

day, to send another person to do your work?—Yes; if we were poorly, we had liberty to send another person in our place.

207. If you wished to rest for half a day, you could send another man in your place?—I was once poorly, and I sent another workman, and they let me have the job again; now that I have been ill six months, they will not let me have the job again. . . .

217. Do you think you would be able to stand your work?—I should like to try; I cannot bear to go wandering about the streets. . . .

220. Is being a gigger harder than the others?—Yes, gigging is very hard work; the fleeces are so heavy and full of water, and you have to stand in this position [*describing it*] to support them and turn the fleece over; if you are not over strong it makes you rather deformed in your legs.

221. At what age do people generally begin gigging?—Some begin about 15, 16 or 17, and some lads begin when about 14.

222. At what age did your father die?—He was 60 when he died.

223. Have you seen the man lately who is doing your work at Mr. Brown's?—Yes.

224. Is he in good health?—I do not know; I must not say a thing that I do not know; it is a good while since I saw him.

225. Was your father a tall or a short man?—He stood about five feet seven.

226. And you are five feet?—Yes.

227. Have you any brothers or sisters?—Two brothers and a sister.

228. Do they work in the same trade?—I have a brother working now at the same trade; he was seventeen the 14th of last February.

229. Has he good health?—He had not over good health when I came from Leeds.

Source 10 from Sidney Pollard and Colin Holmes, editors, Documents in European Economic History, *vol. 2,* Industrial Power and National Rivalry *(New York: St. Martin's, 1972), pp. 322–323. Copyright © 1972 by St. Martin's Press. Reprinted with permission of St. Martin's Press, Inc., and Sidney Pollard.*

10. Working Conditions of a Female Textile Worker in Germany, 1880s and 1890s

In the weaving sheds the girls work in an atmosphere which, on the third day of my work there, gave me bad lung catarrh; tiny flakes of the twisted wool fill the air, settle on dress and hair, and float into nose and mouth; the machines have to be swept clean every two hours; the dust is breathed in by the girls, since they are not allowed to open the windows. To this has to be added the terrible nerve-racking noise of the rattling machines so that no one can hear himself speak. No communication with one's neighbour is possible except by shouting on the top of one's voice. In consequence, all the girls have screeching, irritating voices: even when the shop has gone quiet, at the end of the working day, on the street, at home, they never converse quietly like other people, their conversation is a constant yelling, which produces the impression among outsiders that they are quarrelling.

It is truly a miracle that so many girls still look fresh and blooming, and that they still feel like singing at work, usually sentimental folk songs. . . .

Many girls work happily, particularly those weaving small carpets or curtains woven as one piece who can observe the building up of the pattern. They love their machines like loving a faithful dog; they polish them, and tie coloured ribbons, little pictures of saints and all sorts of gaudy tinsel given to them by their sweethearts at the summer fairs, to the crossbars.

The girls work hard, very hard, and quite a few told me how they collapsed with the exertion of the first four weeks of work, and how most of them suffer for months with irritations of the lung and throat until they get used to the dust. To this has to be added the poor, miserable food, the short periods of rest in rooms which don't deserve the name of "dwelling"—and yet the girls remain cheerful, healthy, lively and enterprising.

I have always watched this with admiration; I could not have stood this for long. I could not take anything in the morning beside coffee; only in the evening I hurried, totally exhausted, to my hotel, to swallow some nourishing food with great difficulty. . . .

No one would dream of stopping work and taking a rest even when suffering from violent headache or toothache, not even a quarter of an hour of being late was tolerated without a substantial fine at the end of the week. . . .

The work of the carpet weavers should not be underrated, it is anything but monotonous or repetitive. When working the complex Turkish patterns, the weaver has to catch the exact moment for changing the different coloured reels. She has to think and coordinate, calculate and pay attention and concentrate all her thoughts. This work requires far more mental activity and sense of responsibility than the crochet work and needlework done by hundreds of girls of society, year after year, in expectation of the shining knight who would one day come and rescue them.

Most factories start work at half past six, pause for breakfast from 8 to 8.30, dinner 12–1; at 4 there are 20–30 minutes for tea, and work goes on until 7. On Saturdays work ends at 5.30, in order to give time to the workers to clean the machines thoroughly and to oil them by 6; Mondays, work starts half an hour later probably because all the girls have a hangover from Sunday.

Source 11 from British Parliamentary Papers: Reports from Commissioners: Children's Employment (Mines), *vol. 17,* Appendix to the First Report of the Commissioners (Mines) *(London: William Clowes for Her Majesty's Stationery Office, 1842), pp. 39, 103, 107–108.*

11. Report on the Employment of Children in British Mines, 1841–1842

May 14, 1841.

No. 49. Mr. *Joseph Staley,* Managing Partner in Coal-works at Yate Common, in the parish of Yate (Two Pits), carried on under the firm of *Staley* and *Parkers:*

Employ from 30 to 35 hands; not more than five or six boys under 13; the two youngest are from eight to nine years old, who work with their father; perhaps three boys not more than 10 years of age; they assist in cutting and carting out the coal from a one-foot seam; no doorboys employed, because there is sufficient ventilation without being particular about closing them; the carters generally manage the doors as they pass; the boys earn from 6s. to 9s. per week when they get handy at cutting; have not more than three or four under 18; all over 15 are earning nearly men's wages—say 15s. per week; the men earn from 18s. to 20s.; considers two tons a fair day's work; wages paid in money every Saturday; the older boys receive their own; the boys, in carting out the coals from the *googs* [narrow inclined planes up which the coal is pulled by a chain and windlass], when short distances, draw by the *girdle* or *lugger, i.e.* a rope round the waist, with an iron hook depending in front, to which a chain, passing between the legs, is attached; if for longer distances, they use wheeled-carriages on a railway; no horses are employed under ground at present; the smaller boys do not tug more than 1 cwt.[39] at a time; the carts generally hold about 2 cwt. each; the thickest vein is two feet six inches, and is worked by the young men; the boys cart through a two feet six inches passageway; the young men have four feet, there being a bed of soft stuff above the coal, to cut away before they come to the roof; the shaft is 45 fathoms,[40] worked by a steam-engine, and strong-plaited rope; thinks rope decidedly safer than chain, as it gives more timely notice of any defect, by a strand or two giving way, whereas a link of iron is sometimes near breaking, a good while before it is discovered, and then separates on a sudden. Has had many years' experience in Staffordshire and Derbyshire, having been brought up a collier; say for 40 years; has been engaged 23 years in this coal-field; the work-

39. **cwt.:** hundredweight, i.e., 100 pounds.
40. **fathom:** a fathom equals 6 feet; the shaft of 45 fathoms thus extended 270 feet below the earth's surface.

ings are quiet dry; a pumping-engine of 60-horse power, is constantly at work when there is water; three or four days a-week is sufficient in summer; hours of work average eight to nine hours a-day; no night-work at present; always employ two sets when it occurs.

Some of the boys and young persons attend the Church Sunday-school, and others the Dissenting Sunday-school; most of them can read a little; look clean and tidy on Sundays; thinks there are no healthier boys in the country.

MESSRS. WILLSON, HOLMES, AND STOCKS, QUARRY-HOUSE PIT.

No.6. *William Jagger*, aged 11.   May 6:

I am a hurrier[41] for my father, Benjamin Jagger; have been in here four years and upwards; I come to work at seven o'clock, and go home at four, five, and six; I get breakfast afore I come down; I get my dinner down here, I get it about one o'clock; I don't know how long I am taking it; I get it as I can; I go to work directly after; I get currant-cake and buttered cake sometimes, never any meat; I get a bit of meat for supper when I go up. I went to day-school often; I comed to work about half a year; I go to Sunday-school now at church; I cannot read or write. I have got to hurry a corve 400 yards; I don't know what weight it is [$2\frac{1}{2}$ cwt.]; it runs upon rails; I push the corves; some of the boys push when there is no rail. I do not oft hurt my feet; I never met with an accident. The men serve me out sometimes—they wallop me; I don't know what for, except 'tis when I don't hurry fast enough; I like my work very well; I would rather hurry than set cards.

The mainway of this pit is 3 feet 6 inches high and 400 yards in length; seams 17 inches thick; gear in good order; shaft not walled up. At the moment of stepping out of the corve at the pit's bottom, a stone weighing from five to seven pounds fell in the water close by my feet from the unlined shaft near the top, or from the bank, a circumstance at once illustrative of the importance of protecting persons in their descent, by walling up the sides of the shaft, and thereby preventing loose measures from falling.

41. Mining vocabulary:
   hurrier: a person who drew a wagon loaded with coal through mine tunnels to the shaft up which the load would be raised to the earth's surface.
   corve: small wagon for carrying coal or ore in a mine.
   getter: a person who cut the coal from the seam. Young male hurriers, who often suffered stunted growth because of their excessive labor in moving coal as children, often graduated to the occupation of getter. Short stature was an asset in the restricted spaces of mine tunnels. The mining commission report from which this testimony is drawn notes that getters described themselves as "mashed up."

MR. JOSEPH STOCKS, BOOTH TOWN PIT, HALIFAX.

No. 26. *Patience Kershaw,* aged 17.   May 15:

My father has been dead about a year; my mother is living and has ten children, five lads and five lasses; the oldest is about thirty, the youngest is four; three lasses go to mill; all the lads are colliers, two getters and three hurriers; one lives at home and does nothing; mother does nought but look after home.

All my sisters have been hurriers, but three went to the mill, Alice went because her legs swelled from hurrying in cold water when she was hot. I never went to day-school; I go to Sunday-school, but I cannot read or write; I go to pit at five o'clock in the morning and come out at five in the evening; I get my breakfast of porridge and milk first; I take my dinner with me, a cake, and eat it as I go; I do not stop or rest any time for the purpose; I get nothing else until I get home, and then have potatoes and meat, not every day meat. I hurry in the clothes I have now got on, trousers and ragged jacket; the bald place upon my head is made by thrusting the corves; my legs have never swelled, but sisters' did when they went to mill; I hurry the corves a mile and more under ground and back; they weigh 3 cwt.; I hurry 11 a-day; I wear a belt and chain at the workings to get the corves out; the getters that I work for are *naked* except their caps; they pull off all their clothes; I see them at work when I go up; sometimes they beat me, if I am not quick enough, with their hands; they strike me upon my back; the boys take liberties with me sometimes, they pull me about; I am the only girl in the pit; there are about 20 boys and 15 men; all the men are naked; I would rather work in mill than in coal-pit.

This girl is an ignorant, filthy, ragged, and deplorable-looking object, and such a one as the uncivilized natives of the prairies would be shocked to look upon.[42]

QUESTIONS TO CONSIDER

Let us bring together your findings on the old and new labor of European working men and women. Your goal is to understand the changes affecting them in the late eighteenth and nineteenth centuries and how these changes came about. You may want to review the questions in Sources and Method before continuing your study of the evidence.

First, consider the length of time workers devoted to labor. Was the preindustrial workday much different in length from the early-industrial-age workday? Note especially the

42. This comment by the mine commissioners is amplified elsewhere in their report, where they note that Kershaw worked in a mine whose tunnels contained 3 or 4 inches of water at all times and that she moved her corve 1,800 to 2,000 yards on each trip.

findings of the Sadler Committee on the workdays of William Cooper, employed in industrial labor, and his father, a craftsman of the old school. Next, consider the number of workdays per year. Both old and new labor generally required a six-day workweek. But reexamine the holidays at Lille, remembering to punctuate the work year with a liberal number of "holy Mondays." On how many days per year did Vauban estimate his workers were employed in agriculture? Compare this quantity of work with that demanded of William Cooper. Like many nineteenth-century miners, this textile worker could probably have looked forward to holidays only on Christmas, Easter Monday, and the Monday after Pentecost. What other time off from work could he have expected? What effect did the Industrial Revolution have on the annual quantity of work for many laborers?

Those employed in both old and new styles of labor certainly worked hard. But the quality, pace, and discipline of their respective work situations certainly vary. Let us first consider the quality or nature of the old labor. What sort of variety characterized the work of agricultural workers like those described by Vauban and Mrs. Britton? Where was much of their work carried on? Where did most industrial-age labor take place? Why do you think Mrs. Britton testified that she preferred physically taxing agricultural work to factory labor? Why do you think William Cooper would have preferred the craftsman's work of his father to industrial labor? How do you think the necessity of

working with machinery would have shaped Cooper's opinion? What basic qualitative differences distinguished the old from the new labor?

Consider the pace of work. Who set the pace for guild members? Who set the pace in the putting-out system, the factory, and the mine? Notice the discipline of the industrial-era workplace, too. What sort of punishments and incentives prodded employees to work quickly? Considering the conditions of preindustrial labor, why do you think the specific regulations in Source 8 were necessary? Recall the statement by Andrew Ure that opened this chapter. What were management's goals in imposing this kind of discipline?

Other changes in labor also accompanied the Industrial Revolution. What do the testimonies from the coal miners and the records of French and German textile workers tell us about the labor of women in the industrial age? Reexamine Mrs. Britton's testimony. In what setting did she labor after her marriage? What effect might female and child industrial labor have had on the family? What educational opportunities existed for boys and girls in industrial labor?

Finally, let us consider the health and safety of workers under both the old and the new systems. Which style of labor do you think Mrs. Britton and William Cooper would have considered more healthful? What hazards awaited textile workers like Cooper and miners like William Jagger and Patience Kershaw?

In other ways, old and new labor were not quite so different. Ideally, any job should provide some security of continuing employment. How did the Prussian guild regulations seek to protect the markets and incomes of the textile workers? Did any other workers, old or new, benefit from such efforts to protect job security? Consider the problems of Mr. Britton and Vauban's workers, the effect of cycles of economic prosperity and depression on William Cooper and his fellow textile workers, and the experiences of putting-out workers described in the song. Did any of them have hopes of continuing employment opportunity?

Consider, too, the problems all these workers confronted when illness, injury, or economic conditions denied them employment. What recourse did Mrs. Britton and her family have in the face of poverty? Did William Cooper have any additional resources to draw on when illness struck? Were they sufficient for his needs?

Your comparative analysis of this chapter's sources provides one more insight into the industrialization of Western Europe. Economic historians speak of *proto-industrialization,* a process that paved the way for industrialization by organizing production into larger units employing traditional technologies. Industrial capitalists later combined experience in such organization with new machines to produce the Industrial Revolution. To understand this process, consider what the factory system meant: large units of production, controlled by capitalists who were prepared to organize labor and resources for a profit, and competition among producers who sought worldwide markets. What evidence of modern industrial organization do you find in the putting-out system? In what ways did it occupy a transitional role? Were its methods of production old or new? Was its organization of production old or new? How were its labor-management relations similar to those of the industrial age? Compare the discipline Andrew Ure advocated for industrial managers with the alleged goal of the clothiers in the popular song. What significance do you attach to the putting-out workers' complaint that they could no longer buy land? Would you say that they were slipping into a work status similar to that of later industrial workers?

Now you are ready to provide detailed answers to the main questions of this chapter: What was the nature of the new labor? How did it evolve? How did it differ from the old labor? Be sure to base your responses on the evidence you have assessed.

EPILOGUE

A combination of developments served to improve conditions for later generations of workers. Early industrial workers won such improvements in their lot only slowly and with considerable struggle, however. The right to take part in government by voting was one common demand of nineteenth-century workers in a Europe that accorded a political voice only to the wealthy and privileged, if it accorded one to anyone at all.

Workers in England began to win the vote only in 1867 after considerable agitation; a revolution in France in 1848 established the right of universal suffrage for men. Elsewhere the vote came more slowly, and Russian workers lacked voting rights until 1906.

In the more democratic Western European nations, a widened right to vote in the nineteenth century made political institutions more responsive to workers' needs. During that century, several European parliaments passed legislation that sought to regulate working conditions for women and children, to establish minimum safety standards, and to begin to provide the accident, health, and old age insurance plans that protect modern workers. Real improvements, however, often lagged behind such legislation. Early wage, hour, and safety regulations ran counter to an important political philosophy of the nineteenth century, liberalism (see Chapter 7), which viewed such legislation as interference in freedom of management. Thus, when early regulations were passed, there frequently were not enough officials to enforce them by comprehensive factory inspections. If you refer to William Cooper's testimony, you will find him completely unaware of a parliamentary act to regulate work hours, eloquent proof of this early lack of enforcement. Governments were slow to create the machinery necessary to enforce these rules.

The nineteenth century also witnessed an often bitter struggle by workers to form their own organizations promoting their common welfare. Because unions and strikes, as we have seen, were illegal in many countries, the first worker organizations of the early nineteenth century often were self-help groups such as the one that aided William Cooper. Only after much struggle did governments in countries like England and France legalize labor unions and the right to strike.

The legalization of unions, however, allowed industrial workers to take collective action in strikes to win better wages and conditions. Early strikes often produced bloody conflict between labor on one side and management, sometimes backed by police or the army in the name of keeping order, on the other. The first major victory for a noncraft union, however, occurred in the London dockworkers' strike of 1889. Twentieth-century developments have improved the lot of workers in other ways, especially through increased leisure time, realized in the forty-hour workweek and paid vacations.

Improvements in wages and working conditions, however, did not change the basic nature of modern factory labor. In the industrial workplace, the pace of work continued to be set by machines, granting little independence to the individual worker, who remained a human cog in the greater modern industrial machine. Though most workers adjusted to this kind of labor, manifestations of their discontent have not disappeared entirely. In 1968, as you will see in Chapter 14, millions of French workers went on strike and occupied their factories. One of their chief demands was for a concept they called *autoges-*

tion, that is, some voice in the workplace decisions that governed their lives on the job.

Such demands by employees have not gone entirely unheeded by management. There have been efforts to reintroduce some worker input into the production process through such practices as quality circles, in which workers engaged in the same phases of production meet periodically to discuss their jobs and to make sugges-tions for improving the production process. Other experiments in such industries as automobile assembly have sought to involve individual workers in several phases of the production process as a way of mitigating the monotony of assembly-line work. Nevertheless, for the majority of Western workers today, the basic nature of industrial employment, as symbolized by the production line, remains unchanged.

CHAPTER SIXTEEN

TWO PROGRAMS FOR

SOCIAL AND POLITICAL

CHANGE: LIBERALISM

AND SOCIALISM

"Workingmen of all countries unite!" proclaimed Karl Marx and Friedrich Engels in *The Communist Manifesto* of 1848, urging working people to overthrow the capitalist system and end the working conditions of the early Industrial Revolution, which we explored in Chapter 6. Marx and Engels were partisans in a nineteenth-century ideological clash in which they and other proponents of socialism opposed liberalism, the dominant doctrine among the rising class of factory owners and managers. Nineteenth-century liberals and socialists differed greatly in their views on such issues as the definition of freedom and democracy, the role of government, and their visions of the future.

We must be careful in this chapter to understand liberalism in its nineteenth- and not its twentieth-century sense. For most twentieth-century Americans, *liberalism* describes an ideology that calls for an activist role for government in assuring the basic needs of its citizens in a variety of areas, including civil rights, material wants, and health and safety protection. In the nineteenth century, liberals sought to maximize the freedom of the individual from government control. Drawing on traditions restricting royal authority that dated back to medieval times, liberals saw in the French Revolution the essential victory they sought to win all over Europe. In destroying the Old Regime, with its absolute monarchy and privilege for the aristocratic few, the Revolution had created a new political order based on individual freedom. Everywhere, liberals sought to draft constitutions that would limit royal authority and ensure basic individual rights. The citizen was to be safe from arbitrary arrest and was to enjoy freedom of speech, assembly, religion, and the press.

*Two Programs
for Social
and Political
Change:
Liberalism
and Socialism*

For the early or classical liberals, however, individual freedom did not mean political democracy, a voice for all in government. The constitutional arrangements created by liberals usually included some sort of property qualification for voting. Most liberals were members of the middle classes and believed that, to exercise the right to vote, a citizen had to have some stake in the existing social and economic order in the form of property. The majority lacked sufficient wealth to vote in all early-nineteenth-century countries under liberal rule. But one liberal French minister, François Guizot, noted that the poor possessed full freedom to increase their wealth so that they could acquire property and participate in political life! Extreme as this view may seem to us, it does express the liberal faith that peaceful political change was possible. The key to the success of such a system of government was the establishment of a society of laws protecting individual freedoms.

Liberal economic thought was also a doctrine of absolute freedom. Liberals opposed the guild and aristocratic privileges that had limited career opportunities in Old Regime Europe. Thus, individual economic opportunity, embodied in the opening of all careers to citizens on the basis of their talents, not their titles, became the central liberal economic tenet. But liberals' faith in economic freedom had far greater implications.

Liberals believed that immutable natural laws, like supply and demand, regulated economic life. Government interference in economic life, they believed, violated not only these laws

but individual freedom as well. Based in large part on the writings of such classical liberal economists as the Englishmen Adam Smith (1723–1790), Thomas Malthus (1766–1834), and David Ricardo (1772–1823), liberal economic thought defended the right of early industrial employers to be free of government regulation. Their doctrine was summed up in the French phrase *laissez-faire* (literally, "leave it alone").

Socialists differed from liberals in that they saw the French Revolution of 1789 as simply the first step in revamping Europe's old order. The Revolution had established individual freedom but not political democracy. More important for socialists, the Revolution had not brought social democracy. To achieve this goal, they advocated a more equitable distribution of society's wealth. Their message, as you might imagine, had considerable appeal to those workers employed in the mills, factories, and mines of the early Industrial Revolution whose lot we explored in Chapter 6.

Some early socialist thinkers expressed the view that economic equality could be realized by peaceful evolutionary change. Karl Marx applied the label "utopian" to those thinkers because of the impracticality, in his view, of their schemes. Charles Fourier (1771–1837) advocated a restructuring of society around essentially agricultural communities that represented an attempt to turn the clock back to a preindustrial economy. Louis Blanc (1811–1882) advocated state assistance in the creation of worker-owned units of production, which was difficult to imagine in a Europe dominated by the liberal ideology of government noninterference in economic life. But some utopian socialists, notably Robert Owen (1771–1858), who created a model industrial town around his textile mills in New Lanark, Scotland, achieved real improvements for working people.

Utopian socialism did not transform society. Some of its ideas, however, did influence other socialist thinkers, including Karl Marx, who advocated a revolutionary transformation of society. Indeed, revolutionary socialism gained large numbers of working-class followers and by the middle and late nineteenth century threatened Western Europe's liberal political leaders with the possibility of a complete overhaul of society in the name of political and social democracy.

Nineteenth-century liberalism and socialism both produced important thinkers who analyzed the ills of their society and advanced not only plans for change but critiques of the opposing ideology. What visions of the future did liberals and socialists propose? How did they hope to realize their ideals? How did their ideologies differ? Your task in this chapter is to answer these questions by examining the ideas of two nineteenth-century political and social theorists.

SOURCES AND METHOD

Liberalism and socialism each had large numbers of eloquent proponents in the nineteenth century. This chapter presents you with samples of liberal and socialist thought in the nineteenth century drawn from the writings of but one advocate of each cause. Your sources in this chapter are the works of the liberal Alexis de Tocqueville and the revolutionary socialist Karl Marx. These two thinkers have been selected because they expressed strikingly different views on similar subjects: the historical development of the West, the nature of democracy, and the role of revolution. Tocqueville and Marx also analyzed the French Revolution of 1848, a topic you may wish to review in your textbook. Their contrasting views on the same issues will provide the basis for your answers to the general questions on liberalism and socialism.

In analyzing the works of Tocqueville and Marx, you must understand that these works were polemic in character—that is, they were all written to advocate the causes espoused by their authors. All such works may be expected to emphasize their authors' viewpoints and summarily dismiss opposing points of view that may have considerable validity. Because each theorist was an eloquent advocate of his cause, some examination of their separate backgrounds and viewpoints is necessary to permit you to analyze their ideas fruitfully.

Alexis Charles Henri Clérel de Tocqueville was born in 1805, the son of an aristocratic father who hoped for the restoration of the French monarchy destroyed by the Revolution of 1789. When Napoleon's fall from power finally brought a restored monarchy, the Tocquevilles rose to positions of importance in govern-

Two Programs
for Social
and Political
Change:
Liberalism
and Socialism

ment. Alexis de Tocqueville's talents gained early recognition with his appointment as a judge at the youthful age of twenty-one. It was not as a jurist that Tocqueville gained fame, however, but rather as a liberal political theorist and as an early student of what we would call today sociology and political science.

In 1831 Tocqueville and his longtime friend Gustave de Beaumont undertook a fact-finding tour in the United States to study that country's pioneering penitentiary system. For nine months Tocqueville and Beaumont traveled through the United States, observing prisons and much more. The fruit of their trip was a study of prisons written largely by Beaumont and Tocqueville's observations on American society and government, published as *Democracy in America* (1835–1840). Tocqueville's keen analysis of American society in the latter work gained him immediate international recognition, and he received an honor unusual for a person of his age: election to the French Academy in 1841.[1]

In 1839 Tocqueville had already won election to the French Chamber of Deputies, which permitted him an active role in French politics. He joined the opposition to the government of King Louis Philippe and rejected es-

pecially the monarchy's restriction of the right to vote to wealthy Frenchmen. As a deputy, Tocqueville wrote a report on slavery that contributed to its abolition in France's colonies. Further, in a speech to the Chamber of Deputies in January 1848 during a period of apparent political calm, his analysis of social conditions led him to predict the imminence of revolution. Indeed, revolution broke out less than four weeks later.

Despite his opposition to Louis Philippe, Tocqueville long had criticized revolution, perceiving a danger that individual liberty could be lost in revolutionary enthusiasm. Nevertheless, he was elected to the legislature of the new Second Republic created by the Revolution of 1848 and took part in the drafting of its constitution, arguing unsuccessfully against a directly elected president. He correctly foresaw the possibility that an ambitious demagogue could sway the people to gain election and threaten democracy. In December 1848, the victor in the presidential elections was Louis-Napoleon Bonaparte. This nephew of Emperor Napoleon I destroyed the republic in favor of an authoritarian empire, naming himself Emperor Napoleon III.[2] Tocqueville retired permanently from public life after Bonaparte's seizure of power,

1. **French Academy:** an association of scholars, writers, and intellectual leaders founded in 1635 to maintain the purity of the French language and establish standards of correct usage. The Academy has only forty members, called the "immortals," who vote to fill vacancies in their ranks caused by deaths of members. The dignity of such election is usually confined to persons of advanced years and long-proven merit.

2. **Emperor Napoleon III:** Bonapartists recognize the son of Emperor Napoleon I (ruled 1804–1814, 1815) as Napoleon II. But Napoleon II never actually ruled France. Aged three years when his father abdicated, he was taken to Vienna by his maternal grandfather, the Emperor of Austria, and spent his brief life there until his death in 1832.

unable to support the new, undemocratic regime.

Returning to writing, Tocqueville produced two more important works before his death from tuberculosis in 1859. The first was his *Recollections* of the Revolution of 1848 and the Second Republic, based on his experiences in Paris in 1848 and 1849; the second was a study of the French Revolution of 1789, *The Old Regime and the Revolution*. Both works demonstrate again Tocqueville's liberal ideology and political astuteness.

In reading the selections by Tocqueville, you should ascertain the nature of his liberal thought. In Source 1, what does Tocqueville identify as the main trend in historical development? What implications did this trend, which he found strong in America, have for Europe's existing class structure? What problems does Tocqueville, in Source 2, find accompanying American democracy? What threatened the individual? What danger did centralized authority pose? In Source 3, Tocqueville treats revolution. Why does he see the danger of revolution diminishing with the advance of political democracy? Does he find revolution justified at times?

Sources 3 and 4 provide you with summations of Tocqueville's political thought and his view of the future. Under what sort of government had he spent his youth? What did it contribute to his political thought?

Born in Germany in 1818, thirteen years after Tocqueville, Karl Marx was the advocate of a very different political order, one of socialist revolution. The son of a successful attorney, Marx enjoyed an excellent edu-

cation. He studied law first and then philosophy, a field in which he completed the doctoral degree that normally would have led to an academic career. Young Marx, however, was an advocate of political and economic democracy whose growing radicalism and atheism precluded such a career. When he turned instead to journalism, his ideas quickly offended the Prussian censors, who suppressed his newspaper.

Marx left Germany in 1843 for Paris, a city in which there was considerable discussion of utopian socialist ideas. Perhaps the greatest single event in Marx's two-year stay in Paris was his meeting with a young businessman, Friedrich Engels, with whom he was to enjoy a lifelong friendship. Engels shared Marx's socialist ideas, gave him intellectual support, and provided financial aid that allowed Marx to devote his life to writing.

French authorities expelled Marx for his radical political ideas in 1845. He moved to Brussels, Belgium, where he and Engels wrote *The Communist Manifesto*, an abstract declaration of war between the working class and its capitalist exploiters. Belgian authorities ultimately also expelled Marx. Back in Paris by March 1848, Marx, like Tocqueville, based his writings on some firsthand experience of the French Revolution of 1848. He also returned to Germany during 1848 before settling in England in 1849, where he spent the rest of his life.

Marx's poor command of spoken English and his illegible handwriting precluded his employment in

*Two Programs
for Social
and Political
Change:
Liberalism
and Socialism*

white-collar jobs, and he and his family often lived in poverty when there were delays in Engels's generosity. In England, Marx drew on his own excellent education, his knowledge of French socialist thought from his Paris days, and his daily research in the British Museum Library to refine his views on socialist revolution. He wrote studies of contemporary events, including *Class Struggles in France* and *The Eighteenth Brumaire of Louis Bonaparte,* which dealt with the French Revolution of 1848 and its aftermath. The final product of his labors was the first volume of *Capital* (1867), a work Engels completed after Marx's death in 1883.

Marx was not to witness the implementation of his ideals during his life. His chief attempt at revolutionary organization, the International Workingmen's Association or First International, founded in 1864, broke up as a result of ideological disputes in 1876. In those disputes, the always irascible Marx found his viewpoints challenged by another revolutionary activist, Mikhail Bakunin (1814–1876). Marx, who prided himself on what he believed was the scientific certainty of his ideas, found Bakunin insufficiently "scientific" and ruptured socialist unity in securing the latter's expulsion from the association. Bakunin went on to become one of the founders of modern anarchism, a movement advocating the destruction of all institutions of modern society. Marx spent the few years remaining before his death in 1883 drained

and embittered by his struggle in the International and by family problems. He died believing that his ideas would have little impact. Nevertheless, his writings became the basis for the international socialist movement.

As you read the selections by Marx, you should answer a number of questions to aid you in formulating your responses to the central problems of this chapter. Marx, like Tocqueville, had a definite view of history. Examine Source 5, a selection from *The Communist Manifesto*. What basic event, according to Marx, has characterized and shaped all historical development? Why does Marx find the latest phase of history, modern middle-class ("bourgeois") capitalism, particularly oppressive? What is Marx's view of the free economy advocated by nineteenth-century liberals?

In Source 6, Marx deals with the French Revolution of 1848. That revolution, of course, failed to bring the working classes to power. Whom did it bring to power in France? In Source 7 we have Marx's statement of his ideals in government. Marx proclaims that he advocates democracy. How does that democracy differ from the kind of democracy acceptable to liberals like Tocqueville?

Now you are ready to read the selections with an eye to answering the main questions of this chapter: What were Tocqueville's and Marx's separate political visions? How did they hope to see their visions realized? How did these two thinkers and their liberal and socialist ideologies differ?

THE EVIDENCE

ALEXIS DE TOCQUEVILLE

Sources 1 and 2 from Alexis de Tocqueville, Democracy in America, *edited by J. P. Mayer and Max Lerner, translated by George Lawrence (New York: Harper & Row, 1965), pp. 3–5, 610–611, 613, 618; pp. 231–233, 665, 667–669. English translation copyright © 1965 by Harper & Row Publishers, Inc. Copyright renewed. Reprinted by permission of HarperCollins Publishers, Inc.*

1. Tocqueville's View of History

No novelty in the United States struck me more vividly during my stay there than the equality of conditions. It was easy to see the immense influence of this basic fact on the whole course of society. It gives a particular turn to public opinion and a particular twist to the laws, new maxims to those who govern and particular habits to the governed.

I soon realized that the influence of this fact extends far beyond political mores and laws, exercising dominion over civil society as much as over the government; it creates opinions, gives birth to feelings, suggests customs, and modifies whatever it does not create.

So the more I studied American society, the more clearly I saw equality of conditions as the creative element from which each particular fact derived, and all my observations constantly returned to this nodal point.

Later, when I came to consider our own side of the Atlantic, I thought I could detect something analogous to what I had noticed in the New World. I saw an equality of conditions which, though it had not reached the extreme limits found in the United States, was daily drawing closer thereto; and that same democracy which prevailed over the societies of America seemed to me to be advancing rapidly toward power in Europe. . . .

A great democratic revolution is taking place in our midst; everybody sees it, but by no means everybody judges it in the same way. Some think it a new thing and, supposing it an accident, hope that they can still check it; others think it irresistible, because it seems to them the most continuous, ancient, and permanent tendency known to history. . . .

Running through the pages of our history, there is hardly an important event in the last seven hundred years which has not turned out to be advantageous for equality.

The Crusades and the English wars decimated the nobles and divided up their lands. Municipal institutions introduced democratic liberty into the heart of the feudal monarchy; the invention of firearms made villein and noble equal on the field of battle; printing offered equal resources to their

Two Programs
for Social
and Political
Change:
Liberalism
and Socialism

minds; the post brought enlightenment to hovel and palace alike; Protestantism maintained that all men are equally able to find the path to heaven. America, once discovered, opened a thousand new roads to fortune and gave any obscure adventurer the chance of wealth and power.

If, beginning at the eleventh century, one takes stock of what was happening in France at fifty-year intervals, one finds each time that a double revolution has taken place in the state of society. The noble has gone down in the social scale, and the commoner gone up; as the one falls, the other rises. Each half century brings them closer, and soon they will touch.

And that is not something peculiar to France. Wherever one looks one finds the same revolution taking place throughout the Christian world.

WHY GREAT REVOLUTIONS
WILL BECOME RARE

When a people has lived for centuries under a system of castes and classes, it can only reach a democratic state of society through a long series of more or less painful transformations. These must involve violent efforts and many vicissitudes, in the course of which property, opinions, and power are all subject to swift changes.

Even when this great revolution has come to an end, the revolutionary habits created thereby and by the profound disturbances thereon ensuing will long endure.

As all this takes place just at the time when social conditions are being leveled, the conclusion has been drawn that there must be a hidden connection and secret link between equality itself and revolutions, so that neither can occur without the other.

On this point reason and experience seem agreed.

Among a people where ranks are more or less equal, there is no apparent connection between men to hold them firmly in place. None of them has any permanent right or power to give commands, and none is bound by his social condition to obey. Each man, having some education and some resources, can choose his own road and go along separately from all the rest.

The same causes which make the citizens independent of each other daily prompt new and restless longings and constantly goad them on.

It therefore seems natural to suppose that in a democratic society ideas, things, and men must eternally be changing shape and position and that ages of democracy must be times of swift and constant transformation.

But is this in fact so? Does equality of social conditions habitually and permanently drive men toward revolutions? Does it contain some disturbing principle which prevents society from settling down and inclines the citizens constantly to change their laws, principles, and mores? I do not think so. The subject is important, and I ask the reader to follow my argument closely.

Almost every revolution which has changed the shape of nations has been made to consolidate or destroy inequality. Disregarding the secondary causes which have had some effect on the great convulsions in the world, you will almost always find that equality was at the heart of the matter. Either the poor were bent on snatching the property of the rich, or the rich were trying to hold the poor down. So, then, if you could establish a state of society in which each man had something to keep and little to snatch, you would have done much for the peace of the world. . . .

Such men are the natural enemies of violent commotion; their immobility keeps all above and below them quiet, and assures the stability of the body social.

I am not suggesting that they are themselves satisfied with their actual position or that they would feel any natural abhorrence toward a revolution if they could share the plunder without suffering the calamities; on the contrary, their eagerness to get rich is unparalleled, but their trouble is to know whom to despoil. The same social condition which prompts their longings restrains them within necessary limits. It gives men both greater freedom to change and less interest in doing so.

Not only do men in democracies feel no natural inclination for revolutions, but they are afraid of them.

Any revolution is more or less a threat to property. Most inhabitants of a democracy have property. And not only have they got property, but they live in the conditions in which men attach most value to property. . . .

Therefore the more widely personal property is distributed and increased and the greater the number of those enjoying it, the less is a nation inclined to revolution.

Moreover, whatever a man's calling and whatever type of property he owns, one characteristic is common to all.

No one is fully satisfied with his present fortune, and all are constantly trying a thousand various ways to improve it. Consider any individual at any period of his life, and you will always find him preoccupied with fresh plans to increase his comfort. Do not talk to him about the interests and rights of the human race; that little private business of his for the moment absorbs all his thoughts, and he hopes that public disturbances can be put off to some other time.

This not only prevents them from causing revolutions but also deters them from wanting them. Violent political passions have little hold on men whose whole thoughts are bent on the pursuit of well-being. Their excitement about small matters makes them calm about great ones. . . .

There are also other, and even stronger, reasons which prevent any great change in the doctrines of a democratic people coming about easily. I have already indicated them at the beginning of this book.

Whereas, in such a nation, the influence of individuals is weak and almost nonexistent, the power of the mass over each individual mind is very great. . . .

Whenever conditions are equal, public opinion brings immense weight to bear on every individual. It surrounds, directs, and oppresses him. The basic constitution of society has more to do with this than any political laws. The

Two Programs
for Social
and Political
Change:
Liberalism
and Socialism

more alike men are, the weaker each feels in the face of all. Finding nothing that raises him above their level and distinguishes him, he loses his self-confidence when he comes into collision with them. Not only does he mistrust his own strength, but even comes to doubt his own judgment, and he is brought very near to recognizing that he must be wrong when the majority hold the opposite view. There is no need for the majority to compel him; it convinces him.

Therefore, however powers within a democracy are organized and weighted, it will always be very difficult for a man to believe what the mass rejects and to profess what it condemns.

This circumstance is wonderfully favorable to the stability of beliefs.

2. Tocqueville on the Problems of Democracy

TYRANNY OF THE MAJORITY

I regard it as an impious and detestable maxim that in matters of government the majority of a people has the right to do everything, and nevertheless I place the origin of all powers in the will of the majority. Am I in contradiction with myself?

There is one law which has been made, or at least adopted, not by the majority of this or that people, but by the majority of all men. That law is justice.

Justice therefore forms the boundary to each people's right.

A nation is like a jury entrusted to represent universal society and to apply the justice which is its law. Should the jury representing society have greater power than that very society whose laws it applies?

Consequently, when I refuse to obey an unjust law, I by no means deny the majority's right to give orders; I only appeal from the sovereignty of the people to the sovereignty of the human race. . . .

Omnipotence in itself seems a bad and dangerous thing. I think that its exercise is beyond man's strength, whoever he be, and that only God can be omnipotent without danger because His wisdom and justice are always equal to His power. So there is no power on earth in itself so worthy of respect or vested with such a sacred right that I would wish to let it act without control and dominate without obstacles. So when I see the right and capacity to do all given to any authority whatsoever, whether it be called people or king, democracy or aristocracy, and whether the scene of action is a monarchy or a republic, I say: the germ of tyranny is there, and I will go look for other laws under which to live.

My greatest complaint against democratic government as organized in the United States is not, as many Europeans make out, its weakness, but rather its irresistible strength. What I find most repulsive in America is not the extreme freedom reigning there but the shortage of guarantees against tyranny.

When a man or a party suffers an injustice in the United States, to whom can he turn? To public opinion? That is what forms the majority. To the legislative body? It represents the majority and obeys it blindly. To the executive power? It is appointed by the majority and serves as its passive instrument. To the police? They are nothing but the majority under arms. A jury? The jury is the majority vested with the right to pronounce judgment; even the judges in certain states are elected by the majority. So, however iniquitous or unreasonable the measure which hurts you, you must submit.[3]

But suppose you were to have a legislative body so composed that it represented the majority without being necessarily the slave of its passions, an executive power having a strength of its own, and a judicial power independent of the other two authorities; then you would still have a democratic government, but there would be hardly any remaining risk of tyranny.

WHAT SORT OF DESPOTISM
DEMOCRATIC NATIONS HAVE TO FEAR

I noticed during my stay in the United States that a democratic state of society similar to that found there could lay itself peculiarly open to the establishment of a despotism. And on my return to Europe I saw how far most of our princes had made use of the ideas, feelings, and needs engendered by such a state of society to enlarge the sphere of their power. . . .

---

3. [Tocqueville's note:] At Baltimore during the War of 1812 there was a striking example of the excesses to which despotism of the majority may lead. At that time the war was very popular at Baltimore. A newspaper which came out in strong opposition to it aroused the indignation of the inhabitants. The people assembled, broke the presses, and attacked the house of the editors. An attempt was made to summon the militia, but it did not answer the appeal. Finally, to save the lives of these wretched men threatened by the fury of the public, they were taken to prison like criminals. This precaution was useless. During the night the people assembled again; the magistrates having failed to bring up the militia, the prison was broken open; one of the journalists was killed on the spot and the others left for dead; the guilty were brought before a jury and acquitted.

I once said to a Pennsylvanian: "Please explain to me why in a state founded by Quakers and renowned for its tolerance, freed Negroes are not allowed to use their rights as citizens? They pay taxes; is it not right that they should vote?"

"Do not insult us," he replied, "by supposing that our legislators would commit an act of such gross injustice and intolerance."

"So, with you, Negroes do have the right to vote?"

"Certainly."

"Then how was it that at the electoral college this morning I did not see a single one of them in the meeting?"

"That is not the fault of the law," said the American. "It is true that Negroes have the right to be present at elections, but they voluntarily abstain from appearing."

"That is extraordinarily modest of them."

"Oh! It is not that they are reluctant to go there, but they are afraid they may be maltreated. With us it sometimes happens that the law lacks force when the majority does not support it. Now, the majority is filled with the strongest prejudices against Negroes, and the magistrates do not feel strong enough to guarantee the rights granted to them by the lawmakers."

"What! The majority, privileged to make the law, wishes also to have the privilege of disobeying the law?"

Two Programs
for Social
and Political
Change:
Liberalism
and Socialism

Our contemporaries are ever a prey to two conflicting passions: they feel the need of guidance, and they long to stay free. Unable to wipe out these two contradictory instincts, they try to satisfy them both together. Their imagination conceives a government which is unitary, protective, and all-powerful, but elected by the people. Centralization is combined with the sovereignty of the people. That gives them a chance to relax. They console themselves for being under schoolmasters by thinking that they have chosen them themselves. Each individual lets them put the collar on, for he sees that it is not a person, or a class of persons, but society itself which holds the end of the chain.

Under this system the citizens quit their state of dependence just long enough to choose their masters and then fall back into it.

A great many people nowadays very easily fall in with this brand of compromise between administrative despotism and the sovereignty of the people. They think they have done enough to guarantee personal freedom when it is to the government of the state that they have handed it over. That is not good enough for me. I am much less interested in the question who my master is than in the fact of obedience. . . .

Subjection in petty affairs is manifest daily and touches all citizens indiscriminately. It never drives men to despair, but continually thwarts them and leads them to give up using their free will. It slowly stifles their spirits and enervates their souls, whereas obedience demanded only occasionally in matters of great moment brings servitude into play only from time to time, and its weight falls only on certain people. It does little good to summon those very citizens who have been made so dependent on the central power to choose the representatives of that power from time to time. However important, this brief and occasional exercise of free will will not prevent them from gradually losing the faculty of thinking, feeling, and acting for themselves, so that they will slowly fall below the level of humanity.

I must add that they will soon become incapable of using the one great privilege left to them. Those democratic peoples which have introduced freedom into the sphere of politics, while allowing despotism to grow in the administrative sphere, have been led into the strangest paradoxes. For the conduct of small affairs, where plain common sense is enough, they hold that the citizens are not up to the job. But they give these citizens immense prerogatives where the government of the whole state is concerned. They are turned alternatively into the playthings of the sovereign and into his masters, being either greater than kings or less than men. When they have tried all the different systems of election without finding one to suit them, they look surprised and go on seeking for another, as if the ills they see did not belong much more to the constitution of the country itself than to that of the electoral body.

It really is difficult to imagine how people who have entirely given up managing their own affairs could make a wise choice of those who are to do that for them. One should never expect a liberal, energetic, and wise government to originate in the votes of a people of servants.

First document in Source 3 from Alexis de Tocqueville, Democracy in America, *edited by J. P. Mayer and Max Lerner, translated by George Lawrence (New York: Harper & Row, 1965), pp. 674–675. English translation copyright © 1965 by Harper & Row Publishers, Inc. Copyright renewed. Reprinted by permission of HarperCollins Publishers, Inc. Second document from J. P. Mayer, editor, Alexander Teixeira De Mattos, translator,* The Recollections of Alexis de Tocqueville *(New York: Meridian, 1959), pp. 63, 68–71. Reprinted with permission of Columbia University Press, 562 W. 113th St., New York, NY 10025, via Copyright Clearance Center, Inc.*

3. Tocqueville on Revolution

[*The general danger of revolution*]

There are some habits, some ideas, and some vices which are peculiar to a state of revolution and which any prolonged revolution cannot fail to engender and spread, whatever may be in other respects its character, object, and field of action.

When in a brief space of time any nation has repeatedly changed its leaders, opinions, and laws, the men of that nation will in the end acquire a taste for change and grow accustomed to see all changes quickly brought about by the use of force. Then they will naturally conceive a scorn for those formalities of whose impotence they have been daily witnesses, and they will be impatient to tolerate the sway of rules which they have so often seen infringed.

As ordinary ideas of equity and morality are no longer enough to explain and justify all the innovations daily introduced by revolution, men fall back on the principle of social utility, political necessity is turned into a dogma, and men lose all scruples about freely sacrificing particular interests and trampling private rights beneath their feet in order more quickly to attain the public aim envisaged.

Such habits and ideas, which I call revolutionary since all revolutions give rise to them, are seen as much in aristocracies as among democratic peoples. But in the former case they are often less powerful and always less permanent, because there they come up against habits, ideas, faults, and eccentricities which are opposed to them. They therefore vanish of their own accord when the revolution is at an end and the nation recovers its former political ways. However, that is not always the case in democratic countries, for in them there is always a danger that revolutionary instincts will mellow and assume more regular shape without entirely disappearing, but will gradually be transformed into mores of government and administrative habits.

Hence, I know of no country in which revolutions are more dangerous than in a democracy, because apart from the accidental and ephemeral ills which they are ever bound to entail, there is always a danger of their becoming permanent, and one may almost say, eternal.

I think that resistance is sometimes justified and that rebellion can be legitimate. I cannot therefore lay it down as an absolute rule that men living in times of democracy should never make a revolution. But I think that they, more than others, have reason to hesitate before they embark on such an enterprise and that it is far better to put up with many inconveniences in their present state than to turn to so dangerous a remedy.

Two Programs
for Social
and Political
Change:
Liberalism
and Socialism

[*Tocqueville on the Revolution of 1848
in France*]

*My Explanation of the 24th of February and My Thoughts as to Its
Effects upon the Future*[4]

And so the Monarchy of July[5] was fallen, fallen without a struggle, and before rather than beneath the blows of the victors, who were as astonished at their triumph as were the vanquished at their defeat. . . .

I had spent the best days of my youth amid a society which seemed to increase in greatness and prosperity as it increased in liberty; I had conceived the idea of a balanced, regulated liberty, held in check by religion, custom and law; the attractions of this liberty had touched me; it had become the passion of my life; I felt that I could never be consoled for its loss, and that I must renounce all hope of its recovery.

I had gained too much experience of men to be able to content myself with empty words; I knew that, if one great revolution is able to establish liberty in a country, a number of succeeding revolutions make all regular liberty impossible for very many years.

I could not yet know what would issue from this last revolution, but I was already convinced that it could give birth to nothing that would satisfy me; and I foresaw that, whatever might be the lot reserved for our posterity, our own fate was to drag on our lives miserably amid alternate reactions of licence and oppression. . . .

I spent the rest of the day with Ampère, who was my colleague at the Institute,[6] and one of my best friends. He came to discover what had become of me in the affray, and to ask himself to dinner. I wished at first to relieve myself by making him share my vexation. . . .

I saw that he not only did not enter into my view, but that he was disposed to take quite an opposite one. Seeing this, I was suddenly impelled to turn against Ampère all the feelings of indignation, grief and anger that had been accumulating in my heart since the morning; and I spoke to him with a violence of language which I have often since recalled with a certain shame, and which none but a friendship so sincere as his could have excused. I remember saying to him, *inter alia*.[7]

---

4. On Thursday, February 24, 1848, King Louis Philippe abdicated the throne in the face of the Paris revolution and fled the capital for England.

5. **Monarchy of July:** the term often used for the regime of King Louis Philippe because that government came to power in July 1830.

6. **Institute:** Institut de France, the cultural institution including the French Academy, of which Tocqueville was a member. **Jean-Jacques Ampère** (1800–1864): a philologist and professor of French literature.

7. **inter alia:** Latin, "among other things."

"You understand nothing of what is happening; you are judging like a poet or a Paris cockney.[8] You call this the triumph of liberty, when it is its final defeat. I tell you that the people which you so artlessly admire has just succeeded in proving that it is unfit and unworthy to live a life of freedom. Show me what experience has taught it! Where are the new virtues it has gained, the old vices it has laid aside? No, I tell you, it is always the same, as impatient, as thoughtless, as contemptuous of law and order, as easily led and as cowardly in the presence of danger as its fathers were before it. Time has altered it in no way, and has left it as frivolous in serious matters as it used to be in trifles."

After much vociferation we both ended by appealing to the future, that enlightened and upright judge who always, alas! arrives too late.

Source 4 from Roger Boesche, editor, James Toupin and Roger Boesche, translators, Alexis de Tocqueville: Selected Letters on Politics and Society *(Berkeley: University of California Press, 1985), pp. 112–113. Copyright © 1985 The Regents of the University of California. Reprinted with permission.*

4. Tocqueville's Ideals of Government (letter to Eugène Stoffels)[9]

I do not think that in France there is a man who is less revolutionary than I, nor one who has a more profound hatred for what is called the revolutionary spirit (a spirit which, parenthetically, is very easily combined with the love of an absolute government). What am I then? And what do I want? Let us distinguish, in order to understand each other better, between the end and the means. What is the end? What I want is not a republic, but a hereditary monarchy. I would even prefer it to be legitimate rather than elected like the one we have, because it would be stronger, especially externally. What I want is a central government energetic in its own sphere of action. Energy from the central government is even more necessary among a democratic people in whom the social force is more diffused than in an aristocracy. Besides our situation in Europe lays down as imperative law for us in what should be a thing of choice. But I wish that this central power had a clearly delineated sphere, that it were involved with what is a necessary part of its functions and not with everything in general, and that it were forever subordinated, in its tendency, to public opinion and to the legislative power that represents this public opinion. I believe that the central power can be invested with very great

8. **Cockney:** generally a person of the lower classes born in London's East End. In this context, it refers to someone from that same class in Paris.

9. **Eugène Stoffels** (1805–1852): an official in Metz, France, and a friend of Tocqueville from their days together in secondary school.

Two Programs
for Social
and Political
Change:
Liberalism
and Socialism

prerogatives, can be energetic and powerful in its sphere, and that at the same time provincial liberties can be well developed. I think that a government of this kind can exist, and that at the same time the majority of the nation itself can be involved with its own affairs, that political life can be spread almost everywhere, the direct or indirect exercise of political rights can be quite extensive. I wish that the general principles of government were liberal, that the largest possible part were left to the action of individuals, to personal initiative. I believe that all these things are compatible; even more, I am profoundly convinced that there will never be order and tranquility except when they are successfully combined.

As for the means: with all those who admit that we must make our way gradually toward this goal, I am very much in accord. I am the first to admit that it is necessary to proceed slowly, with precaution, with legality. My conviction is that our current institutions are sufficient for reaching the result I have in view. Far, then, from wanting people to violate the laws, I profess an almost superstitious respect for the laws. But I wish that the laws would tend little and gradually toward the goal I have just indicated, instead of making powerless and dangerous efforts to turn back. I wish that the government would itself prepare mores and practices so that people would do without it in many cases in which its intervention is still necessary or invoked without necessity. I wish that citizens were introduced into public life to the extent that they are believed capable of being useful in it, instead of seeking to keep them away from it at all costs. I wish finally that people knew where they wanted to go, and that they advanced toward it prudently instead of proceeding aimlessly as they have been doing almost constantly for twenty years.

KARL MARX

Source 5 from Karl Marx and Friedrich Engels, The Communist Manifesto, *translated by Samuel Moore (New York: Penguin, 1977), pp. 79–83, 85–92, 95–96.*

5. Marx's View of History

1
BOURGEOIS AND PROLETARIANS[10]

The history of all hitherto existing society is the history of class struggles.

Freeman and slave, patrician and plebeian, lord and serf, guild-master[11] and journeyman, in a word, oppressor and oppressed, stood in constant op-

---

10. **bourgeois, proletarian:** "By bourgeoisie is meant the class of modern Capitalist, owners of the means of social production and employers of wage labour. By proletariat, the class of modern wage-labourers who, having no means of production of their own, are reduced to selling their labour power in order to live" (note by Engels to the English edition, 1888).

11. **guild-master:** "that is, a full member of a guild, a master within, not a head of a guild" (note by Engels to the English edition, 1888).

position to one another, carried on an uninterrupted, now hidden, now open fight, a fight that each time ended, either in a revolutionary reconstitution of society at large, or in the common ruin of the contending classes.

In the earlier epochs of history, we find almost everywhere a complicated arrangement of society into various orders, a manifold gradation of social rank. In ancient Rome we have patricians, knights, plebeians, slaves; in the Middle Ages, feudal lords, vassals, guild-masters, journeymen, apprentices, serfs; in almost all of these classes, again, subordinate gradations.

The modern bourgeois society that has sprouted from the ruins of feudal society has not done away with class antagonisms. It has but established new classes, new conditions of oppression, new forms of struggle in place of the old ones.

Our epoch, the epoch of the bourgeoisie, possesses, however, this distinctive feature: it has simplified the class antagonisms. Society as a whole is more and more splitting up into two great hostile camps, into two great classes directly facing each other: Bourgeoisie and Proletariat.

From the serfs of the Middle Ages sprang the chartered burghers of the earliest towns. From these burgesses the first elements of the bourgeoisie were developed.

The discovery of America, the rounding of the Cape, opened up fresh ground for the rising bourgeoisie. The East-Indian and Chinese markets, the colonization of America, trade with the colonies, the increase in the means of exchange and in commodities generally, gave to commerce, to navigation, to industry, an impulse never before known, and thereby, to the revolutionary element in the tottering feudal society, a rapid development.

The feudal system of industry, under which industrial production was monopolized by closed guilds, now no longer sufficed for the growing wants of the new markets. The manufacturing system took its place. The guild-masters were pushed on one side by the manufacturing middle class; division of labour between the different corporate guilds vanished in the face of division of labour in each single workshop.

Meantime the markets kept ever growing, the demand ever rising. Even manufacture no longer sufficed. Thereupon, steam and machinery revolutionized industrial production. The place of manufacture was taken by the giant, Modern Industry, the place of the industrial middle class, by industrial millionaires, the leaders of whole industrial armies, the modern bourgeois.

Modern industry has established the world market, for which the discovery of America paved the way. This market has given an immense development to commerce, to navigation, to communication by land. This development has, in its turn, reacted on the extension of industry; and in proportion as industry, commerce, navigation, railways extended, in the same proportion the bourgeoisie developed, increased its capital, and pushed into the background every class handed down from the Middle Ages.

Two Programs
for Social
and Political
Change:
Liberalism
and Socialism

We see, therefore, how the modern bourgeoisie is itself the product of a long course of development, of a series of revolutions in the modes of production and of exchange.

Each step in the development of the bourgeoisie was accompanied by a corresponding political advance of that class. An oppressed class under the sway of the feudal nobility, an armed and self-governing association in the medieval commune;[12] here independent urban republic (as in Italy and Germany), there taxable "third estate" of the monarchy (as in France), afterwards, in the period of manufacture proper, serving either the semi-feudal or the absolute monarchy as a counterpoise against the nobility, and, in fact, cornerstone of the great monarchies in general, the bourgeoisie has at last, since the establishment of Modern Industry and of the world market, conquered for itself, in the modern representative State, exclusive political sway. The executive of the modern State is but a committee for managing the common affairs of the whole bourgeoisie.

The bourgeoisie, historically, has played a most revolutionary part.

The bourgeoisie, wherever it has got the upper hand, has put an end to all feudal, patriarchal, idyllic relations. It has pitilessly torn asunder the motley feudal ties that bound man to his "natural superiors," and has left remaining no other nexus between man and man than naked self-interest, than callous "cash payment." It has drowned the most heavenly ecstasies of religious fervour, of chivalrous enthusiasm, of philistine sentimentalism, in the icy water of egotistical calculation. It has resolved personal worth into exchange value, and in place of the numberless indefeasible chartered freedoms, has set up that single, unconscionable freedom—Free Trade. In one word, for exploitation, veiled by religious and political illusions, it has substituted naked, shameless, direct, brutal exploitation.

The bourgeoisie has stripped of its halo every occupation hitherto honoured and looked up to with reverent awe. It has converted the physician, the lawyer, the priest, the poet, the man of science, into its paid wage-labourers.

The bourgeoisie has torn away from the family its sentimental veil, and has reduced the family relation to a mere money relation. . . .

The bourgeoisie cannot exist without constantly revolutionizing the instruments of production, and thereby the relations of production, and with them the whole relations of society. Conservation of the old modes of production in unaltered form, was, on the contrary, the first condition of existence for all earlier industrial classes. Constant revolutionizing of production, uninterrupted disturbance of all social conditions, everlasting uncertainty and agita-

12. **commune:** "the name taken, in France, by the nascent towns even before they had conquered from their feudal lords and masters local self-government and political rights as the 'Third Estate.' Generally speaking, for the economical development of the bourgeoisie, England is here taken as the typical country; for its political development, France" (note by Engels to the English edition, 1888). "This was the name given their urban communities by the townsmen of Italy and France, after they had purchased or wrested their initial rights of self-government from their feudal lords" (note by Engels to the German edition, 1890).

tion distinguish the bourgeois epoch from all earlier ones. All fixed, fast-frozen relations, with their train of ancient and venerable prejudices and opinions are swept away, all new-formed ones become antiquated before they can ossify. All that is solid melts into air, all that is holy is profaned, and man is at last compelled to face with sober senses, his real conditions of life, and his relations with his kind.

The need of a constantly expanding market for its products chases the bourgeoisie over the whole surface of the globe. It must nestle everywhere, settle everywhere, establish connexions everywhere. . . .

Modern bourgeois society with its relations of production, of exchange and of property, a society that has conjured up such gigantic means of production and of exchange, is like the sorcerer, who is no longer able to control the powers of the nether world whom he has called up by his spells. For many a decade past the history of industry and commerce is but the history of the revolt of modern productive forces against modern conditions of production, against the property relations that are the conditions for the existence of the bourgeoisie and of its rule. It is enough to mention the commercial crises that by their periodical return put on its trial, each time more threateningly, the existence of the entire bourgeois society. In these crises a great part not only of the existing products, but also of the previously created productive forces, are periodically destroyed. In these crises there breaks out an epidemic that, in all earlier epochs, would have seemed an absurdity—the epidemic of over-production. . . .

And how does the bourgeoisie get over these crises? On the one hand by enforced destruction of a mass of productive forces; on the other, by the conquest of new markets, and by the more thorough exploitation of the old ones. That is to say, by paving the way for more extensive and more destructive crises, and by diminishing the means whereby crises are prevented.

The weapons with which the bourgeoisie felled feudalism to the ground are now turned against the bourgeoisie itself.

But not only has the bourgeoisie forged the weapons that bring death to itself; it has also called into existence the men who are to wield those weapons—the modern working class—the proletarians.

In proportion as the bourgeoisie, i.e., capital, is developed, in the same proportion is the proletariat, the modern working class, developed—a class of labourers, who live only so long as they find work, and who find work only so long as their labour increases capital. These labourers, who must sell themselves piecemeal, are a commodity, like every other article of commerce, and are consequently exposed to all the vicissitudes of competition, to all the fluctuations of the market.

Owing to the extensive use of machinery and to division of labour, the work of the proletarians has lost all individual character, and, consequently, all charm for the workman. He becomes an appendage of the machine, and it is only the most simple, most monotonous, and most easily acquired knack, that

Two Programs
for Social
and Political
Change:
Liberalism
and Socialism

is required of him. Hence, the cost of production of a workman is restricted, almost entirely, to the means of subsistence that he requires for his maintenance, and for the propagation of his race. . . .

Modern industry has converted the little workshop of the patriarchal master into the great factory of the industrial capitalist. Masses of labourers, crowded into the factory, are organized like soldiers. As privates of the industrial army they are placed under the command of a perfect hierarchy of officers and sergeants. Not only are they slaves of the bourgeois class, and of the bourgeois State; they are daily and hourly enslaved by the machine, by the overlooker, and, above all, by the individual bourgeois manufacturer himself. The more openly this despotism proclaims gain be its end and aim, the more petty, the more hateful and the more embittering it is. . . .

The proletariat goes through various stages of development. With its birth begins its struggle with the bourgeoisie. At first the contest is carried on by individual labourers, then by the work-people of a factory, then by the operatives of one trade, in one locality, against the individual bourgeois who directly exploits them. They direct their attacks not against the bourgeois conditions of production, but against the instruments of production themselves; they destroy imported wares that compete with their labour, they smash to pieces machinery, they set factories ablaze, they seek to restore by force the vanished status of the workman of the Middle Ages.

At this stage the labourers still form an incoherent mass scattered over the whole country, and broken up by their mutual competition. If anywhere they unite to form more compact bodies, this is not yet the consequence of their own active union, but of the union of the bourgeoisie, which class, in order to attain its own political ends, is compelled to set the whole proletariat in motion, and is moreover yet, for a time, able to do so. At this stage, therefore, the proletarians do not fight their enemies, but the enemies of their enemies, the remnants of absolute monarchy, the landowners, the non-industrial bourgeois, the petty bourgeoisie. Thus the whole historical movement is concentrated in the hands of the bourgeoisie; every victory so obtained is a victory for the bourgeoisie.

But with the development of industry the proletariat not only increases in number; it becomes concentrated in greater masses, its strength grows, and it feels that strength more. The various interests and conditions of life within the ranks of the proletariat are more and more equalized, in proportion as machinery obliterates all distinctions of labour, and nearly everywhere reduces wages to the same low level. The growing competition among the bourgeois, and the resulting commercial crises, make the wages of the workers ever more fluctuating. The unceasing improvement of machinery, ever more rapidly developing, makes their livelihood more and more precarious; the collisions between individual workmen and individual bourgeois take more and more the character of collisions between two classes. Thereupon the workers begin to form combinations (Trades Unions) against the bourgeois; they club together in order to keep up the rate of wages; they found permanent associations in order to make provision beforehand for these occasional revolts. Here and there the contest breaks out into riots.

Now and then the workers are victorious, but only for a time. The real fruit of their battles lies, not in the immediate result, but in the ever-expanding union of the workers. This union is helped on by the improved means of communication that are created by modern industry and that place the workers of different localities in contact with one another. It was just this contact that was needed to centralize the numerous local struggles, all of the same character, into one national struggle between classes. But every class struggle is a political struggle. And that union, to attain which the burghers of the Middle Ages, with their miserable highways, required centuries, the modern proletarians, thanks to railways, achieve in a few years. . . .

Of all the classes that stand face to face with the bourgeoisie today, the proletariat alone is a really revolutionary class. The other classes decay and finally disappear in the face of modern industry; the proletariat is its special and essential product.

The lower middle class, the small manufacturer, the shopkeeper, the artisan, the peasant, all these fight against the bourgeoisie, to save from extinction their existence as fractions of the middle class. They are therefore not revolutionary, but conservative. Nay more, they are reactionary, for they try to roll back the wheel of history. . . .

In the conditions of the proletariat, those of old society at large are already virtually swamped. The proletarian is without property; his relation to his wife and children has no longer anything in common with the bourgeois family relations; modern industrial labour, modern subjection to capital, the same in England as in France, in America as in Germany, has stripped him of every trace of national character. Law, morality, religion, are to him so many bourgeois prejudices, behind which lurk in ambush just as many bourgeois interests.

All the preceding classes that got the upper hand sought to fortify their already acquired status by subjecting society at large to their conditions of appropriation. The proletarians cannot become masters of the productive forces of society, except by abolishing their own previous mode of appropriation, and thereby also every other previous mode of appropriation. They have nothing of their own to secure and to fortify; their mission is to destroy all previous securities for, and insurances of, individual property.

All previous historical movements were movements of minorities, or in the interest of minorities. The proletarian movement is the self-conscious, independent movement of the immense majority, in the interest of the immense majority. The proletariat, the lowest stratum of our present society, cannot stir, cannot raise itself up, without the whole superincumbent strata of official society being sprung into the air.

Two Programs
for Social
and Political
Change:
Liberalism
and Socialism

2

PROLETARIANS AND COMMUNISTS

In what relation do the Communists stand to the proletarians as a whole?

The Communists do not form a separate party opposed to other working-class parties.

They have no interests separate and apart from those of the proletariat as a whole.

They do not set up any sectarian principles of their own, by which to shape and mould the proletarian movement.

The Communists are distinguished from the other working-class parties by this only: 1. In the national struggles of the proletarians of the different countries, they point out and bring to the front the common interests of the entire proletariat, independently of all nationality. 2. In the various stages of development which the struggle of the working class against the bourgeoisie has to pass through, they always and everywhere represent the interests of the movement as a whole.

The Communists, therefore, are on the one hand, practically, the most advanced and resolute section of the working-class parties of every country, that section which pushes forward all others; on the other hand, theoretically, they have over the great mass of the proletariat the advantage of clearly understanding the line of march, the conditions, and the ultimate general results of the proletarian movement.

The immediate aim of the Communists is the same as that of all the other proletarian parties: formation of the proletariat into a class, overthrow of the bourgeois supremacy, conquest of political power by the proletariat.

The theoretical conclusions of the Communists are in no way based on ideas or principles that have been invented, or discovered, by this or that would-be universal reformer.

They merely express, in general terms, actual relations springing from an existing class struggle, from a historical movement going on under our very eyes. The abolition of existing property relations is not at all a distinctive feature of Communism.

All property relations in the past have continually been subject to historical change consequent upon the change in historical conditions.

The French Revolution, for example, abolished feudal property in favour of bourgeois property.

The distinguishing feature of Communism is not the abolition of property generally, but the abolition of bourgeois property. But modern bourgeois private property is the final and most complete expression of the system of producing and appropriating products, that is based on class antagonisms, on the exploitation of the many by the few.

In this sense, the theory of the Communists may be summed up in the single sentence: Abolition of private property.

Source 6 from Karl Marx, The Class Struggles in France *(1848–1850), edited by C. P. Dutt (New York: International Publishers, 1964), pp. 33–34, 39–40, 50–52, 55, 56, 58–59. Used by permission of International Publishers.*

6. Marx on the Revolution of 1848 in Paris

1
FROM FEBRUARY TO JUNE 1848

With the exception of a few short chapters, every important part of the annals of the revolution from 1848 to 1849 carries the heading: Defeat of the revolution!

But what succumbed in these defeats was not the revolution. It was the pre-revolutionary traditional appendages, results of social relationships, which had not yet come to the point of sharp class antagonisms—persons, illusions, conceptions, projects, from which the revolutionary party before the February Revolution was not free, from which it could be freed, not by the victory of February, but only by a series of defeats.

In a word: revolutionary advance made headway not by its immediate tragi-comic achievements, but on the contrary by the creation of a powerful, united counter-revolution, by the creation of an opponent, by fighting whom the party of revolt first ripened into a real revolutionary party.

To prove this is the task of the following pages.

I. THE DEFEAT OF JUNE 1848

After the July Revolution, when the Liberal banker, Laffitte, led his godfather, the Duke of Orleans, in triumph to the Hôtel de Ville,[13] he let fall the words: "From now on the bankers will rule." Laffitte had betrayed the secret of the revolution. . . .

It was not the French bourgeoisie that ruled under Louis Philippe, but a fraction of it, bankers, Stock Exchange kings, railway kings, owners of coal and iron works and forests, a section of landed proprietors that rallied around them—the so-called finance aristocracy. It sat on the throne, it dictated laws in the Chambers, it conferred political posts from cabinet portfolios to the tobacco bureau.

The real industrial bourgeoisie formed part of the official opposition, *i.e.*, it was represented only as a minority in the Chambers. . . .

The petty bourgeoisie of all degrees, and the peasantry also, were completely excluded from political power. Finally, in the official opposition or

13. **Hôtel de Ville:** City Hall. The Duke of Orleans emerged from the July Revolution as King Louis Philippe.

Two Programs
for Social
and Political
Change:
Liberalism
and Socialism

entirely outside the *pays légal*,[14] there were the ideological representatives and spokesmen of the above classes, their savants, lawyers, doctors, etc., in a word: their so-called talents. . . .

The Provisional Government which emerged from the February barricades, necessarily mirrored in its composition the different parties which shared in the victory.[15] It could not be anything but a compromise between the different classes which together had overturned the July throne, but whose interests were mutually antagonistic. A large majority of its members consisted of representatives of the bourgeoisie. . . . The working class had only two representatives, Louis Blanc and Albert. . . .

Up to noon on February 25, the republic had not yet been proclaimed; on the other hand, the whole of the Ministries had already been divided among the bourgeois elements of the Provisional Government and among the generals, bankers and lawyers of the *National*. But the workers were this time determined not to put up with any swindling like that of July 1830. They were ready to take up the fight anew and to enforce the republic by force of arms. With this message, Raspail betook himself to the Hôtel de Ville. In the name of the Parisian proletariat he commanded the Provisional Government to proclaim the republic; if this order of the people were not fulfilled within two hours, he would return at the head of 200,000 men. The bodies of the fallen were scarcely cold, the barricades were not yet cleared away, the workers not yet disarmed, and the only force which could be opposed to them was the National Guard. Under these circumstances the prudent state doubts and juristic scruples of conscience of the Provisional Government suddenly vanished. The interval of two hours had not expired before all the walls of Paris were resplendent with the tremendous historical words:

République française! Liberté, Egalité, Fraternité![16]. . .

The proletariat, by dictating the republic to the Provisional Government and through the Provisional Government to the whole of France, stepped into the foreground forthwith as an independent party, but at the same time challenged the whole of bourgeois France to enter the lists against it. What it won

14. **pays légal:** literally, "legal country." Here Marx refers to the fact that the monarchy established by the July Revolution created a very limited right to vote. One had to possess a substantial amount of property to qualify for the right to vote, with the result that only 170,000 men, out of a population of about 30,000,000, qualified to vote for the Chamber of Deputies in the 1830s.

15. In his work *The Eighteenth of Brumaire of Louis Bonaparte* (New York: International Publishers, 1935), p. 101, Marx referred to the participation of a broad spectrum of social groups in the February Revolution as the "Universal brotherhood swindle." This means that, in his view, the lower classes were seduced into revolutionary action by bourgeois promises of democracy that were unfilled in the postrevolutionary government.

16. **République française: Liberté, Egalité, Fraternité:** "The French Republic: Liberty, Equality, Fraternity," the motto of the Revolution of 1789.

was the terrain for the fight for its revolutionary emancipation, but in no way this emancipation itself! . . .

A hundred thousand workers thrown on the streets through the crisis and the revolution were enrolled by the Minister Marie in so-called National *Ateliers*![17] Under this grand name was hidden nothing but the employment of the workers on tedious, monotonous, unproductive earthworks at a wage of 23 sous.[18] English *workhouses* in the open—that is what these National *Ateliers* were. . . .

All the discontent, all the ill humour of the petty bourgeois was simultaneously directed against these National *Ateliers,* the common target. With real fury they reckoned up the sums that the proletarian loafers swallowed, while their own situation became daily more unbearable. A state pension for sham labour, that is socialism! they growled to themselves. They sought the basis of their misery in the National *Ateliers,* the declarations of the Luxembourg,[19] the marches of the workers through Paris. And no one was more fantastic about the alleged machinations of the Communists than the petty bourgeoisie who hovered hopelessly on the brink of bankruptcy.[20] . . .

In the National Assembly all France sat in judgment on the Paris proletariat. It broke immediately with the social illusions of the February Revolution; it roundly proclaimed the bourgeois republic, nothing but the bourgeois republic. It at once excluded the representatives of the proletariat, Louis Blanc and Albert, from the Executive Commission appointed by it; it threw out the proposal of a special Labour Ministry,[21] and received with stormy applause the statement of the Minister Trélat: "The question is merely one of bringing labour back to its old conditions."

17. **Atelier:** workshop. The National Ateliers were government-funded projects to provide work to the unemployed.

18. **23 sous:** The sou was a French coin worth 5 centimes (100 centimes to 1 franc). Thus Marx cites a wage of a little over 1 **franc** per day for the labor. Initially, wages in the workshops were 2 francs per day for laborers and 1 franc per day for those unemployed for whom labor could not be found. Even 2 francs per day was less than the usual wage for skilled artisans like tailors and shoemakers.

19. **The Luxembourg:** the revolutionary government established a commission to study labor problems; chaired by the socialist Louis Blanc and composed of representatives of various trades, it was headquartered in the Luxembourg Palace. The commission secured the government's enactment of a ten-hour workday in Paris and a twelve-hour workday in the provinces. This reform would have reduced most workers' hours of labor had it been enforced by government supervision.

20. One of the causes of the Revolution of 1848 was a general European economic crisis in 1846–1848 that had its origins in agricultural problems. Potato harvests were disastrously deficient in Ireland and other countries in 1845–1848 because of a blight. Weather factors conspired to reduce wheat harvests in these same years, creating rising food prices and general distress in the economies of most European countries.

21. The National Assembly, elected by universal manhood suffrage in April 1848, had a moderate to conservative majority: Of the 900 members, about 500 were moderate republicans and 300 were monarchists. In such a chamber, proposals for a Ministry of Labor and for a guaranteed right to work, proposed by Louis Blanc, gained little support.

Two Programs
for Social
and Political
Change:
Liberalism
and Socialism

But all this was not enough. The February republic was won by the workers with the passive support of the bourgeoisie. The proletarians regarded themselves, and rightly, as the victors of February, and they made the proud claims of victors. They had to be vanquished on the streets, they had to be shown that they were worsted as soon as they fought, not with the bourgeoisie, but against the bourgeoisie. Just as the February republic, with its socialist concessions, required a battle of the proletariat, united with the bourgeoisie, against monarchy, so a second battle was necessary in order to sever the republic from the socialist concessions, in order to officially work out the bourgeois republic as dominant. The bourgeoisie had to refute the demands of the proletariat with arms in its hands. And the real birthplace of the bourgeois republic is not the February victory; it is the June defeat. . . .

The Executive Commission began by making entry into the National *Ateliers* more difficult, by turning the day wage into a piece wage, by banishing workers not born in Paris to Sologne, ostensibly for the construction of earthworks. These earthworks were only a rhetorical formula with which to gloss over their expulsion, as the workers, returning disillusioned, announced to their comrades. Finally, on June 21, a decree appeared in the *Moniteur*,[22] which ordered the forcible expulsion of all unmarried workers from the National *Ateliers*, or their enrolment in the army.

The workers were left no choice: they had to starve or start to fight. They answered on June 22 with the tremendous insurrection in which the first great battle was joined between the two classes that split modern society. It was a fight for the preservation or annihilation of the bourgeois order. The veil that shrouded the republic was torn to pieces.

It is well known how the workers, with unexampled bravery and talent, without chiefs, without a common plan, without means and, for the most part, lacking weapons, held in check for five days the army, the Mobile Guard, the Parisian National Guard, and the National Guard that streamed in from the provinces. It is well known how the bourgeoisie compensated itself for the mortal anguish it underwent by unheard of brutality, and massacred over 3,000 prisoners.[23] . . .

By making its burial place the birth place of the bourgeois republic, the proletariat compelled the latter to come out forthwith in its pure form as the state whose admitted object is to perpetuate the rule of capital, the slavery of labour. With constant regard to the scarred, irreconcilable, unconquerable enemy—unconquerable because its existence is the condition of its own life—bourgeois rule, freed from all fetters, was bound to turn immediately into

22. **Moniteur:** a journal that published parliamentary debate and government decrees.

23. Marx does not wildly exaggerate the losses here. Casualties in the actual fighting and in the retribution following it were high.

bourgeois terrorism. With the proletariat removed for the time being from the stage and bourgeois dictatorship recognised officially, the middle sections, in the mass, had more and more to side with the proletariat as their position became more unbearable and their antagonism to the bourgeoisie became more acute. Just as earlier in its upsurge, so now they had to find in its defeat the cause of their misery. . . .

Only through the defeat of June, therefore, were all conditions created under which France can seize the initiative of the European revolution. Only after baptism in the blood of the June insurgents did the tricolour[24] become the flag of the European revolution—the red flag.

And we cry: *The revolution is dead!—Long live the revolution!*

Source 7 *from Karl Marx and Friedrich Engels,* The Communist Manifesto, *translated by Samuel Moore (New York: Penguin, 1977), pp. 104–105.*

7. Marx's Ideals of Government and Economy

We have seen above, that the first step in the revolution by the working class, is to raise the proletariat to the position of ruling class, to win the battle of democracy.

The proletariat will use its political supremacy to wrest, by degrees, all capital from the bourgeoisie, to centralize all instruments of production in the hands of the State, i.e., of the proletariat organized as the ruling class; and to increase the total of productive forces as rapidly as possible.

Of course, in the beginning, this cannot be effected except by means of despotic inroads on the rights of property, and on the conditions of bourgeois production; by means of measures, therefore, which appear economically insufficient and untenable, but which, in the course of the movement, outstrip themselves, necessitate further inroads upon the old social order, and are unavoidable as a means of entirely revolutionizing the mode of production.

These measures will of course be different in different countries.

Nevertheless, in the most advanced countries, the following will be pretty generally applicable:

1. Abolition of property in land and application of all rents of land to public purposes.

2. A heavy progressive or graduated income tax.

3. Abolition of all right of inheritance.

4. Confiscation of the property of all emigrants and rebels.

24. **tricolor:** the three-colored flag, composed of vertical stripes of blue, white, and red, adopted in the 1789 Revolution and today the flag of France.

413

Two Programs

for Social

and Political

Change:

Liberalism

and Socialism

5. Centralization of credit in the hands of the State, by means of a national bank with State capital and an exclusive monopoly.

6. Centralization of the means of communication and transport in the hands of the State.

7. Extension of factories and instruments of production owned by the State; the bringing into cultivation of wastelands, and the improvement of the soil generally in accordance with a common plan.

8. Equal liability of all to labour. Establishment of industrial armies, especially for agriculture.

9. Combination of agriculture with manufacturing industries; gradual abolition of the distinction between town and country, by a more equable distribution of the population over the country.

10. Free education for all children in public schools. Abolition of children's factory labour in its present form. Combination of education with industrial production, &c., &c.

When, in the course of development, class distinctions have disappeared, and all production has been concentrated in the whole nation, the public power will lose its political character. Political power, properly so called, is merely the organized power of one class for oppressing another. If the proletariat during its contest with the bourgeoisie is compelled, by the force of circumstances, to organize itself as a class, if, by means of a revolution, it makes itself the ruling class, and, as such, sweeps away by force the old conditions of production, then it will, along with these conditions, have swept away the conditions for the existence of class antagonisms and of classes generally, and will thereby have abolished its own supremacy as a class.

In place of the old bourgeois society, with its classes and class antagonisms, we shall have an association, in which the free development of each is the condition for the free development of all.

QUESTIONS TO CONSIDER

Tocqueville and Marx pose different responses to many of the same issues in the selections presented in this chapter. Your basic task in answering the main questions of this chapter is to compare their ideas.

Central to the thought of both men is a certain vision of historical evolution. Indeed, Marx called himself a "scientific socialist" because, in his view, he had discovered the im-mutable course of historical development. What was this historical process for Marx? What patterns of history did Tocqueville identify? As you continue your study of modern Western history in this course, consider which of these thinkers' ideas seem most adequately to have predicted the political and economic development of the West.

Both Marx and Tocqueville address the problem of revolution in the selections that you have read. First consider Tocqueville. What threats to democracy did he see emerging in the West? Why did he believe that revolution was not likely to be a threat to democracy? What dangers, according to Tocqueville, did revolution pose when it did erupt? Did Tocqueville's liberal principles admit any circumstances under which society should resort to revolution as a means of change? Recall Tocqueville's attitude toward the government of King Louis Philippe in Source 3. Why did Tocqueville oppose the Revolution of 1848 despite this view?

Now analyze Marx's ideas on revolution. Examine the historical role for revolution that Marx believed he had found. Why did Marx see the middle class, those who owned the factories and embraced liberal ideas, as revolutionary? In what ways, according to Marx, was capitalism sowing the seeds of its destruction? What class would challenge the factory owners in revolution? What vision of the future did that class have, according to Marx? Did they want the political democracy Tocqueville was prepared to accept or a broader reorganization of society? How did Marx and Tocqueville differ in their views of the desirability of revolution?

Both authors also wrote on the same revolution, the French uprising of 1848, providing us a further opportunity to contrast their views. As your study of the 1848 revolutions no doubt has demonstrated, it is impossible to consider the uprising of that year a success. Whether revolutionaries' goals were nationalist or liberal, the revolutions ended in defeat everywhere. This was certainly the case in France, where the conflict of June 1848 between the government of the Second Republic and the Parisian unemployed created the political climate for the election of Louis-Napoleon Bonaparte.

How did each author view the revolution of 1848? What guiding emotion do you detect in Tocqueville's *Recollections* of February 24, 1848? What was its source? In formulating your answer, consult the selection in which Tocqueville discusses general aspects of revolution and expresses his ideals of government. What was Marx's view of the failure of the June 1848 revolt? Why was the victory that emerged in 1848 an essential step for Marx toward the final revolution?

Finally, let us compare the political and economic ideals advocated by the liberal Tocqueville and the socialist Marx. Your task here is made more challenging by the assertion of both these political thinkers that they advocated democracy. To understand the differences between them, review their writings to determine how each defined "democracy." Is Tocqueville's conception of democracy expressed primarily in terms of political participation? Is there any room in his thought for social democracy, that is, a more egalitarian distribution of society's wealth? How does Tocqueville characterize his political thought in Source 4? Recall France's history of recurring revolution. Why might he accept a monarch in Europe and an elected head of government in America?

Sources 5 through 7 express especially clearly Marx's democratic philosophy. Does Marx believe in political democracy? How is he concerned

Two Programs
for Social
and Political
Change:
Liberalism
and Socialism

with social democracy? Who would control property, credit, and the means of production in his ideal society? What answers does Marx have to such abuses of industrialization as child labor? What impact would his system have on the lives of its citizens?

Finally, consider the two thinkers' views on the role of government. What role in the lives of its citizens does Tocqueville assign to the government? How does that view mark him as a nineteenth-century liberal? What sort of postrevolutionary government does Marx envision? How does it differ from Tocqueville's ideal? Are there areas where Marx and Tocqueville might agree?

With answers to these fairly specific questions in mind, you are now ready to answer the general questions presented earlier in this chapter: What visions of the future did liberals and socialists propose? How did they hope to realize their ideals? How did their ideologies differ?

EPILOGUE

The selections in this chapter present two contrasting nineteenth-century visions of Western society. Most of what you have read appeared around the middle of the nineteenth century, much of it in the midst of the West's last general outbreak of revolution in 1848. Because both authors wrote about that event and had a definite view of revolution, perhaps it is appropriate to examine briefly how their predictions fared after 1848.

The events of 1848 shook Tocqueville's faith in the growth of democracy founded on limited government and increasing equality of property as well as in political stability and evolutionary change based on respect for the rule of law. Indeed, in 1850 he wrote to his friend Eugène Stoffels of events in France with considerable despair:

> What is clear to me is that for sixty years we have fooled ourselves by believing that we could see the end of revolution. The revolution was thought to have finished at 18 *brumaire*, the same was thought in 1814; I thought myself in 1830 that it could well be at an end . . . I was wrong. It is clear today . . . not only that we have not seen the end of the immense revolution which started before our time, but that today's child will probably not see it.[25]

Tocqueville died in 1859 questioning his vision of the future, and Marx lived on until 1883, also disillusioned, as we have noted, by his own apparent failure decisively to affect the socialist movement. Events after their deaths would have surprised both men. Political change in much of Europe proved to be far more evolution-

25. Tocqueville to Eugène Stoffels, quoted in Jack Lively, *The Social and Political Thought of Alexis de Tocqueville* (Oxford: Clarendon Press, 1962), p. 211. The radical leaders of the French Revolution of 1789–1799 had sought to break with the traditional Western calendar and its Christian observances. Thus they created a new calendar devoid of Christian holidays and with renamed months. The date 18 *brumaire* was the day in 1799 that marked Napoleon's seizure of power in France; 1814 was the year of the restoration of the French monarchy after Napoleon's fall; 1830, of course, was the year King Louis Philippe came to power.

ary than revolutionary in the years after 1848, thanks to several developments predicted neither by Tocqueville nor by Marx.

The liberal ideology represented by Tocqueville became less and less a narrow doctrine of individual freedom. Later liberals, such as the Englishman John Stuart Mill (1806–1873), emphasized that economic liberty reached its limits when it allowed employers to abuse their employees with the low wages and poor working conditions we examined in Chapter 6. Consequently, they supported legislation to rectify many of the worst abuses of industrial employment. Such liberals also believed in political democracy and won extended franchises in countries like England and Italy.

Communist revolution occasionally did break out, as Marx had predicted. But he utterly misjudged the historical developments that produced such revolutions. Writing from the vantage point of the early Industrial Revolution, Marx assumed that working-class misery would intensify and produce communist revolution only in the most industrialized nations. Instead, Marx's revolution broke out in places where he never would have expected it. Peasant populations in countries either on the threshold of industrialization, like Russia in 1917, or not yet industrialized, like China and Vietnam in the 1940s and 1950s, have been the chief adherents of communist revolution. Marx had believed peasants incapable of such ideological mobilization, counting them a politically inert

"sack of potatoes." And, contrary to Marx's prediction that communism would constitute the final stage of human development, such regimes, like that in the former Soviet Union, were breaking down by the early 1990s.

In much of the industrialized West, the widened right to vote, in fact, engendered a new kind of evolutionary socialism quite distinct from Marx's revolutionary socialism. The German Eduard Bernstein (1850–1932) was among the first to recognize that working-class voting rights eliminated the need for Marx's class warfare and revolution. Armed with the vote, Bernstein emphasized, workers could elect parliaments favoring their needs and peacefully win a better life through legislation. The need for revolution was at an end.

In the twentieth century, socialist parties committed to political democracy, sometimes allied with liberals, have been instrumental in bringing greater social equality for working people in much of Western Europe. In modern England, France, Italy, Germany, and other nations, legislation improving working conditions and wages as well as establishing the protection of health and unemployment insurance and old age pensions stands as monument to the widened vote created by liberals and the use of that vote by democratic socialists. The consequent improvement in working-class conditions ultimately resulted in the decline in the broad popular appeal of Marxian revolutionary socialists in much of the West.

CHAPTER SEVENTEEN

TO THE AGE ITS ART,[1]

1870–1920

THE PROBLEM

During World War I, a small group of writers and artists came together in Zurich, Switzerland, to form the core of a movement they called Dada.[2] They chose the name intentionally, precisely because it is a meaningless, nonsensical word conveying their reaction to a West capable of the carnage of the Great War. Dadaists saw everything in Western civilization as absurd and futile, the products of a world become increasingly mechanistic, and they gave form to their vision in startling literary and artistic innovations designed to mock conventional modes of expression. A dadaist poet cut words randomly from newspapers, dropped them into a bag and shook them up, then drew them out and assembled them in the order they emerged as a nonsensical poem.[3] A dadaist artist displayed his version of Leonardo da Vinci's *Mona Lisa*, faithful to the original save for a mustache added, an act that at the time appeared shockingly disrespectful of artistic conventions.[4] In such ways did dadaists call into question all traditional values and modes of expression.

Although the Dada movement had spent itself by 1924, it was nonetheless a highly significant cultural phenomenon, marking the culmination of a number of developments in Western thought that, taken together,

1. "To the age its art": Part of the inscription on the façade of the House of the Secession in Vienna, Austria, built in 1898 as a gallery home for the work of the group of artists calling themselves the Secession because of their break with artistic conventions of the late nineteenth century. The full inscription is: "To the age its art. To the art its freedom."

2. **Dada:** the precise origin of this term has been explained in various ways. It means "hobbyhorse" in French, and one version of its origin holds that it was selected by a random opening of a French dictionary at the word *dada*. Others explain "Dada" as the "Da, Da," that is "Yes, Yes," of the Romanian conversation of one of its founders. Whatever its actual origins, the term was nonsensical to most Europeans in 1918. The original Dada *Manifesto* issued in Berlin in 1918 is reprinted in Hans Richter, *Dada: Art and Anti-Art*, trans. David Britt (New York: Oxford University Press, 1978), pp. 104–107.

3. Tristan Tzara (1896–1963).

4. Marcel Duchamp (1887–1968).

419

represented for many an intellectual crisis, a real challenge to traditional values and beliefs during the period from about 1870 to 1920.

The traditional values and beliefs of most nineteenth-century Westerners were founded on the tenets of Judeo-Christian religion and the legacy of the eighteenth-century Enlightenment. From the Bible, most Westerners derived their faith in a Creator. From the Enlightenment, they drew a belief in the rational nature of humans and their ability to use their intellectual gifts to understand and master the physical world (see Chapter 3). In the last years of the nineteenth century and the first years of the twentieth century, however, the findings of physical and social scientists called traditional values and beliefs into question while failing to advance an alternative faith. At the same time, as we will see, the art of the age reflected an increasing knowledge of the physical world and the diminished authority of old standards of thought and behavior. We will note here only the more important late-nineteenth-century developments in Western knowledge that contradicted traditional thought, some aspects of which continue to stir controversy a century later.

Western religious beliefs met challenges on several fronts after 1870. The pioneering English biologist Charles Darwin (1809–1882) had presented his theory of evolution as it applied to animals in his 1859 classic, *On the Origin of Species*. In 1871 Darwin published what was for many a more disturbing work, *Descent of Man*, in which he applied his evolu-

tionary theories to mankind.[5] Educated Westerners suddenly found that their religious beliefs, grounded on the story of the Creation in the Bible's book of Genesis, conflicted with the rational framework of the natural science in which they also put great stock. The result was a crisis of belief that still manifests itself in parts of the West in struggles over the content of public school biology courses.

At the same time that Darwin's work challenged one basic article of the Judeo-Christian faith, archaeological and biblical studies diminished the uniqueness of the Judeo-Christian heritage. Increasing Western knowledge of ancient Middle Eastern civilization, for example, revealed a great cultural kinship between the Hebrews of the Old Testament and the Babylonians and other ancient peoples. Similarly, scholars of the New Testament period found remarkable parallels to the story of the life of Christ in non-Christian cultures. Was the Judeo-Christian heritage, based on a belief in the Jews as God's chosen people and in a Savior of humankind, as unique as it had previously seemed? The debate still continues between religious fundamentalists and those who accept an increasing body of knowledge founded on scholarship and not faith.

As modern scholarship challenged traditional religious thought, it also raised doubts about the intellectual legacy of the eighteenth century. A central tenet of the Enlightenment held

5. The full titles of these works were *On the Origin of Species by Means of Natural Selection or the Preservation of Favored Races in the Struggle for Life* and *The Descent of Man in Relation to Sex*.

that reason was the supreme and exclusive achievement of human-kind. The work by psychological and biological researchers in the late nineteenth and early twentieth centuries, however, cast increasing doubt on the validity of that belief. Wilhelm Wundt (1832–1920) opened the first experimental psychology laboratory at the University of Leipzig in 1870. His purpose was to conduct experiments on animal subjects to demonstrate that the animal mind and the human mind were fundamentally similar. The Russian physiologist Ivan Pavlov (1849–1936), conducting similar laboratory experiments with dogs in the 1890s, determined that certain responses in his subjects could be conditioned—that is, learned and unlearned. The emerging behaviorist school of psychology to which Pavlov's experiments contributed held that most human actions and emotions, like those of the laboratory dogs, could be similarly conditioned. The human mind suddenly seemed quite similar to that of the animal. Such a concept did not accord with the Enlightenment belief in human rationality. Even more destructive of reason as the cornerstone of human behavior was the work of the Austrian physician Sigmund Freud (1856–1939).

Freud began his pioneering work in mental disorders in the 1880s, achieving success with a therapeutic process in which he allowed his patients to talk freely about their childhood memories, their emotions, and their fantasies. The result of his work was the modern school of psychoanalysis and a very unsettling view of the human mind. Freud and other psychological researchers posited the existence of the human unconscious, an irrational and inaccessible portion of the psyche that exerted tremendous influence, through feelings and impulses repressed from consciousness, on human behavior. Indeed, for Freud, the unconscious was a virtual battleground of conflicting inner forces. The *id* embodied base and instinctual drives, such as sex and violence, which demanded immediate, hedonistic gratification. The *superego*, on the other hand, embraced the conventions of society and the strictures of religion that aimed at repressing such impulses. Between these two extremes was the *ego*, the mediating point of consciousness in which some sort of balance between the hedonistic drives of the id and the repressive tendencies of the superego had to be achieved for the well-balanced mind. The goal of Freud's psychoanalysis was to defuse potentially dangerous unconscious impulses by making them conscious, that is, drawing them into the patient's field of awareness, where they could then be examined and treated.

After Freud, reason could no longer be upheld as the motivating principle of human behavior. The optimistic view of progress—that is, that history and human development moved toward better and better forms—also declined as a result of the work of two pioneering sociologists, the Frenchman Emile Durkheim (1858–1917) and the German Max Weber (1864–1920). In examining his society, Durkheim found that modern times in the West were not necessarily an improvement over the past. In medieval and early modern Europe, social station was determined at birth and traditional social values and religious strictures dictated the individual's comportment within his or her station. In the modern Western world, however, the individual enjoyed greater freedom at the same time that the force of traditional religious and social controls waned. Anarchy threatened society, and *anomie*, a loss of personal direction resulting from the collapse of moral guidelines, afflicted the individual and contributed, Durkheim said, to the West's high rate of suicide. Consequently, he believed, the modern world required a new, secular moral order.

Max Weber examined the results of the Enlightenment effort to explain the physical world scientifically and to organize governments rationally around constitutions and bureaucratic procedures. The results had been high scientific accomplishment and stable government won at the cost of human creativity and personal freedom. The modern institutions of the state and corporations aim at domination of the individual. Thus Weber pessimistically concluded his essay "Politics as a Vocation" with the words: "Not summer's bloom lies ahead of us, but rather a polar night of icy darkness and hardness. . . ."[6] Progress, for Weber and others, was a mixed blessing.

Other social theorists advanced a different but equally disturbing view

6. Quoted in H. H. Gerth and C. Wright Mills, editors and translators, *From Max Weber: Essays in Sociology* (New York: Oxford University Press, 1946), p. 128.

of the world, one marked by strife, violence, and conflict. Marxists, as we saw in Chapter 7, found human existence to be dominated by class conflict; other thinkers advanced equally unsettling visions of human conflict. An important tenet of Enlightenment thought was the basic equality of all humans. Yet some nineteenth-century thinkers, in their enthusiasm for the new scientific discoveries of the age, applied Darwin's biological theory of evolution to society as a whole. Emphasizing the struggle for existence that they found in Darwin's work, they claimed that a process of "survival of the fittest" characterized modern human society. All people were not created equal; rather, the stronger or more intelligent had a right to triumph and survive in life's struggle, whereas others did not. Such an application of Darwin's ideas, known as Social Darwinism, could be used, for example, to justify imperialism on the grounds that a "superior" people had a right to rule an "inferior" people (see Chapter 9). According to this view, despite the progressive improvement predicated by Enlightenment thinkers, human beings still were engaged in a primal struggle for existence.

Philosophers, too, joined in the criticism of the Christian tradition, the Enlightenment, and the modern world. Indeed, the German philosopher Friedrich Nietzsche (1844–1900) offered the most thoroughgoing rebuttal of Enlightenment thought and everything associated with it. Nietzsche saw the modern world in decay because its elevation of reason had undermined the capacity to feel passionately, to will, and to be creative. But if he attacked the Enlightenment tradition, Nietzsche was equally hostile to Christianity. An atheist, he proclaimed that "God is dead," people's belief in the supernatural having been effectively destroyed by generations of rational scientific thinking. And yet, Nietzsche maintained, Christianity continued to exert a large and harmful influence, and its moral dictates still inhibited people's will to act spontaneously and creatively. Nietzsche also deplored the growth of democratic government, which in his view subjected the creative few to the authority of the mediocre majority—the common herd. Nietzsche advocated instead the leadership of a few superior persons, or *Übermenschen* ("overmen" or "higher men"), philosopher-rulers whose wills would be unencumbered by the controls of rational thought, Christianity, or democratic rule.

Even the work of the Scientific Revolution, which formed the basis for the Enlightenment (see Chapter 3), came under attack in the half-century from 1870 to 1920. Nineteenth-century science was based on Newtonian physics, which held that the human intellect could discern the basic laws that structured the physical world. With such knowledge, scientists confidently believed that they could ultimately predict the development of the physical world. The result of scientific research in our period, however, has proved instead the existence of a highly unpredictable world.

In classical physics, the atom was considered a solid, indivisible particle and the basis of all matter. In a number of scientific breakthroughs, however, this concept, along with certain laws of Newtonian physics, was disproved. In 1897 Joseph John Thomson (1856–1940), an English physicist, discovered that the atom is not solid but composed of electrons revolving around a nucleus. Niels Bohr (1855–1962), a Danish physicist, found in 1913 that the electrons do not adhere to Newton's laws of motion. The German physicist Werner Heisenberg (1901–1976) summed up this and other work in modern atomic physics shortly after 1920 in his *uncertainty principle*, which posited that modern physicists could only attempt to describe what occurrences were probable in subatomic matter. Nothing was absolutely certain, some people concluded. Heisenberg's principle prompted one distinguished traditional scientist of the era to exclaim in disbelief, "I refuse to believe that God plays dice with the world!"

The work of Albert Einstein (1879–1955) marked the culmination of research in the physical sciences in our period. Einstein dislodged another cornerstone of traditional science, the notion that time, space, and matter were absolute and measurable phenomena. In Einstein's *relativity theory,* time and space became relative, not absolute concepts. Moreover, energy and matter might be converted into each other. Expressed in the famous equation E (energy) $= m$ (mass) $\times c^2$ (speed of light squared), this concept was to have literally earth-shattering results when the splitting of the atom allowed the conversion of matter into vast and potentially destructive amounts of energy. Einstein's work brought the world to the threshold of the atomic age while discrediting the long-held tenets of absolute time and space.

The greatest challenge to the world view of nineteenth-century Westerners, however, came not as abstract theory but as devastating reality: World War I (see Chapter 11). Many intellectuals and artists initially joined their fellow citizens in welcoming a war that they believed would revitalize the West. In that conflagration, however, every belligerent government harnessed modern science and industry to its war effort. The result was bloodletting on an unprecedented scale that caused intellectuals and artists to despair of traditional values—the mood represented by the Dada movement. As the Dada *Manifesto* declared: "After the carnage, we keep only the hope of a purified humanity."

By the early decades of the twentieth century, then, the patterns of nineteenth-century Western thought seemed under assault on every front. As old ways of thinking fell to the new discoveries in the physical and social sciences, Western artistic expression cast off old norms as well, often with provocative results. To take the example of music, a number of composers of the early twentieth century abandoned traditional harmonies in their compositions, producing a new dissonant sound. The first performance in 1913 of a ballet, *The Rite of Spring,* by one of these composers, Igor Stravinsky (1882–1971), almost provoked a Paris audience to riot. To composers like Stravinsky, harmony no longer seemed appropriate in a world of discord.

Reflecting the trends of the period 1870 to 1920, another art form, painting, also abandoned traditional conventions during this time of intellectual crisis. Your goal in this chapter is to examine the magnitude of the transformations in Western thought of this period by analyzing the works of a group of major painters. How do the paintings reflect a break with traditional artistic standards? What trends can be traced from each artist's work? How did artists reveal the intellectual currents of the period in their works?

SOURCES AND METHOD

This chapter introduces you to a primary source historians traditionally have used in studying a past era—its art. Analysis of a period's works of art can provide the historian with an excellent entry into the intellectual life of that epoch because art often reflects the thought of its age. But we must be clear about what is and is not part of the analytical process you must carry out with this chapter's evidence.

The evidence should not be the object of your aesthetic analysis, that is, your attempt to determine which paintings express your individual concept of beauty. We all have opinions and preferences regarding art, especially the modern art this chapter presents. Consequently, you might be inclined simply to dismiss some of the paintings reproduced here as "strange looking" because they do not accord with your individual taste.

You should, however, analyze the paintings in the context of their times. To help focus your analysis, the paintings selected all have a common subject, the human form, to enable you to appreciate the different visions artists brought to the problem of portraying their fellow humans. They also are arranged roughly chronologically to show you both traditional nineteenth-century art before 1870 and some of its main trends over the half-century from 1870 to 1920. You should attempt to assess the impact that these works would have had on their contemporary viewers. Try to imagine yourself as an educated Western European born about 1850 and living until 1920. You would have reached maturity about 1870 and, in the course of your lifetime, would have experienced tremendous change. Materially, you would have been born in an age in which most people traveled by foot or horse and carriage and would have lived to see people traveling by train, automobile, and airplane. Your messages in later life would be carried by telephone and telegraph, and the diseases that threatened your parents would be only a memory by your middle years. In the course of your lifespan of seventy years, then, your material world would have been totally transformed. So, too, would have been your culture's art. Would you have found this transformation unsettling? To supplement your analysis, a brief introduction to the artists whose work this chapter presents is necessary.

Sources 1 and 2, representing two conventional styles of nineteenth-century art, are works whose style would have seemed familiar to their viewers. They are the starting point for your analysis of artistic trends. The French painter Jean-Auguste Dominique Ingres (1780–1867) was an exponent of the neoclassical style of painting. Art historians apply the label "neoclassical" to Ingres and other artists of his period who found much of their inspiration in classical subjects. In the execution of their works, these artists sought to duplicate the harmony, balance, and realism they found in Greek and Roman art. They also often presented classical themes in their works. Source 1, *The Apotheosis of Homer,* is an example of such a work and of the techniques of many early-nineteenth-century artists. In Source 1 Ingres presents his vision of the reception of the Greek poet Homer into the ranks of the gods, symbolized in the painting by his coronation. What do you notice about Ingres's conception of this scene that illustrates classical values of harmony and balance? What in the artist's technical execution of this mythical scene would lead you to characterize his efforts as almost photographic in detail?

Source 2, *Greece Expiring on the Ruins of Missolonghi,* by Eugène Delacroix (1798–1863), is an example of nineteenth-century romanticism. Romanticism arose in large part as a reaction to the Enlightenment with its emphasis on a rational interpretation of the human experience. In literature

425

and art, exponents of the romantic impulse sought to recover the emotion and drama of life. In thus approaching art, many romantic artists were in conscious revolt against the formalism of neoclassical artists like Ingres. The Greek rebellion of the 1820s against Turkey excited European romantics because it was the war for independence of the land of Homer and Plato; and one English romantic poet, Lord Byron, died in Greece seeking to join the rebel cause. Delacroix's painting shows a Greek fighter crushed in the ruins of the city of Missolonghi, where the Greek defenders succumbed in 1826 to a long siege by the Turks. (Missolonghi, not inconsequentially, was the site of Byron's death.) The woman's gesture of defenseless resignation reflects Greek martyrdom. What view of the world and the role of human beings in it did Delacroix convey? What view of the individual does the image of "Greece" convey to you? Compare the paintings of Delacroix and Ingres. Certainly the artists reflected two very different philosophies. Nevertheless, what similarities do you find in their portrayal of the human form?

As your analysis moves beyond Source 2, you must be careful to assess the paintings in light of the intellectual breakthroughs we have just examined. Remember, too, that by 1850 the invention of the camera, with its ability to produce accurate images, obliged artists to make a serious reevaluation of the function of their art. What was the purpose of the labor involved in re-creating the details in Sources 1 and 2 in portraits when a photograph would capture an even more accurate image?

In Source 3 we encounter the work of an artistic movement that reflected the late nineteenth century's interest in science and the reassessment of the artistic function prompted by the camera. With the impressionist artists who flourished especially in France in the 1870s and 1880s, we see a reconsideration of the whole function of painting that relegated portraiture to the photographer. We also find a systematic attempt, much in the vein of modern science, to portray the artist's subjects with an accuracy that would convey to the viewer the subtle effects of light and shadow as they actually appeared to the human eye.

Some impressionists executed their works with large splashes of color. Georges Seurat (1859–1891) moved beyond this technique to a postimpressionism that he called pointilism in which he created pictures with intricate arrangements of tiny dots of color, the result of his study of scientific theories of color perception. *A Sunday Afternoon on the Island of La Grande Jatte* shows excursioners on an island in the river Seine near Paris. What was the artist's purpose in this painting? Why did he pay so little apparent attention to developing the individual characteristics of the persons in his painting? How would you characterize the figures in *La Grande Jatte*?

In the 1870s many viewed impressionism and the work of Seurat as a dramatic revolt against artistic conventions, but far more was to come. The Dutchman Vincent van Gogh (1853–1890) studied the impressionists and moved beyond them. He gloried in the use of broad brush strokes to express his excitement and emotions in a picture, distorting images in that quest. His work thus makes him an early exponent of another style of art, expressionism. A deeply religious man, van Gogh sought to express his personal vision of his subjects while also seeking in them what he called "that something of the eternal which the halo used to symbolize."[7] Source 4, his portrait *La Berceuse* (The Cradle Rocker), employs startling colors: The woman's hair is orange, her dress green, the wallpaper background green and pink flowers, and the floor red. What feelings did the artist seek to express here? Compare *La Berceuse* with the work of Ingres. Why did van Gogh engage in such obvious distortions of the human shape?

Paul Gauguin (1848–1903) also emerged from the impressionists to create a style called symbolism. Gauguin had two careers, first as a successful Parisian stockbroker, then as an impoverished artist. Indeed, he left his family and business for his art in 1883. In rejecting his middle-class past, he also rejected much of modern industrial society. Gauguin found that Westerners had lost much of life's emotions and mystery in their progress toward the industrial age with its concern for material gain. Western art, he believed, reflected this loss, and he sought to reinfuse the missing

emotion into his paintings by studying the art of non-Western peoples. Gauguin spent most of his last years in the South Pacific trying to capture the spirit of non-Western art. A number of artists followed Gauguin's lead in exploring non-Western art, especially after World War I, which convinced them of the bankruptcy of Western culture and values. Indeed, later artists sought non-Western inspiration more widely than Gauguin; many, for example, incorporated African art forms in their work. In Source 5, Gauguin's painting *Manao Tupapau—The Spirit of the Dead Watches*, how has he added non-Western elements in achieving his artistic goal? How did he inject a fantastic element into Western art?

Source 6, *The Dream*, is the work of Frenchman Henri Rousseau (1844–1910). A self-taught artist, Rousseau spent the first half of his adulthood as a government customs inspector, and his paintings reflect his lack of traditional training. *The Dream* is a fantastic, impossible, and highly detailed scene that conveys Rousseau's view of life. What does the choice of a dream as his subject tell you about the artist's outlook? Does the artist present a realistic group of figures in the nude, the lions, and the snake charmer? Why might you think that Rousseau sought to paint the same natural and non-Western settings that Gauguin did?

The work of the Norwegian artist Edvard Munch (1863–1948) reflected the influence of van Gogh, Gauguin, and the philosophical thought of his day. His *The Scream*, Source 7, is an expressionist work. Even more than

7. Quoted in H. W. Janson, *History of Art: A Survey of the Major Visual Arts from the Dawn of History to the Present Day* (New York: Harry N. Abrams and Prentice-Hall, 1962), p. 507.

van Gogh, however, Munch subordinated detail and character study to a strong message. What sentiments does the central figure convey in *The Scream*? How does the artist's treatment of the background magnify the feelings of the central character? What might the artist be saying about the central figure's relationships with other people?

The work of van Gogh and Gauguin influenced other artists as well. Exhibits of their works in Paris during the first years of the twentieth century inspired a group of young artists to break so much with artistic conventions that their contemporaries called them *les Fauves,* or "The Wild Beasts." And in Vienna, a group of artists calling themselves "The Secession" to reflect their abandonment of traditional modes of artistic expression flourished in the last decades of the nineteenth century and in the twentieth century prior to World War I. The leading artist in this group was Gustav Klimt (1862–1918), a contemporary of Freud, in whom we can plainly see the intellectual and artistic turmoil of this period. Like other artists, Klimt challenged stylistic convention. But what really made his work especially controversial was his apparent rejection of the norms of morality and good taste embraced by late-nineteenth- and early-twentieth-century middle- and upper-class Europeans and his negation of that group's faith in the eventual triumph of liberal ideas and scientific progress (see Chapter 7).

Controversy engulfed Klimt when he was commissioned by the government to provide paintings for the ceremonial hall ceilings of the new University of Vienna building (see Chapter 8). Klimt's commission was to portray "Philosophy," "Medicine," and "Jurisprudence," and his work was expected to have reflected the nineteenth century's scientific and intellectual triumphs and the growth of political liberalism with its concern for justice for all. Instead, Klimt provided paintings, controversial in the extreme because they were to have been paid for with public funds, that offered primitive sexuality and death, the expression of all the dark forces that questioned the very idea of progress. The government rejected the paintings, for not only did they question the progress of the age, they also caused many in the public to charge Klimt with creating pornography.

Source 8 presents one of Klimt's best-known paintings, *The Kiss,* a work completed in 1907–1908 after the university controversy. This painting reflects Klimt's rebellion in several ways. Its background color is gold, demonstrating Klimt's interest in pre-twentieth-century media, especially Byzantine gold mosaics. What else do you notice about it? Why would its divorce from reality lead you to consider this abstract art? The painting contains a great deal of symbolism, too. How do you think many in early-twentieth-century audiences responded to the rectangles on the cloak of the male figure and the ovals on that of the female when you understand that these forms were generally taken to symbolize the genital organs of each figure? Why do you think Klimt's art might have been the most controversial of all?

A young Spanish artist, Pablo Picasso (1881–1973), moved to Paris in 1900 and immediately reflected in his work the influence of many of the artists we have discussed. Yet Picasso went beyond them in the extent of his break with artistic tradition. Source 9, *Les Demoiselles d'Avignon*, shocked Picasso's audiences in several ways in 1907. First, its subject is a group of prostitutes on Avignon Street in Barcelona. Second, it is an early expression of the cubist style in art, in which the artist used a variety of wedges and angles to create his picture.

In *Les Demoiselles d'Avignon*, Picasso abandoned traditional rules of perspective as well as any effort to portray the human form accurately. Some found his cubism almost an attempt to portray his subjects geometrically; others remarked that Picasso's women looked like arrangements of broken pieces of glass. Certainly, too, this work represents Picasso's exploration of forms of artistic expression from Africa and parts of the non-Western world. Why do you think Picasso abandoned artistic conventions? Can you discern any parallels between Picasso's art and the physical science of Einstein and others? What trend in modern art is reflected in the two faces on the picture's right?

Picasso was one of a number of abstract artists at work early in the twentieth century. Abstract art puts primary emphasis on the structure, not the subject, of the picture. Another abstract artist was the German George Grosz (1893–1959), who joined the Dada movement after World War I. Grosz's works show cubist influences in a type of collage technique; they also frequently have a social message, as in Source 10, *Germany, A Winter's Tale*. Completed amid the famine and defeat that overtook Germany in the last days of World War I, this painting presents Grosz's views on the war and the society that produced it. The central figure is an "average" German surrounded by a kaleidoscope of Berlin scenes. What do you notice about the plate in front of him? What comment does this make on the Germany of 1918? What social groups do the three figures at the bottom represent? What roles did they play in pre-1918 German society, according to the artist? What vision of German society in 1918 does the background convey?

The final artist whose work appears in our evidence is the Frenchman Marcel Duchamp (1887–1968). Duchamp joined the Dada movement in despair after World War I, and it was he who created the *"Mona Lisa"* with the mustache that we described earlier in this chapter. Even before the war, however, his work challenged all artistic conventions. Source 11, *Nude Descending a Staircase, Number 1*, challenged traditionalists, who found little here resembling a human being. It also challenged the artistic rebels of the day; cubists, accustomed to presenting static forms, rejected the obvious motion of Duchamp's figure. Cubists forced the picture's removal from the major modern art exhibit in Paris in 1912, and traditionalists were scandalized when the picture appeared at the Armory Show of modern art in New York in 1913. Why do you think the artist rejected any attempt to portray the human form accurately? What manner of comment on the machine age might this work be making? How and why were artists like Duchamp striving for a new and more subjective reality?

Using this background on the painters, turn now to the evidence. As you look at the paintings, seek to assess the magnitude of the changes in Western thought in the period 1870–1920. How do the paintings reflect a break with traditional artistic standards? What trends can be traced from each artist's work? How did the artists reveal the intellectual currents of the period in their works?

THE EVIDENCE

1. Jean-Auguste Dominique Ingres, *The Apotheosis of Homer*, 1827

Source 2 from the Musée des Beaux Arts, Bordeaux/Cliché des Musées Nationaux-Paris.

2. Eugène Delacroix, *Greece Expiring on the Ruins of Missolonghi*, 1827

3. Georges Seurat, A Sunday Afternoon on the Island of La Grande Jatte, 1884–1886

Source 4 from the Stichting Kröller-Müller, Otterlo.

4. Vincent van Gogh, *La Berceuse,* 1889

Source 5 from the Albright-Knox Art Gallery, Buffalo, New York (A. Conger Goodyear Collection). Oil on burlap mounted on canvas, 28½″ × 38⅜″.

5. Paul Gauguin, *Manao Tupapau—The Spirit of the Dead Watches*, 1892

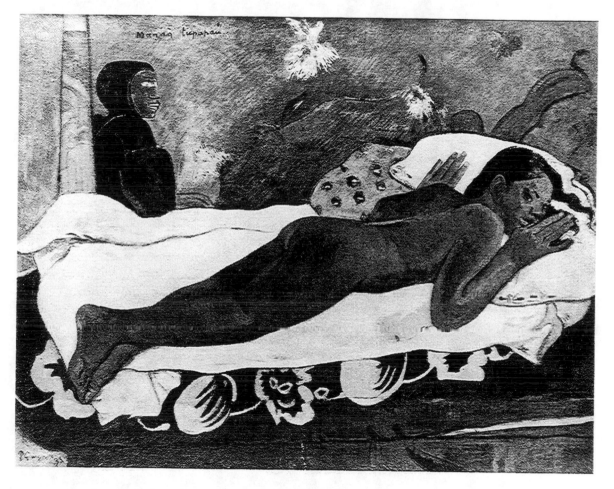

Source 6 from Collection, The Museum of Modern Art, New York (Gift of Nelson A. Rockefeller).
6'8½" × 9'9½".

6. Henri Rousseau, *The Dream*, 1910

Source 7 from the Nasjonalgalleriet, Oslo. Photograph by J. Lathion.

7. Edvard Munch, *The Scream*, 1893

8. Gustav Klimt, *The Kiss*, 1907–1908

9. **Pablo Picasso,** *Les Demoiselles d'Avignon,* 1907

Source 10 formerly from the Collection Garvens, Hanover, Germany (painting has been lost).

10. George Grosz, Germany, A Winter's Tale, 1918

11. Marcel Duchamp, *Nude Descending a Staircase, Number 1, 1911*

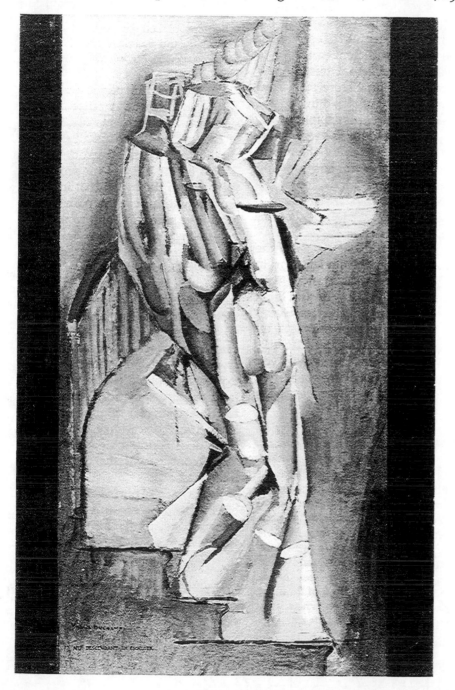

QUESTIONS TO CONSIDER

As we saw in Chapter 8, free public education was becoming more widely available in Western Europe by the late nineteenth century. The number of people with sufficient education to understand intellectual trends grew rapidly in the years before 1920. Consequently, the shifts in thinking we are examining in this chapter were evident to a considerably larger audience than that of the Enlightenment (Chapter 3). Many in this growing educated class must have found the upheavals in the natural sciences, philosophy, and art of their day unpredictable and disturbing.

At the most basic level, consider the changes in art in the period 1870 to 1920. Contrast Sources 1 and 2 with the art that follows. How do you think nineteenth-century audiences would have received the impressionists' offerings after a steady diet of works like Sources 1 and 2? How would you account for the following reaction in 1876 by one French journalist to an early impressionist exhibit?

The Rue le Peletier is a road of disasters. After the fire at the Opera, there is now yet another disaster there. An exhibition has just been mounted at Durand-Ruel [gallery] which allegedly contains paintings. I enter and my horrified eyes behold something terrible. Five or six lunatics, among them a woman, have joined together and exhibited their works. I have seen people rock with laughter in front of these pictures, but my heart bled when I saw them. These would-be artists call themselves revolutionaries, "Impressionists." They take a piece of canvas, colour and brush, daub a few patches of colour on them at random, and sign the whole thing with their name. It is a delusion of the same kind as if the inmates of Bedlam picked up stones from the wayside and imagined they had found diamonds.[8]

But the art of the period was the result of an aesthetic impulse far more significant than change for the sake of change, and perhaps all the more significant for that reason. Art reflected a new view of the world and the place of the individual in it. You must now examine the paintings reproduced here in light of the emerging intellectual outlook we examined at the outset of this chapter. How did the impressionists respond to the great faith in science that characterized their age? Why do you find in the work of the postimpressionist Seurat far less emphasis on the individual than in the work of Ingres and Delacroix? What vision of life does Seurat express? What philosophical changes (and responses by educated persons to those changes) might this diminished importance have represented? How does Seurat's view of the individual contrast with that of later artists like Picasso?

Van Gogh's portrait *La Berceuse* offered its viewers an expression of the artist's sentiments. Why was van Gogh expressing his own feelings

8. Quoted in E. H. Gombrich, *The Story of Art* (New York: Phaidon, 1971), pp. 392–393. **Bedlam:** the early English institution for the insane.

through the medium of another individual rather than creating a photolike replica of that person? What developments in nineteenth-century thought did he reflect in this study of his subject?

In the works of Gauguin we find a search for an art with more meaning than that produced by Western civilization, which the artist found sterile. How would those familiar with the work of Nietzsche, Durkheim, Weber, and perhaps Marx have interpreted Gauguin's work? Remember, too, that Gauguin painted during the age of imperialism (see Chapter 9). How does his art stand in relation to his age's avowed belief in the superiority of Western civilization, the rallying point of the Social Darwinists?

Munch's *The Scream* brings together in one work of art many tendencies in late-nineteenth- and early-twentieth-century thought. Recall the ideas of Durkheim and Weber. Why did Munch portray his subject as a solitary individual? What do you think provoked the agonized scream? Although Munch's work predated most of Freud's great writings, why might you think that Munch and Freud shared a common view of the human psyche?

Consider next Klimt's *The Kiss*. Why do you think Freud's work on the human mind might have influenced Klimt? Many viewers of Klimt's work would have seen it as an attack. What was the artist attacking? George Grosz satirized the world in which he lived. Recall particularly the ideas of the pioneering German sociologist Max Weber and the steril-

ity he found in an increasingly bureaucratized world. What elements of Weber's thought do you find embodied in Grosz's response to German society?

You may find that Picasso's *Les Demoiselles d'Avignon* reflects several trends in Western thought. What is the significance of mathematical and geometric relationships in the cubist approach to the human form? What contrasting message is given by the masklike faces on the right of the picture? How do they reflect some of the same influences Gauguin experienced? What was the effect of the age's ideas on Picasso?

Consider Rousseau's *The Dream*. In one of his most significant works, *The Interpretation of Dreams* (1900), Freud sought to understand the irrational side of the human psyche, the unconscious, by explaining the psychological meaning of dreams. How does Rousseau's vision of reality coincide with Freud's? What significance might you ascribe to the nude and the powerful lions in the context of Freud's work?

The final painting is Duchamp's nude. Review our findings on the paintings that precede his chronologically. Why are you probably not surprised to find in his work a painting totally devoid of anything resembling the human form? What trends in art culminate in Duchamp's work? Remember that he eventually became a dadaist. Can you detect in the nude a message about the machine age and its impact on the individual?

As you answer these questions, you should gain a better understanding

443

of the sweeping intellectual changes that overtook the late-nineteenth- and early-twentieth-century Western world. The dadaist outlook on Western civilization, described in the introduction to this chapter, embodied one extreme reaction to those changes, and the art we have studied presents other responses. You should now be able to answer the central questions of this chapter: How did the paintings reflect a break from traditional artistic standards? What trends can be identified in each artist's work? Finally, how did the artists collectively reveal the intellectual currents of the period?

EPILOGUE

In a sense, this chapter presents a turning point in the history of Western civilization. The West after 1920 was in many ways a far less secure place than the West of the eighteenth and nineteenth centuries, when Europe had been equally secure in its world power and its world view. The nineteenth century in particular had produced a standard of living in the West higher than ever before enjoyed by people anywhere. Westerners were convinced of their primacy.

As the nineteenth century drew to a close, however, many Europeans looked to a disturbing future. Certainly the trends in art we have observed here continued. Dadaism gave way to surrealism, which drew on the artist's unconscious. Later, abstract expressionism and other styles would also develop to present viewers with even greater challenges to their interpretive skills. Other undercurrents were even more distressing, however. Intellectually, the authority of the old faiths and tenets that long had guided Westerners eroded for many persons, and the consequent questioning of traditional values and practices invaded every area of human endeavor. Internationally, the strength of the European powers was challenged by the rise of non-European nations like the United States and Japan. Politically, the nineteenth-century faith in democracy would be challenged by twentieth-century totalitarian movements that reminded many of the threat Max Weber saw in an irrational but charismatic leader (see Chapter 13). Technologically, humankind's progress meant that it had developed unprecedented ability to destroy life (see Chapter 11). Economically, nineteenth-century bourgeois capitalism faced the challenge of communist revolution. The art of the period 1870–1920 reflected all these disturbing developments.

Indeed, the art produced after 1920 by surrealist, abstract expressionist, and other modern artists mirrored the changes in the West that came with accelerating speed after the period we have examined in this chapter. Einstein's work unlocked the destructive possibilities of the atom, and Western science was to create technologies of war far in excess of those employed in World War I. In the giant corporations that came to dominate the Western economy, the individual's significance diminished still further. Using the analytical technique you have mastered in this chapter, you may wish to continue exploring the ideological messages of modern art beyond the period 1870–1920.

CHAPTER EIGHTEEN

WORLD WAR I:

TOTAL WAR

THE PROBLEM

In the first days of August 1914, every major capital city in Europe was the scene of enthusiastic patriotic demonstrations in favor of the declarations of war that began World War I. All confidently predicted victory for their own nation, and all expected a short war. Emperor William II (Kaiser Wilhelm II) told German troops departing for the front, "You will be home before the leaves have fallen from the trees." The war indeed ended in autumn, but it was the autumn of 1918, not 1914. Previous military history did not prepare Europeans in any way for the war they were to undertake in 1914.

Europe's last general war had ended in 1815 with Napoleon's defeat at Waterloo. Subsequent nineteenth-century conflicts never involved all the great powers, and they were invariably short wars. The Prussians, for example, had defeated Austria in six weeks during the Austro-Prussian War of 1866. In the last nineteenth-century conflict involving major powers, the Franco-Prussian War of 1870–1871, France and Prussia had signed an armistice after a little over twenty-seven weeks of combat.

These nineteenth-century wars after Waterloo were also highly limited conflicts, involving relatively small professional armies whose weapons and tactics differed little from those of the Napoleonic era. Civilian populations seldom felt much impact from such conflicts, although Paris endured a siege of eighteen weeks in the Franco-Prussian War.

The war on which Europeans so enthusiastically embarked in 1914 proved far different from the 1870–1871 conflict. The prewar alliance system meant that, for the first time in a century, all the great powers were at war, making the scope of the hostilities greater than in any recent fighting. Moreover, the conflict quickly became a world war as the belligerents fought one another outside Europe and as non-European powers such as Japan and the United States joined the ranks of warring nations.

Even more significant than the number of nations engaged in the conflict, however, was the nature of the war they fought. The Industrial Revolution of the nineteenth century had brought technical changes to warfare that were to transform the 1914 conflict into the Western world's first modern, total war. This would be a war of tremendous cost to both soldiers and civilians, a struggle requiring effort and sacrifice by every citizen of the warring countries.

Modern railroads and motorized transport permitted belligerent nations to bring the full weight of their new industrial strengths to the battlefields of World War I. Both sides for the first time made extensive use of the machine gun as well as new, longer-range heavy artillery. Whole new weapons systems included flame throwers, poison gas, the tank, the airplane, the lighter-than-air dirigible, and the submarine.

Generals trained in an earlier era of warfare failed at first to understand the increased destructive capacity of these new weapons and practiced military tactics of 1870 in fighting the war's first battles. As before, they attacked the enemy with massed infantrymen armed with bayonets fixed, flags flying, drums sounding, and led by officers in dress uniforms complete with white gloves. This was the kind of war Europeans had enthusiastically anticipated in 1914, but because of modern firepower, casualties in such attacks were extremely heavy—indeed, completely unprecedented.

Especially in Western Europe, such losses resulted in increased reliance on what has been called the "infantryman's best friend," the shovel. To avoid the firepower of the new modern weaponry, opposing armies dug into the earth, and by Christmas 1914 they opposed each other in 466 miles of trenches stretching through France from the English Channel to the border of Switzerland. These trenches represented stalemate. They were separated by "No Man's Land," the open space an attacker had to cross to reach the enemy. Swept with machine gun and artillery fire and blocked by barbed wire and other obstacles, "No Man's Land" was an area that an attacking force could cross only with great losses. In such circumstances, neither side could achieve the traditional decisive breakthrough into the enemy's lines. Field Marshal Horatio Kitchener, an experienced commander of the old school of warfare and British Secretary for War until 1916, expressed the frustration of many about such combat: "I don't know what is to be done—this isn't war."

In their efforts to achieve victory, generals and statesmen sought to break the stalemate in a number of ways that extended the impact of World War I. The warring nations mobilized unprecedented numbers of men; over 70 million were called to military service. Never before had so large a part of Europe's population been put in uniform: England mobilized 53 percent of its male population of military age in 1914–1918, and France and Germany called on the service of some 80 percent of their males of draft age.

Each government involved took unprecedented steps to meet its forces' needs for food, material, and ammunition. Governments rationed consumer goods to provide for their armies. England and Germany asserted extraordinary government control over raw materials, privately owned production facilities, and civilian labor in the name of war production.

Civilians felt the war in other ways, too. The stalemate meant a long war, and governments soon recognized that they could not maintain their war efforts during a long conflict if civilian morale broke. Each warring government therefore attempted to exert total control over news and public opinion, often at the expense of its citizens' rights. They censored the press, used propaganda to maintain civilian morale, and placed critics under surveillance or arrest.

Each warring nation also recognized the equal importance of the home front to their enemies in achieving victory. As a result, civilians experienced the war in unprecedented ways. Blockades by surface fleets and submarine attacks on shipping aimed at slowing war production and destroying civilian morale by cutting off vital shipments of raw materials and food to enemy countries. New weapons systems also placed civilians in actual physical danger. Warring nations dropped bombs on their enemies' cities from dirigibles and primitive bomber aircraft, and long-range artillery rained shells on population centers miles from battlefronts.

This was the world's first total war; until the outbreak of another such war in 1939, participants remembered it as the "Great War." Your task in this chapter is to assess the all-encompassing nature of modern warfare through several different kinds of sources. Why was World War I different from previous wars? What impact did it have on the soldiers at the front? How did it affect civilians at home?

SOURCES AND METHOD

As we have seen in Chapter 10, artists and intellectuals at first joined other Europeans in welcoming World War I. They believed that the conflict would sweep away a decadent cultural life and replace it with one that was more vital. Many talented and well-educated men sought to hasten this cultural transformation by volunteering for military service. Front-line combat, however, soon showed these young men that they were caught up in a war unlike any previous struggle. Conscious of the uniqueness of their battlefield experience and aware that their front-line service would leave them forever changed, many made an effort to record their experiences. Letters, diaries, autobiographical works, paintings, and sketches by individual soldiers all supplement the dry official records kept by war ministries of the participating countries and give the historian an excellent sense of battlefield realities and their impact. Your main sources in this chapter comprise creative works, in the form of poetry and fiction, in which a number of talented soldiers sought to convey the experience of modern war and its effect on them.

Literature can be a valuable source for the student of history in understanding the past. We must, however, stay fully aware of its limits as well as its value. The utility of literature as a historical source is somewhat limited by its very nature: As the product of an individual, it reflects personal and social perspectives that must be identified. Most of the authors represented here, for example, came from the middle or upper classes because such individuals, not the sons of the working classes, had the education to write works of enduring significance. With such a social background, many served as officers, and the conditions they endured were in some ways better than those of the enlisted men: The war was often significantly worse for a private than for a captain.

Individuals have opinions, too, and opinions often invade war literature. The soldier often portrayed himself as a victim of forces beyond his control: a powerful government, modern technology, or the military authorities. As historians, we must note these opinions because they convey to us the individual's reaction to the war, but we must look beyond them as well to discern the objective wartime conditions the author was recording.

Not all chroniclers of the war were equally well placed to understand the war. We must ask if each work was based on actual front-line experience. If not, we should discount it as historical evidence. We must also ask if an author's work was written in the midst of war, in which case it may reflect the passions of the moment. If the work was written after the war, the author's selective memory for certain facts may have influenced his or her work. The evidence in this chapter presents works by front-line authors written both at the time of their experiences and after the war. Indeed, the great majority of literary works on the war appeared, like the literature on Vietnam, about a decade after the cessation of hostilities. Perhaps a gestation period is necessary for the minds of many to analyze the combat experience. If that is the case, we must recognize the frailty of the human memory and measure the message of postwar literature against those writings composed in the heat of battle.

Once the various viewpoints and perspectives are identified, however, a student of history can obtain an excellent sense of World War I through works of poetry and fiction. These works present the war in human terms far more vividly than do government reports and statistics. To assist your reading, some information on each of the writers presented here is in order.

Rupert Brooke (1887–1915), the author of Source 1, was a graduate of Cambridge University and one of England's most promising young poets when he enlisted in September 1914 as a sublieutenant in the Royal Naval Division, a land force attached to the British Navy. After brief service in Belgium in 1914, his unit was dispatched to the Middle East in 1915 as part of the British and French attack on the Turks at Gallipoli—a strategy designed to open the straits to the Black Sea so that Western supplies could reach Russia. (The attack itself, in which many Australian and New Zealand troops perished, was generally deemed a disaster.) Not quite twenty-eight years of age, Brooke died of blood poisoning en route to Gallipoli and was buried on the island of Skyros, Greece, home of Achilles of the ancient Homeric myths. The selection by Brooke presented here, the poem "Peace," reflects the romanticism characteristic of much prewar English poetry but also expresses Brooke's response to the war. What were his sensations as he watched the war engulf Europe? How does he characterize the spirit of pre-World War I Europe? What will awaken that spirit? Why do you think his poem suggests that Brooke would welcome death?

A remarkable Frenchman, Charles Péguy (1873–1914), wrote Source 2, "Blessed Are." Péguy was a talented poet and essayist, much of whose work expresses his nationalism as well as his concern for the poor and the cause of social justice. His writings also reflect a remarkable spiritual journey. Raised a Catholic, his dislike for the authoritarian character of the Church grew by the time he reached adulthood, and he declared himself an atheist about 1893. In 1908, however, he rediscovered a deep religious faith, though he kept his distance from the institutional

Church and probably never participated in its sacramental life. Péguy's later writings bear witness to this religiosity as well as to his continued concern for his fellow man and his French nationalism.

Péguy was forty-one when war broke out in 1914, and he therefore qualified for the army reserve, not front-line duty. Always a man of action, however, he volunteered for active service. Commissioned a lieutenant of infantry, he died leading his men in an attack on September 5, 1914. Remember the details of his life as you read "Blessed Are." What elements of Péguy's thought does the poem combine? What was his view of war? Although Péguy's national and religious background was different from that of the English Protestant Brooke, what ideas did he share with Brooke? Why do you think other intellectuals also drew on the romanticism and nationalism of the late nineteenth and early twentieth centuries to welcome war?

Source 3, the "Hymn of Hate," is the work of the German poet Ernst Lissauer (1882–1937), who served as a private in the German army. Composed as the war broke out, the poem was soon set to music and became very popular in Germany. To appreciate its significance fully, you may wish to review in your textbook the sections on nineteenth-century nationalism and on the international rivalries that contributed to World War I. Which nation do the Germans see as their archenemy? Why, after consulting your textbook, do you think this country was so hated in Germany?

Novelists also drew on their wartime experiences. Henri Barbusse (1873–1935), the author of *Under Fire,* worked as a French government employee and a journalist before World War I. Politically a socialist, he was swept up by the general surge of patriotism in 1914 and volunteered for military service. He served in the French army from 1914 through the early days of the great Battle of Verdun in 1916, when he was wounded and left the service. In *Under Fire,* which was written in the trenches, he attempted to portray realistically the physical and psychological impact of modern war. The novel was recognized early as an important work and received France's most prestigious literary award, the Goncourt Prize, in 1916. The excerpt presented as Source 4 describes an attack on the Germans by veteran French infantrymen led by their trusted Corporal Bertrand. How does Barbusse describe modern warfare?

Excerpts from a second novel, *All Quiet on the Western Front* (Source 5), offer us the view of the losing side in the war. Its author, Erich Maria Remarque (1898–1970), grew up the son of a German bookbinder. Drafted at the age of eighteen, he served in the German army from 1916 to the war's end. Remarque had already begun to write before his military service, and his *All Quiet on the Western Front* represented such a realistic picture of the war that many perceived it as an attack on German patriotism. As a consequence, the novel was among the first batch of books burned by the Nazis in 1933. How does Remarque describe the experience of modern warfare? What effect did it have on the many youthful front-line soldiers like the main character, Paul Baumer? What impact did that war have on German civilians?

Two poems conclude our literary evidence on World War I. Source 6, "Dulce et Decorum Est" ("It is sweet and fitting"), is the work of Wilfred Owen (1893–1918). Owen studied briefly at the University of London before the war, intending a career in the clergy. He enlisted in the British army in 1915, aged twenty-two, and as an infantry lieutenant served in France in the great Battle of the Somme. Owen was wounded three times in 1917 and recuperated in England, where he met Siegfried Sassoon, author of the next selection, who encouraged Owen in his writing. After recovering from his wounds, Owen again served on the western front. He received the Military Cross for bravery in October 1918 and died leading his men in an attack on November 4, 1918, one week before the war's end.

Owen's battlefield experiences shaped his poetry. "Dulce et Decorum Est" is titled with a phrase from the Roman poet Horace, whose work would have been familiar to all upper-class English schoolboys of Owen's day. How would you summarize Owen's view of the war, especially his opinion of those on the home front who blindly supported it?

Siegfried Sassoon (1886–1967), author of "The General" (Source 7), was seven years older than his friend Owen, and his poetic response to the war is the reaction of one with greater experience of life and its problems. A Cambridge graduate like Rupert Brooke, he had written poetry since his boyhood. The war transformed Sassoon from an upper-class young man who enjoyed the hunt to a postwar social activist and socialist. Although he served with great bravery as a front-line officer, he experienced an increasingly bitter sense of the war's futility. Wounded in 1917, he had a long convalescence in England and went through an emotional crisis as he attempted to balance his growing pacifism with his enduring sense of duty and the comradeship he felt with those still on the front line. Sassoon's response was to throw away his Military Cross awarded for bravery and to draft a letter of protest of the war to his commanding officer. Stating that a war undertaken as one of defense had become a war of conquest, he declared, "I can no longer be a party to prolong those sufferings for ends which I believe to be evil and unjust." Such a letter from an officer in wartime would normally have resulted in court-martial. Intervention of friends on his behalf led instead to Sassoon's treatment for shell shock, a common psychological problem among front-line troops. It was during his hospitalization for this treatment that Sassoon met Owen. Returning to service in 1918, Sassoon was wounded again but lived to survive the war. His poem, "The General," is very brief, but it reflects Sassoon's attitude toward the war. How does Sassoon view the general?

Participants in the war left other personal records of the conflict in the form of letters and autobiographical works. The letters in Sources 8 and 9 record such remarkable events in the midst of total war that people then, as now, tended to doubt they ever occurred. Nevertheless, the stories of these two anonymous German soldiers can be verified in the writings of their battlefield opponents. How had initial enthusiasm for the war and hatred of the enemy fared at the front? Why?

World War I was the first conflict to demand great participation in the war effort from women. Yet, oddly, few left extensive written records of the war's effect on them. Source 10, drawn from the Englishwoman Vera Brittain's (1893–1970) *The Testament of Youth,* is one of the few works we have by a woman. A student at Oxford when England declared war, Brittain left her studies shortly after for service as a nurse, and her book in part records the war from that vantage point. It also gives us a sense of the war's impact on those at the home front. What kind of warfare does Brittain describe the Germans as practicing? What was their objective in such warfare? What effect did the war have on Brittain?

Sources 11 through 15 are evidence of a nonpersonal nature, reports and statistics amassed by modern governments of the kind we have examined in earlier chapters. Nevertheless, such material will allow you to amplify your understanding of the impact of total warfare. Source

11, taken from the official record compiled by the U.S. Army's forces occupying the Rhineland area of Germany at the war's end, describes the rations for Germany's civilian population during the last days of the war in 1918. These rations reflect the effects of a British naval blockade of the ports of Germany, established to cut the country off from imported food and strategic raw materials. Because prewar Germany was not self-sufficient in food production, the effect of such a blockade was great.

In analyzing this ration information, we must, as students of history, recognize that the supplies shown here may not completely reflect the German dietary situation. Rationing presumes that producers placed all foodstuffs at their government's disposal. In practice they did not, because rationing was based on government-regulated prices that were invariably lower than free market prices in a period of shortage. The result was a lively black market trade in foodstuffs for those who could pay higher prices.

Still, the evidence here does indicate the basic ration for many Germans. Analyze this record. What dietary basics do you find lacking or in short supply? What did German civilians eat a great deal of during the war? What cumulative effect do you think such a diet, imposed by total war, had on German civilians?

The strain of warfare was not only a matter of food and other material restrictions, however. As we noted earlier, warring governments tried to gauge and influence public opinion because they knew that total warfare would become untenable if civilian spirit broke. In Source 12 you will read a report to French police officials from the area of Grenoble in southeastern France in 1917. What does that report show about public opinion? In calling millions of men for military service, total war created tremendous labor shortages and yet another strain on civilians in all countries. Who filled the jobs vacated by men in England, according to Source 13? How did governments pay for modern warfare, according to Source 15?

The ultimate cost of the war can be measured in human lives lost. Official casualty figures, however, present considerable problems of analysis. We must first understand that all such figures are approximate. Deficiencies in wartime record keeping are part of the problem, but governments manipulated figures, too. During the war, security considerations led to consistent understatements of losses by each warring nation to prevent the enemy from knowing its manpower resources. At the war's end, some victorious governments allegedly inflated figures as a basis for postwar claims on their defeated enemies.

The figures for military deaths in Source 14 are taken from a recent study attempting to determine the best estimates of war losses from several sources, not just governmental records. Though we still must accept those figures as only approximations, they do allow a good sense of the relative losses of each country. Which suffered the greatest numerical losses? In which armies did a man mobilized for military service have the greatest chance of being killed? What do the high casualty rates of certain Eastern European countries tell you about those nations' capacities to wage modern warfare? Among the great powers, which nation lost the greatest portion of its population?

As you now read the evidence for this chapter, keep all these questions in mind. They should aid you in answering the central questions posed: Why was World War I different from previous wars? What impact did it have on soldiers at the front? How did it affect civilians at home?

THE EVIDENCE

THE FRONT LINES

Source 1 from Geoffrey Keynes, editor, The Poetical Works of Rupert Brooke *(London: Faber and Faber, 1960), p. 19.*

1. Rupert Brooke, "1914 Sonnet: I. Peace," 1914

Now, God be thanked Who has matched us with His hour,
   And caught our youth, and wakened us from sleeping,
With hand made sure, clear eye, and sharpened power,
   To turn, as swimmers into cleanness leaping,
Glad from a world grown old and cold and weary,
   Leave the sick hearts that honour could not move,
And half-men, and their dirty songs and dreary,
   And all the little emptiness of love!

Oh! we, who have known shame, we have found release there,
   Where there's no ill, no grief, but sleep has mending,
     Naught broken save this body, lost but breath;
Nothing to shake the laughing heart's long peace there
   But only agony, and that has ending;
     And the worst friend and enemy is but Death.

Source 2 from Charles Péguy, Basic Verities: Prose and Poetry, *translated by Ann and Julian Green (New York: Pantheon, 1943), pp. 275–277.*

2. Charles Péguy, "Blessed Are," 1914

Blessed are those who died for carnal earth
Provided it was in a just war.
Blessed are those who died for a plot of ground.
Blessed are those who died a solemn death.

Blessed are those who died in great battles,
Stretched out on the ground in the face of God.
Blessed are those who died on a final high place,
Amid all the pomp of grandiose funerals.

Blessed are those who died for carnal cities.
For they are the body of the city of God.
Blessed are those who died for their hearth and their fire,
And the lowly honors of their father's house. . . .

Blessed are those who died, for they have returned
Into primeval clay and primeval earth.
Blessed are those who died in a just war.
Blessed is the wheat that is ripe and the wheat that is gathered in sheaves.

Source 3 from Ernst Lissauer, Jugend (1914). *Translated by Barbara Henderson,* New York Times, *October 15, 1914.*

3. Ernst Lissauer, "Hymn of Hate," 1914

French and Russian they matter not,
A blow for a blow and a shot for a shot;
We love them not, we hate them not,
We hold the Weichsel and Vosges-gate,[1]
We have but one—and only hate,
We love as one, we hate as one,
We have one foe and one alone.

1. The Germans possessed defensible boundaries against the Russians and the French. In the east, they held the Vistula (*Weichsel*) River in Poland as a barrier to Russian attack. In the west, they blocked the French attack with their possession of the Vosges Mountains.

He is known to you all, he is known to you all,
He crouches behind the dark grey flood,
Full of envy, of rage, of craft, of gall,
Cut off by waves that are thicker than blood.
Come, let us stand at the Judgment place,
An oath to swear to, face to face,
An oath of bronze no wind can shake,

An oath for our sons and their sons to take.
Come, hear the word, repeat the word,
Throughout the Fatherland make it heard.
We will never forego our hate,
We have all but a single hate,
We love as one, we hate as one,
We have one foe, and one alone—

ENGLAND!

In the Captain's mess, in the banquet hall,
Sat feasting the officers, one and all,
Like a sabre-blow, like the swing of a sail,
One seized his glass held high to hail;
Sharp-snapped like the stroke of a rudder's play,
Spoke three words only: "To the Day!"[2]
Whose glass this fate?
They had all but a single hate.
Who was thus known?
They had one foe, and one alone—

ENGLAND!

Take you the folk of the Earth in pay,
With bars of gold your ramparts lay,
Bedeck the ocean with bow on bow,
Ye reckon well, but not well enough now.
French and Russian they matter not,
A blow for a blow, a shot for a shot,
We fight the battle with bronze and steel,
And the time that is coming Peace will seal.

You will hate with a lasting hate,
We will never forego our hate,
Hate by water and hate by land,
Hate of the head and hate of the hand,
Hate of the hammer and hate of the crown,

2. **To the Day!:** in German naval officers' messes before World War I, it was customary to offer a
   toast to "the Day," that is, the day England would be defeated.

Hate of seventy millions, choking down.
We love as one, we hate as one,
We have one foe, and one alone—

ENGLAND!

Source 4 from Henri Barbusse, Under Fire: The Story of a Squad, *translated by Fitzwater Wray (New York: E. P. Dutton, 1917), pp. 250–259.*

4. From Henri Barbusse, *Under Fire: The Story of a Squad,* 1916

We are ready. The men marshal themselves, still silently, their blankets crosswise, the helmet-strap on the chin, leaning on their rifles. I look at their pale, contracted, and reflective faces. They are not soldiers, they are men. They are not adventurers, or warriors, or made for human slaughter, neither butchers nor cattle. They are laborers and artisans whom one recognizes in their uniforms. They are civilians uprooted, and they are ready. They await the signal for death or murder; but you may see, looking at their faces between the vertical gleams of their bayonets, that they are simply men.

Each one knows that he is going to take his head, his chest, his belly, his whole body, and all naked, up to the rifles pointed forward, to the shells, to the bombs piled and ready, and above all to the methodical and almost infallible machine-guns—to all that is waiting for him yonder and is now so frightfully silent—before he reaches the other soldiers that he must kill. They are not careless of their lives, like brigands, nor blinded by passion like savages. In spite of the doctrines with which they have been cultivated they are not inflamed. They are above instinctive excesses. They are not drunk, either physically or morally. It is in full consciousness, as in full health and full strength, that they are massed there to hurl themselves once more into that sort of madman's part imposed on all men by the madness of the human race. One sees the thought and the fear and the farewell that there is in their silence, their stillness, in the mask of tranquillity which unnaturally grips their faces. They are not the kind of hero one thinks of, but their sacrifice has greater worth than they who have not seen them will ever be able to understand.

They are waiting; a waiting that extends and seems eternal. Now and then one or another starts a little when a bullet, fired from the other side, skims the forward embankment that shields us and plunges into the flabby flesh of the rear wall. . . .

A man arrives running, and speaks to Bertrand, and then Bertrand turns to us—

"Up you go," he says, "it's our turn."

All move at once. We put our feet on the steps made by the sappers, raise ourselves, elbow to elbow, beyond the shelter of the trench, and climb on to the parapet.

Bertrand is out on the sloping ground. He covers us with a quick glance, and when we are all there he says, "*Allons*, forward!"[3]

Our voices have a curious resonance. The start has been made very quickly, unexpectedly almost, as in a dream. There is no whistling sound in the air. Among the vast uproar of the guns we discern very clearly this surprising silence of bullets around us—

We descend over the rough and slippery ground with involuntary gestures, helping ourselves sometimes with the rifle. . . . On all sides the slope is covered by men who, like us, are bent on the descent. On the right the outline is defined of a company that is reaching the ravine by Trench 97—an old German work in ruins. We cross our wire by openings. Still no one fires on us. Some awkward ones who have made false steps are getting up again. We form up on the farther side of the entanglements and then set ourselves to topple down the slope rather faster—there is an instinctive acceleration in the movement. Several bullets arrive at last among us. Bertrand shouts to us to reserve our bombs and wait till the last moment.

But the sound of his voice is carried away. Abruptly, across all the width of the opposite slope, lurid flames burst forth that strike the air with terrible detonations. In line from left to right fires emerge from the sky and explosions from the ground. It is a frightful curtain which divides us from the world, which divides us from the past and from the future. We stop, fixed to the ground, stupefied by the sudden host that thunders from every side; then a simultaneous effort uplifts our mass again and throws it swiftly forward. We stumble and impede each other in the great waves of smoke. With harsh crashes and whirlwinds of pulverized earth, towards the profundity into which we hurl ourselves pell-mell, we see craters opened here and there, side by side, and merging in each other. Then one knows no longer where the discharges fall. Volleys are let loose so monstrously resounding that one feels himself annihilated by the mere sound of the downpoured thunder of these great constellations of destruction that form in the sky. One sees and one feels the fragments passing close to one's head with their hiss of red-hot iron plunged in water. The blast of one explosion so burns my hands, that I let my rifle fall. I pick it up again, reeling, and set off in the tawny-gleaming tempest with lowered head, lashed by spirits of dust and soot in a crushing downpour like volcanic lava. The stridor of the bursting shells hurts your ears, beats you on the neck, goes through your temples, and you cannot endure it without a cry. The gusts of death drive us on, lift

3. **Allons:** "Let's go!"

us up, rock us to and fro. We leap, and do not know whither we go. Our eyes are blinking and weeping and obscured. The view before us is blocked by a flashing avalanche that fills space.

It is the barrage fire. We have to go through that whirlwind of fire and those fearful showers that vertically fall. We are passing through. We are through it, by chance. Here and there I have seen forms that spun round and were lifted up and laid down, illumined by a brief reflection from over yonder. I have glimpsed strange faces that uttered some sort of cry—you could see them without hearing them in the roar of annihilation. A brasier full of red and black masses huge and furious fell about me, excavating the ground, tearing it from under my feet, throwing me aside like a bouncing toy. I remember that I strode over a smoldering corpse, quite black, with a tissue of rosy blood shriveling on him; and I remember, too, that the skirts of the great-coat flying next to me had caught fire, and left a trail of smoke behind. On our right, all along Trench 97, our glances were drawn and dazzled by a rank of frightful flames, closely crowded against each other like men.

Forward!

Now, we are nearly running. I see some who fall solidly flat, face forward, and others who founder meekly, as though they would sit down on the ground. We step aside abruptly to avoid the prostrate dead, quiet and rigid, or else offensive, and also—more perilous snares!—the wounded that hook on to you, struggling.

The International Trench! We are there. The wire entanglements have been torn up into long roots and creepers, thrown afar and coiled up, swept away and piled in great drifts by the guns. Between these big bushes of rain-damped steel the ground is open and free.

The trench is not defended. The Germans have abandoned it, or else a first wave has already passed over it. Its interior bristles with rifles placed against the bank. In the bottom are scattered corpses. From the jumbled litter of the long trench, hands emerge that protrude from gray sleeves with red facings, and booted legs. In places the embankment is destroyed and its woodwork splintered—all the flank of the trench collapsed and fallen into an indescribable mixture. In other places, round pits are yawning. . . .

We have spread out in the trench. The lieutenant, who has jumped to the other side, is stooping and summoning us with signs and shouts—"Don't stay there; forward, forward!"

We climb the wall of the trench with the help of the sacks, of weapons, and of the backs that are piled up there. In the bottom of the ravine the soil is shot-churned, crowded with jetsam, swarming with prostrate bodies. Some are motionless as blocks of wood; others move slowly or convulsively. The barrage fire continues to increase its infernal discharge behind us on the ground that we have crossed. But where we are at the foot of the rise it is a dead point for the artillery.

A short and uncertain calm follows. We are less deafened and look at each other. There is fever in the eyes, and the cheek-bones are blood-red. Our breathing snores and our hearts drum in our bodies.

In haste and confusion we recognize each other, as if we had met again face to face in a nightmare on the uttermost shores of death. Some hurried words are cast upon this glade in hell—"It's you!"—"Where's Cocon?"—"Don't know."—"Have you seen the captain?"—"No."—"Going strong?"—"Yes."

The bottom of the ravine is crossed and the other slope rises opposite. We climb in Indian file by a stairway rough-hewn in the ground: "Look out!" The shout means that a soldier half-way up the steps has been struck in the loins by a shell-fragment; he falls with his arms forward, bareheaded, like the diving swimmer. We can see the shapeless silhouette of the mass as it plunges into the gulf. I can almost see the detail of his blown hair over the black profile of his face.

We debouch upon the height. A great colorless emptiness is outspread before us. At first one can see nothing but a chalky and stony plain, yellow and gray to the limit of sight. No human wave is preceding ours; in front of us there is no living soul, but the ground is peopled with dead—recent corpses that still mimic agony or sleep, and old remains already bleached and scattered to the wind, half assimilated by the earth.

As soon as our pushing and jolted file emerges, two men close to me are hit, two shadows are hurled to the ground and roll under our feet, one with a sharp cry, and the other silently, as a felled ox. Another disappears with the caper of a lunatic, as if he had been snatched away. Instinctively we close up as we hustle forward—always forward—and the wound in our line closes of its own accord. The adjutant stops, raises his sword, lets it fall, and drops to his knees. His kneeling body slopes backward in jerks, his helmet drops on his heels, and he remains there, bareheaded, face to the sky. Hurriedly the rush of the rank has split open to respect his immobility.

But we cannot see the lieutenant. No more leaders, then—— Hesitation checks the wave of humanity that begins to beat on the plateau. Above the trampling one hears the hoarse effort of our lungs. "Forward!" cries some soldier, and then all resume the onward race to perdition with increasing speed.

"Where's Bertrand?" comes the laborious complaint of one of the foremost runners. "There! Here!" He had stooped in passing over a wounded man, but he leaves him quickly, and the man extends his arms toward him and seems to sob.

It is just at the moment when he rejoins us that we hear in front of us, coming from a sort of ground swelling, the crackle of a machine-gun. It is a moment of agony—more serious even than when we were passing through the flaming earthquake of the barrage. That familiar voice speaks to us across the plain, sharp and horrible. But we no longer stop. "Go on, go on!"

Our panting becomes hoarse groaning, yet still we hurl ourselves toward the horizon.

"The Boches![4] I see them!" a man says suddenly.

"Yes—their heads, there—above the trench—it's there, the trench that line. It's close. Ah, the hogs!"

We can indeed make out little round gray caps which rise and then drop on the ground level, fifty yards away, beyond a belt of dark earth, furrowed and humped. Encouraged they spring forward, they who now form the group where I am. So near the goal, so far unscathed, shall we not reach it? Yes, we will reach it! We make great strides and no longer hear anything. Each man plunges straight ahead, fascinated by the terrible trench, bent rigidly forward, almost incapable of turning his head to right or to left. I have a notion that many of us missed their footing and fell to the ground. I jump sideways to miss the suddenly erect bayonet of a toppling rifle. Quite close to me, Farfadet jostles me with his face bleeding, throws himself on Volpatte who is beside me and clings to him. Volpatte doubles up without slackening his rush and drags him along some paces, then shakes him off without looking at him and without knowing who he is, and shouts at him in a breaking voice almost choked with exertion: "Let me go, let me go, *nom de Dieu!*[5] They'll pick you up directly—don't worry."

The other man sinks to the ground, and his face, plastered with a scarlet mask and void of all expression, turns in every direction; while Volpatte, already in the distance, automatically repeats between his teeth, "Don't worry," with a steady forward gaze on the line.

A shower of bullets spurts around me, increasing the number of those who suddenly halt, who collapse slowly, defiant and gesticulating, of those who dive forward solidly with all the body's burden, of the shouts, deep, furious, and desperate, and even of that hollow and terrible gasp when a man's life goes bodily forth in a breath. And we who are not yet stricken, we look ahead, we walk and we run, among the frolics of the death that strikes at random into our flesh.

The wire entanglements—and there is one stretch of them intact. We go along to where it has been gutted into a wide and deep opening. This is a colossal funnel-hole, formed of smaller funnels placed together, a fantastic volcanic crater, scooped there by the guns.

The sight of this convulsion is stupefying; truly it seems that it must have come from the center of the earth. Such a rending of virgin strata puts new edge on our attacking fury, and none of us can keep from shouting with a solemn shake of the head—even just now when words are but painfully torn from our throats—"Ah, Christ! Look what hell we've given 'em there! Ah, look!"

4. **Boches:** a derogatory term applied by the French to German soldiers, originating from the French *caboche,* or blockhead.

5. **nom de Dieu:** "Name of God!"

Driven as if by the wind, we mount or descend at the will of the hollows and the earthy mounds in the gigantic fissure dug and blackened and burned by furious flames. The soil clings to the feet and we tear them out angrily. The accouterments and stuffs that cover the soft soil, the linen that is scattered about from sundered knapsacks, prevent us from sticking fast in it, and we are careful to plant our feet in this débris when we jump into the holes or climb the hillocks.

Behind us voices urge us—"Forward, boys, forward, *nom de Dieu!*"

"All the regiment is behind us!" they cry. We do not turn round to see, but the assurance electrifies our rush once more.

No more caps are visible behind the embankment of the trench we are nearing. Some German dead are crumbling in front of it, in pinnacled heaps or extended lines. We are there. The parapet takes definite and sinister shape and detail; the loopholes—we are prodigiously, incredibly close!

Something falls in front of us. It is a bomb. With a kick Corporal Bertrand returns it so well that it rises and bursts just over the trench.

With that fortunate deed the squad reaches the trench.

Pépin has hurled himself flat on the ground and is involved with a corpse. He reaches the edge and plunges in—the first to enter. Fouillade, with great gestures and shouts, jumps into the pit almost at the same moment that Pépin rolls down it. Indistinctly I see—in the time of the lightning's flash—a whole row of black demons stooping and squatting for the descent, on the ridge of the embankment, on the edge of the dark ambush.

A terrible volley bursts point-blank in our faces, flinging in front of us a sudden row of flames the whole length of the earthen verge. After the stunning shock we shake ourselves and burst into devilish laughter—the discharge has passed too high. And at once, with shouts and roars of salvation, we slide and roll and fall alive into the belly of the trench!

Source 5 from Erich Maria Remarque, All Quiet on the Western Front *(New York: Fawcett Crest, 1969), pp. 167–171, 174–175. "Im Westen Nichts Neues" copyright 1928 by Ullstein A.G.; copyright renewed 1956 by Erich Maria Remarque. "All Quiet on the Western Front" copyright 1929, 1930 by Little, Brown and Company; copyright renewed 1957, 1958 by Erich Maria Remarque.*

5. From Erich Maria Remarque, *All Quiet on the Western Front*, 1928

We have been able to bury Müller, but he is not likely to remain long undisturbed. Our lines are falling back. There are too many fresh English and American regiments over there. There's too much corned beef and white wheaten bread. Too many new guns. Too many aeroplanes.

But we are emaciated and starved. Our food is so bad and mixed up with so much substitute stuff that it makes us ill. The factory owners in Germany have grown wealthy;—dysentery dissolves our bowels. The latrine poles are always densely crowded; the people at home ought to be shown these grey, yellow, miserable, wasted faces here, these bent figures from whose bodies the colic wrings out the blood, and who with lips trembling and distorted with pain, grin at one another and say: "It is not much sense pulling up one's trousers again—"

Our artillery is fired out, it has too few shells and the barrels are so worn that they shoot uncertainly, and scatter so widely as even to fall on ourselves. We have too few horses. Our fresh troops are anæmic boys in need of rest, who cannot carry a pack, but merely know how to die. By thousands. They understand nothing about warfare, they simply go on and let themselves be shot down. A single flyer routed two companies of them for a joke, just as they came fresh from the train—before they had ever heard of such a thing as cover.

"Germany ought to be empty soon," says Kat.

We have given up hope that some day an end may come. We never think so far. A man can stop a bullet and be killed; he can get wounded, and then the hospital is his next stop. There, if they do not amputate him, he sooner or later falls into the hands of one of those staff surgeons who, with the War Service Cross in his buttonhole, says to him: "What, one leg a bit short? If you have any pluck you don't need to run at the front. The man is A1.[6] Dismiss!"

Kat tells a story that has travelled the whole length of the front from the Vosges to Flanders;—of the staff surgeon who reads the names on the list, and when a man comes before him, without looking up says: "A1. We need soldiers up there." A fellow with a wooden leg comes up before him, the staff surgeon again says A1—"And then," Kat raises his voice, "the fellow says to him: 'I already have a wooden leg, but when I go back again and they shoot off my head, then I will get a wooden head made and become a staff surgeon.' " This answer tickles us all immensely.

There may be good doctors, and there are, lots of them; all the same, every soldier some time during his hundreds of inspections falls into the clutches of one of these countless hero-grabbers who pride themselves on changing as many C3's and B3's as possible into A1's.

There are many such stories, they are mostly far more bitter. All the same, they have nothing to do with mutiny or lead-swinging. They are merely honest and call a thing by its name; for there is a very great deal of fraud, injustice, and baseness in the army.—Is it nothing that regiment after regiment returns again and again to the ever more hopeless struggle, that attack follows attack along the weakening, retreating, crumbling line?

From a mockery the tanks have become a terrible weapon. Armoured they come rolling on in long lines, and more than anything else embody for us war's horror.

---

6. **A1**: the highest category of physical fitness, that is, qualified for front-line duty.

We do not see the guns that bombard us; the attacking lines of the enemy infantry are men like ourselves; but these tanks are machines, their caterpillars run on as endless as the war, they are annihilation, they roll without feeling into the craters, and climb up again without stopping, a fleet of roaring, smoke-belching armour-clads, invulnerable steel beasts squashing the dead and the wounded—we shrivel up in our thin skin before them, against their colossal weight our arms are sticks of straw, and our hand-grenades matches.

Shells, gas clouds, and flotillas of tanks—shattering, starvation, death.

Dysentery, influenza, typhus—murder, burning, death.

Trenches, hospitals, the common grave—there are no other possibilities.

In one attack our company commander, Bertinck, falls. He was one of those superb front-line officers who are foremost in every hot place. He was with us for two years without being wounded, so that something had to happen in the end.

We occupy a crater and get surrounded. The stink of petroleum or oil blows across with the fumes of powder. Two fellows with a flame-thrower are seen, one carries the tin on his back, the other has the hose in his hands from which the fire spouts. If they get so near that they can reach us we are done for, we cannot retreat at the moment.

We open fire on them. But they work nearer and things begin to look bad. Bertinck is lying in the hole with us. When he sees that we cannot escape because under the sharp fire we must make the most of this cover, he takes a rifle, crawls out of the hole, and lying down propped on his elbows, he takes aim. He fires—the same moment a bullet smacks into him, they have got him. Still he lies and aims again;—once he shifts and again takes his aim; at last the rifle cracks. Bertinck lets the gun drop and says: "Good," and slips back into the hole. The hindermost of the two flame-throwers is hit, he falls, the hose slips away from the other fellow, the fires squirts about on all sides and the man burns.

Bertinck has a chest wound. After a while a fragment smashes away his chin, and the same fragment has sufficient force to tear open Leer's hip. Leer groans as he supports himself on his arm, he bleeds quickly, no one can help him. Like an emptying tube, after a couple of minutes he collapses.

What use is it to him now that he was such a good mathematician at school?

The months pass by. The summer of 1918 is the most bloody and the most terrible. The days stand like angels in gold and blue, incomprehensible, above the ring of annihilation. Every man here knows that we are losing the war. Not much is said about it, we are falling back, we will not be able to attack again after this big offensive, we have no more men and no more ammunition. . . .

There are so many airmen here, and they are so sure of themselves that they give chase to single individuals, just as though they were hares. For every one German plane there come at least five English and American. For one hungry, wretched German soldier come five of the enemy, fresh and fit.

For one German army loaf there are fifty tins of canned beef over there. We are not beaten, for as soldiers we are better and more experienced; we are simply crushed and driven back by overwhelmingly superior forces.

Behind us lie rainy weeks—grey sky, grey fluid earth, grey dying. If we go out, the rain at once soaks through our overcoat and clothing;—and we remain wet all the time we are in the line. We never get dry. Those who still wear high boots tie sand bags round the top so that the mud does not pour in so fast. The rifles are caked, the uniforms caked, everything is fluid and dissolved, the earth one dripping, soaked, oily mass in which lie the yellow pools with red spiral streams of blood and into which the dead, wounded, and survivors slowly sink down.

The storm lashes us, out of the confusion of grey and yellow the hail of splinters whips forth the childlike cries of the wounded, and in the night shattered life groans wearily to the silence.

Our hands are earth, our bodies clay and our eyes pools of rain. We do not know whether we still live. . . .

It is autumn. There are not many of the old hands left. I am the last of the seven fellows from our class.

Everyone talks of peace and armistice. All wait. If it again proves an illusion, then they will break up; hope is high, it cannot be taken away again without an upheaval. If there is not peace, then there will be revolution.

I have fourteen days' rest, because I have swallowed a bit of gas; in a little garden I sit the whole day long in the sun. The armistice is coming soon, I believe it now too. Then we will go home.

Here my thoughts stop and will not go any farther. All that meets me, all that floods over me are but feelings—greed of life, love of home, yearning of the blood, intoxication of deliverance. But no aims.

Had we returned home in 1916, out of the suffering and the strength of our experiences we might have unleashed a storm. Now if we go back we will be weary, broken, burnt out, rootless, and without hope. We will not be able to find our way any more.

And men will not understand us—for the generation that grew up before us, though it has passed these years with us here, already had a home and a calling; now it will return to its old occupations, and the war will be forgotten—and the generation that has grown up after us will be strange to us and push us aside. We will be superfluous even to ourselves, we will grow older, a few will adapt themselves, some others will merely submit, and most will be bewildered;—the years will pass by and in the end we shall fall into ruin.

But perhaps all this that I think is mere melancholy and dismay, which will fly away as the dust, when I stand once again beneath the poplars and listen to the rustling of their leaves. It cannot be that it has gone, the yearning that made our blood unquiet, the unknown, the perplexing, the oncoming things, the thousand faces of the future, the melodies from dreams and from books, the whispers and divinations of women, it cannot be that this has vanished in bombardment, in despair, in brothels.

Here the trees show gay and golden, the berries of the rowan stand red among the leaves, country roads run white out to the sky-line, and the canteens hum like beehives with rumours of peace.

I stand up.

I am very quiet. Let the months and years come, they bring me nothing more, they can bring me nothing more. I am so alone, and so without hope that I can confront them without fear. The life that has borne me through these years is still in my hands and my eyes. Whether I have subdued it, I know not. But so long as it is there it will seek its own way out, heedless of the will that is within me. . . .

He fell in October 1918, on a day that was so quiet and still on the whole front, that the army report confined itself to the single sentence: All quiet on the Western Front.

He had fallen forward and lay on the earth as though sleeping. Turning him over one saw that he could not have suffered long; his face had an expression of calm, as though almost glad the end had come.

Source 6 from C. Day Lewis, editor, The Collected Poems of Wilfred Owen *(New York: New Directions, 1964), p. 55.*

6. Wilfred Owen,
"Dulce et Decorum Est,"
ca 1917

Bent double, like old beggars under sacks,
Knock-kneed, coughing like hags, we cursed through sludge,
Till on the haunting flares we turned our backs
And towards our distant rest began to trudge.
Men marched asleep. Many had lost their boots
But limped on, blood-shod. All went lame; all blind;
Drunk with fatigue; deaf even to the hoots
Of tired, outstripped Five-Nines[7] that dropped behind.

Gas! Gas! Quick, boys!—An ecstasy of fumbling,
Fitting the clumsy helmets just in time;

7. **Five-Nines:** one of the types of artillery used by the Germans was the 5.9-inch howitzer, which projected a very large shell in a high arc. As the barrels of such guns became worn, their accuracy was impaired.

But someone still was yelling out and stumbling
And flound'ring like a man in fire or lime . . .
Dim, through the misty panes and thick green light,
As under a green sea, I saw him drowning.

In all my dreams, before my helpless sight,
He lunges at me, guttering, choking, drowning.

If in some smothering dreams you too could pace
Behind the wagon that we flung him in,
And watch the white eyes writhing in his face,
His hanging face, like a devil's sick of sin;
If you could hear, at every jolt, the blood
Come gargling from the froth-corrupted lungs,
Obscene as cancer, bitter as the cud
Of vile, incurable sores on innocent tongues,—
My friend, you would not tell with such high zest
To children ardent for some desperate glory,
The old Lie: Dulce et decorum est
Pro patria mori.[8]

Source 7 from Siegfried Sassoon, Collected Poems, 1908–1956 *(London: Faber and Faber, 1961), p. 75.*

7. Siegfried Sassoon, "The General," ca 1917

'Good-morning; good-morning!' the General said
When we met him last week on our way to the line.
Now the soldiers he smiled at are most of 'em dead,
And we're cursing his staff for incompetent swine.
'He's a cheery old card,' grunted Harry to Jack
As they slogged up to Arras[9] with rifle and pack.

But he did for them both by his plan of attack.

8. From Horace, *Odes*, III, 2, 3: "It is sweet and fitting to die for one's country."

9. **Arras:** city of northeastern France that was the site of a major British attack in April 1917. With heavy artillery bombardment and the element of surprise, the British were able to break through German lines. Unfortunately, excessive caution on the part of British commanders in exploiting their costly initial successes permitted the Germans time to regroup and deprived the British of a sweeping victory.

Source 8 from Rudolf Hoffman, editor, Der deutscher Soldat: Briefe aus dem Weltkrieg *(Munich: 1937), pp. 297–298. Translated and quoted in Hanna Hafkesbrink,* Unknown Germany: An Inner Chronicle of the First World War Based on Letters and Diaries *(New Haven, Conn.: Yale University Press, 1948), p. 141.*

8. New Year's Eve, 1914: Letter from a Former German Student Serving in France

On New Year's Eve we called across to tell each other the time and agreed to fire a salvo at 12. It was a cold night. We sang songs, and they clapped (we were only 60–70 yards apart); we played the mouth-organ and they sang and we clapped. Then I asked if they haven't got any musical instruments, and they produced some bagpipes (they are the Scots guards, with the short petti-coats and bare legs) and they played some of their beautiful elegies on them, and sang, too. Then at 12 we all fired salvos into the air! . . . It was a real good "Sylvester,"[10] just like in peace-time!

Source 9 from A. F. Wedd, editor and translator, German Students' War Letters, *from the original edition by Philipp Witkop (London: Methuen, 1929), p. 36. Quoted in Hanna Hafkesbrink,* Unknown Germany: An Inner Chronicle of the First World War Based on Letters and Diaries *(New Haven, Conn.: Yale University Press, 1948), pp. 141–142.*

9. Christmas Eve, 1916: Letter from a German Soldier Serving in France

There I stood for four hours in the trench on Christmas Eve, up to my ankles in water and slime, and armed with hand grenades and signal shells. My thoughts were far away, my eyes sought the silhouette of the enemy trench. Then suddenly at 12 o'clock there was a solemn pause. From our reserve po-sition came the sound of a quartette singing Christmas carols. Singing in God's out-of-doors as in peacetime, actually only 60 meters[11] away from an embittered enemy. Was this possible? I know of no hour so uplifting and solemn as was this one. Now several Englishmen ventured to sing a lovely song. Yes, this was peace on the battlefield, peace as one had not known it for two and a half years. Neither infantry nor artillery fire disturbed this night of peace. Lost in meditation we stood in the trench and listened to the singing.

10. **Sylvester:** Roman Catholics observe December 31 as the feast of Saint Sylvester.
11. **60 meters:** 198 feet.

THE HOME FRONT

Source 10 from Vera Brittain, The Testament of Youth: An Autobiographical Study of the Years 1900–1925 *(London: Gollancz, 1981), pp. 365–366.*

10. Vera Brittain:
A London Air Raid,
June 13, 1917

Although three out of the four persons were gone who had made all the world that I knew,[12] the War seemed no nearer a conclusion than it had been in 1914. It was everywhere now; even before Victor was buried, the daylight air-raid of June 13th "brought it home," as the newspapers remarked, with such force that I perceived danger to be infinitely preferable when I went after it, instead of waiting for it to come after me.

I was just reaching home after a morning's shopping in Kensington High Street when the uproar began, and, looking immediately at the sky, I saw the sinister group of giant mosquitoes sweeping in close formation over London. My mother, whose temperamental fatalism had always enabled her to sleep peacefully through the usual night-time raids, was anxious to watch the show from the roof of the flats, but when I reached the doorway my father had just succeeded in hurrying her down to the basement; he did not share her belief that destiny remained unaffected by caution, and himself derived moral support in air-raids from putting on his collar and patrolling the passages.

The three of us listened glumly to the shrapnel raining down like a thunder-shower upon the park—those quiet trees which on the night of my return from Malta[13] had made death and horror seem so unbelievably remote. As soon as the banging and crashing had given way to the breathless, apprehensive silence which always followed a big raid, I made a complicated journey to the City[14] to see if my uncle had been added to the family's growing collection of casualties.

When at last, after much negociation [sic] of the crowds in Cornhill and Bishopsgate, I succeeded in getting to the National Provincial Bank, I found him safe and quite composed, but as pale as a corpse; indeed, the whole staff of men and women resembled a morose consignment of dumb spectres newly transported across the Styx.[15] The streets round the bank were terrifyingly

---

12. Vera Brittain lost her fiancée and two other male friends in World War I. The fourth person, her brother Edward, was still alive in June 1917, but perished while serving with the British army in Italy later in 1917.

13. Brittain had served as a military nurse on the British island of Malta in the Mediterranean.

14. **the City:** the financial district of London.

15. **Styx:** in Greek mythology, the river that the souls of the dead must cross as they leave the world of the living.

quiet, and in some places so thickly covered with broken glass that I seemed to be wading ankle-deep in huge unmelted hailstones. I saw no dead nor wounded, though numerous police-supervised barricades concealed a variety of gruesome probabilities. Others were only too clearly suggested by a crimson-splashed horse lying indifferently on its side, and by several derelict tradesman's carts bloodily denuded of their drivers.

These things, I concluded, seemed less inappropriate when they happened in France, though no doubt the French thought otherwise.

Source 11 from the American Military Government of Occupied Germany, 1918–1920, Report of the Officer in Charge of Civil Affairs, Third Army and American Forces in Germany (Washington, D.C.: U.S. Government Printing Office, 1943), pp. 155–156.

11. German Wartime Civilian Rations, 1918

Conditions on arrival of Third Army.—When the Third Army entered its area of occupation, it found the principal foodstuffs rationed, as had been the case for several years. In brief, the situation may be outlined thus, prior to the war, the average food consumption for the German population, expressed in calories, was about 3500 calories per person per day. According to German figures, this had shrunk to 3000 calories in 1914, 2000 in 1915, 1500 in 1916, and to 1200 in the winter of 1917–1918.

All the principal foodstuffs had been rationed during the war, and, on paper at least, every resource of the Empire in the way of food was entirely under control and carefully distributed.

The ration at the beginning of the occupation was essentially as follows:

Bread	260 grams per head per day[16]
Potatoes	500 grams per head per day

The main reliance for sustenance was placed on the above two foods and, except in the large cities, where the supply was subject to much fluctuation, the amounts indicated, or more, were fairly consistently provided during the whole of the year 1919.

In addition, the following substances constituted a part of the ration in the amounts indicated:

16. To convert grams to ounces, multiply grams by 0.035. Thus the German bread ration was a little over 9 ounces per day per person, and the potato ration was 17.5 ounces per person per day.

Meat	200 grams per head per week. Frequently reduced in amount, and often not issued at all.
Fat	150–200 grams per head per week. Later became very scarce.
Butter	20 grams per head per week. Practically never issued in the ration.
Sugar	600–750 grams per head per month.
Marmalade	200 grams per head per week. Often unavailable.
Milk	Not issued at all to the population in general, on account of its scarcity. Issued only to children under 6 years of age and, on physician's certificates, to the sick, nursing mothers, pregnant women and the aged. One half to one litre per day.

Fresh vegetables, in general, were not rationed and were fairly plentiful. Additional substances, such as rice, oats, grits, margarine, sausage, "Ersatz" (substitute) coffee, eggs, and additional flour, were added to the ration from time to time when available.

Source 12 from Jean-Jacques Becker, The Great War and the French People, *translated by Arnold Pomerans (New York: St. Martin's, 1986), pp. 232–234. Reprinted by permission of Berg Publishers.*

12. Report on French Public Opinion in the Department of the Isère

Grenoble, 17 June 1917

The Prefect[17] of the Department of Isère to the Minister of the Interior[18]

Office of the Sûreté Générale[19]

I have the honour to reply herewith to the questions contained in your confidential telegram circulated on *10 June inst.*:[20]

The inquiry I have myself conducted, or with the help of colleagues, to test the opinion of certain leading personages has shown that the morale of the people of Isère is far from satisfactory and that their exemplary spirit has suffered a

17. **prefect:** since the Revolution of 1789, France has been divided into departments. The chief administrative officer in each department, since the time of Napoleon, has been the prefect. The prefect historically has been an appointee of the central government and thus responsible to it and not to local interests.

18. **Minister of the Interior:** most police services in France are under the control of the central government's Ministry of the Interior.

19. **Sûreté Général:** the central police command charged with criminal investigations.

20. **inst.:** An archaic use of "instant" to mean "current." Here it is used to express "June 10th of the current year."

general decline during the past two months. Today there is weariness bordering on dejection, a result less of the curtailment of the public diet and supply difficulties than of the disappointment caused by the failure of our armies in April,[21] the feeling that military blunders have been made, that heavy losses have been sustained without any appreciable gains, that all further offensives will be both bloody and in vain. The inactivity of Russia, whose contribution now seems highly doubtful, has accentuated the decline in morale.[22] The remarks of soldiers coming back from the front are the major cause of this decline: these remarks, made in the trains, in the railway stations, in the cafés on the way home, and then in the villages, convey a deplorable picture of the mentality of a great number of servicemen. Each one tells of and amplifies this or that unpleasant incident, this or that error committed by his commander, this or that useless battle, this or that act of insubordination presented as so many acts of courage and determination. These remarks, listened to with a ready ear by those who are already nervous or depressed enough as it is, are then peddled about and exaggerated with the result that discontent and anxiety are increased further. Each day, incidents in public places, particularly in the large railway stations and on the trains, reflect the most deplorable attitude in the minds of servicemen.

In the countryside, the restive mood is less obvious than it is in the towns; the peasants work, but they do not hide the fact that 'it's been going on too long'; they are tired of their continuous over-exertion in the fields, of the lack of hands and of the very heavy burden of the requisitions. They are growing more and more suspicious and indifferent to the idea of collective effort and mutual solidarity, and to patriotic appeals, and can think only of their immediate interests and their own safety.

Growers increasingly complain about price rises, even though they probably suffer less than others from the cost of living and even though their produce is sold at ever higher prices.

Nevertheless, it is among the rural populations that one finds the greatest composure and resignation.

In the towns, and particularly in the industrial centres, the more impressionable and hence more excitable population—the workers, the ordinary

---

21. In April 1917, the French army had received a new commander, General Nivelle, who launched a massive and costly offensive to break through German lines and end the war. The offensive failed and, coming after great French losses at Verdun in 1916, provoked a mutiny in the army in which soldiers refused orders to attack until August 1917. The mutinies placed the entire French war effort at risk. Order was restored only by a new commander, General Pétain, and a new and authoritarian prime minister, Georges Clemenceau.

22. Russia had experienced a revolution in February 1917 that toppled Tsar Nicholas II from power and replaced him with a republic under a Provisional Government. Although the leaders of this government were committed to Russia's war against Germany, disorganization of Russian armies by the revolution prevented effective Russian action. Because the Russian collapse accompanied Germany's unrestricted submarine warfare against all shipping around England and the disastrous defeat of the Italian armies at Caporetto in October, 1917 was the great year of crisis for France and its allies.

people—are upset about the duration of the struggle, impatient with the increasing cost of living, irritated by the considerable profits being made out of the war by the big industrialists in their neighbourhood, and increasingly taken in by the propagandists of the united Socialist Party and their internationalist ideas. Under the influence of the Russian Revolution they already dream of workers' and soldiers' committees and of social revolution. These sentiments are aired frequently at workers' meetings, called ostensibly to discuss economic or union matters, and in their paper, *Le Droit du Peuple*,[23] which is waging a very skillful anti-war and internationalist campaign.

This attitude, together with the constant rise in the cost of living, has fuelled a widespread demand for wage increases which the employers have quietly met to a large degree. Unfortunately, the calm following these increases has been momentary only. The cost of living keeps rising further and it is painful to watch each wage increase being followed directly by a corresponding increase in the price of food and the cost of board and lodging. Already those workers engaged on national defence contracts are finding that the new wage scales agreed less than two months ago for Grenoble and district have become inadequate; they are presently asking for a cost-of-living allowance of 2 francs a day and have made it quite clear that if their demand is not met there will be trouble in the streets; some of them have even gone so far as to declare that they know where to find the necessary arms, alluding to the shell and explosives factories in the suburbs of Grenoble. I know perfectly well that these remarks were presumably made in order to intimidate the citizens, but it is nevertheless symptomatic that they should have been made in the first place. When they lack the courage to speak out themselves, the factory propagandists use the women working beside them who, running smaller risks, are less restrained in their threats. The demands of the reservists in the munitions factories have been forwarded to the ministry of supply and a number of agitators have been sent away—not to the front, which would have been dangerous, but to other factories in various parts of the area. Calm has therefore been restored, but there are fears that the present lull may be temporary.

If working-class militancy were to make itself felt in the munitions factories in Grenoble and in the industrial centres of the department, it would be very difficult and extremely risky to try to control it by force: the local police force would prove inadequate, even if it were reinforced by gendarmes. It is clearly necessary to strengthen the police contingent, but this can only be done through the deferment of professional policemen serving in the territorial army or the reserve. The auxiliary policemen drawn from the ranks of the retired are admittedly men of goodwill, but they are physically and mentally worn out, and their contribution and energy are inadequate. The relocation, or rather the transfer, of some gendarmerie brigades would be very useful,

---

23. **Le Droit du Peuple:** the *Right of the People.*

but the consequent changes in domicile would involve cumbersome formalities. . . . It would not be unhelpful if an intelligent, serving special commissioner were put in charge, with particular emphasis on the surveillance of aliens who continue to move about freely in the department and can undermine the morale of our people even as these aliens go about the business of gathering information useful to the enemy.

In conclusion, I believe that the present situation, both in respect of morale and also of social stability, while not giving cause for alarm, is far from satisfactory and that it ought to be considered serious enough to call for precautionary measures, and if necessary for energetic intervention.

What is really needed to lift flagging courage and to restore confidence in the future is a military success by our armies, a major Russian offensive, or just a German retreat.

Source 13 from Report of the War Cabinet Committee on Women in British Industry *(London: His Majesty's Stationery Office, 1919).*

13. Employment of Women in Wartime British Industry

Trades	Est. Number Females Employed in July 1914	Est. Number Females Employed in July 1918	Difference Between Numbers of Females Employed in July 1914 and July 1918	Percentage of Females to Total Number Workpeople Employed July 1914	July 1918	Est. Number Females Directly Replacing Males in Jan. 1918
Metal	170,000	594,000	+424,000	9	25	195,000
Chemical	40,000	104,000	+ 64,000	20	39	35,000
Textile	863,000	827,000	− 36,000	58	67	64,000
Clothing	612,000	568,000	− 44,000	68	76	43,000
Food, drink, and tobacco	196,000	235,000	+ 39,000	35	49	60,000
Paper and printing	147,500	141,500	− 6,000	36	48	21,000
Wood	44,000	79,000	+ 35,000	15	32	23,000
China and earthenware	32,000 ⎫					
Leather	23,100 ⎬	197,100	+ 93,000	4	10	62,000
Other	49,000 ⎭					
Government establishments	2,000	225,000	+223,000	3	47	197,000
Total	2,178,600	2,970,600	+792,000	26	37	704,000

475

WAR COSTS

Source 14 from J. M. Winter, The Great War and the British People (Cambridge, Mass.: Harvard University Press, 1986), p. 75. Reprinted by permission.

14. Estimated Military Casualties, by Nation

Country	Total Killed or Died	Total Mobilized (in thousands)	Prewar Male Pop. 15–49	Total Prewar Pop.	Total Killed		
					Per 1,000 Mobilized	Per 1,000 Males 15–49	Per 1,000 People
Britain, Ireland	723	6,147	11,540	45,221	118	63	16
Canada	61	629	2,320	8,100	97	26	8
Australia	60	413	1,370	4,900	145	44	12
New Zealand	16	129	320	1,100	124	50	15
South Africa	7	136	1,700	6,300	51	4	1
India	54	953	82,600	321,800	57	1	0
France	1,327	7,891	9,981	39,600	168	133	34
French colonies	71	449	13,200	52,700	158	5	1
Belgium	38	365	1,924	7,600	104	20	5
Italy	578	5,615	7,767	35,900	103	75	16
Portugal	7	100	1,315	6,100	70	5	1
Greece	26	353	1,235	4,900	73	21	5
Serbia	278	750	1,225	4,900	371	227	57
Rumania	250	1,000	1,900	7,600	250	132	33
Russia	1,811	15,798	40,080	167,000	115	45	11
United States	114	4,273	25,541	98,800	27	4	1
Allied Total	5,421	45,001	204,018	812,521	120	27	7
Germany	2,037	13,200	16,316	67,800	154	125	30
Austria-Hungary	1,100	9,000	12,176	58,600	122	90	19
Turkey	804	2,998	5,425	21,700	268	148	37
Bulgaria	88	400	1,100	4,700	220	80	19
Central Powers' Total	4,029	25,598	35,017	152,800	157	115	26
Total Overall	9,450	70,599	239,035	965,321	134	40	10

Source 15 from Felix Gilbert, *The End of the European Era, 1890 to the Present, 3rd ed.* *(New York: Norton, 1984), p. 161. Used by permission of W. W. Norton & Company Inc.*

15. War Indebtedness to the United States, Through 1918

Great Britain	$3,696,000,000
France	1,970,000,000
Italy	1,031,000,000

QUESTIONS TO CONSIDER

Now that you have read the selections, try to consider them collectively, drawing out the effects of war on the people of Western Europe. First, consider the initial reaction to war. We saw in The Problem that war was universally greeted with patriotic enthusiasm. What forms did that enthusiasm assume in the poems of Brooke, Péguy, and Lissauer? What previous experience had these authors with modern warfare?

Next, assess the experience of front-line service as it is expressed in the literary and other sources. Why do you think the initial ardor for warfare wore off quickly? On whom or what did the writers lay the blame for the horrors of war? How radical was their discontent? Compare their literary reactions to the war with the artistic responses we examined in Chapter 10. Consider again the casualty figures in Source 14 and the descriptions of trench warfare in Sources 4 and 5. Remember that Barbusse wrote during the war and Remarque a decade later. Do their descriptions of modern warfare differ

substantially? What do you think was uppermost in the minds of men subjected to such conditions?

The war inflicted unprecedented battle losses on every belligerent country, but societal groups within the warring countries did not suffer equally. In any combat situation, the highest casualty rate affects noncommissioned and junior officers— the sergeants, lieutenants, and captains who lead attacks at the front of their units. What social groups does Remarque's *All Quiet on the Western Front* suggest made up the officer corps of each warring nation? What postwar effect do you think the loss of such men might have?

The front-line experience had costs for those who survived, too. Why might you conclude from the German soldiers' accounts of the holidays in 1914 and 1916 that one of the war's first casualties was patriotic devotion to its cause? As the war wore on, other reactions to combat became widespread among soldiers. Barbusse said that the war created two separate Frances, front-line and civilian. Does the character of Baumer in Remarque's novel reflect a similar division in Germany? Do you think a sense of alienation was a common reaction among veterans? How would it affect adjustment to postwar civilian life? Finally, assess the poems of Wilfred Owen and Siegfried Sassoon. How might you describe the sentiments expressed in those poems? What view of military authority does Sassoon's poem express? How old were Owen and Sassoon when they began military service? Are sentiments such as theirs usual in persons so young? What was the source for these views?

World War I affected civilian populations in ways no previous conflict had. Drawing on the German ration data, how do you think you would have found German wartime conditions? Why do you think Germans suffered nutritional deficiencies? Did such shortages also affect the German military, according to Source 5?

Every belligerent country recognized that the home front was essential to victory. The areas the Germans attacked in the London bombing described by Vera Brittain certainly lacked obvious military value. The Germans also launched long-range attacks on Paris, and one shell fell on a crowded church on Good Friday, 1918, killing or injuring 200 people. What was the goal of such attacks on targets of no military value? Recall the report to the French police on public opinion in the Grenoble area. What ideas were current among civilians? Why were French authorities so concerned about public opinion?

The war had a deep impact on women, too, Source 13 clearly shows a great spurt in the employment of Englishwomen in many industries.

In which industries especially did they find employment? How were these jobs probably related to the war effort? Women left certain jobs, too. Which did they abandon? Many of the industries they left traditionally offered low-paying employment for unskilled or semiskilled workers. How did wartime conditions allow women to improve their economic positions in England and, indeed, in all the warring nations? Do you think women's wartime contributions (remember that the nursing efforts of Vera Brittain and other women are not reflected in Source 13) would argue for improved postwar status for women?

The effects of World War I would be felt long after the armistice that ended hostilities in 1918. Refer to the table in Source 14. Notice the total numbers of men mobilized, recalling that in countries like France and Germany 80 percent of the military-age male population was in uniform. What effect do you think the absence of so many young men from their homes had on the birth rate during the years 1914–1918? What enduring impact did the deaths of many of these men have on their countries' birth rates? What implications could all these factors have had for future defense considerations? Among the great powers, which country suffered the greatest proportional war losses? What do you predict the public attitudes in this country might be when war threatened again within twenty years of World War I's end? Do you think the costs of war would evoke the same response in all countries?

Finally, consider the economic costs of war. Wartime expenses outstripped tax revenues for all governments. All borrowed to pay for their war efforts. You must understand the figures in Source 15 in terms of the value of dollars during that period. Viewed in this light, the British debt represented almost five times the entire annual expenditure of the U.S. government in the years preceding the war's outbreak. From whom did the British and their allies borrow? What effect would this new creditor status have on the lender? How would such vast indebtedness affect European countries?

And what of Germany and Austria-Hungary, which lost the war, or Italy, which was on the winning side but failed to achieve all of its wartime goals? These countries made sacrifices comparable to those of the winning side. How would they view their war costs?

Your examination of all these issues should now allow you to answer the main questions of this chapter: Why was World War I different from previous wars? What impact did it have on the soldiers at the front? How did it affect civilians at home?

EPILOGUE

World War I permanently changed Europe and the world. As this chapter demonstrated, the conflict introduced a new kind of warfare, a total warfare that inflicted suffering on the civilian citizens of belligerent countries as well as on their men in military service. But World War I permanently changed much else, too.

The political old order of Europe expired in the trenches along with a generation of young men. The stress of modern warfare meant that no government survived politically when its war effort ended in defeat. At the war's end revolutions overthrew the old monarchies in Russia, Germany, Austria-Hungary, Bulgaria, and Turkey. The governmental change was most dramatic in Russia, where that country's wartime problems led to revolution and eventually to the world's first communist dictatorship, but everywhere defeat meant political collapse. That political collapse also contributed to numerous changes in national boundaries. The breakdown of governmental authority in many defeated countries permitted national minorities in these states to seek independence. Austria-Hungary and Turkey disappeared from the map as large, multinational empires as their subject peoples declared independence at war's end. And the Russian empire lost a large part of its western territory as Finns, Poles, Latvians, Lithuanians, Estonians, and Romanians used the moment of tsarist collapse to escape Russian rule.

World War I also facilitated the transformation of Western society. Women's labor in war industries, their work in nursing, and their

479

participation in uniformed auxiliary services of the armed forces sustained the prewar demands of women for a political voice. In most Western countries, women gained the right to vote after World War I, a major step in attaining a status equal to that of males.

The war changed Europe economically, too. The financial needs of total warfare forced every government to borrow. The most obvious change was that the United States emerged from the war as the greatest creditor nation, but other economic changes occurred as well. As warring nations purchased raw materials and manufactured goods in the Americas and Asia during the conflict, the West's wealth began to shift out of Europe. In addition, Western European nations, particularly France, faced tremendous war-related property damage whose repair would consume funds for years to come.

Another cost of the war in both economic and human terms was found among its victims. The injured and crippled had to be treated, rehabilitated, and paid pensions. The situation of England illustrates the extent of the problem. When the government finalized its pension rolls in 1929, 2,424,000 men were receiving some sort of disability pension, about 40 percent of all the soldiers who had served in the British army in the war.

The war's unhappiest result, however, was that it did not become what U.S. President Woodrow Wilson called "a war to end all wars."

Rather, seeds for the next conflict were sown by the events and consequences of World War I. Total war created the desire for total victory, and the peace treaties reflected animosities produced by four years of bloody conflict. The Treaty of Versailles presented Germany with a settlement that would produce a desire for revision of the peace terms and even revenge. At the same time, the great losses of life in World War I engendered in many people in victorious nations a "never again" attitude that would lead them to seek to avoid another war at all costs. This attitude would in part result in efforts to appease a resurgent and vengeful Germany under Adolf Hitler (see Chapter 13) in the 1930s.

The alienation of former soldiers from civilian life led many to search out civilian opportunities for renewing the comradeship of the front, such as veterans' groups and paramilitary organizations. Especially in the defeated countries or in those victorious countries disappointed with their gains, this impulse had dangerous consequences. In Italy and Germany, veterans enlisted in great numbers in the ranks of uniformed right-wing organizations that became the power base for the brutal armed supporters of the dictators Mussolini and Hitler (see Chapter 13). Pledged to winning back the losses in their nations' defeats in World War I, such leaders as Hitler and Mussolini seized political power by exploiting postwar problems and resentments. Their policies were to breed a second global conflict.

CHAPTER NINETEEN

THE PERILS OF PROSPERITY:

THE UNREST OF

YOUTH IN THE 1960s

THE PROBLEM

Commuters just emerging from subway exits in the university district of Paris on the evening of Friday, May 3, 1968, must have been bewildered. They stepped out into a neighborhood transformed since morning into a war zone in which police and students battled over the future of France's governmental and economic systems. These commuters witnessed a conflict in which French students, like students in many other countries in 1968, called into question a material prosperity purchased, in their view, with a loss of individual liberty in the face of the power of the modern state and giant industrial concerns.

The postwar Western world indeed was experiencing unprecedented prosperity by the late 1960s. The United States enjoyed the world's highest living standard. In Western Europe, the European Economic Community (or EEC), also called the Common Market, served as a key instrument for economic recovery and growth for war-ravaged France, West Germany, Italy, Belgium, the Netherlands, and Luxembourg. Non-EEC countries, including Great Britain and the Scandinavian nations, also shared in this economic success. Even in communist Eastern Europe, war damage was repaired and the socialist economies of the region produced standards of living for their peoples substantially improved over those of the early postwar years.

Behind the façade of material success, however, were a number of problems that led to widespread unrest, especially among the young, in the 1960s. Part of the basis for this discontent may be found in the very economic success of the postwar period. Several Western countries, including France and Great Britain, encouraged growth by government intervention in the economy or national ownership of industries. The economic life of Communist Eastern Europe, of course, was entirely

482

under government control. The result was a growing state economic bureaucracy in which the individual had little voice. The nature of the economic growth was unsettling, too. The West was entering a new phase of industrialization. New and sophisticated industries, such as computers and electronics, flourished; the service sector of the economy grew while older heavy industries declined in importance. The result was deep concern among many workers, who found little demand for their traditional skills and who felt powerless to avoid unemployment or underemployment. Worker dissatisfaction with the existing system only increased with economic recessions like that of 1968 in France, which added to unemployment and reduced the buying power of those who retained their jobs. Economic growth, for many, was not an unqualified success.

Many European students were dissatisfied with the system of higher education. A partial reason may be found in the West's great population growth after World War II. The postwar baby boom of 1946–1964, which affected both Europe and America, coincided with a prosperity that permitted Western democracies to provide their youth with greater educational opportunity than had been offered any earlier generation. In two decades student populations vastly increased. From 1950 to 1970, university enrollments increased from 123,000 to 651,000 in France; from 190,000 to 561,000 in Italy; from 117,000 to 410,000 in West Germany; and from 67,200 to 250,000 in Great Britain.[1] But often the quality of the educational experience declined as the system strained to cope with unprecedented enrollments. University faculty and facilities failed to grow as fast as their student bodies, resulting in crowded lecture halls and student-faculty ratios that went as high as 105 to 1 in Italy and rendered professors inaccessible to students.

Other problems also affected the student population. University curricula often provided a traditional education that did little to prepare a student to succeed in the new service-oriented economy. When European governments decreed half-hearted curriculum reforms to respond to economic change, they often, as in France, extended a student's course of study. The university also seemed divorced from the real problems of society, such as poverty and crime, a fact reflected in the rarity of sociology courses dealing with those problems.

These curricular problems and the impersonal nature of the modern university led to student demands for sweeping change in the educational establishment. The students wished a voice in the decisions that affected them. They increasingly demanded a say in what was taught, who taught, and how the universities were administered. As we will see, such demands also reflected the feelings of many nonstudents who bitterly felt their inability to affect the modern institutions that controlled their lives.

1. B. R. Mitchell, ed., *European Historical Statistics,* abridged ed. (New York: Columbia University Press, 1978), pp. 396–400.

Students of the 1960s were disappointed and angered by educational shortcomings, but they were even more frustrated by their inability to effect political change. The student generation of the 1960s was physically more mature than any previous generation, thanks to improved nutrition. Their sense of adulthood was heightened by the spread of techniques of birth control that freed women from the fear of pregnancy outside of marriage and fostered a youthful revolt against traditional sexual mores. That revolt could have political ramifications; a slogan frequently heard among French students in 1968 was: "Every time I make love I want to make the revolution; every time I make the revolution I want to make love." But these self-consciously mature young people could change little around them. Everywhere, those under twenty-one were eligible for military service but had no right to vote. Nor had students even a voice in their universities' governance. Typically, European governments controlled universities through centralized bureaucracies. In France, for example, such minor events as student dances had to be approved by the Ministry of Education.

Yet for all the dissatisfaction among students and workers, traditional twentieth-century political ideologies offered scant appeal. The cold war had polarized Europe for twenty years, and neither of the opposing doctrines—Russian communism or the democratic capitalism of the United States—offered real answers to student demands. Indeed, in a political sense both doctrines increasingly lost credibility for students. For some, the democratic ideals of the United States no longer seemed attractive because of that nation's increasingly unpopular war in Vietnam. Many saw that Southeast Asian conflict, which engaged about 500,000 American servicemen by 1968, as a war to uphold a favored minority in South Vietnam through military involvement. Those who looked toward a communist vision of a better world similarly were disappointed. The Soviet Union, with its regimented society, inefficient economy, and forceful crushing of dissent in its East German, Polish, and Hungarian satellites in the 1950s, was hardly the best advertisement for Marxian socialism.

Ideological disillusionment led a minority of students to radical doctrines rejecting orthodox Marxism as well as liberal democracy. The ideas of Leon Trotsky, a Marxist who rejected the need for a bureaucracy in a socialist state, attracted some. The example of Mao Zedong, the Chinese revolutionary, stirred other students to reject all authority and to attempt to rally working people to the cause of revolutionary change. Still others were attracted by nineteenth-century anarchist thought that rejected any hierarchy of control over the individual. Some also found inspiration in the revolutionary activism of Cuba's Fidel Castro and Che Guevara. Common to all was the belief that the institutions of society favored the rich, manipulated the poor, and substituted materialism bred of postwar economic growth for individual liberty and any high-minded questioning of the established order. Everywhere student demands could be summed up as calls for participation by individuals in all the decisions that shaped their lives, a concept that French students labeled *autogestion*.

Whatever their ideology, student radicals sought confrontation with established governmental and educational authority in the hope of garnering a mass following for change among the nonrevolutionary majority of students, workers, and others. The radicals increasingly found student followers in many countries. Unrest due to the Vietnam War was widespread on campuses in the United States from the mid-1960s. In Europe, riots began in Italy in 1965 at the universities of Milan and Trento as students demanded a voice in academic policy. Italian unrest continued into the late 1960s, when student radicals combined ideas for a complete overthrow of traditional society with their demands for educational change. Incidents rooted in the desire for political change were common to German and British universities, too. In most of these countries, however, youthful radicals generated little support beyond their campuses. France was the only Western European country in which youthful unrest spread beyond students and thus threatened the existence of the government.

In 1968 France had been led for ten years by President Charles de Gaulle, the seventy-eight-year-old hero of World War II whose imperial style of government only increased the extreme state centralization traditional in that country. Signifi-cantly, too, France was suffering an economic recession that heightened the discontent of many workers. Problems began at the new Nanterre campus of the University of Paris. Placed amid slums housing immigrant workers, this modern university center seemed to radicals a dramatic illustration of the failings of modern consumer society. Led by the anarchist Daniel Cohn-Bendit in a protest of university regulations, Nanterre students forced the closing of their campus in the spring of 1968.

Nanterre radicals next focused their attention on the main campus of the University of Paris, at the Sorbonne, after university authorities had begun disciplinary action against Cohn-Bendit and others on May 3, 1968. As police removed protesting student radicals from the Sorbonne, antipolice violence erupted among crowds of students around the university. The very appearance of the police on university grounds provoked student anger. University confines were normally beyond the jurisdiction of the police, who had last entered the Sorbonne in 1791. The crowd threw rocks and, more dangerously, the heavy cobblestones of Paris streets. Police beat students brutally, and the broadcast of such scenes on the evening television news generated widespread support for the radicals, who now demanded a change in France's government.

For the next two weeks, the university district of Paris was the scene of street fighting between police and students that drew on the traditions of a Paris that had often defied government in the past.[2] Ominously for the government, the student unrest spread to other parts of society. On May 13, 1968, unions scheduled a twenty-four-hour general strike to protest police brutality, despite the opposition of the large French Communist party, which feared the unorthodoxy of the spreading revolt. On May 14 workers began to occupy factories and to refuse to work, the young among them demanding, like the students, a voice in decisions affecting them. For other workers, improved wages were a demand. Within a week, perhaps as many as 10 million workers nationwide had seized their factories and were on strike. Even professionals in broadcasting, sports, and other fields joined the strike. The country was paralyzed, and the government seemed on the brink of collapse as opposition leaders began to discuss alternative regimes.

As the government faltered, both sides in the confrontation clearly saw the significance of the growing revolt. Cohn-Bendit characterized it as "a whole generation rising against a certain sort of society— bourgeois society." A leader of the establishment, France's Prime Minister Georges Pompidou, defined the revolt as one against modern society itself. Even the authoritarian de Gaulle heard the message, con- ceding on May 19, "Reform yes, anarchy no."[3]

Prime Mister Pompidou began to defuse the crisis by offering wage increases to the striking unions. Faced with destroying the consumer society or enjoying more of its benefits, many striking workers quickly chose the latter option. Then, on May 29, de Gaulle flew to West Germany, assured himself of the support of French army units stationed there in case of the need of force, and returned to Paris to end the crisis. Addressing the nation on radio the next day, the president refused to resign as the protesters demanded and instead dissolved the National Assembly, calling for new elections to that body. The maneuver saved the government's cause. The protesters could not call repressive a government that was willing to risk its control of the legislature in elections called ahead of schedule. Although student radicals tried to continue the revolt, most workers accepted proffered pay increases and new elections and returned to work. De Gaulle's supporters won a majority of the seats in the National Assembly on June 23, 1968, and the president retained the power to govern.

As students and workers battled police in France, equally dramatic events were moving to a climax across Europe in Czechoslovakia.

---

2. Students fought much as Parisians had in the eighteenth and nineteenth centuries, tearing up paving stones and piling them with overturned vehicles and fallen trees to create street barricades from behind which they fought police. When the student revolt ended, the government paved cobblestone streets with asphalt.

3. In the present context, *anarchy* is probably the best English word to convey briefly what de Gaulle meant. De Gaulle probably sought a certain effect by using an army colloquialism, *chien lit*, which even the French press had difficulty expressing adequately. It means making "a mess in one's own bed"; in other words, "fouling one's own nest."

Although unrest in democratic France and one-party Czechoslovakia displayed differences, the revolts in both countries had common roots in a rejection of highly centralized and unresponsive authority.

Czechoslovakia, an industrialized country with Western democratic traditions, experienced a coup in 1948 that established a communist government. The leaders of that regime, party First Secretaries Klement Gottwald (1948–1953) and Antonín Novotný (1953–1968) were steadfast followers of authoritarian Stalinist communism, even though the Soviet Union itself began a process of "de-Stalinization" after 1956. But by 1967 Novotný's style of communism was becoming increasingly unacceptable to Czechoslovakians in two chief regards. The most basic problem concerned the nation's two largest ethnic groups: the Czechs and the Slovaks. For a long time the Slovaks had been unhappy with Czech domination of both the Communist party and the state apparatus. The Novotný regime perpetuated this Czech domination as the Slovaks clamored for a stronger voice in national affairs.

Even more fundamental than the regime's ethnic difficulties, however, was its rigid and authoritarian Stalinist communism. Economically, this meant a managed economy, oriented toward heavy industrial goods rather than consumer items, that was hampered by centralized control, no profit motive, and low productivity. The nation had experienced serious economic problems since 1962. Politically, Novotný's government gave the country rigid control by a small party inner circle sustained by a secret police, press censorship, and extreme curbs on intellectual freedom.

A series of events led to change in Czechoslovakia through the efforts of the younger generation of party officials, intellectuals, and students. As in France, loss of support for the regime began among those who were being groomed in the educational system as future leaders, not with the materially deprived. Pressure for change in the country's highest leadership mounted as Novotný's authoritarian style of government resisted reform and economic problems persisted.

In 1963 the Slovak branch of the Communist party named a new First Secretary, the reform-minded Alexander Dubček. In a country where literature long had been politicized, writers began to desert the regime; at the Congress of Czechoslovak Writers in June 1967, they demanded an end to censorship and freedom for their craft. Other intellectuals also grew restive with the regime. But, as in France, it was young people who brought matters to a crisis point. Cries of "We want freedom, we want democracy" and "A good communist is a dead communist" punctuated traditional student May Day observances in 1966 and resulted in arrests by policemen whom the students called "Gestapo," after the Nazi security police. The government responded forcefully, expelling from the universities and drafting into the army leaders of student organizations who had called for more freedom. Nonetheless, opposition to the Novotný regime not only continued but increased, especially after the events of October 31, 1967. On that night, as on numerous previous occasions, an electrical failure left the large complex of student dormitories in Prague, the capital, without light. Students took up candles and began a procession chanting "We want light," a phrase that could indicate far more than their need for electric power. The brutal acts of the police in confronting the students outraged public opinion, thus strengthening reform elements in the party's Central Committee sufficiently for them to gain a majority in that body. On January 5, 1968, the reformers replaced Novotný with the Slovak Alexander Dubček as first secretary of the national Communist party. On March 22, 1968, war hero Ludvik Svoboda replaced Novotný as president of the nation. A bloodless revolution had occurred in Prague.

The spring of 1968 was an exhilarating one for the people of Czechoslovakia. Dubček announced his intention to create "socialism with a human face," a socialism that would allow "a fuller assertion of the personality than any bourgeois democracy," a socialism that would be "profoundly democratic." Rigid press censorship ended, as did other controls on the individual. But Dubček soon found himself in a difficult position. Permitted freedom of expression for the first time in twenty years, Czechoslovaks demanded far more, including even a free political system with a role for noncommunist parties. Such developments, however, threatened neighboring communist dictatorships in East Germany and Poland and risked depriving the So-

viet Union of strategically located Czechoslovakia in its Warsaw Pact alliance system.

On August 21, after having watched developments in Prague for months with growing alarm, the Soviet Union acted. Troops from the Soviet Union, East Germany, Hungary, Poland, and Bulgaria entered Czechoslovakia. In the largest movement of troops in Europe since 1945, they forcibly ended the "Prague Spring" experiment.

The Soviets were met with widespread passive nationalist resistance. The majority of the population seemed to wish continuation of reform, but earlier unrest in Eastern Europe, as in the failed Hungarian revolt of 1956, had demonstrated the futility of civilians' active opposition to Soviet arms. Students again took part in resistance, however, and two, Jan Palach and Jan Zajíc, burned themselves alive in early 1969 in protest. Force prevailed, however, and Soviet pressure assured the gradual replacement of Dubček and his reform leadership with men more subservient to Moscow's wishes. Soviet party First Secretary Leonid Brezhnev announced that events in Czechoslovakia represented an expression of what came to be called the "Brezhnev Doctrine"—that is, the Soviet Union's policy to act against any threat to the stability of an East European communist regime.

Those supporting change in both France and Czechoslovakia were acutely aware of the need to sway public opinion in their favor. This task was made difficult by government controls of the media: In

France, the radio and television systems were state-controlled; in Czechoslovakia, the regime controlled not only electronic media but the press as well. Your problem in this chapter is to analyze events in France and Czechoslovakia in 1968 by examining the materials issued by those who sought to rally support for change. Deprived of media controlled by the political establishment, proponents of change issued leaflets, posters, and cartoons designed to win support. What aspects of the modern state and economy provoked the events of 1968? What vision of the future did the leaders of the French and Czechoslovakian movements embrace? How did they propose to achieve it?

SOURCES AND METHOD

Modern political causes seek to mobilize support in various ways. Because posters, pamphlets, and other publications as well as simple slogans scrawled on walls all aim to energize support for a movement by publicizing its ideas, analyzing such materials provides a broad understanding of the goals and methods of any cause. In this chapter we have assembled two groups of evidence, one relating to the French disorders and the other to the Czechoslovakian reform movement of 1968.

Let us consider the French evidence first. Source 1 is a pamphlet distributed to striking workers by the March 22 Movement, a student group whose name commemorated the student upheaval at the Nanterre campus. It appeared on May 21, 1968. What were the students' goals for the future society and economy of France? What were the aims of workers in their strike? How did student leaders try to unify student and worker causes in this pamphlet? Source 2, a leaflet that appeared on May 22, 1968, was issued by a number of student and worker groups. Consider the views expressed here about President de Gaulle, the government, and the economy. Would the authors have been satisfied only with the departure of de Gaulle from the political scene? What do you deduce from their refusal of "summit negotiations" with government and management? To whom does the leaflet appeal? What vision of the future does it advocate?

You must analyze the language of Source 3 to understand the message it seeks to convey. This is a list of slogans that the student Sorbonne Occupation Committee suggested to its followers on May 16, 1968. Note the locations proposed for such slogans. The one advocating the end of bureaucrats was painted across a large mural in the Sorbonne administration building. How did this and some of the other suggested locations reflect student attitudes toward authority? Now turn to the words themselves. Slogans are important in politics; as we noted in Chapter 13, the simpler they are, the more easily they can be spread to influence large numbers of people. Each side of the 1968 confrontations sought to dismiss the validity of the other's ideas by extreme and often inaccurate name calling. In France as well as in the United States and other countries, students referred to policemen as "pigs" or "fascists." French students' chants of "CRS—SS!" likened the riot police, the CRS (*Compagnies Républicaines de Securité*), to the Nazi SS (*Schutz Staffeln* or security echelon, whose insignia resembled a sharp double S). The students' opponents responded in kind, often calling them "commies." What views of their opponents do the students convey in these slogans? What sort of society do they advocate? What methods do they advocate for their cause?

With the French Sources 4 through 12, you must analyze pictorial attempts to mobilize opinion. The artists conveyed these messages graphically in pictures, with a minimum of words. Here you must ascertain the nature of the message and the goals of the students and workers.

The visual evidence is of several types. In 1968 posters appeared all over the university district of Paris in defiance of long-standing laws against posters on public buildings. Often they were fairly sophisticated in execution because many advanced art students put their skills in the service of the May revolt. The political cartoon also flourished in a number of new radical publications in Paris. The cartoons presented here originated in *L'enragé* (*"The Madman"*), a publication that consisted entirely of cartoons critical of established authority in France.

Cartoons and posters often magnify the physical characteristics of public figures, sometimes to ridicule but also to make perfectly clear the subject of the message. Thus you will find the prominent nose of President de Gaulle quite exaggerated, as well as certain poses. De Gaulle often embellished his speeches by raising both arms, the same gesture he used when leading the singing of the national anthem, *La Marseillaise*, a frequent occurrence after a public address. This pose is duplicated in the cartoons and posters along with his uniform of a French general, complete with the cylindrical cap known as a *kepi*, making him instantly recognizable. Artists further identified de Gaulle by including in their pictures the Cross of Lorraine, the symbol of his World War II resistance movement, with its two transverse bars.

In analyzing the material, remember that political posters and cartoons, though based on real events, are not intended to report those occurrences accurately. They are meant instead to affect public opinion. By carefully examining the posters and cartoons, you can discover the artists' views of events and how they wished to sway public opinion. What action does each picture represent? What message is the artist trying to convey? What reaction does he or she wish to evoke in viewers? What do the pictures tell you about the participants, methods, and aspirations of the French movement?

Now let us examine the Czechoslovakian sources. The Czechoslovakian writings should be examined with the same methods you applied to the French. Source 13 is a tract that circulated illegally in Czechoslovakian literary circles as early as April 1967 and was republished in a Prague student publication in March 1968. Notice first the use of language. What effect do the authors seek in condemning their opponents as "knaves"? What view does the statement as a whole express toward established ideologies, both Soviet Marxist and U.S. capitalist? What methods for change are advocated? Did young Czechoslovakians follow the course of action recommended in the tenth commandment? Why should the intellectuals, students, and professors be the leaders in change?

Source 14 is an extract from a statement that appeared in an influential publication, *Literární Listy* (*Literary Papers*), the journal of the Czechoslovakian Writers' Union. *Literární Listy* was the chief forum in 1968 in which intellectuals expressed their views on reform. It had a large circulation (300,000 copies in June 1968), and it published the manifesto for change, "Two Thousand Words." Source 14 appeared on March 5, 1968, as one of a number of replies to the question of the nation's political future posed by the editors: "Wherefrom, with Whom, and Whither?" The answer reprinted here was made by Ivan Sviták, a philosophy professor and reform leader. Notice his choice of language. Who, in his view, was the enemy of change? How does he characterize these people? What sort of social and political system did Czechoslovakian intellectuals seek?

Sources 15 through 20 are cartoons drawn from *Literární Listy* and its successor, *Listy*. Use the same methods of analysis here as you employed with the French posters and cartoons. You again will note exaggeration of certain physical features to clarify the cartoon's message. Alexander Dubček had a large nose, as de Gaulle did, and it was exaggerated by Czechoslovak cartoonists, just as French artists exaggerated de Gaulle's nose.

The Czechoslovakian cartoonists represented here also used symbols to illuminate their messages. The Phrygian cap worn by the woman in Source 15, for example, represents revolution and liberty. Dubček is depicted in Source 16 as Jánašík, a legendary Slovak "Robin Hood." Source 19 shows the Soviet president Leonid Brezhnev as Saint Florian. Old statues of this saint stand in many Czechoslovakian villages because he was thought to offer protection from fire.

Using the analytical methods described here, you should be able to answer the central questions of this chapter: What aspects of the modern state and economy provoked the events of 1968? What vision of the future did leaders of the French and Czechoslovakian movements embrace? How did they propose to achieve it?

THE EVIDENCE

FRANCE

Sources 1 through 3 from Vladimir Fišera, editor, Writing on the Wall, May 1968: A Documentary Anthology *(London: Allison & Busby, 1978), pp. 133–134; p. 137; pp. 125–126. Reprinted by permission of W. H. Allen Publishers.*

1. The March 22 Movement, "Your Struggle Is Our Struggle," May 21, 1968

We are occupying the faculties, you are occupying the factories. Aren't we fighting for the same thing? Higher education only contains 10 percent workers' children. Are we fighting so that there will be more of them, for a democratic university reform? That would be a good thing, but it's not the most important. These workers' children would just become like other students. We are not aiming for a worker's son to be a manager. We want to wipe out segregation between workers and management.

There are students who are unable to find jobs on leaving university. Are we fighting so that they'll find jobs, for a decent graduate employment policy? It would be a good thing, but it is not vital. Psychology or sociology graduates will become the selectors, the planners and psychotechnicians who will try to organise your working conditions; mathematics graduates will become engineers, perfecting maximum-productivity machines to make your life even more unbearable. Why are we, students who are products of a middle-class life, criticising capitalist society? The son of a worker who becomes a student leaves his own class. For the son of a middle-class family, it could be his opportunity to see his class in its true light, to question the role he is destined for in society and the organisation of our society. We refuse to become scholars who are out of touch with real life. We refuse to be used for the benefit of the ruling class. We want to destroy the separation that exists between those who organise and think and those who execute their decisions. We want to form a classless society; your cause is the same as ours.

You are asking for a minimum wage of 1,000 francs in the Paris area, retirement at sixty, a 40-hour week for 48 hours' pay.

These are long-standing and just demands: nevertheless, they seem to be out of context with our aims. Yet you have gone on to occupy factories, take your managers as hostages, strike without warning. These forms of struggle have been made possible by perseverance and lengthy action in various enterprises, and because of the recent student battles.

These struggles are even more radical than our official aims, because they go further than simply seeking improvements for the worker within the capitalist system, they imply the destruction of the system. They are political in the true sense of the word: you are fighting not to change the Prime Minister, but so that your boss no longer retains his power in business or society. The form that your struggle has taken offers us students the model for true socialist activity: the appropriation of the means of production and of the decision-making power by the workers.

Our struggles converge. We must destroy everything that seeks to alienate us (everyday habits, the press, etc.). We must combine our occupations in the faculties and factories.

Long live the unification of our struggles!

2. "Producers, Let Us Save Ourselves," May 22, 1968

To ten million strikers, to all workers:

No to parliamentary solutions, with de Gaulle going and the bosses staying.

No to summit negotiations which give only a new lease of life to a moribund capitalism.

No more referenda. No more spectacles.

Don't let anybody speak for us. Maintain the occupation of all workplaces.

To continue the struggle, let us put all the sectors of the economy which are hit by the strike at the service of the fighting workers.

Let us prepare today our power of tomorrow (direct food-supplies, the organisation of public services: transport, information, housing, etc.).

In the streets, in the local committees, wherever we are, workers, peasants, wage-earners, students, teachers, school students, let us organise and coordinate our struggles.

FOR THE ABOLITION OF THE EMPLOYERS, FOR WORKERS' POWER.

3. Sorbonne Occupation Committee, Slogans to Be Circulated by Any Means, May 16, 1968

(leaflets—announcements over microphones—comics—songs—painting on walls—texts daubed over the paintings in the Sorbonne—announcements in the cinema during the film, or stopping it in the middle—texts written on the posters in the underground—whenever you empty your glass in the bistro—before making love—after making love—in the lift)

Occupy the factories.

Power to the workers' councils.

Abolish class society.

Down with a society based on commodity production and the spectacle.

Abolish alienation.

An end to the university.

Mankind will not be happy until the last bureaucrat has been strung up by the guts of the last capitalist.

Death to the pigs.

Free the four people arrested for looting on 6 May.

THE ENEMY

Sources 4 through 8 from *Bibliothèque Nationale,* Les Affiches de Mai 68 ou l'imagination graphique *(Paris: Bibliothèque Nationale, 1982), p. 64; p. 15, p. 9; p. 63; p. 47.*

4. Poster, May 1968

6. Poster: "Light Salaries, Heavy Tanks," May 1968

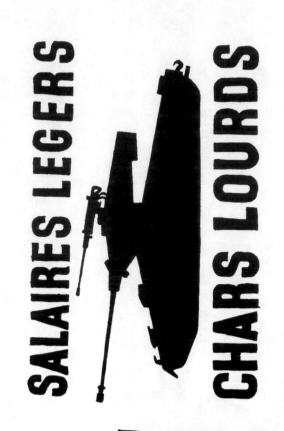

SALAIRES LEGERS

CHARS LOURDS

5. Poster: "Let Us Smash the Old Gears!"
May 1968

BRISONS
LES VIEUX ENGRENAGES

REVOLUTIONARY METHODS

7. Poster: "Beauty Is in the Street!," May 1968

8. Poster: "Less than 21 Years of Age: Here Is Your Ballot!," May 1968

497

Source 9 from Jean-Jacques Pauvert, editor, L'enragé: collection complète des 12 numéros introuvables, mai–novembre 1968 *(Paris: Jean-Jacques Pauvert, 1978).*

9. Cartoon, June 10, 1968

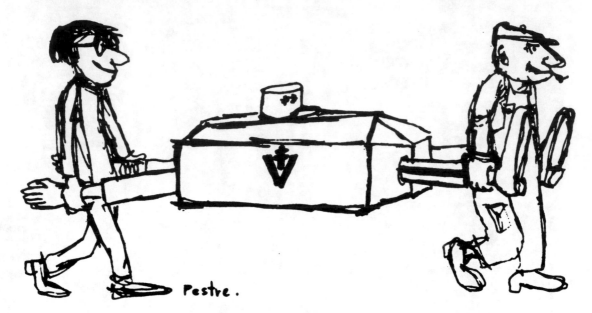

THE STUDENTS' VISION

Sources 10 and 11 from Bibliothèque Nationale, Les Affiches de Mai 68 ou l'imagination graphique, *p. 10; p. 24.*

10. Cartoon: "Each One of Us Is the State," May 1968

11. Cartoon: "Popular Power," May 1968

THE STUDENTS IN DEFEAT

Source 12 from Pauvert, L'enragé: collection complète des 12 numéros introuvables, mai–novembre 1968.

12. Cartoon, June 17, 1968

CZECHOSLOVAKIA

Sources 13 and 14 from Ivan Sviták, The Czechoslovak Experiment, 1968-1969 (New York: Columbia University Press, 1971), pp. 17-18; p. 16. Reprinted by permission of the author.

13. "Ten Commandments for a Young Czechoslovak Intellectual," March 1968

There are no more knaves than before; it is only that their field of activity is larger. . . . And so all of us are living in close collaboration with a few knaves.

LUDVÍK VACULÍK, in *Orientation, 1967*[4]

1. Do not collaborate with knaves. If you do, you inevitably become one of them. Engage yourself against the knaves.

2. Do not accept the responsibility forced upon you by the knaves for their own deeds. Do not believe such arguments as "we are all responsible," or the social problems touch "all of us," or "everyone has his share of guilt." Openly and clearly dissociate yourself from the deeds of the knaves and from arguments that you are responsible for them.

3. Do not believe any ideology that consists of systems of slogans and words which only speculate about your feelings. Judge people, political parties, and social systems concretely, according to the measure of freedom they give, and according to how tolerable the living conditions are. Judge them according to results, not words.

4. Do not solve only the narrow generational problems of youth; understand that the decisive problems are common to all human beings. You cannot solve them by postulating the demands of young men, but by vigorously defending the problems of all people. Do not complain about the privileges of one generation, but fight for human rights.

5. Do not consider the given social relations as constant. They are changing in your favor. Look forward. If you do not want to be wrong today, you must think from the point of view of the year 2000.

6. Do not think only as a Czech or a Slovak, but consider yourself a *European*. The world will sooner adapt to Europe (where Eastern Europe belongs) than to fourteen million Czechs and Slovaks. You live neither in America nor in the Soviet Union; you live in Europe.

---

4. **Ludvík Vaculík:** a novelist and one of the leaders of the Czechoslovakian reform movement; he also drafted the manifesto "Two Thousand Words."

7. Do not succumb to utopias or illusions; be dissatisfied and critical. Have the sceptical confidence of a negotiator, but have confidence in the purpose of your negotiations. The activity has its own value.

8. Do not be afraid of your task in history and be courageous in intervening in history. The social changes and transformations of man take place, no doubt, without regard to you, but to understand these changes and to influence them with the limited possibilities of an individual is far better than to accept the fatal inevitability of events.

9. Do not negotiate out of good motives alone; negotiate with sound arguments and with consideration of what you can achieve. A good deed can rise from a bad motive and vice versa. The motives are forgotten, but deeds remain.

10. Do not let yourself be *shot* in the fight between the interests of the power blocs. *Shoot* when in danger. Are you not in danger right now when you collaborate with the few knaves? Are you a knave?

14. Ivan Sviták, "Wherefrom, with Whom, and Whither?," March 5, 1968

From totalitarian dictatorship toward an open society, toward the liquidation of the power monopoly and toward the effective control of the power elite by a free press and by public opinion. From the bureaucratic management of society and culture by the "hard-line thugs" (C. Wright Mills)[5] toward the observance of fundamental human and civil rights, at least to the same extent as in the Czechoslovakia of bourgeois democracy. With the labor movement, without its *apparatchiks*;[6] with the middle classes, without their groups of willing collaborators; and with the intelligentsia in the lead. The intellectuals of this country must assert their claim to lead an open socialist society toward democracy and humanism.

5. **C. Wright Mills** (1916–1962): a Columbia University sociologist, the author of influential books including *White Collar* and *The Power Elite* and a severe critic of modern institutions.

6. **apparatchik**: a Russian word describing an individual who is part of the existing power structure.

THE PEOPLE'S VISION

Sources 15 and 16 from Literární Listy, *in Sviták,* The Czechoslovak Experiment, 1968–1969, *p. 2; p. 51.*

15. Cartoon: "If There Are No Complications the Child Should Be Born in the Ninth Month," 1968

16. Cartoon, 1968

THE ENEMY

Source 17 from Literární Listy, *in Robin Alison Remington, editor,* Prague in Winter: Documents on Czechoslovak Communism in Crisis *(Cambridge, Mass.: M.I.T. Press, 1969), p. 289.*

17. Cartoon, "Workers of All Countries Unite—Or I'll Shoot!," August 28, 1968

Sources 18 and 19 from Literární Listy, *in Sviták,* The Czechoslovak Experiment, 1968–1969, p. 196; p. 155.

18. Cartoon: "Liberté, Egalité, Freundschaft!" ("Liberty, Equality, Friendship!"), 1968

IN DEFEAT

19. Cartoon: "But There Is No Fire!," 1969

Source 20 from Listy, *in Remington,* Prague in Winter, *p. 373.*

20. Cartoon: "It Is Only a Matter of a Few Tactical Steps Back," January 30, 1969

JDE JENOM O NĚKOLIK
TAKTICKÝCH ÚSTUPKŮ.

Vladimír Jiránek

QUESTIONS TO CONSIDER

France and Czechoslovakia are two very different countries at opposite ends of Europe. Let us compare the events of 1968 as they unfolded in these two locations. Do they illustrate a common response to problems basic to modern life in the noncommunist and communist West?

Consider first the demands of French and Czechoslovakian protest leaders. Examine again the written and visual evidence, and consider the protesters' views on working conditions in France. What problems do they identify in Sources 1, 2, and 3? How are these problems defined graphically? Why do you think that the artist in Source 4 portrayed modern capitalism as a puppeteer? What is the significance of the puppeteer's appearance? Why did the artist show de Gaulle as part of the industrial gears of France in Source 5? Turn next to the Czechoslovakian statements on working conditions. Notice particularly Source 14, with its references to management by "hard-line thugs" and "apparatchiks." What great lie about communism (whose slogan is, "Workers of the World Unite!") do the Czechoslovakians discern in Source 17? What common theme do you find in French and

Czechoslovakian protesters' ideas on the conditions of labor in the modern economy?

Next consider the political vision of the 1968 activists. Take the French first. What sort of government did the formulators of Source 3 envision? How is that idea amplified in Sources 9, 10, and 11? These cartoons spell their messages in words, but their art contains a message, too. Look closely at Source 10. How does the artist see the individual faring against big government, industrial giants, and powerful unions? What solution does the artist propose in the caption? Which groups did the creator of Source 11 hope would seize political power? Does the same message appear in Source 9? Who is being buried? What does his body represent? Notice the clothing and grooming of the pallbearers. Can you identify the occupational groups that the artist hopes will seize power after the burial?

The Czechoslovakians also had a political vision. Review Sources 13 and 14. What political outlook do these statements express? What groups did Czechoslovakian reformers expect to lead change? Combine this message with Source 15. How do the reformers regard their chances for success? How were the political visions of the French and Czechoslovakian reformers similar?

Both movements also expressed images of their opponents and the methods to be employed in their struggles. What sort of action does the artist of Source 7 recommend to the French? What secondary message do you think underlies the portrayal of the fighter as a woman? Source 8

shows a close-up view of a Parisian paving stone. What message do you find in its accompanying statement? In Sources 6 and 12, we find some statements of the reformers' view of the opposition and its power. Why do you think the artist pictured a silhouette of a tank in Source 6? The final French selection, Source 12, is a cartoon that appeared on the cover of *L'enragé* after the defeat of the students and workers. What significance do you find in the portrayal of de Gaulle? What has crippled him? What supports him? What view of the government does the shape of his crutches convey?

The Czechoslovakian sources also characterize the reformers' opposition and their chances of success. In Source 15 what does the woman's obvious pregnancy represent? When does Dubček predict the birth? How long did the Czechoslovakian experiment in greater democracy actually last? What does Dubček's strange activity in Source 16 convey about the artist's view of the future? Sources 18 and 19 are cartoons that appeared as the Soviet Union and its Warsaw Pact allies invaded Czechoslovakia. The inspiration for Source 18 is the painting by Eugène Delacroix, *Liberty Leading the People,* in which a bare-breasted female Liberty (in a Phrygian cap) leads revolutionaries to freedom. In our cartoon, however, the artist portrays Liberty as Walter Ulbricht, the head of the East German Communist party. What is the artist's view of the friendship of this Liberty? The cartoon also employs a modified version of the motto of the French Revolution of 1789, *"Liberté,*

Égalité, Fraternité" ("Liberty, Equality, Brotherhood"), rendered as *"Liberté, Egalité, Freundschaft"* (German for "friendship"). Considering the preceding twenty-five years of European history, why might the artist have used French for "Liberty" and "Equality" while using German for the last word? Why is Brezhnev/Florian in Source 19 pouring water on a house representing Czechoslovakia (CSSR: Czechoslovak Socialist Republic)? Why does Dubček object? What significance do you ascribe to the difference in the two figures' sizes?

The last cartoon, Source 20, reflects Czechoslovakia in defeat. Many alleged that making peace with the country's Russian conquerors would be simple: "It is only a matter of a few tactical steps back!" Where do the steps backward lead in this case? What does this tell us about the fate of the reform movement? What common sentiment do you detect in the French and Czechoslovakian evidence regarding the reformers' chances for meaningful success in the face of the modern state?

Answering these questions should prepare you to formulate your replies to the central questions of this chapter: What aspects of the modern state and economy provoked the events of 1968? What vision of the future did leaders of the French and Czechoslovakian movements embrace? How did they propose to achieve it?

EPILOGUE

As you continue your reading on the history of Western civilization through the events of the 1970s, 1980s, and 1990s, it will become clear that the student unrest in France and other parts of Western Europe as well as events in Czechoslovakia is of enduring importance.

Perhaps in partial response to this agitation, significant political changes occurred in much of the West in the 1970s and 1980s. In most Western democracies, eighteen-year-olds won the vote. In many countries, too, at least a partial reversal of political centralization began, perhaps in some measure stemming from youthful demands for more "power to the people." This impulse to diminish state authority defied ideological labels: In France and Sweden it was begun by socialist governments, whereas in the United States it has been the work of conservative administrations. No country, however, has yet approached the French students' vision of autogestion.

In France, where student movements amassed the broadest nonstudent support, other changes occurred. His power tarnished by the events of 1968, de Gaulle resigned within a year of the student strikes over a minor issue of government reform. Universities and their curricula were radically restructured in an attempt to meet some student demands, and working conditions in the factories were improved. Even in France, however, fundamental educational and industrial policy remained firmly in the hands of government officials and corporate managers. Student political activism and bitter labor disputes, many originating in issues raised in 1968, persist.

Elsewhere, the student revolt garnered less support, produced fewer changes, and led some frustrated student radicals to turn their energies from protest to brutal political violence in the 1970s. In West Germany, some student radicals formed terrorist groups like the Baader-Meinhof gang, which lashed out violently at West German symbols of the conservative consumer society and American military installations. The Red Brigades terrorist groups in Italy had the same roots and objectives.

In the 1980s youthful discontent in Western Europe partially manifested itself in the Green movement. Especially strong in West Germany, this movement represents the continued alienation of many from the West's industrial economy and modern society. The Green movement attacks the effects of modern industry on our environment and particularly the failure of traditional governing parties effectively to address environmental issues. The Greens in West Germany also advocated an end to their country's participation in the North Atlantic Treaty Organization (NATO). While not always well organized, Greens entered the political life of a number of countries and by 1992 had elected members to parliaments in Germany and Switzerland as well as to the European Parliament. Indeed, in 1998, the Greens became part of the governing coalition (with the Social Democratic party) in Germany, and

the party's leader became foreign minister. Such a governing role led the Greens to accept NATO membership for Germany.

Eastern Europe felt the effects of Soviet actions in Czechoslovakia in 1968 for two decades, as those seeking political, economic, and social change in that region consciously confined reform within the boundaries established by the Brezhnev Doctrine. Discontent with communist rule and Soviet domination, however, grew in the 1980s, led by the rise in Poland of an independent, noncommunist labor movement, Solidarity. By the late 1980s, events in the Soviet Union also actually fostered change in Eastern Europe. Soviet President Mikhail Gorbachev (1985–1991) proclaimed a policy of *glasnost* (openness) and *perestroika* (restructuring) and abandoned the Brezhnev Doctrine, allowing Eastern European nations to determine their own destinies. The result was a largely peaceful revolution in 1989, when one-party communist political systems collapsed in Poland, Hungary, East Germany, Romania, and Czechoslovakia. Indeed, by the end of 1991, the ultimate result of Gorbachev's new path was the dissolution of the Soviet Union and its one-party communist political system, replaced by the Commonwealth of Independent States. Events in Czechoslovakia provide an example of the rapidity of Eastern European change in 1989 and remind us of the enduring importance of the events of 1968 in promoting that change.

In Czechoslovakia the rigid, one-party communist rule reimposed by Soviet arms in 1968 proved particu-